Myasthenia Gravis

Disease Mechanisms and Immune Intervention

Second Edition

EDITED BY

Premkumar Christadoss

UNIVERSITY OF TEXAS MEDICAL BRANCH, GALVESTON

Linus
Publications, Inc.

Published by Linus Publications, Inc.

Deer Park, NY 11729

ISBN : 1-60797-060-0

Printed in the United States of America.

Print Numbers 5 4 3 2 1

Table of Contents

VI. CLINICAL TRIALS IN MYASTHENIA GRAVIS

Preface

This book will present the current concept of autoimmune myasthenia gravis (MG) pathogenesis and strategy for specific therapy or cure for MG. MG is a classical autoimmune disease of the nervous system for which the target antigen, nicotinic acetylcholine receptor, has been cloned, sequenced and biochemically characterized. Antibodies to acetylcholine receptors and complement destroy acetylcholine receptor at the neuromuscular junction, thus leading to defective neuromuscular transmission, muscle fatigue and weakness. Target antigens have been characterized for only a very few other autoimmune diseases. Therefore, MG serves as a prototype for other autoimmune diseases, especially antibody-and/or complement-mediated autoimmune diseases (e.g., Graves disease, SLE, hemolytic anemia, pemphigus, etc.)

In the last few years, rapid advances have been made in unraveling the cellular and molecular mechanisms involved in the pathogenesis of MG, both in the animal model of experimental autoimmune MG (EAMG), and in human MG. Significant advances are being made in characterizing the cells and molecules involved in the autoimmune response to the acetylcholine receptor (AChR) and the MUSK protein. Preclinical and clinical trials have been performed utilizing the information gained in basic research. These advances are leading to the development of specific methods of immune intervention for MG.

Since there are rapid advances and numerous publications on MG and EAMG, it is important to compile the literature on MG research containing a timely review of specific topics. Thus, this book focuses on recent published data and how it is integrated into the present knowledge of MG. The chapters in this book have been contributed by world-renowned authors in US, Europe and China working in the area of MG.

Part I of the book chapters focuses on the clinical features, diagnosis, lab investigation, immunopathogenesis and current treatment of all forms of MG. Included in Part I are chapters on the genetics of MG and the role of thymus and BAFF in MG pathogenesis. Lambert Eaton syndrome and congenital MG are discussed in Parts II and III, respectively. Part IV deals with the role of T cells, B cells, complement, cytokines and chemokines in the experimental autoimmune MG. Further the immunopathogenesis of the new mouse model of MUSK-induced EAMG is discussed. The pre-clinical trial section is Part V. Here the role of regulatory cells, dendritic cells, IV Ig and Pixantrone in immune modulation is reviewed. Other avenues of treatment of MG by blocking classical complement pathway and IL-6 and antigen specific apheresis are also discussed. Also there is a chapter on antisense cholinesterase inhibitor. The book concludes with a clinical trial section in Part VI. Clinical trials on etanercept and retuximab are presented.

The target audience consists of basic scientists and clinical scientists in the university, as well as clinicians, industry researchers, graduate students, medical students and postdoctoral fellows interested in autoimmune disease or neuroimmunology research. The purpose is to educate the physician on the newest clinical trials and to educate the scientists on the complexity of the immune system in antibody-and complement-mediated diseases. Medical students and clinicians will learn the current diagnosis and treatment of MG. Graduate students will not only be interested in reading the latest in EAMG/MG research, but also will find information to help them develop a future strategy to unravel the precise mechanism of disease and development specific therapy. Further, the book will be an ideal tool to apply basic and clinical knowledge gained in MG research to other autoimmune disease research. I would like to dedicate this book in memory of my mother Sarojini Christadoss.

Premkumar Christadoss, M.B.B.S.

I

Myasthenia Gravis

Myasthenia Gravis Clinical Features, Diagnosis and Lab Investigations

Amelia Evoli M.D.

INTRODUCTION

1. MYASTHENIA GRAVIS: A DISEASE OF THE NEUROMUSCULAR JUNCTION

The impulse transmission from motor nerve to muscle (neuromuscular transmission - NMT) is a highly efficient process, as in healthy subjects even the most intense muscle exertion does not lead to transmission failure. Such a property is ensured by the functional organization of a specialized synapse, the neuromuscular junction (NMJ). At normal NMJ (Figure 1), the nerve terminal and muscle post-synaptic membrane are tightly juxtaposed. In-between there is a 50-nm-thick synaptic cleft, comprised of a basal lamina to which the enzyme acetylcholinesterase (ACHE) as well as other synaptic specific proteins are associated. The nerve terminal contains a large number of synaptic vesicles, packed at special sites of the pre-synaptic membrane (active zones) where voltage-gated calcium channels (VGCCs) are linearly arranged. Each synaptic vesicle contains 5,000-10,000 molecules of acetylcholine (ACh) and is referred to as a quantum. The post-synaptic membrane is folded into many secondary synaptic folds which greatly increase its area. At the crest of the folds, the acetylcholine receptors (AChRs) are assembled at a high density ($10,000$-$20,000/\mu m^2$), anchored to the dystroglycan complex through rapsyn (1-2). The AChR clustering which is essential for the NMJ function and the maintenance of the post-synaptic apparatus requires the interaction of nerve-derived factors (such as agrin and neuregulins), and muscle proteins like rapsyn and MuSK (muscle-specific kinase) (1-2).

When an action potential (AP) depolarizes the nerve terminal, the opening of VGCCs results in a rapid increase of the intra-nerve Ca²⁺concentration, which triggers the exocytosis of 50-300 synaptic vesicles. The released ACh traverses the synaptic space, but, as it is rapidly cleaved by ACHE, only 50% of the neurotransmitter discharged from the motor axon actually reaches the postsynaptic receptors (3). The binding of two ACh molecules leads to a conformational change in the AChR and opens the ion channel; the influx of cations (mainly Na⁺) results in a local membrane depolarization, end plate potential (EPP), which is greatest in the depths of secondary folds where voltage-gated sodium channels (VGSC) are concentrated (4). When the EPP is adequate to open these channels, a propagated muscle AP ensues. The small muscle membrane depolarization produced by the occasional release of a single quantum is called miniature end-plate potential (MEPP).

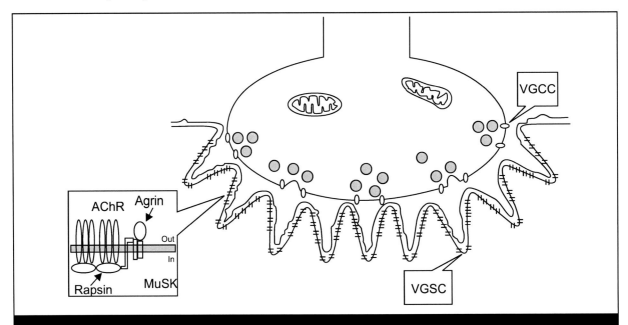

Figure 1. Schematic View of the Neuromuscular Junction. AChR: acetylcholine receptor; MuSK: muscle specific kinase; VGSC: voltage-gated sodium channel; VGCC; voltage-gated calcium channel

The number of ACh quanta released by each nerve impulse is considerably greater than the amount required to depolarize the muscle membrane to the threshold for AP generation, i.e. EPP amplitude largely exceeds the limit for VGSC activation. This corresponds to the so called safety factor of NMT, which is a dynamic measure and is influenced by morphological and functional changes in the NMJ constituents (5).

The diseases affecting the NMJ are characterized by an alteration, generally a reduction, of the safety factor. They are related to three mechanisms: autoimmune (antibodies against end-plate transmembrane proteins), genetic (mutations of genes encoding for different synaptic proteins) and pharmacological (the NMJ is vulnerable to a number of drugs and toxins) (3,6).

Myasthenia gravis (MG) is the most common among these disorders. It is an antibody (Ab) mediated disease, in which the autoimmune attack causes morphologic alterations and functional impairment of the post-synaptic membrane, responsible for a reduced safety factor of NMT. Signs and symptoms are due to fatigable weakness of voluntary muscles.

Two main antigens have been recognized in MG: in most cases, the Ab target is the AChR, while, in a minority of patients, Abs to MuSK are present. Thymus alterations, such as follicular hyperplasia and thymoma are frequently associated with MG, especially with the anti-AChR positive disease.

The immunopathogenic mechanisms of autoimmune MG will be reviewed in chapter 2. This chapter will focus on the clinical aspects, laboratory tests to confirm a suspected MG and differential diagnosis.

2. EPIDEMIOLOGY

MG has a world-wide distribution and can occur at any age from infancy to the nineties. It typically shows two peak ages of onset, with predominance of women among early-onset cases (between the 2nd and 4th decade) and of men in a more advanced age (7). The pattern is quite different in Asian populations characterized by a high frequency of pediatric cases with no clear differences in gender distribution (8).

Although MG is still a rare disease, its frequency has steadily increased in the past two decades: the annual incidence which was estimated of 9-10 new cases/million in the eighties (9) was found to be 21/million in a more recent study (10), while prevalence increased from 60/million to the present rate approaching 200/million (7). Interestingly, the recent rise in the disease frequency appears to be mostly related to a higher diagnosis rate in elderly subjects. Different factors such as improvement of diagnosis, reduced mortality for MG and increased longevity of population can account for this finding. Figure 2 shows how age at the disease onset has changed overtime in two MG series, each including 200 consecutive patients, diagnosed at our center (Catholic University, Roma, Italy). Although a bimodal pattern is recognizable in both populations, a shift of the age of onset towards later decades is present in the group of patients diagnosed more recently.

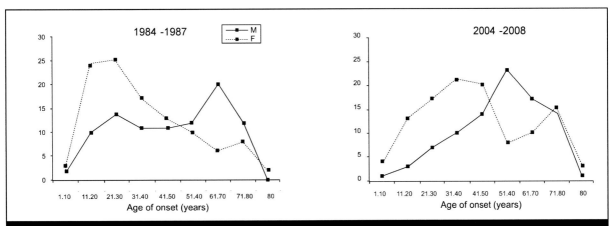

Figure 2. Changes in the age of onset in myasthenia gravis patients diagnosed in different periods with an interval of 20 years.

Epidemiological studies have generally been conducted irrespectively of the patients' Ab status. Consequently, their estimates mainly reflect the distribution of MG with anti-

AChR Abs (AChR-MG) which includes the great majority of patients. MG with Abs to MuSK (MuSK-MG) is a comparatively new and much more rare disease. This clinical form shows a striking predominance in women and a less broad age range than AChR-MG for the rare occurrence of anti-MuSK Abs in patients with disease onset after the age of 60. The prevalence of MuSK-MG among anti-AChR negative patients shows a remarkable variability in different countries, from 0% to over 40%; it appears to be higher at a latitude around 40° north of the equator, which includes a large area of the United States and the Mediterranean countries (11).

3. CLINICAL ASPECTS

The hallmark of MG is fatigable weakness of skeletal muscles, with marked variability in the extension and severity of clinical signs. Fatigability is the most specific feature; weakness is usually present on examination although, in mildly affected cases, it may become evident only on exertion. MG is characterized by symptom fluctuations which may occur daily (weakness is typically relieved by rest and worsened by exercise), or over longer periods, with relapse and remission phases. The disease course is highly variable, as weakness can remain localized to certain muscle groups or become generalized; some patients experience only mild disability through the whole duration of their disease, while, in others, symptoms may rapidly progress to respiratory failure within few weeks after onset. Although all voluntary muscles can be affected, some muscle groups are more frequently involved than others, so that the clinical pattern is fairly typical in the majority of cases.

3.1. Clinical features

The involvement of extrinsic ocular muscles (EOM) is very frequent in MG, both at the onset and in the subsequent course of the disease, and results in binocular diplopia and ptosis. Diplopia may be due to paresis of one eye muscle, but more commonly multiple pareses occur. Usually, in the first stages, double vision is intermittent, as patients become aware of it (or just of blurred vision) in the evening or after driving or reading, later, it tends to become more constant. Ptosis can be monolateral and, when present in both eyes, it is usually asymmetrical (Figure 3, b and c); fluctuations are commonly seen, even when eyelid drooping is nearly complete. In mildly affected cases, ocular disturbances may not be evident on clinical examination and appear only on provocative tests (i.e. sustained upward gaze). The asymmetric involvement of EOM and the variability of symptoms are typical of MG; however, patients with long-standing disease can develop nearly complete ophthalmoplegia (12); at this stage, diplopia disappears and fluctuations become less evident.

In most patients presenting with purely ocular disease weakness spreads to other muscle groups. Progression of MG is observed in 80% of these cases within 2 years from the first symptoms, later the chance of generalization decreases, and after 3 years from the onset it is around 10% (12-14). Subjects who complain of purely ocular symptoms for the entire course of the disease represent 15-20% of the whole MG population (12-14), with a higher proportion among Chinese patients (8). See chapter 3 for clinical and immunopathogenic features of purely ocular MG.

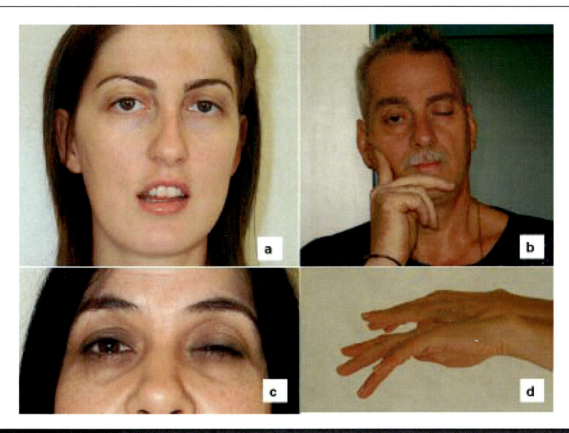

Figure 3. Clinical features of myasthenia gravis. Mild symmetrical ptosis and marked facial weakess with vertical laugh (a): because of extensor neck weakness the patient is supporting his head, asymmetrical ptosis is also present (b): marked ptosis on the left eye (c): asymmetrical drooping of fingers when the patient keeps her arms extended (d).

Reduced strength of facial muscles is common in MG and is responsible for difficulties in closing eyes, blowing cheeks and whistling. Patients often complain of a reduced facial expression and avoid laughing, as the orbicularis oris muscle weakness produces a characteristic vertical laugh ("myasthenic snarl") (Figure 3, a). Oro-pharingeal weakness results in "bulbar" symptoms, so-called as they are due to the involvement of muscles innervated by motor-neurons in the medulla oblongata. Fatigability in chewing and swallowing manifests with progressive difficulty through the meal, a more prominent weakness results in persistent eating problems often causing significant weight loss, and severe dysfagia requires the positioning of a naso-gastric tube. Dysarthria is prevalently due to pharyngeal weakness and is apparent as nasal voice on exertion (reading or counting aloud), until speech becomes unintelligible in severely affected cases. Weakness of the tongue contributes to speaking and eating difficulties and, when long standing, may evolve into a characteristic atrophy with two lateral and one medial furrows (triple furrowed tongue) (15). Involvement of laryngeal muscles with vocal cord paralysis is relatively infrequent and must be regarded as a potentially life-threatening event. It is associated with a hoarse voice and, when severe, it causes exertional breathlessness with stridor (16).

Limb weakness is more marked in proximal muscles and generally symmetrical. Patients complain of inability to keep their arms raised in performing daily activities, and of heaviness of their lower limbs with difficulty in climbing steps or walking long-distance. Leg involvement is especially frequent in young patients, in whom sudden falls often represent the onset of symptom. Among distal muscles, finger extensors are the most commonly affected with drooping of one or two fingers on each side when the patient keeps his arms stretched (Figure 3,d); weakness of foot extensors occurs more rarely. Both extensor and flexor neck muscles can be involved: extensor weakness is responsible for the patient's difficulty in holding up his/her head (Figure 3, b) and, when severe, it causes a "dropped head"; patients are less aware of neck flexor involvement, which can be tested on clinical examination (asking a supine subject to lift his head and to maintain this position). Some female patients complain of urine incontinence, likely due to reduced strength of pelvic floor muscles and of the external sphincter of the bladder; this problem usually resolves with MG treatment.

A reduction of the respiratory function, as a decreased forced vital capacity on spirometry, is quite common in patients with moderate to severe symptoms; however, in about 20% of cases, the disease progresses to respiratory insufficiency (the so called myasthenic crisis) which is a medical emergency requiring assisted ventilation. Breathing difficulties in MG can arise from airway obstruction as in the case of vocal cord paralysis, but more commonly, failure of ventilation is caused by weakness of the diaphragm and intercostal muscles, while patients' upper airways, although patent, are obstructed by bronchial secretions as coughing is not valid, and by saliva aspiration due to the impairment of palatal function. In an impending MG crisis, respiratory distress (dyspnoea, restlessness, hypertension, tachycardia) is always associated with bulbar weakness, which suggests the diagnosis. Respiratory crises are infrequent in the first stages of the disease; they can be precipitated by infections, surgery, iodinated contrast administration, withdrawal or excessive dosage of ACHE inhibitors (ACHE-Is), and can occur in the initial phase of prednisone treatment.

3.2. Scoring systems and Disease course

Several systems have been devised to evaluate the extension and severity of MG signs. Basically, all these systems make a distinction between patients with purely ocular myasthenia from those with generalized disease and, in the latter group, differentiate mild, moderate and severe clinical forms. The Osserman classification, first published in 1958 and later modified (17-18), which has been in use for more than 40 years, also considered the rate of disease progression. More recently, a Task Force of the MG Foundation of America (MGFA) proposed a new scale, now generally used, which takes into account, for each class of disease severity, the weakness pattern according to the prevalent involvement of limb or bulbar muscles (19). These clinical scales are shown in Table 1.

It is important to note that these classifications broadly define disease types and are used to describe, also retrospectively, a patient's status at a certain point of his/her disease. They can not measure muscle weakness and are therefore not suited to assess changes of disease severity in individual cases. In order to overcome these limitations, quantitative scores, based on the evaluation of sentinel muscle groups, have been devised, to be used in patients' follow-up and in the assessment of the effect of treatments (20-21). The MGFA quantitative MG (QMG) score for disease severity is a validated clinical scale including 13 test items (19). Currently, it is largely employed both in daily clinical practice and in therapeutical trials (22).

Table 1

Modified Osserman Classification		MGFA Classification	
Group1	Purely Ocular	Group I	Any ocular muscle weakness
Group 2A	Mild Generalized (ocular and limb, no prominent bulbar signs)	Group II	Mild Weakness affecting other than ocular muscles
Group 2B	Moderate Generalized (ocular and limb, and bulbar involvement, no crises)	II a	Predominantly affecting limb, axial muscles, or both
Group 3	Acute Generalized with prominent bulbar involvement and crises	II b	Predominantly affecting bulbar, respiratory muscles, or both
Group 4	Late Severe Generalized with pro minent bulbar signs and crises	Group III	Moderate weakness affecting other than ocular muscles
		III a	Predominantly affecting limb, axial muscles or both
		III b	Predominantly affecting bulbar, respiratory muscles, or both
		Group IV	Severe weakness affecting other than ocular muscles
		IV a	Predominantly affecting limb, axial muscles, or both
		IV b	Predominantly affecting bulbar, respiratory, muscles, or both
		Group V	Defined by intubation, with or without mechanical ventil ation, except when employed during routine postoperative management.

A few reports have analyzed the natural course of MG, mostly in patient series diagnosed before the mid 1960s. At that time the great majority of patients were treated only with ACHE-Is, which are assumed not to influence the disease history. In these cohorts, MG progressed to the maximum severity in the first three to seven years from the onset; deaths for myasthenic crises occurred in 25-33% of patients, mostly in the first three years; in the survivors, the disease tended to stabilize and, in the long-term course, 15-29% of cases remained unchanged and 11-20% went into complete remission (13, 23-25); patients with a thymoma generally had severe disease and a high death rate (25). There is no doubt that the modern treatment and improved intensive care assistance have changed the natural course of MG, as proved by the dramatic reduction in the mortality rate (< 5% in recent reports) (22). Moreover, the early use of immunotherapy appears to reduce the disease progression to the most severe clinical manifestations, as shown by a reduced frequency of respiratory crises (20% or less) in recent reports (26), in comparison with earlier series (25).

3.3. Clinical forms

In the great majority of patients MG is associated with serum Abs to AChR. AChR-MG encompasses all clinical forms, from purely ocular to severe generalized disease, and features which are considered characteristic of MG (symptom fluctuations, highly variable course, typical weakness distribution) are commonly detected in this entity. Generalized AChR-MG includes an early-onset disease (age of onset < 50 years), prevalent in female patients and very frequently associated with thymus follicular hyperplasia, a late-onset disease, more common in male subjects, and thymoma-associated MG (10-15% of whole MG population) which occurs most frequently in the fifth and sixth decade (27).

Anti-AChR Abs are not detectable, at least by the standard immunoassay, in about 10% of patients with generalized MG and in 50% of cases with symptoms restricted to ocular muscles. Abs to MuSK are present in a proportion of these subjects; in the remaining patients with neither anti-AChR nor anti-MuSK Abs the disease is called seronegative MG (SNMG). SNMG is thought to belong to the same spectrum as AChR-MG, since low-affinity anti-AChR IgG1 Abs have recently been described in a proportion of these patients, including a few cases with ocular disease (28). Clinical studies support this view as SNMG features appear undistinguishable from those of AChR-MG, with an increased frequency of mild forms (29-30). Moreover, thymus hyperplasia has been described in 35-50% of early-onset SNMG patients (31-32), while the association with a thymoma is very rare (33).

MuSK-MG has been recognized as a distinct clinical entity in the past few years. Anti-MuSK Abs are usually associated with a generalized disease, of which three phenotypes have been described. The most frequent is a severe form prevalently involving bulbar muscles (29-30, 35). Ocular symptoms are frequent at the onset, then the disease rapidly progresses to dysphagia, dysarthria, marked facial and neck weakness, while limb fatigue is less severe and inconsistent. Daily fluctuations are less common than in typical MG, but, especially in the first years from the onset, the disease has a brittle course with repeated deterioration phases and a high frequency of respiratory crises (29,35-36). In spite of treatment, some patients develop over the years permanent facial and pharyngeal weakness (with nasal speech), together with atrophy of facial muscles and the tongue (29, 37). Such localized muscle atrophy, which can also be seen in long-standing AChR-MG (15), appears to be more frequent in anti-MuSK positive patients (37). A second clinical pattern is characterized by a predominant involvement of neck, shoulder, and respiratory muscles without ocular weakness; finally, in some cases the clinical picture does not differ from AChR-MG (38-39). In MuSK-MG the thymus is generally normal and hyperplastic changes are distinctly uncommon (31-32); a unique thymoma case has been so far described (40).

3.4. MG in pregnancy and in newborns from myasthenic mothers

MG often occurs in women in fertile age and in most cases does not contraindicate child-bearing. A close cooperation between neurologist, obstetrician and neonatologist is required to secure good management during gestation and delivery. The course of MG is variable during pregnancy (approximately 1/3 of patients deteriorate, 1/3 remain unchanged and 1/3 improve), although the first trimester and the post-partum period appear to be critical for disease exacerbations (41). On the other hand, MG influences the outcome of pregnancy, being associated with abortion, premature labor, prolonged delivery and an increased rate of operative interventions (42).

Neonatal MG is a transient disease affecting about 10-15% of newborns to MG women, due to Ab placental transfer. It has been described mostly in association with maternal AChR-MG, but there are also reports of affected babies born to SNMG and MuSK-MG women (43-44). Symptoms (weak sucking, impaired swallowing, feeble cry, hypotonia and, in some cases, respiratory difficulty) are evident within the first two days of life and generally last 2-4 weeks. A few children, born to women with AChR-MG, were reported with persistent weakness of facial and pharyngeal muscles (facial diplegia and dysarthria). This clinical picture is thought to be due to a localized myopathic process, resulting from inactivation of fetal AChR during muscle development (45-46). An early exposure to fetal AChR to Abs could also be responsible for arthrogryposis multiplex congenita, a severe complication of maternal MG, resulting from lack of fetal movements in utero (45-46).

4. DIAGNOSIS

The clinical diagnosis of MG relies on typical history and signs of fluctuating muscle weakness. In mildly affected patients, fatigability may appear only on exertion, with the use of quantitative tests on selected muscle groups (19). Neurological examination is otherwise normal; pain and autonomic disturbances are absent; muscle atrophy is uncommon, and, when present, it is restricted to single districts (mostly tongue and facial muscles).

The clinical diagnosis is then confirmed by positive results on: (a) pharmacological testing; (b) electrophysiological testing; (c) serum anti-AChR and anti-MuSK Ab assay. Through the first two approaches, the patient's weakness is recognized as due to a post-synaptic defect of the NMT, detection of anti-AChR or anti-MuSK Abs confirms the diagnosis of autoimmune MG.

4.1. Pharmacological testing

ACHE-Is enhance the safety factor of NMT by increasing the availability of ACh and a positive response to these drugs strongly supports the clinical suspect of MG. For diagnostic purposes, parenterally-given short-acting agents are preferred. Tensilon test consists in the intravenous injection of edrophonium chloride (Tensilon), starting with a dose of 2 mg; if there is no response and in the absence of adverse effects, after one minute, another 2 -5 mg are given; clinical reaction is evident within 10-60 seconds from the injection and lasts for 1.5 to 10 minutes (47). In order for this test to be considered positive, the improvement must be unequivocal. Therefore, the response should be evaluated in weak muscles whose function can be quantified (see Figure 4), avoiding to rely upon the patient's impression (a placebo test should be performed first).

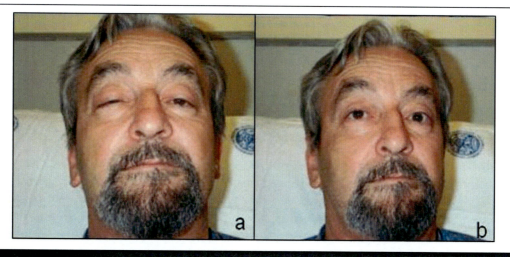

Figure 4. Severe bilateral ptosis prevalent on the right side (a) markedly relieved by the injection of 4 mg of edrophonium chloride (Tensilon)

Edrophonium administration is commonly associated with lacrimation, sweating and fasciculation. As severe side effects, such as bronchoconstriction and bradycardia, may also occur, Tensilon test should not be performed before patient's clinical information and an ECG are available, and atropine must always be kept at hand. Neostigmine (Prostigmine) 1mg i.m. can be used as an alternative to edrophonium, being associated with fewer cholinergic side effects. In this case, the clinical response appears 15-30 minutes after the injection. Edrophonium/ neostigmine testing is generally considered to be highly sensitive in MG diagnosis, with a 90% rate of positive responses (48). An important exception is represented by patients with anti-MuSK Abs. In these subjects, ACHE-Is injection often precipitates marked nicotinic side effects, such as cramps and widespread fasciculations, clinical improvement is significantly less common than in AChR-MG (< 70%) and worsening of weakness can be observed (29, 49).

A positive reaction to Tensilon can be found in other disorders of NMT, such as congenital myasthenic syndromes (CMS) and, less frequently, in the Lambert-Eaton myasthenic syndrome (LEMS). "False" responses have been observed in amyotrophic lateral sclerosis (ALS), Guillain-Barrè syndrome (50) and in patients with intracranial lesions (48).

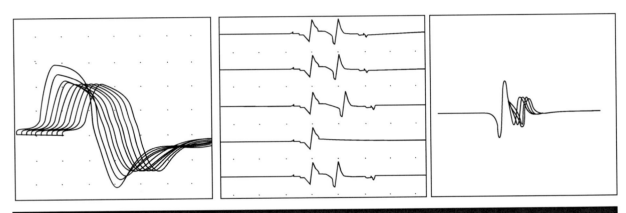

Figure 5. EMG features in myasthenia gravis. 3/sec RNS of the ulnar nerve showing 34% decrement in the amplitude of the CMAP recorded from the abductor digiti quinti muscle (a): SF-EMG (orbicularis oculi muscle): in the first three traces, jitter progressively increases until the 2nd potential is blocked (b): SF-EMG (orbicularis oculi muscle): increased jitter as second action potential wave group (c).

4.2. Electrophysiological testing

4.2.1. Repetitive nerve stimulation (RNS)

The routine test consists in a supramaximal repetitive stimulation of the motor nerve at 2-3/sec (low-rate RNS), recording the compound muscle action potential (CMAP) from the muscle with surface electrodes. A decremental response with a difference >10% in the CMAP amplitude between first and fourth or fifth stimulus is the typical finding in MG (Figure 5, a).
This pattern is the electrophysiological equivalent of clinical fatigability. During repetitive motor nerve firing (which also occurs in the course of sustained muscle exertion), the quantal release at NMJ is physiologically reduced. This is of little consequence in normal individuals, in whom the EPP value remains above the threshold to elicit, for each nerve depolarization, a muscle AP. In

MG, owing to the reduced safety factor of NMT, low-rate RNS leads to transmission failure at an increasing number of NMJs, which results in CMAP decrement.

The diagnostic sensitivity of RNS depends on weakness extension. It is quite low in ocular myasthenia (51), while in patients with generalized disease the positivity rate is around 70% (47) when both distal and proximal limb muscles are tested. The diagnostic yield can be further increased by muscle warming to 35°C and by delivery RNS after maximum voluntary contraction (7, 26). In patients with MuSK-MG, owing to the prevalent involvement of the cranial muscles, RNS is often negative unless facial muscles are tested (52).

A decremental response on low-rate RNS is also present in other disorders of NMT and, to a lesser extent, in ALS (48); specificity for MG is improved by post-tetanic exhaustion (53).

4.2.2. Single-fiber electromyography (SF-EMG)

SF-EMG identifies APs generated by individual muscle fibers and can selectively record potential pairs from two fibers belonging to the same motor unit. The time interval between the two APs has a certain variability, which is called "jitter" and is expressed as mean consecutive difference (MCD) of successive inter-potential intervals. Moreover, "fiber density" which is a measure of local concentration of muscle fibers, and is then indicative of rearrangements within the motor unit, is calculated (54). When NMT is altered as in MG, jitter is pathologically increased and intermittent transmission failure, seen as "blocking" of the second potential, can occur (Figure 5, b and c). In evaluating jitter measurement, different parameters are taken into account, such as 1) the mean jitter value (as MCD) in the fiber pairs examined, 2) the percent blocking, and 3) the percent of pairs in which jitter exceeds the normal limit for that muscle (54). SF-EMG is usually performed in the extensor communis digitorum (ECD), and, in the case of negative results, on facial muscles (most commonly in the frontalis and in the orbicularis oculi). It is the most sensitive diagnostic test for MG, and, provided that both limb and facial districts are examined, positive results are recorded in more than 90% of cases (53-54). Moreover, when performed in cranial muscles SF-EMG can detect NMT abnormalities in patients with focal symptoms, such as subjects with purely ocular MG (55) or MuSK-MG (29, 35-36). However, an increased jitter is far from specific for MG as, apart from other diseases of NMT, it can be found in several neurogenic and myopathic conditions. Measure of fiber density (which is normal in MG) can assist in reaching the correct diagnosis (54).

4.3. Anti-AChR and anti-MuSK Ab assay

Serum anti-AChR Abs measured in routine practice (also called binding anti-AChR Abs) are detected with an immunoprecipitation assay, using human AChR labeled with I^{125}-a-bungarotoxin as antigen. Positive results on this standard test are found in 90% of patients with generalized MG (including nearly all thymoma cases) and in a lower proportion (40-70%) of subjects with purely ocular symptoms (51). Sensitivity is reduced by immunosuppressive therapy at the time of testing (56) and, to a lesser extent, after thymectomy in patients with a hyperplastic thymus (57). Therefore, for diagnostic purposes, it is relevant that the serological assay is performed, as far as possible, before therapeutic interventions. On the other hand, anti-AChR Abs can be undetectable in the first stages of the disease and become positive afterwards (seroconversion) (56). Although patients with ocular myasthenia tend to have lower levels than those with generalized weakness, in the general MG population the Ab titer does not correlate with disease severity and is often increased in individuals in full remission (57). The diagnostic accuracy of the standard anti-AChR assay is high, ranging from 97% to 99% (51), as positive results in non-MG patients are distinctly rare (48). Other serological tests are available to detect blocking (58) and modulating anti-AChR Abs (56), but although the latter may slightly increase the diagnostic yield, these additional assays are not used routinely.

Abs to MuSK, which are detected through immunoprecipitation assay using human recombinant I^{125}-labeled-MuSK as antigen, were first described in 2001 (59) and since then have gained a relevant role in MG diagnosis. These Abs have been detected in a proportion of anti-AChR negative MG patients ranging from 23 to 49% (with an average around 35%), with the lowest frequency rates in China and in Scandinavian countries (8, 60). The Ab serum level is markedly reduced by immunosuppressive therapy, while it remains unaltered after thymectomy (61). Although no formal studies have addressed their diagnostic accuracy, anti-MuSK Abs appear to be specific for anti-AChR negative MG (30), the co-existence of the two Abs having seldom been reported (62).

4.4. Additional testing

Serum Abs which bind skeletal muscle with a striatonal pattern (anti-striatonal Abs) have been recognized in MG since the sixties. Later, these Abs were found to react with two intracellular muscle antigens, i.e. the giant protein titin and the ryanodine receptor (RyR) (63-64). Anti-titin and anti-RyR Abs are generally found in AChR-MG, where they are strongly associated with thymoma (anti-titin are positive in 95% and anti-RyR Abs in 75% of thymoma patients), are also present in nearly 50% of late-onset non-thymoma patients, while are very uncommon in early-onset MG (65). The presence of these Abs correlates with disease severity. Specifically, anti-titin Abs could be responsible for a thymoma-associated myositis, while anti-RyR are frequently found in subjects with invasive thymoma and could be related to cardiac involvement and sudden death in these cases (65).

Mediastinal computerized tomography (CT) is the procedure of choice for thymus imaging, although magnetic resonance (MR) is increasingly being used in this application. In MG patients, a radiological study of the mediastinum is indicated to detect a possible thymoma, which represents an obvious indication to surgery. In this task, CT and MR proved to be roughly equivalent, i.e. both are fairly accurate in diagnosing a thymoma and in predicting its invasiveness (66), even though capsule infiltration and focal invasion appear to be more evident on MR imaging (67). On the other hand, both these techniques showed a lower accuracy in distinguishing between a normal and a hyperplastic thymus, especially in young patients (66). Moreover, it should be taken into account that iodinated contrast administration can occasionally precipitate worsening of MG symptoms (68).

4.5. Diagnostic strategy

In establishing the diagnosis of MG, the order in which pharmacological, electrophysiological and serological tests are given, depends on clinical presentation and practical considerations. Anti-AChR and anti-MuSK Abs are highly specific and their detection in patients with congruent clinical findings, in practice, confirms the diagnosis; in these cases edrophonium/neostigmine test and EMG exams are not indeed necessary.

In patients with mild symptoms it is justified to wait for serological results; if Ab assays are negative, other tests should be performed. The choice between RNS and SF-EMG depends on their relative sensitivity in relation to weakness extension: SF-EMG has a stronger indication in subjects with purely ocular symptoms and in those with mild weakness; RNS is generally adequate in patients with more relevant generalized symptoms. A clearly positive response on short-acting ACHE-Is is an additional support to the diagnosis. On the other hand, in severely ill patients who require prompt diagnosis, pharmacological and EMG tests have great clinical value, as they are easy to administer and give immediate results. A clinical picture of marked bulbar weakness, with negative RNS on limb muscles and no response to Tensilon should arouse the suspicion of MuSK-MG and prompt the search for these Abs.

A radiological study of the mediastinum should be performed in all patients, although the presence of a thymoma is uncommon in ocular myasthenia, and very rare in children, MuSK-MG and SNMG. The exclusion of a thymoma must be especially careful in patients at higher risk for such an association, i.e. anti-AChR positive adult subjects. Anti-titin and anti-RyR Abs are strongly indicative of an underlying thymoma in young patients, while their predictive value is much lower in patients older than 50. In these cases, if the initial evaluation is negative, it can be worthwhile to perform another CT/MR after a few months, as a small thymoma may escape radiological detection.

As MG frequently coexists with thyroid autoimmune disease, specific Abs and hormones should be tested. Moreover, especially in the elderly, a screening for medical conditions (chronic infections, diabetes, arterial hypertension, glaucoma, osteoporosis) which could complicate treatment for MG is indicated.

5.1. Differential diagnosis

Differential diagnosis, in practice, concerns SNMG which must be differentiated from other conditions that can simulate MG. In patients with generalized symptoms, other NMT diseases, namely LEMS and CMS, must first be considered, as they share with MG similar clinical findings (including the response to Tensilon) and EMG patterns, both on low-rate RNS and SF-EMG. LEMS is a presynaptic disorder, in which the number of ACh vesicles released by each nerve depolarization is reduced from normal; it is morphologically characterized by paucity and disorganization of active zones on the nerve terminal caused by Abs to P/Q type VGCCs (69). LEMS should be suspected in adult-onset cases, with prominent weakness in proximal muscles of the leg, mild ocular and bulbar symptoms, hypoactive tendon reflexes (which increase after a brief muscle contraction) and autonomic disturbances. LEMS diagnosis can be confirmed by typical EMG findings, i.e. a small CMAP amplitude at rest with an incremental response (facilitation) during high-rate RNS or after a brief contraction, and by detection of specific anti-VGCC Abs (70). See chapter 10 for clinical and immunopathological features of LEMS.

In the pediatric age, the differential diagnosis mainly involves CMS which constitute a heterogeneous group of inherited disorders affecting the NMJ at presynaptic, synaptic and postsynaptic level (71). Most of these conditions present at birth or during the first year of life and some have characteristic clinical and EMG features (72). However, it must be taken into account that clinical presentation is highly variable, symptoms may become evident in childhood and even in early adulthood, and family history can be negative (most CMS are inherited as autosomal recessive diseases). These patients can be easily misdiagnosed as having SNMG, running the risk of useless and potentially harmful treatment. Once a CMS is suspected, the identification of the specific NMT defect will require gene mutation analysis and, in some patients, muscle biopsy followed by morphological, *in vitro* electrophysiological and molecular genetic studies (72).

Botulism and tick paralysis both cause acute ophthalmoplegia and weakness of bulbar and limb muscles, but, differently from MG, autonomic disturbances are usually present. On EMG studies, these conditions are characterized by low CMAP amplitude at rest; in botulism, a decremental pattern at 2-3/sec RNS and facilitation on high-rate stimulation are typically found (73), while in tick paralysis RNS elicits a normal response (74).

ALS patients with clinically isolated bulbar symptoms may be erroneously diagnosed with MG. These patients can show a mild reaction to ACHE-Is, as well as a decremental response on RNS and increased jitter. However, clear symptom fluctuations are absent and the finding of an increased fiber density (indicative of reinnervation) on SF-EMG (54) usually prompts a needle EMG which clarifies the diagnosis.

Even though myasthenic patients frequently complain of weakness of extensor neck muscles, an isolated involvement of this district is rare in MG (75); furthermore, in subjects presenting with a "dropped head syndrome" several myopathic and neurogenic conditions must be considered as alternative diagnoses (76). In general, a "chronic fatigue syndrome" can be easily differentiated from MG, as it is associated more with diffuse tiredness and muscle pain than with weakness involving specific muscle groups; SF-EMG shows minor jitter abnormalities together with a moderately increased fiber density, pointing to myogenic abnormalities rather than to a primary NMT defect (77-78).

In patients showing exclusive or predominant weakness of EOM, with bilateral ptosis and ophthalmoparesis, a mitochondrial disease causing progressive external ophthalmoplegia (PEO) should be considered. PEO is characterized by slowly developing, symmetrical ptosis with no (or very limited) fluctuations; diplopia is absent, although it may occur in the initial stages of the disease; weakness may extend to facial, axial and limb muscles (79); an increased jitter on SF-EMG can be present (80). Additional clinical features, including hearing loss, cataracts, neuropathy and ataxia, when present, are highly indicative of a mitochondrial disorder; a differentiation from MG concerns cases with pure muscle weakness. The association of mitochondrial myopathy with MG has occasionally been reported (81).

Miller Fisher syndrome is a variant of acute inflammatory demyelinating neuropathy characterized by the triad of ophthalmoparesis, ataxia and loss of tendon reflexes (82). The differential diagnosis with MG may be difficult when ataxia is not evident and opthalmoparesis is asymmetrical (83); besides, in these patients, SF-EMG commonly shows marked NMT alterations as increased jitter and blocking, due to the effect of anti-GQ1b Abs at the motor nerve terminal (82).

Thyroid ophthalmopathy is a relatively common cause of diplopia without ptosis and can be confused with ocular myasthenia in the initial stage of the disease, when proptosis and orbital congestion are not yet evident. In these patients, eyelid retraction on one side may give the false impression of contralateral ptosis. Graves ophthalmopathy can be associated with MG and can be overlooked when it occurs without obvious thyroid dysfunction (84); the diagnosis relies on the demonstration of eye muscle enlargement on the CT scan of the orbits (84).

Lastly, in few patients with ocular and /or bulbar weakness, diagnosed with SNMG on the basis of clinical improvement with ACHE-Is or a decremental response on RNS (85-86), brain-stem lesions were found on CT/MRI of the brain. These reports suggest caution in the evaluation of pharmacological and electrophysiological tests in SNMG, and recommend neuroradiological investigations in patients with focal symptoms, atypical presentation or a rapidly progressive disease.

In the absence of anti-AChR and anti-MuSK Abs, the diagnostic confirmation of MG requires a careful ruling out of other conditions and should be based more on the clinical context than on positive results on one single test.

REFERENCES

1. Sanes, J.R., and J.W. Lichtman. 2001. Induction, assembly, maturation and maintenance of a postsynaptic apparatus. *Nat. Rev. Neurosci.* 2:791–805.

2. Hughes, B.W., L.L. Kusner, and H.J. Kaminski. 2006. Molecular architecture of the neuromuscular junction. *Muscle Nerve* 33:445-461.

3. Hirsch, N.P. 2007. The neuromuscular junction in health and disease. *Br. J Anaesth.* 99:132-138.

4. Ruff, R.L. 2003. Neurophysiology of the neuromuscular junction: Overview. *Ann. N.Y. Acad. Sci.* 998:1-10.

5. Wood, S. J., and C.R. Slater. 2001. Safety factor at the neuromuscular junction. *Prog. Neurobiol.* 64:393-429.

6. Lewis, R.L., and L. Gutmann. 2004. Snake venoms and the neuromuscular junction. *Semin. Neurol.* 24:175-179.

7. Keesey, J.C. 2004 Clinical evaluation and management of myasthenia gravis. *Muscle Nerve* 29:484-505.

8. Zhang, X., M. Yang, J. Xu, M. Zhang, B. Lang, W. Wang, and A. Vincent. 2007. Clinical and serological study of myasthenia gravis in HuBei Province, China. *J Neurol Neurosurg Psychiatry* 78:386-390.

9. Phillips, L.H., 2nd. 2003. The epidemiology of myasthenia gravis. *Ann. N.Y. Acad. Sci.* 998:407-412.

10. Aragonès, J.M., I. Bolíbar, X. Bonfill, E. Bufill, A. Mummany, F. Alonso, and I. Illa. 2003. Myasthenia gravis: a higher than expected incidence in the elderly. *Neurology* 60:1024-1026.

11. Vincent, A., M.I. Leite, M.E. Farruggia, S. Jacob, S. Viegas, H. Shiraishi, O. Benveniste, P.B. Morgan, D. Hilton-Jones, J. Newsom-Davis, D. Beeson, and N. Willcox. 2008. Myasthenia gravis seronegative for acetylcholine receptor antibodies. *Ann. N.Y. Acad. Sci.* 1132:84-92.

12. Evoli, A., P. Tonali, E. Bartoccioni, and M. Lo Monaco. 1988. Ocular myasthenia: diagnostic and therapeutical problems. *Acta Neurol. Scand.* 77:31-35.

13. Grob, D., N. Brunner, T. Namba, and M. Pagala. 2008. Lifetime course of myasthenia gravis. *Muscle Nerve* 37:141–149.

14. Luchanok, U., and H.J. Kaminski. 2008. Ocular myasthenia: diagnostic and treatment recommendations and the evidence base. *Curr. Opin. Neurol.* 21:8-15.

15. Oosterhuis, H.J.G.H. 1997 In Myasthenia gravis. Groningen Neurol. Press, pp.26-30.

16. Hanson, A., C. J. Lueck, and D. J. Thomas. 1996. Myasthenia gravis presenting with stridor. *Thorax* 51:108-109.

17. Osserman, K.E. 1958. Clinical aspects. In: Myasthenia gravis. K.E. Osserman, editor. New York, NY: Grune & Stratton, pp79–80.

18. Osserman, K.E., and G. Genkins. 1971. Studies in myasthenia gravis: review of a twenty-year experience in over 1200 patients. *Mt. Sinai J. Med.* 38:497-537.

19. Jaretzki, A 3rd, R.J. Barohn, R.M. Ernstoff, H.J. Kaminski, J.C. Keesey, A.S. Penn, and D.B. Sanders. 2000. Myasthenia gravis: recommendations for clinical research standards. Task Force of the Medical Scientific Advisory Board of the Myasthenia Gravis Foundation of America. *Ann. Thorac. Surg.* 70:327-334.

20. Besinger, U.A., K.V. Toyka, M. Homberg, R. Hohlfeld, and A. Fateh-Moghadam. 1983. Myasthenia gravis: long-term correlation of binding and bungarotoxin blocking antibodies against acetylcholine receptor with changes in disease severity. *Neurology* 33:1316–1321.

21. Mantegazza, R., C. Antozzi, D. Peluchetti, A. Sghirlanzoni , and F. Cornelio. 1988. Azathioprine as a single drug or in combination with steroids in the treatment of myasthenia gravis. *J. Neurol.* 235:449-453.

22. Hampton, T. 2007. Trials assess myasthenia gravis therapies. *JAMA* 298:29-30.

23. Grob, D., N.G. Brunner, and T. Namba. 1981. The natural course of myasthenia gravis and effects of therapeutic measures. *Ann. N. Y. Acad. Sci.* 377:352-369.

24. Cohen, M.S., and Y. David. 1981. Aspects of the natural history of myasthenia gravis: crisis and death. *Ann. N. Y. Acad. Sci.* 377:670-677.

25. Oosterhuis H.J.G.H. 1989. The natural course of myasthenia gravis: a long term follow up study. *J. Neurol. Neurosurg. Psychiatry* 52:1121-1127.

26. Juel, V.C., and J.M. Massey. 2007. Myasthenia gravis. *Orphanet J. Rare Dis.* 6:44.

27. Vincent, A. 2002. Unravelling the pathogenesis of myasthenia gravis. *Nature Rev. Immunol.* 2:797-804.

28. Leite, M.I., S. Jacob, S. Viegas, J. Cossins, L. Clover, B.P. Morgan, D. Beeson, and A. Vincent. 2008. IgG1 antibodies to acetylcholine receptors in 'seronegative' myasthenia gravis. *Brain* 131:1940-1952.

29. Evoli, A., P. Tonali, L. Padua, M. Lo Monaco, F. Scuderi, A.P. Batocchi, M. Marino, and E. Bartoccioni. 2003. Clinical correlates with anti-MuSK antibodies in generalized seronegative myasthenia gravis. *Brain* 126:2304-2311.

30. Vincent, A., and M.I. Leite. 2005. Neuromuscular junction autoimmune disease: muscle specific kinase antibodies and treatments for myasthenia gravis. *Curr. Opin. Neurol.* 18:519-525.

31. Lauriola, L., F. Ranelletti, N. Maggiano, M. Guerriero, C. Punzi, F. Marsili, E. Bartoccioni, and A. Evoli. 2005. Thymus changes in anti-MuSK-positive and -negative myasthenia gravis. *Neurology* 64:536-538.

32. Leite, M.I., P. Ströbel, M. Jones, K. Micklem, R. Moritz, R. Gold, E.H. Niks, S. Berrih-Aknin, F. Scaravilli, A. Canelhas, A. Marx, J. Newsom-Davis, N. Willcox, and A. Vincent. 2005. Fewer thymic changes in MuSK antibody-positive than in MuSK antibody-negative MG. *Ann. Neurol.* 57:444-448.

33. Maggi, L., F. Andreetta, C. Antozzi, P. Gonfalonieri, F. Cornelio, V. Scaioli, and R. Mantegazza. 2008. Two cases of thymoma-associated myasthenia gravis without antibodies to the acetylcholine receptor. *Neuromuscul. Disord.* 18:678-680.

34. Caress, J.B., C.H. Hunt, and S.D. Batish. 2005. Anti-MuSK myasthenia gravis presenting with purely ocular findings. *Arch. Neurol.* 62: 1002-1003.

35. Lavrnic D., M. Losen, A. Vujic, M. De Baets, L.J. Hajdukovic, V. Stojanovic, R. Trikic, P. Djukic, S. Apostolski. 2005. The features of myasthenia gravis with autoantibodies to MuSK. *J. Neurol. Neurosurg. Psychiatry* 76:1099-1102.

36. Deymeer, F., O. Gungor-Tuncer, V. Yilmaz, Y. Parman, P. Serdaroglu, C. Ozdemir, A. Vincent, and G. Saruhan-Direskeneli. 2007. Clinical comparison of anti-MuSK- vs anti-AChR-positive and seronegative myasthenia gravis. *Neurology* 68:609-611.

37. Farrugia, M.E., M.D. Robson, L. Clover , P. Anslow, J. Newsom-Davis, R. Kennett, D. Hilton-Jones, P.M. Matthews, and A. Vincent. 2006. MRI and clinical studies of facial and bulbar muscle involvement in MuSK antibody-associated myasthenia gravis. *Brain* 129:1481-1492.

38. Zhou, L., J. McConville, V. Chaudhry, R.N. Adams, R.L. Skolasky, A. Vincent, and D.B. Drachman. 2004. Clinical comparison of muscle-specific tyrosine kinase (MuSK) antibody-positive and -negative myasthenic patients. *Muscle Nerve* 30:55-60.

39. Sanders, D. B., K. El-Salem, J.M. Massey, J. McConville, and A. Vincent. 2003. Clinical aspects of MuSK antibody positive seronegative MG. *Neurology* 60:1978-1980.

40. Taka, E., M.A. Topcuoglu, B. Akkaya, A. Galati, M.Z. Onal, and A.Vincent. 2005. Thymus changes in anti-MuSK-positive and -negative myasthenia gravis. *Neurology* 65:782-783.

41. Batocchi, A.P., L. Majolini, A. Evoli, M.M. Lino, C. Minisci, and P. Tonali. 1999. Course and treatment of myasthenia gravis during pregnancy. *Neurology* 52:447- 452.

42. Hoff, J.M., A.K. Daltveit, and N.E. Gilhus. 2003. Myasthenia gravis. Consequences for pregnancy, delivery and the newborn. *Neurology* 61:1362–1366.

43. Melber, D. 1988. Maternal-fetal transmission of myasthenia gravis with negative acetylcholine receptor antibody. *N Engl. J. Med.* 318:996.

44. Niks, E.H., A. Verrips, B.A. Semmekrot, M.J.J. Prick, A. Vincent, M.J.D. van Tol, C.M. Jol-van der Zijde, and J.J.G.M. Verschuuren. 2008. A transient neonatal myasthenic syndrome with anti-MuSK antibodies. *Neurology* 70:1215-1216.

45. Jeannet, P.-Y., J.-P. Marcoz, T. Kuntzer, and E. Roulet-Perez. 2008. Isolated facial and bulbar paresis: a persistent manifestation of neonatal myasthenia gravis. *Neurology* 70:237-238.

46. Oskoui, M., L. Jacobson, W.K. Chung, J. Haddad, A. Vincent, P. Kaufmann, and D.C. De Vivo. 2008. Fetal acetylcholine receptor inactivation syndrome and maternal myasthenia gravis. *Neurology* 71: 2010-2012.

47. Evoli, A., A.P. Batocchi, and P. Tonali. 1996. A practical guide to the recognition and management of myasthenia gravis. *Drugs* 52: 662-670.

48. Phillips, L.H. 2nd, and P.A. Melnick. 1990. Diagnosis of myasthenia gravis in the 1990s. *Semin. Neurol.* 10:62-69.

49. Hatanaka, Y., S. Hemmi, M.B. Morgan, M.L. Scheufele, G.C. Claussen, G.I. Wolfe, and S.J. Oh. 2005. Nonresponsiveness to anticholinesterase agents in patients with anti-MuSK-antibody-positive MG. *Neurology* 65:1508-1509.

50. Oh, S.J., and H.K. Cho 1990. Edrophonium responsiveness not necessarily diagnostic of myasthenia gravis. *Muscle Nerve* 13:187-191.

51. Benatar, M. 2006. A systematic revue of diagnostic studies in myasthenia gravis. *Neuromuscul. Disord.* 16:459-467.

52. Oh, S.J., Y. Hatanaka, S. Hemmi, A.M. Young, M.A. Scheufele, S.P. Nations, L. Liang, G.C. Claussen, and G.I. Wolfe. 2006. Repetitive nerve stimulation of facial muscles in MuSK antibody-positive myasthenia gravis. *Muscle Nerve* 33:500-504.

53. Howard, J.F., D.B. Sanders, and J.M. Massey. 1994. The electrodiagnosis of myasthenia gravis and the Lambert-Eaton myasthenic syndrome. *Neurol. Clin.* 12:305-330.

54. Sander, D.B., and E. V. Stålberg. 1996. AAEM Minimonograph # 25: Single-fiber electromyography. *Muscle Nerve* 19: 1069-1083.

55. Sanders, D.B. 2002. The clinical impact of single-fiber electromyography. *Muscle Nerve* 11: S15–S20.

56. Chan, K.H., D.H. Lachance, C.M. Harper, and V.A. Lennon. 2007. Frequency of seronegativity, in adult-acquired generalized myasthenia gravis. *Muscle Nerve* 36:651–658.

57. Limburg, P.C., H. The, E. Hummel-Tappel, and H.J.G.H. Oosterhuis. 1983. Anti-acetylcholine receptor antibodies in myasthenia gravis. Part 1. Relation to clinical parameters in 250 patients. *J. Neurol. Sci.* 58:357-370.

58. Hara, H., K. Hayachi, K. Ohta, N. Itoh, H. Niscitani, and M. Ohta. 1993. Detection and characterization of blocking-type anti-acetylcholine receptor antibodies in sera from patients with myasthenia gravis. *Clin. Chem.* 39:2053-2057.

59. Hoch, W., J. McConville, S. Helms, J. Newsom-Davis, A. Melms, and A. Vincent. 2001. Auto-antibodies to the receptor tyrosine kinase MuSK in patients with myasthenia gravis without acetylcholine receptor antibodies. *Nat. Med.* 7:365-368.

60. Wolfe, G.I., and A.J. Oh. 2008. Clinical phenotype of muscle-specific tyrosine kinase-antibody-positive myasthenia gravis. *Ann. N.Y. Acad Sci.* 1132:71-75.

61. Bartoccioni, E., F. Scuderi, G.M. Minicuci, M. Marino, F. Ciaraffa, and A. Evoli. 2006. Anti-MuSK antibodies: correlation with myasthenia gravis severity. *Neurology* 67:505-507.

62. Díaz-Manera. J., R. Rojas-García, E. Gallardo, C. Juárez, A. Martínez-Domeño, S. Martínez-Ramírez, J. Dalmau, R. Blesa, and I. Illa. 2007. Antibodies to AChR, MuSK and VGKC in a patient with myasthenia gravis and Morvan's syndrome. *Nat. Clin. Pract. Neurol.* 3:405-410.

63. Aarli, J.A., K. Stefansson, L.S. Marton, and R.L. Wollmann. 1990. Patients with myasthenia gravis and thymoma have in their sera IgG autoantibodies against titin. *Clin. Exp. Immunol.* 82:284-288.

64. Mygland, A., O.B. Tysnes, P. Volpe, J.A. Aarli, and N.E. Gilhus. 1992. Ryanodine receptor autoantibodies in myasthenia gravis patients with a thymoma. *Ann. Neurol.* 32:589-591.

65. Skeie, G.O., J.A. Aarli, and N.E. Gilhus. 2006 Titin and ryanodine receptor antibodies in myasthenia gravis. *Acta Neurol. Scand.* 113 (S183):19–23.

66. Batra, P., C. Jr. Herrmann, and D. Mulder. 1987. Mediastinal imaging in myasthenia gravis: correlation of chest radiography, CT, MR, and surgical findings. *Am. J. Roentgenol.* 148:515-519.

67. Sadohara, J., K. Fujimoto, N. L. Müller, S. Kato, S. Takamori , K. Ohkuma, H. Terasaki, and N. Hayabuchi. 2006. Thymic epithelial tumors: comparison of CT and MR imaging findings of low-risk thymomas, high-risk thymomas, and thymic carcinomas. *Eur. J. Radiol.* 60:70-79.

68. Chagnac, Y., M. Hadanin, and Y Goldhammer. 1985. Myasthenic crisis after intravenous administration of iodinated contrast agent. *Neurology* 35:1219-1220.

69. Vernino, S. 2007. Autoimmune and paraneoplastic channelopathies. *Neurotherapeutics* 4:305-314.

70. Sanders, D.B. 2003. Lambert-Eaton myasthenic syndrome. Diagnosis and treatment. *Ann. N.Y. Acad. Sci.* 998:500-508.

71. Engel, A.G., and S.M. Sine. 2005. Current understanding of congenital myasthenic syndromes. *Curr. Opin. Pharmacol.* 5:308-321.

72. Engel, A.G. 2007. The therapy of congenital myasthenic syndromes. *Neurotherapeutics* 4:252–257.

73. Gorson, K.C. 2005. Approach to neuro-muscular disorders in the intensive care unit. *Neurocrit. Care* 3:195-212.

74. Grattan-Smith, P.J., J.G. Morris, H.M. Johnston, C. Yannikas, R. Malik, R. Russel, and R.A. Ouvrier. 1997. Clinical and neurophysiological features of tick paralysis. *Brain* 120:1975-1987.

75. Yaguchi, H., A. Takei, S. Honma, I. Yamashita, S. Doi, and T. Hamada. 2007. Dropped head sign as the only symptom of myasthenia gravis. *Intern. Med.* 46:743-745.

76. Kastrup, A., H.-J. Gdynia, T. Nägele, and A. Riecker. 2008. Dropped-head syndrome due to steroid responsive focal myositis: a case report and review of the literature. *J. Neurol. Sci.* 267:162-165.

77. Roberts, L., and E. Byrne. 1994. Single-fiber EMG studies in chronic fatigue syndrome: a reappraisal. *J. Neurol.(Neurd.in the text) Neurosurg. Psychiatry* 57: 375-376.

78. Connolly, S., and C.J. Fowler. 1994. Single-fiber EMG studies in chronic fatigue syndrome: a reappraisal. *J. Neurol. (Neurd.in the text) Neurosurg. Psychiatry* 57: 1157.

79. Bohlega, S., F.M. Santorelli, M. Hirano, A. al-Jishi, K. Tanji, and S. Di Mauro. 1996. Multiple mitochondrial DNA deletions associated with autosomal recessive ophthalmoplegia and severe cardiomyopathy. *Neurology* 46:1329-1334.

80. Krendel, D.A., D.B. Sanders, and J.M. Massey. 1987. Single fiber electromyography in chronic progressive external ophthalmoplegia. *Muscle Nerve* 10:299-302.

81. Chakraborty, P.P., S.K. Mandal, S.R. Chodury, D. Bandyopadhyay, and R. Bhattacharjee. 2007. Mitochondrial myopathy associated with myasthenia gravis in a young man. *J. Clin. Neurosci.* 14:705-708.

82. Overell, J.R. and H.J. Willinson. Recent developments in Miller Fisher syndrome and related disorders. 2005. *Curr. Opin Neurol.* 18:562-566.

83. Ichikawa, H., Y. Kamiya, K. Susuki, M. Susuki, N. Yuli, and M. Kawamura. 2002. Unilateral oculomotor nerve palsy associated with anti-GQ1b IgG antibody. *Neurology* 59:957.

84. Bartalena, L., and M.L. Tanda. 2009. Clinical practice. Graves' ophthalmopathy. *N. Engl J. Med.* 360:994-1001.

85. Shams, P.N., A. Waldman, and G.Y. Plant. 2002. B cell lymphoma of the brain stem masquerading as myasthenia. *J. Neurol. Neurosurg. Psychiatry* 72: 271-273.

86. Akkaya, Ö.F., H. A.Şayn, A.Şenel, B. Ertas, K. Kinay, and M.K. Onar. 2005. Brain stem lesion mimicking myasthenia gravis. *Clin. Neurol. Neurosurg.* 107:246-248.

Pathogenic Mechanisms in Myasthenia Gravis

Erdem Tûzûn, MD & Angela Vincent, MBBS, MSc, FRCPath, FRCP, FMedSci.

1. INTRODUCTION

Myasthenia gravis (MG) is a relatively uncommon disease caused by dysfunction of the post-synaptic part of the nerve-muscle junction and consequent impairment in neuromuscular transmission, resulting in fluctuating muscle weakness and fatigability (1-3). The clinical features, diagnosis and lab investigation of MG (generalized and ocular forms) are discussed in detail in Chapter 1 and 3. In most cases, fluctuating muscle weakness and fatigability seen in MG is caused by autoantibodies specific for the nicotinic acetylcholine receptor (AChR) of the muscle, a ligand-gated ion channel which is located at the post-synaptic region of the neuromuscular junction (NMJ). The AChR binds acetylcholine (ACh), after its release from the motor nerve, and is essential for neuromuscular transmission. Around 20% MG patients with generalised muscle weakness do not have AChR-specific antibodies. Antibodies to a muscle specific kinase (MuSK) are involved in the pathogenesis of these MG patients (4,5). Today, we are aware of several myasthenic disorders other than MG, some also caused by autoimmunity against the pre-synaptic part of the NMJ (Lambert-Eaton myasthenic syndrome) (Chapter 11), and others by toxins/medications or congenital mutations of AChR or other NMJ proteins (Chapter 12). However, MG is not only the most common disorder of neuromuscular transmission but also the first identified antibody-mediated neurological disease and, therefore, has been the role model in unravelling the pathogenesis of many other central and peripheral autoimmune diseases. Here, we will first review the experimental findings leading to understanding of the autoimmune nature of MG and then discuss the immunological mechanisms of the disease with a special emphasis on some recent findings.

2. EVIDENCE FOR AUTOIMMUNE PATHOGENESIS

Neuromuscular transmission is achieved by release of ACh in packets or quanta from the presynaptic nerve terminal and the interaction of released ACh with the AChR on the postsynaptic membrane resulting in miniature endplate potentials. Earliest studies on MG pathogenesis demonstrated that muscle specimens from MG patients exhibit reduced miniature endplate potentials (6) and decreased postsynaptic binding sites for alpha-bungarotoxin (α-BTx) (7), a snake toxin that irreversibly binds to AChR. These observations strongly suggested that the neuromuscular defects in MG were caused by reduced numbers of AChRs, rather than as a result of reduced release of ACh as had been previously suggested.

Evidence supporting the autoimmune basis for MG pathogenesis started accumulating in the early 60s (1,8,9). The presence of other autoimmune disorders in patients and their families, increased risk of acquiring the disease in monozygotic twins and detection of thymic abnormalities suggested that MG could be an autoimmune disorder (see 8,9). Moreover, altered serum complement and immune complex levels, and development of MG in the neonates of myasthenic mothers (implicating induction of disease by passive transfer of antibodies from the mother) indicated an antibody-mediated pathogenesis (1,9-11).

Purification of AChR on neurotoxin columns in the 70s enabled induction of an MG-like disease (experimental autoimmune myasthenia gravis, EAMG) in rabbits and then rodents by AChR immunization, further corroborating the role of autoimmunity in MG. Following AChR immunisation, animals developed severe muscle weakness with loss of back curvature, lowered heads, spewed limbs and often dribbling. Notably, muscle weakness was reversible by anti-cholinesterases due to increased availability of the neurotransmitter acetylcholine (12). The initial immunisation experiments were followed by studies demonstrating that the neurophysiological and pathological aspects of EAMG also bore a resemblance to MG (see 13-15 for reviews). In the 70s, another line of evidence supporting immune pathogenesis emerged, as it was demonstrated that early-onset MG was associated with HLA alleles B8 and DR3 (eg. 16).

Rigorous research of the last few decades has shown that AChR loss in MG is the result of an autoimmune attack directed against the AChRs, or in some cases MuSK (see below), mediated principally by humoral immunity. Antibodies and the complement cascade are the most important constituents of this autoimmune attack, directly inducing pathological changes at the NMJ and disturbing neuromuscular transmission. In addition, the antibodies can directly block AChR function, or lead to down-regulation of surface AChRs. The thymus and T cells are essential ingredients in the development of MG not by inducing pathological changes but rather by establishing a robust immune response against the AChR (1-3).

3. HUMORAL IMMUNITY

Fundamental elements of humoral immunity causing the MG are serum antibodies directed against the NMJ antigens and complement factors. Antibodies will be reviewed in this chapter and the role of the complement system will be discussed in greater detail in a separate chapter. Around 80-90% of MG patients have pathogenic serum antibodies directed against the nicotinic AChR of the muscle (AChR-MG) (3). AChR-specific antibodies cannot be detected in about 10-20% of patients with MG and some of these patients have antibodies to another NMJ protein, muscle specific kinase (MuSK). From 0% to more than 40% of anti-AChR antibody negative MG patients have been reported to have anti-MuSK antibodies (3,5). Frequency of MuSK antibody positive MG (MuSK-MG) varies with geographical location, and is maximal at around 40 degrees north of the equator in the northern hemisphere (Vincent unpublished results). With the exception of very rare cases (17), MG patients display either AChR or MuSK-specific antibodies (5). The rest of the patients without either AChR- or MuSK antibodies make up the current "seronegative group" (SNMG), but over 60% of these patients have recently been shown to display low-affinity anti-AChR antibodies, placing them in the AChR-MG subgroup (18). Even taking this new finding into consideration, around 5% of MG patients still do not have a serological diagnosis.

3.1. AChR Antibodies

Anti-AChR antibodies are high affinity polyclonal IgGs. They generally bind to the extracellular domain of the receptor and react with different AChR epitopes, although a variable but generally high proportion of these are within the "main immunogenic region" which is found on each of the two α-subunits of the receptor (Figure 1). AChR-specific antibodies can be detected by radioimmunoprecipitation (RIA) of ^{125}I-α-BTx-labelled AChRs extracted from human muscle or from human muscle-like cell lines (19,20). Since the majority of the AChR-specific antibodies recognize the native conformation of the AChR, they usually cannot be detected by assays that involve recombinant or synthetic peptide fragments of the protein (21).

AChR-specific antibodies appear to possess great pathogenic significance in MG. Passive transfer of sera from AChR-MG patients or from AChR-immunised rodents to naïve rodents

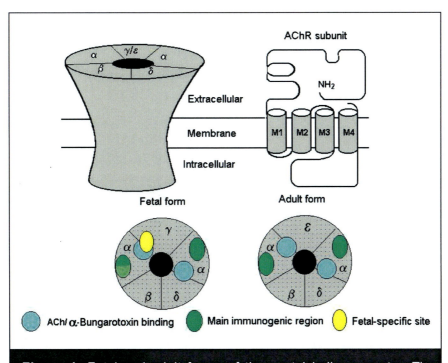

Figure 1: Fetal and adult forms of the acetylcholine receptor. The acetylcholine receptor (AChR) is a pentameric membrane protein. Each of the subunits comprises an extracellular domain, four transmembrane regions and a cytoplasmic domain. The receptor consists of $(\alpha)_2$, β, ε and δ subunits in the fetal form and $(\alpha)_2$, β, ε and δ subunits in the adult form..

cause muscle weakness and reduced AChR content at the NMJ, implying that antibodies rather than immune cells are primarily responsible from MG development (22). Moreover, AChR-MG patients significantly benefit from plasma exchange which clears antibodies, complements and other humoral immune factors from the circulation (23). One observation that initially raised questions about the pathogenicity of AChR-specific antibodies is that their levels do not correlate with the clinical severity of MG. This is probably due to the fact that MG patients have an array of antibodies differing widely in their pathogenicity, as well as the presence of host factors that modify the pathogenicity. For instance it may be that only part of the circulating AChR-specific antibodies are capable of binding critical epitopes on the AChR, that would change the AChR functions, and that the proportions of these antibodies vary from one patient to another, making it futile to compare anti-AChR levels between different MG patients (21). Nevertheless, within an individual patient, clinical severity of MG is reduced in correlation with a decrease in serum antibody levels (24).

AChR-specific antibodies are predominantly complement-fixing IgG1 and IgG3 isotypes (Table I). In both MG and EAMG, immunoglobulin, complement and MAC deposits are detected at the NMJs and they co-localise with AChRs that are visualised by α-BTx (25,26). Moreover, both inborn deficiencies of the complement factors and inhibition of the complement cascade significantly reduce the incidence and severity of muscle weakness in experimental animals with EAMG (27,28). These findings suggest that AChR antibodies cause muscle weakness primarily by activating the complement cascade, resulting in the formation of MACs which lyse the postsynaptic membrane and thus reduce AChR numbers. Alternatively, some antibodies crosslink AChRs, increase their endocytosis and degradation and thus decrease the number of available AChRs and others simply prevent ACh binding to AChR (29,30). These two latter mechanisms are probably less important than the complement-associated mechanism in most patients, but individuals may.well differ in the relative contributions of the three mechanisms.

3.2. SNMG

It is now clear that patients who do not have typical AChR antibodies detected by the RIA ("seronegative" MG) are heterogeneous in nature. Some of these patients are now known to have MuSK-specific antibodies, and these patients tend to have somewhat different clinical features, although they respond well to plasma exchange indicating that they do have an antibody-mediated disease. By contrast, those that are negative for both AChR and MuSK antibodies (SNMG patients) are largely clinically and pathophysiologically similar to patients with AChR antibodies. Serum samples of SNMG patients induce transmission defects in the NMJ, when injected into mice, and mothers with SNMG can have babies with neonatal myasthenia (4,31-33). In vitro studies showed that plasma/serum samples of SNMG patients inhibit AChR currents in a manner very similar to that observed with a monoclonal anti-AChR antibody (34). Many of these patients exhibit reduced NMJ AChR numbers (35) and thymic pathologies (36) that are similar to those of AChR-MG patients. All of these observations suggested that they may have AChR antibodies that cannot be detected by conventional assays. A recent study identified that many patients who do not display AChR- or MuSK-specific antibodies by routine RIAs, have low affinity anti-AChR antibodies that can only be detected by a cell-based assay. This assay utilises human embryonic kidney (HEK 293) cells expressing AChR molecules that are clustered by co-transfected rapsyn (18).

The "low affinity" AChR antibodies are similar to those detected by RIA. The AChR antibodies are IgG1 and capable of activating the complement cascade and inducing complement deposition on binding to clusters of AChRs on HEK-293 cells. All these findings suggest that antibody-mediated disease mechanisms are also in play in these MG forms (18). Nevertheless, other electrophysiological studies suggest that there are also non-IgG factor(s) in sera of SNMG patients that affect AChR functions by binding to a non-AChR muscle receptor and increasing phosphorylation (37). The identity of this putative target is not known.

3.3. MuSK antibodies

Among all MG forms, MuSK-MG patients probably make up the most distinct entity by means of antibody type and pathogenicity. MuSK knock-out mice display poorly structured NMJs and die shortly after birth confirming that MuSK is an essential mediator of agrin-dependent AChR clustering during development (38). Congenital myasthenic syndrome patients with MuSK mutations show reduced AChR and MuSK numbers at the NMJ (39), suggesting that even in adult life, MuSK plays an important role in maintaining the high density of AChRs at the NMJ. This was best shown by inhibition of MuSK in a mouse model by RNA interference that resulted in declustering of the AChR and disruption of the NMJs. Interestingly, this took more than two weeks, but demonstrated that the acquired loss of MuSK functions in the adult muscle, by antibody-mediated attack, might also impair the neuromuscular transmission (40).

MuSK-MG patients show a very good response to plasma exchange (41) suggesting that MuSK-MG is an antibody mediated disorder. In in vitro studies, MuSK antibody positive sera reduced the number of AChR clusters of myotubes but showed no substantial effect on surface AChR numbers or mRNA expression of AChR subunits (42). However, in vivo, MuSK-specific antibodies do not appear to be associated with reduced AChR numbers at the NMJ. In a single study examining AChR loss at the end-plates of biceps brachii biopsies from MG patients, AChR-MG patients showed great reduction of NMJ AChR numbers as expected, whereas no significant AChR reduction was observed in MuSK-MG patients (34).

Similarly, in contrast with AChR-specific antibodies, MuSK-specific antibodies do not appear to primarily exert their pathogenicity via complement activation. A previous report on muscle pathology showed NMJ complement deposition only in a small fraction of MuSK-MG patients (34). Moreover, a muscle biopsy specimen from a patient with MuSK-specific antibodies was reported to show reduced miniature endplate potentials despite the absence of complement deposition or AChR loss (43). In line with these findings, the dominant MuSK-antibody isotype in MuSK-MG is the non-complement fixing IgG4 (44) (Table I). Nevertheless, some MuSK-MG patients do have complement activating IgG1 antibodies that bind MuSK molecules expressed at high density by HEK-293 cells and subsequently activate the complement cascade resulting in C3b deposition on the cells (18). It is possible that complement activation might not be operational in vivo since NMJs express MuSK at a relatively low density. The current data suggest that complement-mediated NMJ destruction is a

Table I. Human IgG subclasses.

Name	Complement activation	Mouse equivalent
IgG1, IgG3	High	IgG2a, IgG2b
IgG2	Partial	IgG3
IgG4	Minimal	IgG1

possible pathogenic mechanism but may occur selectively in those muscles that express higher concentrations of MuSK at the NMJ. In other respects, there is no clear evidence for how the antibodies cause a defect in neuromuscular transmission.

MuSK antibodies also appear to inhibit the function of MuSK on cultured cells. When MuSK antibody positive plasmas are applied to MuSK expressing mouse muscle cells, they inhibit agrin-induced AChR clustering resulting in reduced stability of the post-synaptic membrane architecture (45). Also, in mice and rabbits, MuSK immunisation results in MuSK-specific antibody production, which is associated with mild clinical weakness, altered neuromuscular junction morphology and reduced miniature end-plate potentials (46,47). These findings suggest that MuSK antibodies might induce clinical muscle weakness in MG patients by directly harming the muscle fibers and/or disordering the AChR distribution of the post-synaptic NMJ.

One additional mechanism might be a direct effect of MuSK IgG on muscle fibers. Some MuSK antibody positive patients exhibit particularly severe facial and tongue muscle atrophy that is difficult to treat with immunosuppressive therapies (48,49). Electromyography and MRI studies suggest that this atrophy might be caused by a myopathic process (50,51). Notably, anti-MuSK IgGs enhance the expression of at least two proteins that are upregulated in muscles undergoing atrophy (striated muscle RING-finger protein-1 (MURF-1) and atrogin) in cultured muscle cells (52,53). Likewise, injection of anti-MuSK IgGs into mice enhances MURF-1 expression in facial muscles that are frequently affected in MuSK-MG but not in the leg muscles that are less affected (52). More studies are required to reproduce these findings and to explore further how MuSK-specific antibodies may induce muscle atrophy.

3.4. Antibodies in Ocular MG

In ocular MG, muscle weakness is restricted to the extraocular muscles. Only 40-60% of ocular MG patients display high affinity AChR antibodies and around 30% of the remaining patients display low affinity AChR antibodies (2,18). Whether ocular MG patients have MuSK antibodies is open to debate. Most MG patients present with purely ocular symptoms at the first manifestation of the disease but electromyography and muscle biopsy studies indicate that other muscles are also affected. In fact, most of these patients develop generalised MG in the following 2 years. A patient is generally considered as ocular MG if the symptoms are confined to the ocular muscles for longer than 2 years, because the risk of development of generalised muscle weakness after that period is very low. Whereas MuSK positive patients may initially present with pure ocular involvement, as do most MG patients, they usually develop generalised muscle weakness within months (45,54). Reported ocular MG patients with MuSK-specific antibodies have been followed for less than 2 years (55) and MuSK-specific antibodies have only been reported in a single patient in association with persistent ocular MG (56).

3.5. Antibodies to Fetal AChRs

The pentameric AChR exists in two forms; $\alpha_2\beta\gamma\delta$ subunits in fetal or denervated muscle and $\alpha_2\beta\gamma\delta\varepsilon$ in adult muscle (1) (Figure 1). Newborns of the mothers with MG may suffer from a clinical condition called neonatal myasthenia (11). This condition is caused by placental passive transfer of AChR-specific antibodies that are mostly directed against the α-subunits. Alternatively, some mothers with MG can give birth to babies with arthrogryposis multiplex congenita (AMC) as well as neonatal MG, characterized with fetal muscle paralysis and severe bone and joint deformities often causing death (57). These women have antibodies mainly directed against the fetal isoform of the AChR that inhibit its functions in vitro (58). When these serum antibodies are injected into pregnant mice, the offsprings are born with AMC-like features such as oddly fixed joints, scoliosis and cranial defects (59). A few non-myasthenic mothers, who have given birth to healthy babies or babies with AMC, develop MG later, either during a pregnancy or afterwards. In contrast with the antibodies of other MG patients, these mothers' AChR antibodies show higher reactivity with fetal AChR relative to adult AChR, suggesting that fetal AChR might be inducing MG in these mothers (60). Rarely, mothers of some neonates with AMC may display no clinical signs or symptoms of MG but still have antibodies to the fetal isoform of the AChR. They are asymptomatic presumably because their fetal AChR antibodies do not show an appreciable reaction with the adult isoform of the AChR (60,61). These findings suggest that all mothers who have given birth to AMC neonates in the past, or whose fetuses display reduced or lost movements during gestation, should be checked for AChR antibodies, whether they have MG or not.

4. CELLULAR IMMUNITY

4.1. T cells

Muscle biopsy specimens of MG patients exhibit very little or no cellular infiltration at the NMJ, and in general, pathological alterations in MG are restricted to the NMJs. In MG, NMJs look elongated and the postsynaptic membrane that contains the AChRs is more simplified and shorter than in a healthy NMJ. Otherwise, muscle fibers of MG patients look fairly unaffected (26). Likewise, neurophysiological studies cannot detect any signs of myopathy in the vast majority of MG patients. Therefore, in MG, T cells do not appear to exert a direct harmful effect on the muscle fibers, as they do in polymyositis, for instance.

Nevertheless, in autoimmune disorders, T cells are important in the presentation of self antigens to B cells via HLA and costimulatory molecules, and consequent production of the high affinity autoantibodies (this probably applies also to the antibodies termed "low affinity" since they are IgG1 and clearly able to bind specifically to their membrane target (18)). T cells also aid in establishing a robust immune response against antigens by releasing several proinflammatory cytokines and other soluble factors (62). EAMG studies have shown that T helper cells, in particular, play a vital role in MG pathogenesis by presenting AChR fragments to B cells and thus instigating high affinity AChR-specific antibody production. Loss of T cell functions causes a substantial reduction in the incidence of EAMG induced by AChR immunization, demonstrating the importance of T cells in priming B cells against AChR. Likewise, deficiency of cytokines released by T cells is associated with decreased EAMG incidence and severity (13-15).

In line with the experimental findings, peripheral blood lymphocytes of MG patients show enhanced proliferation and cytokine production in the presence of the whole AChR molecule (native conformation) or its fragments (synthetic peptides), indicating that these cells have been formerly primed with the AChR molecule. Lymphocytes show variable proliferation responses to different AChR peptides and these responses are restricted by MHC class II molecules (63,64). Whether T cells play an equally important role in MuSK-MG remains to be investigated.

Table II. Subgroups of myasthenia gravis and the associated antibodies.

	Early-onset	Late-onset	Thymoma	MuSK (+)	Seronegative	Ocular
Sex ratio	F>M	M>F	M=F	F>M	F>M	M>F
Age at onset	<40 years	>40 years	Any	Any	Any	Any
AChR antibody	Positive	Positive	Positive	Negative, very rarely positive	Negative or low-affinity antibodies	~50% high, %30 low affinity
Thymic pathology	Hyperplasia	Normal or atrophy	Thymoma	Atrophy, hyperplasia uncommon	Hyperplasia in some	Minimal but not often available
Titin antibody	Negative	Often positive	Usually positive	Negative	Negative	Negative
MuSK antibody	Negative	Negative	Negative	Positive	Negative	Negative

4.2. Thymus

The aetiology of MG is still largely unknown and presumably different causative factors are in operation for different clinical forms of the disease. Currently, the only well-known aetiological factors for MG are thymic abnormalities. MG patients may have thymoma (30–60% of thymoma patients have MG and about 10% of MG patients have thymoma), thymic hyperplasia, an atrophic thymus or a normal thymus (3,8). Earliest reports of thymic changes and thymectomy-based treatment go back to early 20th century (65). A classification of different forms of MG (Table II) based on thymic pathology, age at onset and serum antibodies further epitomize the fact that MG is not a single entity and thymus plays an important role in MG pathogenesis. See chapter 7 and 8 for an in depth review on thymic pathology seen in MG.

Thymic hyperplasia is frequently observed in younger female patients (40 years-old), most of whom have AChR-specific serum antibodies. About 60% of these early-onset patients are HLA-B8 and DR3 positive (16). In this group of patients, the thymus shows lymphocytic infiltrates with germinal centres, B cells and T cells, often in close proximity to thymic myoid cells (66). AChR-specific T cells can be cloned from the thymus, thymic lymphocytes produce AChR-specific antibodies, and serum AChR antibody levels fall following thymectomy (67-69). While the epithelial and myoid cells of both normal and myasthenic thymi express AChR, thymi of normal individuals do not exhibit increased germinal centres or AChR antibody production (70). AChR molecules expressed by the thymic cells have been proposed to play a central role in the breakdown of tolerance to NMJ and sensitisation of the immune cells to AChR. The presence of complement deposits on epithelial and myoid cells of thymus obtained from both AChR-MG and SNMG patients at an early stage of disease substantiates this hypothesis (71). This finding also confirms that similar pathogenic mechanisms are involved in AChR-MG and patients with low affinity AChR antibodies (18,71).

Thymoma patients (around 10% of MG patients) are older (usually 40-60 ages), do not show gender predominance, benefit much less from thymectomy and almost always have AChR-specific antibodies. There are no clear HLA associations in this form (72). While MG-associated thymomas are usually lymphoepithelial and benign in nature, in about 10% of the patients, mediastinal or pleural metastases may occur. Metastases outside the chest cavity are extremely rare (73).

Thymomas display infiltrating CD4+ and CD8+ T cells (74,75) and only express individual AChR subunits and not the whole AChR in its native conformation (76). In this form of MG, the immune response to AChR appears to be primarily conveyed by peripheral lymphoid tissues rather than the thymus (77). Recently, it has been shown that thymoma tissue is capable of generating mature CD4+ and CD8+ T cells. Presumably, AChR epitopes expressed by thymic epithelial cells activate T cells, which are then exported from the thymus and initiate an antibody response to AChRs by activating B cells in the periphery. Since these cells have long life spans, they can persist after removal of the thymoma and continue inducing autoantibody production. They also rapidly increase in number following the recurrence of the tumor (74).

The majority of MG patients with thymoma have high affinity neutralizing antibodies to IFN-α and IL-12, while antibodies to other cytokines are very rarely detected. Levels of these two anti-cytokine antibodies correlate with the clinical severity of MG and tend to show a striking increase with the recurrence of the tumor. Also, cultured thymoma cells spontaneously produce anti-IFN-α and IL-12 antibodies without requiring a B cell activator. The presence of these antibodies suggests that there are plasma cells present in the thymoma that secrete IFN-α and IL-12. Since these cytokines favor Th1 type T cell activation, thymoma cells might be aiding in the activation of immune cells and thus support AChR antibody production (78,79).

A particularly important group are those who develop MG later in life. Late onset MG (>40 years old) shows a slight male predominance and the thymus is usually not enlarged or is atrophic (probably normal for age). There is an HLA association with B7 and DR2 (80). Antibodies to titin, ryanodin and other intracellular striated muscle antigens (e.g. actin, α-actinin, myosin and connectin) are detected in MG patients with thymoma and late-onset MG. Titin antibodies are present in 80% of patients with thymoma and they can be used as a thymoma marker in MG patients (81). Whether these antibodies play a significant pathogenic role in MG pathogenesis remain to be elucidated.

Studies on thymus tissue taken at thymectomy have shown that pathological features of thymi from AChR-MG and SNMG patients show substantially similar features that differ from those of MuSK-MG patients. Seronegative patients often present with thymic hyperplasia just as AChR-MG patients. Thymus specimens of SNMG patients exhibit frequent lymphocytic infiltrates with germinal centres but in lesser amounts than those of AChR-MG patients (82,83).

Alternatively, MG patients with MuSK-specific antibodies often have thymic atrophy (normally involuted thymus) or a normal thymus. Thymi of MuSK-MG patients usually lack germinal centres or lymphocytic infiltrates that are frequently observed in AChR-MG patients but thymic hyperplasia can occasionally be observed (35). Thymoma has only been demonstrated once in a MuSK-MG patient (84) and while MuSK is expressed by both myoid and epithelial cells of the thymus (85), there is no report on the expression of MuSK by thymomas. In contrast with other forms of generalised MG, complement deposits are rarely observed in thymi of MuSK-MG patients (71,86). In general, the role of thymus is much less understood in MuSK-MG pathogenesis and thymus may not be directly involved in the development of anti-MuSK autoimmunity.

5. CONCLUSION

Meticulous work on MG over the past 40 years have led to elucidation of the immunopathogenic mechanisms of an antibody-mediated autoimmune disease. While the earliest studies have established the fundamental pathological features and main players of the disease, the experimental and clinical findings of the last decade have shed light on several novel aspects of autoimmunity in MG and uncovered some of the complexity of this disease. Most importantly, MuSK-MG have emerged as a distinct form of MG, differing somewhat in clinical and pathophysiological features from AChR-MG and SNMG. Nevertheless, the immunopathogenic features of MuSK-MG are still not clearly understood and further studies are required to delineate the exact pathogenic mechanisms by which serum antibodies and thymus are involved in MuSK-MG. Alternatively, the recent discovery of low-affinity anti-AChR antibodies and demonstration of thymic lymphocytic infiltrates and increased germinal centres in previously "SNMG" patients suggest that AChR-MG and SNMG are similar and justify thymectomy in the mainstream treatment of SNMG. Important work that remains to be done is to define the target antigens in the remaining generalised or purely ocular SNMG patients, to elucidate better the immunopathogenic mechanisms that lead to muscle weakness in MuSK-MG, and to find ways by which it can be interrupted.

REFERENCES

1. Vincent, A. 2002. Unravelling the pathogenesis of myasthenia gravis. *Nat. Rev. Immunol.* 2:797-804.

2. Vincent, A., J. Palace, and D. Hilton-Jones. 2001. Myasthenia gravis. *Lancet.* 357:2122-2128.

3. Vincent, A., and M.I. Leite. 2005. Neuromuscular junction autoimmune disease: muscle specific kinase antibodies and treatments for myasthenia gravis. *Curr. Opin. Neurol.* 18:519-525.

4. Vincent, A., J. McConville, M.E. Farrugia, J. Bowen, P. Plested, T. Tang, A. Evoli, I. Matthews, G. Sims, P. Dalton, L. Jacobson, A. Polizzi, F. Blaes, B. Lang, D. Beeson, N. Willcox, J. Newsom-Davis, and W. Hoch. 2003. Antibodies in myasthenia gravis and related disorders. *Ann. N. Y. Acad. Sci.* 998:324-335.

5. Vincent, A., M.I. Leite, M.E. Farrugia, S. Jacob, S. Viegas, H. Shiraishi, O. Benveniste, B.P. Morgan, D. Hilton-Jones, J. Newsom-Davis, D. Beeson, and N. Willcox. 2008. Myasthenia gravis seronegative for acetylcholine receptor antibodies. *Ann. N. Y. Acad. Sci.* 1132:84-92.

6. Elmqvist, D., W.W. Hofmann, J. Kugelberg, and D.M. Quastel. 1964. An electrophysiological Investigation of neuromuscular transmission in myasthenia gravis. *J. Physiol.* 174:417-434.

7. Fambrough, D.M., D.B. Drachman, and S Satyamurti. 1973. Neuromuscular junction in myasthenia gravis: decreased acetylcholine receptors. *Science.* 182:293-295.

8. Oosterhuis, H.J. 1989. The natural course of myasthenia gravis: a long term follow up study. *J. Neurol. Neurosurg. Psychiatry.* 52:1121-1127.

9. Grob, D. 1999. Natural history of myasthenia gravis. In: Engel AG, ed. Myasthenia gravis and myasthenic disorders. Oxford: Oxford University Press. Contemporary Neurology Series: 131–145.

10. Nastuk, W.L., O.J. Plescia, and K.E. Osserman. 1960. Changes in serum complement activity in patients with myasthenia gravis. *Proc. Soc. Exp. Biol. Med.* 105:177-184.

11. Gans, B., and D.H. Forsdick. 1953. Neonatal myasthenia gravis; report of a case. *Br. Med. J.* 1:314-316.

12. Patrick, J., and J. Lindstrom. 1973. Autoimmune response to acetylcholine receptor. *Science.* 180:871-872.

13. Yang, H., E. Goluszko, C. David, D.K. Okita, B. Conti-Fine, T.S. Chan, M.A. Poussin, and P. Christadoss. 2002. Mapping myasthenia gravis-associated T cell epitopes on human acetylcholine receptors in HLA transgenic mice. *J. Clin. Invest.* 109:1111-1120.

14. Link, H., and B.G. Xiao. 2001. Rat models as tool to develop new immunotherapies. *Immunol. Rev.* 184:117-128.

15. Christadoss, P., M. Poussin, and C. Deng. 2000. Animal models of myasthenia gravis. *Clin. Immunol.* 94:75-87.

16. Compston, D.A., A. Vincent, J. Newsom-Davis, and J.R. Batchelor. 1980. Clinical, pathological, HLA antigen and immunological evidence for disease heterogeneity in myasthenia gravis. *Brain.* 103:579-601.

17. Díaz-Manera, J., R. Rojas-García, E. Gallardo, C. Juárez, A. Martínez-Domeño, S. Martínez-Ramírez, J. Dalmau, R. Blesa, and I. Illa. 2007. Antibodies to AChR, MuSK and VGKC in a patient with myasthenia gravis and Morvan's syndrome. *Nat. Clin. Pract. Neurol.* 3:405-410.

18. Leite, M.I., S. Jacob, S. Viegas, J. Cossins, L. Clover, B.P. Morgan, D. Beeson, N. Willcox, and A. Vincent. 2008. IgG1 antibodies to acetylcholine receptors in 'seronegative' myasthenia gravis. *Brain.* 131:1940-1952.

19. Lindstrom, J.M., M.E. Seybold, V.A. Lennon, S. Whittingham, and D.D. Duane. 1976. Antibody to acetylcholine receptor in myasthenia gravis. Prevalence, clinical correlates, and diagnostic value. *Neurology.* 26:1054-1059.

20. Beeson, D., L. Jacobson, J. Newsom-Davis, and A. Vincent. 1996. A transfected human muscle cell line expressing the adult subtype of the human muscle acetylcholine receptor for diagnostic assays in myasthenia gravis. *Neurology.* 47:1552-1555.

21. Tzartos, S.J., T. Barkas, M.T. Cung, A. Mamalaki, M. Marraud, P. Orlewski, D. Papanastasiou, C. Sakarellos, M. Sakarellos-Daitsiotis, P. Tsantili, and V. Tsikaris. 1998. Anatomy of the antigenic structure of a large membrane autoantigen, the muscle-type nicotinic acetylcholine receptor. *Immunol. Rev.* 163:89-120.

22. Toyka, K.V., D.B. Brachman, A. Pestronk, and I. Kao. 1975. Myasthenia gravis: passive transfer from man to mouse. *Science.* 190:397-399.

23. Pinching, A.J, and D.K. Peters. 1976. Remission of myasthenia gravis following plasma-exchange. *Lancet.* 2:1373-1376.

24. Newsom-Davis, J., A.J. Pinching, A. Vincent, and S.G. Wilson. 1978. Function of circulating antibody to acetylcholine receptor in myasthenia gravis: investigation by plasma exchange. *Neurology.* 28:266-272.

25. Sahashi, K., A.G. Engel, E.H. Lambert, and F.M. Howard, Jr. 1980. Ultrastructural localization of the terminal and lytic ninth complement component (C9) at the motor end-plate in myasthenia gravis. *J. Neuropathol. Exp. Neurol.* 39:160-172.

26. Engel, A.G., E.H. Lambert, and F.M. Howard. 1977. Immune complexes (IgG and C3) at the motor end-plate in myasthenia gravis: ultrastructural and light microscopic localization and electrophysiologic correlations. *Mayo Clin. Proc.* 52:267-280.

27. Tüzün, E., B.G. Scott, E. Goluszko, S. Higgs, and P. Christadoss. 2003. Genetic evidence for involvement of classical complement pathway in induction of experimental autoimmune myasthenia gravis. *J. Immunol.* 171:3847-3854.

28. Soltys, J., L.L. Kusner, A. Young, C. Richmonds, D. Hatala, B. Gong, V. Shanmugavel, and H.J. Kaminski. 2009. Novel complement inhibitor limits severity of experimentally myasthenia gravis. *Ann. Neurol.* 65:67-75.

29. Tzartos, S.J., M.E. Seybold, and J.M. Lindstrom. 1982. Specificities of antibodies to acetylcholine receptors in sera from myasthenia gravis patients measured by monoclonal antibodies. *Proc. Natl. Acad. Sci. U S A.* 79:188-192.

30. Drachman, D.B., C.W. Angus, R.N. Adams, J.D. Michelson, and G.J. Hoffman. 1978. Myasthenic antibodies cross-link acetylcholine receptors to accelerate degradation. *N. Engl. J. Med.* 298:1116-1122.

31. Evoli, A., A.P. Batocchi, M. Lo Monaco, S. Servidei, L. Padua, L. Majolini, and P. Tonali. 1996. Clinical heterogeneity of seronegative myasthenia gravis. *Neuromuscul. Disord.* 6:155-161.

32. Burges, J., D.W. Wray, S. Pizzighella, Z. Hall, and A. Vincent. 1990. A myasthenia gravis plasma immunoglobulin reduces miniature endplate potentials at human endplates in vitro. *Muscle Nerve.* 13:407-413.

33. Mier, A.K., and C.W. Havard. 1985. Diaphragmatic myasthenia in mother and child. *Postgrad. Med. J.* 61:725-727.

34. Spreadbury, I., U. Kishore, D. Beeson, and A. Vincent. 2005. Inhibition of acetylcholine receptor function by seronegative myasthenia gravis non-IgG factor correlates with desensitisation. *J. Neuroimmunol.* 162:149-156.

35. Shiraishi, H., M. Motomura, T. Yoshimura, T. Fukudome, T. Fukuda, Y. Nakao, M. Tsujihata, A. Vincent, and K. Eguchi. 2005. Acetylcholine receptors loss and postsynaptic damage in MuSK antibody-positive myasthenia gravis. *Ann. Neurol.* 57:289-293.

36. Lauriola, L., F. Ranelletti, N. Maggiano, M. Guerriero, C. Punzi, F. Marsili, E. Bartoccioni, and A. Evoli. 2005. Thymus changes in anti-MuSK-positive and –negative myasthenia gravis. *Neurology.* 64:536-538.

37. Plested, C.P., T. Tang, I. Spreadbury, E.T. Littleton, U. Kishore, and A. Vincent. 2002. AChR phosphorylation and indirect inhibition of AChR function in seronegative MG. *Neurology.* 59:1682-1688.

38. DeChiara, T.M., D.C. Bowen, D.M. Valenzuela, M.V. Simmons, W.T. Poueymirou, S. Thomas, E. Kinetz, D.L. Compton, E. Rojas, J.S. Park, C. Smith, P.S. DiStefano, D.J. Glass, S.J. Burden, and G.D. Yancopoulos. 1996. The receptor tyrosine kinase MuSK is required for neuromuscular junction formation in vivo. *Cell.* 85:501-512.

39. Chevessier, F., B. Faraut, A. Ravel-Chapuis, P. Richard, K. Gaudon, S. Bauché, C. Prioleau, R. Herbst, E. Goillot, C. Ioos, J.P. Azulay, S. Attarian, J.P. Leroy, E. Fournier, C. Legay, L. Schaeffer, J. Koenig, M. Fardeau, B. Eymard, J. Pouget, and D. Hantaï. 2004. MUSK, a new target for mutations causing congenital myasthenic syndrome. *Hum. Mol. Genet.* 13:3229-3240.

40. Kong, X.C., P. Barzaghi, and M.A. Ruegg. 2004. Inhibition of synapse assembly in mammalian muscle in vivo by RNA interference. *EMBO Rep.* 5:183-188.

41. Evoli, A., M.R. Bianchi, R. Riso, G.M. Minicuci, A.P. Batocchi, S. Servidei, F. Scuderi, and E. Bartoccioni. 2008. Response to therapy in myasthenia gravis with anti-MuSK antibodies. *Ann. N. Y. Acad. Sci.* 1132:76-83.

42. Farrugia, M.E., D.M. Bonifati, L. Clover, J. Cossins, D. Beeson, and A. Vincent. 2007. Effect of sera from AChR-antibody negative myasthenia gravis patients on AChR and MuSK in cell cultures. J. Neuroimmunol. 185:136-144.

43. Selcen, D., Fukuda, T., Shen, X.M., and A.G. Engel. 2004. Are MuSK antibodies the primary cause of myasthenic symptoms? *Neurology.* 62:1945-1950.

44. McConville, J., M.E. Farrugia, D. Beeson, U. Kishore, R. Metcalfe, J. Newsom-Davis, and A. Vincent. 2004. Detection and characterization of MuSK antibodies in seronegative myasthenia gravis. *Ann. Neurol.* 55:580-584.

45. Hoch, W., J. McConville, S. Helms, J. Newsom-Davis, A. Melms, and A. Vincent. 2001. Auto-antibodies to the receptor tyrosine kinase MuSK in patients with myasthenia gravis without acetylcholine receptor antibodies. *Nat. Med.* 7:365-368.

46. Jha, S., K. Xu, T. Maruta, M. Oshima, D.R. Mosier, M.Z. Atassi, and W. Hoch. 2006. Myasthenia gravis induced in mice by immunization with the recombinant extracellular domain of rat muscle-specific kinase (MuSK). *J. Neuroimmunol.* 175:107-117.

47. Shigemoto, K., S. Kubo, N. Maruyama, N. Hato, H. Yamada, C. Jie, N. Kobayashi, K. Mominoki, Y. Abe, N. Ueda, and S. Matsuda. 2006. Induction of myasthenia by immunization against muscle-specific kinase. *J. Clin. Invest.* 116:1016-1024.

48. Sanders, D.B., K. El-Salem, J.M. Massey, J. McConville, and A. Vincent. 2003. Clinical aspects of MuSK antibody positive seronegative MG. *Neurology.* 60:1978-1980.

49. Evoli, A., P.A. Tonali, L. Padua, M.L. Monaco, F. Scuderi, A.P. Batocchi, M. Marino, and E. Bartoccioni. 2003. Clinical correlates with anti-MuSK antibodies in generalized seronegative myasthenia gravis. *Brain.* 126:2304-2311.

50. Farrugia, M.E., M.D. Robson, L. Clover, P. Anslow, J. Newsom-Davis, R. Kennett, D. Hilton-Jones, P.M. Matthews, and A. Vincent. 2006. MRI and clinical studies of facial and bulbar muscle involvement in MuSK antibody-associated myasthenia gravis. *Brain.* 129:1481-1492.

51. Farrugia, M.E., R.P. Kennett, D. Hilton-Jones, J. Newsom-Davis, and A. Vincent. 2007. Quantitative EMG of facial muscles in myasthenia patients with MuSK antibodies. *Clin. Neurophysiol.* 118:269-277.

52. Benveniste, O., L. Jacobson, M.E. Farrugia, L. Clover, and A. Vincent. 2005. MuSK antibody positive myasthenia gravis plasma modifies MURF-1 expression in C2C12 cultures and mouse muscle in vivo. *J. Neuroimmunol.* 170:41-48.

53. Boneva, N., M. Frenkian-Cuvelier, J. Bidault, T. Brenner, and S. Berrih-Aknin. 2006. Major pathogenic effects of anti-MuSK antibodies in myasthenia gravis. *J. Neuroimmunol.* 177:119-131.

54. Zhou, L., J. McConville, V. Chaudhry, R.N. Adams, R.L. Skolasky, A. Vincent, and D.B. Drachman. 2004. Clinical comparison of muscle-specific tyrosine kinase (MuSK) antibody-positive and -negative myasthenic patients. *Muscle Nerve.* 30:55-60.

55. Caress, J.B., C.H. Hunt, and S.D. Batish. 2005. Anti-MuSK myasthenia gravis presenting with purely ocular findings. *Arch. Neurol.* 62:1002-1003.

56. Hanisch, F., K. Eger, and S. Zierz. 2006. MuSK-antibody positive pure ocular myasthenia gravis. *J. Neurol.* 253:659-660.

57. Vincent, A., C. Newland, L. Brueton, D. Beeson, S. Riemersma, S.M. Huson, and J. Newsom-Davis. 1995. Arthrogryposis multiplex congenita with maternal autoantibodies specific for a fetal antigen. *Lancet.* 346:24-25.

58. Riemersma, S., A. Vincent, D. Beeson, C. Newland, S. Hawke, B. Vernet-der Garabedian, B. Eymard, and J. Newsom-Davis. 1996. Association of arthrogryposis multiplex congenita with maternal antibodies inhibiting fetal acetylcholine receptor function. *J. Clin. Invest.* 98:2358-2363.

59. Jacobson, L., A. Polizzi, G. Morriss-Kay, and A. Vincent. 1999. Plasma from human mothers of fetuses with severe arthrogryposis multiplex congenita causes deformities in mice. *J. Clin. Invest.* 103:1031-1038.

60. Matthews, I., G. Sims, S. Ledwidge, D. Stott, D. Beeson, N. Willcox, and A. Vincent. 2002. Antibodies to acetylcholine receptor in parous women with myasthenia: evidence for immunization by fetal antigen. *Lab. Invest.* 82:1407-1417.

61. Brueton, L.A., S.M. Huson, P.M. Cox, I. Shirley, E.M. Thompson, P.R. Barnes, J. Price, J. Newsom-Davis, and A. Vincent. 2000. Asymptomatic maternal myasthenia as a cause of the Pena-Shokeir phenotype. *Am. J. Med. Genet.* 92:1-6.

62. Male, D., J. Brostoff, D.B. Roth, and I. Roitt. 2006. Immunology, 7th Edition. Mosby Publishing.

63. Link, H., O. Olsson, J. Sun, W.Z. Wang, G. Andersson, H.P. Ekre, T. Brenner, O. Abramsky, and T. Olsson. 1991. Acetylcholine receptor-reactive T and B cells in myasthenia gravis and controls. *J. Clin. Invest.* 87:2191-2196.

64. Hawke, S., H. Matsuo, M. Nicolle, G. Malcherek, A. Melms, and N. Willcox. 1996. Autoimmune T cells in myasthenia gravis: heterogeneity and potential for specific immunotargeting. *Immunol. Today.* 17:307-311.

65. Buzzard, E.F. 1905. The clinical history and postmortem examination of five cases of myasthenia gravis. *Brain.* 28:438–483.

66. Alpert, L.I., A. Papatestas, A. Kark, R.S. Osserman, and K. Osserman. 1971. A histologic reappraisal of the thymus in myasthenia gravis. A correlative study of thymic pathology and response to thymectomy. *Arch. Pathol.* 91:55-61.

67. Melms, A., B.C. Schalke, T. Kirchner, H.K. Müller-Hermelink, E. Albert, and H. Wekerle. 1988. Thymus in myasthenia gravis. Isolation of T-lymphocyte lines specific for the nicotinic acetylcholine receptor from thymuses of myasthenic patients. *J. Clin. Invest.* 81:902-908.

68. Scadding, G.K., A. Vincent, J. Newsom-Davis, and K. Henry. 1981. Acetylcholine receptor antibody synthesis by thymic lymphocytes: correlation with thymic histology. *Neurology.* 31:935-943.

69. Kuks, J.B., H.J. Oosterhuis, P.C. Limburg, and T.H. The. 1991. Anti-acetylcholine receptor antibodies decrease after thymectomy in patients with myasthenia gravis. Clinical correlations. *J. Autoimmun.* 4:197-211.

70. Schluep, M., N. Willcox, A. Vincent, G.K. Dhoot, and J. Newsom-Davis. 1987. Acetylcholine receptors in human thymic myoid cells in situ: an immunohistological study. *Ann. Neurol.* 22:212-222.

71. Leite, M.I., M. Jones, P. Ströbel, A. Marx, R. Gold, E. Niks, J.J. Verschuuren, S. Berrih-Aknin, F. Scaravilli, A. Canelhas, B.P. Morgan, A. Vincent, and N. Willcox. 2007. Myasthenia gravis thymus: complement vulnerability of epithelial and myoid cells, complement attack on them, and correlations with autoantibody status. *Am. J. Pathol.* 171:893-905.

72. Müller-Hermelink, H.K., and A. Marx. 2000. Thymoma. *Curr. Opin. Oncol.* 12:426-433.

73. Tandan, R., R. Taylor, D.P. DiCostanzo, K. Sharma, T. Fries, and J. Roberts. 1990. Metastasizing thymoma and myasthenia gravis. Favorable response to glucocorticoids after failed chemotherapy and radiation therapy. *Cancer.* 65:1286-1290.

74. Buckley, C., D. Douek, J. Newsom-Davis, A. Vincent, and N. Willcox. 2001. Mature, long-lived CD4+ and CD8+ T cells are generated by the thymoma in myasthenia gravis. *Ann. Neurol.* 50:64-72.

75. Hoffacker, V., A. Schultz, J.J. Tiesinga, R. Gold, B. Schalke, W. Nix, R. Kiefer, H.K. Müller-Hermelink, and A. Marx. 2000. Thymomas alter the T-cell subset composition in the blood: a potential mechanism for thymoma-associated autoimmune disease. *Blood.* 96:3872-3879.

76. Marx, A., T. Kirchner, F. Hoppe, R. O'Connor, B. Schalke, S. Tzartos, and H.K. Müller-Hermelink. 1989. Proteins with epitopes of the acetylcholine receptor in epithelial cell cultures of thymomas in myasthenia gravis. *Am. J. Pathol.* 134:865-877.

77. Vincent, A., N. Willcox, M. Hill, J. Curnow, C. MacLennan, and D. Beeson. 1998. Determinant spreading and immune responses to acetylcholine receptors in myasthenia gravis. *Immunol. Rev.* 164:157-168.

78. Shiono, H., Y.L. Wong, I. Matthews, J.L. Liu, W. Zhang, G. Sims, A. Meager, D. Beeson, A. Vincent, and N. Willcox. 2003. Spontaneous production of anti-IFN-alpha and anti-IL-12 autoantibodies by thymoma cells from myasthenia gravis patients suggests autoimmunization in the tumor. *Int. Immunol.* 15:903-913.

79. Zhang, W., J.L. Liu, A. Meager, J. Newsom-Davis, and N. Willcox. 2003. Autoantibodies to IL-12 in myasthenia gravis patients with thymoma; effects on the IFN-gamma responses of healthy CD4+ T cells. *J. Neuroimmunol.* 139:102-108.

80. Aarli, J.A., F. Romi, G.O. Skeie, and N.E. Gilhus. 2003. Myasthenia gravis in individuals over 40. *Ann. N. Y. Acad. Sci.* 998:424-431.

81. Yamamoto, A.M., P. Gajdos, B. Eymard, C. Tranchant, J.M. Warter, L. Gomez, C. Bourquin, J.F. Bach, and H.J. Garchon. 2001. Anti-titin antibodies in myasthenia gravis: tight association with thymoma and heterogeneity of nonthymoma patients. *Arch. Neurol.* 58:885-890.

82. Willcox, N., M. Schluep, M.A. Ritter, and J. Newsom-Davis. 1991. The thymus in seronegative myasthenia gravis patients. *J. Neurol.* 238:256-261.

83. Verma, P.K., and J.J. Oger. 1992. Seronegative generalized myasthenia gravis: low frequency of thymic pathology. *Neurology.* 42:586-589.

84. Saka, E., M.A. Topcuoglu, B. Akkaya, A. Galati, M.Z. Onal, and A. Vincent. 2005. Thymus changes in anti-MuSK-positive and -negative myasthenia gravis. *Neurology.* 65:782-783.

85. Mesnard-Rouiller, L., J. Bismuth, A. Wakkach, S. Poëa-Guyon, and S. Berrih-Aknin. 2004. Thymic myoid cells express high levels of muscle genes. *J. Neuroimmunol.* 148:97-105.

86. Leite, M.I., P. Ströbel, M. Jones, K. Micklem, R. Moritz, R. Gold, E.H. Niks, S. Berrih-Aknin, F. Scaravilli, A. Canelhas, A. Marx, J. Newsom-Davis, N. Willcox, and A. Vincent. 2005. Fewer thymic changes in MuSK antibody-positive than in MuSK antibody-negative MG. *Ann. Neurol.* 57:444-448.

Ocular Myasthenia: Diagnosis, Treatment and Pathogenesis

Uladzimir Luchanok, MD, PhD, Henry J. Kaminski, MD, Linda L. Kusner, PhD

1. INTRODUCTION

Ocular myasthenia gravis (MG) is clinically defined as muscle weakness confined to the extraocular muscles and levator palpebrae superioris. The MG Foundation of America classification includes weakness of eye closure within the definition of ocular myasthenia, Class 1 by the categorization system. MG prevalence is about 400 per million with ocular myasthenia contributing about 20 percent to that number and affecting both sexes throughout the lifespan (1-4). The classic statement of the disease being of old men and young women is true, with an age distribution being bimodal with incidence peaks in the 20s for women and rising for men after age 40 (3,5-7). Ocular myasthenia is more common among Oriental populations with a higher frequency of onset prior to puberty (8). A higher incidence and prevalence was found among African–Americans than in the corresponding Caucasian population with ocular myasthenia comprising 25% (2), while a study from South Africa indicated that the Black population was more likely to have treatment resistant ocular myasthenia compared to Whites (9). Such epidemiological studies suggest genetic risk to ocular myasthenia and also would support consideration of ocular myasthenia as a distinct disease.

2. CLINICAL MANIFESTATIONS OF OCULAR MYASTHENIA

The majority of patients with MG initially complain of droopy eyelids or double vision (10-12). The hallmark feature of MG, including its ocular manifestations, is the variability of weakness. Symptoms can range in severity over a day and over months with periods of complete resolution.

The clinical pattern both assists in diagnosis and complicates clinical recognition of ocular myasthenia, since patients may lack manifestations during physician visits. About half of patients who present with ocular myasthenia develop general weakness within six months and about 80 percent will generalize within 2 years (13-15). If weakness remains restricted to ocular muscles for two years, generalization of weakness is unlikely, but has been described to occur, even decades later (6,15,16).

Ptosis is the most common manifestation of ocular myasthenia, may be its only sign, and may be unilateral or bilateral. Its severity is variable and may differ between lids. Rare patients may not event appreciate lid droop and complain only of blurred vision because of the lid's obstruction of the pupil; however friends and family will usually mention lid droop or appearance of sleepiness to the patient.

Several physical examination signs support the diagnosis of MG:

Enhanced ptosis, lid retraction and related signs. Enhanced ptosis is appreciated by manual elevation of the ptotic lid and coincidentally the contralateral, less affected, lid drops. This observation supports Hering's law of equal innervation, which stipulates that synergic ocular muscles receive equal innervation. The attempt to overcome ptosis in the affected lid leads to increased neuronal stimulation to both levators. Once the stimulus for the innervational pulse is relieved by elevation of the more severely affected lid, the contralateral lid droops. If significant asymmetry exists, the contralateral lid may be hyper-retracted. Synchronous disinhibition of the orbicularis oculi or sympathetic inhibition of Müller's muscle may serve to limit ptosis severity (17,18). In some patients, lid retraction with subsequent ocular irritation may be so prominent that becomes a greater complaint than ptosis (19). Co-existent thyroid ophthalmopathy may contribute to apparent lid retraction (10). As with enhancement of ptosis, manual elevation of the ptotic lid will allow the retracted lid to return to a more normal position, revealing the compensatory origin of the retraction (10).

"Paradoxical" reversal of ptosis, in which ptosis alternates lids during a day, can be observed in MG both after the rest and after administration of edrophonium (20). Such an observation eliminates consideration of any other disease in diagnosis.

The fatigue recovery test may be useful in diagnosis. If a patient develops enchanced ptosis after looking up, then voluntary maximal contraction of the antagonistic orbicularis oculi muscle for 10 seconds may improve the strength of the previously fatigued levator palpebrae muscle, leading to a temporary improvement of lid opening (21).

Cogan's lid twitch sign. Cogan's lid twitch sign may be observed by having a patient look down for ten seconds, and then make a saccade back to primary position (22). The sign is observed when the ptotic lid elevates excessively during the repositioning, occasionally causing a transient lid retraction. It then twitches or slowly droops back to a ptotic position. The sign is thought to be caused by the rapid recovery of levator palpebrae strength after rest in downgaze, coupled with its susceptibility to fatigue with contraction, leading to the droop after return to the primary position. A small study of the Cogan lid twitch sign found only 50% sensitivity with a positive predictive value of 25%. These poor results may be in part due to diurnal fluctuation of weakness (23). Cogan's sign has been reported in a patient with a dorsal midbrain astrocytoma (24).

Peek sign of orbicularis oculi fatigue. After the examiner has applied gentle opposition to the sustained lid closure, orbicularis oculi weakness is appreciated by separation of the lid margins with resultant scleral exposure. The patient thus appears to "peek" at the examiner (25).

Ophthalmoparesis is the second most common manifestation of ocular myasthenia. Most MG patients complain of frank double vision; however, ocular motility symptoms may include dizziness, gait instability, or visual blurring, and may be more prominent than double vision. The patient will appreciate improvement in symptoms with closure of one eye. Up to 90% of patients who present with diplopia have associated ptosis, and the combination should immediately bring to consideration the diagnosis of MG (10,12,26). Any extraocular muscle may be involved by MG. Perhaps the elevator muscles (superior rectus and inferior oblique) are more often involved and more severely affected, especially in long-standing ocular myasthenia (27,28). However, such observations are not helpful in diagnosis of the individual patient.

The eye movement abnormalities of MG mimic central or peripheral nervous system eye movement abnormalities, and the degree of weakness varies from complete paralysis to subtle weakness with isolated nystagmus. Dissociated gaze-evoked nystagmus contralateral to a paretic eye may be observed, which represents adaptive increases in innervational pulse. Highly suggestive of MG are saccadic velocities, which are preserved or increased within a limited range of movement, or intrasaccadic fatigue, which is appreciated when a saccade suddenly slows in mid-flight (29).

2.1 Differential Diagnosis.

There are few disorders that may be confused with ocular myasthenia. Graves ophthalmopathy may mimic ocular myasthenia by restrictive extraocular weakness but ptosis is absent, and if the patient is thyrotoxic, lid retraction may be present. Ptosis in a patient with Graves disease suggests coexistent MG (10). Thyroid disease occurs more commonly in patients with MG, particularly in the presence of acetylcholine receptor antibodies (30). Also, patients with both MG and Graves disease are more likely to develop ophthalmoparesis even in the euthyroid state as compared to patients with Graves disease alone (31).

Ocular myasthenia may mimic any pupil-sparing ocular motility disorder including fourth, sixth, and partial third nerve palsies, and central gaze disorders, such as internuclear ophthalmoplegia, the one and a half syndrome, and chronic progressive external ophthalmoplegia (12,32). However, brainstem pathology will usually have associated cranial nerve or long track signs. Chronic progressive external opthalmoplegia produces symmetric ptosis and ophthalmoparesis, but with slow saccades, which should distinguish it from ocular MG (32-34). Horner's syndrome is identified by miosis and elevation of the lower lid, whereas clinically evident pupilary abnormalities never occur in MG. Senile ptosis and levator dehiscence are readily differentiated by absence of significant fluctuation.

Other neuromuscular junction disorders, such as Lambert-Eaton myasthenic syndrome, botulism, or organophosphate poisoning disorders, may mimic ocular myasthenia, but purely ocular presentations of these disorders are rare. Appropriate history, physical examination, and ancillary testing should distinguish these conditions from MG.

3. DIAGNOSTIC TESTING

The diagnosis of ocular myasthenia often may be made purely on its characteristic presentation, but most clinicians and patients appreciate diagnostic confirmation and accept therapeutic decisions with more objective confirmations of the diagnosis. Diagnostic tests must be used with an appreciation of their limitations

3.1. Edrophonium Test

The edrophonium test involves intravenous infusion of edrophonium chloride, which inhibits the action of acetylcholinesterase (AChE). Procedures for edrophonium intravenous infusion are not standardized and sensitivity assessments vary. Edrophonium is administered slowly over a few minutes to a maximum of 10mg and the examiner looks for improvement in strength of a weak muscle, which occurs 30-60 sec after administration (35). Subjective improvement is not evidence of a positive test (35,36). To limit adverse effects, edrophonium infusion should stop after a positive response is achieved. Kupersmith et al. (14) found that all patients who had a positive test required at most 7mg.

The sensitivity has been reported to be 60-97%; however, the studies are small with variable rigor, and in clinical practice its sensitivity is likely to be much lower than 97%. Improvement in ptosis may be a more sensitive endpoint than evaluation of EOM weakness (14,16,35,37). Positive responses are observed in other neuromuscular transmission disorders, such as Lambert–Eaton syndrome and botulism. False positive tests are reported with Guillain–Barre syndrome, compressive cranial neuropathies and brain stem pathology (12, 35).

The frequency of serious complications that include bradycardia, syncope, seizure, respiratory failure, or transient ischemic attack is low, 0.16 percent by one survey (38). Some hospitals require cardiac monitoring during the procedure, but the authors do not think this is necessary. Beyond muscarinic side effects of tearing, salivation, sweating, abdominal cramps and nausea, the test has limited morbidity (12,35). Cardiac dysrhythmias and bronchial asthma are relative contraindications for performance of edrophonium testing.

3.2. Other Clinical Evaluations

The ice pack, rest, and sleep tests are non-pharmacological evaluations that were developed to avoid the adverse effects associated with edrophonium. The ice test is performed by placement of a cooling pack across the eyes for 2 to 5 minutes followed by the examiner's assessment for improvement of eye movement or ptosis deficit (38,39). Some patients may have difficulty tolerating the ice pack. Sensitivity and specificity of ice test was estimated to be 94 and 97 percent, respectively (40). A small, randomized trial compared the ice test to the rest test and found that the median improvement of ptosis with the rest test was 2 mm and with the ice test 4.5 mm, but no improvement was found in nonmyasthenic patients (41).

The rest test involves having the patient close their eyelids for 2 to 5 minutes. A positive test is considered to be a 2 mm or greater improvement of ptosis. For the sleep test, the patient lies with eyes closed in a quiet, dark room for 30 minutes and then ptosis and ophthalmoparesis are assessed. Sensitivity and specificity of the sleep test are reported to be 99 percent and 91 percent (40,42). The drawback of all these evaluations is that sensitivity and specificity assessments have been performed with small sample sizes. Inter-observer reliability has not been assessed (40).

3.3. Serum Autoantibody Evaluation

Acetylcholine receptor (AChR) antibody assessment is performed concurrently or in lieu of the clinical tests (43). Three methods are used to identify AChR antibodies. The binding AChR antibody is the most sensitive test, but about half of ocular myasthenia patients will be negative. Testing for modulating AChR antibody may increase the diagnostic yield slightly; however, it has a higher rate of false positives. The blocking AChR antibody has limited diagnostic utility since it is identified in only 1% of MG patients without binding AChR antibodies. Assessments of the sensitivity of AChR antibody testing for ocular myasthenia ranges between 39 and 71%

with a specificity of 95–100% (40). False-positive detection of AChR antibodies occurs in autoimmune liver disease, systemic lupus erythematosus, rheumatoid arthritis, Lambert–Eaton syndrome, inflammatory neuropathies, amyotrophic lateral sclerosis, thyroid ophthalmopathy, thymoma patients, patients taking D-penicillamine, and first-degree relatives of MG patients (44). Some studies suggest a correlation between AChR antibody seropositivity in ocular myasthenia patients and risk of generalization of MG. However, studies are not consistent, and the predictive values of AChR antibodies for generalization is not high (14,45).

Rare cases of ocular myasthenia in association with antibodies to the muscle-specific kinase (MuSK) have been described (46-48), but large case series of MuSK antibody-positive patients have not identified ocular myasthenia patients (49-51). Preliminary data summarized from the International Seronegative MG Survey showed that the vast majority of MuSK antibody-positive patients have generalized MG (52). It appears that MuSK antibody determination is not necessary when the diagnosis of ocular myasthenia can be supported clinically with clinical tests or electrodiagnostics.

3.4. Electrodiagnosis

Electrodiagnositic testing is commonly used in suspected ocular myasthenia, since clinical assessments may be equivocal and AChR antibodies negative. Routine nerve conduction studies and needle electromyography are usually performed to rule other neuromuscular diseases; however, when ocular myasthenia is the diagnostic consideration, these studies are usually negative (53,54). The needle EMG findings are nonspecific and may include short-duration, low-amplitude and polyphasic motor unit action potentials.

Repetitive nerve stimulations are used to identify a neuromuscular transmission defect. Their reported sensitivity for ocular myasthenia is poor (11–39%), but specificity is high (89–98%). The sensitivity of repetitive nerve stimulation of the radial nerve with recording from the anconeus is eleven percent and may reach 34 percent with stimulation of the truncus primaris superior with deltoid recording (40). Although evaluation of the orbicularis oculi, orbicularis oris or nasalis increases the percentage of abnormalities identified, these studies are difficult for patients to tolerate. An increase in the quantity of nerve-muscle pairs tested does not improve the sensitivity for ocular myasthenia (55). Of note, appreciation of a decremental response to repetitive stimulation in an extremity muscle does not predict progression to generalized weakness.

Single-fiber electromyography (SFEMG) can be performed using usual volitional technique or as a stimulated jitter investigation. The sensitivity and specificity of SFEMG for ocular myasthenia performed on the frontalis muscle is 86 percent and 73 percent respectively, and 97 percent and 92 percent when orbicularis oculi is investigated (40,56,57). One hundred percent sensitivity may be achieved when the lower orbucularis oculi is tested (58). SFEMG with stimulated jitter investigation in the masseter muscles was reported to be 100 percent sensitive for ocular myasthenia based on increased number of unstable pairs and 67 percent sensitive based on abnormal mean jitter (59).

3.5. Other Considerations

Additional testing is necessary when the diagnosis of MG is made. Thyroid dysfunction is a common co-morbidity and may complicate diagnosis, as described above. Correction to a euthyroid state may improve weakness in ocular myasthenia. Therefore, it is appropriate to screen all ocular myasthenia patients for hypo- or hyperthyroidism, and orbital imaging may be necessary to rule out ophthalmopathy. If clinically indicated the co-existence of other autoimmune disorders should be evaluated, in particular pernicious anemia, which may not be clinically manifest. Chest imaging should be performed to exclude thymoma, although its presence is rare in ocular myasthenia. In anticipation of immunosuppressive treatments, screening for tuberculosis is appropriate.

4. TREATMENT

The goal of all therapy is to eliminate patient symptoms within the limits of the adverse effects of treatments and ultimately to achieve complete stable remission. The physician must also monitor for the potential progression to generalized MG. Prospective, controlled trials do not exists to guide treatment of ocular myasthenia patients (60), and the recommendations listed below are based largely on retrospective studies and clinical experience (figure 1).

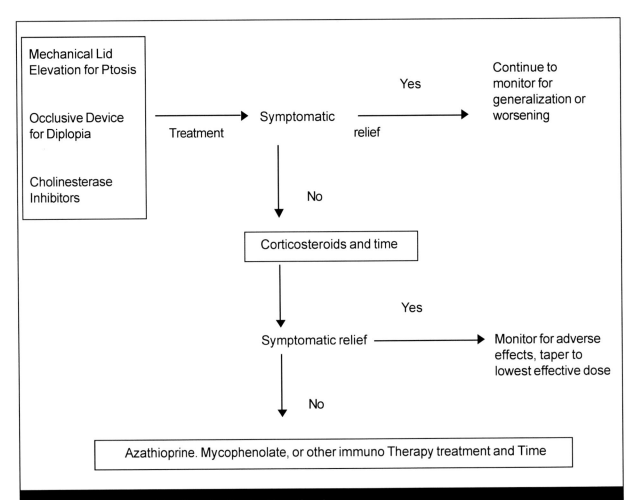

Figure 1. Treatment Algorithm for Ocular Myasthenia

4.1. Non-Pharmaceutical Treatment Options

It is important for the clinician to appreciate that some patients have adequate relief with non-pharmacological treatments and prefer them to drugs. Consideration of non-pharmacological therapies need to be placed into the context of the drug therapies to allow the patient make an informed choice.

Eyelid tape or lid crutches may be used to correct ptosis. Their drawback is scleral irritation due to exposure and patient discomfort. Visual occlusive devices, such as eye patches or opaque contact lenses, can be used to correct double vision but they also will cover a part of patient's visual field. Prisms, often used to correct diplopia in different conditions, are less successful in OM because of the varying nature of alignment of the visual axes. It leads to the need in frequent correction of the prism, which is usually not very effective. Eye muscle surgery may be beneficial in rare patients when a fixed strabismus occurs and non-variable ptosis develops (61,62). Botulinum toxin has been used for ocular alignment. However, it needs to be used cautiously given the potential for systemic neuromuscular transmission blockade.

4.2. Pharmaceutical Treatment

Pharmaceutical treatment options are divided into AChE inhibitors that enhance neuromuscular transmission or immunosuppressive therapy to moderate the autoimmune abnormality. A report of the Quality Standards Subcommittee of the American Academy of Neurology on the medical treatment of ocular myasthenia concluded that given the absence of robust therapeutic evaluations, it is not possible to make any evidence-based recommendations regarding the use of cholinesterase inhibitors, corticosteroids, or other immunosuppressive agents in improving the manifestations of ocular myasthenia or in reducing the risk of progression to generalized MG. The decision to use such agents should be weighed against the potential for harmful side effects (60). Our comments are based on retrospective evaluations, other expert opinion, and personal experience (figure 1).

4.2.1. Acetylcholesterase Inhibition.

Inhibitors of AChE are used first to alleviate the visual deficit of ocular myasthenia. They may be effective for treatment of ptosis, but often do not benefit double vision (63-65). An improvement of unilateral ptosis may occasionally 'unmask' double vision, which may be more debilitating for the patient (12). A recent retrospective study suggested that patients with ocular myasthenia with an initial presentation of concurrent ptosis and diplopia may have a decreased response to pyridostigmine (66). In one report, AChE therapy achieved improvement in close to 30% of patients (67); however, other studies indicate lower success rates (65). Many patients with ocular myasthenia will move to other therapies (65), but given the potential for symptomatic benefit and the low frequency of serious adverse events, they are an appropriate first-line approach to therapy (67).

Typically, pyridostigmine therapy is initiated at doses of 30–60 mg three times per day and increased as tolerated to 90–120 mg every 3–4 h per day. Mean daily doses of 270-300 mg are reported with some patients using 720 mg per day (65,67). Complications are primarily related to muscarinic effects, in particular abdominal cramps, nausea, vomiting and diarrhea, which occur in at least a third of patients (11) and possibly all patients to some extent.

4.2.2. Immunosuppressive Treatment.

Prednisone is commonly used to treat ocular myasthenia, except when it is contraindicated or patients refuse due to concerns of complications. It was shown to resolve diplopia and other symptoms of ocular myasthenia more frequently than pyridostigmine alone with much better long term results (65). Given that prednisone is more effective than pyridostigmine and even in moderate dosages is associated with a reasonably high frequency of adverse events, prednisone therapy should be offered to the patients with poor response to pyridostigmine. Patients should be informed of side effects and appropriate measures taken to mitigate them (65). Retrospective studies suggest reduced rates of generalization among patients with ocular myasthenia treated with corticosteriods (from 36 to 7 percent at two years in one study), but the authors feel there is not enough evidence to recommend corticosteroids only for prevention of generalized MG (14,68-70).

A typical starting dose is 10–20mg of prednisone once a day followed by an increase of 5–10mg every three days until ptosis and double vision are significantly improved or resolved, which usually happens in the first few weeks of therapy, or until a maximum dose of 60–80 mg/day is achieved (14,68,71) [14, 68, 71]. Slow taper at a rate of 5–10 mg/day every 2 weeks is instituted usually after symptom resolution is maintained for 1 month. Rapid tapers often lead to recurrence of symptoms, but even with gradual dose reductions about 40 percent of patients will have symptom recurrence (67).

Most patients require maintenance doses of prednisone for years. The lowest possible dose that prevent symptoms should be used (often 10 mg or less daily). Patients may need intermittent increases when symptoms recur. Significant improvement with 'good' results in 72–96 percent of patients is reported, and about twenty percent of patients treated with prednisone may have remission of all manifestations lasting more than 6 months after therapy is discontinued (16,65,65,72). The frequency of diplopia in primary gaze decreases from 95 percent to about a quarter after one month of therapy with prednisone. Although some patients do well with every other day dosing of prednisone, which is thought to reduce corticosteroid complications, there are reports that exacerbations may be more common with alternate day therapy (16,65). There is no reason to administer prednisone in daily divided doses and patients should be instructed to take a single morning dose, which mimics the diurnal peak of endogenous corticosteroids.

Other immunosuppressant therapy may be considered in some patients with significant visual disability or with intolerable adverse effects from corticosteroid treatment (72). Thymectomy is not generally indicated. Of course, patients with a thymoma should undergo tumor removal and co-incident removal of the remainder of the thymus. Azathioprine was demonstrated to reduce corticosteroid requirements in a randomized, placebo-controlled trial of generalized MG patients, and retrospective analyses support its efficacy in ocular myasthenia. However, there is limited data on efficacy of immunosuppressive treatment in ocular myasthenia, and the evidence base relies on data from the generalized disease and expert opinion. Recent Cochrane reviews identified seven randomized controlled trials of immunosuppressants in generalized MG and concluded that the limited conclusion could be reached that cyclosporine (alone or with corticosteroids) or cyclophosphamide (with corticosteroids) lead to the significant improvement of generalized MG within 1 year compared with placebo. There is limited evidence of any significant benefit from treatment with azathioprine (as monotherapy or with corticosteroids), mycophenolate mofetil (as monotherapy with either corticosteroids or cyclosporin) or tacrolimus (with corticosteroids or plasma exchange or both) within 1 year. Also, there was insufficient data on the long term efficacy, steroid-sparing effect and safety of immunosuppressants in MG (73-75). However, see the more detailed discussion in Chapter 4.

5. PATHOPHYSIOLOGY

MG is caused by the failure of skeletal muscle to respond appropriately to nerve stimulation due to antibody-induced injury (76). The antibodies are produced by auto-sensitized B cells by a T cell dependent mechanism and induce neuromuscular transmission compromise by blocking the AChR, increasing its rate of internalization, or the predominant mechanism of complement-mediated injury. In ocular myasthenia patients, the concentration of antibody is lower or absent than in patients with generalized MG. Although absolute correlation of antibody concentration and severity of weakness is poor (77,78), the low titers of antibody support the clinical impression that ocular muscle is more susceptible to autoantibody injury. The properties that may mediate this susceptibility include antibody targets, the immune response, and the safety factor of the neuromuscular junctions (Figure 2).

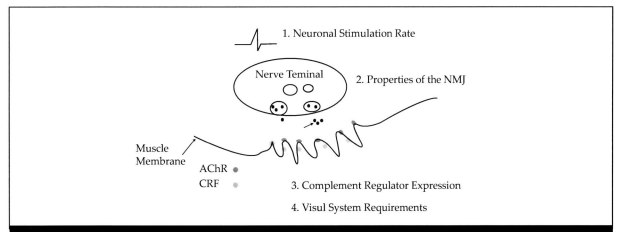

1. Neuronal Stimulation Rate

Nerve Teminal

2. Properties of the NMJ

Muscle Membrane

AChR

CRF

3. Complement Regulator Expression

4. Visul System Requirements

Figure 2. Illustration of Extraocular Musde Susceptibility to Myasthenia Gravis. 1) Ocular motor neurons fire at extremely high rates, such high repetitive could make the junctions susceptible to transmission failure. 2) The post synaptic folds are simplified compared to junctions of other skeletel muscle, which suggest a lower safety factor for transmission. 3) Complement inhibitors are expressed at lower levels at EOM synapses. 4) The eyes must be perfectly aligned to assure clear vision. even slight weakness of an extraocular could produce dramatic symptoms. See text for further details.

Ocular myasthenia patients demonstrate distinct differences from generalized MG patients in antibody production and T-cell response. The lower levels or absence of AChR antibodies seen with ocular myasthenia (77,78) suggests a greater sensitivity to the antibodies produced either through a higher exposure to the AChR target, an epitope that is specific to ocular muscle (79,80), or reduced ability to moderate complement attack due to lower levels of the complement regulators or some combination of all three factors (81,82). The *in vitro* response of the T-cells to AChR is lower in ocular patients than patients with generalized MG and this activity fluctuates over time (83). The end result is that a limited autoimmune response is insufficient to produce generalized weakness but does lead to compromised ocular muscle function.

5.1. Physiological and Structural Considerations.

Genomic expression studies performed on human, rat and mice of extraocular muscle(EOM) identified that the extraocular muscles represent a unique allotype. The results identified significant numbers of differentially expressed genes in extraocular muscle ranging in number from approximately 100 to 350 genes (82,84-86). The studies found expression differences compared to other skeletal muscle of genes involved in intermediary metabolism, excitation-contraction coupling, structural organization, transcriptional regulation, and myogenesis. A few genes of interest (discussed below) have begun to emerge that may lead to a greater understanding of disease susceptibilities.

Structural and signaling proteins of the NMJ of the extraocular muscle are the same that have been identified in other skeletal muscle fiber types (87). The majority of extraocular muscle fibers are singly innervated fibers (SIF) and share similar endplate morphology with other skeletal muscles having a single en plaque neuromuscular junction. These fibers have less prominent synaptic folds, and therefore one would predict fewer AChR and sodium channels on the post-synaptic membrane (88-90). The EOM miniature endplate potential amplitudes are similar to those of leg muscle junctions indicating that AChR density is similar at these synapses. The lower degree of synaptic folding and the greater number of endplates may allow for a greater number of exposed target sites for antibody attack.

Molecular organization of two members of the dystrophin-glycoprotein complex, alpha-dystrobrevin and syntrophin beta1 maintain differences in extraocular muscle compared to other skeletal muscle (90). This difference in the expression contribute to the lack of junctional folds at some NMJ. Elevated rapsyn expression reduces disease severity in experimental MG by increasing the functional integrity of the NMJ (91). The result suggests that a more structurally stable NMJ decreases membrane loss. Although no reduction in expression or changes in localization of rapsyn has been uncovered in extraocular muscle, the lack of junctional folds could suggest that the integrity of the NMJ EOM may be less and more susceptible to injury by MG.

EOM vascularity is much higher compared to other skeletal muscle and it likely necessary because of its greater metabolic needs (92,93). The increase in blood-flow would also include the increase in circulating T cells, B cells and macrophages to the muscle and would increase antibody delivery to the EOM junctions.

5.2. Complement and Immune Factors.

The complement cascade is responsible for the destruction of the NMJ after antibody targeting. DAF is a regulator of the complement-mediated injury by blocking the cascade at the C3 level (94). DAF was found by genomic profiling studies to be lower in expression level in the extraocular muscles which lead to the suggestion that greater membrane attack complex deposition and greater lysis of the muscle membrane could occur (81,82,95). Studies on DAF knockout mice have shown an increase susceptibility to experimental MG than the control littermates (95,96).

Production of anti-AChR CD4+ cells is required for the development of MG due to their role in driving antibody production (97). The CD4+ T cell responds to a large number of epitopes on the AChR and few differences are identified between the response of T cells from generalized MG and ocular myasthenia patients. T cells from ocular myasthenia do have a wider range of activation from the gamma subunit of the AChR and a limited response from the epsilon subunit. Another difference in the T cell response is the variation that occurs over time suggestd that the

T cells are not stable as in generalized MG (83). The instability of the response may indicate that the T-cells themselves are not stimulated in ocular myasthenia patients to the degree observed in in the generalized disease.

5.3. Neuromuscular Transmission.

Firing frequencies of ocular motor neurons may reach peaks of 400-600 Hz during saccades. In contrast, the rapid movement of a limb would be the result of a firing frequency of 150 Hz from the spinal motor neuron. In most skeletal muscles, a safety factor allows for a wide range of firing frequencies to produce an action potential without fatigue (98). However, in extraocular muscle there is reason to believe that the safety factor is low or absent making them more susceptible to any neuromuscular transmission disorder, including the one produced by MG (90).

While most NMJ of skeletal muscle function as a slave to the firing of the motor neuron, the NMJ of EOM has its own unique response. Ocular motor neuron firing frequency correlates with eye position. As well, force appears be controlled by the motor neuron firing rates rather than having additional motor units recruited to generate additional force. Multi-innervated fibers (MIF) act in a tonic fashion, similar to slow or tonic fibers of amphibians, with no safety factor and no action potentials. Force generation is directly proportional to the membrane depolarization caused by the endplate potential and action potentials are not generated. Therefore, a safety factor does not exist for MIF and any reduction of endplate potential induced by a loss of AChR would decrease contractile force of these fibers.

The contraction and relaxation properties of orbital fibers vary along their length. These fibers contract in a graded fashion in the region of the MIF endplates and in a twitch pattern around the SIF endplates. The motor neurons innervating the MIF lie in the periphery of ocular motor nuclei and are innervated by premotor neurons that control smooth pursuit, vergence, and gaze holding. This pattern of innervation suggests that these fibers are likely to be proprioceptors. Any alteration in the response of the MIF might drastically change the ability to maintain appropriate eye position.

A unique finding in ocular myasthenia is the presence of fast saccades despite a reduced range of eye movement. Only the pale global fibers of extraocular muscle have substantial synaptic folding, which would serve to improve their safety factor. Peak velocity of saccades among ocular myasthenia patients was found to be similar, or even greater than, controls, even though later in the eye movement saccades slowed. The finding suggests that the global fibers because of a higher safety factor are spared in MG (29).

5. CONCLUSION

A focused review of diagnosis and treatment of ocular myasthenia was provided and the significant limitations of the literature were highlighted. As long as physician is suspicious of ocular myasthenia the confirmation of the diagnosis is generally straightforward. Although expert opinion would suggest that treatment is highly effective, significant knowledge gaps exist as to severity of treatment complications and the quality of life of ocular myasthenia patients. Only through prospective trials or multi-center, rigorously constructed outcome databases will improvements in treatment be achieved. Studies of the cell and molecular biology have led to greater understanding of the differential susceptibility of extraocular muscle to disease. It is possible that therapeutics, such as complement inhibition or enhancement of NMJ stability, could be particularly beneficial for treatment of ocular myasthenia.

REFERENCES

1. MacDonald BK, Cockerell OC, Sander JW, Shorvon SD. The incidence and lifetime prevalence of neurological disorders in a prospective community-based study in the UK. *Brain* 2000;123 (Pt 4):665-676.
2. Phillips LH, 2nd, Torner JC, Anderson MS, Cox GM. The epidemiology of myasthenia gravis in central and western Virginia. *Neurology* 1992;42:1888-1893.
3. Phillips LH, 2nd, Torner JC. Epidemiologic evidence for a changing natural history of myasthenia gravis. *Neurology* 1996;47:1233-1238.
4. Somnier FE, Keiding N, Paulson OB. Epidemiology of myasthenia gravis in Denmark. A longitudinal and comprehensive population survey. *Arch Neurol* 1991;48:733-739.
5. Vincent A, Clover L, Buckley C, Grimley Evans J, Rothwell PM. Evidence of underdiagnosis of myasthenia gravis in older people. *J Neurol Neurosurg Psychiatry* 2003;74:1105-1108.
6. Grob D. Natural History of Myasthenia Gravis. In: Engel AG (ed), *Myasthenia Gravis and Myasthenic Disorders.* New York: Oxford University Press; 1999:131-154.
7. Mantegazza R, Baggi F, Antozzi C, et al. Myasthenia gravis (MG): epidemiological data and prognostic factors. *Ann N Y Acad Sci* 2003;998:413-423.
8. Chiu HC, Vincent A, Newsom-Davis J, Hsieh KH, Hung T. Myasthenia gravis: population differences in disease expression and acetylcholine receptor antibody titers between Chinese and Caucasians. *Neurology* 1987;37:1854-1857.
9. Heckmann JM, Owen EP, Little F. Myasthenia gravis in South Africans: racial differences in clinical manifestations. *Neuromuscul Disord* 2007;17:929-934.
10. Barton JJ, Fouladvand M. Ocular aspects of myasthenia gravis. *Semin Neurol* 2000;20:7-20.
11. Beekman R, Kuks JB, Oosterhuis HJ. Myasthenia gravis: diagnosis and follow-up of 100 consecutive patients. *J Neurol* 1997;244:112-118.
12. Daroff R. Ocular Myasthenia. In: Kaminski HJ (ed), *Myasthenia Gravis and Related Disorders.* Totowa, NJ: Humana Press; 2003:115-128.
13. Bever CT, Jr., Aquino AV, Penn AS, Lovelace RE, Rowland LP. Prognosis of ocular myasthenia. *Ann Neurol* 1983;14:516-519.
14. Kupersmith MJ, Latkany R, Homel P. Development of generalized disease at 2 years in patients with ocular myasthenia gravis. *Arch Neurol* 2003;60:243-248.
15. Oosterhuis HJ. The natural course of myasthenia gravis: a long term follow up study. *J Neurol Neurosurg Psychiatry* 1989;52:1121-1127.
16. Evoli A, Tonali P, Bartoccioni E, Lo Monaco M. Ocular myasthenia: diagnostic and therapeutic problems. *Acta Neurol Scand* 1988;77:31-35.
17. Kusner LL, Puwanant A, Kaminski HJ. Ocular myasthenia: diagnosis, treatment, and pathogenesis. *Neurologist* 2006;12:231-239.
18. Schmidtke K, Buttner-Ennever JA. Nervous control of eyelid function. A review of clinical, experimental and pathological data. *Brain* 1992;115 Pt 1:227-247.
19. Kansu T, Subutay N. Lid retraction in myasthenia gravis. *J Clin Neuroophthalmol* 1987;7:145-150.

20. Komiyama A, Hirayama K. Paradoxical reversal of ptosis in myasthenia gravis by edrophonium administration. *J Neurol Neurosurg Psychiatry* 1988;51:315.
21. Toyka KV. Ptosis in myasthenia gravis: extended fatigue and recovery bedside test. *Neurology* 2006;67:1524.
22. Cogan DG. Myasthenia Gravis: A Review of the Disease and a Description of Lid Twitch as a Characteristic Sign. *Arch Ophthalmol* 1965;74:217-221.
23. Van Stavern GP, Bhatt A, Haviland J, Black EH. A prospective study assessing the utility of Cogan's lid twitch sign in patients with isolated unilateral or bilateral ptosis. *J Neurol Sci* 2007;256:84-85.
24. Ragge NK, Hoyt WF. Midbrain myasthenia: fatigable ptosis, 'lid twitch' sign, and ophthalmoparesis from a dorsal midbrain glioma. *Neurology* 1992;42:917-919.
25. Osher RH, Griggs RC. Orbicularis fatigue: the 'peek' sign of myasthenia gravis. *Arch Ophthalmol* 1979;97:677-679.
26. Elrod RD, Weinberg DA. Ocular myasthenia gravis. *Ophthalmol Clin North Am* 2004;17:275-309; v.
27. Weinberg DA, Lesser RL, Vollmer TL. Ocular myasthenia: a protean disorder. *Surv Ophthalmol* 1994;39:169-210.
28. Cleary M, Williams GJ, Metcalfe RA. The pattern of extra-ocular muscle involvement in ocular myasthenia. *Strabismus* 2008;16:11-18.
29. Khanna S, Liao K, Kaminski HJ, Tomsak RL, Joshi A, Leigh RJ. Ocular myasthenia revisited: insights from pseudo-internuclear ophthalmoplegia. *J Neurol* 2007;254:1569-1574.
30. Toth C, McDonald D, Oger J, Brownell K. Acetylcholine receptor antibodies in myasthenia gravis are associated with greater risk of diabetes and thyroid disease. *Acta Neurol Scand* 2006;114:124-132.
31. Marino M, Barbesino G, Pinchera A, et al. Increased frequency of euthyroid ophthalmopathy in patients with Graves' disease associated with myasthenia gravis. *Thyroid* 2000;10:799-802.
32. Leigh RJ, Zee DS. *The Neurology of Eye Movements*. 3 ed. Philadelphia: F.A. Davis; 1999.
33. Barton JJ, Jama A, Sharpe JA. Saccadic duration and intrasaccadic fatigue in myasthenic and nonmyasthenic ocular palsies. *Neurology* 1995;45:2065-2072.
34. Hirano M, DiMauro S. ANT1, Twinkle, POLG, and TP: new genes open our eyes to ophthalmoplegia. *Neurology* 2001;57:2163-2165.
35. Pascuzzi RM. The edrophonium test. *Semin Neurol* 2003;23:83-88.
36. Daroff RB. The office Tensilon test for ocular myasthenia gravis. *Arch Neurol* 1986;43:843-844.
37. Nicholson GA, McLeod JG, Griffiths LR. Comparison of diagnostic tests in myasthenia gravis. *Clin Exp Neurol* 1983;19:45-49.
38. Ing EB, Ing SY, Ing T, Ramocki JA. The complication rate of edrophonium testing for suspected myasthenia gravis. *Can J Ophthalmol* 2000;35:141-144; discussion 145.
39. Golnik KC, Pena R, Lee AG, Eggenberger ER. An ice test for the diagnosis of myasthenia gravis. *Ophthalmology* 1999;106:1282-1286.
40. Benatar M. A systematic review of diagnostic studies in myasthenia gravis. *Neuromuscul Disord* 2006;16:459-467.
41. Kubis KC, Danesh-Meyer HV, Savino PJ, Sergott RC. The ice test versus the rest test in myasthenia gravis. *Ophthalmology* 2000;107:1995-1998.

42. Odel JG, Winterkorn JM, Behrens MM. The sleep test for myasthenia gravis. A safe alternative to Tensilon. *J Clin Neuroophthalmol* 1991;11:288-292.

43. Howard FM, Jr., Lennon VA, Finley J, Matsumoto J, Elveback LR. Clinical correlations of antibodies that bind, block, or modulate human acetylcholine receptors in myasthenia gravis. *Ann N Y Acad Sci* 1987;505:526-538.

44. Lennon VA. Serologic profile of myasthenia gravis and distinction from the Lambert-Eaton myasthenic syndrome. *Neurology* 1997;48:S23-S27.

45. Seybold ME. Diagnosis of myasthenia gravis. In: Engel AG (ed), *Myasthenia gravis and myasthenic disorders.* New York: Oxford University Press; 1999:146-166.

46. Caress JB, Hunt CH, Batish SD. Anti-MuSK myasthenia gravis presenting with purely ocular findings. *Arch Neurol* 2005;62:1002-1003.

47. Chan JW, Orrison WW. Ocular myasthenia: a rare presentation with MuSK antibody and bilateral extraocular muscle atrophy. *Br J Ophthalmol* 2007;91:842-843.

48. Bennett DL, Mills KR, Riordan-Eva P, Barnes PR, Rose MR. Anti-MuSK antibodies in a case of ocular myasthenia gravis. *J Neurol Neurosurg Psychiatry* 2006;77:564-565.

49. Evoli A, Tonali PA, Padua L, et al. Clinical correlates with anti-MuSK antibodies in generalized seronegative myasthenia gravis. *Brain* 2003;126:2304-2311.

50. Zhou L, McConville J, Chaudhry V, et al. Clinical comparison of muscle-specific tyrosine kinase (MuSK) antibody-positive and -negative myasthenic patients. *Muscle Nerve* 2004;30:55-60.

51. Evoli A, Bianchi MR, Riso R, et al. Response to therapy in myasthenia gravis with anti-MuSK antibodies. *Ann N Y Acad Sci* 2008;1132:76-83.

52. Vincent A, Leite MI, Farrugia ME, et al. Myasthenia gravis seronegative for acetylcholine receptor antibodies. *Ann N Y Acad Sci* 2008;1132:84-92.

53. Meriggioli MN, Sanders DB. Myasthenia gravis: diagnosis. *Semin Neurol* 2004;24:31-39.

54. Katirji B, Kaminski HJ. Electrodiagnostic approach to the patient with suspected neuromuscular junction disorder. *Neurol Clin* 2002;20:557-586, viii.

55. Costa J, Evangelista T, Conceicao I, de Carvalho M. Repetitive nerve stimulation in myasthenia gravis—relative sensitivity of different muscles. *Clin Neurophysiol* 2004;115:2776-2782.

56. Ukachoke C, Ashby P, Basinski A, Sharpe JA. Usefulness of single fiber EMG for distinguishing neuromuscular from other causes of ocular muscle weakness. *Can J Neurol Sci* 1994;21:125-128.

57. de Entrambasaguas M, Lopez-Bernabe R, Lopez-Alemany M. [Ocular myasthenia gravis: diagnostic aspects and evolution]. *Rev Neurol* 2007;44:397-403.

58. Papathanasiou ES, Zamba-Papanicolaou E. Differential orbicularis oculi involvement in neuromuscular junction dysfunction. *J Clin Neurophysiol* 2008;25:293-298.

59. Khuraibet AJ, Rousseff RT, Behbehani R, al-Shubaili AF, Khan RA. Single-fiber electromyography of masseter muscle in myasthenia gravis. *Muscle Nerve* 2008;37:522-525.

60. Benatar M, Kaminski HJ. Evidence report: the medical treatment of ocular myasthenia (an evidence-based review): report of the Quality Standards Subcommittee of the American Academy of Neurology. *Neurology* 2007;68:2144-2149.

61. Ohtsuki H, Hasebe S, Okano M, Furuse T. Strabismus surgery in ocular myasthenia gravis. *Ophthalmologica* 1996;210:95-100.

62. Bentley CR, Dawson E, Lee JP. Active management in patients with ocular manifestations of myasthenia gravis. *Eye* 2001;15:18-22.

63. Sommer N, Melms A, Weller M, Dichgans J. Ocular myasthenia gravis. A critical review of clinical and pathophysiological aspects. *Doc Ophthalmol* 1993;84:309-333.

64. Sommer N, Sigg B, Melms A, et al. Ocular myasthenia gravis: response to long-term immunosuppressive treatment. *J Neurol Neurosurg Psychiatry* 1997;62:156-162.

65. Kupersmith MJ, Ying G. Ocular motor dysfunction and ptosis in ocular myasthenia gravis: effects of treatment. *Br J Ophthalmol* 2005;89:1330-1334.

66. Chirapapaisan N, Tanormrod S, Chuenkongkaew W. Factors associated with insensitivity to pyridostigmine therapy in Thai patients with ocular myasthenia gravis. *Asian Pac J Allergy Immunol* 2007;25:13-16.

67. Bhanushali MJ, Wuu J, Benatar M. Treatment of ocular symptoms in myasthenia gravis. *Neurology* 2008;71:1335-1341.

68. Mee J, Paine M, Byrne E, King J, Reardon K, O'Day J. Immunotherapy of ocular myasthenia gravis reduces conversion to generalized myasthenia gravis. *J Neuroophthalmol* 2003;23:251-255.

69. Monsul NT, Patwa HS, Knorr AM, Lesser RL, Goldstein JM. The effect of prednisone on the progression from ocular to generalized myasthenia gravis. *J Neurol Sci* 2004;217:131-133.

70. Wakata N, Iguchi H, Sugimoto H, Nomoto N, Kurihara T. Relapse of ocular symptoms after remission of myasthenia gravis—a comparison of relapsed and complete remission cases. *Clin Neurol Neurosurg* 2003;105:75-77.

71. Papapetropoulos TH, Ellul J, Tsibri E. Development of generalized myasthenia gravis in patients with ocular myasthenia gravis. *Arch Neurol* 2003;60:1491-1492.

72. Tackenberg B, Hemmer B, Oertel WH, Sommer N. Immunosuppressive treatment of ocular myasthenia gravis. *BioDrugs* 2001;15:369-378.

73. Hart IK, Sharshar T, Sathasivam S. Immunosuppressant drugs for myasthenia gravis. *J Neurol Neurosurg Psychiatry* 2009;80:5-6; discussion 6.

74. A trial of mycophenolate mofetil with prednisone as initial immunotherapy in myasthenia gravis. *Neurology* 2008;71:394-399.

75. Sanders DB, Hart IK, Mantegazza R, et al. An international, phase III, randomized trial of mycophenolate mofetil in myasthenia gravis. *Neurology* 2008;71:400-406.

76. Hughes BW, Moro De Casillas ML, Kaminski HJ. Pathophysiology of myasthenia gravis. *Semin Neurol* 2004;24:21-30.

77. Howard FJ, Lennon V, Finley J, Matsumoto J, Elveback L. Clinical correlations of antibodies that bind, block, or modulate human acetylcholine receptors in myasthenia gravis. *Ann NY Acad Sci* 1987;505:526-538.

78. Limburg PC, The TC, Hummel-Teppel E, Oosterhuis H. Anti-acetylcholine receptor antibodies in myasthenia gravis. I. Relation to clinical parameters in 250 patients. *J Neurol Sci* 1983;58:357-370.

79. Gunji K, Skolnick C, Bednarczuk T, et al. Eye muscle antibodies in patients with ocular myasthenia gravis: Possible mechanism for eye muscle inflammation in acetylcholine receptor antibody-negative patients. *Clin Immunol Immunopathol* 1998;87:276-281.

80. Kaminski HJ, Kusner LL, Block CH. Expression of acetylcholine receptor isoforms at extraocular muscle endplates. *Invest Ophthalmol Vis Sci* 1996;37:345-351.

81. Kaminski HJ, Li Z, Richmonds C, Lin F, Medof ME. Complement regulators in extraocular muscle and experimental autoimmune myasthenia gravis. *Exp Neurol* 2004;189:333-342.

82. Porter JD, Khanna S, Kaminski HJ, et al. Extraocular muscle is defined by a fundamentally distinct gene expression profile. *Proc Natl Acad Sci U S A* 2001;98:12062-12067.

83. Wang Z, Diethelm-Okita B, Okita D, Kaminski H, Howard J, Conti-Fine B. T-cell recognition of muscle acetylcholine receptor in ocular myasthenia gravis. *J Neuroimmunol* 2000;108:29-39.

84. Cheng G, Porter JD. Transcriptional profile of rat extraocular muscle by serial analysis of gene expression. *Invest Ophthalmol Vis Sci* 2002;43:1048-1058.

85. Fischer MD, Gorospe JR, Felder E, et al. Expression profiling reveals metabolic and structural components of extraocular muscles. *Physiol Genomics* 2002;9:71-84.

86. Fischer MD, Budak MT, Bakay M, et al. Definition of the unique human extraocular muscle allotype by expression profiling. *Physiol Genomics* 2005;22:283-291.

87. Khanna S, Porter JD. Conservation of synapse-signaling pathways at the extraocular muscle neuromuscular junction. *Ann N Y Acad Sci* 2002;956:394-396.

88. Spencer RF, Porter JD. Structural organization of the extraocular muscles. In: Buttner-Ennever J (ed), *Neuroanatomy of the oculomotor system*. Amsterdam: Elsevier; 1988:33-79.

89. Spencer RF, Porter JD. Biological organization of the extraocular muscles. *Prog Brain Res* 2005;151:43-80.

90. Kaminski HJ, Li Z, Richmonds C, Ruff RL, Kusner L. Susceptibility of ocular tissues to autoimmune diseases. *Ann N Y Acad Sci* 2003;998:362-374.

91. Losen M, Stassen MH, Martinez-Martinez P, et al. Increased expression of rapsyn in muscles prevents acetylcholine receptor loss in experimental autoimmune myasthenia gravis. *Brain* 2005;128:2327-2337.

92. Wooten GF, Reis DJ. Blood flow in extraocular muscle of cat. *Arch Neurol* 1972;26:350-352.

93. Wilcox LM, Keough EM, Connolly RJ, Hotte CE. Comparative extraocular muscle blood flow. *J Exp Zool* 1981;215:87-90.

94. Nicholson-Weller A, Wang CE. Structure and function of decay accelerating factor CD55. *J Lab Clin Med* 1994;123:485-491.

95. Kaminski HJ, Kusner LL, Richmonds C, Medof ME, Lin F. Deficiency of decay accelerating factor and CD59 leads to crisis in experimental myasthenia. *Exp Neurol* 2006;202:287-293.

96. Lin F, Kaminski H, Conti-Fine B, Wang W, Richmonds C, Medof M. Enhanced Susceptibility to Experimental Autoimmune Myasthenia Gravis in the Absence of Decay-Accelerating Factor Protection. *J Clin Invest* 2002;110:1269-1274.

97. Conti-Fine BM, Kaminski HJ. Autoimmune Neuromuscular Transmission Disorders: Myasthenia Gravis and Lambert-Eaton Myasthenic Syndrome. *Continuum* 2001;7:56-93.

98. Wood SJ, Slater CR. Safety factor at the neuromuscular junction. *Prog Neurobiol* 2001;64:393-429.

4

Myasthenia Gravis Therapy and Thymectomy

Jaya R. Trivedi, M.D. & Gil I. Wolfe, M.D.

1. INTRODUCTION

Myasthenia gravis (MG) is the most frequently encountered autoimmune disease of the neuromuscular junction (NMJ). The immune-mediated nature of MG was suspected as early as 1960 when Simpson speculated that MG was an autoimmune disease with antibodies directed against the nicotinic skeletal muscle acetylcholine receptor (AChR) (1). This hypothesis was confirmed in the 1970s when Lindstrom and colleagues developed an animal model of experimental autoimmune myasthenia gravis (EAMG) by immunizing rabbits and rats with highly purified AChR from the electric organ of the eel (2). Not only did the animals develop weakness, but they responded to anticholinesterase medications and showed typical decremental responses on repetitive nerve stimulation (3). These animals also had high serum AChR antibodies. Subsequently, AChR antibodies were found in the serum of MG patients, and passive transfer of the neuromuscular block occurred by injecting animals with IgG obtained from MG patients (4). AChR antibodies have been shown to reduce the number of functional AChR by several mechanisms: accelerated turnover by cross-linking, complement-dependent lysis of the postsynaptic membrane, and direct blockade of acetycholine (ACh) binding sites (5). In light of the relatively well characterized immune-mediated nature of MG, it is not surprising that immunosuppressive therapy plays a key role in its effective management.

Treatment of MG has improved dramatically over the last few decades, with an increasing number of immunotherapies used in management. In general, the objective of therapy is to return patients to normal function as expeditiously as possible, while limiting side effects and costs. With optimal therapy, most patients can return to productive lives, and there is essentially no mortality (5). The treatment focuses on anticholinesterases, immunosuppressive agents, thymectomy, and short-term interventions such as plasma exchange and intravenous immunoglobulin (IVIG). Treatment should be individualized, and there is no single regimen that is appropriate for all patients (6). The aggressiveness of management should be weighed relative to a number of factors including disease severity, distribution of involvement, rate of progression, degree of functional impairment, lifestyle and career choices, coexisting disease, and patient age and sex. The prognosis with treatment is generally favorable. In a recent survey, only 4% of patients followed for at least 12 months had moderate or severe disability, although some degree of ocular or generalized weakness persisted in the majority (7).

2. ANTICHOLINESTERASE AGENTS

Rational therapeutic use of cholinesterase inhibitors dates back to the second half of the 19th century, when Calabar bean abstract was given as an antidote for atropine poisoning (8) and physostigmine was first used to treat glaucoma (9). In 1934, Walker (10) introduced the use of physostigmine for MG when she reported that physostigmine salicylate injections produced dramatic, though temporary, improvement in a 56 year-old woman with generalized disease. Today, the synthetic quaternary ammonium compounds pyridostigmine and neostigmine are the mainstays of anticholinesterase therapy in MG because of their limited central nervous system toxicity.

2.1. Clinical use

Cholinesterase inhibitors are often the initial intervention in MG. These agents inhibit the enzymatic hydrolysis of ACh at the synapse, allowing the neurotransmitter to accumulate at the NMJ, prolonging its activity, and increasing the number of neurotransmitter-receptor interactions. Pyridostigmine bromide is the preferred cholinesterase inhibitor as it has a longer half-life and a more favorable side-effect profile than neostigmine bromide. A clinical response to pyridostigmine generally begins in 15 to 30 minutes and last up to 3 to 4 hours, although a "wearing-off" effect may occur before then. Initial doses of 30 to 60 mg every 4 to 6 hours are typical (11). Individual doses can be titrated upward to 90 and even 120 mg to maximize the clinical response, but regimens exceeding 120 mg every 3 hours are unlikely to have added benefit and will likely produce serious cholinergic side effects (12). Dosing equivalents and pediatric doses for other

Table 1. Equivalent Dosing of Acetylcholinesterase Inhibitors*

AchE Inhibitor	Oral dose	IM dose	IV dose	Pediatric oral dose
Pyridostigmine bromide (Mestinon)	60 mg	2.0 mg	0.7 mg	1.0 mg/kg; up to 7.0 mg/kg/d in divided doses
Neostigmine (Prostigmin)	15 mg (bromide)	1.5 mg (methylsulfate)	0.5 mg (methylsulfate)	0.3 mg/kg; up to 2 mg/kg/d in divided doses
Ambenonium chloride (Mytelase)	7.5 mg			0.15-0.3 mg/kg; up to 1.5 mg/kg/d in divided doses

* These values are approximate and may need to be adjusted depending on clinical response.

cholinesterase inhibitors are shown in Table 1. A 60mg/5ml elixir of pyridostigmine and 2 mg injection (equivalent to 60 mg administered orally) (13) are also available. Mestinon Timespan, a timed-release 180 mg pyridostigmine tablet, is occasionally prescribed at bedtime for patients who awaken in the middle of the night or in the morning with myasthenic symptoms such as dysphagia (14). Absorption of the timed-release preparation is unpredictable, however, and many MG experts do not recommend its frequent or daytime use.

Proper dosing of pyridostigmine requires individualization. With experience, patients often learn to self-adjust the dose for optimal benefit. Such initiative should not be discouraged as long as the patient has insight into the drug's onset of action and side effects. A proper dose should produce an improvement that begins within 45 minutes and is wearing off before the next dose is taken.

2.2. Side effects

The most common adverse events of the cholinesterase inhibitors are muscarinic in nature, including gastrointestinal cramps, diarrhea, nausea and vomiting, increased lacrimal, salivary and bronchial secretions, and sweating (11). Oral glycopyrrolate (1 mg), hyoscyamine sulfate (0.125 mg), atropine (0.4 mg) or over-the-counter loperamide can be prescribed either on an as-needed basis or prophylactically at the same time as a pyridostigmine dose to limit these side effects. Nicotinic toxicity includes muscle cramping, fasciculations, and weakness. Consumption of large amounts of bromide can lead to bromism and acute psychosis. Patients allergic to bromide may develop a rash; in such settings ambenonium chloride is a therapeutic alternative.

Unfortunately, a large number of MG patients cannot be controlled on anticholinesterase medications alone (12). At that point, thymectomy and immunosuppressive therapies need to be considered and initiated.

3. CORTICOSTEROIDS

Corticosteroids, the first immunosuppressants to be widely used in MG, produce marked improvement in 80% or more of patients (15,16). Despite the absence of controlled, randomized studies, corticosteroids are considered by many MG experts as the most effective oral immunosuppressive agents for MG and a mainstay of therapy (17). In a study of 116 patients, prednisone produced remission in 28%, marked improvement in 53% (minor symptoms; return to activities of daily living), moderate improvement in 15% (functional limitations), and no improvement in only 5% (16). The clinical response is relatively rapid, observed within the first 2 to 4 weeks on dosing of approximately 1 to 1.5 mg/kg/d (Table 2). If a positive response is apparent in this timeframe, patients can be switched to an alternate day regimen of 1 to 1.5 mg/kg/d after 4 weeks (18). More refractory patients require daily dosing for 2-3 months before a slower alternate-day taper can commence. The mean response to maximum benefit is 5-6 months.

A recent study of 35 MG patients demonstrated that prednisone was superior to pyridostigmine in improving ocular symptoms and signs using ocular items of the Quantitative MG (QMG) score as the outcome measure (p=0.0021) (19). Complete resolution of ocular symptoms was seen in only 29% of patients on anticholinesterase agents alone versus 70% of those taking prednisone. In another study, prednisone reduced the incidence of disease generalization at 2 years in a retrospective analysis of patients presenting with pure ocular MG (20). Only 7% of ocular MG patients receiving prednisone developed generalized disease, compared to 36% receiving pyridostigmine alone or taking no medication.

3.1. Transient worsening

The main concern when initiating high doses of prednisone is the transient worsening that occurs in one-third to one-half of MG patients (15,16). In the series of Pascuzzi et al.,(16) 8.6% of patients experiencing transient worsening required intubation. Thus, an advised practice is to admit MG patients to the hospital for 5 to 7 days when initiating high-dose prednisone. A common regimen used to avoid these transient exacerbations is to begin with low-dose prednisone on alternate days, starting at 10-25 mg, increasing the dose by 10-20 mg every few days to a peak dose of 1.5 mg/kg on alternate days (21). This is a useful strategy in patients with milder disability where a slower response is acceptable. For instance, a slow ramp-up is often used in patients with ocular MG.

3.2. Tapering

After patients have achieved significant improvement, there should not be a rush to taper off the corticosteroid (22). Premature or rapid tapering is a common management error. It is best to taper slowly, reducing the dose no faster than 5 mg every 2 weeks. Once a dose of 20 mg every other day has been reached, tapering at even slower rates is advisable. Although an effort should be made to taper off the prednisone completely, many patients will require chronic low-dose therapy. In the series of Pascuzzi et al. (16) only 14% of patients were able to discontinue prednisone and maintain improvement. Other immunosuppressants to be discussed later can be added to prednisone as "steroid sparers" to assist with tapering efforts (23). Prior thymectomy does not appear to influence the likelihood of a successful prednisone taper (24).

3.3. Side effects

Side effects of corticosteroids are common and significant (Table 2), occurring in two-thirds of patients (16), with greater severity when high doses are used for more than a month. Side effects can subside at doses below 20 mg every other day. Exercise, dietary modification, and calcium and vitamin D supplementation are important prophylactic measures. The addition of bisphosphonate therapy has been recommended by medical societies to prevent bone loss in patients receiving long-term or newly initiated cortocosteroid therapy (25). It is the side effects that lead some to question whether corticosteroids are overutilized in myasthenia gravis (26). Still, the lower cost and apparent greater efficacy of steroids compared to other immunosuppressive agents provide a strong argument for their continued use in MG (27). A multi-center survey from Japan indicates that the proportion of MG patients treated with corticosteroids actually increased from 50% in 1987 to 64% in 1999-2000 (7).

4. OTHER IMMUNOTHERAPIES

4.1. Azathioprine

Azathioprine inhibits purine metabolism and blocks cell proliferation, thereby affecting rapidly dividing cell populations including lymphocytes. Although a relatively weak immunosuppressive drug, it is the best established "steroid-sparing" agent in MG. In addition to its use in patients who have had a relapse during a corticosteroid taper or who are experiencing adverse events from chronic steroid use, azathioprine also is used as a first-line agent (28). Retrospective studies demonstrate that 70-90% of MG patients improve on azathioprine (28, 29). However, its role is hampered by a delayed onset of action; benefit may begin as early as 2 months (28), but may not be seen for 10 months (29), and a maximal effect may not be reached for 12 to 24 months (23).

A randomized, double-blind trial compared the use of oral prednisolone plus azathioprine 2.5 mg/kg/d versus prednisolone alone, providing useful insight into its role in MG (30). Once patients reached remission, prednisolone was tapered by blinded personnel to the minimal dose that maintained remission. Due to low overall recruitment and withdrawals in older patients, only 18 patients completed the 36-month trial. Median prednisolone dosing did not differ between the two arms at 12 months, but was significantly lower in the combined therapy group at 24 and 36 months, with a steroid-sparing effect first discernable at 15 months. Patients receiving azathioprine had fewer relapses, longer remissions, and fewer side effects with less weight gain. At 3 years, 63% of patients receiving azathioprine had been completely tapered off of prednisolone, compared to 20% who had received prednisolone alone (30). In another study, relapses occurred in the majority of patients who discontinued azathioprine (31). However, these patients did respond favorably to azathioprine upon reinitiation.

Initial and maintenance dosing and adverse events for azathioprine are listed in Table 2. Should hepatotoxicity or leukopenia develop, the dose should be reduced by 50 to 100 mg a day. Once normalized, the dose can be increased in 25 to 50 mg increments. If the white blood cell count falls below $3 \times 10^9/L$, azathioprine should be held until the count recovers to $4 \times 10^9/L$, and then restarted at a lower dose. Development of an idiosyncratic flu-like syndrome or skin rash with drug fever are reasons to permanently discontinue azathioprine.

4.2. Cyclosporin

Cyclosporin potently inhibits T cell-dependent immune responses via disruption of calcineurin signaling, reduced production and secretion of cytokines such as interleukin-2, and impaired T helper cell activation. Cyclosporin is one of the few agents to have been subjected to randomized, double-blinded, placebo-controlled trials in MG (31-33). A total of 39 patients were randomized in the larger study, 20 to cyclosporin (5 mg/kg/d) and 19 to placebo (32). An unblinded investigator adjusted dosing to achieve morning trough levels of 300-500 nm/mL without impairing renal function. Patients were evaluated monthly with the QMG. By 6 months, patients receiving cyclosporin demonstrated significantly improved strength, reduced symptoms, and greater reduction in AChR antibodies than patients on placebo. Also observed was a trend toward more successful steroid tapering in patients receiving the active drug. Clinical improvement with cyclosporin is usually observed between 4 and 12 weeks (34). A preliminary report of a double-blind trial suggested that azathioprine 2.5 mg/kg/d and cyclosporin 5 mg/kg/d were equally effective (35). Improvement with cyclosporin is observed in patients who have been refractory to other agents (32, 34).

Side effects of hypertension and nephrotoxicity are common with cyclosporin, and clinical experience suggests the drug is less well tolerated than either azathioprine or mycophenolate mofetil. Over one-quarter of patients will have serum creatinine levels increase between 30-70% above baseline levels (34). In the randomized trial, at 36 month follow-up of 18 patients initially randomized to cyclosporin, 55% had discontinued the medication (32). Leading causes were nephrotoxicity in 10%, headache or psychiatric symptoms in 10%, gastrointestinal symptoms in 10%, and infection in 5%. Patients at increased risk for nephrotoxicity are those over age 50 with preexisting hypertension or renal dysfunction (33). Higher initial dosing and blood levels also increase the likelihood of nephrotoxicity. As with azathioprine and other immunosuppressive agents, there is concern that cyclosporin increases the incidence of skin cancer and other malignancies over time.

Dosing, adverse event, and lab monitoring information for cyclosporin are listed in Table 2. Current dosing recommendations for ongoing therapy are lower than the 5-6 mg/kg/d used in earlier studies. Long-term disease control is possible in many patients with dosing at 3 mg/kg/d or less (34). Trough blood levels of 100-150 µg/L tend to correlate with clinical improvement (34). It is important not to mix different cyclosporin preparations as the different brands are not bioequivalent. Concurrent use of other medications with potential renal toxicity such as diuretics should be avoided. Cyclosporin has numerous problematic drug interactions including aminoglycosides, vancomycin, amphotericin B, ketoconazole, bactrim, H_2 blockers, colchicine, and several nonsteroidal anti-inflammatory drugs.

4.3. Mycophenolate mofetil

Mycophenolate mofetil is the latest immunosuppressive agent to enter routine use in MG, having shown promise in several uncontrolled, open series demonstrating favorable responses in two-thirds of patients (36-37). The most common dosing regimen is 1 gm twice daily.

Mycophenolate blocks inosine monophosphate dehydrogenase, resulting in selective inhibition of B and T lymphocyte proliferation by impairing purine synthesis. It is routinely used in allogeneic transplant patients and has been well tolerated in the MG population (36, 37).[7] Main side effects are diarrhea, vomiting, increased risk for infection, and relatively rare leukopenia. Long-term safety for mycophenolate is still in question, but malignancy rates do not appear higher in the transplant population. However, a single case report of primary CNS lymphoma in an 83 year-old MG patient successfully treated with mycophenalate for 3 years was recently published (38). She had documented lymphocytopenia (<500/µL) that had earlier required mycophenolate dose adjustments. Dramatic remission of the lymphoma was observed after mycophenolate was stopped and intravenous rituximab was administered. Also of concern are recent reports from the Food and Drug Administration of progressive multifocal encephalopathy in solid organ transplant recipients or in patients with systemic lupus erythematosus who were receiving mycophenolic acid.

In a recent retrospective analysis of 85 patients that employed MG Foundation of America (MGFA) postintervention classifications, 73% achieved pharmacologic remission, minimal manifestation status, or improvement with mycophenolate (39). Patients with severe weakness (MG Foundation of America Class IV) were somewhat less likely to respond. Mycophenolate had a relatively rapid onset of action, with improvement observed at a mean of 9-11 weeks and maximal improvement by approximately 6 months (39). However, in some subjects the initial response lagged up to 40 weeks. Only 6% of patients discontinued therapy because of side effects, with gastrointestinal intolerance being the leading cause.

With its more rapid onset of action and favorable side effects profile, mycophenolate has replaced azathioprine as the first-line "steroid sparer" in many MG clinical centers. However, recent data from two randomized, controlled trials of mycophenolate have raised questions regarding its use in this manner. Neither study succeeded in demonstrating that mycophenolate plus prednisone was more successful than prednisone alone in reducing QMG scores (40) attaining minimal manifestation status (41), or improving various secondary outcome measures. Several explanations have been forwarded for these negative results: the generally mild disease status of patients, the better-than-expected response to relatively low doses of prednisone, and the duration of the studies. Nevertheless, the available data do raise questions regarding the actual efficacy of mycophenolate as a steroid-sparing agent, at least in the first year of use.

4.4. Cyclophosphamide

The use of cyclophosphamide, a nitrogen mustard alkylating agent that blocks cell proliferation, is mainly reserved for refractory MG patients. Reported use is limited. Perez et al. (42) reported 42 patients treated with cyclophosphamide; 33 were also receiving corticosteroids. At the time of retrospective analysis, 25 (60%) were asymptomatic and 12 were in complete remission off all medications, a higher strictly defined remission rate than for other MG treatments.

In a randomized, placebo-controlled double-blinded study, monthly intravenous pulses of cyclophosphamide 500 mg/m² were given to 23 MG patients with severe, refractory disease or steroid-related side effects (43). At month 12, the cyclophosphamide arm had significantly improved muscle strength on quantitative MG scoring. At both 6 and 12 months, steroid doses were significantly lower in the cyclophosphamide group. Similarly, impressive therapy responses were seen in three refractory MG patients who received high-dose (50 mg/kg) intravenous cyclophosphamide for 4 days followed by "rescue" with granulocyte colony stimulating factor. Marked improvement in strength without disease recurrence over several years was observed (44). Of note, one of these patients was anti-muscle specific tyrosine kinase (MuSK)-antibody positive.

Cyclophosphamide has a high rate and severity of toxicity. Alopecia can occur in 75%, leukopenia in 35%, and nausea and vomiting in 25%. The increased risk of bladder and lymphoreticular malignancy with prolonged administration of cyclophosphamide should be of particular concern. Intravenous, pulsed cyclophosphamide may be safer than daily oral delivery, as a result of lower total cumulative doses (Table 2) (43,44). Based on recent work, pulsed therapy appears to be a rational option in carefully selected refractory patients.

4.5. Intravenous immunoglobulin

Intravenous immunoglobulin (IVIg) is frequently used by neurologists for various immune-mediated neuromuscular diseases including MG. In an analysis of eight published retrospective

MG studies, a response rate to IVIg of 73% was calculated, with clinical responses seen in 4 to 5 days (45). The effect can persist for several weeks to several months. A randomized, double-blinded, placebo-controlled trial of IVIg in generalized MG was initiated but was terminated before an adequate number of subjects could be enrolled (46). In the open-label IVIg extension, favorable trends in quantitative strength and electrophysiologic outcome measures were seen in patients who had initially received placebo, in line with qualitative improvement seen in prior reports (46).

A recent randomized, double-blinded, placebo-controlled trial enrolled 51 patients and found a meaningful improvement in the QMG score 14 days after a 2 gm/kg dose of IVIg versus D5W placebo (47). The treatment effect persisted through day 28, although the change in QMG barely missed statistical significance (p–0.055). The response appeared independent of age, sex, disease duration, and antibody status since seronegative and anti-MuSK MG patients were also enrolled. When stratifying patients, it was determined that only those with more severe disease at entry (QMG scores e" 11) benefited from IVIg. The authors concluded that patients with

Table 2. Commonly Used Immunosuppressant Agents for MG

Agent (Trade names)	Initial dose	Maintenance dose	Onset of Action	Major Adverse Events	Lab Monitoring	Comments
Prednisone	15-20 mg qd, increasing by 5 to 10 mg q2-3 days	1.5 mg/kg a day, followed by slow alternate day taper (taper by 5-10 mg a month)	2-4 weeks	Hypertension, diabetes, weight gain, bone loss, cataracts, GI ulcers, psychologic disorders	Potassium, glucose every few months; bone density monitoring	Administer in single am dose; if starting with high doses (1.5 mg/kg) watch for early worsening seen in up to 1/2 of pts
Azathioprine (Imuran)	50 mg day	Increase by 50 mg increments q 2-4 weeks to target of 2-3 mg/kg	2-10 months for initial response. Up to 24 months for peak	Fever, abdominal pain, nausea, vomiting, anorexia, leukopenia, hepatotoxic, skin rash	CBC, LFTs 2-4 times in first month, then monthly	10% of patients cannot tolerate because of flu-like reaction; major drug interaction with allopurinol
Cyclosporin (Sandimmune, Neoral, Gengraf)	100 mg bid	Increase slowly as needed to 3-6 mg/kg on bid schedule	1-3 months	Hirsuitism, tremor, gum hyperplasia, hypertension, hepatotoxic, nephrotoxic	CBC, LFTs, BUN/Cr monthly. Follow trough drug levels	Bioequivalence differs between preparations; avoid brand switching when possible
Mycophenolate Mofetil (CellCept)	250 to 500 mg bid	1000 to 1500 mg po bid	2-12 months	Diarrhea, vomiting, leukopenia	CBC weekly for 4 weeks, q2 weeks for 4 weeks, then monthly	Diarrhea may resolve by switch to tid dosing

Cyclophos-phamide (Cytoxan)	3-5 mg/kg a day. Can be preceded by intravenous pulse	2-3 mg/kg a day	2-6 months	Alopecia, leukopenia, nausea and vomiting, skin discoloration, anorexia hemorrhagic cystitis, malignancy	CBC, chemistry panel, urinalysis every 2-4 weeks	Intravenous pulse therapy may be less toxic
Tacrolimus/ FK-506 (Prograf)	3-5 mg a day or 0.1 mg/kg/day	Increase up to 5 mg a day following trough levels (see last column)	1-3 months	Hypergly-cemia, hypertension, headache, hyperkalemia, nephrotoxicity, diarrhea, nausea and vomiting	BUN/Cr, glucose, potassium, trough levels every few weeks initially, then less regularly	Insulin-dependent diabetes mellitus developed in 20% of post-renal transplant patients. Trough levels of 8-9 ng/ml have been effective in MG
Rituximab (Rituxan)	375 mg/m^2 IV every 1-2 wk for 4 wk	None or 375 mg/m^2 every 4-10 wk for a few months	1-3 mo	Pruritus, nausea, vomiting, dizziness, headache, angina, cardiac dysrhythmia, anemia, leukopenia, thrombocyto-penia	CBC regularly in first month of therapy, cardiac monitoring in patients with pre-existing disease	Tumor lysis syndrome should not be an issue in the MG population; premedicate with acetaminophen and diphenhydra-mine
Etanercept (Enbrel)	25 mg SQ twice weekly	25 mg SQ twice weekly	2-6 mo	Injection site reactions, vomiting, rhinitis, upper respiratory tract infection, anemia, pancytopenia, vasculitis, central demyelination	CBC	Reactivation of hepatitis B and granulomatous disease (TB) is of concern; avoid in patients with heart failure
IVIg (Carimune, Flebogamma, Gammagard, Gamunex, Octagam)	2 gm/kg over 2-5 days	0.4-1 gm/kg every 4 weeks; can attempt to decrease frequency over time	1-2 weeks	Headache, aseptic meningitis, nephrotoxic, ischemic events, fluid overload	BUN/Cr	Avoid in patients with recent ischemia

64

minor symptoms or with pure ocular disease clinically and on quantitative scoring are unlikely to benefit from IVIg. For these patients who fail anticholinesterase therapy, immunosuppressive agents should be considered. No serious adverse events were observed, although 75% of subjects randomized to IVIg reported headache.

Indications for IVIg include: reducing perioperative morbidity prior to thymectomy, inducing rapid improvement in patients with severe disease or in crisis, and for chronic management in selected refractory patients. IVIg demonstrated similar efficacy to plasmapheresis in MG exacerbations (48), although some reports suggest it is less effective than plasma exchange in true crisis scenarios.

Complication rates tend to be lower for IVIg than for plasma exchange. IVIg is a particularly attractive alternative to plasma exchange in patients with poor venous access, hemodynamic instability or other contraindications to plasmapheresis. Standard IVIg regimens and adverse events are listed in Table 2. For a detailed description of IVIg therapy in MG and its mechanisms of action see chapter 6.

4.6. Plasma exchange

Plasma exchange was first used in MG in 1976 (49), and is primarily employed in the short-term, acute management of severe disease including crisis and in readying weak patients for thymectomy (50). It produces rapid improvement in a matter of days when used in clinical situations similar to those mentioned for IVIg. It is presumed that elimination of circulating AChR antibodies and other humoral factors of pathological significance account for the beneficial effects of plasma exchange (51).

A course of plasmapheresis consists of four to six exchanges in which approximately 50 ml/kg of plasma (one plasma volume) is removed at each treatment. The plasma is replaced by albumin or plasma protein fractions. There is no risk of disease transmission if blood products other than albumin and plasma protein fractions are avoided. Regional anticoagulation with citrate is typically used (52). Decisions regarding the number of exchanges and total amount removed are largely driven by the status of the patient including clinical response and tolerability of the large hemodynamic shifts from the procedure. Improvement is often seen within 48 hours after the first or second exchange. Treatments can be performed daily or every other day in the acute setting. Long-term bimonthly or monthly exchanges are used in selected refractory patients as part of a chronic treatment program.

The main limitations of plasma exchange are:
- intravenous access since large-bore, double-lumen catheters are often required;
- complications such as perioral and/or limb paresthesias due to chelation of ionized calcium by citrate (citrate reaction) (53);
- infections, pneumothorax, hypotension, sepsis, and pulmonary embolism;
- expense and inavailablilty in many community hospital settings;
- the relatively brief clinical response when not combined with immunosuppressive agents (54).

See chapter 5 for clinical trial on plasma exchange and IgG immunoabsorption and chapter 23 for preclinical studies on anti-AChR antibody immunoabsorption during plasma exchange.

5. NEWER IMMUNOTHERAPIES

5.1. Tacrolimus

Case reports (55) and open trials (56-60) have demonstrated efficacy for tacrolimus as monotherapy, adjuvant therapy when added to immunosuppresive agents, and in refractory MG. In a trial of 19 patients, approximately half improved on either quantitative strength or symptom scales at 16 weeks (57). Long-term observation in 12 patients for up to 2 years showed continued benefit without serious side effects. Favorable responses to tacrolimus were recently confirmed in a randomized, though unblinded, prednisolone-controlled study (maximum dose 20 mg/day) of 36 *de novo* MG patients (60). Plasma exchange and high dose intravenous methylprednisolone were added as needed for disease control. Patients in both arms of the study improved significantly. The number of plasma exchange and methylprednisolone treatments were significantly lower in patients treated with tacrolimus both in early phases of therapy and through one-year of follow-up ($p<0.05$). Likewise, prednisolone doses were significantly lower for patients who were on tacrolimus at one year ($p<0.05$). Four patients maintained minimal manifestation status on tacrolimus alone. Tacrolimus was well tolerated, with increased serum creatinine levels observed in only one patient who also had hypertension.

In the largest report of 212 patients, tacrolimus was given at a dosage of 0.1 mg/kg per day in 2 divided doses, later adjusted for plasma drug concentrations between 7 and 8 mg/mL (61). Approximately half of the patients were on prednisone or were cyclosporin dependent. The mean follow-up time was nearly 50 months (range12-79 months). With the addition of tacrolimus, prednisone could be withdrawn in 95% of patients. Quantitative MG scores fell significantly from 20.5 at baseline to less than 1.0 at the final visit, and muscle strength improvement was evident as early as 1 month after treatment initiation. More than 85% of patients achieved complete stable remission or pharmacologic remission at the end of follow-up, with another 5% reaching minimal manifestation status. Impressive remission results were observed regardless of whether patients had undergone thymectomy and irrespective of whether patients had thymoma, although complete stable remission was less likely in thymomatous MG. Tacrolimus was well tolerated overall, with hypertension in 1.9% of patients, nephrotoxicity in 2.9%, neurotoxicity such as tremor or paresthesia in 5.9%, and diabetes in 1.4%.

Doses of 3-5 mg a day or 0.1 mg/kg/d have been used in various studies. Tacrolimus is in the same immunosuppressant class as cyclosporin, has a similar onset of action, but may be less nephrotoxic. Hyperglycemia is a well-recognized complication (Table 2). Large-scale, double-blind, placebo-controlled studies of tacrolimus for MG are currently underway in Japan.

5.2. Rituximab

Rituximab, a chimeric monoclonal antibody directed against the B cell surface membrane antigen CD20 that induces depletion of B lymphocytes, has produced clinical improvement within 4 weeks in case reports of adults and children (62-64). No complications or side effects were observed. Several ongoing studies and pilot trials that have enrolled a total of 14 MG patients have also documented efficacy for the agent, including in patients with antibodies to MuSK (65-67). In these preliminary reports, infusions were given weekly to every other week for the first month. Treatment may cease at that point or be followed by repeated infusions every 4 to 10 weeks, depending on the protocol. In a prospective study of 6 MG patients (three with anti-MuSK antibodies) who had failed two or three lines of conventional immunosuppressive agents in association with oral corticosteroids, all six successfully stopped steroids at a 2 year follow-up (68). There is considerable interest in studying rituximab further in MG, especially in the anti-MuSK population.

In addition to the adverse events listed in Table 2, rituximab has been associated with the development of progressive multifocal encephalopathy in the non–Hodgkin lymphoma population for which it is indicated. Clinical trials and the mechanisms of action of rituximab is discussed in depth in chapter 27.

5.3. Etanercept

This soluble, recombinant tumor necrosis factor-alpha (TNFα) receptor blocker, was studied in a prospective pilot trial in 11 patients with corticosteroid-dependent MG (69). Eight patients completed the 6-month trial, receiving 25 mg subcutaneously twice a week. Prednisone was tapered according to a standardized protocol. Of the three patients who did not complete the study, one withdrew due to a generalized rash. The two others dropped out because of disease worsening, which in one case was severe, occurring after 3 weeks of etanercept treatment and requiring plasma exchange. Of note, this patient had a nearly 300-fold elevation in TNFα levels with treatment — a proinflammatory response seen in other autoimmune diseases — perhaps upregulating the cytokine response and leading to the exacerbation. Of the remaining 8 patients, 5 improved on QMG by at least 3 points, the primary measure of efficacy. It took between 2 to 6 months to see significant improvement on the various outcome measures. At study exit, prednisone had been reduced by a mean of 80.4%.

In a satellite study, etanercept treatment raised the levels of most plasma complement and cytokine levels, including C3, interleukins (IL), and IFN-γ (70). Patients who responded best to etanercept had either small increases or actual decreases in cytokine levels during the pilot study. The investigators surmised that in some patients, etanercept might worsen disease control, especially in subjects with high baseline IL-6 and IFN-ã levels. Routine use of etanercept in MG is not currently recommended. The detailed clinical trial of etanercept is reported in chapter 26.

6. THYMECTOMY

Thymectomy has been regularly performed for MG both in thymoma and non-thymoma cases for nearly 70 years. In 1939, Blalock et al (71) reported improvement of generalized MG in a 21 year-old woman following removal of a cystic thymic tumor. In a subsequent study by Blalock (72), of six MG patients who underwent thymectomy, one became symptom-free, two significantly improved, and two had mild benefit. Additional favorable reports followed, and the surgery became an accepted therapy.

6.1. Effect of thymectomy

Thymectomy, with or without the presence of thymoma, has gained wide acceptance as a key component of MG management. There is a general consensus that generalized MG patients between puberty and 60 years of age will benefit from thymectomy (73). However, randomized studies of thymectomy that control for medical therapy have never been performed. In a 1977 analysis, remission rates compiled from some of the larger series of surgical and non-surgical patients did not portray a significant difference between the two treatment groups (Table 3). It should be kept in mind that the non-surgical series in this table were mostly published prior to the routine use of corticosteroids and other medical immunotherapies (74).

Table 3. Remission Rates With and Without Thymectomy[74]

Surgical therapy		Non-surgical therapy	
Author Year	n (% in remission)	Author Year	n (% in remission)
Simpson 1958	258 (21)	Kennedy et al. 1937	87 (31)
Perlo et al. 1971	267 (34)	Grob 1953	202 (23)
Mulder et al. 1974	73 (36)	Simpson 1958	99 (16)
Emeryk et al. 1976	112 (23)	Oosterhuis 1964	180 (31)
Papatestas et al. 1975	111 (25)	Perlo et al. 1971	417 (17)
Total	821 (28)	Total	985 (24)

A recent evidence-based practice parameter from the American Academy of Neurology analyzed retrospective, controlled, non-randomized studies of thymectomy in MG. A total of 28 studies published between 1953 and 1998 were identified (75). The effect of surgery was broadly favorable in most series. However, the benefit of surgery was generally small. For example, the median relative rate favoring surgery over non-surgical treatment for achieving remission was 2.1 (a modest gain when considering that the median remission rate in the non-thymectomized groups was 10%). Other median relative rates were 1.6 for asymptomatic status, 1.7 for improvement , and 1.1 for survival. Patient subgroup analysis indicated that only those MG patients with moderate weakness (Osserman 2b) or greater showed a significant improvement following thymectomy compared to controls. Importantly, the modest benefits ascribed to thymectomy were confounded by baseline differences between the surgical and non-surgical groups as well as limited thymic resections performed in a significant percent of the patients. No study included blinded assessments. In those few studies that employed a matched design with an attempt to control for multiple confounding variables, a consistent benefit from thymectomy was not observed. As a result, the authors expressed uncertainty as to whether claims of improved MG outcomes were a result of thymectomy or related to differences in baseline characteristics between surgical and non-surgical groups. The AAN practice parameter concluded that thymectomy be considered a treatment *option* in patients without thymoma (75). To address this uncertainty, an international, NIH-supported, prospective, single-blinded, randomized trial controlling for medical therapy has been organized in non-thymomatous MG (76) and began enrolling subjects in late 2006.

6.2. Extent of resection

Transsternal thymectomy approaches are still the standard and preferred surgical technique since they permit greater tissue removal, although transcervical and infraaxillary video-assisted approaches are also used. There is some evidence to support the view that the greater the resection, the better the long-term results (77). Using a "maximal" thymectomy approach that includes both transcervical and transsternal incisions, life-table analyses demonstrated an 81% remission rate at 7.5 years (78). Comparative remission rates for transcervical approaches have been in the 30-45% range at 7 years (79), and approximately 50% at 6 years using either an extended transsternal or a video-assisted thorascopic procedure that includes a transverse cervical incision (80). It should be noted that remission rates in surgical series often have unexpectedly high remission rates. Definitions of remission as well as their duration vary between studies, and the retrospective determination of these outcomes is certainly open to bias (75,77).

Table 4 provides estimates of the extent of thymic removal for the most common resections. No matter the approach, thymectomy should not be performed as an emergent procedure. Plasma exchange or IVIg can be used to stabilize patients with more severe disease prior to surgery. The extended transsternal procedure is being studied in the prospective international trial mentioned earlier.

Table 4. Rough Estimates of the Extent of Thymic Remova (77)

Thymectomy approach	Percent resected
"Maximal" transcervical-transsternal	98-100
Extended transsternal	85-95
Video-assisted thorascopic (VATS)	80-85
Extended transcervical	75-80
Transsternal	70-75
Transcervical	40-50

6.3. Patient approach

The presence of a thymoma (10-15% of MG patients) is the one absolute indication for thymectomy. All newly diagnosed MG patients must undergo a chest CT or MRI to look for evidence of thymoma. Of note, routine chest radiographs may not detect up to 25% of thymic tumors. But in most cases of MG where there is no thymoma, there are uncertainties surrounding the role of thymectomy. At this point, it is reasonable to relay to patients that more likely than not they will improve after thymectomy. However, such statements should be balanced by informing them that potential benefits have not been established in rigorous clinical studies, and that remission and improvement are known to occur without thymectomy. Furthermore, it would be misleading to guarantee improvement after thymectomy or give a fixed timetable for clinical benefit.

Thymectomy is generally not a first or second-line approach in patients with pure ocular MG. It is probably less effective in the elderly, and most MG experts do not advocate its use in this group, with cutoff ages ranging between 50 and 70 years (median 60 years) (73). Post-thymectomy patients who continue to have significant disability from MG despite the use of cholinesterase inhibitors should be started on immunosuppressive therapy. Thymectomy has been performed with favorable results in childhood (81) - even in patients less than 5 years of age (82-83). Its use, however, remains controversial in the youngest children, with recommended lower age limits ranging from 1 year to puberty (73).

7. NOVEL APPROACHES

7.1. Monarsen

Formerly known as EN101, this experimental oral antisense oligonucleotide against acetylcholinesterase mRNA is in early investigational studies. In a recently reported open trial, 13 of 15 patients who discontinued pyridostigmine demonstrated symptomatic improvement on QMG (84). The improvement was dramatic, with a mean 6.13 point reduction after only 4 days of therapy. Fourteen patients reported subjective improvement compared to their status on pyridostigmine. Four patients continued Monarsen for 4 weeks with continued benefit, although two resumed use of daily pyridostigimine (60-120 mg). A favorable effect from Monarsen lasted up to 48 hours, in contrast to the transient effect of pyridostigmine. Monarsen has been well tolerated in studies. In the trial, 56% experienced transient dry mouth or eyes (84). Further investigation is underway. See chapter 25 for the pre-clinical and clinical trial of Monarsen

7.2. Terbutaline

Although adrenergic agonists such as ephedrine were used in the past to treat MG, they are rarely used today. Catecholamines may have direct effects on neuromuscular transmission and also may regulate lymphocyte proliferation and antibody synthesis. A pilot, double-blinded, placebo-controlled crossover study (2 week treatment periods) demonstrated that terbutaline, a β2 agonist, produced at least a 3-point improvement on the QMG in 5 of 8 patients (63%) (85). Decrements on repetitive nerve stimulation also improved. No such benefit was seen with placebo. The terbutaline dose of 2.5 mg tid was well tolerated. This study was small and brief, and further investigation is warranted before sympathomimetic compounds are routinely used in MG.

8. MANAGEMENT OF MG CRISIS

Myasthenic crisis refers to an exacerbation severe enough to endanger life, generally related to respiratory failure from either diaphragmatic or intercostal muscle weakness or airway compromise related to bulbar dysfunction. It occurs in approximately 15-20% of all patients with MG, primarily in the first two years after disease onset. Management of MG crisis should take place in an intensive care setting to allow for close monitoring. Intercurrent infections, a common trigger, should be managed aggressively. Patients with marked bulbar weakness or low baseline vital capacities of <20-25 ml/kg are especially at risk for respiratory failure. Paradoxical breathing or dyspnea in a supine position may provide additional warning signs.

Because of its rapid onset of action within days, plasma exchange is a favored treatment for MG crisis. A course of plasmapheresis consists of 4 to 6 exchanges in which approximately 50 ml/kg of plasma are removed at each treatment. However, it should be stressed that there is no exact science to the number of exchanges or the amount removed. The treatments can be done daily or every other day in the hospital so that the full course is completed in 7 to 10 days. Since the response to plasma exchange is short-lived, high-dose corticosteroids are routinely administered in crisis settings. Although parenteral pyridostigmine is available (2mg IM = 60 mg po), it is generally withheld while patients are intubated since the anticholinesterase may complicate management of airway secretions and is unlikely to play a contributing role in successful weaning from the ventilator. IVIg has demonstrated similar efficacy to plasmapheresis in MG exacerbations (48), although some reports suggest it is less effective than plasma exchange in true crisis scenarios. Complication rates tend to be lower for IVIg than for plasma exchange.

9. TREATMENT OF OCULAR MG

9.1. Non-pharmacologic

Local treatments represent an option in selected ocular MG patients where conservative, non-pharmacologic therapy is preferred. Such clinical scenarios might include very limited symptoms or disability, failure of medical management, patient preferences, or intolerable side effects from pharmacologic agents. Ptosis, for instance, can be managed with a crutch attached to an eyeglass frame or with small adhesive tapestrips (86). Ptosis tape has a double-sided adhesive that is placed in the crease of the eyelid to hold it open. Both crutches and ptosis tape require a period of adjustment by the patient. Although these local interventions may be uncomfortable and result in eye irritation due to excessive exposure, they are well tolerated on occasion. Eyelid surgery for ptosis is an option in patients who are refractory to prosthetic and pharmacological measures, but is complicated by corneal exposure. Surgery is most often reserved for patients with stable disease and fixed deficits (86).

For patients with rare, intermittent diplopia, no therapy may be the wisest approach. Double vision that is more persistent may be corrected with prisms, especially when the deviation is relatively fixed. Alternate patching of one eye, spectacle lens occluders, and opaque contact lens are other options, especially for short, intermittent episodes of diplopia. Due to characteristic disease fluctuations and the occasional spontaneous remission, extraocular muscle surgery is rarely recommended for diplopia (87).

9.2. Pharmacologic

Medical treatment usually begins with anticholinesterase agents as described earlier in the chapter. In general, ptosis responds better than double vision, and these agents usually will not completely eliminate diplopia. In settings of severe, unilateral ptosis, anticholinesterase agents may unmask double vision by raising the lowered lid, and this may prove to be even more disabling for the patient (88). Overall, only 20-40% of ocular MG patients respond satisfactorily to anticholinesterases.

For patients with persistent ocular symptoms, corticosteroids are usually the next option. Prednisone was superior to pyridostigmine in improving ocular symptoms and signs in a recent study (19). The low-dose titration previously described in Section 3.1 — beginning at doses of 10-20 mg and gradually increasing by 10 mg increments every few days until symptoms are controlled — offers a good strategy in ocular MG. As mentioned earlier, retrospective data suggest that early corticosteroid treatment may reduce the risk of disease generalization (20), but a prospective trial is still needed. Whether corticosteroids alter the progression or simply mask symptoms also needs to be addressed.

Experience with other immunosuppressive agents in ocular MG is limited. Sommer et al. (88) reported improvement in 3 of 4 patients on azathioprine monotherapy. With its favorable side-effects profile and more rapid onset of action, mycophenolate mofetil appears to be a rational choice for ocular MG, although it has not been studied specifically in this population. Notably, an AAN Quality Standards Subcommittee evidence-based review failed to uncover high-quality study data on which to base recommendations for the pharmacological treatment of ocular MG (89). The report also concluded that corticosteroids and azathioprine are of uncertain benefit in reducing the risk of progression to generalized MG.

10. SPECIAL POPULATIONS

10.1. MG and pregnancy

While cholinesterase inhibitors are safe, most immunosuppressive agents are potential teratogens. These agents should be discontinued prior to conception. Corticosteroids, plasma exchange, and IVIG have been used safely during pregnancy. There is rarely a pressing need to perform thymectomy during pregnancy. Surgery can be entertained following delivery.

10.2. Juvenile MG

As in adults, treatment should be individualized. Corticosteroids retard growth and increase the risk for later osteoporosis, requiring utmost caution in their chronic use in children. Thymectomy (81) and various immunosuppressants (90,91) have been used successfully in children.

10.3. Neonatal MG

Transient neonatal MG, as the terminology suggests, is self-limited, with symptoms usually resolving within one month. If there is no significant respiratory or bulbar dysfunction, medications are not necessary. In more severely affected infants, treatment is supportive, including ventilator support and nasogastric feeding. Pyridostigmine (7 mg/kg/d) in divided doses 30 minutes prior to feedings may be helpful (22).

10.4 Seronegative and MuSK-antibody positive MG

Seronegative patients are more likely to have purely ocular MG, and when generalized, their disease tends to be less severe. Seronegative patients have improved with corticosteroids, immunosuppressive agents, plasmapheresis, and thymectomy (92). A subgroup of seronegative patients with prominent ocular and bulbar involvement may not respond favorably to immunosuppressants, but do improve with plasma exchange (93).

A distinctive subset of "seronegative" MG patients express antibodies to muscle-specific tyrosine kinase (MuSK). These patients often have prominent oculobulbar involvement that is more refractory to conventional treatment (94). A poor response to anticholinesterase agents was observed in 70% of subjects (95). Absence of benefit following thymectomy was noted in a

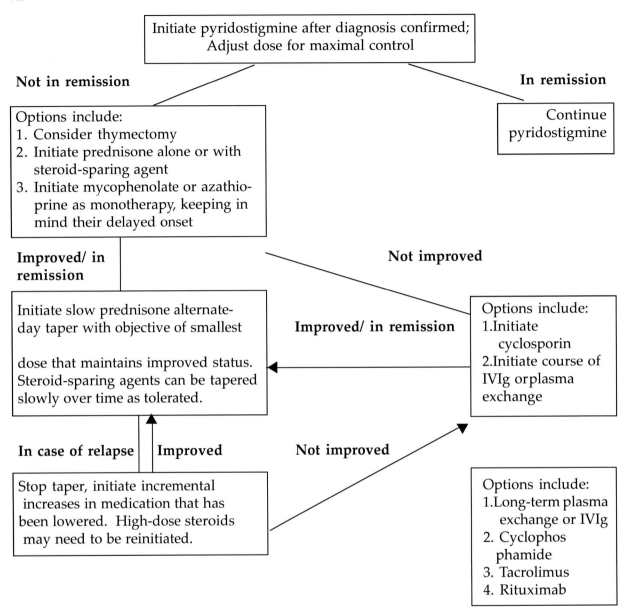

Initiate pyridostigmine after diagnosis confirmed;
Adjust dose for maximal control

Not in remission

In remission

Options include:
1. Consider thymectomy
2. Initiate prednisone alone or with steroid-sparing agent
3. Initiate mycophenolate or azathioprine as monotherapy, keeping in mind their delayed onset

Continue pyridostigmine

Improved/ in remission

Not improved

Initiate slow prednisone alternate-day taper with objective of smallest dose that maintains improved status. Steroid-sparing agents can be tapered slowly over time as tolerated.

Improved/ in remission

Options include:
1. Initiate cyclosporin
2. Initiate course of IVIg or plasma exchange

In case of relapse **Improved**

Not improved

Stop taper, initiate incremental increases in medication that has been lowered. High-dose steroids may need to be reinitiated.

Options include:
1. Long-term plasma exchange or IVIg
2. Cyclophosphamide
3. Tacrolimus
4. Rituximab

recent report of 12 anti-MuSK patients - five with typical MG findings and seven with proximal neck/shoulder or respiratory muscle weakness but without ocular involvement (96). Effective therapies in these 12 patients included plasma exchange in 10, daily prednisone in five, and cyclosporin or mycophenolate mofetil in nine. Five of nine benefitted from pyridostigmine in this series, but none of four patients on azathioprine improved. A 48 year-old woman with anti-MuSK antibodies and severe bulbar and respiratory weakness responded to immunoablative cyclophosphamide infusions (50 mg/kg/d for 4 days) after proving refractory to IVIg, prednisone, cyclosporin, azathioprine, mycophenolate, tacrolimus, rituximab, and ongoing plasma exchange (97). The dramatic and durable clinical improvement in this woman mirrors a prior report (44). Rituximab 375 mg/m² given weekly for 4 weeks and then once every 4 to 10 weeks eliminated the need for plasma exchange in another woman with refractory anti-MuSK MG (65). Although MuSK MG patients are often challenging in the early stages, requiring plasma exchange for frequent exacerbations, over three-quarters will eventually reach a favorable classification of improved, minimal manifestations status, or remission through persistent, aggressive management (98).

11. TREATMENT ALGORITHM

Taking into account the caveat that MG treatment must be individualized, the flow chart below summarizes an approach to management suitable for many patients with generalized disease. If a thymoma is found, thymectomy would be a requisite component of early intervention.

12. CONCLUSIONS

MG is a well-characterized autoimmune disease of the NMJ that responds favorably to medical management. Pharmacotherapy options include anticholinesterase agents, corticosteroids, and steroid-sparing immunomodulating agents. Therapy choices should be individualized and are guided by several factors including age, side effect profile, disease severity, co-morbid illness, and cost. Cholinesterase inhibitors are often started as first-line agents. However, most patients will require additional treatment, at which time immunotherapy or thymectomy are generally considered.

Due to low cost and a relatively rapid onset of action, corticosteroids are widely considered a first-line immunotherapy in MG. However, other immunosuppressants are often used in conjunction with corticosteroids in an effort to reduce side effects. In some patients, such immunosuppressants are used as monotherapy, although their delayed onset of action must be taken into consideration. With their rapid onset of action, plasmapheresis and IVIg are the mainstays of treatment for myasthenic crisis and can be used preoperatively to prepare patients for thymectomy. They may also be used on a chronic basis in severe, refractory patients.

The outcome for MG patients is very favorable. A large single-center report on nearly 2000 patients followed between 1940 and 2000 demonstrated significant advances in outcomes over time (99). Compared to 1940-57 data, the percent of patients classified as improved has essentially doubled since 1986, with significant declines in death rates. In a recent multicenter survey of specialized MG clinics in Japan that included 470 patients with a mean follow-up of 8 years, 30% entered remission, 35% had only ocular manifestations, and 35% had generalized disease (100). Of the generalized group, only 4% were classified as having moderate or severe disability from MG. In general, clinicians and their patients can expect that 90-95% of the time directed therapy will yield a favorable clinical outcome.

REFERENCES

1. Simpson J. Myasthenia gravis: a new hypothesis. *Scot Med J* 1960;5:419-436.
2. Lindstrom JM, Lennon VA, Seybold ME, Whittingham S. Experimental autoimmune myasthenia gravis and myasthenia gravis: biochemical and immunochemical aspects. *Ann NY Acad Sci* 1976;274:254-274.
3. Seybold ME, Lambert EH, Lennon VA, Lindstrom JM. Experimental autoimmune myasthenia: clinical, neurophysiologic and pharmacologic aspects. *Ann NY Acad Sci* 1976;274:275-282.
4. Toyka KV, Drachman DB, Griffin DE, Pestronk A, Winkelstein JA, Fishbeck KH and Kao I. Myasthenia gravis: study of humoral immune mechanisms by passive transfer to mice. *N Engl J Med* 1977;296:125-131.
5. Vincent A, Drachma n DB. Myasthenia gravis. In: Pourmand R, Harati Y, editors. Advances in Neurology: Neuromuscular Disorders. Philadelphia: Lippincott Williams & Wilkins, 2002:159-188.
6. Kaminski HJ. Myasthenia gravis. In: Katirji B, Kaminski HJ, Preston DC, Ruff RL, Shapiro BE, editors. Neuromuscular Disorders in Clinical Practice. Boston: Butterworth-Heinemann, 2002: 916-930.
7. Kawaguchi N, Kuwabara S, Nemoto Y, Fukutake T, Satomura Y, Arimura K, Osame M, and Hattori T; The Study Group of Myasthenia Gravis in Japan. Treatment and outcome of myasthenia gravis: retrospective multi-center analysis of 470 Japanese patients, 1999-2000. *J Neurol Sci* 2004;224:43-47.
8. Kleinwächter. Beobachtung über die wirkung des calabar-extracts gegen atropin-vergiftung. *Berl Klin Wochensch* 1864;38:369-371.
9. Laqueur L. Ueber atropin und physostigmin und ihre wirkung auf den intraocularen druck. Ein beitrag zur therapie des glaucoms. Graefe Arch Clin Exp Ophthalmol 1877;23:149-176.
10. Walker MB. Treatment of myasthenia with physostigmine. Lancet 1934;1:1200- 1201.
11. Wolfe GI, Barohn RJ, Galetta SL. Drugs for the diagnosis and treatment of myasthenia gravis. In: Zimmerman T, Kooner K, Sharir M, Fechtner RD, editors. Textbook of Ocular Pharmacology. Philadelphia: Lippincott-Raven Press, 1997:837-848.
12. Drachman DB. Myasthenia gravis. *N Engl J Med* 1994;330:1797-1810.
13. Reynolds J, editor. Martindale: The extra pharmacopoeia. 30th ed. London: The Pharmaceutical Press; 1993.
14. Sanders DB, Scoppetta C. The treatment of patients with myasthenia gravis. Neurol Clin 1994;12:343-368.
15. Johns TR. Long-term cortocosteroid treatment of myasthenia gravis. *Ann NY Acad Sci* 1987;505:568-583.
16. Pascuzzi RM, Coslett HB, Johns TR. Long-term corticosteroid treatment of myasthenia gravis: report of 116 patients. *Ann Neurol* 1984;15:291-298.
17. Richman DP, Agius MA. Treatment principles in the management of autoimmune myasthenia gravis. *Ann NY Acad Sci* 2003;998:457-472.
18. Warmolts J, Engel A. Benefit from alternate-day prednisone in myasthenia gravis. *N Engl J Med* 1972;286:17-20.
19. Bhanushali MJ, Wuu J, Benatar M. Treatment of ocular symptoms in myasthenia gravis. *Neurology* 2008;71:1335-1341.

20. Kupersmith MJ, Latkany R, Homel P. Development of generalized disease at 2 years in patients with ocular myasthenia gravis. *Arch Neurol* 2003;60:243-248.

21. Seybold ME, Drachman DB. Gradually increasing doses of prednisone in myasthenia gravis: reducing the hazards of treatment. *N Engl J Med* 1974;290:81-84.

22. Wolfe GI, Barohn RJ. Neuromuscular junction disorders of childhood. In: Swaiman KF, Ashwal S, Ferriero DM, editors. Pediatric Neurology: Principles and Practice. 4th ed. Philadelphia: Mosby Elsevier, 2006:1941-1968.

23. Massey JM. Treatment of acquired myasthenia gravis. Neurology 1997;48 (Suppl 5):S46-S51.

24. Miano MA, Bosley TM, Heiman-Patterson TD, Reed J, Sergott RC, Savino PJ, and Schatz NJ. Factors influencing outcome of prednisone dose reduction in myasthenia gravis. *Neurology* 1991;41:919-921.

25. American College of Rheumatology Ad Hoc Committee on Glucocorticoid-Induced Osteoporosis. Recommendations for the prevention and treatment of glucocorticoid-induced osteoporosis. Arthritis Rheumatism 2001;44:1496-1503.

26. Rivner MH. Steroid treatment for myasthenia gravis: steroids are overutilized. *Muscle Nerve* 2002;25:115-117.

27. Bedlack RS, Sanders DB. Steroid treatment for myasthenia gravis: steroids have an important role. *Muscle Nerve* 2002;25:117-121.

28. Mantegazza R, Antozzi C, Peluchetti D, Sghirlanzoni A and Cornelio F. Azathioprine as a single drug or in combination with steroids in the treatment of myasthenia gravis. *J Neurol* 1988;235:449-453.

29. Witte AS, Cornblath DR, Parry GJ, Lisak RP, and Schatz NJ. Azathioprine in the treatment of myasthenia gravis. *Ann Neurol* 1984;15:602-605.

30. Palace J, Newsom-Davis J, Lecky B, Myasthenia Gravis Study Group. A randomized double-blind trial of prednisolone alone or with azathioprine in myasthenia gravis. *Neurology* 1998;50:1778-1783.

31. Mertens HG, Hertel G, Reuther P, Ricker K. Effect of immunosuppressive drugs (azathioprine). *Ann NY Acad Sci* 1981;337:691-698.

32. Tindall RS, Phillips JT, Rollins JA, Wells L, and Hall K. A clinical therapeutic trial of cyclosporine in myasthenia gravis. *Ann NY Acad Sci* 1993;681:539-551.

33. Tindall RS, Rollins JA, Phillips JT, Greenlee RG, Wells L, and Belendiuk G. Preliminary results of a double-blind, randomized, placebo-controlled trial of cyclosporin in myasthenia gravis. *N Engl J Med* 1987;316:719-724.

34. Ciafaloni E, Nikhar NK, Massey JM, Sanders DB. Retrospective analysis of the use of cyclosporin in myasthenia gravis. *Neurology* 2000;55:448-450.

35. Schalke B, Kappos L, Dommasch D, Rohrbach E, and Mertens HG. Cyclosporin A treatment of myasthenia gravis: initial results of a double-blind trial of cyclosporin A versus azathioprine. *Ann NY Acad Sci* 1987;505:872-875.

36. Chaudhry V, Cornblath DR, Griffin JW, O'Brien R, and Drachman DB. Mycophenolate mofetil: a safe and promising immunosuppressant in neuromuscular diseases. *Neurology* 2001;56:94-96.

37. Ciafaloni E, Massey JM, Tucker-Lipscomb B, Sanders DB. Mycophenolate mofetil for myasthenia gravis: an open-label study. *Neurology* 2001;56:97-99.

38. Vernino S, Salomao DR, Habermann TM, O'Neill BP. Primary CNS lymphoma complicating treatment of myasthenia gravis with mycophenolate mofetil. *Neurology* 2005;65:639-641.

39. Meriggioli MN, Ciafaloni E, Al-Hayk KA, Rowin J, Tucker-Lipscomb B, Massey JM, and Sanders DB. Mycophenolate mofetil for myasthenia gravis: an analysis of efficacy, safety, and tolerability. *Neurology* 2003;61:1438-1440.

40. The Muscle Study Group. A trial of mycophenolate mofetil with prednisone as initial immunotherapy in myasthenia gravis. *Neurology* 2008;71:394-399.

41. Sanders DB, Hart IK, Mantegazza R, Shukla SS, Siddiqui ZA, De Baets MH, Melms A, Nicolle MW, Solomons N, and Richman DP. An international, phase III, randomized trial of mycophenolate mofetil in myasthenia gravis. *Neurology* 2008;71:400-406.

42. Perez MC, Buot WL, Mercado-Danguilan C, Bagabaldo ZG, and Renales LD. Stable remissions in myasthenia gravis. *Neurology* 1981;31:32-37.

43. Gustavo de Feo L, Schottlender J, Martelli NA, Molfino NA. Use of intravenous pulsed cyclophosphamide in severe, generalized myasthenia gravis. *Muscle Nerve* 2002;26:31-36.

44. Drachman DB, Jones RJ, Brodsky RA. Treatment of refractory myasthenia: "rebooting" with high-dose cyclophosphamide. *Ann Neurol* 2003;53:29-34.

45. Arsura EL. Experience with intravenous immunoglobulin in myasthenia gravis. *Clin Immunol Immunopathol* 1989;53:S170-S179.

46. Wolfe GI, Barohn RJ, Foster BM, Jackson CE, Kissel JT, Day JW, Thornton CA, Nations SP, Bryan WW, Amato AA, Freimer ML, and Parry GJ; Myasthenia Gravis–IVIG Study Group. Randomized, controlled trial of intravenous immunoglobulin in myasthenia gravis. *Muscle Nerve* 2002;26:549-552.

47. Zinman L, Ng E, Bril V. IV immunoglobulin in patients with myasthenia gravis: a randomized controlled study. *Neurology* 2007;68:837-841.

48. Gajdos P, Chevret S, Clair B, Tranchant C, and Chastang C. Clinical trial of plasma exchange and high-dose intravenous immunoglobulin in myasthenia gravis. *Ann Neurol* 1997;41:789-796.

49. Pinching A, Peters DK, Newsom-Davis J. Remission of myasthenia gravis following plasma exchange. *Lancet* 1976;2:1373-1376.

50. Behan PO, Shakir RA, Simpson JA, Burnett AK, Allan TL, and Haase G. Plasma-exchange combined with immunosuppressive therapy in myasthenia gravis. *Lancet* 1979;2:438-440.

51. Lehmann, HC, Hartung HP, Hetzel GR, Stuve O, Kieseier BC. Plasma exchange in neuroimmunological disorders. Part 2. Treatment of neuromuscular disorders. *Arch Neurol* 2006;63:1066-1071.

52. Assessment of plasmapheresis. Report of the Therapeutics and Technology Assessment Subcommittee of the American Academy of Neurology. *Neurology* 1996;47:840-843.

53. Rodnitzky RL, Goeken JA. Complications of plasma exchange in neurological patients. *Arch Neurol* 1982;39:350-354.

54. Seybold ME. Plasmapheresis in myasthenia gravis. *Ann NY Acad Sci* 1987;505:584-587.

55. Evoli A, Di Schino C, Marsili F, Punzi C. Successful treatment of myasthenia gravis with tacrolimus. *Muscle Nerve* 2002;25:111-114.

56. Kawaguchi N, Yoshiyama Y, Nemoto Y, Munakata S, Fukutake T, and Hattori T. Low-dose tacrolimus treatment in thymectomised and steroid-dependent myasthenia gravis. *Curr Med Res Opin* 2004;20:1269-1273.

57. Konishi T, Yoshiyama Y, Takamori M, Yagi K, Mukai E, and Saida T; Japanese FK5O6 MG Study Group. Clinical study of FK506 in patients with myasthenia gravis. *Muscle Nerve* 2003;28:570-574.

58. Ponseti JM, Azem J, Fort JM, Codina A, Montoro JB, and Armengol M. Benefits of FK506 (tacrolimus) for residual, cyclosporin- and prednisone-resistant myasthenia gravis: one year follow-up of an open-label study. *Clin Neurol Neurosurgery* 2005;107:187-190.

59. Nagaishi A, Yukitake M, Kuroda Y. Long-term treatment of steroid-dependent myasthenia gravis patients with low-dose tacrolimus. *Intern Med* 2008;47:731-736.

60. Nagane Y, Utsugisawa K, Obara D, Kondoh R, and Terayama Y. Efficacy of low-dose FK506 in the treatment of myasthenia gravis-a randomized pilot study. Eur *Neurol* 2005;53:146-150.

61. Ponseti JM, Gamez J, Azem J, Lopez-Cano M, Vilallonga R, and Armengol M. Tacrolimus for myasthenia gravis: a clinical study of 212 patients. *Ann N Y Acad Sci* 2008;1132:254-263.

62. Zaja F, Russo D, Fuga G, Perella G, and Baccarani M. Rituximab for myasthenia gravis developing after bone marrow transplant. *Neurology* 2000;55:1062-1063.

63. Gajra A, Vajpayee N, Grethlein SJ. Response of myasthenia gravis to rituximab in a patient with non-Hodgkin lymphoma. *Am J Hematol* 2004;77:196-197.

64. Wylam ME, Anderson PM, Kuntz NL, Rodriguez V. Successful treatment of refractory myasthenia gravis using rituximab: a pediatric case report. *J Pediatr* 2003;143:674-677.

65. Illa I, Diaz-Manera J, Rojas-Garcia R, Pradas J, Rey A, Blesa R, Juarez C, and Gallardo E. Rituximab in refractory myasthenia gravis: a follow-up study of patients with anti-AChR or anti-MuSK antibodies [abstract]. *Neurology* 2008;70:A301.

66. Tandan R, Potter C, Bradshaw D. Pilot trial of rituximab in myasthenia gravis [abstract]. *Neurology* 2008;70:A301.

67. Gardner R, Pestronk A, Al-Lozi M. Intractable myasthenia gravis responding to riuximab treatment [abstract]. *Neurology* 2008;70:A301.

68. Lebrun C, Bourg V, Tieulie N, Thomas P. Successful treatment of refractory generalized myasthenia gravis with rituximab. *Eur J Neurol* 2009;16:246-250.

69. Rowin J, Meriggioli MN, Tuzun E, Leurgans S, and Christadoss P. Etanercept treatment in corticosteroid-dependent myasthenia gravis. Neurology 2004;63:2390-2392.

70. Tüzün E, Meriggioli MN, Rowin J, Yang H, and Christadoss P. Myasthenia gravis patients with low plasma IL-6 and IFN-ã benefit from etanercept treatment. J Autoimmunity 2005;24:261-268.

71. Blalock A, Mason MF, Morgan HJ, Riven SS. Myasthenia gravis and tumors of the thymic region: report of a case in which the tumor was removed. Ann Surgery 1939;110:544-561.

72. Blalock A, Harvey AM, Ford FR, Lilienthal JL. The treatment of myasthenia gravis by removal of the thymus gland. JAMA 1941;117:1529-1533.

73. Lanska DJ. Indications for thymectomy in myasthenia gravis. Neurology 1990;40:1828-1829.

74. McQuillen MP, Leone MG. A treatment carol: thymectomy revisited. *Neurology* 1977;27:1103-1106.

75. Gronseth GS, Barohn RJ. Thymectomy for non-thymomatous autoimmune myasthenia gravis (an evidence-based review). *Neurology* 2000;55:7-15.

76. Wolfe GI, Kaminski HJ, Jaretzki III A, Swan A, and Newsom-Davis J. Development of a thymectomy trial in nonthymomatous myasthenia gravis patients receiving immunosuppressive therapy. *Ann NY Acad Sci* 2003;998:473-480.

77. Jaretzki III A. Thymectomy for myasthenia gravis: analysis of the controversies regarding technique and results. *Neurology* 1997;48 (suppl 5):S52-S63.

78. Jaretzki III A, Wolff M. Maximal thymectomy for myasthenia gravis: surgical anatomy and operative technique. *J Thorac Cardiovasc Surg* 1988;96:711-716.

79. Jaretzki III A, Aarli JA, Kaminski HJ, Phillips LH 2nd, and Sanders DB; Medical/ Scientific Advisory Board, Myasthenia Gravis Foundation of America, Inc. Thymectomy for myasthenia gravis: evaluation requires controlled prospective studies. *Ann Thorac Surg* 2003;76:1-3.

80. Mantegazza R, Baggi F, Bernasconi P, Antozzi C, Confalonieri P, Novellino L, Spinelli L, Ferro MT, Beghi E, and Cornelio F. Video-assisted thoracoscopic extended thymectomy and extended thymectomy (T-3b) in non-thymomatous myasthenia gravis patients: remission after 6 years of follow-up. *J Neurol Sci* 2003;212:31-36.

81. Rodriguez M, Gomez MR, Howard FM, Taylor WF. Myasthenia gravis in children: long-term follow-up. *Ann Neurol* 1983;13:504-510.

82. Adams C, Theodorescu D, Murphy EG, Shandling B. Thymectomy in juvenile myasthenia gravis. *J Child Neurol* 1990;5:215-218.

83. Lakhoo K, De Fonseca J, Rodda J, Davies MRQ. Thymectomy in black children with juvenile myasthenia gravis. Pediatr Surg Int 1997;12:113-115.

84. Argov Z, McKee D, Agus S, Brawer S, Shlomowitz N, Yoseph OB, Soreq H, and Sussman JD. Treatment of human myasthenia gravis with oral antisense suppression of acetylcholinesterase. *Neurology* 2007;69:699-700.

85. Soliven B, Rezania K, Gundogdu B, Harding-Clay B, Oger J, and Arnason BG. Terbutaline in myasthenia gravis: a pilot study. *J Neurol Sci* 2009;277:150-154.

86. Weinberg DA, Lesser RL, Vollmer TL. Ocular myasthenia: a protean disorder. Surv Ophthalmol 1994;39:169-210.

87. Miller NR. Myopathies and disorders of neuromuscular transmission. Walsh and Hoyt's Clinical Neuro-Ophthalmology. 4th ed. Baltimore: Williams & Wilkins, 1985:840-862.

88. Sommer N, Sigg B, Melms A, Weller M, Schepelmanm K, Herzau V, and Dichgans J. Ocular myasthenia gravis: response to long term immunosuppressive treatment. *J Neurol Neurosurg Psychiatry* 1997;62:156-162.

89. Benatar M, Kaminski HJ. Evidence report: the medical treatment of ocular myasthenia (an evidence-based review). *Neurology* 2007;68:2144-2149.

90. Badurska B, Ryniewicz B, Strugalska H. Immunosuppressive treatment for juvenile myasthenia gravis. *Eur J Pediatr* 1992;151:215-217.

91. Carter B, Harrison R, Lunt GG, Behan PO, and Simpson JA. Antiacetylcholine receptor antibody titers in the sera of myasthenia patients treated with plasma exchange combined with immunosuppressive therapy. *J Neurol Neurosurg Psychiatry* 1980;43:397-402.

92. Soliven BC, Lange DJ, Penn AS, Younger D, Jaretzki III A, Lovelace RE, and Rowland LP. Seronegative myasthenia gravis. *Neurology* 1988;38:514-517.

93. Evoli A, Batocchi AP, Lo Monaco M, Servidei S, Padua L, Majolini L, and Tonali P. Clinical heterogeneity of seronegative myasthenia gravis. *Neuromusc Disord* 1996;6:155-161.

94. Scuderi F, Marino M, Colonna L, Mannella F, Evoli A, Provenzano C, and Bartoccioni E. Anti-P110 autoantibodies identify a subtype of "seronegative" myasthenia gravis with prominent oculobulbar involvement. *Lab Invest* 2002;82:1139-1146.

95. Hatanaka Y, Hemmi S, Morgan MB, Scheufele ML, Claussen GC, Wolfe GI, and Oh SJ. Nonresponsiveness to anticholinesterase agents in patients with MuSK-antibody-positive MG. *Neurology* 2005;65:1508-1509.

96. Sanders DB, El-Salem K, Massey JM, McConville J, and Vincent A. Clinical aspects of MuSK antibody positive seronegative MG. *Neurology* 2003;60:1978-1980.

97. Lin PT, Martin BA, Weinacker AB, So YT. High-dose cyclophosphamide in refractory myasthenia gravis with MuSK antibodies. *Muscle Nerve* 2006;33:433-435.

98. Wolfe GI, Trivedi JR, Oh SJ. Clinical review of muscle-specific tyrosine kinase-antibody positive myasthenia gravis. *J Clin Neuromusc Dis* 2007;8:217-224.

99. Grob D, Bruner N, Namba T, Pagala M. Lifetime course of myasthenia gravis. *Muscle Nerve* 2008;37:141-149.

100. Kawaguchi N, Kuwabara S, Nemoto Y, Fukutake T, Satomura Y, Arimura K, Osame M, and Hattori T; The Study Group for Myasthenia Gravis in Japan. Treatment and outcome of myasthenia gravis: retrospective multi-center analysis of 470 Japanese patients, 1999-2000. *J Neurol Sci* 2004;224:43-47.

Plasma Exchange And Immunoadsorption For Myasthenia Gravis

Carlo Antozzi M.D. & Renato Mantegazza M.D.

1. INTRODUCTION

Since the first report by Pinching and Newsom-Davis in 1976 (1), therapeutic plasma exchange (TPE) represents a critical therapeutic tool for myasthenia gravis (MG) (2). Along the last twenty years considerable improvement has been achieved on technical aspects of plasmatic treatment for autoimmune disorders; on the other hand, controlled studies are lacking, standardization of clinical protocols is limited and several questions remain open. Nevertheless, MG remains the best candidate disorder because of the definite role of specific autoantibodies against the acetylcholine receptor (AChR-Ab) or muscle-specific tyrosine kinase (MuSK-Ab), the two antigenic targets of the neuromuscular junction reported so far in this disease (3). The technique of TPE has been introduced as a short-term therapy for acute worsening of MG, a clinical condition that remains the main indication to its application. However, improvement of apheresis devices, reduction of side effects as well as introduction of selective apheretic techniques have increased the use of plasma treatment as a long-term immunomodulatory option for treatment-resistant MG.

2. THERAPEUTIC APHERESIS IN MG

In 1986, a Consensus Conference held by the NIH discussed the use of TPE in MG and concluded that PE is effective in the short-term and that a placebo-controlled trial would not be feasible nor ethically justified (4,5). Therefore, no evidence-based information is available in the literature.

The analysis of the open studies reported is difficult due to their heterogeneity. In particular, exchange protocols differed considerably among studies and in the majority of the patients were submitted to a variable number of exchange sessions. The analysis is also complicated by the fact that treated patients were either in myasthenic crisis or prolonged worsening; the effect of ongoing treatments with steroids and disease duration might also have influenced the results. Methodological flaws related to these studies have been underlined in the Cochrane review on this topic (6). Nevertheless, open studies showed that TPE was effective in at least 60-70% of treated patients and that improvement was strictly related in time with plasma removal. The heterogeneity of treatment protocols in terms of number of sessions is so wide that a definite conclusion on the optimal number of sessions to be performed cannot be achieved. In some studies the number was fixed while in others patients were submitted to a number of exchange sessions apparently dependent on the achievement of a detectable clinical improvement. In clinical practice, we still adopt a conservative approach consisting of a short protocol of two exchanges every other day with removal of one plasma volume per session; in our hands this protocol was effective in 70% of treated patients, all affected with bulbar MG (7). We routinely evaluate the patient within seven days and repeat the same protocol in case of failure. We favour a conservative approach that can be effective in a short period of time instead of performing several exchanges as default. This is important considering the patient's tolerability, particularly when vascular accesses are poor. The majority of authors usually recommend three to six exchanges removing 1-1.5 plasma volumes with saline and 5% albumin replacement, performed every other day. We prefer the alternate days schedule because of the immunoglobulin backflow from the extravascular to the intravascular space. From a technical standpoint, PE is performed by means of computerized continuous flow cell separators; alternatively, plasma can be separated by filtration. Two vascular accesses are needed, the first for blood inflow, and the second one for reinfusion of cells mixed with the replacement fluid. Venous accesses are preferable; the use of central venous or arterial catheters should be limited to selected patients since it is an invasive procedure, with higher costs and potential side effects, particularly when they must be maintained for several days. A single needle approach is also feasible with some apheretic devices, even though more time consuming.

2.1. Indications to therapeutic plasma exchange in MG

The main indication to TPE in MG is the acute worsening of the disease (either severe generalized or bulbar) or myasthenic crisis. Other indications include worsening during the start of corticosteroids, and preparation to thymectomy in symptomatic patients. On the basis of our experience we think there is no need to perform TPE immediately before thymectomy when MG is well controlled by pharmacological treatment. The chronic use of TPE in MG has never been addressed with a definite protocol. Nevertheless, TPE can be used at repeated intervals in selected patients in case of frequent relapses, when the response to pharmacological treatment is unsatisfactory after an adequate clinical follow-up, or in patients that have major contraindications to long-terms corticosteroids. Limitations to the use of chronic TPE are the need for good vascular accesses and the obvious effects on several plasma components in case of intensive protocols. Therefore, the number of sessions and interval between them must be tailored on each patient taking into account the general clinical conditions, severity of MG, and potential side effects. Because of these limitations, selective apheresis should be the technique of choice in severe immunosuppression-resistant patients requiring chronic treatments (8-11).

2.2 Therapeutic plasma exchange and MuSK-MG

Recently, antibodies to MuSK have been reported in a proportion of patients in which anti-AChR antibodies were not detectable (12). These patients can be differentiated on clinical grounds from those with anti-AchR antibodies. Their clinical picture is characterized by a typical "oculo-bulbar" involvement and more frequent respiratory compromise and incidence of myasthenic crisis. The disease in these patients is frequently refractory to standard immunosuppressive regimens; nevertheless, MuSK-positive MG shows a dramatic response to PE (or intravenous immunoglobulins) (13). This feature is of particular importance in the effort to overcome the prolonged bulbar involvement that frequently occurs in this subset of MG patients. The reason for this clinical behaviour is still unclear but is likely related to the activity of anti-MuSK antibodies that do not bind complement, as occurs with anti-AChR antibodies, and therefore might cause a different kind of damage to the neuromuscular junction. Treatment protocols are similar to those reported above for AChR-positive MG.

3. THERAPEUTIC PLASMA EXCHANGE AND INTRAVENOUS IMMUNOGLOBULINS

The use of TPE in MG must also be considered in comparison with intravenous immunoglobulins (IVIG) that represent an alternative to TPE and share the same indications. Several uncontrolled studies appeared in the literature (14). One randomized trial comparing the two treatments has been reported by the Myasthenia Gravis Clinical Study Group in France in 1997 (15). The study compared PE and IVIG in patients with acute forms of the disease and concluded that IVIG (400 mg/kg for 3 or 5 days) was as effective as TPE (3 sessions of 1.5 plasma volumes each). More recently, no significant superiority of 2 g/kg over1 g/kg was observed in the treatment of MG exacerbations (16). Therefore, IVIG can be considered as a safe and effective alternative treatment option when TPE is not readily available, or feasible due to inadequate vascular access, in patients with contraindications to extracorporeal circulation, and in children.

4. SELECTIVE APHERETIC TECHNIQUES

The ideal apheretic approach should remove only the specific autoantibody involved in the pathogenesis of the disease under treatment, leaving all the other plasma components unaltered. Such a specific approach is not yet available for clinical practice. A compromise is represented by circulating immunoglobulin G (IgG) immunoadsorption (IA), a procedure able to remove IgG and hence the specific autoantibody. Two different ligands are available for clinical use in IgG-mediated disorders. The first to be introduced was protein A. Protein A is a component of the staphylococcal cell wall and has the particular feature of binding human IgG with high affinity; the binding is thought to be mediated by the Fc fragment of IgG. Moreover, protein A has several other features that make it an ideal candidate for IA: the protein has a negligible interaction with other plasma components, is stable to wide variations in temperature and pH, and can be easily regenerated (17). A second method involves the use of polyclonal sheep anti-human IgG that removes directly circulating IgG by means of an immunological interaction (18). In both cases, plasma must be separated by centrifugation, and is then passed on-line through a set of two filters filled with either protein A or sheep anti-human IgG. The filters are operated by dedicated monitors and work alternatively; while the first filter removes immunoglobulins, the second one is washed, submitted to the elution process to remove the adsorbed IgG, and finally filled with a buffer solution, ready for the next adsorption cycle. These particular features make these techniques suitable for treatment of unlimited amounts of plasma since no replacement fluid is needed and the interaction with coagulation factors is negligible. Moreover, the dilution effect of replacement fluids does not occur with selective techniques compared with TPE. From a technical standpoint IA is more complicated and expensive then TPE. The procedure takes several hours since at least two plasma volumes are treated during each session to fully exploit the binding capacity of the filters. Our treatment protocol consists of three sessions of at least two plasma volumes each, performed every other day. Again, considering the IgG backflow from the extra to the intravascular space we favour the alternate day regimen. More intensive protocols can be performed safely since no replacement fluid is required. Afterwards, we usually perform one maintenance session every four to six weeks; when clinical improvement between consecutive sessions remains stable and the interval between them can be increased to more than two months we usually stop IA treatment. Because of the complexity of the procedure, duration, and costs, the indications to IA are different from that of PE that remains the first line option for acute exacerbations of MG. We favour the use of IA in patients with treatment-resistant MG after adequate clinical follow-up, patients that require frequent PE to keep a satisfactory improvement, or patients that have major contraindications to the use of high dose corticosteroids or other immunosuppressive drugs.

During the last decade we submitted to IA 19 treatment-resistant MG patients; the severity of the disease ranged from IIIA to IVB according to the Myasthenia Gravis Foundation of America (MGFA) classification. Patients were treated periodically for a mean of 16 months. Improvement up to minimal manifestations or pharmacological remission was recorded in 18 out of 19. It is of interest that IA was effective in 6 patients after failure of TPE or IVIG. The mean corticosteroid reduction at the end of the treatment period was 42%. The absence of detectable antiAChR or MuSK antibodies is not a contraindication to start IA that was indeed dramatically effective in a "double-negative" patient.

A different affinity-type semiselective method using tryptophan-linked polyvinyl alcohol gel has been proposed and used to treat MG patients with promising initial results in terms of clinical improvement (19,20). The binding is mediated by a chemical interaction and is less selective than protein A or sheep anti-human IgG since other plasma components are retained, particulary fibrinogen and complement. A variable range of reduction of IgG and specific antibodies has been reported. The procedure does not seem to be more clinically effective than PE and further studies should be perfomed.

4.1. Mechanism of action of IA.

The effect of IA, and its superiority compared with PE or IVIG, is likely related to the massive removal of IgG to an extent that cannot be achieved with standard PE. After treatment of two plasma volumes we observed a mean 71% of total IgG and 82% reduction of specific autoantibodies (mean of 51 sessions) (9). A representative example of the first induction course and subsequent maintenance protocol is shown in the figure. Anti-AChR Ab levels before and after IA in a representative patient were reduced up to 93%; both IgG and anti-AChR antibody levels increase after treatment, but their synthesis does not seem to be increased by repeated removal; on the contrary, the time course of autoantibody recovery is consistent with IgG half-life.

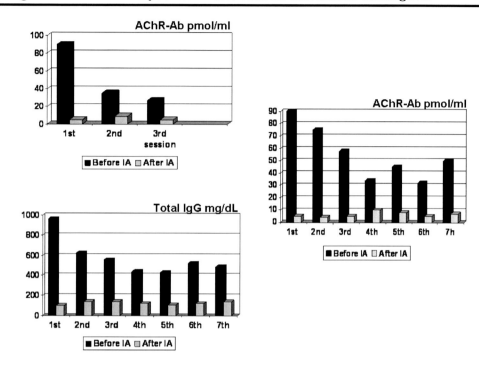

Moreover, as shown by Goldammer and colleagues, the synthesis of free light chains, a marker of current antibody synthesis, is not increased by IA (21). We also measured the potential influence of IA on different circulating cytokines in patients affected with MG or Lambert Eaton syndrome and found increased levels of IL-10 and reduced levels of IL-18 in post-IA plasma samples (22). Interestingly, IL-18 plays a role in the pathogenesis of experimental MG since the in vivo blockade of IL-18 activity suppressed the clinical manifestations of the disease (23); moreover, serum levels of IL-18 were found to be increased in MG patients and clinical improvement correlated with its reduction (24). Therefore, the effects of IA on the immunological homeostasis might be wider and more complex than the mere mechanical removal of circulating antibodies, and deserve further clinical and laboratory investigations.

5. CONCLUSIONS

The introduction and improvement of apheretic techniques for MG modified considerably the management of the disease either in case of acute worsening or in patients with prolonged unresponsiveness to immunosuppression. The incidence of respiratory insufficiency and duration of stay in the intensive care have been reduced by plasmapheresis. In parallel, selective apheresis can be particularly helpful for long-term immunomodulation otherwise not easily achievable with TPE. However, studies are needed with the aim of a better standardization of apheretic protocols and their application in conjunction with corticosteroids/immunosuppressive drugs.

Interest has been raised in recent in years on the possibility of antigen-specific removal of pathogenic autoantibodies in MG using new immunoadsorbents with immobilized recombinant subunits of the AchR, with interesting results in vitro. We hope that this new approach will soon be tested for clinical application after the necessary scaling up. A detailed review of this new approach is reported in this book by Dr. Tzartos (25) in Chapter 23.

References

1. Pinching A.J., Peters D.K., Newsom-Davis J. Remission of myasthenia gravis following plasma exchange. *Lancet* 1976;1373-1376.
2. Richman D.P., Agius M.A. Treatment of autoimmune myasthenia gravis. Neurology 2003; 61:1652-1661.
3. Conti-FineB.M., Milani M., Kaminski H.J. Myasthenia gravis: past, present and future. *J. Clin. Invest.* 116:2843-2854.
4. NIH Consensus Conference. The utility of therapeutic plasmapheresis for neurological disorders. *Natl. Inst. Health Consens Dev. Conf. Consens. Statement* 1986: 6:1-7.
5. Assessment of plasmapheresis. Report of the Therapeutics and Technology Assessment Subcommittee of the American Academy of Neurology. *Neurology* 1996;47:840-843.
6. Gajdos P., Chevret S., Toyka K. Plasma exchange for myasthenia gravis. *Cochrane Database of Systematic Reviews* 2002, Issue 4.Art.No.: CD002275. DOI:10.1002/14651858.CD002275.
7. Antozzi C., Gemma M., Regi B., Berta E., Confalonieri P., Peluchetti D., Mantegazza R., Marconi M., Fiacchino F., Cornelio F. A short plasma exchange protocol is effective in severe myasthenia gravis. *J. Neurol.* 1991;238:103-107.
8. Antozzi C., Berta E., Confalonieri P., Zuffi M., Cornelio F., Mantegazza R. Protein-A immunoadsorption in immunosuppression-resistant myasthenia gravis. *Lancet.* 1994;34:124.
9. Berta E, Confalonieri P., Simoncini O., Bernardi G., Busnach G., Mantegazza R., Cornelio F., Antozzi C. Removal of anticetylcholine receptor antibodies by protein-A immunoadsorption in myasthenia gravis. *Int. J. Artif. Organs* 1994;17:603-608.
10. Benny W.B., Sutton D.M.C., Oger J., Bril V., McAteer, Rock G. Clinical evaluation of a staphylococcal protein A immunoadsorption system in the treatment of myasthenia gravis. *Transfusion* 1999;39:682-687.
11. Haas M., Mayr N., Zeitholfer J., Goldammer A, Derfler K. Long-term treatment of myasthenia gravis with immunoadsorption. *J. Clin. Apher.* 2002;17:84-87.
12. Hoch W., McConville J., Helms S., Newsom-Davis J., Melms A., Vincent A. Autoantigens to the receptor tyrosine kinase MuSK in patients with myasthenia gravis without acetylcholine receptor antibodies. *Nat. Med.* 2001 7;365-368.
13. Evoli A., Tonali P.A., Padua L., Monaco M.L., Scuderi F., Batocchi A.P., Marino M., Bartoccioni E. Clinical correlates with anti-MuSK antibodies in generalized seronegative myasthenia gravis. *Brain* 2003;126;2304-2311.
14. Gajdos P., Chevret S., Toyka K.V. Intravenous immunoglobulins for myasthenia gravis. *Cochrane Database of Systematic Reviews* 2008, Issue 1.Art. No.:CD002277. DOI: 10.1002/14651858.CD002277.pub3.
15. Gajdos P., Chevret S., Clair B., Tranchant C., Chastang C. Clinical trial of plasma exchange and high dose immunoglobulin in myasthenia gravis. *Ann Neurol* 1997;41:789-796.
16. Gajdos P., Tranchant C., Clair B., Bolgert F., Eymard B., Stojkovic T., Attarian S., Chevret S., for the Myasthenia Gravis Clinical Study Group. *Arch. Neurol* 2005;62:1689-1693.
17. Samuelsson G. Extracorporeal immunoadsorption with proteina A: technical aspects and clinical results. *J. Clin. Apher.* 2001;16:49-52.

18. Bosch T. Therapeutic apheresis. State of the art in the year 2005. *Ther. Apher. Dial* 2005;9:459-468.

19. Shibuya N., Sato T., Osame M., Takegami T., Doi S., Kawanami S. Immunoadsorption therapy for myasthenia gravis. *J Neurol Neurosurg Psych* 1994;57:578-581.

20. Grob D., Simpson D., Mitsumoto H., Hoch B., Mokhtarian F., Bender A., Greenberg M., Koo A., Nakayama S. Treatment of myasthenia gravis by immunoadsorption of plasma. *Neurology* 1995;45;338-344.

21. Goldammer A., Derfler K., Herkner K., Bradwell A.R. Horl W.H., Haas M. Influence of plasma immunoglobulin level on antibody synthesis. *Blood* 2002;100:353-355.

22. Baggi F., Ubiali F., Nava S., Nessi V., Andreetta F., Rigamonti A., Maggi L., Mantegazza R., Antozzi C. Effect of IgG immunoadsorption on serum cytokines in MG and LEMS patients. *J Neuroimmunol* 2008;201-202:104-110.

23. Im S.H., Barchan D., Maiti P.K., Raveh L:, Souroujon M.C., Fuchs S. Suppression of experimental myasthenia gravis, a B cell-mediated autoimmune disease, by blockade of IL-18. *FASEB J.* 2001;15:2140-2148.

24. Jander S., Stoll G. Increased serum levels of the interferon-gamma-inducing cytokine interleukin-18 in myasthenia gravis. Neurology 2002;59:287-289.

25. Zisimopoulou P., Lagoumintzis G., Kostelidou K., Bitzopoulou K., Kordas G., Trakas N., Poulas K., Tzartos S.J. Towards antigen-specific apheresis of pathogenic autoantibodies in the treatment of myasthenia gravis by plasmapheresis. *J. Neuroimmunol.* 2008: 201-202:95-103.

Evidence-based Efficacy of Intravenous Immunoglobulin Therapy in Human Myasthenia Gravis and Mechanisms of Action

Marinos C. Dalakas. M.D.

1. INTRODUCTION

Myasthenia gravis (MG) is the prototypic autoimmune disease because it fulfils the following criteria: the antigen, the acetylcholine receptor (AChR), is known; antibodies against the AChRs are detected and measured in the patients' serum; the patients' IgG binds to the AChRs at the postsynaptic region and, by fixing complement or crosslinking, results in internalization or degradation of the AChRs and simplification of the postsynaptic junctional folds; the IgG antibodies are pathogenic because they transmit the disease to experimental animals and cause destruction of the AChRs in cultured myotubes; immunization of healthy animals with AChRs leads to clinical signs of myasthenia which can be subsequently passed to other animals with purified IgG; and removal of the pathogenic autoantibodies results in clinical improvement (1-4).

All the above make MG an attractive candidate disease for effective management with immunosuppressive or immunomodulating drugs. Although MG is no longer "gravis" because it responds fairly well to the available therapies, we still do not have a cure for the disease. Treatment begins with anticholinesterases, which are helpful early in the disease, followed by long-term steroid administration along with immunosuppressive therapies such as azathioprine, cyclosporine or Mycophenolate Mofetil. Plasmapheresis may be required for periods of crisis or as temporary relief to patients with difficult disease or until the aforementioned agents take effect (1-5). Given the chronicity of the disease, the long-term use of these therapeutic modalities needs to be curtailed because of their cumulative adverse side effects. The need for another effective immunomodulating therapy without long-term side effects has prompted experimentation with high-dose IVIg, an immunomodulating drug that is expensive but relatively safe compared to the other therapies. Considering the multiple mechanisms of action of IVIg in modifying the immune response, as discussed later, IVIg can be a useful modality in the treatment of certain patients with MG at a given state of their illness.

This review provides an evidence-based, critical assessment on the role of IVIg in the management of MG and summarizes the present knowledge on the mechanisms of action of IVIg as relate to immunopathogenesis of the disease.

2. MECHANISMS OF ACTION OF IVIG AS RELATE TO THE IMMUNOPATHOGENESIS OF MG

The main mechanisms of actions of IVIg are listed in the Table. The beneficial effect exerted by the IVIg is probably the result of multiple mechanisms that often act in concert with each other (6-9). Among the actions listed in the Table, those most relevant in modifying the immune response in MG patients resulting in a clinical benefit, are discussed below in more detail.

2.1. Effect of IVG on AChR antibodies via the Idiotypic-anti-idiotypic interactions.

Humans normally make small amounts of antibodies to sequences of at least 220 of their own proteins and to anti-idiotypic antibodies directed against Fab, the antigen-binding region of these autoantibodies (10). Because IVIg preparations are derived from a large pool of human donors, they contain antibodies and anti-idiotypic antibodies against the naturally occurring proteins and their autoantibodies, including antibodies against AChR. Electron microscopy has shown that IVIg contains 40% dimers formed by double-arm or single-arm binding between the $F(ab')_2$, domains of the IgG molecules (6-9,11,12) as shown schematically in figure 1. The dimers, which are absent in native IgG, are more likely to be formed within the IVIg preparations and probably represent complexes of idiotypic-anti- idiotypic antibodies (12).

Table. Immunornodulatory actions of IVIg

• Neutralization of pathogenic autoantibodies by anti-idiotypic antibodies
• Downregulation of antibody production
• Inhibition of complement binding and prevention of membranolytic attack complex formation
• Suppression of pathogenic cytokines
• Possible competition for antigen recognition via soluble CD4, CD8, and major histocompatibility complex formation
• Transient lymphopenia, reduction of natural killer cells, and downregulation of lymphocyte function-associated antigen-1 expression on T cells
• Alteration of Fc receptor glycosylation on phagocytic cells and interference with Fc receptor-mediated phagocytosis
• Inhibition of superantigens
• Inhibition of CD8[+] T-cell function via antibodies against a conserved region of the major histocompatibility complex class I antigen

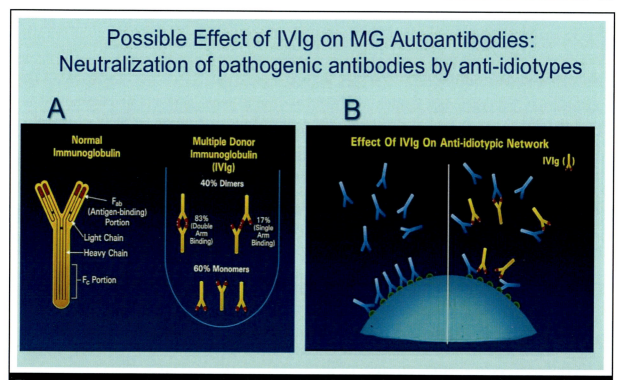

Figure 1. A. Single donor IgG contains anti-idiotypic antibodies in monomers while multiple donor IgG's contain id-anti-id antibodies that form dimers. The larger the pool of donors, the higher the number of F(ab')$_2$ pairs and wider the specrtum of id-anti-id specificities (i.e. AchR). B. The anti-idiotypic antibodies supplied by the IVIg neutralize the pathogenic antibodies directed against the AChR.

According to the network theory (13), normal immune homeostasis is under the control of complementary anti-idiotypes, the lack of which disrupts a steady-state condition, allowing the autoantibodies, eg., against AChRs, to become pathogenic. The repertoire of F(ab')$_2$, dimers within the IVIg, by providing complementary autoantibodies (i.e., against AChR), can restore the connectivity among the autoantibodies of the idiotypic network. Furthermore, as shown schematically in figure 1, the anti-idiotypic autoantibodies against the AChR present in IVIg could bind to antigenic determinants of the circulating pathogenic anti-AChR autoantibodies and, by neutralizing their functional activity, might prevent their interaction with the native AChR at the end- plates. This action, albeit theoretical, is of direct relevance in MG because the circulating antibodies are pathogenic.

2.2. Downregulation of antibody production.

The anti-idiotypic antibodies within the IVIg may also downregulate autoantibody production by binding to membrane-associated IgM and IgG on B lymphocytes, bridging surface immunoglobulin to Fc receptors in an antibody-mediated feedback inhibition (14,15). Moreover, the V regions of the IgG within the IVIg may interact with antigenic determinants on surface immunoglobulins of B cells in an antigen-specific fashion, causing negative signals on B cells. IVIg also contains antibodies to the CD5 molecules (16), normally expressed on an autoantibody-producing CD20+ (B1) subset of B cells (16), contributing further to their functional inactivation and maintenance of self-tolerance. The suppression of autoantibodies by IVIg however remains inconsistent and most of the times minimal.

2.3. Inhibition of complement binding.

In MG, the IgG antibodies against the AChR fix complement, and the membranolytic attack complex (MAC) is present at the motor end-plates (1-4). IVIg forms covalent or noncovalent complexes with the products of complement activation, notably C3b and C4b, and prevents the incorporation of C3 molecules into the C5 convertase assembly (17). This binding diverts the complement fragments, intercepts the assembly of MAC, and prevents MAC-mediated destruction of the target antigen, as discussed elsewhere (6-8,17). The effect of IVIg on the complement activation can prevent the MAC-fixing anti- AChR antibodies from binding to the end-plate region(12).

2.4. Competition for antigen recognition.

The glycoproteins CD4 and CD8, expressed on helper and suppressor/cytotoxic T cells, are the physiological ligands for the MHC-II and MHC-I molecules. Some IVIg preparations have high levels of soluble CD4 and MHC-II (18), which could interfere with the MHC II on the surface of antigen-presenting cells or with antigen recognition by CD4$^+$ cells, suppressing the ongoing immune process. Along these lines, the effect of IVIg on dendritic cells and costimulation is directly relevant in affecting antigen recognition by antigen-presenting cells (8,19).

2.5. Suppression of cytokines.

Cytokines, derived from macrophages or activated T cells, can cause anergic T cells to become responsive to an autoantigen and to participate in antigen recognition by the T cells (6-9,20). IVIg contains specific, high-affinity antibodies against interleukins (IL-la and IL-6) and tumor necrosis factor (TNFα) that neutralize circulating cytokines (21) suppressing the ongoing immune response.

2.6. Alteration of Fc receptor affinity.

After IVIg therapy, the unbound IgG molecules may bind to Fc receptors on the surface of phagocytic cells, altering the affinity of the receptors and causing a dose-dependent competitive inhibition with the IgG antibody complexed to antigens (22,23). In experimental MG this process may, in theory, intercept the Fc receptor-mediated phagocytosis of antigen-bearing end- plates, preventing their destruction by the autoantibodies and inhibiting antibody-dependent, cell-mediated cytotoxicity. Whether this process is relevant in patients with MG is unclear, because macrophages are not present at the end-plate region (1-4).

2.7. Other IVIg actions, of potential relevance in MG patients include:

2.7.1. Modulation of T-cell functions and inhibition of adhesion molecules.

IVIg induces mild lymphopenia (6-9), enhances suppressor T-cell function, reduces CD4+/CD32+ (helper/inducer) subsets and natural killer (NK) cells, and downregulates the expression of intercellular cell adhesion molecule-I (ICAM-I) and lymphocyte function-associated antigen-1 (LFA-1) on activated T cells (24).

2.7.2. Inhibition of superantigens.

Superantigens (bacterial toxins, enterotoxins, or viruses) may be responsible for disrupting self-tolerance and could potentially trigger a flare or an attack in MG, especially for the relapses seen after infections (21). IVIg contains antibodies against epitopes of superantigens (25) that intercept the presentation of superantigens to accessory cells, inhibiting T-cell activation(12).

2.7.3. Inhibition of CD8$^+$ T-cell function.

IVIg contains antibodies against a conserved region of the MHC-I that may inhibit CD8$^+$ cell function, (26) modulating further the ongoing immune response.

3. EFFICACY OF IVIG IN EAMG AND A MECHANISM OF ACTION RELEVANT TO HUMAN MG

The effect of IVIg has been explored in the animal model of rats with EAMG by Dr Fuchs's group (see Chapter 24). It was shown in a series of experiments that IVIg can prevent the induction of EAMG and can suppress the ongoing disease both at its acute and chronic stages (4 weeks after induction) in a dose-dependent fashion (0,4 gm/kg/day for one 5-day course vs two 5 day courses) (27). The AChR-specific IgG antibodies were also reduced after IVIg administration, both in the acute and the chronic stage of treatment. In these experiments, it was shown that IVIg modulated EAMG by suppressing Th1 and B cell proliferation but not by generating regulatory T cells (27). Chromatography of pooled human IVIg on immobilized immunoglobulins isolated either from EAMG or from MG patients, resulted in a complete depletion of the suppressive activity of IVIg. Further, this suppressive effect was recovered upon reconstitution of the activity-depleted IVIg with the eluted minute IVIg fractions adsorbed onto EAMG- or MG-specific columns (28). On this basis, it appears that a disease specific anti-Immunoglobulin fraction, present within the IVIg preparations, is essential for the suppressive effect of IVIg in EAMG and probably human MG (28).

4. EXPERIENCE OF IVG IN MG

4.1. Concerns with the present trials

According to the above, IVIg ought to work in MG patients either during the acute exacerbations, or as a means of managing difficult cases during the chronic phases of the disease (12). The published series on the use of IVIg, however, although promising for the treatment of exacerbations, have not been adequately designed to provide evidence-based answers regarding the use of IVIg in the chronic management of the disease or as a steroid-sparing agent (12). This has been critically summarized in the recent Cochrane review (29). The role of IVIg has not been also explored in myasthenic crises in a controlled study.

4.2. Chronological review of non-randomized trials (12).

In 1986, Arsura et al. (30) treated 12 patients (eight thymectomized and eight receiving steroids) with 2 g/kg IVIg over a 5-day period. The patients' mean age was 50 years and the mean disease duration 42 months. Eleven of the 12 patients improved after 3.6 ± 2.7 days, reaching maximal improvement after 8 ± 4 days and lasting up to 52 ± 37 days. In addition, four of 12 patients were able to reduce steroids by 50%. In a follow-up study of nine patients who responded to IVIg after the initial infusion (31), subsequent infusions resulted in a sustained improvement lasting up to a mean period of 3 months. The antibody titers against AChRs remained unchanged after IVIg.

In 1987, Gajdos et al. (32) treated 21 patients, including some with advanced disease, using 2 g/kg IVIg. Based on a minimum of 20 points required to establish efficacy, the strength improved from 39 to 58 points on day 10 and up to 63 points (normal 100) on day 25 ($p < 0.001$) in 10 of 21 patients. In addition, 10 of 16 patients with an acute exacerbation improved by more than 20 points. In contrast, none of five patients with advanced disease improved. The authors confirmed their earlier findings that IVIg is effective in MG (33).

In 1991, Cosi et al. (34) reported 39 patients treated with 2 g/g IVIg over a 5-day period. Twenty-six of the 39 patients improved by day 21 by one Oosterhuis grade, and 16 patients improved by two grades. Overall, improvement was noted in 70% of the patients by day 12 and persisted in 60% of the patients by day 60. In contrast to the study of Gajdos et al. (32) the response to IVIg was no different between patients in an acute or a chronic phase of the disease. The AChR antibody titers decreased in some patients, but the reduction did not correlate with the clinical response. Although it was stated that the IVIg-related improvement was sustained for as long as 180 days, several patients had received concomitant immunosuppressive treatments.

Various other small, uncontrolled series including those by Ippoliti et al., (35) Edan and Landgraf, (36), Besinger et al., (37) Uchiyama et al., (38) and Cook et al. (39) showed results similar to those described above.

IVIg was also evaluated as a maintenance therapy in chronic MG patients in two uncontrolled studies. In one, Achiron et al (40) evaluated the efficacy of IVIg as a maintenance therapy in an open study of 10 people with severe generalised MG and an acute deterioration unresponsive to conventional treatment with corticosteroids and immunosuppressive drugs. Intravenous immunoglobulin was administered at a loading dose of 2 g/kg over five days, followed by a maintenance treatment at 0.4 g/kg once every six weeks. The mean severity of the disease decreased by 2.5 grades on the Osserman scale after one year ($p < 0.001$) with a parallel reduction of the prednisone and Azathioprine doses. In another trial, Hilkevich et al (41) treated 11patients with generalised MG with severe bulbar involvement. Intravenous immunoglobulin was initiated at a dose of 2 g/kg over five days followed by 0.4 g/kg once monthly for a mean period of 20.3 months. All patients improved. The Oosterhuis grade statistically decreased after IVIg at the end of follow-up period. The prednisone dose was also reduced from 60mg daily to 9.25mg on alternate days ($p < 0.0004$) without any attempt to reduce the Azathioprine dose.

In a small series of four patients, Sticker et al (42) reported that none of four patients in myasthenic crisis responded to IVIg but all four responded to plasmapheresis, which began 48 hr after the IVIg. Caution is needed in interpreting this report however because plasmapheresis began 48 hr after IVIg, which did not allow assessment of the efficacy of IVIg over a 2-day period(12).

4.3. Conclusion and criticisms from the uncontrolled series.

Several conclusions can be drawn from all the aforementioned trials. On the negative side, the studied patients have been heterogeneous regarding disease severity and duration; the effect of other treatments used before initiation of IVIg or concurrently with the IVIg has not been factored in; the number of patients in each series was small; the assessment of efficacy has been heterogenous; and the long-term efficacy of IVIg, especially as a steroid-sparing agent, was not systematically studied (12). On the positive side, it appears that IVIg is promising as a treatment option because the majority of patients (sometimes as high as 78%) may respond to IVIg, at least for a short-time period (12). The improvement seems to occur early, beginning after a mean period of 3 to 10 days, but the duration of effect is unclear, ranging from 30 to 120 days (mean period of 45 days). Some of these concerns have been resolved with the randomized trials discussed below, but others remain still unsettled and require new studies.

4.4. Randomized Controlled Trials with IVIg in Acute exacerbations of MG

Based on RCT discussed chronologically below as also reviewed by the Cochrane database (29), IVIg on a short term basis has the same efficacy as plasma exchange or prednisone for the treatment of MG exacerbations and is superior to placebo for the severe forms of the disease. There has not been a controlled study comparing IVIg to plasma exchange for the MG crises.

A) In 1997, Gajdos et al. (43) conducted the first randomized study involving 87 MG patients in acute exacerbation. The aim was to compare the efficacy and tolerance of IVIg or plasma exchange in MG exacerbations and compare two doses of IVIg. Participants had to fulfil the following criteria:

1) diagnosis of MG based on: (a) acquired weakness of voluntary muscles, including those innervated by cranial nerves; (b) fluctuation of muscle fatigability; (c) anti- AChR antibodies titers greater than 1 nM or a decremental electromyographic response (at least 10%) associated with a positive response to anticholinesterase drugs; and

2) an exacerbation, defined as the appearance of at least one of the following symptoms within the last month: difficulty in swallowing, acute respiratory failure or major functional disability responsible for the discontinuation of physical activity.

Of the enrolled patients, 50% were receiving steroids or azathioprine and most of them were thymectomized. The patients were randomized to receive three courses of plasmapheresis (1.5 volume each) performed once every 2 days, or to IVIg. The IVIg group had two arms; one receiving 0.4g/kg for 3 days (total 1.2 g/kg) and another receiving the traditional dose of 0.4 g/kg given over a 5-day period (total 2 g/kg). Immunosuppressive treatment with corticosteroids or other drugs was continued without any change in dosage. The end point was an improvement in Myasthenic muscle strength scores by day 15. The MMS is the sum of nine independent observations of trunk, limbs, neck and cranial muscles which when added yield an overall numerical rating between 0 for a maximum deficit and 100 for normal strength (32,33). Among the 87 enrolled patients, 41 were randomized to the plasma exchange group and 46 to the IVIg group (23 in the three-day group and 23 in the five-day group). Of interest, five participants in the plasma exchange group and four in the IVIg group were on mechanical ventilation. At day

15, no statistical significant difference was noted among the three groups. Specifically, the mean change in the MMS score was 16.6 in the plasma exchange group and 15.6 in the IVIg group (p = 0.65). In the IVIg group, the mean change was 18.9 in the three-day IVIg group and 12.4 in the five-day IVIg group (p = 0.14).

The mean change in anti-AChR antibodies titre was 13.8% decrease in the plasma exchange group and 16.8% increase in the IVIg group (p = 0.36). The mean change in anti- AChR antibodies titre was not significantly different between the three-day and five-day IVIg groups. It was concluded that IVIg is as effective as plasmapheresis but is preferable to plasmapheresis because of fewer side effects.

B) A second trial, performed by Schuchardt et al in 2002 [cited in the Cohrane review (29)], compared IVIg to oral methylprednisolone in 33 patients with moderate exacerbations of MG. Participants were randomised to receive either IVIg 30 g daily for five consecutive days and placebo tablets, or methylprednisolone 1mg/kg daily increased to 1.5 mg/kg daily on day seven and infusion of one per cent human albumin. The primary end point was the change in the two most affected criteria of the QMGS from day 0 to day 14. Among the 33 participants, 15 were randomized to IVIg group and 18 to the methylprednisolone group. The mean sum of the two most pathological items of the QMGS at day 0 was 3.9 for the IVIg group and 4.2 for the methylprednisolone group. At day 14 these values were 2.9 for the IVIg group and 2.8 for the methylprednisolone group. The time to improvement and to maximum improvement was shorter in the IVIg group, but these differences were not significant (29). The study, although short and underpowered, suggested that after 15 days of treatment, IVIg was as effective as corticosteroids.

C) The third trial was conducted by Gajdos et al (44) comparing two doses of IVIg in 173 patients fulfilling the inclusion criteria of their earlier 1999 trial. Patients were randomized to receive either IVIg 1 g/kg on day one and placebo on day two, or IVIg 1 g/kg on day one and 1 g/kg on day two. The study's endpoint was the change of MMS between randomisation and day 15. Among the 173 participants, 81 were randomized to receive 1 g/kg IVIg and 87 to receive 2 g/kg IVIg. On day 15, the mean MMS change from baseline was 15.49 points in the 1 g/kg IVIg group and 19.33 points in the 2 g/kg IVIg group. The mean MMS change in both groups was similar (p= 0.12); the median time needed to response was also similar in both groups (13.5 days and 12 days in the 2 groups respectively p = 0.48). The study was important because it demonstrated that 2 g/kg, an arguably arbitrary dose but the one most commonly used, is as effective as 1g/kg, providing efficacy at a significant cost-saving.

D) The fourth trial was conducted by Zinman et al (45). This trial compared IVIg to placebo in MG patients who had "worsening weakness" defined as increasing symptoms or signs severe enough (as judged by both the patient and the physician) to warrant a change in therapy. Patients were excluded if they had respiratory distress requiring intensive care, a vital capacity less than 1 L, severe swallowing difficulties, a change in corticosteroid dosage in the two weeks prior to screening or other disorders causing weakness. Fifty one AChR-positive patients were randomized to receive either IVIg 2g/kg or the equivalent volume of dextrose 5% over two days. The main endpoint was the change in QMGS from baseline (day 0) to day 14. An analysis of the IVIg treatment effect was performed by stratifying the patients according to their baseline severity: mild MG (QMGS <10.5) and moderate to severe MG (QMGS > 10.5). Seventeen patients were classified as ocular MG, 23 as mild MG and 28 as moderate to severe MG. On day 14, the mean change in QMGS was -2.5 in the IVIg group and -0.9 in the placebo group (p = 0.047). On day 28, these values were -3 in the IVIg group and -1.2 in the placebo group (p = 0.055). For the mild MG cases, the mean change in QMGS on day 14 was similar in the two groups: -0.7 in the IVIg group and -1.1 in the placebo group. The only significant difference was noted for the moderate to severe MG group where these values were -4.1 in the IVIg group and -0.7 in the placebo group (p = 0.01); that treatment effect was maintained at day 28. None of the electrophysiologic measures showed a significant improvement with IVIg. This study, the latest on the efficacy of the IVIg, has several limitations. First, the effect was modest, as patients improved by 2,54 QMG units compared to 0,89 in the placebo; considering that individual QMG scores usually vary up to 2.6 units, this effect might not have been clinically meaningful. Second, the effect did not reach the 3.5 units cited as clinically significant and used to calculate the sample size. Third, it was statistically significant (by more than 4.1 points) only in a small number of patients with severe MG, suggesting that the study lost power because of including patients with less severe disease. Fourth, the definition of "worsening weakness" was rather subjective.

4.5. Randomized Controlled Trials of IVIg in the chronic management of MG

Two RCTs have addressed the efficacy of IVIg for the treatment of moderate to severe but stable MG, one comparing IVIg to plasma exchange and the other to placebo. None showed a significant difference.

A) In 2001, Roanger et al (29, 46) compared, in a controlled crossover study, the efficacy of IVIg to plasma exchange in 12 patients with moderate to severe MG in a stable phase. Patients were included if : a) they were in Osserman class III to V and were restricted in daily activities or completely dependent on skilled care for support; b) if were treated with prednisone or azathioprine; c) had anti-AChR antibodies; and d) had a significant decrement (15 %) on EMG. Participants were randomly assigned to receive either IVIg 0.4 g/kg on five subsequent days, followed by five plasma exchanges every other day 16 weeks later, or five plasma exchanges first followed by IVIg, 16 weeks later. The main endpoint was the clinical improvement measured before and seven days after each treatment using the quantified MG score (QMGS). The mean fall in QMGS was 0.23 (p < 0.05) after plasma exchange and 0.10 (NS) after IVIg from baseline to one week. From baseline to four weeks, the mean fall in QMGS both after plasma exchange and after IVIg was significant (p < 0.05). The change from baseline to eight or 16 weeks was not significant for either plasma exchange or for IVIg. This was an underpowered cross-over study that does not allow any conclusions regarding the long-term effect of IVIg or plasmapheresis. The same conclusion was drawn by the Cochrane review(29)

B) The second trial was conducted by Wolf et al (47). In this study IVIg was compared to placebo (5% albumin). Patients were included if they had: a) mild or moderate generalised MG and have never received corticosteroids or immunosuppressive therapy; (b) persistent symptoms and signs of generalised MG despite taking prednisone at a dose over 20 mg on alternate days. Participants were randomised to receive either IVIg 1 g/kg or five per cent albumin as placebo on days one and two. A 1 g/kg infusion of IVIg or placebo was repeated on day 22. The primary endpoint was the change in the QMGS from baseline (day 0) to day 42. At day 42 participants were invited into a six-week open label study that followed an identical protocol to the randomised trial. Fifteen participants were included, six in the IVIg arm and nine in the placebo arm. Mean change in the QMGS from day 0 to day 42 was 0.00 in the IVIg group and -1.6 in the placebo group (p = 0.53). In the open-label segment, the change in the QMGS for those patients who initially received placebo was -2.0 from day 0 to day 42 (p = 0.03) and -3.6 from day 0 to day 84 (p= 0.01).

Because of insufficient number of participants and the type of design, the data from this trial is limited to draw any conclusions regarding the role for IVIg in chronic MG.

4.6. Changes in the AChR antibody titers after IVIg therapy.

The changes in the AChR antibody titers have not been consistent after IVIg therapy (12). In four series the titers declined and in three they remained unchanged. In the controlled studies by Gajdos et al (43) and Ronager et al(46), the changes in anti-AChR antibody titre 15 days and 7 days, respectively, after IVIg treatment were not significant.

In an *in vitro* study of 30 samples of MG serum, IVIg interacted with the AChR antibodies and inhibited the antibody activity up to 30% of the pre-incubation level (48). The inhibition was mostly observed in patients with lower titers and was dose-dependent, being higher after incubation with increasing amounts of IVIg. By affinity chromatography, it was further shown that the inhibition was due to direct binding of the AChRs on the insolubilized IgG present within the IVIg preparation.

4.7. IVIg in MuSK-antibody positive patients

Small case series suggest that IVIg may be effective in MuSK-positive MG , but the results are based on anectodal reports. In one study, two patients resistant to steroids, tacrolimus and plasmapheresis started improving within 3 days after IVIg infusions, with benefit lasting up to 3 months (49). In another similar case, the effect of IVIg lasted up to 20 months (50). Whether IVIg is effective in patients with seronegative MG remains unclear.

5. FUTURE PROSPECTS OF IVIG IN MG

IVIg undoubtedly has a role in the treatment of MG, but this role needs to be further assessed with additional control trials (12,29). The main advantages of IVIg are its rapid onset, its lack of long-term toxicity (although rare and sometimes severe side effects can occur) (6-9), and its potential to reduce the required doses of immunosuppressive drugs. The main disadvantages of IVIg include its high cost and the need to repeat the infusions to maintain response (12). The numbers of confounding factors involved in deciding the best therapy of MG at a given state of the disease demand carefully designed studies, clear objectives, accurate assessment of efficacy, and precise control of the concomitant immunosuppressive drugs (12,29). Such studies are difficult today but can be done with proper rescue clauses. The following objectives need to be addressed in the design of future trials:

1. Is IVIg effective in patients with mild to severe but stable MG not adequately controlled with immunosuppressive drugs? If so, when should it be used in relationship to the other drugs and is it cost-effective?
2. Does IVIg have a role as a steroid-sparing drug?
3. Is the effect of IVIg temporary or does it have a long-term benefit?
4. Is IVIg effective in a crisis and is it as good as plasmapheresis?

5. Is there a synergistic effect of IVIg with the other drugs used in the treatment of the disease?
6. What is the mechanism of action of IVIg in MG, and does it have an effect on AChR antibody titers, immunoregulatory T cells or other immune factors?
7. Is IVIg effective in seronegarive MG or in MUSk-positive patients?

6. CONCLUSION

Until further controlled trials are conducted to establish efficacy, IVIg should be used judiciously in MG. There is a paradox with the need for controlled trials in MG because until now the commonly used therapies including Mestinon, plasmapheresis, thymectomy and steroids have been accepted as "effective" solely on the basis of "clinical experience" but not controlled trials. Because there is a clear abuse of IVIg in the chronic management of MG, better studies are needed especially in this form of the disease. In acute exarcerbations, the evidence is more clear that IVIg has benefit and it might be preferable to plasmapheresis because it is easier to use, but whether it is as good as plasmapheresis remains still an open question.

REFERENCES

1. Engel AG. Acquired autoimmune myasthenia gravis. In: Engel AG, Frankni-Armstrong C, eds. Myology. New York: McGraw-Hill, 2006; 1769-1792.

2. Drachman DB. Chapter 8 Therapy of myasthenia gravis. Hand book Clin Neurol. 2008;91:253-72.

3. Penn AS, Richman DP, Ruff RL, Lennon VA. Myasthenia gravis and related disorders. *Ann NY Acad Sci* 1993;681.

4. Vincent A, Rothwell P. Myasthenia gravis. *Autoimmunity.* 2004;37(4):317-9.

5. Dalakas MC. Neuroimmunotherapy: a practical approach to the treatment of immune-mediated neurological diseases. *Semin Neurol* 1994;14:97-105.

6. Dalakas MC. The use of intravenous immunoglobulin in the treatment of autoimmune Neurological Disorders: Evidence-based indications and safety profile. *Pharmacol Therapeutics* 2004;102:177-193.

7. Dalakas MC. Intravenous immunoglobulin in the treatment of autoimmune neuromuscular diseases: present status and practical therapeutic guidelines. *Muscle & Nerve* 1999;22(11):1479–97.

8. Kaveri SV, Lacroix-Desmazes S, Bayry J. The antiinflammatory IgG. *N Engl J Med.* 2008;359(3):307-9.

9. Dalakas MC. Intravenous immunoglobulin in autoimmune neuromuscular diseases. *JAMA.* 2004 May 19;291(19):2367-75.

10. Avrameas S. Natural autoantibodies: from "horror autotoxicus" to "gnothi seauton." Immunol Today 1991;12:154-159.

11. Tankersley DL, Preston MS, Finlayson JS. Immunoglobulin G dimer: an idiotype-anti-idiotype complex. *Mol Immunol* 1988; 25:41-48

12. Experience with IVIg in the treatment of patients with myasthenia gravis. Neurology 48S:64-69;1997.

13. Jerne NK. The immune system: a web of V-domains. New York: Academic Press, 1976.

14. Uher F, Dickler HB. Cooperativity between B lymphocyte membrane molecules: independent ligand occupancy and crosslinking of antigen receptors and Fc gamma receptors downregulates B lymphocyte function. *J Immunol* 1986;137: 3124-3129.

15. Jungi TW, Nydegger VE. Proposed mechanisms of action of intravenous IgG in autoimmune diseases. *Transfus Sci* 1992; 13 :267-290.

16. Vassilev T, Gelin C, Kaveri SV, Zilber MT, Boumsell L, Kaza-tchkine MD. Antibodies to the CD5 molecule in normal human immunoglobulins for therapeutic use (intravenous immunoglobulins, IVIg). *Clin Exp Immunol* 1993;92:369-372.

17. Basta M, Dalakas MC. High-dose intravenous immunoglobulin exerts its beneficial effect in patients with dermatomyositis by blocking endomysial deposition of activated complement fragments. *J Clin Invest* 1994;94:1729-1735.

18. Blasczyk R, Westhoff V, Grosse-Wilde H. Soluble CD,, CD, and HLA molecules in commercial immunoglobulin preparations. *Lancet* 1993;341:789-790.

19. Dasgupta S, Repessé Y, Bayry J, Navarrete AM, Wootla B, Delignat S, Irinopoulou T, Kamaté C, Saint-Remy JM, Jacquemin M, Lenting PJ, Borel-Derlon A, Kaveri SV, Lacroix-Desmazes S. VWF protects FVIII from endocytosis by dendritic cells and subsequent presentation to immune effectors. *Blood.* 2007;109(2):610-2.

20. Svenson M, Hansen MB, Bendtzen K. Binding of cytokines to pharmaceutically prepared human immunoglobulin. *J Clin Invest* 1993;92:2533-2539.

21. Dalakas MC. Basic aspects of neuroimmunology as they relate to immunotherapeutic targets: present and future prospects. A*nn Neurol* 1995;37 (supp1)2-13.

22. Kurlander RJ.Reversible and irreversible loss of Fc receptor function of human monocytes as a consequence of interaction with immunoglobulin G. *J Clin Invest* 1980;66:773-781.

23. Anthony RM, Nimmerjahn F, Ashline DJ, Reinhold VN, Paulson JC, Ravetch JV. Recapitulation of IVIG anti-inflammatory activity with a recombinant IgG Fc. Science. 2008;320(5874):373-6.

24. Engelhard D, Waner JL, Kapoor N, Good RA. Effect of intravenous immune globulin on natural killer cells activity: possible association with autoimmune neutropenia and idiopathic thrombocytopenia. *J Pediatr* 1986;108:77-81.

25. Takei S, Arora YK, Walker SM. Intravenous immunoglobulin contains specific antibodies inhibitory to activation of T cells by staphylococcal toxin superantigens. J *Clin Invest* 1993;91: 602-607.

26. Kaveri S,Vassilev T, Hurez V, et al. Antibodies to a conserved region of HLA class I molecule capable of modulating CD8 T cells mediated function, are present in pooled normal immunoglobulin for therapeutic use. *J Clin Invest* 1996;97:868-869.

27. Zhu KY, Feferman T, Maiti PK, Souroujon MC, Fuchs S. Intravenous immunoglobulin suppresses experimental myasthenia gravis: immunological mechanisms. *J Neuroimmunol.* 2006;176(1-2):187-97.

28. Fuchs S, Feferman T, Meidler R, Margalit R, Sicsic C, Wang N, Zhu KY, Brenner T, Laub O, Souroujon MC. A disease-specific fraction isolated from IVIG is essential for the immunosuppressive effect of IVIG in experimental autoimmune myasthenia gravis. *J Neuroimmunol.* 2008;194(1-2):89-96.

29. Gajdos P, Chevret S, Toyka K. Intravenous immunoglobulin for myasthenia gravis. Cochrane Database Syst Rev. 2008;(1):CD002277.

30. Arsura EL, Bick A, Brunner NG, Namba T, Grob D. High-dose intravenous immunoglobulin in the management of myasthenia gravis. *Arch InterMed* 1986;146:1365-1368.

31. Arsura EL, Bick A, Brunner NG, Grob D. Effects of repeated doses of intravenous immunoglobulin in myasthenia gravis. Am J Med Sci 1988;295:438-443.

32. Gajdos Ph, Outin HD, Morel E, Raphael JC, Goulon M. High dose intravenous gamma globulin for myasthenia gravis: an alternative to plasma exchange? *Ann NY Acad Sci* 1987;505: 843-844.

33. Gajdos Ph, Outin H, Elkharrat D, et al. High-dose intravenous gammaglobulin for myasthenia gravis. *Lancet* 1984;1:406- 407.

34. Cosi V, Lombardi M, Piccolo G, Erbetta A. Treatment of myasthenia gravis with high-dose intravenous immunoglobulin. *Acta Neurol Scand* 1991;84:81-84.

35. Ippoliti G, Cosi V, Piccolo G, Lombardi M, Mantegaz R. High-dose intravenous gammaglobulin for myasthenia gravis. Lancet 1984;2:809.

36. Edan G, Landgraf. Experience with intravenous immunoglobulin in myasthenia gravis: a review. *J Neurol Neurosurg Psychiatry* 1994;57(suppl):55-56.

37. Besinger UA, Fateh-Moghadam A, Knorr-Held S, Wick M, Kissel H, Albiez M. Immunomodulation in myasthenia gravis by high dose intravenous 7-S immunoglobulin. A*nn NY Acad Sci* 1987;505:828-831.

38. Uchiyama M, Ichikawa Y, Takaya M, Moriuchi J, Shimizu H, Arimori S. High dose gamma globulin therapy of generalized myasthenia gravis. *Ann NY Acad Sci* 1987;505:868-870,

39. Cook L, Howard JF, Folds JD. Immediate effects of intravenous IgG administration on peripheral blood B and T cells and polymorphonuclear cells in patients with myasthenia gravis. *J Clin Immunol* 1988;8:23-31.

40. Achiron A, Barak Y, Miron S, Sarova-Pinas I. Immunoglobulin treatment in refractory myasthenia gravis. *Muscle & Nerve* 2000;23(4): 551–5

41. Hilkevich O, Drory VE, Chapman J, Korczyn AD. The use of intravenous immunoglobulin as maintenance therapy in myasthenia gravis. *Clinical Neurophamacology* 2001;24(3):173–6.

42. Sticker RB, Kwiatkowska BJ, Habis JA, Kiprov DD. Myasthenic crisis. Response to plasmapheresis following failure of intravenous ã-globulin. *Arch Neurol* 1993;50:837-840.

43. Gajdos P, Chevret S, Clair B, Tranchant C, Chastang C. Clinical trial of plasma exchange and high dose immunoglobulin inmyasthenia gravis. *Annals of Neurology* 1997;41(6):789–96.

44. Gajdos P, Tranchant C, Clair B, Bolgert F, Eymard B, Stojkovic T, et al.Treatment of myasthenia gravis exacerbation with intravenous immunoglobulin 1g/kg versus 2g/kg: a randomized double blind clinical trial. *Archives of Neurology* 2005; Vol. 62, issue 11:1689–93.

45. Zinman L, Ng E, Bril V. IV immunoglobulin in patients with myasthenia gravis. A randomized controlled trial. *Neurology* 2007;68 (11):837–41.

46. Ronager J, Ravnborg M, Hermansen I, Vorstrup S. Immunoglobulin treatment versus plasma exchange in patients with chronicmoderate to severe myasthenia gravis. *Artificial Organs* 2001;25(12):967–73.

47. Wolfe GI, Barohn RJ, Foster BM, Jackson CE, Kissel JT, Day JW, et al. Randomized, controlled trial of intravenous immunoglobulin in myasthenia gravis. *Muscle & Nerve* 2002;26(4):549–52.

48. Liblau R, Gajdos Ph, Bustardet FA, El Habib R, Bach JF, Morel E. Intravenous gamma globulin in myasthenia gravis: interaction with anti-acetylcholine receptor autoantibodies. *J Clin Immunol* 1991;11:128-131.

49. Takahashi H, Kawaguchi N, Nemoto Y, Hattori T. High-dose intravenous immunoglobulin for the treatment of MuSK antibody-positive seronegative myasthenia gravis. *J Neurol Sci.* 2006;247(2):239-41.

50. Shibata-Hamaguchi A, Samuraki M, Furui E, Iwasa K, Yoshikawa H, Hayashi S, Yamada M. Long-term effect of intravenous immunoglobulin on anti-MuSK antibody-positive myasthenia gravis. *Acta Neurol Scand.* 2007;116(6):406-8.

Genetics of Human Autoimmune Myasthenia Gravis

Henri-Jean Garchon MD, PhD.

1. INTRODUCTION

Unlike congenital myasthenic syndromes that are caused by mutation of genes coding for components of the muscle acetylcholine receptor, the genetics of human autoimmune myasthenia gravis (MG) is complex and multifactorial. Available data, however, shed light on the disease heterogeneity and also provide insight into its pathogenesis. Here, we review important issues specific to MG genetic studies as well as the most significant genetic factors identified to date.

2. ROLE OF GENETIC FACTORS IN MG

Segregation of autoimmune MG in families does not follow a simple pattern. Indeed, there are few reported families with multiple cases of the disease (1-6). As a result, it has not been possible to conduct genome-wide linkage scans of MG susceptibility loci. Nonetheless, the recurrence risk of 2-4% for the relatives of the patients remains considerably greater than the prevalence of the disease in the general population, 1×10^{-4} in Caucasians (7-11). There are also two twin studies that indicated a rate of concordance for the disease higher than expected in monozygotic twin pairs compared to dizygotic ones (12,13). Taken together, these data are consistent with a genetic component playing a significant role in MG susceptibility.

In addition, there is an increased frequency of autoimmune diseases other than MG among the relatives of MG patients (3,14). These are mostly autoimmune diseases of the thyroid and rheumatoid arthritis. These observations strongly suggest that MG and these other autoimmune conditions share a common predisposing genetic background. Conversely, the study of endophenotypes among the relatives of the patients, including electromyographical anomalies and anti-AChR autoantibodies, failed to identify a disease-relevant trait with a greater penetrance than MG that would have been amenable to genetic linkage analysis (15). Finally, the most convincing argument for a role of genetic factors came from their direct identification; among them, the human leukocyte antigens (HLA) have long held the most conspicuous place.

3. HETEROGENEITY OF MG

Although the autoantibodies against the muscle AChR appear to be a common effector mechanism in the majority of the MG patients, their clinical presentation is quite variable (see Chapter 1) and, specifically, the disease is frequently associated with characteristic anomalies of the thymus (discussed in Chapter 2). This suggests the existence of several forms of the disease, each of which most likely corresponds to a different pathogenetic pathway. Accounting for such heterogeneity is an essential step in an analysis of genetic data because it increases the power to detect genetic associations. This is especially critical in genome-wide association scans that aim at identifying variants with modest effects. In MG, several kinds of criteria, including

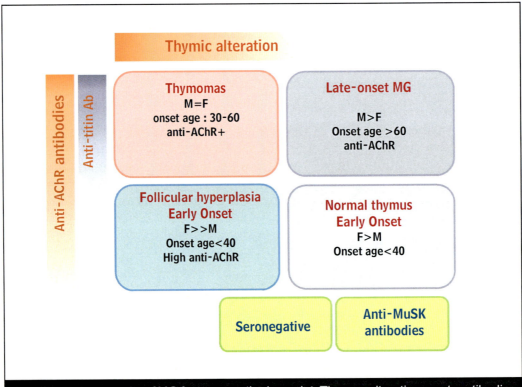

Figure 1. Heterogeneity of MG from a genetic viewpoint. Thymus alterations, autoantibodies against specific antigens, including the AChR, MuSK and titin, age at onset of disease, and the ratio of males (M) and females (F) are used to delineate subgroups of patients.

thymus histopathology, the serum autoantibodies and the age at disease onset, must be considered (Figure 1).

The presence of a thymus alteration, including thymus follicular hyperplasia and thymoma, is a first critical parameter, especially because there is consistent evidence that it plays a key role in breakage of immune tolerance and production of autoantibodies (16,17). Moreover, these alterations correlate remarkably with clinical and biological features (18,19). Thymus hyperplasia is preferentially observed in women with an early onset of disease (before 40 years of age) and with often high, though quite variable, serum titers of anti-AChR autoantibodies. It does not seem to occur in patients with anti-MuSK autoantibodies but has been consistently reported in patients who score negatively for both anti-AChR and anti-MuSK autoantibodies (20-22). Recent work indicates that these seronegative patients indeed express low affinity anti-AChR antibodies requiring a highly sensitive assay for their detection (23).

Conversely, thymomas occur equally in women and men and are often associated with severe clinical symptoms. These patients are consistently positive for anti-AChR auto-antibodies and also for anti-titin antibodies (19,24). Titin is a giant protein (M_r $3'x10^6$) that plays an important role in the elasticity of muscle fibers (25) and is the major molecular target of anti-striated muscle antibodies in MG patients (26). The pathogenetic significance of anti-titin antibodies is presently not known.

Patients whose thymus is normal or who have not been thymectomized form a heterogeneous group. The age at onset of the disease and the presence of serum anti-titin antibodies are useful indicators to categorize them. Thus, anti-titin antibodies are frequently detected also in patients with a normal thymus (verified by computerized tomography) and a late onset of disease (>60 years) (19,27). Conversely, they are exceptionally present in patients with thymic hyperplasia and more generally in patients with an onset age under 40, including those with a normal/atrophic thymus upon histopathologic examination.

Figure 1 summarizes how these criteria can be used and combined to delineate subgroups of MG patients relevant for genetic analyses. Considering more than one criterion is recommended whenever possible to increase the likelihood of dealing with a homogenous group of patients. Moreover, complete information is not always available: decision of thymectomy in non-thymomatous young patients varies with physicians; anti-titin autoantibody assays are specialized and not routinely done; cohorts with differing recruitment protocols may have to be merged. Conversely, information may be unreliable: an immunosuppressive treatment before thymectomy may mask follicular hyperplasia; it is sometimes difficult for the patient to accurately date the first symptoms.

A further critical level of heterogeneity for genetic analysis is the ethnic origin. Firstly, allele frequencies of genetic markers often vary considerably among ethnic groups, an issue that confounds all genetic data analyses and is not specific to MG. Second, there are significant differences in the clinical expression of the disease in Asians and in Blacks compared with Caucasians. The disease seems to be milder, more prevalent among children, more often ocular only and seronegative among Asians than Caucasians (28,29). In contrast, it appears to be more severe in Blacks, especially the ocular localization, and, while the prevalence of anti-AChR antibody negativity is also high in Blacks, the proportion of anti-MuSK positivity is higher than in Whites and Asians (30,31).

4. PANORAMA OF MG GENETIC FACTORS

To date, genetic factors known in MG have been involved by the means of association studies. These compare groups of unrelated patients and controls and seek a correlation between the disease and an allele of a genetic marker. Although there is no definitive knowledge about the nature of the causal DNA variations involved in complex genetic diseases such as MG, these are thought to be primarily common bi-allelic single nucleotide polymorphisms (SNPs) (32). This means that disease-associated alleles of these common SNPs are also present in the healthy population with a significant prevalence, at variance with rare mutations underlying Mendelian diseases such as congenital myasthenic syndromes.

The major histocompatibility complex (MHC) is by far the most important genetic factor, with the largest influence but also with multiple effects on the patient phenotype. Apart from the MHC, a number of MHC-unlinked loci were investigated using a candidate gene approach. Tables 1 and 2 provide their list, including those associated with MG and those reported to be not associated with MG. For the latter, we are now aware that their study was not always conducted with adequate power to make a statistically valid decision; their detailed re-assessment based on an exhaustive analysis of their polymorphism in large enough samples might be necessary to definitively rule out their role. Beyond, a genome-wide association scan relying on a broad international collaboration is underway for a systematic search of common disease variants. Hereafter, the discussion will be focused on the most relevant currently known genetic factors, including the MHC and two causative variants, one in the self-antigen gene CHRNA1, the other in the general autoimmunity gene PTPN22.

5. THE MAJOR HISTOCOMPATIBILITY COMPLEX

5.1. Overview of HLA and the MHC

The human leukocyte antigens (HLA) were discovered owing to their central role in allograft rejection (57). They are now known to be a cornerstone of the immune response, given their function of presentation of antigenic peptides to lymphocytes. They are membrane-bound molecules of the immunoglobulin superfamily of two main types, class I and class II. Genes of the class I, such as HLA-A and HLA-B, and those of the class II, such as DRB1, show several hundreds of alleles and define the most polymorphic genetic system of the human species. This extreme polymorphism together with their function explains why HLA loci have been excellent candidates to account for individual susceptibility to a large number of inflammatory and immune diseases, including autoimmune diseases (58-60).

Subsequently, genetic investigation of HLA culminating with genome sequencing and interspecies comparative mapping revealed that HLA loci belong to a large and conserved region of human chromosome 6p21, termed the Major Histocompatibility Complex (61,62). It extends over 7.8 megabases and harbors the highest density of genes of the human genome (Figure 2). The class II region, on the centromeric side, and the class I region, on the telomeric side, are separated by class III loci and are flanked by the extended class I and class II regions. Numerous genes of the class III encode proteins with essential immune functions, notably complement factors, heat shock proteins, tumor necrosis factor and lymphotoxins, receptors for natural killer cells, in addition to many newly discovered genes that are expressed in the immune system but whose function is not known yet.

Table 1. Non-MHC genes associated with MG [Reprinted from *Ann N Y Acad Sci* 1132:180-192, 2008]

Locus symbol, gene product	Variant or marker	Mechanism	References
CHRNA1, α-subunit of muscle nicotinic acetylcholine receptor	promoter SNP (−478A/G), G allele alters binding of IRF8 transcription factor and response to interferon-γ	Causal, affects the gene promiscuous expression in thymus and tolerization	(33-36)
PTPN22, cellular tyrosine phosphatase 22	Coding (Arg620Trp); Trp allele impairs binding to Csk kinase	Causal, immunoregulatory, increases phosphatase activity and impairs T cell activation, including IL2 production	(37,38)
FCGR2A, type 2A low affinity receptor for IgG	coding (R131H), H variant increases receptor affinity for IgG2	Potentially modifies regulation of B cell activation	(39,40)
CTLA4, cytotoxic T cell late antigen 4	Coding (Thr17Ala), 3'UTR microsatellite; alteration of glycosylation pattern by the signal peptide variant	Molecular and immunological mechanisms debated	(41,42)
CHRNG, CHRND; γ- and δ-subunits of muscle nicotinic acetylcholine receptor	Intronic microsatellite	unknown	(43)
ADRB2, β2-adrenergic receptor	Coding SNP (Gly16Arg)	unknown	(44)
IL10, interleukin-10	Microsatellite, SNPs in upstream region	Potentially upregulates IL10 expression, promoting B-cell growth	(45,46)
IL1B, interleukin-1β	SNP in exon 5	Disease-associated allele associated with 'high-secretor' phenotype	(47)
IFNG, interferon-γ	Non coding SNP (+874A/T), maps to a putative NF-κB binding site	Potentially alters IFN-γ production	(46)
TCRA, T-cell receptor α locus	Restriction fragment length polymorphisms	Antigenic peptide recognition	(48)
IGH, immunoglobulin heavy chain	Gm allotypes	unknown	(49)
IGK, immunoglobulin κ-chain	Coding SNP, conservative change	unknown	(50)

Table 2. Non-MHC loci reported not to be associated with MG

[Reprinted with permission from Ann NY Acad Sci 1132: 180-192,2008]

Locus symbol, gene product	Marker tested	References
CHRNB1, β-subunit of muscle nicotinic acetylcholine receptor	Microsatellite	(51)
CHRNE, ε-subunit of muscle nicotinic acetylcholine receptor	Intronic insertion-deletion polymorphism	(52)
IL1RN, IL1 receptor antagonist	Variable number tandem repeat in intron 2	(47)
IL4, interleukin 4	Variable number tandem repeats	(53)
IL6, interleukin 6	Promoter SNP (-174C/G), alters an estrogen response element	(54)
CCR2, chemokine receptor 2	SNP (Val64Ile)	(55)
CCR5, chemokine receptor 5	32bp deletion in open reading frame	(55)
FCGR3B, type 2B low affinity receptor for IgG	Coding (F158V, NA1/NA2)	(40)
IL12B, interleukin 12 p40 subunit	3'untranslated region SNP	(46)
B7H3, B7 homolog 3	SNPs	(56)

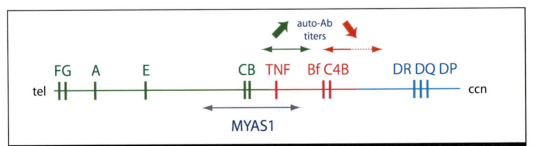

Figure 2. Organization of the MHC on chromosome 6p21 with its three classes, I (green), II (blue) and III (pink) and representative loci for each class. The intervals of the 8.1 MHC haplotype that are associated with MG and thymus hyperplasia (MYAS1) and with modulation of serum auto-antibody titers are also depicted. Tel, telomere; cen, centromere.

5.2. Association of the 8.1 HLA haplotype in MG

Very early in the history of HLA-disease associations, MG was associated with HLA class I loci, including B8 and A1 alleles, and subsequently with HLA class II loci and their DR3 and Dw3 alleles (63-65). Other HLA-linked genes, including a null allele of the complement C4A gene and a promoter polymorphism of the TNFalpha gene were also associated (66,67). Indeed, these polymorphisms are in strong linkage disequilibrium with each other – this means that they are recurrently associated –, despite a physical distance of several megabases separating HLA-A and HLA class II genes. They thus define a stable haplotype that is often termed 8.1 as it consistently harbors the HLA-B8 allele and that is the most frequent one in Caucasian populations with a prevalence of 5% (66,68). Its frequency is markedly and specifically increased up to 60-70% in the MG patients with a thymus hyperplasia or with early disease onset but not in other forms of MG (18,69) and it has been reproducibly observed in all Caucasian MG patients studied to date. However, it has also been involved in several other human autoimmune diseases, including systemic lupus erythematosus, celiac disease, rheumatoid arthritis and autoimmune thyroiditis, in immune phenotypes such as IgA deficiency and in several cancers (70,71). It is not known whether the same genes are involved in these various pathologies.

As mentioned above, too few multiple-case families are available to allow efficient genetic linkage studies in MG. In such situations, family-based methods of association can be alternatively used to test linkage of a genetic region with a disease. Their principle is to assess allelic transmission to MG offspring by their parents. In case of non - association with the disease, a given allele has a 50% probability to be transmitted to a child. A significant deviation from this Mendelian proportion is considered as evidence of association. It also indicates linkage because the method assumes linkage between the tested marker and the disease locus. Using this study design, it was possible to demonstrate a significant distortion of the transmission of HLA-DR alleles to MG patients and therefore to establish linkage of the MHC to the form of the disease presenting with thymus follicular hyperplasia (69). The corresponding locus has been termed MYAS1.

Because the 8.1 haplotype is so prevalent among MG patients, it is difficult to detect an effect of other alleles. To overcome this, an efficient method relies on relative predispositional effects and consists in removing the most significantly associated allele, here DR3, in both patients and controls and starting again an association analysis, proceeding iteratively until no association is detected. Using this approach, two other alleles, DR16 and DR9, were associated positively in a French cohort of MG patients while DR7 was found protective (69).

5.3. Heterogeneity of HLA associations

Subgroups of patients other than those with thymus hyperplasia have been much less investigated. Regarding the patients with thymoma, conflicting data have been reported. Associations with both HLA class II and class I loci were described (72-75). However, because MG with thymoma is a rare pathology, these studies investigated small-size samples. A larger study of 92 French MG patients detected no association with DR alleles (69). However, an association of the HLA-A class I locus was reported by two groups although the associated allele was not the same in both studies (75,76). Even more interestingly, considering the thymoma histotype revealed a strong protection of HLA-A2, the most prevalent HLA-A allele, in the B2 type thymomas (76). This indicates that the thymoma histotype, which influences the clinical outcome, is also a relevant criterion for stratification in future genetic analyses. Of note, somatic loss of heterozygosity at the MHC occurs in thymoma tumors and this further supports a role of the region in this pathology (77).

As for the non-thymoma MG patients with late-onset of disease, a group of growing size as a result of population ageing, a large study of French patients reported an increased prevalence of DR7 (69). Interestingly, an association with DQA1*201, an allele in linkage disequilibrium with DR7, was also described Turkish MG patients with anti-titin antibodies (78). Finally, the patients with anti-MuSK auto-antibodies who form a group that does not overlap with the anti-AChR autoantibody positive patients were reported to be associated with the DQ5 class II allele in two different studies (79,80).

All the data discussed above involved Caucasian patients. Different associations were detected in other ethnic groups: class I alleles were preferentially associated with MG in Blacks (B8) and in Chinese (Bw46), whereas DR9 was associated with mild (including ocular) forms of MG in Chinese and in Japanese patients (28,81-84). Altogether, all these observations concur to emphasize a heterogeneity of genetic associations that correlates with the clinical and biological heterogeneity of the disease, the most striking and consistent association being that of the 8.1 haplotype in MG with thymus follicular hyperplasia.

5.4. Non-HLA MHC loci

The main obstacle that has hindered the fine mapping of the disease locus on the 8.1 haplotype has been the strong linkage disequilibrium between most alleles of this haplotype. Previous reports, however, have indicated that the association of HLA-B8 was predominant over that of DR3 or A1, whose associations were actually secondary to that of B8 (18,85-87). However, the HLA-B locus is still separated from HLA-A (on the telomeric side) and from DR loci (on the centromeric side) by an interval of over 1 million nucleotides that includes a large number of candidate genes, opening the possibility that these also might be actually responsible for the observed HLA associations. Increasing the density of the map of genetic markers was therefore necessary to reconstruct and identify disease-associated haplotypes and then to narrow down the susceptibility interval by looking at ancestrally-recombinant haplotypes (85,88). This approach has been combined with a family-based association analysis to successfully refine the location of the MYAS1 locus in a still large interval of 1.2 Mb at the boundary of class III and proximal class I regions (Figure 2) (87). Remarkably, this interval that encompasses 36 genes excluded the HLA-DRB1 gene, consistent with the earlier reports (18,86). The disease risk followed an additive model, with an odds ratio of 6.5 for a single copy of the 8.1 haplotype and 42 for two copies (P < 1×10^{10}), similar to that previously measured (86,89). It is interesting to note that, as the frequency of the 8.1 haplotype in the control population is ~5%, the predisposing allele at the MYAS1 locus is likely to be a rare one, depending on how long it has emerged after the constitution of the 8.1 ancestral haplotype.

Besides the effect on thymus follicular hyperplasia, the study of Vandiedonck et al. (87) reported a major and composite effect of the 8.1 haplotype on serum titers of anti-AChR autoantibodies: a quantitative trait locus mapping in the MHC central region was associated with 7-8 fold elevated titers of autoantibodies and its effect was suppressed by a locus in *cis* mapping towards the class II region (Figure 2). It is unclear at present whether the locus for thymic follicular hyperplasia and the one controlling autoantibody titers are the same or not.

Altogether, these observations demonstrate the major and recurrent influence of the MHC in disease expression, even though the underlying DNA variation remains to be precisely identified. With the recent major advances of the Human Genome Program, including the characterization of high-resolution polymorphism maps and the full sequencing of the MHC region on several haplotypes, it now becomes possible to increase the resolution of MHC gene mapping considerably and hopefully to eventually identify the disease-causing variants (60,90).

6. THE CHRNA1 LOCUS

This locus encodes the α-subunit of the AChR, a trans-membrane pentamer that is the target of the pathogenic auto-antibodies found in the sera of most patients with generalized MG (91). Conceivably, a polymorphism of the AChR could alter its behavior in response to binding by pathogenic antibodies, therefore affecting the neuromuscular transmission. Alternatively, it is now known that expression of self-antigens in the thymic epithelium, even of the most "tissue-specific" ones such as insulin, is essential to install and maintain immune tolerance of maturing T-cells (92). Given the importance of thymic pathology in MG, this hypothesis is of particular interest to account for an association of an AChR polymorphism in MG (17,93).

Early studies using microsatellite markers indicated an association of the genes encoding the α-subunit, CHRNA1 on chromosome 2q31.1, and of those encoding the γ and δ subunits, CHRNG and CHRND, both located in tandem on 2q37.1, therefore close to the telomere and distant from CHRNA1 (33,34,43). Recently, an exhaustive analysis of the CHRNA1 gene polymorphism, based on re-sequencing and followed by a detailed analysis of SNP associations, led to identify a promoter polymorphism associated with an early onset of the disease in MG patients with thymus hyperplasia (36). Remarkably, the gene shows only one synonymous coding SNP, in exon 7, reflecting tight conservation at the protein level. Analysis of the pattern of linkage disequilibrium among the 43 common variants identified 11 tagging SNPs that were representative of the common polymorphism content of the gene in Caucasians. One of these SNPs was then found to significantly influence the age at onset of the disease in two independent cohorts of early-onset MG cases and controls, one from France and the other from the UK. The predisposing allele increased by more than two-fold the risk of developing the disease before the age of 20 years. Additional approaches combining *in silico* analyses and experimental testing

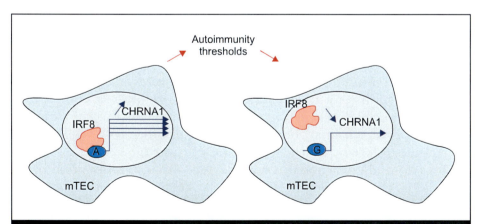

Figure 3. The rs16862847 promoter variant (A or G, circled blue) in the CHRNA1 gene modifies binding of the IRF8 transcription factor and expression level of CHRNA1 in medullary epithelial cells (mTEC). This expression level that is modulated also by the AIRE protein (not shown) is essential to setting of tolerance versus autoimmunity.

were used to eventually identify the causative SNP, *rs16862847*. This is located in the CHRNA1 promoter region and its minor allele, G, disrupts a motif that is consensus for binding the transcription factor IRF8 (interferon regulatory factor 8) (Figure 3). This factor is involved in both the regulation of interferon genes and the response of a number of genes to interferon exposure (94). By using various molecular techniques, this SNP was found to markedly influence CHRNA1 expression, notably in response to interferon, and to control binding of IRF8 to the gene promoter harboring the major A allele.

The significance of the modification of CHRNA1 expression by *rs16862847* could be understood in light of basic studies from the group of Bruno Kyewski on immune tolerance and on the role of promiscuous expression of tissue-restricted antigens in medullary thymic epithelial cells (mTECs)(92): the CHRNA1 mRNA levels in freshly purified mTECs from non-autoimmune subjects were significantly influenced by the *rs16862847* variant; the G allele, associated with early onset of the disease and with loss of IRF8 binding to the promoter, was expressed at significantly lower levels that the A allele. Thus, this promoter sequence point mutation established a link between CHRNA1 expression levels in the thymic epithelium and the autoimmune risk.

Gene expression analysis in mTECs also revealed the level of AIRE message (Autoimmune regulator) as a major factor influencing self-antigen expression. The AIRE gene codes for a nuclear protein that plays an important role in controlling promiscuous expression of a number of tissue-restricted antigens and its mutation in humans causes the type 1 auto-immune polyglandular syndrome (95). How AIRE mediates this effect is not understood yet. The available data, however, suggested that AIRE and IRF8 acted additively and independently on CHRNA1 expression. Altogether, such control of thymic expression of a self-antigen by a disease-modifying regulatory DNA variant emphasizes the role of central tolerance in human autoimmune diseases and opens a new area of investigation of the antigen-specific component of a human autoimmune response.

7. THE PTPN22 GENE

In contrast to the CHRNA1 promoter variant just described, a missense polymorphism in the gene encoding the intracellular protein phosphatase PTPN22 (1858C/T, dbSNP reference: *rs2476601*) provides a perfect example of non antigen-specific factor of autoimmunity. This variant changes an arginine (R, using the one-letter code for amino acids) into a tryptophane (or W) at position 620 of the protein and impairs its binding to the protein tyrosine kinase CSK. This impairs T-cell signaling resulting from ligation of the T-cell antigen receptor and notably inhibits interleukin-2 production (96). Deficiency of this interleukin is known to predispose to autoimmunity (97). Moreover, genetic variants in the interleukin-2 receptor have been associated with type 1 diabetes predisposition and other autoimmune diseases (98). The PTPN22 gene with the minor T allele at *rs2476601*, which encodes the W variant, has been associated initially with type 1 diabetes (96) and subsequently with several other autoimmune diseases, including rheumatoid arthritis, juvenile idiopathic arthritis, systemic lupus erythematosus, autoimmune thyroid diseases, vitiligo, and Addison's disease (see review (99)). Conversely, other diseases such as multiple sclerosis, Crohn's disease, psoriasis and primary Sjögren's syndrome, have appeared not to be associated or only loosely with this variant.

Study of the *PTPN22* risk T allele in a large group of 470 French patients with autoimmune MG compared with 296 population-matched controls has revealed a strong association but only in non-thymoma patients without anti-titin antibodies (37). This subgroup of patients includes the patients with thymus follicular hyperplasia and early onset of disease as discussed above.

The measured odds ratio, 1.97 (95% confidence interval: 1.32-2.97), was among the highest observed in an autoimmune disease. The association was independent of the occurrence of another autoimmune disease such as rheumatoid arthritis or autoimmune thyroiditis, previously shown to be associated with the variant by themselves. It was also independent of the MHC haplotype and of the serum titers of anti-AChR autoantibodies. It was actually observed among anti-AChR "seronegative" patients. Conversely, in this French cohort, the PTPN22 polymorphism was not associated in the patients with anti-titin antibodies and those with a thymoma, again stressing the genetic heterogeneity of MG. A recent study in a large Swedish cohort has replicated these findings, including the heterogeneity of the association and the large effect in patients with young onset age (38). Both the fact that this variant is causal and the magnitude of its effect make it an important reference for future studies in MG, opening the perspective of the search of new genetic factors through pathway interaction analysis.

8. CONCLUSION AND PERSPECTIVES

As seen, known genetic factors, dominated by the MHC, correlate remarkably well with the heterogeneity of MG defined using clinical and biological criteria. Their in-depth study should provide invaluable insight into the pathophysiology of MG. Genotyping microarrays and high-throughput sequencing technology now provide the means to extend the search of these factors to the entire human genome, which should lead to exciting new developments of this field.

REFERENCES

1. Namba, T., N. G. Brunner, S. B. Brown, M. Muguruma, and D. Grob. 1971. Familial myasthenia gravis. Report of 27 patients in 12 families and review of 164 patients in 73 families. *Arch Neurol* 25:49-60.
2. Bundey, S. 1972. A genetic study of infantile and juvenile myasthenia gravis. *J Neurol Neurosurg Psychiatry* 35:41-51.
3. Pirskanen, R. 1977. Genetic aspects in myasthenia gravis. A family study of 264 Finnish patients. *Acta Neurol Scand* 56:365-388.
4. Allen, N., P. Kissel, D. Pietrasiuk, and M. J. Perlow. 1984. Myasthenia gravis in monozygotic twins. Clinical follow-up nine years after thymectomy. *Arch Neurol* 41:994-996.
5. Provenzano, C., O. Arancio, A. Evoli, B. Rocca, E. Bartoccioni, D. de Grandis, and P. Tonali. 1988. Familial autoimmune myasthenia gravis with different pathogenetic antibodies. *J Neurol Neurosurg Psychiatry* 51:1228-1230.
6. Szobor, A. 1989. Myasthenia gravis: familial occurrence. A study of 1100 myasthenia gravis patients. *Acta Med Hung* 46:13-21.
7. Phillips, L. H., 2nd, J. C. Torner, M. S. Anderson, and G. M. Cox. 1992. The epidemiology of myasthenia gravis in central and western Virginia. *Neurology* 42:1888-1893.
8. Robertson, N. P., J. Deans, and D. A. Compston. 1998. Myasthenia gravis: a population based epidemiological study in Cambridgeshire, England. *J Neurol Neurosurg Psychiatry* 65:492-496.
9. Kalb, B., G. Matell, R. Pirskanen, and M. Lambe. 2002. Epidemiology of myasthenia gravis: a population-based study in Stockholm, Sweden. *Neuroepidemiology* 21:221-225.
10. Chung, B., V. Wong, and P. Ip. 2003. Prevalence of neuromuscular diseases in Chinese children: a study in southern China. *J Child Neurol* 18:217-219.
11. Oopik, M., L. Puksa, S. M. Luus, A. E. Kaasik, and J. Jakobsen. 2008. Clinical and laboratory-reconfirmed myasthenia gravis: a population-based study. *Eur J Neurol* 15:246-252.
12. Namba, T., M. S. Shapiro, N. G. Brunner, and D. Grob. 1971. Myasthenia gravis occurring in twins. *J Neurol Neurosurg Psychiatry* 34:531-534.
13. Murphy, J., and S. F. Murphy. 1986. Myasthenia gravis in identical twins. *Neurology* 36:78-80.
14. Kerzin-Storrar, L., R. A. Metcalfe, P. A. Dyer, G. Kowalska, I. Ferguson, and R. Harris. 1988. Genetic factors in myasthenia gravis: a family study. *Neurology* 38:38-42.
15. Pascuzzi, R. M., L. H. Phillips, 2nd, T. R. Johns, and V. A. Lennon. 1987. The prevalence of electrophysiological and immunological abnormalities in asymptomatic relatives of patients with myasthenia gravis. *Ann N Y Acad Sci* 505:407-415.
16. Kao, I., and D. B. Drachman. 1977. Thymic muscle cells bear acetylcholine receptors: possible relation to myasthenia gravis. *Science* 195:74-75.
17. Hohlfeld, R., and H. Wekerle. 2008. Reflections on the "intrathymic pathogenesis" of myasthenia gravis. *J Neuroimmunol* 201-202:21-27.
18. Compston, D. A., A. Vincent, J. Newsom-Davis, and J. R. Batchelor. 1980. Clinical, pathological, HLA antigen and immunological evidence for disease heterogeneity in myasthenia gravis. *Brain* 103:579-601.

19. Yamamoto, A. M., P. Gajdos, B. Eymard, C. Tranchant, J. M. Warter, L. Gomez, C. Bourquin, J. F. Bach, and H. J. Garchon. 2001. Anti-titin antibodies in myasthenia gravis: tight association with thymoma and heterogeneity of nonthymoma patients. *Arch. Neurol.* 58:885-890.

20. Leite, M. I., P. Strobel, M. Jones, K. Micklem, R. Moritz, R. Gold, E. H. Niks, S. Berrih-Aknin, F. Scaravilli, A. Canelhas, A. Marx, J. Newsom-Davis, N. Willcox, and A. Vincent. 2005. Fewer thymic changes in MuSK antibody-positive than in MuSK antibody-negative MG. *Ann Neurol* 57:444-448.

21. Lauriola, L., F. Ranelletti, N. Maggiano, M. Guerriero, C. Punzi, F. Marsili, E. Bartoccioni, and A. Evoli. 2005. Thymus changes in anti-MuSK-positive and -negative myasthenia gravis. *Neurology* 64:536-538.

22. Hayashi, A., H. Shiono, M. Ohta, K. Ohta, M. Okumura, and Y. Sawa. 2007. Heterogeneity of immunopathological features of AChR/MuSK autoantibody-negative myasthenia gravis. *J Neuroimmunol* 189:163-168.

23. Leite, M. I., S. Jacob, S. Viegas, J. Cossins, L. Clover, B. P. Morgan, D. Beeson, N. Willcox, and A. Vincent. 2008. IgG1 antibodies to acetylcholine receptors in 'seronegative' myasthenia gravis. *Brain* 131:1940-1952.

24. Aarli, J. A., K. Stefansson, L. S. Marton, and R. L. Wollmann. 1990. Patients with myasthenia gravis and thymoma have in their sera IgG autoantibodies against titin. *Clin Exp Immunol* 82:284-288.

25. Labeit, S., and B. Kolmerer. 1995. Titins: giant proteins in charge of muscle ultrastructure and elasticity. *Science* 270:293-296.

26. Gautel, M., A. Lakey, D. P. Barlow, Z. Holmes, S. Scales, K. Leonard, S. Labeit, A. Mygland, N. E. Gilhus, and J. A. Aarli. 1993. Titin antibodies in myasthenia gravis: identification of a major immunogenic region of titin. *Neurology* 43:1581-1585.

27. Aarli, J. A., F. Romi, G. O. Skeie, and N. E. Gilhus. 2003. Myasthenia gravis in individuals over 40. *Ann N Y Acad Sci* 998:424-431.

28. Matsuki, K., T. Juji, K. Tokunaga, M. Takamizawa, H. Maeda, M. Soda, Y. Nomura, and M. Segawa. 1990. HLA antigens in Japanese patients with myasthenia gravis. *J Clin Invest* 86:392-399.

29. Zhang, X., M. Yang, J. Xu, M. Zhang, B. Lang, W. Wang, and A. Vincent. 2007. Clinical and serological study of myasthenia gravis in HuBei Province, China. *J Neurol Neurosurg Psychiatry* 78:386-390.

30. Heckmann, J. M., E. P. Owen, and F. Little. 2007. Myasthenia gravis in South Africans: racial differences in clinical manifestations. *Neuromuscul Disord* 17:929-934.

31. Oh, S. J., M. B. Morgan, L. Lu, Y. Hatanaka, S. Hemmi, A. Young, and G. C. Claussen. 2009. Racial differences in myasthenia gravis in Alabama. *Muscle Nerve* 39:328-332.

32. Hirschhorn, J. N., and M. J. Daly. 2005. Genome-wide association studies for common diseases and complex traits. *Nat Rev Genet* 6:95-108.

33. Garchon, H. J., F. Djabiri, J. P. Viard, P. Gajdos, and J. F. Bach. 1994. Involvement of human muscle acetylcholine receptor alpha-subunit gene (CHRNA) in susceptibility to myasthenia gravis. *Proc. Natl. Acad. Sci. USA* 91:4668-4672.

34. Heckmann, J. M., K. E. Morrison, B. Emeryk-Szajewska, H. Strugalska, J. Bergoffen, N. Willcox, and J. Newsom-Davis. 1996. Human muscle acetylcholine receptor alpha-subunit gene (CHRNA1) association with autoimmune myasthenia gravis in black, mixed-ancestry and Caucasian subjects. *J. Autoimmun.* 9:175-180.

35. Giraud, M., G. Beaurain, B. Eymard, C. Tranchant, P. Gajdos, and H. J. Garchon. 2004. Genetic control of autoantibody expression in autoimmune myasthenia gravis: role of the self-antigen and of HLA-linked loci. *Genes Immun* 5:398-404.

36. Giraud, M., R. Taubert, C. Vandiedonck, X. Ke, M. Levi-Strauss, F. Pagani, F. E. Baralle, B. Eymard, C. Tranchant, P. Gajdos, A. Vincent, N. Willcox, D. Beeson, B. Kyewski, and H. J. Garchon. 2007. An IRF8-binding promoter variant and AIRE control CHRNA1 promiscuous expression in thymus. *Nature* 448:934-937.

37. Vandiedonck, C., C. Capdevielle, M. Giraud, S. Krumeich, J. P. Jais, B. Eymard, C. Tranchant, P. Gajdos, and H. J. Garchon. 2006. Association of the PTPN22*R620W polymorphism with autoimmune myasthenia gravis. *Ann Neurol* 59:404-407.

38. Lefvert, A. K., Y. Zhao, R. Ramanujam, S. Yu, R. Pirskanen, and L. Hammarstrom. 2008. PTPN22 R620W promotes production of anti-AChR autoantibodies and IL-2 in myasthenia gravis. *J Neuroimmunol* 197:110-113.

39. Raknes, G., G. O. Skeie, N. E. Gilhus, S. Aadland, and C. Vedeler. 1998. FcgammaRIIA and FcgammaRIIIB polymorphisms in myasthenia gravis. *J Neuroimmunol* 81:173-176.

40. van der Pol, W. L., M. D. Jansen, J. B. Kuks, M. de Baets, F. G. Leppers-van de Straat, J. H. Wokke, J. G. van de Winkel, and L. H. van den Berg. 2003. Association of the Fc gamma receptor IIA-R/R131 genotype with myasthenia gravis in Dutch patients. *J Neuroimmunol* 144:143-147.

41. Wang, X. B., M. Kakoulidou, Q. Qiu, R. Giscombe, D. Huang, R. Pirskanen, and A. K. Lefvert. 2002. CDS1 and promoter single nucleotide polymorphisms of the CTLA-4 gene in human myasthenia gravis. *Genes Immun* 3:46-49.

42. Chuang, W. Y., P. Strobel, R. Gold, W. Nix, B. Schalke, R. Kiefer, A. Opitz, E. Klinker, H. K. Muller-Hermelink, and A. Marx. 2005. A CTLA4high genotype is associated with myasthenia gravis in thymoma patients. *Ann Neurol* 58:644-648.

43. Giraud, M., B. Eymard, C. Tranchant, P. Gajdos, and H. J. Garchon. 2004. Association of the gene encoding the delta-subunit of the muscle acetylcholine receptor (CHRND) with acquired autoimmune myasthenia gravis. *Genes Immun* 5:80-83.

44. Xu, B. Y., D. Huang, R. Pirskanen, and A. K. Lefvert. 2000. beta2-adrenergic receptor gene polymorphisms in myasthenia gravis (MG). *Clin Exp Immunol* 119:156-160.

45. Huang, D. R., Y. H. Zhou, S. Q. Xia, L. Liu, R. Pirskanen, and A. K. Lefvert. 1999. Markers in the promoter region of interleukin-10 (IL-10) gene in myasthenia gravis: implications of diverse effects of IL-10 in the pathogenesis of the disease. *J Neuroimmunol* 94:82-87.

46. Yilmaz, V., Y. Tutuncu, N. Baris Hasbal, Y. Parman, P. Serdaroglu, F. Deymeer, and G. Saruhan-Direskeneli. 2007. Polymorphisms of interferon-gamma, interleukin-10, and interleukin-12 genes in myasthenia gravis. *Hum Immunol* 68:544-549.

47. Huang, D., R. Pirskanen, P. Hjelmstrom, and A. K. Lefvert. 1998. Polymorphisms in IL-1beta and IL-1 receptor antagonist genes are associated with myasthenia gravis. *J Neuroimmunol* 81:76-81.

48. Oksenberg, J. R., M. Sherritt, A. B. Begovich, H. A. Erlich, C. C. Bernard, L. L. Cavalli-Sforza, and L. Steinman. 1989. T-cell receptor V alpha and C alpha alleles associated with multiple and myasthenia gravis. *Proc Natl Acad Sci U S A* 86:988-992.

49. Nakao, Y., H. Matsumoto, T. Miyazaki, H. Nishitani, K. Ota, T. Fujita, and K. Tsuji. 1980. Gm allotypes in myasthenia gravis. *Lancet* 1:677-680.

50. Dondi, E., P. Gajdos, J. F. Bach, and H. J. Garchon. 1994. Association of Km3 allotype with increased serum levels of autoantibodies against muscle acetylcholine receptor in myasthenia gravis. *J Neuroimmunol* 51:221-224.

51. Djabiri, F., P. Gajdos, B. Eymard, L. Gomez, J. F. Bach, and H. J. Garchon. 1997. No evidence for an association of AChR beta-subunit gene (CHRNB1) with myasthenia gravis. *J Neuroimmunol* 78:86-89.

52. Bonifati, D. M., N. Willcox, A. Vincent, and D. Beeson. 2004. Lack of association between acetylcholine receptor epsilon polymorphisms and early-onset myasthenia gravis. *Muscle Nerve* 29:436-439.

53. Huang, D., S. Xia, Y. Zhou, R. Pirskanen, L. Liu, and A. K. Lefvert. 1998. No evidence for interleukin-4 gene conferring susceptibility to myasthenia gravis. *J Neuroimmunol* 92:208-211.

54. Huang, D., C. Zheng, R. Giscombe, G. Matell, R. Pirskanen, and A. K. Lefvert. 1999. Polymorphisms at - 174 and in the 3' flanking region of interleukin-6 (IL-6) gene in patients with myasthenia gravis. *J Neuroimmunol* 101:197-200.

55. Zhao, X., B. Gharizadeh, P. Hjelmstrom, R. Pirskanen, P. Nyren, A. K. Lefvert, and M. Ghaderi. 2003. Genotypes of CCR2 and CCR5 chemokine receptors in human myasthenia gravis. *International journal of molecular medicine* 12:749-753.

56. Sakthivel, P., X. Wang, B. Gharizadeh, R. Giscombe, R. Pirskanen, P. Nyren, and A. K. Lefvert. 2006. Single-nucleotide polymorphisms in the B7H3 gene are not associated with human autoimmune myasthenia gravis. *J Genet* 85:217-220.

57. Dausset, J. 1981. The major histocompatibility complex in man. *Science* 213:1469-1474.

58. Ryder, L. P., A. Svejgaard, and J. Dausset. 1981. Genetics of HLA disease association. *Annu Rev Genet* 15:169-187.

59. Thorsby, E. 1997. Invited anniversary review: HLA associated diseases. *Hum Immunol* 53:1-11.

60. de Bakker, P. I., G. McVean, P. C. Sabeti, M. M. Miretti, T. Green, J. Marchini, X. Ke, A. J. Monsuur, P. Whittaker, M. Delgado, J. Morrison, A. Richardson, E. C. Walsh, X. Gao, L. Galver, J. Hart, D. A. Hafler, M. Pericak-Vance, J. A. Todd, M. J. Daly, J. Trowsdale, C. Wijmenga, T. J. Vyse, S. Beck, S. S. Murray, M. Carrington, S. Gregory, P. Deloukas, and J. D. Rioux. 2006. A high-resolution HLA and SNP haplotype map for disease association studies in the extended human MHC. *Nat Genet* 38:1166-1172.

61. Horton, R., L. Wilming, V. Rand, R. C. Lovering, E. A. Bruford, V. K. Khodiyar, M. J. Lush, S. Povey, C. C. Talbot, Jr., M. W. Wright, H. M. Wain, J. Trowsdale, A. Ziegler, and S. Beck. 2004. Gene map of the extended human MHC. *Nat Rev Genet* 5:889-899.

62. Vandiedonck, C., and J. C. Knight. 2009. The human Major Histocompatibility Complex as a paradigm in genomics research. *Briefings in functional genomics & proteomics*.

63. Fritze, D., C. Herrman, Jr., F. Naeim, G. S. Smith, and R. L. Walford. 1974. HL-A antigens in myasthenia gravis. *Lancet* 1:240-242.

64. Feltkamp, T. E., P. M. van den Berg-Loonen, L. E. Nijenhuis, C. P. Engelfriet, A. L. van Rossum, J. J. van Loghem, and H. J. Oosterhuis. 1974. Myasthenia gravis, autoantibodies, and HL-A antigens. *Br Med J* 1:131-133.

65. Pirskanen, R. 1976. Genetic associations between myasthenia gravis and the HL-A system. *J Neurol Neurosurg Psychiatry* 39:23-33.

66. Dawkins, R. L., F. T. Christiansen, P. H. Kay, M. Garlepp, J. McCluskey, P. N. Hollingsworth, and P. J. Zilko. 1983. Disease associations with complotypes, supratypes and haplotypes. *Immunol Rev* 70:1-22.

67. Hjelmstrom, P., C. S. Peacock, R. Giscombe, R. Pirskanen, A. K. Lefvert, J. M. Blackwell, and C. B. Sanjeevi. 1998. Polymorphism in tumor necrosis factor genes associated with myasthenia gravis. *J Neuroimmunol* 88:137-143.

68. Ahmad, T., M. Neville, S. E. Marshall, A. Armuzzi, K. Mulcahy-Hawes, J. Crawshaw, H. Sato, K. L. Ling, M. Barnardo, S. Goldthorpe, R. Walton, M. Bunce, D. P. Jewell, and K. I. Welsh. 2003. Haplotype-specific linkage disequilibrium patterns define the genetic topography of the human MHC. *Hum Mol Genet* 12:647-656.

69. Giraud, M., G. Beaurain, A. M. Yamamoto, B. Eymard, C. Tranchant, P. Gajdos, and H. J. Garchon. 2001. Linkage of HLA to myasthenia gravis and genetic heterogeneity depending on anti-titin antibodies. *Neurology* 57:1555-1560.

70. Price, P., C. Witt, R. Allcock, D. Sayer, M. Garlepp, C. C. Kok, M. French, S. Mallal, and F. Christiansen. 1999. The genetic basis for the association of the 8.1 ancestral haplotype (A1, B8, DR3) with multiple immunopathological diseases. *Immunol. Rev.* 167:257-274.

71. Candore, G., D. Lio, G. Colonna Romano, and C. Caruso. 2002. Pathogenesis of autoimmune diseases associated with 8.1 ancestral haplotype: effect of multiple gene interactions. *Autoimmun Rev* 1:29-35.

72. Carlsson, B., J. Wallin, R. Pirskanen, G. Matell, and C. I. Smith. 1990. Different HLA DR-DQ associations in subgroups of idiopathic myasthenia gravis. *Immunogenetics* 31:285-290.

73. Spurkland, A., N. E. Gilhus, K. S. Ronningen, J. A. Aarli, and F. Vartdal. 1991. Myasthenia gravis patients with thymus hyperplasia and myasthenia gravis patients with thymoma display different HLA associations. *Tissue Antigens* 37:90-93.

74. Vieira, M. L., S. Caillat-Zucman, P. Gajdos, S. Cohen-Kaminsky, A. Casteur, and J. F. Bach. 1993. Identification by genomic typing of non-DR3 HLA class II genes associated with myasthenia gravis. *J Neuroimmunol* 47:115-122.

75. Machens, A., C. Loliger, U. Pichlmeier, T. Emskotter, C. Busch, and J. R. Izbicki. 1999. Correlation of thymic pathology with HLA in myasthenia gravis. *Clin Immunol* 91:296-301.

76. Vandiedonck, C., C. Raffoux, B. Eymard, C. Tranchant, E. Dulmet, S. Krumeich, P. Gajdos, and H. J. Garchon. 2009. Association of HLA-A in autoimmune myasthenia gravis with thymoma. *J Neuroimmunol* 210:120-123.

77. Inoue, M., A. Marx, A. Zettl, P. Strobel, H. K. Muller-Hermelink, and P. Starostik. 2002. Chromosome 6 suffers frequent and multiple aberrations in thymoma. *Am J Pathol* 161:1507-1513.

78. Saruhan-Direskeneli, G., A. Kilic, Y. Parman, P. Serdaroglu, and F. Deymeer. 2006. HLA-DQ polymorphism in Turkish patients with myasthenia gravis. *Hum Immunol* 67:352-358.

79. Niks, E. H., J. B. Kuks, B. O. Roep, G. W. Haasnoot, W. Verduijn, B. E. Ballieux, M. H. De Baets, A. Vincent, and J. J. Verschuuren. 2006. Strong association of MuSK antibody-positive myasthenia gravis and HLA-DR14-DQ5. *Neurology* 66:1772-1774.

80. Bartoccioni, E., F. Scuderi, A. Augugliaro, S. Chiatamone Ranieri, D. Sauchelli, P. Alboino, M. Marino, and A. Evoli. 2009. HLA class II allele analysis in MuSK-positive myasthenia gravis suggests a role for DQ5. *Neurology* 72:195-197.

81. Christiansen, F. T., M. S. Pollack, M. J. Garlepp, and R. L. Dawkins. 1984. Myasthenia gravis and HLA antigens in American blacks and other races. *J Neuroimmunol* 7:121-129.

82. Hawkins, B. R., M. S. Ip, K. S. Lam, J. T. Ma, C. L. Wy, R. T. Yeung, and R. L. Dawkins. 1986. HLA antigens and acetylcholine receptor antibody in the subclassification of myasthenia gravis in Hong Kong Chinese. *J Neurol Neurosurg Psychiatry* 49:316-319.

83. Chiu, H. C., R. P. Hsieh, K. H. Hsieh, and T. P. Hung. 1987. Association of HLA-DRw9 with myasthenia gravis in Chinese. *J Immunogenet* 14:203-207.

84. Hawkins, B. R., Y. L. Yu, V. Wong, E. Woo, M. S. Ip, and R. L. Dawkins. 1989. Possible evidence for a variant of myasthenia gravis based on HLA and acetylcholine receptor antibody in Chinese patients. *The Quarterly journal of medicine* 70:235-241.

85. Degli-Esposti, M. A., A. Andreas, F. T. Christiansen, B. Schalke, E. Albert, and R. L. Dawkins. 1992. An approach to the localization of the susceptibility genes for generalized myasthenia gravis by mapping recombinant ancestral haplotypes. *Immunogenetics* 35:355-364.

86. Janer, M., A. Cowland, J. Picard, D. Campbell, P. Pontarotti, J. Newsom-Davis, M. Bunce, K. Welsh, A. Demaine, A. G. Wilson, and N. Willcox. 1999. A susceptibility region for myasthenia gravis extending into the HLA-class I sector telomeric to HLA-C. *Hum. Immunol.* 60:909-917.

87. Vandiedonck, C., G. Beaurain, M. Giraud, C. Hue-Beauvais, B. Eymard, C. Tranchant, P. Gajdos, J. Dausset, and H. J. Garchon. 2004. Pleiotropic effects of the 8.1 HLA haplotype in patients with autoimmune myasthenia gravis and thymus hyperplasia. *Proc Natl Acad Sci U S A* 101:15464-15469.

88. Jawaheer, D., W. Li, R. R. Graham, W. Chen, A. Damle, X. Xiao, J. Monteiro, H. Khalili, A. Lee, R. Lundsten, A. Begovich, T. Bugawan, H. Erlich, J. T. Elder, L. A. Criswell, M. F. Seldin, C. I. Amos, T. W. Behrens, and P. K. Gregersen. 2002. Dissecting the genetic complexity of the association between human leukocyte antigens and rheumatoid arthritis. *Am J Hum Genet* 71:585-594.

89. van den Berg-Loonen, E. M., L. E. Nijenhuis, C. P. Engelfriet, T. E. Feltkamp, A. L. van Rossum, and H. J. Oosterhuis. 1977. Segregation of HLA haplotypes in 100 families with a myasthenia gravis patient. *J Immunogenet* 4:331-340.

90. Stewart, C. A., R. Horton, R. J. Allcock, J. L. Ashurst, A. M. Atrazhev, P. Coggill, I. Dunham, S. Forbes, K. Halls, J. M. Howson, S. J. Humphray, S. Hunt, A. J. Mungall, K. Osoegawa, S. Palmer, A. N. Roberts, J. Rogers, S. Sims, Y. Wang, L. G. Wilming, J. F. Elliott, P. J. de Jong, S. Sawcer, J. A. Todd, J. Trowsdale, and S. Beck. 2004. Complete MHC haplotype sequencing for common disease gene mapping. *Genome Res* 14:1176-1187.

91. Tzartos, S. J., T. Barkas, M. T. Cung, A. Mamalaki, M. Marraud, P. Orlewski, D. Papanastasiou, C. Sakarellos, M. Sakarellos-Daitsiotis, P. Tsantili, and V. Tsikaris. 1998. Anatomy of the antigenic structure of a large membrane autoantigen, the muscle-type nicotinic acetylcholine receptor. *Immunol. Rev.* 163:89-120.

92. Kyewski, B., and L. Klein. 2006. A Central Role for Central Tolerance. *Annu Rev Immunol* 24:571-606.

93. Kyewski, B., and R. Taubert. 2008. How promiscuity promotes tolerance: the case of myasthenia gravis. *Ann N Y Acad Sci* 1132:157-162.

94. Tamura, T., H. Yanai, D. Savitsky, and T. Taniguchi. 2008. The IRF family transcription factors in immunity and oncogenesis. *Annu Rev Immunol* 26:535-584.

95. Mathis, D., and C. Benoist. 2007. A decade of AIRE. *Nat Rev Immunol* 7:645-650.

96. Bottini, N., L. Musumeci, A. Alonso, S. Rahmouni, K. Nika, M. Rostamkhani, J. MacMurray, G. F. Meloni, P. Lucarelli, M. Pellecchia, G. S. Eisenbarth, D. Comings, and T. Mustelin. 2004. A functional variant of lymphoid tyrosine phosphatase is associated with type I diabetes. *Nat Genet* 36:337-338.

97. Yamanouchi, J., D. Rainbow, P. Serra, S. Howlett, K. Hunter, V. E. Garner, A. Gonzalez-Munoz, J. Clark, R. Veijola, R. Cubbon, S. L. Chen, R. Rosa, A. M. Cumiskey, D. V. Serreze, S. Gregory, J. Rogers, P. A. Lyons, B. Healy, L. J. Smink, J. A. Todd, L. B. Peterson, L. S. Wicker, and P. Santamaria. 2007. Interleukin-2 gene variation impairs regulatory T cell function and causes autoimmunity. *Nat Genet* 39:329-337.

98. Lowe, C. E., J. D. Cooper, T. Brusko, N. M. Walker, D. J. Smyth, R. Bailey, K. Bourget, V. Plagnol, S. Field, M. Atkinson, D. G. Clayton, L. S. Wicker, and J. A. Todd. 2007. Large-scale genetic fine mapping and genotype-phenotype associations implicate polymorphism in the IL2RA region in type 1 diabetes. *Nat Genet* 39:1074-1082.

99. Bottini, N., T. Vang, F. Cucca, and T. Mustelin. 2006. Role of PTPN22 in type 1 diabetes and other autoimmune diseases. *Seminars in immunology* 18:207-213.

Thymoma Pathology and Thymoma-Associated Myasthenia Gravis

Alexander Marx M.D., Wen-Yu Chuang M.D., & Philipp Ströbel M.D.

1. INTRODUCTION

Thymomas are histologically divers tumors that are composed of neoplastic thymic epithelial cells (TECs) showing minimal to moderate atypia (1). Since the neoplastic TECs of most thymomas keep many functions of normal TECs, almost all thymomas harbour a variable number of non-neoplastic thymic lymphocytes (=thymocytes) with a differentiation that is very akin to thymocytes of the normal thymus (2-4). As a consequence, most thymomas resemble the normal thymus more or less closely (while this is not the case for the more atypical thymic carcinomas). Thymomas show the highest frequency of associated (=paraneoplastic) **autoimmune diseases** (**AID**, up to 50%) (**Table 1**) and autoantibodies (almost 100%) of all human tumors (5). Among the paraneoplastic AIDs encountered in thymoma patients, autoimmune **Myasthenia gravis** (**MG**) due to autoantbodies against the nicotic **acetylcholine receptor (AChR)** at the muscle end plate is by far the most common AID (6,7). Of all MG patients, 10-15% harbour a thymoma, and 20-40% of thymoma patients suffer from MG (= **paraneoplastic MG, p-MG**)

Myasthenia gravis (MG) is a heterogeneous AID mediated by polyclonal autoantibodies that are directed against a spectrum of targets at the postsynaptic membrane of the neuromuscular junction and interfere with its function (8). Presence or absence of autoantibodies against the AChR, various thymic pathologies and the age at disease onset have been taken as criteria to subdivide MG into different, clinically meaningful entities. As to antibodies against the AChR, MG has been subdivided traditionally into seropositive and seronegative types (see Chapter 01., A Evoli). In seropositive MG (~70% of all patients with generalized MG and ~50% of patients with purely ocular MG), the pathogenic, high-affinity autoantibodies are directed against the

Table 1. Paraneoplastic diseases or symptoms of presumed autoimmune pathogenesis reported as associated with thymoma[17,20,131,154,155]. In the majority of these diseases, the immunopathogenesis has not formally been resolved. Myasthenia gravis is by far most common paraneoplastic AID in thymoma patients.

Addison's disease	Myasthenia gravis
Agranulocytosis	Myocarditis
Alopecia areata	Myoclonus
Aplastic anemia	Neuromyotonia
Autoimmune colitis (GvHD-like)	Panhypopituitarism
Autoimmune autonomic neuropathy	Pernicious Anemia
Autoimmun gastrointestinal dysmotility	Polymyositis
(Intestinal pseudo-obstruction)	Pure red cell aplasia
Autoimmune hepatitis	Rheumatoid arthritis
Cognitive impairment	Rippling muscle disease
Cranial nerve dysfunction	Sarcoidosis
Cushing syndrome	Scleroderma
Dyssomnia	Seizures
Encephalitis (limbic and/or cortical)	Sensory motor neuropathy
Glomerulonephritis	Stiff Person syndrome
Hemolytic anemia	Systemic lupus erythematosus
Hypogammaglobulinemia (Good Syndrome)	Thyroiditis

AChR (9,10), while so called seronegative MG (SNMG) is now known to be heterogeneous. Depending on ethnic and geographic backgrounds (11-14), a variable percentage of "SNMG" cases results from autoantibodies (commonly IgG4 but also IgG1) to muscle-specific tyrosine kinase (MuSK) at the neuromuscular endplate (15). Furthermore, the subgroup of patients showing neither high-affinity anti-AChR nor anti-MuSK autoantibodies (12) can now be further subdivided into patients with IgG1 autoantibodies that escape detection by conventional radio-immunoassay since they react only with *clustered* AChRs (16), and still other patients ("triple seronegatives") without any of the before-mentioned antibodies. In practical terms, **>99% of thymoma-associated MG patients are anti-AChR seropositive** and, in addition, show autoantibodies against a broad spectrum of targets (17), including "striational antigens", especially titin (18), and neuronal structures (19-20). Recently, **rare seronegative MG(+) thymoma patients**, including one with anti-MuSK autoantibodies, have been reported (22).

Age per se is no first-line criteria for the subdivision of MG. Thus, **thymoma-associated MG can occur in virtually all age groups**, including rare pediatric patients, although it is most prevalent between 40 to 70 years of age. A wide spectrum of affected age groups is also observed in seronegative MG (23), particularly in anti-MuSK(+) patients (24). On the other hand, the two most common MG subtypes, EOMG and LOMG, show characteristic age associations that likely reflect (among other, e.g. genetic variables) the age-dependent physiology of the thymus, namely a functionally declining, but still quite active thymus up to the age of 40 (-50) years, and massive thymic involution thereafter (25). Consequently, early-onset MG **(EOMG)** is an entity among seropositive, non-thymomatous MG patients that occurs mainly among women up to the age of 40-50 years. An additional hallmark of EOMG is **"thymic follicular hyperplasia" (TFH)**, suggesting a central role of the thymus in EOMG development (26). By contrast, so called late-onset MG **(LOMG)** is a seropositive, non-thymomatous form of MG that shows no sex-predilection, is generally devoid of TFH in the (physiologically) atrophic thymus and is common after the age of 50 years (27). For unknown reasons, the incidence of MG diagnosed in persons over 40 years of age has been increasing during the last decades and accounts now for about 60% of all MG cases diagnosed per year (27,28). Although LOMG patients share a variety of autoimmune phenomena with thymoma patients (e.g. anti-titin (18) and anti-cytokine autoantibodies (29), the role of the thymus in the pathogenesis of LOMG, if any, is unclear. Although thymic involution is a consistent age-related phenomenon, its speed shows remarkable inter-individual variability (25). Therefore, taking TFH (25) and anti-titin antibodies (30,31) into account, it is not surprising that MG patients with a "grey zone age" between ~40 and ~50 years may either show features of EOMG or LOMG (Chuang, unpublished.).

2. THYMIC PATHOLOGY IN MG

2.1. Thymic Follicular Hyperplasia (TFH)

Since **TFH is observed in up to 30% of MG(+) thymoma patients** in the thymic remnants adjacent to the tumor (while it is uncommon in MG(-) thymomas)(32), TFH is shortly described here. It is the most common thymic pathology in MG (~70% of MG patients) and characteristic of patients with EOMG(12,33,34) and "seronegative" MG patients without anti-MuSK autoantibodies (12,16). TFH is characteristic of MG but occurs in other autoimmune diseases (35) and, rarely, in healthy persons as well (36). Histologically, in TFH, the basal membrane between thymic medulla and perivascular spaces adjacent to lymphoid follicles is disrupted (33,34,37-39) and there is an immune attack against **myoid cells** (37). These cells are unique, non-innervated myoblast- and myotube-like cells that occur in the normal thymic medulla and express fetal and adult-type AChR (34,40-42). Myoid cells in TFH are located outside lymphoid follicles (33,34,37), stay MHC class II negative as in normal thymus (43) but show increased proliferation and turn-over (44). What triggers TFH development in EOMG and thymoma-associated MG is incompletely understood (26,45). In EOMG, a contribution of chemokines (e.g. CXCL13) (46) and polymorphisms of genetic background have been considered due to association of MG with MHC class I and II (47-49), IL-1b (50), TNFa (51-53), IL-10 (54) and the AChR alpha- but not beta-subunit (55-57). It is unknown whether hyperexpression of bcl-2 in thymic germinal centers (58) or of FAS in mature thymic T-cells (59,60) are involved in the etiology of TFH.

2.2. Thymus histology in Late-onset MG (LOMG)

Thymus histology in LOMG patients (typically >50 years of age) has traditionally been termed "thymic atrophy". However, morphometric studies have shown that the size of the thymus is essentially normal when compared to age-matched healthy populations (25), and that the number of myoid cells per area of thymic parenchyma is unchanged (34,61). Roughly 70% of MG(+) thymoma patients show age-related involution of the thymus adjacent to the tumor.

2.3. Thymomas: General Considerations

Thymomas and thymic carcinomas are tumors composed of neoplastic counterparts of thymic epithelial cells ("Thymic Epithelial Tumors"; TETs). Because of their derivation from thymic epithelial (stem) cells, TETs are distinguished not only from thymic lymphomas (i.e. neoplasms of thymic lymphocytes) but also from other epithelial tumors occurring in the thymus, e.g. teratomas, embryonal carcinomas or yolk sac tumor that are progeny of germ cells that are entrapped in the thymus during their migration from the yolk sac to the gonads during fetal development (62).

In the context of this book it is important that only a subset (10-40%) of thymomas, but neither thymic carcinomas nor other thymic or extra-thymic tumors exhibit a significant MG-association. Since we believe that this observation gives strong clues to the pathogenesis of thymoma-associated MG (see below), we wish to stress that thymomas are separated from thymic carcinomas by their closer resemblance to normal thymus. In particular, more than 90% of thymomas but no thymic carcinomas, show (variably disturbed) intratumorous thymopoiesis. This is a unique feature among human tumors. However, <10% of thymomas do not show significant intratumorous thymopoiesis (e.g. up to 50% of type A thymomas, and the exceedingly rare metaplastic thymomas (63). Nevertheless, these tumors are considered thymomas because they either resemble their thymopoietically active counterparts (in case of type A thymomas) or show a generally benign clinical course (in case of metaplastic thymomas) that precludes their classsification as thymic carcinomas.

Malignancy is *not* a criteria that distinguishes thymomas from thymic carcinomas: while all thymic carcinomas (by definition) are considered malignant neoplasms, about 50% of thymomas (particularly the WHO B2 and B3 types) exhibit a high risk for a) extensive local infiltration beyond the mediastinal fat, b) metastasis and c) a malignant, i.e. unfavourable clinical course (see below).

Another highly unusual feature of malignant thymomas compared to thymic and most other carcinomas is their lacking propensity to metastasize to lymph nodes. By contrast, pleural spread is the most common type of metastasis in both malignant thymomas and thymic carcinomas. This peculiarity of thymomas led to the development of a unique staging system, the **Masaoka system (64)** that was slight modified later (65) **(Table 2)** and is still recommended by the WHO (66).

The significant associations between different thymic alterations and clinical, epidemiological and genetic findings (5,8,67-69) in generalized seropositive forms of MG are summarized in **Table 3.**

2.4. The WHO Histological Classification of Thymic Epithelial Tumors

The classification of thymomas has been controversial for decades, since the "histogenetic" concept and nomenclature (70,71) was not accepted by the World Health Organiztion (WHO) (72). However, the new WHO classification (66,72) has acknowledged the "histogenetic thymoma subtypes" but replaced the controversial nomenclature by a unique coding system that labels tumors with letters and numbers. By contrast, thymic carcinomas are named like morphologically similar carcinomas

Table 2. Masaoka staging system for thymomas as modified by Koga et al. [65], and corresponding TNM stages[66,156]

Masaoka Stage	Criteria	Corresponding TNM Stage
Stage I	Full encapsulation of tumor	pT1 pN0 pM0
Stage II*	Tumor infiltration *beyond* capsule into mediastinal fat (minimal invasion)	pT2 pN0 pM0
Stage III	Direct tumor infiltration into adjacent organs and structures (lung, pericardi-um, great vessels, thoracic wall) ("wide invasion")	pT3 pN0 pM0
Stage IVa	Pleural dissemination	pT4 pN0 pM0
Stage IVb	Distant metastasis	Any pT pN1 or pM1

* the original staging system by Masaoka et al.[64] suggested invasion *into* the capsule as part of the spectrum of stage II ("IIa"). Like Koga et al.[65] we found no difference between stage I and "IIa" thymomas in terms of survival and, therefore, prefer the use of the "modifies Masaoka system" as shown here[66].

outside the thymus, with the most common one being thymic squamous cell carcinoma (TSCC). The WHO classification has gained world-wide support since 1999 – with few exceptions (73). In addition to being reasonably reproducible, it is clinically meaningful in terms of oncology (see below), immunological features (3.69) and the association with various AIDs, including MG (Table 4). The following MG-associated thymoma subtypes are distinguished in the WHO classification (66):

WHO type A thymomas (formerly: "medullary" (70)),
WHO type AB thymomas ("mixed" (70)),
WHO type B1 thymomas ("predominantly cortical" (70)),
WHO type B2 thymomas ("cortical thymomas" (70)) and
WHO type B3 thymomas (formerly: "Well Differentiated Thymic Carcinoma (71))

The characteristic histological features of MG-associated thymomas are shown in **Fig. 1**. The following short descriptions focus on the key morphological and clinical features of the MG-associated thymoma subtypes.

Type A thymomas, by definition, are epithelial-rich tumors (like B3 thymomas). They are composed of spindle and/or polygonal epithelial cells without atypia. Type A thymomas harbor no or, more commonly, a paucity of thymocytes, the majority of which represent CD3+ CD1a- TdT- mature CD4 and CD8 T cells, while characteristic immature thymocytes (CD1a+, TdT+) are rare or missing. This is a diagnostically important feature (in distinction to WHO type B3 thymomas) as is epithelial expression of the lymphocyte marker CD20 in ~50% of type A thymomas (0% in type B3). Although previously called "medullary" thymoma, typical features of a mature thymic medulla, such as Hassall's corpuscles, expression of the Autoimmune Regulator (AIRE) and its target genes, and high levels of MHC class II genes are absent (17,74). Among the MG-associated thymomas, MG prevalence is lowest in patients with type A thymomas (~10-30%). Type A thymomas are commonly encapsulated or locally infiltrative (>85% Masaoka stages I and II), while Masaoka stages III and IV are rare. Type A thymomas almost always follow a benign clinical course after complete resection.

Table 3: Subtypes of generalized, seropostive MG according to thymus pathology and associated epidemiological, clinical and genetic findings[5,17,49,69,109,157,158].

	EOMG/TFH	Thymoma	LOMG/"A"
Onset of symptoms: age (years)	10–40(-50)*	15-80	(> 40) >50*
Sex m : f	1 : 3	1 : 1	2 : 1
HLA-association	B8; DR3	A25 and A02[0]	DR7
Myoid cells	present	absent	present
Intrathymic/intrathymomatous anti-AChR autoantibody production	present	absent	absent
AIRE expression	normal	absent in 95%[1]	normal
TNFA*T1/B*2 homozygosity	rare	very frequent	frequent
TNFA*T2; TNFB1			
TNFB*1, C4A*QO, C4B*1, DRB1*03	frequent	rare	rare
CTLA4 +49A/G genotype distribution	similar to healthy controls	+49A/A more frequent in MG(+) than MG(-) thymomas	not available
PTPN22 +1858T(+)	increased[2]	increased[3]	increased[4]
Autoantibodies against			
AChR	positive	> 95 %	positive
Striated muscle	10 – 20 %	> 90 %	30 – 60 %
Titin	< 10 %	> 90 %	30 – 40 %
Ryanodine receptor	< 5%	50 – 60 %	20%
IL-12, IFN- , IFN-	absent	63 – 88 %	infrequent

EOMG/TFH: early onset myasthenia gravis/thymic lymphofollicular hyperplasia; LOMG/"A": late onset myasthenia gravis/"atrophy" (meanwhile morphometric studies revealed that LOMG-associated "atrophy" represents normal involution that is adequate for age[25]; p-MG: paraneoplastic MG.

* During an age period between ~40 and 50 years, both EOMG (TFH(+)) or LOMG (without TFH but with anti-titin autoantibodies) can be encountered

[0]A25 reported as increased in all thymomas subtypes; A02 protective in WHO type B2 thymomas in ref.[69] but not in ref.[114] (who reported an association of thymoma-MG with HLA-A24)

[1]~half of the rare WHO type B1 thymomas express AIRE protein[17]

[2]in three different studies[116,117](own observation) but not in a fourth (ref.[118])

[3]in our own cohort of patients but not in ref.[116]

[4]shown in ref.[118] but not in ref.[116]

Type AB thymomas are labelled as such because they are *biphasic* tumors. They show variable proportions of areas resembling type A thymomas, in addition to lymphocyte-rich areas that resemble either type B1 or, rarely, type B2 thymomas, or show the same spindle epithelial cells that occur in type A areas. Like type A thymomas, 50-70% of type AB thymomas express CD20 in the epithelial component (75). The frequency of p-MG is slightly higher (20-40%) than in type A thymomas, while the propensity for minimal (but not wide) invasiveness and the generally favourable clinical course are very similar in type A and AB thymomas (76).

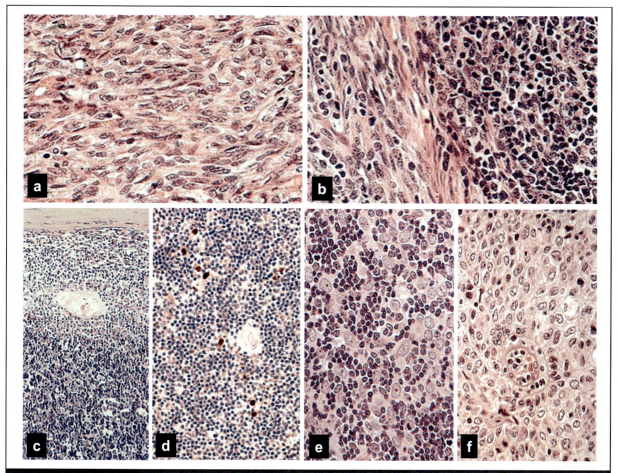

Figure 1. Morphological spectrum of thymomas associated with paraneoplastic MG. a) WHO type A (medullary) thymoma with prominent spindle cells and scarce intermingled lymphocytes that are mostly mature (CD3+, CD1a-, TdT-) by flow-cytometry. b) WHO type AB (mixed) thymoma with features of both WHO type A and lymphocyte-rich areas. c) WHO type B1 thymoma with many immature (CD3+/-, CD1a+, TdT+) T cells; lack of cytologic atypia in epithelial cells; well developed Hassall's corpuscle. d) WHO type B1 thymoma with scattered AIRE-positive epithelial cells (brown nuclei) in a "medullary area" (immunoperoxidase). e) WHO type B2 thymoma showing less T cells but more and larger epithelial cells than the B1 thymoma; prominent nuclei and nucleoli. f) WHO type B3 thymoma with dominance of epithelial cells and formation of a "palisade" around a perivascular space. Few, mostly immature thymocytes. (H&E).

Type B1 thymomas are the most lymphocyte-rich thymomas and have previously been called "predominantly cortical" or "organoid" thymomas, to stress their "thymus-like" histology with a predominance of cortex-like areas. Many B1 thymomas show apparently full maturation of (small) medullary areas as reflected by Hassall's corpusles (~60% of cases) and a high number of medullary B-lymphocytes and mature (medullary) T cells. In addition, type B1 thymomas are the only thymomas showing **expression of AIRE** protein in the medullary areas **(Fig 1d)** (~50% of cases), underlining the particularly high level of mTEC differentiation. Type B1 thymomas in ~50% harbour **myoid cells** (that rarely also occur in type B2 thymomas and thymic carcinomas). Nevertheless, they show a higher frequency of p-MG (20-70%) than type A and AB thymomas

Table 4. Autoimmune diseases with defined autoantigens, pathogenic relevance of autoantibodies or autoreactive T-cells in thymoma and thymic carcinoma (TC) patients and relationship to histological tumor subtype[21,93,159,160].

Autoimmune disease	Autoantigen	Pathogenic relevance of autoantibodies or autoreactive T cells	Preferred thymoma subtype (WHO)
Myasthenia gravis	AChR[1]	YES	WHO Type B> AB>A
	StrA[2]	Probably NO	
	IFN-a, IL12	Probably YES	
Neuromyotonia	VGKC[3]	YES	not established
Peripheral Neuropathy	VGKC	YES	not established
Stiff Person Syndrome	GAD[4]	Unknown	not established
Rippling Muscle Disease	Neuronal AChR	Pobably Yes	WHO Type AB, B
Intestinal Pseudo-obstruction	Neuronal AchR	Probably Yes	not established
Limbic Encephalitis	Neuronal nuclear antigens, glial antigens	Probably YES	not established
Pure Red Cell Aplasia	Unknown	Yes (T cells) (Auto-Abs?)	WHO Type A > B
Neutropenia, Pancytopenia	Unknown	(Auto-Abs?)	not established
Polymyositis Dermatomyositis	Unknown	Unknown	WHO Type B, TC

[1]AChR, Acetylcholine receptor [2]StrA, striational antigens (myosin, titin, ryanodine receptor) [3]VGKC, voltage-gated potassium channel [4]GAD, glutamic acid decarboxylase

(76). Like type A and AB thymomas, type B1 tumors are frequently circumscribed (>90% Masaoka stage I and II) and generally follow a benign clinical course (76). While R0-resection can be achieved in >90% of cases, very late recurrences up to 20 years after surgery have been observed (77).

Type B2 thymomas, previously called "cortical thymomas", by definition belong to the lymphocyte-rich thymomas. They resemble thymic cortex throughout the tumor showing a clear predominance of immature thymocytes. However, tumor cells, their nuclei and nucleoli are much larger and more prominent than their counterparts in normal thymic cortex and in WHO type B1 thymomas. Preliminary studies revealed that B2 thymomas show the most "cortex-like" gene expression signature among thymomas (own observation). In addition, analysis of genetic polymorphisms (MG association with HLA-A02 specifically in B2 thymomas (69)) suggests that B2 thymomas are a distinct thymoma subtype. The associationwith p-MG is also high in B2 thymomas (up to 59%). In contrast to type A, AB and B1 thymomas, type B2 thymomas are clearly malignant neoplasms with a tendency for wide infiltration (Masaoka stage III ~ 38%) and metastasis (stage IVa and IVb ~ 11%). Nevertheless, type B2 thymomas follow a relative protracted clinical course (actuarial survival rate at 10 years ~70-80%). Recurrences are harbingers of a dismal prognosis (76).

Type B3 thymomas, by definition, belong to the epithelial-rich thymomas (like type A thymomas) and have alternatively been called "well differentiated thymic carcinoma" (71) or "atypical thymomas" (78). Although the overall abundance of intratumorous thymocytes is much lower in type B3 than B2 thymomas, the subset composition, particularly the high proportion of immature thymocytes expressing CD1a, CD99 and TdT, is very similar in B3 and B2 thymomas.

This aids to distinguish (the malignant) B3 thymomas from the commonly benign type A thymomas that are virtually devoid of immature thymocytes (see above). In our series, type B3 thymomas exhibit the highest rate of associated p-MG (~50%) and are even more malignant than B2 thymomas (actuarial survival rate at 10 years ~50-70%) (76,79).

2.5. Oncological Relevance of the WHO Thymoma Classification in MG Patients

By most authors, histotype according to the WHO classification has been reported to be an independent prognostic marker(76,79-82). There is unanimity, however, that Masaoka stage is more relevant (75,76,79,83), and that consideration of both histotype and stage can improve therapeutic decision making. By contrast, **p-MG is no longer an adverse but likely a favorable parameter in thymoma patients (83)**, probably through earlier detection of MG-associated thymomas that are generally smaller than MG(-) thymomas at the time of surgery (76, 97). By combining WHO-based histotype and Masaoka stage, the following three risk groups can be distinguished among MG-associated thymomas (76,79,81,84):

Very low risk: a) type A, AB and B1 thymomas in stages I and II[a](very common)

b) type B2 thymomas in stage I (rare)

High risk: a) type B3 in stage III (common)

b) stage IV thymomas (however, type A thymomas may not be fatal)

c) R1 and R2 resection

Intermediate: all other combinations[b].

[a]if complete resection can be achieved; [b]including the very common WHO type B2 and B3 thymomas in Masaoka stage II.

While patients with very low risk thymomas are generally cured by radical surgery alone, patients with high risk thymomas appear to profit from neoadjuvant or adjuvant approaches (85-90). For intermediate risk cases, retrospective studies are less helpful as to treatment decisions; thus, it is not yet clear, whether adjuvant treatment (e.g. radiotherapy) for stage II thymomas is beneficial in cases of type B2 (probably not) and B3 (probably yes) thymomas (76).

3. PATHOGENESIS OF THYMOMA −ASSOCIATED (PARANEOPLASTIC) MG

3.1. Cellular features of thymomas with potential impact on paraneoplastic MG

As summarized in **Table 3**, there is strong evidence that the pathogenesis of thymoma-associated MG differs from TFH-associated MG (5,7,69,91-93). Important differences between TFH and thymomas concerning cellular features are the following:

1.   While the thymic medulla is distorted by lymphoid follicles but principally maintained in TFH, medullary areas are absent (in ~95%) or much smaller in thymomas.

2.   In contrast to prominent intrathymic anti-AChR autoantibody production by plasma cells in TFH, there is no such production in thymomas (94,95), maybe with very few exceptions (96)

3. AChR-expressing myoid cells are numerous in the thymic medulla, where they are targets of an autoimmune attack in TFH (37), while they are absent in almost all thymomas.

4. Thymic epithelial cells in both TFH and normal thymus express high levels of MHC class II antigens, while their expression levels are reduced in thymomas (74, 97-100).

5. A subset of medullary thymic epithelial cells (mTECs) express the autoimmune regulator AIRE (101). Inactivating *AIRE* mutations elicit the autoimmune syndrome APS-1, also called APECED (autoimmune polyendocrinopathy, candidiasis, ectodermal dystrophy) (101,102). AIRE is a strong transcriptional regulator enforcing central tolerance by promoting the 'promiscuous' expression and improved presentation of a subset of peripheral tissue antigens (e.g. insulin and the AChR α-subunit) in mTECs (103-106). Of note, AIRE expression in concert with interferon signaling through IRF8 plays a role in the pathogenesis of EOMG by regulating the expression level of the AChR α-subunit in mTECs (107). By contrast, AIRE is not expressed in the vast majority of thymomas and **AIRE deficiency does not segregate with MG in thymoma** patients (17).

6. Despite normal AIRE expression in TFH but AIRE deficiency in thymomas, the spectrum of autoantibodies in MG patients with thymomas and TFH is very similar (17). Important exceptions are striational (e.g. anti-titin) antibodies, and **antibodies against IL-12, IFN-α and IFN-ω**, the latter being a hallmark of all APECED and 60% of thymoma patients. In contrast to autoantibodies against AChR, those against interferons are produced inside thymomas, occur less commonly in LOMG and are absent in EOMG/TFH (17,29,108,109). Since anti-IFN antibodies have an impact on IFN-dependent gene expression, they may contribute to central tolerance failure (110). However, MG is *not* among the many AIDs encountered in patients with germ line encoded AIRE deficiency, i.e. APECED. Furthermore, AIRE deficiency and anti-IFN autoantibodies occur in both MG(+) and MG(-) thymomas (17,29). While these observations do not exclude a contribution of AIRE deficieny and anti-IFN autoantibodies to the pathogenesis of p-MG (111), these abnormalities *alone* are insufficient to elicit p-MG[17].

7. Thymoma epithelial cells express AChR mRNA (112), with the AChR *ε-subunit* being the most abundantly expressed subunit. Furthermore, there was association between AChR e-subunit expression and WHO histotype: virtually all WHO type A and AB thymomas, but only 45% of type B1-B3 thymomas expressed this subunit. Autoantibodies with preferential binding to adult (i.e. e+) AChRs were particularly prevalent in the patients with the highest ε-subunit expression levels. Therefore, it appears likely that thymoma epithelial cells play a distinctive role in autosensitization in MG-associated thymomas, particularly those of type A or AB (112).

8. Regulatory, CD4+CD25+FoxP3+ T cells (Tregs) have been reported to be functionally impaired in EOMG patients (45), while they are quantitatively reduced inside both MG(+) and MG(-) thymomas (4,113). While deficient Treg production *per se* is insufficient to induce p-MG., we consider it a potentially relevant facet of the autoimmunizing scenario leading to p-MG (see **Fig. 2**).

3.2.. Genetic background contributing to MG in thymomas

In stark contrast to EOMG patients who show a strong association with the HLA-A1-B8-DR3 haplotype, no reproducible HLA association has been reported in p-MG (reviewed in ref. (69)).

Recently, however, a protective effect of HLA-A02 was described in p-MG patients with type B2 thymomas, while HLA-A25 was significantly increased in the whole group of MG(+) thymomas (**Table 3**). An association of p-MG with HLA-A24 as reported previously in German thymoma patients (114) could not be confirmed in a much larger French cohort (69). In addition, recent findings in two other genes, CTLA4 and PTPN22, might hint to non-tolerizing thymopoiesis inside MG(+) thymomas as a mechanism contributes to p-MG. First, a single nucleotide

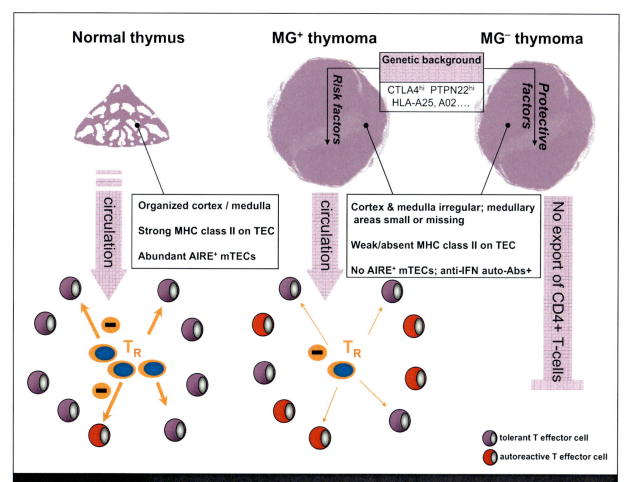

Figure 2. Simplistic unifying model of the pathogenesis of paraneoplastic MG in thymomas with ongoing intratumorous thymopoiesis. As with normal thymus (left), MG-associated thymomas (middle) promote T-cell maturation from immature precursors to fully mature, naïve CD4+ T-cells[4] that are exported to the blood[28]. Exported CD4+ T cells are not properly tolerized in MG(+) thymomas, supposedly due to tumor-specific features (e.g. reduced MHC class II expression) and genetic background (e.g. polymorphisms of HLA-A, CTLA4 etc. genes)[74]. Furthermore, export of non-tolerized CD4+ T effector cells is not balanced by adequate export of CD4+CD25+FoxP3+ regulatory T cells (T_R)[129]. After export to the "periphery" (residual thymus, lymph nodes, bone marrow, muscle?) and following unkown triggering events, naïve T effector cells become activated and finally provide help to autoantibody-producing B-cells in MG(+) thymomas (not shown). According to recent findings, the thymoma might be a place where autoantigen-specific T cell activation could also take place[112]. In MG(-) thymomas, the major difference is their failure to export any CD4+ T cells, including CD4+ T effector cells (right).

polymorphism (SNP) in exon 1 of the T-lymphocyte–associated antigen 4 (CTLA4 +49A/A) was found to be more prevalent in MG(+) than MG(-) thymomas (68). This finding was surprising, since CTLA4 +49A/A confers high CTLA4 levels and is known to be protective in several other autoimmune diseases. CTLA4 is a negative regulator of T-cell activation and competitively interferes with the binding of CD28 to CD80 and CD86 on antigen-presenting cells in the periphery and inside the thymus (115). The seemingly paradoxical association of p-MG with a CTLA4high phenotype implies a unique pathogenesis of thymoma-associated MG. Specifically, we proposed that non-tolerogenic selection inside MG-associated thymomas and subsequent export of autoreactive CD4+ T cells to the periphery might be a key mechanism contributing in p-MG (68) (see below).

As is the case with CTLA4 and p-MG, we think that central tolerance failure is also a contributing mechanism contributing to p-MG associated with another SNP, PTPN22 +1858T+ (74). This SNP was previously found to be associated with many other AIDs, including EOMG (116,117) and anti-titin(+) LOMG (118). Like CTLA4, PTPN22 is an inhibitor of T cell receptor signalling and the MG-prone SNP +1858T+ is an apparently paradoxical *gain-of-function* variant (119). Again, we believe that the paradox can be resolved by assuming that the gain-of-function PTPN22 genotypes interfere with negative selection of CD4+ T cells through inhibition of death promoting T cell receptor signalling (74).

Several other genetic polymorphisms have been proposed to contribute to MG in thymomas but need confirmation in other cohorts of patients (120)

3.3. Somatic genetic and functional features contributing to paraneoplastic MG

As mentioned above, the maintenance of thymopoietic activity in thymomas is now considered a major prerequisite for MG development in the majority of thymomas (maybe not in type A thymomas that are often thymopoietically inactive). Loss of heterozygosity (LOH) of the MHC locus at chromosome 6p21.3 in the neoplastic thymic epithelium appears to be more frequent among MG(+) than MG(-) thymomas. This LOH implies an MHC chimerism between the hemizygous thymoma epithelium (presumed to perform T-cell selection) and MHC-heterozygous intratumorous dendritic cells and the peripheral immune system. However, LOH of the MHC locus is observed in only about 50% of MG-associated thymomas, and MHC chimerism might be just one among other mechanisms of non-tolerogenic T-cell selection in a subset of cases (93,121). Indeed, the consistently reduced levels of MHC class II proteins on thymoma epithelial cells (see above) might *per se* have autoimmunizing potential (135).

3.4. Shared features among MG-associated thymomas

Although the various histological thymoma subtypes show considerable morphological and functional differences, MG-associated thymomas share the following features:

1. All MG-associated thymomas (except for some type A thymomas) share morphological and functional features with the normal thymus. In particular, they provide signals for the homing of immature hematopoietic precursors and promote their differentiation to apparently mature T-cells (3,122,123). Intratumorous maturation of mature naïve CD4+ T-cells appears to be of critical importance in >90% of MG(+) thymomas (types AB, B1, B2,

B3): presence of p-MG is tightly linked to the generation and subsequent export of high numbers of CD4+CD45RA+ naïve T-cells (4,28), while this subset is reduced in MG(-) thymomas. Mature T cells generated by the thymoma can persist in the periphery for several years after removal of the tumour (28). The number of freshly thymoma-derived T cells increases substantially if the tumour recurs (28,124).

2. MG-associated thymomas are enriched for autoreactive T-cells with specificity for the AChR α- and ε-subunit (3, 125-128). There is strong evidence that part of them are generated by intratumorous, non-tolerogenic thymopoiesis (127,128). Not mutually exclusive, the occurrence of autoantibodies with preferential binding to the adult AChR in thymomas with strong AChR ε-subunit expression (112) strongly argues for active immunization of T-cells inside the thymoma, be they generated inside the thymoma or recirculated from the periphery.

3. The production of autoreactive T-cells in thymomas and their activation outside the thymoma may partly reflect inefficient generation of CD4+CD25+FOXP3+ regulatory T-cells that are significantly reduced in thymomas (129).

4. Concurrent autoimmunity against four apparently unrelated types of autoantigens is highly characteristic of paraneoplastic MG. These autoantigens are a) the AChR (21), b) striational muscle antigens, including titin (130), c) neuronal antigens (20,131) and d) cytokines IL-12, IFN-α and IFN-ω (see above). Autoimmunity to the ryanodine receptor is also highly characteristic but less frequent (132,133).

3.5. A pathogenetic model of paraneoplastic myasthenia gravis

Taking the above described features into account, we propose the following model for the development of paraneoplastic MG for the majority (> 95 %) of thymomas in which thympoiesis is encountered: in the pre-myasthenic phase of thymoma growth, the pathogenesis of p-MG might start with abnormal, non-tolerogenic T-cell selection inside the thymoma. This step is followed by export of naïve, potentially intolerant T cells to the extratumorous immune system, i.e. to lymph nodes, normal thymus, spleen and, maybe, bone marrow. At these sites, activation of naïve T cells, interaction between dendritic cells, T cells and B cells and, finally, the production of autoantibodies might occur. Not mutually exclusive, active immunization of T cells against the AChR may occur inside the thymoma (112,134).

In detail, in the context of low epithelial MHC class II expression (and thus weak T-cell receptor:MHC interactions), a CTLA4[high] phenotype or other factors interfering with negative T-cell selection could favor T-cell survival and export and tip the balance towards development of MG, while other polymorphisms or tumor-specific factors that strengthen negative T-cell selection would prevent the intratumorous generation of autoreactive T cells and MG (4,68). Furthermore, it has been shown in mice that tolerance induction is influenced by the quantity and quality of MHC/peptide complexes on thymic epithelial cells (135-138). The MHC level is particularly important when medullary structures (contributing to negative selection under physiological conditions) are reduced (139-140). The latter observations might have a bearing on paraneoplastic MG: hyperexpression of endogenous proteins together with disturbed T-cell selection might favor the generation of thymoma-derived autoreactive T-cells (142) and/or their active immunization inside the thymoma (112). The process of selection and activation of autoreactive,

AChR-reactive T cells (128) in thymoma patients might not be a random process, as suggested by the observation that these T-cells are restricted to the minority HLA isotypes DP14 and DR52a that are infrequent in MG patients without thymoma (127). MG-associated thymomas export mature naïve CD4+ T-cells (28,124) that may not be checked by adequate numbers of regulatory T-cells of appropriate specificities (129). Export of naive T-cells might gradually replace the normally tolerant, thymus-derived T-cell repertoire by a "chimeric" autoimmunity-prone T-cell repertoire derived from both the thymoma and the non-neoplastic residual thymus. In accordance with this model, MG can rarely develop after surgical removal of the thymoma (6) and resection of early stage rather than advanced thymomas is likely to induces complete remisson of p-MG (143) tumors. In order to be pathogenically relevant, the potentially autoantigen-reactive T cells have to become activated in order to provide help for autoantibody producing B-cells outside the thymoma (144) (Fig. 2). At this stage, it can be hypothesized that anti-IL-12 or anti-IFN-α autoantibodies (145) facilitate the CD4 T-cell dependent production of anti AChR autoantibodies.

3.6. ETIOLOGICAL TRIGGERS OF PARANEOPLASTIC MG

The mechanisms that activate the autoimmunity-prone T-cell repertoire outside the thymoma, i.e. the etiologies triggering the MG-provoking autoimmune cascade, remain to be defined. We have observed paraneoplastic MG following pregnancy, unspecific infectious or traumatic "stimuli", but in most cases no major event can be identified (93). The „periphery" outside the thymoma, where exported non-toleraized naïve T effector cells become activated, can be the residual thymus (146) that is frequently enriched in autoreactive T cells and lymphoid follicles, resulting in a TFH-like morphology in many MG-associated thymoma cases. However, other lymphoid organs have to play a role in this process, given that even complete surgical removal of thymoma plus residual thymus is often not followed by a decline of autoantibody titers (147). Events that might activate intolerant CD8+ T cells inside or outside the thymoma are even less clear (6,69).

3.7. Major unresolved questions in paraneoplastic MG

The above model still awaits reconciliation with the following open points:

1. It has remained unclear why MG is so predominant among the autoimmune diseases associated with thymomas. Abnormal proteins that contain AChR-, titin- or ryanodine receptor (RyR)-like epitopes (128,133,148,149) have been described in thymomas, but it is not known whether these proteins are crucial for the development of anti-AChR, anti-titin- or anti-RyR autoimmunity. Alternatively, we speculate that the lack of myoid cells in thymomas could impair intra-tumorous tolerance induction towards striated muscle cell antigens.

2. In spite of absence of AIRE in thymomas and despite the high frequency of various auto-antibodies in the serum of thymoma patients, clinical autoimmune *diseases* other than MG are relatively rare (about 10 % of cases) (17) (**Table 1**). A possible explanation could be that clinical symptoms in MG may be elicited by autoantibodies and complement at even nanomolar concentrations (6), while other autoimmune diseases like type I diabetes may not be autoantibody-mediated, but follow a more complex attack of cytotoxic T-cells (150).

3. The role of AIRE deficiency and of antibodies to IL-12 and type I interferons in the autoimmunization process, if any, requires explanation (111).The presence of these autoantobodies in both MG(+) and, less commonly, MG(-) thymomas does not argue against their pathogenic significance, considering that they interfere with interferon-driven gene expression in humans (110). The respective targets in thymomatous epithelial cells would be important to know. Indeed, APECED and thymoma patients might be indispensible models to resolve these questions since these antibody responses are not encountered in AIRE-deficient mice, in which immunopathology is mainly driven by CD4+ Tells with TH1 functions (151).

4. Another enigma is the occurrence of MG in some patients with type A thymomas. Since this thymoma subtype usually exhibits minimal or virtually no intratumorous thymopoiesis in terms of immature CD4+CD8+ and naïve CD4+ T-cells (123,124), the above pathogenetic model (**Fig. 2**) may not apply to some patients with this subtype. However, type A thymomas are frequently associated with pure red cell aplasia that is believed to result from an attack of cytotoxic T cells on red cell precursors in the bone marrow. Therefore, it might be speculated that CD8+, and not CD4+ T-cells might be relevant in some MG patients with type A thymoma. Indeed, a role of CD8+ T cells may extend beyond type A thymomas considering the recently described association of MHC class I polymorphisms with p-MG, with a (protective) role of HLA-A02 particularly in type B2 thymomas (69).

5) Finally, it has not been elucidated which autoantigens maintain the prolonged autoantibody response after thymoma resection during which the adjacent residual non-neoplastic thymus with its myoid cells is usually removed as well. An obvious candidate is the AChR itself: AChR could be released from skeletal muscle endplates following destruction by autoantibodies or cytotoxic T-cells. Hypothetically, released AChR and striational antigens may be presented to autoreactive T cells by the intramuscular inflammatory infiltrate (152) or by antigen presenting cells in regional lymph nodes (5,153).

REFERENCES

1. Marx A,Ströbel P, Zettl A, et al. Thymic epithelial tumours. Introduction on thymoma and thymic carcinoma. In: Travis WD, Brambilla E, Müller-Hermelink HK, Harris CC, eds. WHO Classification of Tumours of the Lung, Thymus, and Heart Pathology and Genetics. Lyon: IARC Press; 2004:152-153.

2. Fujii Y, Hayakawa M, Inada K, Nakahara K. Lymphocytes in thymoma: association with myasthenia gravis is correlated with increased number of single-positive cells. *Eur J Immunol.* 1990;20:2355-2358.

3. Nenninger R, Schultz A, Hoffacker V, et al. Abnormal thymocyte development and generation of autoreactive T cells in mixed and cortical thymomas. *Lab Invest.* 1998;78:743-753.

4. Ströbel P, Helmreich M, Menioudakis G, et al. Paraneoplastic myasthenia gravis correlates with generation of mature naive CD4+ T cells in thymomas. *Blood.* 2002;100:159-166.

5. Marx A, Wilisch A, Schultz A, Gattenlohner S, Nenninger R, Muller-Hermelink HK. Pathogenesis of myasthenia gravis. *Virchows Arch.* 1997;430:355-364.

6. Vincent A, Willcox N. The role of T-cells in the initiation of autoantibody responses in thymoma patients. *Pathol Res Pract.* 1999;195:535-540.

7. Willcox N, Leite MI, Kadota Y, et al. Autoimmunizing mechanisms in thymoma and thymus. *Ann N Y Acad Sci.* 2008;1132:163-173.

8. Drachman DB. Myasthenia gravis. *N Engl J Med.* 1994;330:1797-1810.

9. Lindstrom JM, Seybold ME, Lennon VA, Whittingham S, Duane DD. Antibody to acetylcholine receptor in myasthenia gravis: prevalence, clinical correlates, and diagnostic value. 1975 [classical article]. *Neurology.* 1998;51:933 and 936 pages following.

10. Tzartos SJ, Barkas T, Cung MT, et al. Anatomy of the antigenic structure of a large membrane autoantigen, the muscle-type nicotinic acetylcholine receptor. *Immunol Rev.* 1998;163:89-120.

11. Lee JY, Sung JJ, Cho JY, et al. MuSK antibody-positive, seronegative myasthenia gravis in Korea. *J Clin Neurosci.* 2006;13:353-355.

12. Leite MI, Strobel P, Jones M, et al. Fewer thymic changes in MuSK antibody-positive than in MuSK antibody-negative MG. *Ann Neurol.* 2005;57:444-448.

13. Yeh JH, Chen WH, Chiu HC, Vincent A. Low frequency of MuSK antibody in generalized seronegative myasthenia gravis among Chinese. *Neurology.* 2004;62:2131-2132.

14. Bartoccioni E, Marino M, Evoli A, Ruegg MA, Scuderi F, Provenzano C. Identification of disease-specific autoantibodies in seronegative myasthenia gravis. *Ann N Y Acad Sci.* 2003;998:356-358.

15. Hoch W, McConville J, Helms S, Newsom-Davis J, Melms A, Vincent A. Auto-antibodies to the receptor tyrosine kinase MuSK in patients with myasthenia gravis without acetylcholine receptor antibodies. *Nat Med.* 2001;7:365-368.

16. Leite MI, Jacob S, Viegas S, et al. IgG1 antibodies to acetylcholine receptors in 'seronegative' myasthenia gravis. *Brain.* 2008;131:1940-1952.

17. Strobel P, Murumagi A, Klein R, et al. Deficiency of the autoimmune regulator AIRE in thymomas is insufficient to elicit autoimmune polyendocrinopathy syndrome type 1 (APS-1). *J Pathol.* 2007;211:563-571.

18. Gautel M, Lakey A, Barlow DP, et al. Titin antibodies in myasthenia gravis: identification of a major immunogenic region of titin. *Neurology*. 1993;43:1581-1585.

19. Dhamija R, Tan KM, Pittock SJ, Foxx-Orenstein A, Benarroch E, Lennon VA. Serologic profiles aiding the diagnosis of autoimmune gastrointestinal dysmotility. *Clin Gastroenterol Hepatol*. 2008;6:988-992.

20. Vernino S, Lennon VA. Autoantibody profiles and neurological correlations of thymoma. *Clin Cancer Res*. 2004;10:7270-7275.

21. Vincent A. Antibodies to ion channels in paraneoplastic disorders. *Brain Pathol*. 1999;9:285-291.

22. Maggi L, Andreetta F, Antozzi C, et al. Two cases of thymoma-associated myasthenia gravis without antibodies to the acetylcholine receptor. *Neuromuscul Disord*. 2008;18:678-680.

23. Evoli A, Batocchi AP, Lo Monaco M, et al. Clinical heterogeneity of seronegative myasthenia gravis. *Neuromuscul Disord*. 1996;6:155-161.

24. Evoli A, Tonali PA, Padua L, et al. Clinical correlates with anti-MuSK antibodies in generalized seronegative myasthenia gravis. *Brain*. 2003;126:2304-2311.

25. Strobel P, Moritz R, Leite MI, et al. The ageing and myasthenic thymus: A morphometric study validating a standard procedure in the histological workup of thymic specimens. *J Neuroimmunol*. 2008;201-202:64-73.

26. Hohlfeld R, Wekerle H. Reflections on the "intrathymic pathogenesis" of myasthenia gravis. *J Neuroimmunol*. 2008;201-202:21-27.

27. Aarli JA. Myasthenia gravis in the elderly: Is it different? *Ann N Y Acad Sci*. 2008;1132:238-243.

28. Buckley C, Douek D, Newsom-Davis J, Vincent A, Willcox N. Mature, long-lived CD4+ and CD8+ T cells are generated by the thymoma in myasthenia gravis. *Ann Neurol*. 2001;50:64-72.

29. Meager A, Wadhwa M, Dilger P, et al. Anti-cytokine autoantibodies in autoimmunity: preponderance of neutralizing autoantibodies against interferon-alpha, interferon-omega and interleukin-12 in patients with thymoma and/or myasthenia gravis. *Clin Exp Immunol*. 2003;132:128-136.

30. Yamamoto AM, Gajdos P, Eymard B, et al. Anti-titin antibodies in myasthenia gravis: tight association with thymoma and heterogeneity of nonthymoma patients. Arch Neurol. 2001;58:885-890.

31. Romi F, Gilhus NE, Varhaug JE, Myking A, Skeie GO, Aarli JA. Thymectomy and anti-muscle autoantibodies in late-onset myasthenia gravis. *Eur J Neurol*. 2002;9:55-61.

32. Quintanilla-Martinez L, Wilkins EW, Jr., Ferry JA, Harris NL. Thymoma—morphologic subclassification correlates with invasiveness and immunohistologic features: a study of 122 cases. Hum Pathol. 1993;24:958-969.

33. Roxanis I, Micklem K, McConville J, Newsom-Davis J, Willcox N. Thymic myoid cells and germinal center formation in myasthenia gravis; possible roles in pathogenesis. *J Neuroimmunol*. 2002;125:185-197.

34. Kirchner T, Schalke B, Melms A, von Kugelgen T, Muller-Hermelink HK. Immunohistological patterns of non-neoplastic changes in the thymus in Myasthenia gravis. *Virchows Arch B Cell Pathol Incl Mol Pathol*. 1986;52:237-257.

35. Muller-Hermelink HK, Marx A, T K. Thymus. In: Damjanov I LJ, ed. Anderson's Pathology (ed 10). St. Louis: *Mosby*; 1996:1218-1243.

36. Middleton G, Schoch EM. The prevalence of human thymic lymphoid follicles is lower in suicides. *Virchows Arch.* 2000;436:127-130.

37. Leite MI, Jones M, Strobel P, et al. Myasthenia gravis thymus: complement vulnerability of epithelial and myoid cells, complement attack on them, and correlations with autoantibody status. *Am J Pathol.* 2007;171:893-905.

38. Roxanis I, Micklem K, Willcox N. True epithelial hyperplasia in the thymus of early-onset myasthenia gravis patients: implications for immunopathogenesis. *J Neuroimmunol.* 2001;112:163-173.

39. Flores KG, Li J, Sempowski GD, Haynes BF, Hale LP. Analysis of the human thymic perivascular space during aging. *J Clin Invest.* 1999;104:1031-1039.

40. Navaneetham D, Penn AS, Howard JF, Jr., Conti-Fine BM. Human thymuses express incomplete sets of muscle acetylcholine receptor subunit transcripts that seldom include the delta subunit. *Muscle Nerve.* 2001;24:203-210.

41. Geuder KI, Marx A, Witzemann V, et al. Pathogenetic significance of fetal-type acetylcholine receptors on thymic myoid cells in myasthenia gravis. *Dev Immunol.* 1992;2:69-75.

42. Schluep M, Willcox N, Vincent A, Dhoot GK, Newsom-Davis J. Acetylcholine receptors in human thymic myoid cells in situ: an immunohistological study. *Ann Neurol.* 1987;22:212-222.

43. Curnow J, Corlett L, Willcox N, Vincent A. Presentation by myoblasts of an epitope from endogenous acetylcholine receptor indicates a potential role in the spreading of the immune response. *J Neuroimmunol.* 2001;115:127-134.

44. Bornemann A, Kirchner T. An immuno-electron-microscopic study of human thymic B cells. *Cell Tissue Res.* 1996;284:481-487.

45. Le Panse R, Cizeron-Clairac G, Cuvelier M, et al. Regulatory and pathogenic mechanisms in human autoimmune myasthenia gravis. *Ann N Y Acad Sci.* 2008;1132:135-142.

46. Meraouna A, Cizeron-Clairac G, Panse RL, et al. The chemokine CXCL13 is a key molecule in autoimmune myasthenia gravis. *Blood.* 2006;108:432-440.

47. Compston DA, Vincent A, Newsom-Davis J, Batchelor JR. Clinical, pathological, HLA antigen and immunological evidence for disease heterogeneity in myasthenia gravis. *Brain.* 1980;103:579-601.

48. Degli-Esposti MA, Andreas A, Christiansen FT, Schalke B, Albert E, Dawkins RL. An approach to the localization of the susceptibility genes for generalized myasthenia gravis by mapping recombinant ancestral haplotypes. *Immunogenetics.* 1992;35:355-364.

49. Giraud M, Vandiedonck C, Garchon HJ. Genetic factors in autoimmune myasthenia gravis. *Ann N Y Acad Sci.* 2008;1132:180-192.

50. Huang D, Shi FD, Giscombe R, Zhou Y, Ljunggren HG, Lefvert AK. Disruption of the IL-1beta gene diminishes acetylcholine receptor-induced immune responses in a murine model of myasthenia gravis. *Eur J Immunol.* 2001;31:225-232.

51. Skeie GO, Pandey JP, Aarli JA, Gilhus NE. TNFA and TNFB polymorphisms in myasthenia gravis. *Arch Neurol.* 1999;56:457-461.

52. Huang DR, Pirskanen R, Matell G, Lefvert AK. Tumour necrosis factor-alpha polymorphism and secretion in myasthenia gravis. *J Neuroimmunol.* 1999;94:165-171.

53. Franciotta D, Cuccia M, Dondi E, Piccolo G, Cosi V. Polymorphic markers in MHC class II/III region: a study on Italian patients with myasthenia gravis. *J Neurol Sci.* 2001;190:11-16.

54. Huang DR, Zhou YH, Xia SQ, Liu L, Pirskanen R, Lefvert AK. Markers in the promoter region of interleukin-10 (IL-10) gene in myasthenia gravis: implications of diverse effects of IL-10 in the pathogenesis of the disease. *J Neuroimmunol.* 1999;94:82-87.

55. Garchon HJ, Djabiri F, Viard JP, Gajdos P, Bach JF. Involvement of human muscle acetylcholine receptor alpha-subunit gene (CHRNA) in susceptibility to myasthenia gravis. Proc Natl Acad Sci U S A. 1994;91:4668-4672.

56. Djabiri F, Gajdos P, Eymard B, Gomez L, Bach JF, Garchon HJ. No evidence for an association of AChR beta-subunit gene (CHRNB1) with myasthenia gravis. *J Neuroimmunol.* 1997;78:86-89.

57. Giraud M, Beaurain G, Yamamoto AM, et al. Linkage of HLA to myasthenia gravis and genetic heterogeneity depending on anti-titin antibodies. *Neurology.* 2001;57:1555-1560.

58. Onodera J, Nakamura S, Nagano I, et al. Upregulation of Bcl-2 protein in the myasthenic thymus. *Ann Neurol.* 1996;39:521-528.

59. Masunaga A, Arai T, Yoshitake T, Itoyama S, Sugawara I. Reduced expression of apoptosis-related antigens in thymuses from patients with myasthenia gravis. *Immunol Lett.* 1994;39:169-172.

60. Moulian N, Bidault J, Truffault F, Yamamoto AM, Levasseur P, Berrih-Aknin S. Thymocyte Fas expression is dysregulated in myasthenia gravis patients with anti-acetylcholine receptor antibody. *Blood.* 1997;89:3287-3295.

61. Sempowski GD, Hale LP, Sundy JS, et al. Leukemia inhibitory factor, oncostatin M, IL-6, and stem cell factor mRNA expression in human thymus increases with age and is associated with thymic atrophy. *J Immunol.* 2000;164:2180-2187.

62. Schneider DT, Schuster AE, Fritsch MK, et al. Multipoint imprinting analysis indicates a common precursor cell for gonadal and nongonadal pediatric germ cell tumors. *Cancer Res.* 2001;61:7268-7276.

63. Chan JKC, Zettl A, Inoue M, De Jong D, Yoneda S. Metaplastic Thymoma. In: Travis WD, Brambilla E, Müller-Hermelink HK, Harris CC, eds. Tumours of the Lung, Pleura, Thymus and Heart Pathology & Genetics. Lyon: *IARC*; 2004:169-170.

64. Masaoka A, Monden Y, Nakahara K, Tanioka T. Follow-up study of thymomas with special reference to their clinical stages. *Cancer.* 1981;48:2485-2492.

65. Koga K, Matsuno Y, Noguchi M, et al. A review of 79 thymomas: modification of staging system and reappraisal of conventional division into invasive and non-invasive thymoma. *Pathol* Int. 1994;44:359-367.

66. Müller-Hermelink HK, Engel P, Kuo TT, et al. Tumours of the thymus: Introduction. In: Travis WD, Brambilla E, Müller-Hermelink HK, Harris CC, eds. Tumours of the Lung, Pleura, Thymus and Heart, Pathology & Genetics. Lyon: IARC; 2004:149-151.

67. Willcox N. Myasthenia gravis. *Curr Opin Immunol.* 1993;5:910-917.

68. Chuang WY, Strobel P, Gold R, et al. A CTLA4high genotype is associated with myasthenia gravis in thymoma patients. *Ann Neurol.* 2005;58:644-648.

69. Vandiedonck C, Raffoux C, Eymard B, et al. Association of HLA-A in autoimmune myasthenia gravis with thymoma. *J Neuroimmunol.* 2009;210:120-123.

70. Marino M, Muller-Hermelink HK. Thymoma and thymic carcinoma. Relation of thymoma epithelial cells to the cortical and medullary differentiation of thymus. *Virchows Arch A Pathol Anat Histopathol.* 1985;407:119-149.

71. Kirchner T, Schalke B, Buchwald J, Ritter M, Marx A, Muller-Hermelink HK. Well-differentiated thymic carcinoma. An organotypical low-grade carcinoma with relationship to cortical thymoma. *Am J Surg Pathol.* 1992;16:1153-1169.

72. Rosai J. Histological typing of tumours of the thymus (ed 2nd). Berlin and Heidelberg: *Springer-Verlag;* 1999.

73. Marchevsky AM, Gupta R, McKenna RJ, et al. Evidence-based pathology and the pathologic evaluation of thymomas: the World Health Organization classification can be simplified into only 3 categories other than thymic carcinoma. *Cancer.* 2008;112:2780-2788.

74. Strobel P, Chuang WY, Chuvpilo S, et al. Common cellular and diverse genetic basis of thymoma-associated myasthenia gravis: role of MHC class II and AIRE genes and genetic polymorphisms. *Ann N Y Acad Sci.* 2008;1132:143-156.

75. Pan CC, Chen WY, Chiang H. Spindle cell and mixed spindle/lymphocytic thymomas: an integrated clinicopathologic and immunohistochemical study of 81 cases. *Am J Surg Pathol.* 2001;25:111-120.

76. Strobel P, Bauer A, Puppe B, et al. Tumor recurrence and survival in patients treated for thymomas and thymic squamous cell carcinomas: a retrospective analysis. *J Clin Oncol.* 2004;22:1501-1509.

77. Palestro G, Chiarle R, Marx A, Müller-Hermelink HK, Sng I. WHO Type B1 Thymoma. In: Travis WD, Brambilla E, Müller-Hermelink HK, Harris CC, eds. Tumours of the Lung, Thymus, and Heart Pathology and Genetics. Lyon: *IARC* Press; 2004.

78. Suster S, Moran CA. Thymoma, atypical thymoma, and thymic carcinoma. A novel conceptual approach to the classification of thymic epithelial neoplasms. *Am J Clin Pathol.* 1999;111:826-833.

79. Quintanilla-Martinez L, Wilkins EW, Jr., Choi N, Efird J, Hug E, Harris NL. Thymoma. Histologic subclassification is an independent prognostic factor. *Cancer.* 1994;74:606-617.

80. Rieker RJ, Muley T, Klein C, et al. An institutional study on thymomas and thymic carcinomas: experience in 77 patients. Thorac Cardiovasc Surg. 2008;56:143-147.

81. Okumura M, Ohta M, Tateyama H, et al. The World Health Organization histologic classification system reflects the oncologic behavior of thymoma: a clinical study of 273 patients. *Cancer.* 2002;94:624-632.

82. Ho FC, Fu KH, Lam SY, Chiu SW, Chan AC, Muller-Hermelink HK. Evaluation of a histogenetic classification for thymic epithelial tumours. *Histopathology.* 1994;25:21-29.

83. Chalabreysse L, Roy P, Cordier JF, Loire R, Gamondes JP, Thivolet-Bejui F. Correlation of the WHO schema for the classification of thymic epithelial neoplasms with prognosis: a retrospective study of 90 tumors. *Am J Surg Pathol.* 2002;26:1605-1611.

84. D'Angelillo RM, Trodella L, Ramella S, et al. Novel prognostic groups in thymic epithelial tumors: assessment of risk and therapeutic strategy selection. *Int J Radiat Oncol Biol Phys.* 2008;71:420-427.

85. Girard N, Mornex F, Van Houtte P, Cordier JF, van Schil P. Thymoma: a focus on current therapeutic management. *J Thorac Oncol.* 2009;4:119-126.

86. Casey EM, Kiel PJ, Loehrer PJ, Sr. Clinical management of thymoma patients. Hematol *Oncol Clin North Am.* 2008;22:457-473.

87. Wright CD, Choi NC, Wain JC, Mathisen DJ, Lynch TJ, Fidias P. Induction chemoradiotherapy followed by resection for locally advanced Masaoka stage III and IVA thymic tumors. *Ann Thorac Surg.* 2008;85:385-389.

88. Giaccone G, Wilmink H, Paul MA, van der Valk P. Systemic treatment of malignant thymoma: a decade experience at a single institution. *Am J Clin Oncol.* 2006;29:336-344.

89. Lucchi M, Melfi F, Dini P, et al. Neoadjuvant chemotherapy for stage III and IVA thymomas: a single-institution experience with a long follow-up. *J Thorac Oncol.* 2006;1:308-313.

90. Chen G, Marx A, Wen-Hu C, et al. New WHO histologic classification predicts prognosis of thymic epithelial tumors: a clinicopathologic study of 200 thymoma cases from China. *Cancer.* 2002;95:420-429.

91. Willcox N, Schluep M, Ritter MA, Newsom-Davis J. The thymus in seronegative myasthenia gravis patients. *J Neurol.* 1991;238:256-261.

92. Vincent A, Willcox N, Hill M, Curnow J, MacLennan C, Beeson D. Determinant spreading and immune responses to acetylcholine receptors in myasthenia gravis. *Immunol Rev.* 1998;164:157-168.

93. Muller-Hermelink HK, Marx A. Thymoma. Curr Opin Oncol. 2000;12:426-433.

94. Newsom-Davis J, Willcox N, Schluep M, et al. Immunological heterogeneity and cellular mechanisms in myasthenia gravis. Ann N Y Acad Sci. 1987;505:12-26.

95. Spuler S, Sarropoulos A, Marx A, Hohlfeld R, Wekerle H. Thymoma-associated myasthenia gravis. Transplantation of thymoma and extrathymomal thymic tissue into SCID mice. *Am J Pathol.* 1996;148:1359-1365.

96. Fujii Y, Monden Y, Nakahara K, Hashimoto J, Kawashima Y. Antibody to acetylcholine receptor in myasthenia gravis: production by lymphocytes from thymus or thymoma. *Neurology.* 1984;34:1182-1186.

97. Willcox N, Schluep M, Ritter MA, Schuurman HJ, Newsom-Davis J, Christensson B. Myasthenic and nonmyasthenic thymoma. An expansion of a minor cortical epithelial cell subset? *Am J Pathol.* 1987;127:447-460.

98. Inoue M, Fujii Y, Okumura M, et al. T-cell development in human thymoma. *Pathol Res Pract.* 1999;195:541-547.

99. Kadota Y, Okumura M, Miyoshi S, et al. Altered T cell development in human thymoma is related to impairment of MHC class II transactivator expression induced by interferon-gamma (IFN- gamma). *Clin Exp Immunol.* 2000;121:59-68.

100. Strobel P, Helmreich M, Kalbacher H, Muller-Hermelink HK, Marx A. Evidence for distinct mechanisms in the shaping of the CD4 T cell repertoire in histologically distinct myasthenia gravis-associated thymomas. *Dev Immunol.* 2001;8:279-290.

101. Heino M, Peterson P, Kudoh J, et al. Autoimmune regulator is expressed in the cells regulating immune tolerance in thymus medulla. Biochem Biophys Res Commun. 1999;257:821-825.

102. Nagamine K, Peterson P, Scott HS, et al. Positional cloning of the APECED gene. *Nat Genet.* 1997;17:393-398.

103. Peterson P, Org T, Rebane A. Transcriptional regulation by AIRE: molecular mechanisms of central tolerance. *Nat Rev Immunol.* 2008;8:948-957.

104. Tykocinski LO, Sinemus A, Kyewski B. The thymus medulla slowly yields its secrets. *Ann N Y Acad Sci.* 2008;1143:105-122.

105. Taubert R, Schwendemann J, Kyewski B. Highly variable expression of tissue-restricted self-antigens in human thymus: implications for self-tolerance and autoimmunity. *Eur J Immunol.* 2007;37:838-848.

106. Anderson MS, Venanzi ES, Chen Z, Berzins SP, Benoist C, Mathis D. The cellular mechanism of Aire control of T cell tolerance. *Immunity.* 2005;23:227-239.

107. Giraud M, Taubert R, Vandiedonck C, et al. An IRF8-binding promoter variant and AIRE control CHRNA1 promiscuous expression in thymus. *Nature.* 2007;448:934-937.

108. Shiono H, Wong YL, Matthews I, et al. Spontaneous production of anti-IFN-alpha and anti-IL-12 autoantibodies by thymoma cells from myasthenia gravis patients suggests autoimmunization in the tumor. *Int Immunol.* 2003;15:903-913.

109. Meager A, Visvalingam K, Peterson P, et al. Anti-interferon autoantibodies in autoimmune polyendocrinopathy syndrome type 1. *PLoS Med.* 2006;3:e289.

110. Kisand K, Link M, Wolff AS, et al. Interferon autoantibodies associated with AIRE-deficiency decrease the expression of IFN-stimulated genes. *Blood.* 2008.

111. Meager A, Peterson P, Willcox N. Hypothetical review: thymic aberrations and type-I interferons; attempts to deduce autoimmunizing mechanisms from unexpected clues in monogenic and paraneoplastic syndromes. *Clin Exp Immunol.* 2008.

112. Maclennan CA, Vincent A, Marx A, et al. Preferential expression of AChR epsilon-subunit in thymomas from patients with myasthenia gravis. *J Neuroimmunol.* 2008;201-202:28-32.

113. Luther C, Poeschel S, Varga M, Melms A, Tolosa E. Decreased frequency of intrathymic regulatory T cells in patients with myasthenia-associated thymoma. *J Neuroimmunol.* 2005;164:124-128.

114. Machens A, Loliger C, Pichlmeier U, Emskotter T, Busch C, Izbicki JR. Correlation of thymic pathology with HLA in myasthenia gravis. Clin Immunol. 1999;91:296-301.

115. Kwon H, Jun HS, Khil LY, Yoon JW. Role of CTLA-4 in the activation of single- and double-positive thymocytes. *J Immunol.* 2004;173:6645-6653.

116. Vandiedonck C, Capdevielle C, Giraud M, et al. Association of the PTPN22*R620W polymorphism with autoimmune myasthenia gravis. *Ann Neurol.* 2006;59:404-407.

117. Lefvert AK, Zhao Y, Ramanujam R, Yu S, Pirskanen R, Hammarstrom L. PTPN22 R620W promotes production of anti-AChR autoantibodies and IL-2 in myasthenia gravis. *J Neuroimmunol.* 2008;197:110-113.

118. Greve B, Hoffmann P, Illes Z, et al. The autoimmunity-related polymorphism PTPN22 1858C/T is associated with anti-titin antibody-positive myasthenia gravis. *Hum Immunol.* 2009.

119. Vang T, Congia M, Macis MD, et al. Autoimmune-associated lymphoid tyrosine phosphatase is a gain-of-function variant. *Nat Genet.* 2005;37:1317-1319.

120. Amdahl C, Alseth EH, Gilhus NE, Nakkestad HL, Skeie GO. Polygenic disease associations in thymomatous myasthenia gravis. Arch Neurol. 2007;64:1729-1733.

121. Zettl A, Ströbel P, Wagner K, et al. Recurrent genetic aberrations in thymoma and thymic carcinoma. *Am J Pathol.* 2000;157:257-266.

122. Takeuchi Y, Fujii Y, Okumura M, Inada K, Nakahara K, Matsuda H. Accumulation of immature CD3-CD4+CD8- single-positive cells that lack CD69 in epithelial cell tumors of the human thymus. *Cell Immunol.* 1995;161:181-187.

123. Nenninger R, Schultz A, Vandekerckhove B, Hünig T, Müller-Hermelink HK, Marx A. Abnormal T lymphocyte development in myasthenia gravis-associated thymomas. New York
London: Plenum Press; 1997.

124. Hoffacker V, Schultz A, Tiesinga JJ, et al. Thymomas alter the T-cell subset composition in the blood: a potential mechanism for thymoma-associated autoimmune disease [In Process Citation]. *Blood*. 2000;96:3872-3879.

125. Sommer N, Harcourt GC, Willcox N, Beeson D, Newsom-Davis J. Acetylcholine receptor-reactive T lymphocytes from healthy subjects and myasthenia gravis patients. *Neurology*. 1991;41:1270-1276.

126. Conti-Fine BM, Navaneetham D, Karachunski PI, et al. T cell recognition of the acetylcholine receptor in myasthenia gravis. *Ann N Y Acad Sci*. 1998;841:283-308.

127. Nagvekar N, Moody AM, Moss P, et al. A pathogenetic role for the thymoma in myasthenia gravis. Autosensitization of IL-4- producing T cell clones recognizing extracellular acetylcholine receptor epitopes presented by minority class II isotypes. *J Clin Invest*. 1998;101:2268-2277.

128. Schultz A, Hoffacker V, Wilisch A, et al. Neurofilament is an autoantigenic determinant in myasthenia gravis. *Ann Neurol*. 1999;46:167-175.

129. Strobel P, Rosenwald A, Beyersdorf N, et al. Selective loss of regulatory T cells in thymomas. *Ann Neurol*. 2004;56:901-904.

130. Aarli JA, Skeie GO, Mygland A, Gilhus NE. Muscle striation antibodies in myasthenia gravis. Diagnostic and functional significance. *Ann N Y Acad Sci*. 1998;841:505-515.

131. Etienne M, Weimer LH. Immune-mediated autonomic neuropathies. *Curr Neurol Neurosci Rep*. 2006;6:57-64.

132. Mygland A, Aarli JA, Matre R, Gilhus NE. Ryanodine receptor antibodies related to severity of thymoma associated myasthenia gravis. *J Neurol Neurosurg Psychiatry*. 1994;57:843-846.

133. Mygland A, Kuwajima G, Mikoshiba K, Tysnes OB, Aarli JA, Gilhus NE. Thymomas express epitopes shared by the ryanodine receptor. J Neuroimmunol. 1995;62:79-83.

134. Shiono H, Roxanis I, Zhang W, et al. Scenarios for autoimmunization of T and B cells in myasthenia gravis. *Ann N Y Acad Sci*. 2003;998:237-256.

135. Fukui Y, Ishimoto T, Utsuyama M, et al. Positive and negative CD4+ thymocyte selection by a single MHC class II/peptide ligand affected by its expression level in the thymus. Immunity. 1997;6:401-410.

136. Ashton-Rickardt PG, Tonegawa S. A differential-avidity model for T-cell selection. *Immunol Today*. 1994;15:362-366.

137. Hogquist KA, Jameson SC, Heath WR, Howard JL, Bevan MJ, Carbone FR. T cell receptor antagonist peptides induce positive selection. *Cell*. 1994;76:17-27.

138. Barton GM, Rudensky AY. Requirement for diverse, low-abundance peptides in positive selection of T cells. Science. 1999;283:67-70.

139. Derbinski J, Kyewski B. Linking signalling pathways, thymic stroma integrity and autoimmunity. Trends *Immunol*. 2005;26:503-506.

140. Laufer TM, Fan L, Glimcher LH. Self-reactive T cells selected on thymic cortical epithelium are polyclonal and are pathogenic in vivo. *J Immunol*. 1999;162:5078-5084.

141. van Meerwijk JP, MacDonald HR. In vivo T-lymphocyte tolerance in the absence of thymic clonal deletion mediated by hematopoietic cells. *Blood*. 1999;93:3856-3862.

142. Sommer N, Willcox N, Harcourt GC, Newsom-Davis J. Myasthenic thymus and thymoma are selectively enriched in acetylcholine receptor-reactive T cells. *Ann Neurol*. 1990;28:312-319.

143. Lucchi M, Ricciardi R, Melfi F, et al. Association of thymoma and myasthenia gravis: oncological and neurological results of the surgical treatment. *Eur J Cardiothorac Surg.* 2009;35:812-816; discussion 816.

144. Marx A, Schultz A, Wilisch A, Helmreich M, Nenninger R, Muller-Hermelink HK. Paraneoplastic autoimmunity in thymus tumors. *Dev Immunol.* 1998;6:129-140.

145. Meager A, Vincent A, Newsom-Davis J, Willcox N. Spontaneous neutralising antibodies to interferon—alpha and interleukin-12 in thymoma-associated autoimmune disease [letter]. *Lancet.* 1997;350:1596-1597.

146. Conti-Tronconi BM, McLane KE, Raftery MA, Grando SA, Protti MP. The nicotinic acetylcholine receptor: structure and autoimmune pathology. *Crit Rev Biochem Mol Biol.* 1994;29:69-123.

147. Somnier FE. Exacerbation of myasthenia gravis after removal of thymomas [see comments]. *Acta Neurol Scand.* 1994;90:56-66.

148. Marx A, O'Connor R, Geuder KI, et al. Characterization of a protein with an acetylcholine receptor epitope from myasthenia gravis-associated thymomas [see comments]. *Lab Invest.* 1990;62:279-286.

149. Marx A, Wilisch A, Schultz A, et al. Expression of neurofilaments and of a titin epitope in thymic epithelial tumors. Implications for the pathogenesis of myasthenia gravis. *Am J Pathol.* 1996;148:1839-1850.

150. Lang KS, Recher M, Junt T, et al. Toll-like receptor engagement converts T-cell autoreactivity into overt autoimmune disease. *Nat Med.* 2005;11:138-145.

151. Devoss JJ, Shum AK, Johannes KP, et al. Effector mechanisms of the autoimmune syndrome in the murine model of autoimmune polyglandular syndrome type 1. *J Immunol.* 2008;181:4072-4079.

152. Maselli RA, Richman DP, Wollmann RL. Inflammation at the neuromuscular junction in myasthenia gravis. *Neurology.* 1991;41:1497-1504.

153. Muller-Hermelink HK, Wilisch A, Schultz A, Marx A. Characterization of the human thymic microenvironment: lymphoepithelial interaction in normal thymus and thymoma. *Arch Histol Cytol.* 1997;60:9-28.

154. Evoli A, Minisci C, Di Schino C, et al. Thymoma in patients with MG: characteristics and long-term outcome. *Neurology.* 2002;59:1844-1850.

155. Tan KM, Lennon VA, Klein CJ, Boeve BF, Pittock SJ. Clinical spectrum of voltage-gated potassium channel autoimmunity. *Neurology.* 2008;70:1883-1890.

156. Yamakawa Y, Masaoka A, Hashimoto T, et al. A tentative tumor-node-metastasis classification of thymoma. *Cancer.* 1991;68:1984-1987.

157. Vandiedonck C, Beaurain G, Giraud M, et al. Pleiotropic effects of the 8.1 HLA haplotype in patients with autoimmune myasthenia gravis and thymus hyperplasia. *Proc Natl Acad Sci* U S A. 2004;101:15464-15469.

158. Giraud M, Beaurain G, Eymard B, Tranchant C, Gajdos P, Garchon HJ. Genetic control of autoantibody expression in autoimmune myasthenia gravis: role of the self-antigen and of HLA-linked loci. *Genes Immun.* 2004;5:398-404.

159. Vernino S, Auger RG, Emslie-Smith AM, Harper CM, Lennon VA. Myasthenia, thymoma, presynaptic antibodies, and a continuum of neuromuscular hyperexcitability. *Neurology.* 1999;53:1233-1239.

160. Pande R, Leis AA. Myasthenia gravis, thymoma, intestinal pseudo-obstruction, and neuronal nicotinic acetylcholine receptor antibody. *Muscle Nerve.* 1999;22:1600-1602.

Dysregulation of the immune system in human Myasthenia Gravis: Possible role in pathogenesis

Frédérique Truffault, Rozen Le Panse, Jacky Bismuth,

Nicole Kerlero de Rosbo PhD, and Sonia Berrih-Aknin PhD

1. INTRODUCTION

Myasthenia Gravis (MG) is an autoimmune disease mediated by antibodies directed to molecules at the neuromuscular junction: antibodies to acetylcholine receptor (AChR) are found in 85% of patients and antibodies against muscle-specific kinase (MuSK) in about 5% of patients (1). These antibodies are highly specific for MG, since they are almost never observed in other autoimmune or neurological diseases or in healthy subjects (2). Anti-AChR antibodies are highly pathogenic. Indeed, injection of the immunoglobulin (Ig) fraction from MG serum containing anti-AChR antibodies induces an experimental form of MG in susceptible laboratory animals (3). Similar results have also been obtained with experimentally raised monoclonal anti-AChR antibodies (4). More recently, animals immunized with the ectodomain of MuSK showed MG-like muscle weakness with a reduction of AChR clustering at the neuromuscular junction (5). Therefore, autoantibodies to AChR and MuSK are clearly key pathogenic factors in these forms of myasthenia, although this does not exclude the possible involvement of other pathogenic components. The mechanisms of action of these antibodies have been studied and it was shown that binding of anti-AChR antibodies to their receptors impairs the neuromuscular transmission essentially by internalization of the AChR and its complement- dependent degradation (6). MG associated with anti-MuSK antibodies was described relatively recently (7) and, as yet, there is only a few publications on this specific form of the disease; while their mechanism of action is not understood, anti-MuSK antibodies appear to have functional effects by inhibiting AChR clustering (5) and decreasing the proliferation of muscle cells *in vitro* (8).

Pathogenic mechanisms in human MG implicate not only the muscle as the target of the autoimmune response, but also the thymus, which is very frequently abnormal. Two major pathologies are common: thymic hyperplasia characterized by the presence of germinal centers (GC) and found in more than 60% of the early-onset patients, and thymoma, tumors of thymic epithelial cells infiltrated with thymocytes, that are present in the older patients (over 40 years old) (9). While the percentage of patients with thymic hyperplasia appears to vary considerably between studies, it should be noted that treatments such as administration of corticosteroids reduce the size and number of germinal centers dramatically (10); discrepant results could therefore be due to the inclusion or exclusion of corticosteroid-treated patients in the cohorts studied. Whether or not other types of therapy, such as plasmapheresis or IVIg administration have an effect on thymic hyperplasia has not been described.

The mechanisms that control the onset of the disease and the initiation of autoantibody production are still unknown. However, it is clear that both genetic predisposition and triggering environmental factors are involved, as also likely in other autoimmune diseases (11). Indeed, there is a high percentage of disease-discordant pairs in monozygotic twins demonstrating the central role of environmental factors in the etiology of MG (12), (13), and the genetic predisposition has been clearly demonstrated, namely HLA genes. It was shown that MG is placed under the control of at least three distinct genes: (1) a class II predisposing gene in the 8.1 ancestral haplotype in early onset female patients with thymic hyperplasia; (2) a thymoma-associated class II allele on the DQB1*0604 haplotype; and (3) a protective allele DR1 (14). See Chapter 7 for a detailed genetic analysis of MG.

Since the studies performed in MG patients are inevitably performed after the onset of the disease, it is difficult to discriminate between the factors involved in the causes and consequences of the autoimmune response. In addition, there is no spontaneous model of myasthenia in rodents. The classical model is based on immunization with torpedo AChR in complete Freund Adjuvant (CFA) to induce a specific response to AChR in an inflammatory environment. Therefore, these models, which are very useful to study the mechanisms downstream of the production of antibodies, are not relevant to the study of the upstream events and triggering factors. The general strategy to progress in the understanding of the pathophysiological mechanisms of MG is to identify molecular events associated with the triggering of the disease and to investigate their potential causal effects in relevant models.

The aim of this publication is to review the dys regulation of the immune system in human MG and to argue their potential role in the pathogenic mechanisms. We will first examine the involvement of the thymus in the pathogenicity of MG. Since Chapter 8 is dedicated to thymoma pathology, this chapter will focus almost exclusively on thymic hyperplasia and the pathological mechanisms associated with its development. We will detail the specific anti-AChR response and the systemic dysregulation of the immune system including the different cell types such as T, B, Treg, thymic epithelial cells as well as pro-inflammatory and anti-viral environments. Finally we will discuss the potential defects of tolerance mechanisms.

2. IMPLICATION OF THE THYMUS IN MG

2.1. Thymic remodeling in subgroups of MG patients

While adult normal thymuses almost never show germinal centers, the thymus in the young female MG patients with anti-AChR antibodies is often filled with germinal centers indicating an active immune response (10). Interestingly, germinal centers could also be found in the target organs in many other autoimmune diseases, such as synovial tissue in rheumatoid arthritis (15) or thyroid in chronic thyroiditis (16). The observation that these germinal centers are considerably smaller and less numerous in corticosteroid-treated MG patients, (Figure 1) in parallel with clinical improvement, brings an additional argument in favor of their role in pathogenesis.

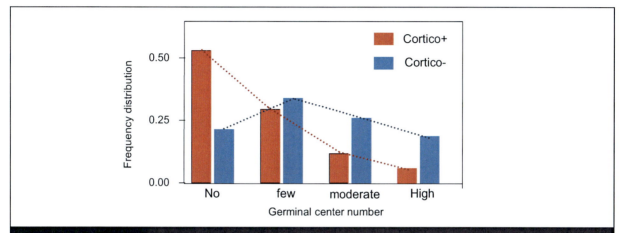

Figure 1: corticotherapy reduces the number of germinal centers in the thymus of MG patients. Corticosteroid treated patients (n=34) have less germinal centers than untreated patients (n=112). $X^2 = 14.21$, p<0.003

There is a relationship between thymus pathology and the anti-AChR antibody titer. Indeed, patients with elevated AChR antibody titers had hyperplastic thymuses, while changes in thymic histology in patients with low or negative antibody titers are limited (17). Confirming this observation, Leite et al. showed that approximately 75% thymic samples from seronegative MG patients (MuSK-neg/AChR-neg) had lymph node-type infiltrates similar to those in AChR+ patients, but with fewer germinal centers (18). However, very recently, it appeared that these seronegative MG patients may have low-affinity anti-AChR antibodies (19), supporting further a relationship between thymic changes and anti-AChR antibodies. The presence of AChR has been searched in the thymus and demonstrated in the different thymic cell types (20, 21). However, the amount of the different AChR subunits, analyzed at the mRNA level, differs from one cell type to another: myoid cells display a high expression of all AChR subunits, while the expression is intermediate in TEC and very low in thymocytes (22).

It is worth mentioning that the role played by the thymus in patients with anti-AChR antibodies is not discernible in patients with anti-MuSK antibodies. Indeed, in MuSK-MG patients, histologic alterations are minimal, an observation which argues against an intrathymic disease pathogenesis (23). In the series of 14 MuSK-MG patients studied by Leite et al, 4 of the thymuses had rare small germinal centers, but overall they were not different from age-matched controls (18). Interestingly, MuSK is expressed in the thymus both in myoid and TEC as are the AChR subunits (22), suggesting that the presence of the antigen in the thymus is not sufficient to induce an autoimmune response. Indeed, our previous work on transgenic mice overexpressing beta-galactosidase in the thymus indicated that the level of tolerance to an antigen expressed in the thymus is highly dependent upon its level of expression (24).

2.2. Implication of the thymus in the anti-AChR autoimmune response

Many reports argue for a specific role of the thymus in the anti-AChR response. These arguments are summarized in Table I.

2.2.1. Anti-AChR T-cell response

T cells isolated from hyperplastic MG thymus gave significantly higher and more consistent responses to AChR than parallel cultures of autologous blood cells, whereas responses to purified protein derivative of Mycobacterium, as a positive control for immune responses in general, showed an opposite trend (25). Similarly, in a series of 10 MG patients undergoing thymectomy, all 10 thymuses contained T lymphocytes reactive against AChR, whereas only 3 of the 10 patients showed significant T cell responses to AChR in the peripheral immune compartment (blood), (26). These results could be explained by a preferential localization of AChR-reactive T cells in the hyperplastic MG thymus and a dilution of the thymic pathogenic cells in the periphery.

2.2.2. Anti-AChR B-cell response

Examination of the production of anti-AChR antibodies by B cells show that the anti-AChR specific production is much higher in the thymus than in the periphery. Fujii et al. who examined the *in vitro* production of anti-AChR antibodies in 13 MG patients (27), reported that the specific activity of the spontaneously produced IgG (anti-AChR/total IgG) was about 10-fold higher in the thymus than in bone marrow, peripheral blood, or lymph node cell cultures. Similar results were described by Yoshikawa et al. (28). In addition, patients whose thymic and peripheral blood B cells secrete antibodies to AChR *in vitro* have a greater decrease than the non-secretors in their need for Mestinon over the 60 months of follow-up after thymectomy, suggesting a relationship between the production of antibodies by thymic cells and clinical status (29). However, since there is no abrupt decrease in anti-AChR antibody titer after thymectomy (30), it is reasonable to propose that extra-thymic B cells contribute also significantly to the anti-AChR antibodies in the serum.

Table I: Comparison of anti-AChR B and T cell responses in the thymus and periphery

	Thymus	Periphery	Ref
Anti-AChR T cell response	Higher for AChR than PPD	Higher for PPD than for AChR	(25)
Anti-AChR T cell response	10/10	3/10	(26)
Serum level of anti-AChR antibodies	Correlation with thymus pathology	No Correlation with CD4/CD8 ratio	(17)
In vitro anti-AChR antibodies	High specific activity	Low specific activity	27),(28), (31)
In vitro anti-AChR antibodies	Up-regulation by TEC	No regulation by TEC	(32)

Several other characteristics of anti-AChR antibody production by thymic cells have been demonstrated:

1. Thymic cell secretion of anti-AChR antibodies parallels serum antibody levels, emphasizing a direct role of the thymus in anti-AChR antibody synthesis (33).
2. Thymic cell secretion of anti-AChR antibodies does not need any polyclonal stimulation. Indeed, while polyclonal activation increases significantly the whole production of Ig by thymic B cells, it does not induce changes in the anti-AChR antibody titer (34) ;
3. Specific anti-AChR antibody production by thymic B cells from MG patients, increases upon contact with thymic epithelial cells, while this does not occur with peripheral B cells (32).
4. Cells isolated from the thymus of patients treated with corticosteroids make significantly less anti-AChR antibodies than cells of untreated patients (33).

Altogether, it appears that the thymus of MG patients is one major site of anti-AChR antibody production, in correlation with clinical status and therapeutics. These results support a preferential localization of AChR B and T cells in the hyperplastic MG thymus and probably a dilution of these thymic pathogenic cells in the periphery. However, these results do not let know whether the initial interaction between naïve T cells and AChR-presenting cells occurred in the thymus or in the periphery.

2.3. Thymic abnormalities: cause or consequence of the autoimmune response?

Although the thymus is hyperplastic in many young female MG patients, the question of whether it is involved at an early step of the disease is difficult to answer. Figure 2 summarizes the various components of the immune system shown to be altered in MG and the presumable cascade of events leading to muscle damage.

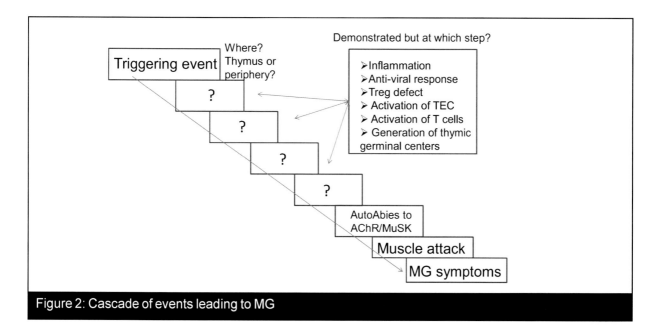

Figure 2: Cascade of events leading to MG

The arguments suggesting that thymic events are implicated in the first or early-intermediate steps in the pathological process are as follows:

1. In animal models induced by immunization with AChR in CFA, the resulting anti-AChR response is not associated with thymic pathology (35), while in animals that develop MG spontaneously, i.e. dogs and cats, may present with abnormal thymuses (36). Anti-AChR antibodies are therefore unlikely to be the causal factor of thymic abnormalities. However, we cannot exclude that because of intrinsic differences between the thymus of rodents and humans, the pathogenic antibodies might reach the human thymus but would not reach the murine thymus.

2. When implanted into immunodeficient mice, human MG thymic tissue or cells induce the formation of antibodies against AChR in the recipients and loss of AChR at the muscle endplates (37) (38), demonstrating that MG thymus contains all the components required for the anti-AChR autoimmune response.

3. Thymectomy is much more beneficial when carried out shortly after onset of clinical symptoms, suggesting that the pathogenic cells are first in the thymus, and then disseminate to the periphery (39).

4. Many of the immune defects observed in MG patients are more clearly detectable in the thymus than in the periphery (40). Thus it seems that pathogenic reactions are more diluted in the periphery than in the thymus.

5. Thymectomy induces changes in the periphery, for example activation molecules, that tend towards normal values (such as soluble IL-2R) in correlation with improvement of clinical symptoms (41).

It is quite reasonable to propose that the autoimmune response could be initiated in the thymus through the effect of a triggering agent that would upregulate AChR expression and induce an inflammatory environment concomitantly.

3. SYSTEMIC ACTIVATION OF THE IMMUNE SYSTEM

3.1. T cells : Th subsets and markers of activation

Expression of cytokines specific to Th subsets has been analyzed at the mRNA level in blood mononuclear cells (MNC). MG patients had elevated numbers of MNC expressing IFN-gamma and IL-4, indicating that both Th1 and Th2 cells are involved in MG pathogenic mechanisms. The expression of these cytokines increased further upon culture of MNC from MG patients in the presence of AChR. An AChR-induced upregulation of TGF-beta was observed in thymectomized patients. rTGF-beta suppressed AChR-induced upregulation of pro-inflammatory cytokines but not IL-10. These results indicate that MG patients have high numbers of *in vivo*-activated and organ-specific antigen-responsive Th1- and Th2-like cells expressing IFN-gamma and IL-4 mRNA, respectively. Upregulation of TGF-beta in MG after thymectomy suggests that TGF-beta has favorable effects in MG (42). Since TGF-beta is involved in Treg generation, this result raises the role of Treg in MG pathogenesis; this point is addressed later. The implication of Th1 cells has also been suggested by the increased number of CXCR3+ cells in the thymus and in CD4+ peripheral cells (43). CXCR3 was also increased in EAMG, suggesting that CXCR3 increase results from the immunization and inflammation processes. Interestingly, molecules inhibiting the binding of the CXCR3 ligand, CXCL10, to its receptor limit the severity of MG, indicating that this could be a new therapeutic approach (44).

A thymocyte subpopulation with strong Fas expression (Fas(hi)) was markedly increased in AChR-MG patients compared to controls. Fas(hi) thymocytes were enriched in activated cells, expressing CD25 (IL-2 receptor alpha subunit) or HLA-DR, showed intermediate CD3 expression, and produced high level of IL-4, suggesting they display a Th2 phenotype. These results indicate that Fas(hi) thymocytes, which accumulate in MG patients with anti-AChR antibodies, could be involved in the AChR-targeted autoimmune response developing in the thymus (40).

T(FH) subset is clearly distinguishable from Th1 and Th2 cells by several criteria, including chemokine receptor expression (CXCR5), location/migration (B cell follicles), and function (B cell help) (45). It appears that this subset is also involved in MG. Indeed, MG patients showed a significantly higher frequency of CXCR5+ CD4+ T cells in the peripheral blood compared with the control group. In addition, the frequency of CXCR5+ CD4+ T cells correlated with disease severity. This subset was also increased in MG patients positive for other autoantibodies together with anti-AChR antibodies compared to those having only anti-AChR antibodies. After thymectomy plus glucorticoids, the CXCR5+ CD4+ T cell percentage decreased gradually to the control level with a significant inverse correlation between the CXCR5+ CD4+ T cell frequency and duration of the therapy (46). Interestingly, major expansions in diverse Vbeta among CD4+ T cells were associated with the CD57+CXCR5+ subset. Furthermore, the expression of markers for activation on these cells, lymphocyte trafficking and B cell-activating ability persisted for more than 3 years, strengthening the hypothesis of a chronic activation. Thus, these data provide evidence for persistent clonally expanded CD4+ B helper T cell populations in the blood of MG patients (47).

Altogether, these data support strongly that in MG disease, Th1, Th2 and T(FH) are involved. Accordingly, several markers of activation related to T-cell function have been associated with MG. Thymic lymphocytes from MG patients have an enhanced sensitivity to recombinant interleukin-2 (48). We showed that serum levels of soluble IL-2R (sIL-2R) were increased in about a third of patients before thymectomy and even more so in severely affected patients. Sequential sampling after thymectomy indicated a significant and progressive decline of sIL-2R levels within two years after surgery, which correlated with clinical improvement or remission (41). In addition, increased sIL-2R titers were significantly associated with generalized and bulbar MG disease, while ocular cases were not different from controls (49), indicating that sIL-2R is a marker of MG severity. MG patients have also higher serum levels of sICAM-1, sVCAM-1 and sTNF-R II than healthy control individuals, and plasmapheresis can induce a substantial decrease in serum levels of sICAM-1 and sVCAM-1 together with a decrease in anti-AChR Ab titer. Patients with high circulating anti- AChR Ab titer had higher serum levels of sICAM-1 and sVCAM-1 than patients with low anti- AChR Ab titer, suggesting a systemic activation of the immune response which is more pronounced in patients with high circulating anti-AChR Ab titer (50).

3.2. B cells: markers of activation and Ig production

We have shown that MG thymus contains B cells expressing high levels of activation markers, such as CD71, 4F2, CD23, and B8.7, indicating that a marked proportion of them are activated. Moreover, addition of B-cell growth factor 12kDa and, to a lesser extent, of rIL-2 induces a spontaneous proliferation of these B-cell populations *in vitro* (34). *In situ* hybridization analysis of MG thymus with the six VH and the 4 VK human family probes has shown that the thymic B-cell repertoire closely reflects the polyclonal VH and the VK family usage of normal peripheral blood lymphocytes, with a preferential utilization of VH3, VK1 and VK3 (51). Altogether, these results suggest that B cells from MG thymus are polyclonal and activated. This assumption was confirmed more recently by microarray analysis of MG thymus which revealed an increased expression in hyperplastic MG thymus of all immunoglobulins (Ig) genes spotted on the array (23 IgL and 11 IgH), as compared to age- and sex-matched healthy control thymus (10). In addition, the activation of B cells was not limited to the thymus since soluble CD23 (sCD23) was significantly raised in MG sera (52). Soluble CD23 (sCD23) reflects B-cell activation and is generally increased by interleukin-4 (IL-4) and decreased by interferon-gamma (IFN-gamma). Therefore, variations in sCD23 may reflect enhanced Th2 activity. The serum B-cell activating factor (BAFF) levels were also analyzed in MG patients and were shown to be significantly higher than those of all the control subjects (53), supporting again a high activation level of B cells from MG patients.

In addition, in the periphery, the total Ig production is apparently higher in MG patients than in age-matched healthy control individuals (28), suggesting that the increase in Ig synthesis is not due only to anti-AChR antibodies. In this context, antibodies against several autoantigens other than AChR have been detected in MG patients, in particular muscle-cell antigens, such as titin or ryanodine receptor (54).

Altogether, the higher markers of activation consistently observed in MG patients support the hypothesis of a systemic and chronic activation that involves the different T helper subsets (Th1, Th2 and T (FH)) as well as B cells. These data raise the potential defects of immunoregulation in MG patients that will be discussed later.

The observation that activation is not restricted to AChR specific T and B cells raise at least two possibilities. 1) Through overactivation of the immune system by an environmental factor, many T cells are activated inducing in turn production of antibodies by B cells, among which some are specific to AChR. Taking into account the high pathogenicity of anti-AChR antibodies, this leads to the induction of MG; and 2) Upon response to an infectious agent, viral or bacterial, AChR-reactive T cells may be selected through molecular mimicry. The bystander effect induced by the specific immune response could secondarily recruit many other T and B cells with diverse specificities.

3.3. Inflammatory and anti-viral signatures

Our DNA microarray analysis has indicated that most genes regulated by the pro-inflammatory cytokine, interferon (IFN)-gamma (or IFN-II), are increased in MG thymic hyperplasia, including genes encoding MHC, beta2 microglobulin, and inflammatory cytokines such as CXCL10 (55). This signature was also observed in the thymus of seronegative MG patients although at a lower extent (10), suggesting similar pathogenic mechanism in this subgroup of patients. The recent findings that seronegative MG patients have also thymic changes, albeit moderate, and display low-affinity anti-AChR antibodies support this hypothesis (18, 19).

The same technology has revealed a clear IFN-I signature in the hyperplastic MG thymus (10). Such a signature being generally associated with an anti-viral reaction, these results raise the possibility that a viral agent played a role in the triggering of the autoimmune reaction. This hypothesis is under investigation not only in MG but also in several other autoimmune diseases. Indeed, the study of animal models has clearly shown that infections may trigger autoimmune diseases, as in the case of Coxsackie B4 virus in type I diabetes and the encephalomyocarditis virus in autoimmune myositis, two models in which viruses are thought to act by increasing immunogenicity of autoantigens secondary to local inflammation. It is possible that unknown viruses may be at the origin of a number of chronic autoimmune diseases, as illustrated by the data incriminating IFN-alpha in the pathophysiology of type I diabetes, systemic lupus erythematosus, or MG (11).

Major attention has recently been drawn to Toll-like receptors (TLRs) that recognize conserved molecular patterns present on pathogens, including bacteria, viruses, fungi and protozoa. Pathogen recognition *via* TLRs activates the innate as well as the adaptive immune responses. Very few studies have explored the potential role of TLR in MG. In one study, the expression of TLRs 2 to 5 was studied in 37 thymuses from MG patients. TLR4 mRNA levels were significantly greater in thymitis (hyperplasia with diffuse B-cell infiltration) and involuted thymus than in germinal center hyperplasia and thymoma. Immunohistochemistry and confocal microscopy showed TLR4 protein mostly on epitheliomorphic (cytokeratin-positive) cells located in close association with clusters of AChR-positive myoid cells in thymic medulla, as well as at the interface between cortical and medullary areas. It is possible that in a subgroup of MG patients, an exogenous or endogenous danger signal may activate the innate immune system and give rise to TLR4-mediated mechanisms contributing to autoimmunity (56).

4. POTENTIAL DEFECTS OF TOLERANCE MECHANISMS IN MG: ROLE OF AIRE AND FOXP3

The thymus plays a major role in the development of T cells and in mechanisms of central tolerance. Indeed, hematopoietic stem cells arising from the bone marrow evolve to mature T cells through mechanisms of thymic selection during which most autoreactive T cells are eliminated and regulatory T cells (Treg cells) are generated. These processes occur via interactions of developing thymocytes with thymic dendritic and epithelial cells. Therefore, these thymic stromal cell populations play a central role in the elimination of autoreactive cells and their functional defects could allow the escape of autoreactive T cells. In an inflammatory environment, such observed in MG thymus, these autoreactive T cells could then be activated and lead to autoimmunity.

4.1. Alteration in thymic stromal cells in MG

4.1.1. Dendritic cells in MG

Very few studies on dendritic cells (DC) in MG patients have been reported. Nagane et al. showed that, in MG thymus, mature DCs were numerous in non-medullary areas, such as the subcapsular/outer cortex, around the germinal centers and in extralobular connective tissue, particularly around blood vessels. They suggested that DCs may migrate into the hyperplastic thymus from the vascular system and present self-antigens, thereby promoting the priming and/or boosting of potentially autoreactive T cells against AChR (57). Another study suggested that DC-induced activation of autologous T cells in the periphery is more pronounced in MG than in healthy controls. This was associated with an increased production of both Th1 (IFN-gamma) and Th2 (IL-10 and IL-4) cytokines by T cells (58). The limited number of studies on DC in MG does not allow to conclude on their implication in MG and the role of these cells deserves further investigation.

4.1.2. Thymic epithelial cells (TECs) in MG

TECs play a major role in the differentiation of T cells *via* direct contact and cytokine production. For example, normal TEC produce IL-1 and IL-6 that are important for regulation of thymopoiesis but these two cytokines are also known to be involved in inflammatory reactions

154

Table II: Summary of the literature data on the status of Treg cells in MG patients

	Number of CD4+ CD25+ cells	Expression of FoxP3 in CD4CD25+ cells	Function of TReg	
PBMC	No change even after thymectomy			(74)
PBMC	Increase in clinically stable patients and after thymectomy			(75)
Thymus	No change	mRNA decrease in CD4+CD25+ cells	Defective	(68)
Thymoma	Decrease in thymoma, No change in periphery			(76)
PBMC	No change		No defect	(69)
Thymus and PBMC	Decrease in untreated patients, and normal in immunosuppressed patients			(70)
Thymus/ Thymoma	Normal in hyperplasia, reduced in thymoma			(65)
Thymus/ Thymoma	No change			(77)
PBMC	Decrease			(78)
PBMC	No change	Decrease of FoxP3 in CD4CD25+ cells	Defective	(71)
PBMC	No change	No change	Defective	(72)

(59) (60). We showed that MG TECs present a striking IL-6 overproduction as compared to controls when stimulated by exogenous signals such as LPS and cytokines (IL-1 beta, TNF-alpha). Our study of IL-1 production by MG TEC yielded similar data; indeed, we demonstrated that TEC from hyperplastic thymuses spontaneously produce higher amounts of IL-1 than control TECs. In addition, we observed an association between the level of hyperplasia and *in vitro* IL-1 production, suggesting a role for IL-1 in the expansion of thymic lymphoid follicles (61). Interestingly, increased IL-1 production by TEC was observed with a physiological signal such as the syngeneic lympho-epithelial cell contact, suggesting that interactions between thymocytes and TEC could stimulate production of inflammatory cytokines by TEC. Other published data confirm the activation status of TEC, in particular Colombara et al. showed that TEC from MG patients not only overproduce IL-6 but also RANTES. In addition, MG-TEC basally overexpress genes coding for p38 and ERK1/2 MAPKs and for components of their signaling pathways. Pharmacological blockage with specific inhibitors confirmed their role in the control of IL-6 and RANTES gene expression (62). Overexpresion of chemokines by TEC from MG patients was also recently shown for CXCL13 (10). Since CXCL13 attracts B

cells efficiently, these results suggest that a high CXCL13 production by TEC could be responsible, at least in part, for germinal center formation in MG thymus.

The demonstration of an overproduction of cytokines and chemokines by MG TECs *in vitro* is quite surprising since TEC are usually several days in culture before analysis. Therefore, altogether, these results suggest that TECs remain in an activated state even when taken away from the activated thymic microenvironment. This raises the possibility that the functional changes in MG TEC are due to a genetic background or to some epigenetic events that occur in vivo and persist *in vitro*.

Another potential role of TECs in tolerance mechanisms is through their relationship with the transcription factor AIRE. Medullary TECs express a diverse set of genes coding for parenchymal organ specific proteins, regulated by the transcription factor, AIRE (63). This phenomenon, termed promiscuous gene expression, has led to the reconsideration of the role of the thymus in central T-cell tolerance to self-antigens and, therefore, in prevention of autoimmunity (64). A possible involvement of AIRE in the development of MG was suggested by the observation that medullary TECs isolated from AIRE-deficient mice contain much lower levels of RNA transcripts for AChR-alpha subunit than their wild-type counterparts (65). A recent study has demonstrated *ex vivo* and through a transactivation assay that AIRE modulates AChR-alpha mRNA levels in human medullary TECs (66). These findings reveal a critical function of AIRE in regulating quantitative expression of this auto-antigen in the thymus, suggesting that AIRE contributes to the threshold for self-tolerance versus autoimmunity. According to this assumption, one would expect a low level of AIRE and of AChR-alpha in MG thymus. However, this hypothesis is quite difficult to confirm since MG thymus is highly activated at the time when thymic tissue is available for investigation through thymectomy, i.e. often a long time after disease onset. Indeed, in the study by Scarpino et al., no difference in expression of AChR and AIRE was observed between healthy and hyperplastic thymuses (65). However, taking into account the major changes in the hyperplasic thymus, one could not exclude that the levels of AIRE and AChR were very low before the triggering event, therefore favoring the escape of autoreactive clones.

4.2. Treg cells

4.2.1. Functional defect in Treg cells from MG patients

CD4C25+ Treg cells have a major role in the control of the autoimmune response, and more generally in the immune response (67). Qualitative or quantitative defects of Treg cells has been demonstrated in many autoimmune diseases. Table II summarizes observations so far made for Treg cells in MG. Thus, the number of Treg cells does not appear to be significantly altered according to the markers CD4+CD25+. We could not detect any changes in the number of CD4+CD25+ or CD4+CD25hi cells in MG thymus (68). In contrast, another group observed a decrease in the number of peripheral CD4+CD25+ T cells in MG (69); however, in another study, the same team reported that there was no difference in peripheral Treg-cell numbers between MG patients and healthy individuals, indicating, that if there are changes in the number of Treg in MG patients, these changes must be very limited (70). However, more recently, Zhang et al. showed that, while the percentage of CD4+CD25+ cells was not changed in MG patients, FoxP3 was dramatically down-regulated in peripheral CD4+CD25+ cells at both mRNA and protein expression levels (71). This discordance could be explained by technical differences, such as the use of anti-FoxP3 antibodies that recognize different epitopes, but it could also be due to biological differences related to different genetic backgrounds of the cohorts tested. Indeed, the study by Zhang et al. was carried out on Chinese patients who have a genetic background clearly different from that of Caucasian patients included in the other studies.

If the markers of Treg cells are still a matter of debate in MG patients, their function appears to be clearly defective. We showed that Treg cells from MG thymus have a defect in their suppressive function when co-cultured with autologous CD4+CD25- T cells (68). This result was confirmed by Zhang et al. (71), and more recently by Luther et al. using peripheral blood cells (72). To address the possibility that this defect may be attributable to the presence of a high number of activated effector cells in the isolated Treg population, we analyzed the expression of CD127, the IL-7 receptor, recently shown to discriminate between regulatory and effector function (73), in CD25-expressing T-cells. MG and control thymocytes did not differ in their CD127 expression, both in CD25+ and CD25++ cells. These results indicate that the defect in suppressive activity of thymic Treg cells in MG patients is probably not due to an excess of effector cells among the CD4+CD25+ population.

4.2.2. Relationship between defect of Treg cells and inflammatory events

Since immunological investigations are, perforce, carried out in MG patients when the disease is well established, it is not clear if, in individuals who develop MG, the Treg cells were defective before or after the disease-triggering event. It is possible that this defect is genetically or epigenetically predetermined, so that, in case of inflammation, the defective Treg cells would be unable to neutralize the inflammatory environment. However, it is also possible that the inflammatory environment influences the functional activity of the Treg cells.

Inflammatory cytokines have been demonstrated to inhibit generation of Treg cells. Indeed, IL-6, an acute phase protein induced during inflammation was shown to inhibit the generation of Foxp3+ Treg cells induced by TGF-beta (79). More recently, it was shown that Treg cells stimulated with TGF-beta exhibit a sustained expression of FoxP3 while in the presence of TGF-beta, IL-6 alone or in combination with IL-1 and IL-23 markedly downregulated FoxP3 expression and increased IL-17 production. Therefore, the Treg program appears to be turned off by IL-6, and Treg cells can be reprogrammed to Th17 in the presence of TGF-beta and IL-6 (80). IL-6, which abrogates suppression by Treg cells, also drives Th17 differentiation in naive cells when paired with IL-1beta and IL-23 in human. Close relationship between CD4+FOXP3+ regulatory Treg cells and proinflammatory IL-17-producing T cells expressing the lineage-specific transcription factor ROR gamma t was recently confirmed by the unexpected finding that human memory FoxP3+ Treg cells secrete IL-17 *ex vivo* and constitutively express ROR gamma t (81). However, this finding is observed essentially in the periphery since it was recently shown that the normal human thymus does not contain IL-17–producing Treg cells (82). In the context described above, whereby MG TEC overproduce IL-6 and IL-1, one could assume that such an environment could modify the balance between functional Treg cells, and inflammatory cells, namely Th17 cells, or, as suggested above, that Treg cells themselves could be driven to secrete the pro-inflammatory IL-17. This aspect needs further investigation.

Therapies such as corticoids or immune suppressors can normalize Treg-cell function in MG (83), (72) suggesting that Treg cells are probably under the influence of the inflammatory environment and that it is necessary to reduce the inflammation to turn them functional again.

5. CONCLUSION

The data presented in this manuscript suggest strongly that patients with MG present several dysregulations of their immune system. We propose that a primary event of yet unknown origin could cause inflammation in the thymus that would induce critical changes leading to MG.

The presence of the autoantigen AChR in the thymus, its high immunogenicity, and the possible regulation of its expression by pro-inflammatory cytokines make this molecule a potential autoimmune target in this highly activated site, which would perpetuate the autoimmune and inflammatory response. Why AChR expressed in the thymus is not properly tolerated in MG patients is not clear. Both interferon-gamma and AIRE are able to regulate AChR-alpha, and a defect of tolerance mechanism would suggest defect of AIRE in MG thymus before the onset of the disease. Since inflammation alters the expression of many genes including AIRE, this hypothesis will be very difficult to prove, since thymic tissues are only available after the onset of the disease.

The initial event(s) leading to an inflammatory response in the thymus could then trigger an increased *in situ* production of various cytokines and chemokines, which in turn would attract B and T cells from the periphery. Whether these cells are already activated when they reach the thymus is not clear. However, since the level of activation of these cells in the thymus is much higher than it is in the periphery (40, 48), we believe that the ongoing activation of the cells occurs in the thymus.

Once T cells are activated in the thymus, one could expect their activation status to be regulated by Treg cells, but, since in MG Treg cells are non-functional, the level of activation and inflammation remains very high. The Treg defect could be linked to the high IL-1 and IL-6 production by MG TEC, since FoxP3(+) cells were shown to be driven to secrete IL-17 under inflammatory conditions. In this context, the upstream question is why TEC overproduce pro-inflammatory cytokines. The triggering event likely contributes to this overproduction, but it is likely that TECs from MG patients have the genetic background that allows a continuous and chronic activation status. Indeed, data showing that TECs kept a high activation status for at least two weeks *in vitro* away from the thymic environment, suggest epigenetic changes in these cells, which deserve further investigation.

In conclusion, we propose that the primary triggering event induces inflammation of the thymus that remains chronic because of defective Treg cells. Therefore, the defect of Treg cells is a major factor that may contribute to the predisposition to MG. The causes of this defect and the potential role of TECs need further investigation.

REFERENCES

1. Evoli, A. 2006. Clinical aspects of neuromuscular transmission disorders. *Acta Neurol Scand Suppl* 183:8-11.

2. Howard, F. M., Jr., V. A. Lennon, J. Finley, J. Matsumoto, and L. R. Elveback. 1987. Clinical correlations of antibodies that bind, block, or modulate human acetylcholine receptors in myasthenia gravis. *Ann N Y Acad Sci* 505:526-538.

3. Lindstrom, J. M., A. G. Engel, M. E. Seybold, V. A. Lennon, and E. H. Lambert. 1976. Pathological mechanisms in experimental autoimmune myasthenia gravis. II. Passive transfer of experimental autoimmune myasthenia gravis in rats with anti-acetylcholine recepotr antibodics. *J Exp Med* 144:739-753.

4. Richman, D. P., C. M. Gomez, P. W. Berman, S. A. Burres, F. W. Fitch, and B. G. Arnason. 1980. Monoclonal anti-acetylcholine receptor antibodies can cause experimental myasthenia. *Nature* 286:738-739.

5. Shigemoto, K., S. Kubo, N. Maruyama, N. Hato, H. Yamada, C. Jie, N. Kobayashi, K. Mominoki, Y. Abe, N. Ueda, and S. Matsuda. 2006. Induction of myasthenia by immunization against muscle-specific kinase. *J Clin Invest* 116:1016-1024.

6. Engel, A. G., and G. Fumagalli. 1982. Mechanisms of acetylcholine receptor loss from the neuromuscular junction. *Ciba Found Symp*:197-224.

7. Hoch, W., J. McConville, S. Helms, J. Newsom-Davis, A. Melms, and A. Vincent. 2001. Auto-antibodies to the receptor tyrosine kinase MuSK in patients with myasthenia gravis without acetylcholine receptor antibodies. *Nat Med* 7:365-368.

8. Boneva, N., M. Frenkian-Cuvelier, J. Bidault, T. Brenner, and S. Berrih-Aknin. 2006. Major pathogenic effects of anti-MuSK antibodies in Myasthenia Gravis. *J Neuroimmunol* 177:119-131.

9. Levine, G. D., and J. Rosai. 1978. Thymic hyperplasia and neoplasia: a review of current concepts. *Hum Pathol* 9:495-515.

10. Meraouna, A., G. Cizeron-Clairac, R. L. Panse, J. Bismuth, F. Truffault, C. Tallaksen, and S. Berrih-Aknin. 2006. The chemokine CXCL13 is a key molecule in autoimmune myasthenia gravis. *Blood* 108:432-440.

11. Bach, J. F. 2005. Infections and autoimmune diseases. J Autoimmun 25 Suppl:74-80.

12. Namba, T., M. S. Shapiro, N. G. Brunner, and D. Grob. 1971. Myasthenia gravis occurring in twins. *J Neurol Neurosurg Psychiatry* 34:531-534.

13. Agafonov, B. V., V. G. Tsuman, D. I. Shagal, O. P. Sidorova, L. G. Sibiriakova, L. L. Lebedeva, A. E. Nalivkin, and S. Fialkovskii. 1997. [Twin studies of myasthenia]. *Zh Nevrol Psikhiatr Im S S Korsakova* 97:18-21.

14. Vieira, M. L., S. Caillat Zucman, P. Gajdos, S. Cohen Kaminsky, A. Casteur, and J. F. Bach. 1993. Identification by genomic typing of non-DR3 HLA class II genes associated with myasthenia gravis. *J-Neuroimmunol* 47:115-122.

15. Berek, C., and H. J. Kim. 1997. B-cell activation and development within chronically inflamed synovium in rheumatoid and reactive arthritis. Semin Immunol 9:261-268.

16. Kasajima, T., M. Yamakawa, and Y. Imai. 1987. Immunohistochemical study of intrathyroidal lymph follicles. *Clin Immunol Immunopathol* 43:117-128.

17. Berrih, S., E. Morel, C. Gaud, F. Raimond, H. Le Brigand, and J. F. Bach. 1984. Anti-AChR antibodies, thymic histology, and T cell subsets in myasthenia gravis. *Neurology* 34:66-71.

18. Leite, M. I., P. Strobel, M. Jones, K. Micklem, R. Moritz, R. Gold, E. H. Niks, S. Berrih-Aknin, F. Scaravilli, A. Canelhas, A. Marx, J. Newsom-Davis, N. Willcox, and A. Vincent. 2005. Fewer thymic changes in MuSK antibody-positive than in MuSK antibody-negative MG. *Ann Neurol* 57:444-448.

19. Leite, M. I., S. Jacob, S. Viegas, J. Cossins, L. Clover, B. P. Morgan, D. Beeson, N. Willcox, and A. Vincent. 2008. IgG1 antibodies to acetylcholine receptors in 'seronegative' myasthenia gravis. *Brain* 131:1940-1952.

20. Wakkach, A., T. Guyon, C. Bruand, S. Tzartos, S. Cohen-Kaminsky, and S. Berrih-Aknin. 1996. Expression of acetylcholine receptor genes in human thymic epithelial cells: implications for myasthenia gravis. *J Immunol* 157:3752-3760.

21. Wakkach, A., S. Poea, E. Chastre, C. Gespach, F. Lecerf, S. De La Porte, S. Tzartos, A. Coulombe, and S. Berrih-Aknin. 1999. Establishment of a human thymic myoid cell line. Phenotypic and functional characteristics. *Am J Pathol* 155:1229-1240.

22. Mesnard-Rouiller, L., J. Bismuth, A. Wakkach, S. Poea-Guyon, and S. Berrih-Aknin. 2004. Thymic myoid cells express high levels of muscle genes. *J Neuroimmunol* 148:97-105.

23. Lauriola, L., F. Ranelletti, N. Maggiano, M. Guerriero, C. Punzi, F. Marsili, E. Bartoccioni, and A. Evoli. 2005. Thymus changes in anti-MuSK-positive and -negative myasthenia gravis. *Neurology* 64:536-538.

24. Salmon, A. M., C. Bruand, A. Cardona, J. P. Changeux, and S. Berrih-Aknin. 1998. An acetylcholine receptor alpha subunit promoter confers intrathymic expression in transgenic mice. Implications for tolerance of a transgenic self-antigen and for autoreactivity in myasthenia gravis. *J Clin Invest* 101:2340-2350.

25. Sommer, N., N. Willcox, G. C. Harcourt, and J. Newsom-Davis. 1990. Myasthenic thymus and thymoma are selectively enriched in acetylcholine receptor-reactive T cells. *Ann Neurol* 28:312-319.

26. Melms, A., B. C. Schalke, T. Kirchner, H. K. Muller-Hermelink, E. Albert, and H. Wekerle. 1988. Thymus in myasthenia gravis. Isolation of T-lymphocyte lines specific for the nicotinic acetylcholine receptor from thymuses of myasthenic patients. *J Clin Invest* 81:902-908.

27. Fujii, Y., J. Hashimoto, Y. Monden, T. Ito, K. Nakahara, and Y. Kawashima. 1986. Specific activation of lymphocytes against acetylcholine receptor in the thymus in myasthenia gravis. *J Immunol* 136:887-891.

28. Yoshikawa, H., K. Satoh, Y. Yasukawa, and M. Yamada. 2001. Analysis of immunoglobulin secretion by lymph organs with myasthenia gravis. *Acta Neurol Scand* 103:53-58.

29. Katzberg, H. D., T. Aziz, and J. Oger. 2002. In myasthenia gravis, clinical and immunological improvement post-thymectomy segregate with results of in vitro antibody secretion by immunocytes. *J Neurol Sci* 202:77-83.

30. Kuks, J. B., H. J. Oosterhuis, P. C. Limburg, and T. H. The. 1991. Anti-acetylcholine receptor antibodies decrease after thymectomy in patients with myasthenia gravis. Clinical correlations. *J Autoimmun* 4:197-211.

31. McLachlan, S. M., L. V. Nicholson, G. Venables, F. L. Mastalgia, D. Bates, B. R. Smith, and R. Hall. 1981. Acetylcholine receptor antibody synthesis in lymphocyte cultures. *Journal of clinical & laboratory immunology* 5:137-142.

32. Safar, D., S. Berrih-Aknin, and E. Morel. 1987. In vitro anti-acetylcholine receptor antibody synthesis by myasthenia gravis patient lymphocytes: correlations with thymic histology and thymic epithelial-cell interactions. *J Clin Immunol* 7:225-234.

33. Yoshikawa, H., and V. A. Lennon. 1997. Acetylcholine receptor autoantibody secretion by thymocytes: relationship to myasthenia gravis. *Neurology* 49:562-567.

34. Leprince, C., S. Cohen-Kaminsky, S. Berrih-Aknin, B. Vernet-Der Garabedian, D. Treton, P. Galanaud, and Y. Richard. 1990. Thymic B cells from myasthenia gravis patients are activated B cells. Phenotypic and functional analysis. *J Immunol* 145:2115-2122.

35. Meinl, E., W. E. Klinkert, and H. Wekerle. 1991. The thymus in myasthenia gravis. Changes typical for the human disease are absent in experimental autoimmune myasthenia gravis of the Lewis rat. *Am J Pathol* 139:995-1008.

36. Day, M. J. 1997. Review of thymic pathology in 30 cats and 36 dogs. *J Small Anim Pract* 38:393-403.

37. Schonbeck, S., F. Padberg, R. Hohlfeld, and H. Wekerle. 1992. Transplantation of thymic autoimmune microenvironment to severe combined immunodeficiency mice. A new model of myasthenia gravis. *J-Clin-Invest* 90:245-250.

38. Aissaoui, A., I. Klingel-Schmitt, J. Couderc, D. Chateau, F. Romagne, F. Jambou, A. Vincent, P. Levasseur, B. Eymard, M. C. Maillot, P. Galanaud, S. Berrih-Aknin, and S. Cohen-Kaminsky. 1999. Prevention of autoimmune attack by targeting specific T-cell receptors in a severe combined immunodeficiency mouse model of myasthenia gravis [see comments]. *Ann Neurol* 46:559-567.

39. Dural, K., E. Yildirim, S. Han, K. Ozisik, N. Ulasan, H. Saygin, and U. Sakinci. 2003. The importance of the time interval between diagnosis and operation in myasthenia gravis patients. *J Cardiovasc Surg* (Torino) 44:125-129.

40. Moulian, N., J. Bidault, F. Truffault, A. M. Yamamoto, P. Levasseur, and S. Berrih-Aknin. 1997. Thymocyte Fas expression is dysregulated in myasthenia gravis patients with anti-acetylcholine receptor antibody. *Blood* 89:3287-3295.

41. Cohen Kaminsky, S., Y. Jacques, C. Aime, D. Safar, E. Morel, and S. Berrih Aknin. 1992. Follow-up of soluble interleukin-2 receptor levels after thymectomy in patients with myasthenia gravis. *Clin-Immunol-Immunopathol* 62:190-198.

42. Link, J. 1994. Interferon-gamma, interleukin-4 and transforming growth factor-beta mRNA expression in multiple sclerosis and myasthenia gravis. *Acta Neurol Scand Suppl* 158:1-58.

43. Feferman, T., P. K. Maiti, S. Berrih-Aknin, J. Bismuth, J. Bidault, S. Fuchs, and M. C. Souroujon. 2005. Overexpression of IFN-Induced Protein 10 and Its Receptor CXCR3 in Myasthenia Gravis. *J Immunol* 174:5324-5331.

44. Feferman, T., R. Aricha, K. Mizrachi, E. Geron, R. Alon, M. C. Souroujon, and S. Fuchs. 2009. Suppression of experimental autoimmune myasthenia gravis by inhibiting the signaling between IFN-gamma inducible protein 10 (IP-10) and its receptor CXCR3. *J Neuroimmunol* 209:87-95.

45. King, C., S. G. Tangye, and C. R. Mackay. 2008. T follicular helper (TFH) cells in normal and dysregulated immune responses. *Annual review of immunology* 26:741-766.

46. Saito, R., H. Onodera, H. Tago, Y. Suzuki, M. Shimizu, Y. Matsumura, T. Kondo, and Y. Itoyama. 2005. Altered expression of chemokine receptor CXCR5 on T cells of myasthenia gravis patients. *J Neuroimmunol* 170:172-178.

47. Tackenberg, B., J. Kruth, J. E. Bartholomaeus, K. Schlegel, W. H. Oertel, N. Willcox, B. Hemmer, and N. Sommer. 2007. Clonal expansions of CD4+ B helper T cells in autoimmune myasthenia gravis. *Eur J Immunol* 37:849-863.

48. Cohen-Kaminsky, S., P. Levasseur, J. P. Binet, and S. Berrih-Aknin. 1989. Evidence of enhanced recombinant interleukin-2 sensitivity in thymic lymphocytes from patients with myasthenia gravis: possible role in autoimmune pathogenesis. *J Neuroimmunol* 24:75-85.

49. Confalonieri, P., C. Antozzi, F. Cornelio, O. Simoncini, and R. Mantegazza. 1993. Immune activation in myasthenia gravis: soluble interleukin-2 receptor, interferon-gamma and tumor necrosis factor-alpha levels in patients' serum. *J-Neuroimmunol* 48:33-36.

50. Tesar, V., E. Jelinkova, M. Jirsa, M. Bakosova, P. Pitha, and V. Chabova. 2000. Soluble adhesion molecules and cytokines in patients with myasthenia gravis treated by plasma exchange. *Blood Purif* 18:115-120.

51. Guigou, V., D. Emilie, S. Berrih-Aknin, F. Fumoux, M. Fougereau, and C. Schiff. 1991. Individual germinal centres of myasthenia gravis human thymuses contain polyclonal activated B cells that express all the Vh and Vk families. *Clin Exp Immunol* 83:262-266.

52. Bansal, A. S., W. Ollier, M. N. Marsh, R. S. Pumphrey, and P. B. Wilson. 1993. Variations in serum sCD23 in conditions with either enhanced humoral or cell-mediated immunity. *Immunology* 79:285-289.

53. Ragheb, S., R. Lisak, R. Lewis, G. Van Stavern, F. Gonzales, and K. Simon. 2008. A potential role for B-cell activating factor in the pathogenesis of autoimmune myasthenia gravis. *Archives of neurology* 65:1358-1362.

54. Romi, F., G. O. Skeie, J. A. Aarli, and N. E. Gilhus. 2000. Muscle autoantibodies in subgroups of myasthenia gravis patients. *J Neurol* 247:369-375.

55. Poea-Guyon, S., P. Christadoss, R. Le Panse, T. Guyon, M. De Baets, A. Wakkach, J. Bidault, S. Tzartos, and S. Berrih-Aknin. 2005. Effects of cytokines on acetylcholine receptor expression: implications for myasthenia gravis. *J Immunol* 174:5941-5949.

56. Bernasconi, P., M. Barberis, F. Baggi, L. Passerini, M. Cannone, E. Arnoldi, L. Novellino, F. Cornelio, and R. Mantegazza. 2005. Increased toll-like receptor 4 expression in thymus of myasthenic patients with thymitis and thymic involution. *Am J Pathol* 167:129-139.

57. Nagane, Y., K. Utsugisawa, D. Obara, M. Yamagata, and H. Tohgi. 2003. Dendritic cells in hyperplastic thymuses from patients with myasthenia gravis. *Muscle Nerve* 27:582-589.

58. Adikari, S. B., A. K. Lefvert, R. Pirskanen, R. Press, H. Link, and Y. M. Huang. 2004. Dendritic cells activate autologous T cells and induce IL-4 and IL-10 production in myasthenia gravis. *J Neuroimmunol* 156:163-170.

59. Le, P. T., D. T. Tuck, C. A. Dinarello, B. F. Haynes, and K. H. Singer. 1987. Human thymic epithelial cells produce interleukin 1. *J Immunol* 138:2520-2526.

60. Le, P. T., S. Lazorick, L. P. Whichard, Y. C. Yang, S. C. Clark, B. F. Haynes, and K. H. Singer. 1990. Human thymic epithelial cells produce IL-6, granulocyte-monocyte-CSF, and leukemia inhibitory factor. *J Immunol* 145:3310-3315.

61. Aime, C., S. Cohen-Kaminsky, and S. Berrih-Aknin. 1991. In vitro interleukin-1 (IL-1) production in thymic hyperplasia and thymoma from patients with myasthenia gravis. *J Clin Immunol* 11:268-278.

62. Colombara, M., V. Antonini, A. P. Riviera, F. Mainiero, R. Strippoli, M. Merola, G. Fracasso, O. Poffe, N. Brutti, G. Tridente, M. Colombatti, and D. Ramarli. 2005. Constitutive activation of p38 and ERK1/2 MAPKs in epithelial cells of myasthenic thymus leads to IL-6 and RANTES overexpression: effects on survival and migration of peripheral T and B cells. *J Immunol* 175:7021-7028.

63. Rizzi, M., F. Ferrera, G. Filaci, and F. Indiveri. 2006. Disruption of immunological tolerance: role of AIRE gene in autoimmunity. *Autoimmun Rev* 5:145-147.

64. Derbinski, J., J. Gabler, B. Brors, S. Tierling, S. Jonnakuty, M. Hergenhahn, L. Peltonen, J. Walter, and B. Kyewski. 2005. Promiscuous gene expression in thymic epithelial cells is regulated at multiple levels. *J Exp Med*.

65. Scarpino, S., A. Di Napoli, A. Stoppacciaro, M. Antonelli, E. Pilozzi, R. Chiarle, G. Palestro, M. Marino, F. Facciolo, E. A. Rendina, K. E. Webster, S. A. Kinkel, H. S. Scott, and L. Ruco. 2007. Expression of autoimmune regulator gene (AIRE) and T regulatory cells in human thymomas. *Clin Exp Immunol* 149:504-512.

66. Giraud, M., R. Taubert, C. Vandiedonck, X. Ke, M. Levi-Strauss, F. Pagani, F. E. Baralle, B. Eymard, C. Tranchant, P. Gajdos, A. Vincent, N. Willcox, D. Beeson, B. Kyewski, and H. J. Garchon. 2007. An IRF8-binding promoter variant and AIRE control CHRNA1 promiscuous expression in thymus. *Nature* 448:934-937.

67. Hori, S., T. Takahashi, and S. Sakaguchi. 2003. Control of autoimmunity by naturally arising regulatory CD4+ T cells. *Adv Immunol* 81:331-371.

68. Balandina, A., S. Lecart, P. Dartevelle, A. Saoudi, and S. Berrih-Aknin. 2005. Functional defect of regulatory CD4(+)CD25+ T cells in the thymus of patients with autoimmune myasthenia gravis. *Blood* 105:735-741.

69. Battaglia, A., C. Di Schino, A. Fattorossi, G. Scambia, and A. Evoli. 2005. Circulating CD4+CD25+ T regulatory and natural killer T cells in patients with myasthenia gravis: a flow cytometry study. *J Biol Regul Homeost Agents* 19:54-62.

70. Fattorossi, A., A. Battaglia, A. Buzzonetti, F. Ciaraffa, G. Scambia, and A. Evoli. 2005. Circulating and thymic CD4 CD25 T regulatory cells in myasthenia gravis: effect of immunosuppressive treatment. *Immunology* 116:134-141.

71. Zhang, Y., H. B. Wang, L. J. Chi, and W. Z. Wang. 2009. The role of FoxP3+CD4+CD25hi Tregs in the pathogenesis of myasthenia gravis. *Immunol Lett* 122:52-57.

72. Luther, C., E. Adamopoulou, C. Stoeckle, V. Brucklacher-Waldert, D. Rosenkranz, L. Stoltze, S. Lauer, S. Poeschel, A. Melms, and E. Tolosa. 2009. Prednisolone treatment induces tolerogenic dendritic cells and a regulatory milieu in myasthenia gravis patients. *J Immunol* 183:841-848.

73. Liu, W., A. L. Putnam, Z. Xu-Yu, G. L. Szot, M. R. Lee, S. Zhu, P. A. Gottlieb, P. Kapranov, T. R. Gingeras, B. Fazekas de St Groth, C. Clayberger, D. M. Soper, S. F. Ziegler, and J. A. Bluestone. 2006. CD127 expression inversely correlates with FoxP3 and suppressive function of human CD4+ T reg cells. J Exp Med 203:1701-1711.

74. Huang, Y. M., R. Pirskanen, R. Giscombe, H. Link, and A. K. Lefvert. 2004. Circulating CD4CD25 and CD4CD25 T Cells in Myasthenia Gravis and in Relation to Thymectomy. *Scand J Immunol* 59:408-414.

75. Sun, Y., J. Qiao, C. Z. Lu, C. B. Zhao, X. M. Zhu, and B. G. Xiao. 2004. Increase of circulating CD4+CD25+ T cells in myasthenia gravis patients with stability and thymectomy. *Clin Immunol* 112:284-289.

76. Luther, C., S. Poeschel, M. Varga, A. Melms, and E. Tolosa. 2005. Decreased frequency of intrathymic regulatory T cells in patients with myasthenia-associated thymoma. *J Neuroimmunol* 164:124-128.

77. Fattorossi, A., A. Battaglia, A. Buzzonetti, G. Minicuci, R. Riso, L. Peri, G. Scambia, and A. Evoli. 2008. Thymopoiesis, regulatory T cells, and TCRVbeta expression in thymoma with and without myasthenia gravis, and modulatory effects of steroid therapy. *J Clin Immunol* 28:194-206.

78. Li, X., B. G. Xiao, J. Y. Xi, C. Z. Lu, and J. H. Lu. 2008. Decrease of CD4(+)CD25(high)Foxp3(+) regulatory T cells and elevation of CD19(+)BAFF-R(+) B cells and soluble ICAM-1 in myasthenia gravis. *Clin Immunol* 126:180-188.

79. Bettelli, E., Y. Carrier, W. Gao, T. Korn, T. B. Strom, M. Oukka, H. L. Weiner, and V. K. Kuchroo. 2006. Reciprocal developmental pathways for the generation of pathogenic effector TH17 and regulatory T cells. *Nature* 441:235-238.

80. Yang, X. O., R. Nurieva, G. J. Martinez, H. S. Kang, Y. Chung, B. P. Pappu, B. Shah, S. H. Chang, K. S. Schluns, S. S. Watowich, X. H. Feng, A. M. Jetten, and C. Dong. 2008. Molecular antagonism and plasticity of regulatory and inflammatory T cell programs. *Immunity* 29:44-56.

81. Ayyoub, M., F. Deknuydt, I. Raimbaud, C. Dousset, L. Leveque, G. Bioley, and D. Valmori. 2009. Human memory FOXP3+ Tregs secrete IL-17 ex vivo and constitutively express the T(H)17 lineage-specific transcription factor RORgamma t. *Proceedings of the National Academy of Sciences of the United States of America* 106:8635-8640.

82. Voo, K. S., Y. H. Wang, F. R. Santori, C. Boggiano, Y. H. Wang, K. Arima, L. Bover, S. Hanabuchi, J. Khalili, E. Marinova, B. Zheng, D. R. Littman, and Y. J. Liu. 2009. Identification of IL-17-producing FOXP3+ regulatory T cells in humans. *Proceedings of the National Academy of Sciences of the United States of America* 106:4793-4798.

83. Braitch, M., S. Harikrishnan, R. A. Robins, C. Nichols, A. J. Fahey, L. Showe, and C. S. Constantinescu. 2009. Glucocorticoids increase CD4CD25 cell percentage and Foxp3 expression in patients with multiple sclerosis. *Acta Neurol Scand* 119:239-245.

The Role of BAFF in Autoimmunity and MG

Samia Ragheb Ph.D., Robert Lisak M.D., Felicitas Gonzales B.S. &
Yanfeng Li M.S.

1. INTRODUCTION

Autoimmune myasthenia gravis (MG) is a disease in which dysregulation of the immune system promotes the survival, activation, and maturation of autoreactive B-cells. Yet, we do not understand the molecular pathways that allow autoreactive B-cells to persist. BAFF is a potent B-cell survival factor and it plays an essential role in B-cell homeostasis. On the B-cell surface, various receptors for BAFF deliver stimulatory or inhibitory signals. Thus, the interaction of BAFF with its various receptors regulates B-cell function. When over-expressed, BAFF protects B-cells from apoptosis, thereby contributing to autoimmunity. BAFF may play an important role in the pathogenesis of MG.

For MG, and other immune-mediated diseases, there is a need to develop new therapies that target specific pathways in the immune system. BAFF and its receptors are attractive targets for the therapy of B-cell mediated diseases. The use of antagonists of the BAFF pathway has great potential as a new treatment option for MG and for other B-cell mediated diseases of the neuromuscular junction, such as Lambert-Eaton syndrome. BAFF antagonists may well provide new treatment options for these patients.

2. BAFF AND B-CELL BIOLOGY

B-cell activating factor (BAFF), also known as B lymphocyte stimulator (BLyS), is a member of the tumor necrosis factor (TNF) superfamily: TNFSF 13b. In humans, BAFF is mapped to chromosome 13q32-34 [1,2]. In the peripheral immune system, myeloid cells (neutrophils, monocytes, macrophages, and myeloid-derived dendritic cells) are the primary producers of soluble BAFF [3-6]. A membrane-bound form of BAFF is also expressed on the surface of myeloid cells. Full-length BAFF is a 285 aa type II transmembrane protein. Similar to other ligands of the TNF superfamily, BAFF contains a conserved region within the extracellular domain. A furin family protease cleaves the membrane form of BAFF to generate soluble BAFF (sBAFF), which contains the extracellular 152 amino acids (aa 134 – 285). The structure of sBAFF is a jelly roll-like β-pleated sheet with homomultimeric interactions. sBAFF is a homotrimer, and it interacts with its receptors in its trimeric form [7-9]. BAFF is highly conserved. The aa identity of soluble human BAFF is 86% with mouse, 93% with pig, 91% with cow, 90% with rabbit, 78% with duck, 78% with quail, 77% with goose, and 76% with chicken. Because of this homology, BAFF displays functional cross-reactivity across species [2, 10-16].

BAFF transgenic animals exhibit hypergammaglobulinemia, lymphoproliferation, B-cell hyperplasia, splenomegaly, and develop autoimmune disease [17-19]. Manifestations that are similar to those in systemic lupus erythematosus and in Sjogren's syndrome include an increased production of autoantibodies, and immune complex mediated glomerulonephritis. As they age, BAFF transgenic mice also have a propensity to develop B-cell lymphomas [17]. Conversely, in BAFF deficient animals, there is a marked reduction in the B-cell lineage with depletion of marginal zone and follicular B-cells. Defects in peripheral B-cell maturation are accompanied by hypogammaglobulinemia [20,21]. Therefore, BAFF plays an essential role in B-cell homeostasis. It is a potent survival factor for B-cells, and is necessary for peripheral B-cell differentiation [22-26]. It plays an essential role in the maintenance and maturation of peripheral B-cells. BAFF regulates follicular B-cell numbers. Long-lived plasma cells are also dependent on BAFF for their survival [27,28]. BAFF differentially regulates Bcl-2 family members in a manner consistent with pro-survival and attenuation of apoptosis [29-32]. These anti-apoptotic effects are mediated by upregulation of Bcl-2 and inhibition of Bim [33]. When over-expressed, BAFF protects B-cells from apoptosis, thereby contributing to autoimmunity and malignancy.

Because BAFF is a crucial and potent factor for the survival and growth of B-cells, both normal and autoreactive B-cells compete for available BAFF. BAFF levels appear to regulate the survival threshold for B-cells. Because autoreactive B-cells are poorly competitive for survival, they appear to be more dependent on BAFF for their survival [34-37]. An environment of excess BAFF promotes the survival and maturation of autoreactive B-cells, thereby breaking immune self-tolerance. Therefore, BAFF levels can alter the selection of autoreactive B-cells. BAFF costimulates B-cell activation/proliferation via the B-cell receptor (BCR) or via CD40, and it mediates the survival of these activated B-cells [1,2]. Furthermore, coupling of BCR signaling and BAFF-R expression has been demonstrated [38,39]. This leads to the intriguing concept that follicular B-cell selection, activation, and survival are linked. Therefore, the type and strength of signals that are received via the BCR, CD40, and receptors for BAFF affect and control the fate of B-cells, whether they are normal or autoreactive [40,41].

3. BAFF-BINDING RECEPTORS

Three functional receptors for BAFF have been identified. They are BCMA (B-cell maturation antigen, TNFRSF 17, CD269), TACI (transmembrane activator and cyclophilin ligand interactor, TNFRSF 13b, CD267), and BAFF-R (BAFF receptor, BR3, TNFRSF 13c, CD268). All three receptors lack signal sequences and are classified as type III transmembrane proteins. Both BCMA and

TACI can also bind to the BAFF-related molecule APRIL (A Proliferation Inducing Ligand). The BAFF-R binds BAFF exclusively. Expression of the receptors is primarily restricted to B-cells [42-46], although activated and memory T-cells are reported to express TACI and BAFF-R [47,48].

BAFF-R deficient mice have a marked reduction in the B-cell compartment, and lack both marginal zone and follicular B-cells [49,50]. Wild type mice in which the interaction of BAFF with the BAFF-R is blocked by decoy receptors (fusion proteins of BAFF-R-Fc, TACI-Fc, or BCMA-Fc) also have a marked reduction in the B-cell compartment [51]. The B-lymphopenic A/WySnJ mice have a mutant signaling-deficient form of the BAFF-R. They have a similar phenotype to that of BAFF deficient mice. They exhibit a loss of peripheral B-cells and decreased levels of circulating immunoglobulins [52-55]. Data on receptor expression in humans and mice show that the BAFF-R is the predominant receptor on circulating B-cells [48]. In B-cells, the pro-survival signals of BAFF are mediated by the BAFF-R.

Conversely, TACI deficient mice have a higher number of hyper-responsive B-cells in the periphery, they develop autoimmune disease, exhibit lymphoproliferation, and develop lymphoma [56-58]. The interaction of BAFF with TACI appears to deliver inhibitory signals such that signaling through TACI decreases the size of the B-cell pool. For humans, the role of TACI is more ambiguous. On the one hand, TACI expression is upregulated after B-cell stimulation, and TACI is found primarily on marginal zone B-cells and on CD27+ memory B-cells [59]. TACI appears to be a negative regulator/terminator of the B-cell response. On the other hand, in humans, TACI mutations are associated with immunoglobulin deficiency [60-62]; TACI mutations are associated with familial combined variable immunodeficiency (CVID) and with selective IgA deficiency. This would appear to suggest that TACI plays a positive role in terminal B-cell differentiation. However, TACI mutations do not lead to a complete loss of protein expression and TACI may still be functional in these patients. Furthermore, although TACI mutations have been associated with antibody deficiency, it is not clear that they are the cause.

BCMA deficient mice lack an obvious phenotype [21,63]. BCMA expression is restricted to the end stages of B-cell differentiation. BCMA expression is upregulated in germinal center cells and in plasmablasts, and it serves an essential survival and maturation function as B-cells differentiate into plasma cells [27,28,64].

Mature human B-cells, at all stages of differentiation, express one (or more) of the BAFF-binding receptors and are BAFF-dependent [65,66]. The BAFF-R is the main receptor to mediate BAFF signals in naïve B-cells. Following activation, and during differentiation, BAFF-R expression is down modulated while TACI expression is upregulated. BCMA expression is upregulated at the terminal stages of B-cell differentiation and appears to be restricted to antibody-producing cells. A recent study demonstrates that IL-17 may synergize with BAFF to enhance the survival and maturation of human B-cells [67]. This study demonstrates the potential involvement of IL-17 in B-cell biology, and highlights the potential for other cytokine signals to enhance or antagonize BAFF-mediated signaling. BAFF levels, and the interaction of BAFF with its three receptors, regulate peripheral B-cell homeostasis and function, and regulate the immune self-tolerance of B-cells [46, 68-70]. Dysregulation of this signaling alters peripheral immune self-tolerance and leads to the development of autoimmune disease.

4. SIGNALING VIA BAFF-R

The human BAFF-R gene maps to chromosome 22. The BAFF-R is expressed on all peripheral B-cells and it binds BAFF exclusively. The signaling events downstream of the BAFF-R that lead to

B-cell survival are not well defined. It is apparent that BAFF-mediated survival is through differential regulation of Bcl-2 family members. Signaling downstream of the BAFF-R leads to B-cell survival through activation of NF-κB [68]. Activation of the NF-κB transcription factor normally proceeds either through the canonical pathway which is dependent on NEMO (NF-κB Essential Modulator), or through the alternate pathway which is NEMO independent [71]. Both pathways have been shown to be utilized in BAFF-R signaling [72-74]. Act 1 is an adaptor molecule which appears to play a negative regulatory role in BAFF-R signaling. Act 1 deficiency results in a dramatic increase of peripheral B-cells, splenomegaly, hypergammaglobulinemia, and production of autoantibodies. Mice that are deficient in Act 1 develop systemic autoimmune disease with manifestations of lupus-like glomerulonephritis and Sjogren's syndrome [75,76].

5. BAFF AND T-CELL BIOLOGY

In vitro, BAFF costimulates human T-cell activation which has been shown to be mediated by the BAFF-R [48,77]. *In vivo*, BAFF transgenic animals exhibit enhanced cutaneous delayed-type hypersensitivity (DTH) responses, which are considered to be classical TH-1-mediated immune responses [78]. Another study suggests that BAFF may also play a role in TH-17-mediated immune responses. In mouse models of collagen-induced arthritis, both T- and B-cells are necessary for disease induction and progression. When *Lam et al.* use shRNA to silence the BAFF gene, intra-articular injection of shRNA suppresses the development of disease by inhibiting the generation of plasma cells and TH-17 cells [79]. Furthermore, in a comparison of wild type and IL-17 $^{-/-}$ mice, recombinant BAFF exacerbates disease in the wild type animals, but not in the IL-17 $^{-/-}$ animals. These studies highlight the previously unrecognized role of BAFF in T-cell mediated immune responses.

6. BAFF IN IMMUNE-MEDIATED DISEASES

6.1. Systemic Lupus Erythematosus (SLE)

SLE is the prototype of systemic autoimmune diseases. The disease is characterized by the production of autoantibodies against an array of nuclear antigens. Multiple organ systems may become affected, and the deposition of immune complexes leads to glomerulonephritis, kidney damage, and possible renal failure. Approximately 50% of patients with SLE have increased levels of BAFF in the blood. BAFF levels appear to correlate with the anti-dsDNA titer, but not with disease activity [80-82].

Two murine models of lupus, the NZB/W F1 mouse and the MRL-lpr/lpr mouse are prototypical models for SLE nephritis. These genetically susceptible mouse strains develop disease spontaneously. In these models, the increased levels of BAFF in the serum correlate with the titers of anti-dsDNA antibodies and with proteinuria. The treatment of lupus-prone mice with soluble decoy receptors that block BAFF reduces disease incidence and severity, inhibits B-cell activation, reduces the titers of autoantibodies, and increases survival [42, 83-85].

6.2. Rheumatoid Arthritis (RA)

RA is a chronic systemic autoimmune disease characterized by inflammation that targets the synovial membrane, cartilage, and bone, ultimately leading to joint damage. Both T- and B-cells

The Role of BAFF ... ■ Samia Ragheb, Robert Lisak, Felicitas Gonzales and Yanfeng Li.

169

mediate disease pathogenesis [86]. Patients with RA are reported to have increased levels of BAFF in the circulation which correlate with the titer of rheumatoid factor and with clinical disease activity [80,87]. In patients with RA, increased BAFF levels are also found in the joint synovial fluid [88].

In animal models of collagen-induced arthritis (CIA), both T- and B-cells are necessary for disease induction and progression. In the CIA model, increased serum levels of BAFF correlate with the titer of anti-collagen antibodies [89]. *In vitro*, macrophages and dendritic cells express high levels of BAFF, and recombinant BAFF reduces the apoptosis of B-cells. In another study using the CIA model, treatment with TACI-Fc inhibits the development of disease and reduces joint pathology [90]. In yet another study, the use of shRNA to silence the BAFF gene inhibits both the onset and progression of disease [79].

6.3. Sjogren's Syndrome (SS)

SS is a chronic inflammatory disorder characterized by lymphocyte infiltration of the lacrimal and salivary glands, leading to secretory malfunction of these exocrine glands. SS can develop alone (Primary Sjogren's) or in association with other autoimmune diseases, namely RA and SLE [91]. The two most common autoantibodies in SS patients are the SS-A/Ro and SS-B/La antibodies. The disease is characterized by B-cell hyperactivity, and SS patients have an increased risk of developing B-cell non-Hodgkin's lymphoma.

As they age, mice that over express BAFF develop Sjogren's-like symptoms with decreased saliva production and destruction of glands [19]. Sjogren's patients have increased levels of BAFF in the circulation and also have increased BAFF expression in the inflamed salivary glands [92,93]. It is not clear whether this increased BAFF expression is from the infiltrating mononuclear cells or from resident cells. The increased BAFF levels in the serum of SS patients correlate with the titer of autoantibodies (anti-SS-A, anti-SS-B, and rheumatoid factor) [92]. Peripheral blood B-cells from SS patients have increased expression of Bcl-2 and reduced apoptosis [94].

6.4. Myasthenia Gravis (MG)

Autoimmune MG is a B-cell mediated disease in which the target autoantigen is the acetylcholine receptor (AChR) at the neuromuscular junction [95,96]. Patients with generalized MG have circulating anti-AChR antibodies [97-99]. These antibodies are responsible for the pathology of MG, leading to impaired neuromuscular transmission and subsequent muscle weakness. In MG patients with thymoma, there are also autoantibodies to other skeletal muscle antigens, which include the ryanodine receptor and titin [100]. At present, the role of these antibodies in disease pathogenesis is not known. Some MG patients who are seronegative for anti-AChR have circulating antibodies to muscle-specific kinase (MuSK) [101,102]. Although these antibodies do not appear to fix complement, MuSK-specific antibodies are pathogenic nevertheless [103-106].

In some patients, the myasthenic thymus is implicated in initiating or perpetuating the disease process [107-110]. Approximately 60 – 80% of patients with autoimmune MG have thymic follicular hyperplasia in the medulla. Germinal centers in the thymic perivascular space are similar to those found in lymph nodes. In MG, it is thought that the thymic germinal center environment is providing signals that promote autoreactive B-cell survival, activation, and maturation. Yet, these signals are not known. Patients with thymic follicular hyperplasia tend to have higher serum titers of anti-AChR antibodies [111], and show evidence of enhanced B-cell activation [112-114]. Furthermore, in the MG thymus with follicular hyperplasia, germinal center B-cells over-express Bcl-2 [115,116], an indicator of enhanced survival. A recent study shows that, in the myasthenic thymus with hyperplasia, macrophages express BAFF and germinal center B-cells express the BAFF-R [117].

Serum BAFF levels in patients with MG are significantly higher than those in non-myasthenic control subjects [118,119]. However, there is no association between the serum BAFF level and the extent or severity of disease. This is not surprising as previous studies have shown that there is no correlation between the serum titer of anti-AChR antibodies and disease severity [111,120]. There is a trend for BAFF levels to be higher in patients who are seropositive for AChR-specific antibodies [118,119]. There is no correlation between the serum BAFF level and the concentration of total IgG, IgA, or IgM [119]. In one study, the frequency of B-cells that express the BAFF-R appears to be higher in patients with MG [121]. However, in another study, there is no difference in the percentage of B-cells that express BCMA, BAFF-R, or TACI between patients with MG and healthy controls [122].

6.5. Graves Disease

This disease manifests itself as hyperthyroidism that is mediated by agonistic autoantibodies to the thyroid-stimulating hormone (TSH) receptor. In a murine model, the soluble decoy receptor BAFF-R-Fc inhibits disease and decreases autoantibody levels. This is accompanied by a reduction in the serum thyroid hormone levels [123].

6.6. Insulin-Dependent Diabetes Mellitus (IDDM)

In patients with type 1 diabetes and in the non-obese diabetic (NOD) mouse, autoimmune disease is due to the loss of T-cell and B-cell tolerance to islet-specific antigens, leading to the destruction of insulin-producing cells [124]. In the NOD mouse, neutralization of BAFF reduces the incidence of spontaneous diabetes, decreases the severity of islet inflammation, and abrogates insulin autoantibodies in the serum [125].

6.7. Multiple Sclerosis (MS)

MS is an inflammatory demyelinating disease in which components of the immune system target and attack the myelin sheath in the central nervous system (CNS) [126-128]. Various components of the immune system work in concert to destroy myelin, the myelin-producing oligodendrocytes, and in some cases also damage the nerve. T-cells play a central role in initiating and orchestrating the inflammatory process [127,129]. Although the immunopathogenesis of MS is generally considered to be T-cell mediated, there is compelling evidence of B-cell involvement. B-cells and plasma cells are also found in the MS lesion, and autoantibodies potentiate disease pathophysiology and contribute to demyelination and axonal degeneration [130-132]. Furthermore, lymphoid follicle-like structures are found in the brain meninges of some MS patients [133,134].

BAFF is expressed in the normal human brain, and BAFF expression is upregulated in MS plaques [135]. However, serum BAFF levels in MS patients are not significantly different from those in healthy subjects [119], and the cell-surface expression of BAFF-binding receptors on CD19[+] B-cells is not different between MS patients and healthy controls [122]. In animal models,

The Role of BAFF ... ∎ Samia Ragheb, Robert Lisak, Felicitas Gonzales and Yanfeng Li.

171

BAFF expression is upregulated in the CNS in the meninges, which is the site of ectopic lymphoid follicle development in experimental autoimmune encephalomyelitis (EAE) [136]. In one EAE study, the soluble decoy receptor BCMA-Fc decreases CNS inflammation and demyelination, and reduces antibody titers [137]. In another EAE study, a BAFF vaccine that induces high titers of anti-BAFF antibodies is protective [138].

6.8. Coeliac Disease

Coeliac disease is an inflammatory autoimmune disorder of the small intestine. Gliadin, a gluten glycoprotein, is the target of the autoimmune response. Both T-cells and B-cells contribute to the pathophysiology of the disease [139]. Patients with coeliac disease are reported to have increased levels of BAFF in the circulation [140]. These levels decrease after the introduction of a gluten-free diet.

6.9. Inflammatory Airway Diseases

Patients with chronic rhino sinusitis have increased expression of BAFF mRNA and BAFF protein in nasal polyps [141], and mucosal epithelial cells are a major source of BAFF in nasal mucosa. In patients with IgE-mediated allergy, BAFF levels in the bronchoalveolar lavage rise after allergen challenge [142]. In patients with asthma, increased serum levels of BAFF correlate with the severity of asthmatic symptoms, regardless of whether the disease is IgE- or non-IgE-mediated [143].

6.10. Inflammatory Skin Diseases

Serum levels of BAFF are reported to be elevated in patients with bullous pemphigoid, an autoimmune blistering disease [144]. A subset of patients with alopecia areata, a tissue-specific autoimmune disease of hair follicles, have higher levels of BAFF in the serum [145,146].

7. BAFF AND B-CELL CANCER

7.1. B-cell Chronic Lymphocytic Leukemia (B-CLL)

B-CLL is characterized by the presence and accumulation of CD5[+] B-cells that are resistant to apoptosis and have prolonged survival. BAFF levels are higher in the serum of patients with B-CLL. B-CLL cells express BAFF-binding receptors. In some patients, B-CLL cells also express BAFF. Therefore, an autocrine pathway appears to protect these cells from apoptosis [147-149].

7.2. Non-Hodgkin's Lymphoma (NHL)

NHL is characterized by the transformation and clonal expansion of mature B-cells at various stages of differentiation. In patients with aggressive non-Hodgkin's lymphoma, serum BAFF levels are elevated [150,151]. NHL cells express BAFF-binding receptors. BAFF is also expressed by the tumors, and the expression level increases as the tumors transform to a more aggressive phenotype. High BAFF levels correlate with a poor prognosis for NHL patients [151]. BAFF promotes the survival of NHL [151,152]. A recent report suggests that single nucleotide polymorphisms in the BAFF gene are associated with increased BAFF expression in NHL [153]. Bone marrow stromal cells also express BAFF which promotes the survival of lymphoma cells and protects them from apoptosis [154]. Therefore, BAFF promotes the survival of NHL through autocrine and paracrine pathways.

7.3. Multiple Myeloma (MM)

MM is characterized by the accumulation of malignant plasma cells in the bone marrow. Serum levels of BAFF are elevated in patients with MM [155]. BAFF-R, TACI, and BCMA are expressed by multiple myeloma cells, and BAFF can promote their survival and proliferative capacity [155,156]. BAFF is also expressed by MM cells and by bone marrow stromal cells, which express and secrete soluble BAFF [156,157]. As is the case for other B-cell cancers, for MM cells, both paracrine and autocrine pathways attenuate apoptosis. Approximately 78% of cases of B-cell lymphoproliferative disorders are BAFF-R+ [158].

8. MOLECULAR SIGNALS THAT REGULATE BAFF PRODUCTION

Within the immune system, the primary source of soluble BAFF is the myeloid lineage. Recently, BAFF has also been found to be expressed and secreted by cells that are known to be targets of the autoimmune response: these include synoviocytes in RA [159] and salivary gland epithelial cells in primary Sjogren's syndrome [160]. These findings underscore the importance of resident cells in the target organs in perpetuating autoimmunity.

The signals that modulate BAFF expression are not fully understood. Resting monocytes constitutively express a low level of membrane-bound BAFF; this expression is upregulated by IFN-γ, IFN-α, and IL-10. These cytokines augment BAFF expression in monocytes, macrophages, and dendritic cells. Bacterial components such as lipopolysaccharide (LPS) also upregulate BAFF expression [3,4,161]. Therefore, signals from both the innate and adaptive immune response can modulate BAFF production by myeloid cells. TGF-β has also been shown to upregulate BAFF expression in mouse macrophages, [in vitro162]. *In vivo* therapy in human patients has shown that IFN-α and IFN-β upregulate BAFF expression in patients with melanoma and MS, respectively [163,164]. Interestingly, IFN-γ and the type I interferons (IFN-α and IFN-β) which are known to have opposite effects on myeloid cell function, have similar effects on BAFF expression.

Suppressor of cytokine signaling-1 (SOCS-1) plays a critical role in the negative regulation of IFN-γ signaling. In SOCS-1 deficient mice, IFN-γ-stimulated dendritic cells are hyper-responsive. SOCS-1 deficiency also leads to higher BAFF production by dendritic cells, and leads to systemic autoimmune-like disease in mice [165].

The autoimmune regulator (AIRE) gene is primarily expressed in the thymus in medullary cells, and in the periphery on antigen presenting cells [166,167]. AIRE plays a role in both the central and peripheral immune self-tolerance mechanisms for T-cells. AIRE deficiency leads to higher numbers of antigen presenting cells [168]. AIRE deficient mice also have higher serum levels of BAFF than wild type mice, and this is associated with increased expression of membrane-bound BAFF on the surface of dendritic cells. Aging AIRE $^{-/-}$ mice have a similar phenotype to that of BAFF transgenic mice [169,170].

9. BAFF PATHWAY-TARGETED THERAPY

It has been ten years since BAFF was first discovered. BAFF plays a role in a diverse array of human B-cell diseases that include autoimmunity, malignancy, and immunodeficiency [171]. Identification and understanding of the molecules that participate in the BAFF pathway can potentially identify new targets for therapy. Four different antagonists of the BAFF pathway have been developed for clinical use thus far. The first is an anti-BAFF neutralizing antibody (LymphoStat-B, Belimumab); it targets human soluble BAFF and has a half-life of 8.5 – 14 days [172]. The second is anti-BAFF-R [173], which blocks the interaction of BAFF with the BAFF-R/BR3 and it also kills BAFF-R expressing cells. The third is the decoy receptor BR3-Fc, which is a humanized fusion protein of the extracellular domain of human BAFF-R with the Fc portion of human IgG1 [174]. Because BAFF, but not APRIL, binds to the BAFF-R, these three antagonists offer a method of selective BAFF blockade. APRIL would still be available to bind to TACI and BCMA. The fourth antagonist is TACI-Ig (Atacicept), a fusion protein of the extracellular domain of human TACI with the Fc portion of human IgG1 [175]. Its half-life is 7 days. TACI-Ig offers a non-selective method of BAFF blockade, because it would interfere with both BAFF and APRIL signaling.

Clinical trials of Belimumab and Atacicept are ongoing in patients with SLE and RA [176-178]. Because BAFF blockade deprives B-cells from a crucial survival factor, the effect of BAFF blockade appears to be mediated mainly *via* B-cell depletion. Mature B-cells, at all stages of differentiation (from naïve to plasmablast), are dependent on BAFF, and are potentially susceptible to BAFF blockade. This blockade would affect the survival and maturation of all B-cells, whether they are normal or autoreactive. BAFF pathway-targeted therapy may offer an advantage over Rituximab therapy. Rituximab is a monoclonal antibody that targets and depletes CD20+ B-cells [179]. It does not target plasma cells, which do not express cell-surface CD20. Therapies that target the BAFF pathway would affect the survival of long-lived plasma cells, thereby reducing autoantibody production. One of the consequences of B-cell depletion therapies is that homeostatic mechanisms will kick in to promote B-cell survival. It is known that Rituximab therapy leads to increased BAFF production [180,181]. Once therapy is stopped, compensatory BAFF over-expression may lead to a resurgence of autoreactive B-cells. Therefore, the optimal clinical therapeutic benefit of BAFF antagonism may require combination with other therapeutic agents [182].

BAFF itself may be therapeutic in primary immunodeficiencies that affect the B-cell compartment [183], and BAFF may be used to enhance the efficacy of vaccines aimed at boosting the humoral immune response [184,185]. The discovery of the BAFF pathway has opened a new chapter in the manipulation of the B-cell response.

REFERENCES

1. Moore PA, Belvedere O, Orr A, Pieri K, LaFleur DW, Feng P, Soppet D, Charters M, Gentz R, Parmelee D, Li Y, Galperina O, Giri J, Roschke V, Nardelli B, Carrell J, Sosnovtseva S, Greenfield W, Ruben SM, Olsen HS, Fikes J, Hilbert DM. Blys: Member of the tumor necrosis factor family and B lymphocyte stimulator. *Science* 1999; 285: 260-263.

2. Schneider P, MacKay F, Steiner V, Hofmann K, Bodmer J-L, Holler N, Ambrose C, Lawton P, Bixler S, Acha-Orbea H, Valmori D, Romero P, Werner-Favre C, Zubler RH, Browning JL, Tschopp J. BAFF, a novel ligand of the tumor necrosis factor family, stimulates B cell growth. *J Exp Med* 1999; 189: 1747-1756.

3. Nardelli B, Belvedere O, Roschke V, Moore PA, Olsen HS, Migone TS, Sosnovtseva S, Carrell JA, Feng P, Giri JG, Hilbert DM. Synthesis and release of B-lymphocyte stimulator from myeloid cells. *Blood* 2001; 97: 198-204.

4. Craxton A, Magaletti D, Ryan EJ, Clark EA. Macrophage- and dendritic cell-dependent regulation of human B-cell proliferation requires the TNF family ligand BAFF. *Blood* 2003; 101: 4464-4471.

5. Gorelik L, Gilbride K, Dobles M, Kalled SL, Zandman D, Scott ML. Normal B cell homeostasis requires B cell activation factor production by radiation-resistant cells. *J Exp Med* 2003; 198: 937-945.

6. Scapini P, Nardelli B, Nadali G, Calzetti F, Pizzolo G, Montecucco C, Cassatella MA. G-CSF-stimulated neutrophils are a prominent source of functional BLyS. *J Exp Med* 2003; 197: 297-302.

7. Karpusas M, Cachero TG, Qian F, Boriack-Sjodin A, Mullen C, Strauch K, Hsu YM, Kalled SL. Crystal structure of extracellular human BAFF, a TNF family member that stimulates B lymphocytes. *J Mol Biol* 2002; 315: 1145-1154.

8. Liu Y, Xu L, Opalka N, Kappler J, Shu HB, Zhang G. Crystal structure of sTall-1 reveals a virus-like assembly of TNF family ligands. *Cell* 2002; 108: 383-394.

9. Oren DA, Li Y, Volovik Y, Morris TS, Dharia C, Das K, Galperina O, Gentz R, Arnold E. Structural basis of BLyS receptor recognition. *Nat Struct Biol* 2002; 9: 288-292.

10. Schneider K, Kothlow S, Schneider P, Tardivel A, Gobel T, Kaspers B, Staeheli P. Chicken BAFF – a highly conserved cytokine that mediates B cell survival. *Int Immunol* 2004; 16: 139-148.

11. Dan WB, Guan ZB, Zhang C, Li BC, Zhang J, Zhang SQ. Molecular cloning, in vitro expression and bioactivity of goose B-cell activating factor. *Vet Immunol Immunopathol* 2007; 118: 113-120.

12. Guan Z-B, Dan W-B, Shui Y, Ye J-L, Zhang S-Q. cDNA cloning, expression and bioactivity of porcine BAFF. *Dev Comp Immunol* 2007; 31: 1211-1219.

13. Guan Z-B, Shui Y, Zhang S-Q. Two related ligands of the TNF family, BAFF and APRIL, in rabbit: Molecular cloning, 3D modeling, and tissue distribution. *Cytokine* 2007; 39: 192-200.

14. Guan Z-B, Ye J-L, Dan W-B, Yao W-J, Zhang S-Q. Cloning, expression and bioactivity of duck BAFF. *Mol Immunol* 2007; 44: 1471-1476.

15. Guan Z-B, Shui Y, Zhang J-X, Zhang S-Q. Molecular cloning, genomic organization and expression analysis of the gene encoding bovine (Bos taurus) B-cell activating factor belonging to the TNF family (BAFF). *Gene* 2008; 425: 17-22.

The Role of BAFF ... ∎ Samia Ragheb, Robert Lisak, Felicitas Gonzales and Yanfeng Li.

175

16. Chen CM, Ren WH, Yang G, Zhang CS, Zhang SQ. Molecular cloning, in vitro expression and bioactivity of quail BAFF. Vet Immunol Immunopathol 2009; E-pub.

17. Mackay F, Woodcock SA, Lawton P, Ambrose C, Baetscher M, Schneider P, Tschopp J, Browning JL. Mice transgenic for BAFF develop lymphocytic disorders along with autoimmune manifestations. *J Exp Med* 1999; 190: 1697-1710.

18. Khare SD, Sarosi I, Xia X-Z, McCabe S, Miner K, Solovyev I, Hawkins N, Kelley M, Chang D, Van G, Ross L, Delaney J, Wang L, Lacey D, Boyle WJ, Hsu H. Severe B cell hyperplasia and autoimmune disease in TALL-1 transgenic mice. Proc Natl Acad Sci USA 2000; 97: 3370-3375.

19. Groom J, Kalled SL, Cutler AH, Olson C, Woodcock SA, Schneider P, Tschopp J, Cachero TG, Batten M, Wheway J, Mauri D, Cavill D, Gordon TP, Mackay CR, Mackay F. Association of BAFF/Blys overexpression and altered B cell differentiation with Sjogren's syndrome. *J Clin Invest* 2002; 109: 59-68.

20. Gross JA, Dillon SR, Mudri S, Johnston J, Littau A, Roque R, Rixon M, Schou O, Foley KP, Haugen H, McMillen S, Waggie K, Schreckhise RW, Shoemaker K, Vu T, Moore M, Grossman A, Clegg CH. TACI-Ig neutralizes molecules critical for B cell development and autoimmune disease: impaired B cell maturation in mice lacking Blys. *Immunity* 2001; 15: 289-302.

21. Schiemann B, Gommerman JL, Vora K, Cachero TG, Shulga-Morskaya S, Dobles M, Frew E, Scott ML. An essential role for BAFF in the normal development of B cells through a BCMA-independent pathway. *Science* 2001; 293: 2111-2114.

22. MacLennan ICM, Vinuesa CG. Dendritic cells, BAFF, and APRIL: innate players in adaptive antibody responses. *Immunity* 2002; 17: 235-238.

23. Rolink AG, Tschopp J, Schneider P, Melchers F. BAFF is a survival and maturation factor for mouse B cells. *Eur J Immunol* 2002; 32: 2004-2010.

24. Mackay F, Schneider P, Rennert P, Browning J. BAFF and APRIL: a tutorial on B cell survival. Ann Rev Immunol 2003; 21: 231-264.

25. Cancro MP. Peripheral B-cell maturation: the intersection of selection and homeostasis. *Immunol Rev* 2004; 197: 89-101.

26. Jego G, Pascual V, Palucka AK, Banchereau J. Dendritic cells control B cell growth and differentiation. *Curr Dir Autoimmun* 2005; 8: 124-139.

27. O'Connor BP, Raman VS, Erickson LD, Cook WJ, Weaver LK, Ahonen C, Lin LL, Mantchev GT, Bram RJ, Noelle RJ. BCMA is essential for the survival of long-lived bone marrow plasma cells. *J Exp Med* 2004; 199: 91-98.

28. Benson MJ, Dillon SR, Castigli E, Geha RS, Xu S, Lam K-P, Noelle RJ. Cutting Edge: The dependence of plasma cells and independence of memory B cells on BAFF and APRIL. *J Immunol* 2008; 180: 3655-3659.

29. Do RKG, Hatada E, Lee H, Tourigny MR, Hilbert D, Chen-Kiang S. Attenuation of apoptosis underlies B lymphocyte stimulator enhancement of humoral immune response. *J Exp Med* 2000; 192: 953-964.

30. Hsu BL, Harless SM, Lindsley RC, Hilbert DM, Cancro MP. Blys enables survival of transitional and mature B cells through distinct mediators. *J Immunol* 2002; 168: 5993-5996.

31. Tardivel A, Tinel A, Lens S, Steiner Q-G, Sauberli E, Wilson A, Mackay F, Rolink AG, Beermann F, Tschopp J, Schneider P. The anti-apoptotic factor Bcl-2 can functionally substitute for the B cell survival but not for the marginal zone B cell differentiation activity of BAFF. *Eur J Immunol* 2004; 34: 509-518.

32. Craxton A, Draves KE, Gruppi A, Clark EA. Baff regulates B cell survival by downregulating the BH3-only family member Bim via the ERK pathway. *J Exp Med* 2005; 202: 1363-1374.

33. Cory S. Regulation of lymphocyte survival by the BCL-2 gene family. *Ann Rev Immunol* 1995; 13: 513-543.

34. Hartley SB, Cooke MP, Fulcher DA, Harris AW, Cory S, Basten A, Goodnow CC. Elimination of self-reactive B lymphocytes proceeds in two stages: Arrested development and cell death. *Cell* 1993; 72: 325-335.

35. Cyster JG, Hartley SB, Goodnow CC. Competition for follicular niches excludes self-reactive cells from the recirculating B-cell repertoire. *Nature* 1994; 371: 389-395.

36. Lesley R, Xu Y, Kalled SL, Hess DM, Schwab SR, Shu H-B, Cyster JG. Reduced competitiveness of autoantigen-engaged B cells due to increased dependence on BAFF. *Immunity* 2004; 20: 441-453.

37. Thien M, Phan TG, Gardam S, Amesbury M, Basten A, Mackay F, Brink R. Excess BAFF rescues self-reactive B cells from peripheral deletion and allows them to enter forbidden follicular and marginal zone niches. *Immunity* 2004; 20: 785-798.

38. Smith SH, Cancro MP. Cutting Edge: B cell receptor signals regulate BLys receptor levels in mature B cells and their immediate progenitors. *J Immunol* 2003; 170: 5820-5823.

39. Hase H, Kanno Y, Kojima M, Hasegawa K, Sakurai D, Kojima H, Tsuchiya N, Tokunaga K, Masawa N, Azuma M, Okumura K, Kobata T. BAFF/BLys can potentiate B-cell selection with the B-cell coreceptor complex. *Blood* 2004; 103: 2257-2265.

40. Noelle RJ, Erickson LD. Determinations of B cell fate in immunity and autoimmunity. *Curr Dir Autoimmun* 2005; 8: 1-24.

41. Stadanlick JE, Cancro MP. BAFF and the plasticity of peripheral B cell tolerance. *Curr Opin Immunol* 2008; 20: 158-161.

42. Gross JA, Johnston J, Mudri S, Enselman R, Dillon SR, Madden K, Xu W, Parrish-Novak J, Foster D, Lofton-Day C, Moore M, Littau A, Grossman A, Haugen H, Foley K, Blumberg H, Harrison K, Kindsvogel W, Clegg CH. TACI and BCMA are receptors for a TNF homologue implicated in B-cell autoimmune disease. *Nature* 2000; 404: 995-999.

43. Yan M, Marsters SA, Grewal IS, Wang H, Ashkenazi A, Dixit VM. Identification of a receptor for Blys demonstrates a crucial role in humoral immunity. *Nat Immunol* 2000; 1: 37-41.

44. Yu G, Boone T, Delaney J, Hawkins N, Kelley M, Ramakrishnan M, McCabe S, Qiu W, Kornuc M, Xia X-Z, Guo J, Stolina M, Boyle WJ, Sarosi I, Hsu H, Senaldi G, Theill LE. APRIL and TALL-1 and receptors BCMA and TACI: system for regulating humoral immunity. *Nat Immunol* 2000; 1: 252-256.

45. Thompson JS, Bixler SA, Qian F, Vora K, Scott ML, Cachero TG, Hesslon C, Schneider P, Sizing ID, Mullen C, Strauch K, Zafari M, Benjamin CD, Tschopp J, Browning JL, Ambrose C. BAFF-R, a newly identified TNF receptor that specifically interacts with BAFF. *Science* 2001; 293: 2108-2111.

46. Kalled SL, Ambrose C, Hsu YM. The biochemistry and biology of BAFF, APRIL and their receptors. *Curr Dir Autoimmun* 2005; 8: 206-242.

47. von Bulow GU, Bram RJ. NF-AT activation induced by a CAML-interacting member of the tumor necrosis factor receptor superfamily. *Science* 1997; 278: 138-141.

48. Ng LG, Sutherland APR, Newton R, Qian F, Cachero TG, Scott ML, Thompson JS, Wheway J, Chtanova T, Groom J, Sutton IJ, Xin C, Tangye SG, Kalled SL, Mackay F, Mackay CR. B cell-activating factor belonging to the TNF family (BAFF)-R is the principal BAFF receptor facilitating BAFF costimulation of circulating T and B cells. *J Immunol* 2004; 173: 807-817.

49. Sasaki Y, Casola S, Kutok JL, Rajewsky K, Schmidt-Supprian M. TNF family member B cell-activating factor (BAFF) receptor-dependent and –independent roles for BAFF in B cell physiology. *J Immunol* 2004; 173: 2245-2252.

50. Shulga-Morskaya S, Dobles M, Walsh ME, Ng LG, Mackay F, Rao SP, Kalled SL, Scott ML. B cell-activating factor belonging to the TNF family acts through separate receptors to support B cell survival and T cell-independent antibody formation. J *Immunol* 2004; 173: 2331-2341.

51. Pelletier M, Thompson JS, Qian F, Bixler SA, Gong D, Cachero T, Gilbride K, Day E, Zafari M, Benjamin C, Gorelik L, Whitty A, Kalled SL, Ambrose C, Hsu Y-M. Comparison of soluble decoy IgG fusion proteins of BAFF-R and BCMA as antagonists of BAFF. *J Biol Chem* 2003; 278: 33127-33133.

52. Miller DJ, Hayes CE. Phenotypic and genetic characterization of a unique B lymphocyte deficiency in strain A/WySnJ mice. *Eur J Immunol* 1991; 21: 1123-1130.

53. Harless SM, Lentz VM, Sah AP, Hsu BL, Clise-Dwyer K, Hilbert DM, Hayes CE, Cancro MP. Competition for BLyS-mediated signaling through Bcmd/BR3 regulates peripheral B lymphocyte numbers. *Curr Biol* 2001; 11: 1986-1989.

54. Yan M, Brady JR, Chan B, Lee WP, Hsu B, Harless S, Cancro M, Grewal IS, Dixit VM. Identification of a novel receptor for B lymphocyte stimulator that is mutated in a mouse strain with severe B cell deficiency. *Curr Biol* 2001; 11: 1547-1552.

55. Rahman ZSM, Rao SP, Kalled SL, Manser T. Normal induction but attenuated progression of germinal center responses in BAFF and BAFF-R signaling-deficient mice. *J Exp Med* 2003; 198: 1157-1169.

56. von Bulow GU, van Deursen JM, Bram RJ. Regulation of the T-independent humoral response by TACI. *Immunity* 2001; 14: 573-582.

57. Yan M, Wang H, Chan B, Roose-Girma M, Erickson S, Baker T, Tumas D, Grewal IS, Dixit VM. Activation and accumulation of B cells in TACI-deficient mice. *Nat Immunol* 2001; 2: 638-643.

58. Seshasayee D, Valdez P, Yan M, Dixit VM, Tumas D, Grewal IS. Loss of TACI causes fatal lymphoproliferation and autoimmunity, establishing TACI as an inhibitory BLyS receptor. *Immunity* 2003; 18: 279-288.

59. Sakurai D, Kanno Y, Hase H, Kojima H, Okumura K, Kobata T. TACI attenuates antibody production costimulated by BAFF-R and CD40. *Eur J Immunol* 2007; 37: 110-118.

60. Castigli E, Wilson SA, Garibyan L, Rachid R, Bonilla F, Schneider L, Geha RS. TACI is mutant in common variable immunodeficiency and IgA deficiency. *Nat Genet* 2005; 37: 829-834.

61. Salzer U, Chapel HM, Webster AD, Pan-Hammarstrom Q, Schmitt-Graeff A, Schlesier M, Peter HH, Rockstroh JK, Schneider P, Schaffer AA, Hammarstrom L, Grimbacker B. Mutations in TNFRSF13B encoding TACI are associated with common variable immunodeficiency in humans. *Nat Genet* 2005; 37: 820-828.

62. Poodt AEJ, Driessen GJA, de Klein A, van Dongen JJM, van der Burg M, de Vries E. TACI mutations and disease susceptibility in patients with common variable immunodeficiency. *Clin Exp Immunol* 2009; 156: 35-39.

63. Xu S, Lam KP. B-cell maturation protein, which binds the tumor necrosis factor family members BAFF and APRIL, is dispensable for humoral immune responses. *Mol Cell Biol* 2001; 21: 4067-4074.

64. Avery DT, Kalled SL, Ellyard JI, Ambrose C, Bixler SA, Thien M, Brink R, Mackay F, Hodgkin PD, Tangye SG. BAFF selectively enhances the survival of plasmablasts generated from human memory B cells. *J Clin Invest* 2003; 112: 286-297.

65. Zhang X, Park CS, Yoon SO, Li L, Hsu YM, Ambrose C, Choi YS. BAFF supports human B cell differentiation in the lymphoid follicles through distinct receptors. *Int Immunol* 2005; 17: 779-788.

66. Darce JR, Arendt BK, Wu X, Jelinek DF. Regulated expression of BAFF-binding receptors during human B cell differentiation. J Immunol 2007; 179: 7276-7286.

67. Doreau A, Belot A, Bastid J, Riche B, Trescol-Biemont M-C, Ranchin B, Fabien N, Cochat P, Pouteil-Noble C, Trolliet P, Durieu I, Tebib J, Kassai B, Ansieau S, Puisieux A, Eliaou J-F, Bonnefoy-Berard N. Interleukin 17 acts in synergy with B cell-activating factor to influence B cell biology and the pathophysiology of systemic lupus erythematosus. *Nat Immunol* 2009; 10: 778-785.

68. Bossen C, Schneider P. BAFF, APRIL and their receptors: Structure, function and signaling. *Sem Immunol* 2006; 18: 263-275.

69. Brink R. Regulation of B cell self-tolerance by BAFF. Sem in Immunol 2006; 18: 276-283.

70. Kalled SL. Impact of the BAFF/BR3 axis on B cell survival, germinal center maintenance and antibody production. *Sem Immunol* 2006; 18: 290-296.

71. Bonizzi G, Karin M. The two NF-κB activation pathways and their role in innate and adaptive immunity. *Trends Immunol* 2004; 25: 280-288.

72. Claudio E, Brown K, Park S, Wang H, Siebenlist U. BAFF-induced NEMO-independent processing of NF-κB2 in maturing B cells. *Nat Immunol* 2002; 3: 958-965.

73. Enzler T, Bonizzi G, Silverman GJ, Otero DC, Widhopf GF, Anzelon-Mills A, Rickert RC, Karin M. Alternative and classical NF-κB signaling retain autoreactive B cells in the splenic marginal zone and result in lupus-like disease. *Immunity* 2006; 25: 403-415.

74. Sasaki Y, Derudder E, Hobeika E, Pelanda R, Reth M, Rajewsky K, Schmidt-Supprian M. Canonical NF-κB activity, dispensable for B cell development, replaces BAFF-receptor signals and promotes B cell proliferation upon activation. *Immunity* 2006; 24: 729-739.

75. Qian Y, Qin J, Cui G, Naramura M, Snow EC, Ware CF, Fairchild RL, Omori SA, Rickert RC, Scott M, Kotzin BL, Li X. Act 1, a negative regulator in CD40- and BAFF-mediated B cell survival. *Immunity* 2004; 21: 575-587.

76. Qian Y, Giltiay N, Xiao J, Wang Y, Tian J, Han S, Scott M, Carter R, Jorgensen TN, Li X. Deficiency of Act 1, a critical modulator of B cell function, leads to development of Sjogren's syndrome. *Eur J Immunol* 2008; 38: 2219-2228.

77. Huard B, Arlettaz L, Ambrose C, Kindler V, Mauri D, Roosnek E, Tschopp J, Schneider P, French LE. BAFF production by antigen-presenting cells provides T cell co-stimulation. *Int Immunol* 2004; 16: 467-475.

The Role of BAFF ... ■ Samia Ragheb, Robert Lisak, Felicitas Gonzales and Yanfeng Li.

179

78. Sutherland APR, Ng LG, Fletcher CA, Shum B, Newton RA, Grey ST, Rolph MS, Mackay F, Mackay CR. BAFF augments certain Th1-associated inflammatory responses. *J Immunol* 2005; 174: 5537-5544.

79. Lam QLK, Ko OKH, Zheng B-J, Lu L. Local BAFF gene silencing suppresses Th17-cell generation and ameliorates autoimmune arthritis. *Proc Natl Acad Sc*i (USA) 2008; 105: 14993-14998.

80. Cheema GS, Roschke V, Hilbert DM, Stohl W. Elevated serum B lymphocyte stimulator levels in patients with systemic immune-based rheumatic diseases. *Arthr & Rheum* 2001; 44: 1313-1319.

81. Zhang J, Roschke V, Baker KP, Wang Z, Alarcon GS, Fessler BJ, Bastian H, Kimberly RP, Zhou T. Cutting edge: A role of B lymphocyte stimulator in systemic lupus erythematosus. *J Immunol* 2001; 166: 6-10.

82. Stohl W, Metyas S, Tan S-M, Cheema GS, Oamar B, Xu D, Roschke V, Wu Y, Baker KP, Hilbert DM. B lymphocyte stimulator overexpression in patients with systemic lupus erythematosus. Longitudinal observations. *Arthritis Rheu*m 2003; 48: 3475-3486.

83. Kayagaki N, Yan M, Seshasayee D, Wang H, Lee W, French DM, Grewal IS, Cochran AG, Gordon NC, Yin J, Starovasnik MA, Dixit VM. BAFF/BLyS receptor 3 binds the B cell survival factor BAFF ligand through a discrete surface loop and promotes processing of NF-κB2. *Immunity* 2002; 17: 515-524.

84. Liu W, Szalai A, Zhao L, Liu D, Martin F, Kimberly RP, Zhou T, Carter RH. Control of spontaneous B lymphocyte autoimmunity with adenovirus-encoded soluble TACI. *Arth Rheum* 2004; 50: 1884-1896.

85. Ramanujam M, Wang X, Huang W, Schiffer L, Grimaldi C, Akkerman A, Diamond B, Madaio MP, Davidson A. Mechanism of action of transmembrane activator and calcium modulator ligand interactor-Ig in murine systemic lupus erythematosus. *J Immunol* 2004; 173: 3524-3534.

86. Firestein GS. Evolving concepts of rheumatoid arthritis. Nature 2003; 423: 356-361.

87. Bosello S, Youinou P, Daridon C, Tolusso B, Bendaoud B, Pietrapertosa D, Morelli A, Ferraccioli G. Concentrations of BAFF correlate with autoantibody levels, clinical disease activity, and response to treatment in early rheumatoid arthritis. *J Rheumatol* 2008; 35: 1256-1264.

88. Tan S-M, Xu D, Roschke V, Perry JW, Arkfeld DG, Ehresmann GR, Migone T-S, Hilbert DM, Stohl W. Local production of B lymphocyte stimulator protein and APRIL in arthritic joints of patients with inflammatory arthritis. *Arthr & Rheum* 2003; 48: 982-992.

89. Zhang M, Ko KH, Lam QL, Lo CK, Srivastava G, Zheng B, Lau YL, Lu L. Expression and function of TNF family member B cell-activating factor in the development of autoimmune arthritis. *Int Immunol* 2005; 17: 1081-1092.

90. Wang H, Marsters SA, Baker T, Chan B, Lee WP, Fu L, Tumas D, Yan M, Dixit VM, Ashkenzazi A, Grewal IS. TACI-ligand interactions are required for T cell activation and collagen-induced arthritis in mice. *Nat Immunol* 2001; 2: 632-637.

91. Jonsson R, Moen K, Vestrheim D, Szodoray P. Current issues in Sjogren's syndrome. *Oral Dis* 2002; 8: 130-140.

92. Mariette X, Roux S, Zhang J, Bengoufa D, Lavie F, Zhou T, Kimberly R. The level of Blys (BAFF) correlates with the titre of autoantibodies in human Sjogren's syndrome. *Ann Rheum Dis* 2003; 62: 168-171.

93. Lavie F, Miceli-Richard C, Quillard J, Roux S, Leclerc P, Mariette X. Expression of BAFF (BLyS) in T cells infiltrating labial salivary glands from patients with Sjogren's syndrome. *J Pathol* 2004; 202: 496-502.

94. Szodoray P, Jellestad S, Alex P, Zhou T, Wilson PC, Centola M, Brun JG, Jonsson R. Programmed cell death of peripheral blood B cells determined by laser scanning cytometry in Sjogren's syndrome with a special emphasis on BAFF. J *Clin Immunol* 2004; 24: 600-611.

95. Patrick J, Lindstrom J. Autoimmune response to acetylcholine receptors. *Science* 1973; 180: 871-872.

96. Ragheb S, Lisak RP. The immunopathogenesis of acquired (autoimmune) myasthenia gravis. In: Handbook of Myasthenia Gravis and Myasthenic Syndromes. 1994; p. 239-276. Dekker. New York.

97. Appel SH, Almon RR, Levy NR. Acetylcholine receptor antibodies in myasthenia gravis. *N Engl J Med* 1975; 293: 760-761.

98. Lennon VA, Jones G, Howard FM, Elveback L. Autoantibodies to acetylcholine receptors in myasthenia gravis. *N Engl J Med* 1983; 308: 402-403.

99. Drachman DB, De Silva S, Ramsay D, Pestronk A. Humoral pathogenesis of myasthenia gravis. *Ann NY Acad Sci* 1987; 505: 90-105.

100. Skeie GO, Aarli JA, Gilhus NE. Titin and ryanodine receptor antibodies in myasthenia gravis. *Acta Neurol Scand Suppl* 2006; 183: 19-23.

101. Evoli A, Tonali PA, Padua L, Monaco ML, Scuderi F, Batocchi AP, Marino M, Bartoccioni E. Clinical correlates with anti-MuSK antibodies in generalized seronegative myasthenia gravis. *Brain* 2003; 126: 2304-2311.

102. Sanders DB, El-Salem K, Massey JM, McConville J, Vincent A. Clinical aspects of MuSK antibody positive seronegative MG. *Neurology* 2003; 60: 1978-1980.

103. Shiraishi H, Motomura M, Yoshimura T, Fukudome T, Fukuda T, Nakao Y, Tsujihata M, Vincent A, Eguchi K. Acetylcholine receptors loss and postsynaptic damage in MuSK antibody-positive myasthenia gravis. *Ann Neurol* 2005; 57: 289-293.

104. Jha S, Xu K, Maruta T, Oshima M, Mosier DR, Atassi MZ, Hoch W. Myasthenia gravis induced in mice by immunization with the recombinant extracellular domain of rat muscle-specific kinase (MuSK). *J Neuroimmunol* 2006; 175: 107-117.

105. Shigemoto K, Kubo S, Maruyama N, Hato N, Yamada H, Jie C, Kobayashi N, Mominoki K, Abe Y, Ueda N, Matsuda S. Induction of myasthenia by immunization against muscle-specific kinase. *J Clin Invest* 2006; 116: 1016-1024.

106. Cole RN, Reddel SW, Gervasio OL, Phillips WD. Anti-MuSK patient antibodies disrupt the mouse neuromuscular junction. *Ann Neurol* 2008; 63: 782-789.

107. Castleman B. The pathology of the thymus gland in myasthenia gravis. Ann NY *Acad Sci* 1966; 135: 496-503.

108. Goldstein G. Myasthenia gravis and the thymus. *Ann Rev Med* 1971; 22: 119-124.

109. Wekerle H, Ketelsen UP, Zurn AP, Fulpius BW. Intrathymic pathogenesis of myasthenia gravis: transient expression of acetylcholine receptors on thymus-derived muscle cells. *Eur J Immunol* 1978; 8: 579-583.

110. Ragheb S, Lisak RP. The thymus and myasthenia gravis. In: Chest Surgery Clinics of North America. The Thymus. 2001; p. 311-327. Saunders. Philadelphia.

111. Lindstrom JM, Seybold ME, Lennon VA, Whittingham S, Duane D. Antibody to acetylcholine receptor in myasthenia gravis: prevalence, clinical correlates and diagnostic value. *Neurology* 1976; 26: 1054-1059.

112. Scadding GK, Vincent A, Newsom-Davis J, Henry K. Acetylcholine receptor antibody synthesis by thymic lymphocytes: correlation with thymic histology. *Neurology* 1983; 31: 935-943.

113. Levinson AI, Zweiman B, Lisak RP, Dziarski A, Moskovitz AR. Thymic B-cell activation in myasthenia gravis. *Neurology* 1984; 34: 462-468.

114. Sims GP, Shiono H, Willcox N, Stott DI. Somatic hypermutation and selection of B cells in thymic germinal centers responding to acetylcholine receptor in myasthenia gravis. *J Immunol* 2001; 167: 1935-1944.

115. Onodera J, Nakamura S, Nagano I, Tobita M, Yoshioka M, Takeda A, Oouchi M, Itoyama Y. Upregulation of bcl-2 in the myasthenic thymus. *Ann Neurol* 1996; 39: 521-528.

116. Shiono H, Fujii Y, Okumura M, Takeuchi Y, Inoue M, Matsuda H. Failure to down-regulate Bcl-2 protein in thymic germinal center B cells in myasthenia gravis. *Eur J Immunol* 1997; 27: 805-809.

117. Thangarajh M, Masterman T, Helgeland L, Rot U, Jonsson MV, Eide GE, Pirskanen R, Hillert J, Jonsson R. The thymus is a source of B-cell-survival factors – APRIL and BAFF – in myasthenia gravis. *J Neuroimmunol* 2006; 178: 161-166.

118. Kim JY, Yang Y, Moon J-S, Lee EY, So SH, Lee H-S, Park KD, Choi Y-C. Serum BAFF expression in patients with myasthenia gravis. *J Neuroimmunol* 2008; 199: 151-154.

119. Ragheb S, Lisak R, Lewis R, Van Stavern G, Gonzales F, Simon K. A potential role for B-cell activating factor in the pathogenesis of autoimmune myasthenia gravis. *Arch Neurol* 2008; 65: 1358-1362.

120. Roses AD, Olanow CW, McAdams MW, Lane RJM. No direct correlation between serum anti-acetylcholine receptor antibody levels and clinical state of individual patients with myasthenia gravis. *Neurology* 1981; 31: 220-224.

121. Li X, Xiao B-G, Xi J-Y, Lu C-Z, Lu J-H. Decrease of CD4⁺CD25^high^Foxp3⁺ regulatory T cells and elevation of CD19⁺ BAFF-R⁺ B cells and soluble ICAM-1 in myasthenia gravis. *Clin Immunol* 2008; 126: 180-188.

122. Thangarajh M, Kisiswa L, Pirskanen R, Hillert J. The expression of BAFF-binding receptors is not altered in multiple sclerosis or myasthenia gravis. *Scand J Immunol* 2007; 65: 461-466.

123. Gilbert JA, Kalled SL, Moorhead J, Hess DM, Rennert P, Li Z, Khan MZ, Banga JP. Treatment of autoimmune hyperthyroidism in a murine model of Grave's disease with TNF-family ligand inhibitors suggests a key role for BAFF in disease pathology. Endocrinology 2006; Epub.

124. Silveira PA, Grey ST. B cells in the spotlight: innocent bystanders or major players in the pathogenesis of type 1 diabetes. Trends Endocrinol Metab 2006; 17: 128-135.

125. Zekavat G, Rostami SY, Badkerhanian A, Parsons RF, Koeberlein B, Yu M, Ward CD, Migone T-S, Yu L, Eisenbarth GS, Cancro MP, Naji A, Noorchashm H. In vivo BLyS/BAFF neutralization ameliorates islet-derived autoimmunity in nonobese diabetic mice. *J Immunol* 2008; 181: 8133-8144.

126. Wingerchuk DM, Lucchinetti CF, Noseworthy JH. Multiple sclerosis: current pathophysiological concepts. *Lab Invest* 2001; 81: 263-281.

127. Sospedra M, Martin R. Immunology of multiple sclerosis. Ann Rev Immunol 2005; 23: 683-747.

128. Frohman EM, Racke MK, Raine CS. Multiple sclerosis – The plaque and its pathogenesis. *N Engl J Med* 2006; 354: 942-955.

129. Chitnis T. The role of CD4 T cells in the pathogenesis of multiple sclerosis. *Int Rev Neurobiol* 2007; 79: 43-72.

130. Cross AH, Trotter JL, Lyons J-A. B cells and antibodies in CNS demyelinating disease. *J Neuroimmunol* 2001; 112: 1-14.

131. Nikbin B, Bonab MM, Khosravi F, Talebian F. Role of B cells in the pathogenesis of multiple sclerosis. *Int Rev Neurobiol* 2007; 79: 13-42.

132. Vyshkina T, Kalman B. Autoantibodies and neurodegeneration in multiple sclerosis. *Lab Invest* 2008; 88: 796-807.

133. Prineas JW. Multiple sclerosis: presence of lymphatic capillaries and lymphoid tissue in the brain and spinal cord. *Science* 1979; 203: 1123-1125.

134. Serafini B, Rusicarelli B, Magliozzi R, Shigliano E, Aloisi F. Detection of ectopic B-cell follicles with germinal centers in the meninges of patients with secondary progressive multiple sclerosis. *Brain Pathol* 2004; 14: 164-174.

135. Krumbholz M, Theil D, Derfuss T, Rosenwald A, Schrader F, Monoranu C-M, Kalled SL, Hess DM, Serafini B, Aloisi F, Wekerle H, Hohlfeld R, Meinl E. BAFF is produced by astrocytes and up-regulated in multiple sclerosis lesions and primary central nervous system lymphoma. *J Exp Med* 2005; 201: 195-200.

136. Magliozzi R, Columba-Cabezas S, Serafini B, Aloisi F. Intracerebral expression of CXCL13 and BAFF is accompanied by formation of lymphoid follicle-like structures in the meninges of mice with relapsing experimental autoimmune encephalomyelitis. *J Neuroimmunol* 2004; 148: 11-23.

137. Huntington ND, Tomioka R, Clavarino C, Chow AM, Linares D, Mana P, Rossjohn J, Cachero TG, Qian F, Kalled SL, Bernard CC, Reid HH. A BAFF antagonist suppresses experimental autoimmune encephalomyelitis by targeting cell-mediated and humoral immune responses. *Int Immunol* 2006; 18: 1473-1485.

138. Xue X, Feng G, Li M, Qin X, Wu S, Zhang C, You Y, Wang W, Ziang C, Liu Y, Zhu W, Ran Y, Zhang Z, Yan Z, Han W, Zhang Y. Amelioration of experimental autoimmune encephalomyelitis by BLyS autovaccine. *Vaccine* 2008; 26: 2873-2881.

139. Briani C, Samaroo D, Alaedini A. Celiac disease: from gluten to autoimmunity. *Autoimmun Rev* 2008; 7: 644-650.

140. Fabris M, Visentini D, De Re V, Picierno A, Maieron R, Cannizzaro R, Villalta D, Curcio F, De Vita S, Tonutti T. Elevated B cell-activating factor of the tumor necrosis family in coeliac disease. *Scand J Gastroenterol* 2007; 42: 1434-1439.

141. Kato A, Peters A, Suh L, Carter R, Harris KE, Chandra R, Conley D, Grammer LC, Kern R, Schleimer RP. Evidence of a role for B cell-activating factor of the TNF family in the pathogenesis of chronic rhinosinusitis with nasal polyps. *J Allergy Clin Immunol* 2008; 121: 1385-1392.

142. Kato A, Xiao H, Chustz RT, Liu MC, Schleimer RP. Local release of B cell-activating factor of the TNF family after segmental allergen challenge of allergic subjects. *J Allergy Clin Immunol* 2009; 123: 369-375.

143. Kang JS, Yoon YD, Ahn JH, Kim SC, Kim KH, Kim HM, Moon EY. B cell-activating factor is a novel diagnosis parameter for asthma. *Int Arch Allergy Immunol* 2006; 141: 181-188.

144. Asashima N, Fujimoto M, Watanabe R, Nakashima H, Yazawa N, Okochi H, Tamaki K. Serum levels of Baff are increased in bullous pemphigoid but not in pemphigus vulgaris. *Br J Dermatol* 2006; 155: 330-336.

The Role of BAFF ... ▮ Samia Ragheb, Robert Lisak, Felicitas Gonzales and Yanfeng Li.

183

145. Alexis AF, Dudda-Subramanya R, Sinha AA. Alopecia areata: autoimmune basis of hair loss. *Eur J Dermatol* 2004; 14: 364-370.

146. Kuwano Y, Fujimoto M, Watanabe R, Ishiura N, Nakashima H, Ohno Y, Yano S, Yazawa N, Okochi H, Tamaki K. Serum BAFF and APRIL levels in patients with *alopecia areata*. J Dermatol Sci 2008; 50: 236-239.

147. Novak AJ, Bram RJ, Kay NE, Jelinek DF. Aberrant expression of B-lymphocyte stimulator by B chronic lymphocytic leukemia cells: a mechanism for survival. *Blood* 2002; 100: 2973-2979.

148. Kern C, Cornuel J-F, Billard C, Tang R, Rouillard D, Stenou V, Defrance T, Ajchenbaum-Cymbalista F, Simonin P-Y, Feldblum S, Kolb J-P. Involvement of BAFF and APRIL in the resistance to apoptosis of B-CLL through an autocrine pathway. Blood 2004; 103: 679-688.

149. Haiat S, Billard C, Quiney C, Ajchenbaum-Cymbalista F, Kolb JP. Role of BAFF and APRIL in human B-cell chronic lymphocytic leukemia. *Immunology* 2006; 118: 281-292.

150. Briones J, Timmerman JM, Hilbert DM, Levy R. BLyS and BLyS receptor expression in non-Hodgkin's lymphoma. *Exp Hematol* 2002; 30: 135-141.

151. Novak AJ, Grote DM, Stenson M, Ziesmer SC, Witzig TE, Habermann TM, Harder B, Ristow KM, Bram RJ, Jelinek DF, Gross JA, Ansell SM. Expression of BLys and its receptors in B-cell non-Hodgkin lymphoma: correlation with disease activity and patient outcome. *Blood* 2004; 104: 2247-2253.

152. He B, Chadburn A, Jou E, Schattner EJ, Knowles DM, Cerutti A. Lymphoma B cells evade apoptosis through the TNF family members BAFF/BLys and APRIL. *J Immunol* 2004; 172: 3268-3279.

153. Novak AJ, Slager SL, Fredericksen ZS, Wang AH, Manske MM, Ziesmer S, Liebow M, Macon WR, Dillon SR, Witzig TE, Cerhan JR, Ansell SM. Genetic variation in B-cell-activating factor is associated with an increased risk of developing B-cell non-Hodgkin lymphoma. *Cancer Res* 2009; 69: OF1-8.

154. Lwin T, Crespo LA, Wu A, Dessureault S, Shu H, Moscinski LC, Sotomayor E, Dalton WS, Tao J. Lymphoma cell adhesion-induced expression of B cell-activating factor of the TNF family in bone marrow stromal cells protects non-Hodgkin's B lymphoma cells from apoptosis. *Leukemia* 2009; 23: 170-177.

155. Moreaux J, Legouffe E, Jourdan E, Quittet P, Reme T, Lugagne C, Moine P, Rossi J-F, Klein B, Tarte K. BAFF and APRIL protect myeloma cells from apoptosis induced by interleukin 6 deprivation and dexamethasone. *Blood* 2004; 103: 3148-3157.

156. Novak AJ, Darce JR, Arendt BK, Harder B, Henderson K, Kindsvogel W, Gross JA, Greipp PR, Jelinek DF. Expression of BCMA, TACI, and BAFF-R in multiple myeloma: a mechanism for growth and survival. *Blood* 2004; 103: 689-694.

157. Tai YT, Li XF, Breitkreutz I, Song W, Neri P, Catley L, Podar K, Hideshima T, Chauhan D, Raje N, Schlossman R, Richardson P, Munshi NC, Anderson KC. Role of B-cell activating factor in adhesion and growth of human multiple myeloma cells in the bone marrow microenvironment. *Cancer* Res 2006; 66: 6675-6682.

158. Rodig SJ, Shahsafaei A, Li B, Mackay CR, Dorfman DM. BAFF-R, the major B cell-activating factor receptor, is expressed on most mature B cells and B-cell lymphoproliferative disorders. *Hum Pathol* 2005; 36: 1113-1119.

159. Ohata J, Zvaifler NJ, Nishio M, Boyle DL, Kalled SL, Carson DA, Kipps TJ. Fibroblast-like synoviocytes of mesenchymal origin express functional B cell-activating factor of the TNF family in response to proinflammatory cytokines. *J Immunol* 2005; 174: 864-870.

160. Ittah M, Miceli-Richard C, Eric Gottenberg J, Lavie F, Lazure T, Ba N, Sellam J, Lepajolec C, Mariette X. B cell-activating factor of the tumor necrosis factor family (BAFF) is expressed under stimulation by interferon in salivary gland epithelial cells in primary Sjogren's syndrome. *Arth Res Ther* 2006; 8: R51.

161. Zhou L, Zhong R, Hao W, Wang H, Fan X-X, Zhang L, Qingmei M. Interleukin-10 and interferon-γ up-regulate the expression of B-cell activating factor in cultured human promyelocytic leukemia cells. *Exp Mol Pathol* 2009; E-pub.

162. Kim H-A, Jeon S-H, Seo G-Y, Park J-B, Kim P-H. TGF-β1 and IFN-γ stimulate mouse macrophages to express BAFF via different signaling pathways. *J Leukoc Biol* 2008; 83: 1431-1439.

163. Krumbholz M, Faber H, Steinmeyer F, Hoffmann L-A, Kumpfel T, Pellkofer H, Derfuss T, Ionescu C, Starck M, Hafner C, Hohlfeld R, Meinl E. Interferon-β increases BAFF levels in multiple sclerosis: implications for B cell autoimmunity. *Brain* 2008; 131: 1455-1463.

164. Gandhi KS, McKay FC, Schibeci SD, Arthur JW, Heard RN, Stewart GJ, Booth DR. BAFF is a biological response marker to IFN-beta treatment in multiple sclerosis. *J Interferon Cytokine Res* 2008; 28: 529-539.

165. Hanada T, Yoshida H, Kato S, Tanaka K, Masutani K, Tsukada J, Nomura Y, Mimata H, Kubo M, Yoshimura A. Suppressor of cytokine signaling-1 is essential for suppressing dendritic cell activation and systemic autoimmunity. *Immunity* 2003; 19: 437-450.

166. Heino M, Peterson P, Kudoh J, Nagamine K, Lagerstedt A, Ovod V, Ranki A, Rantala I, Nieminen M, Tuukkanen J, Scott HS, Antonarakis SE, Shimizu N, Krohn K. Autoimmune regulator is expressed in the cells regulating immune tolerance in thymus medulla. *Biochem Biophys Res Comm* 1999; 257: 821-825.

167. Kogawa K, Nagafuchi S, Katsuta H, Kudoh J, Tamiya S, Sakai Y, Shimizu N, Harada M. Expression of AIRE gene in peripheral monocyte/dendritic cell lineage. *Immunol Lett* 2002; 80: 195-198.

168. Ramsey C, Hassler S, Marits P, Kampe O, Surh CD, Peltonen L, Winqvist O. Increased antigen presenting cell-mediated T cell activation in mice and patients without the autoimmune regulator. *Eur J Immunol* 2006; 36: 305-317.

169. Hassler S, Ramsey C, Karlsson MC, Larsson D, Herrmann B, Rozell B, Backheden M, Peltonen L, Kampe O, Winqvist O. Aire-deficient mice develop hematopoetic irregularities and marginal zone B-cell lymphoma. *Blood* 2006; 108: 1941-1948.

170. Lindh E, Lind SM, Lindmark E, Hassler S, Perheentupa J, Peltonen L, Winqvist O, Karlsson MCI. AIRE regulates T-cell-independent B-cell responses through BAFF. Proc Natl Acad Sci (USA) 2008; 105: 18466-18471.

171. Tangye SG, Bryant VL, Cuss AK, Good KL. BAFF, APRIL and human B cell disorders. *Sem in Immunol* 2006; 18: 305-317.

172. Baker KP, Edwards BM, Main SH, Choi GH, Wager RE, Halpern WG, Lappin PB, Riccobene T, Abramian D, Sekut L, Sturm B, Poortman C, Minter RR, Dobson CL, Williams E, Carmen S, Smith R, Roschke V, Hilbert DM, Vaughan TJ, Albert VR.

The Role of BAFF ... ■ Samia Ragheb, Robert Lisak, Felicitas Gonzales and Yanfeng Li.

185

Generation and characterization of LymphoStat-B, a human monoclonal antibody that antagonizes the bioactivities of B lymphocyte stimulator. *Arthr & Rheum* 2003; 48: 3253-3265.

173. Lin WY, Gong Q, Seshasayee D, Lin Z, Ou Q, Ye S, Suto E, Shu J, Lee WP, Lee CW, Fuh G, Leabman M, Iyer S, Howell K, Gelzleichter T, Beyer J, Danilenko D, Yeh S, DeForge LE, Ebens A, Thompson JS, Ambrose C, Balazs M, Starovasnik MA, Martin F. Anti-BR3 antibodies: a new class of B-cell immunotherapy combining cellular depletion and survival blockade. *Blood* 2007; 110: 3959-3967.

174. Vugmeyster Y, Seshasayee D, Chang W, Storn A, Howell K, Sa S, Nelson T, Martin F, Grewal I, Gilkerson E, Wu B, Thompson J, Ehrenfels BN, Ren S, Song A, Gelzleichter TR, Danilenko DM. A soluble BAFF antagonist, BR3-Fc, decreases peripheral blood B cells and lymphoid tissue marginal zone and follicular B cells in cynomolgus monkeys. *Am J Pathol* 2006; 168: 476-489.

175. Carbonatto M, Yu P, Bertolino M, Vigna E, Steidler S, Fava L, Daghero C, Roattino B, Onidi M, Ardizzone M, Peano S, Visich J, Janszen D, Dillon S, Ponce R. Nonclinical safety, pharmacokinetics, and pharmacodynamics of atacicept. *Toxicol Sci* 2008; 105: 200-210.

176. Dall'Era M, Chakravarty E, Wallace D, Genovese M, Weisman M, Kavanaugh A, Kalunian K, Dhar P, Vincent E, Pena-Rossi C, Wofsy D. Reduced B lymphocyte and immunoglobulin levels after atacicept treatment in patients with systemic lupus erythematosus: results of a multicenter, phase Ib, double-blind, placebo-controlled, dose-escalating trial. *Arth Rheum* 2007; 56: 4142-4150.

177. Furie R, Stohl W, Ginzler EM, Becker M, Mishra N, Chatham W, Merrill JT, Weinstein A, McCune WJ, Zhong J, Cai W, Freimuth W; Belimumab Study Group. Biologic activity and safety of belimumab, a neutralizing anti-B-lymphocyte stimulator (BLyS) monoclonal antibody: a phase I trial in patients with systemic lupus erythematosus. *Arth Res Ther* 2008; 10: R109.

178. Tak PP, Thurlings RM, Rossier C, Nestorov I, Dimic A, Mircetic V, Rischmueller M, Nasonov E, Schmidt E, Emery P, Munafo A. Atacicept in patients with rheumatoid arthritis: results of a multicenter, phase Ib, double-blind, placebo-controlled, dose-escalating, single- and repeated-dose study. *Arth Rheum* 2008; 58: 61-72.

179. Reff ME, Carner K, Chambers KS, Chinn PC, Leonard JE, Raab R, Newman RA, Hanna N, Anderson DR. Depletion of B cells in vivo by a chimeric mouse human monoclonal antibody to CD20. *Blood* 1994; 83: 435-445.

180. Cambridge G, Stohl W, Leandro MJ, Migone T-S, Hilbert DM, Edwards JCW. Circulating levels of B lymphocyte stimulator in patients with rheumatoid arthritis following rituximab treatment. *Arth Rheum* 2006; 54: 723-732.

181. Lavie F, Miceli-Richard C, Ittah M, Sellam J, Gottenberg JE, Mariette X. Increase of B cell-activating factor of the TNF family (BAFF) after rituximab: insights into a new regulating system of BAFF production. *Ann Rheum Dis* 2007; 66: 700-703.

182. Ramanujam M, Davidson A. BAFF blockade for systemic lupus erythematosus: will the promise be fulfilled. *Immunol Rev* 2008; 223: 156-174.

183. Stewart DM, Mc Avoy MJ, Hilbert DM, Nelson DL. B lymphocytes from individuals with common variable immunodeficiency respond to B lymphocyte stimulator (BLys protein) in vitro. *Clin Immunol* 2003; 109: 137-143.

184. Chen L, Ran MJ, Shan XX, Cao M, Cao P, Yang XM, Zhang SQ. BAFF enhances B-cell-mediated immune response and vaccine-protection against a very virulent IBDV in chickens. *Vaccine* 2009; 27: 1393-1399.

185. Tertilt C, Joh J, Krause A, Chou P, Schneeweiss K, Crystal RG, Worgall S. Expression of B cell activating factor enhances protective immunity of a vaccine against *P. aeruginosa*. Infect Immun 2009; E-pub.

II

Lambert -Eaton Myasthenic Syndrome

Lambert-Eaton Myasthenic Syndrome

Vern C. Juel, M.D. and Donald B. Sanders, M.D.

1. INTRODUCTION

Lambert-Eaton syndrome (LES) is a rare autoimmune disorder characterized by muscle weakness, fatigue, and autonomic dysfunction resulting from antibody mediated attack against the P/Q-type voltage-gated calcium channels (VGCC) on presynaptic cholinergic nerve terminals at the neuromuscular junction and in autonomic ganglia. Although LES was initially described as a paraneoplastic disorder (CA-LES) in a patient with small cell lung carcinoma (SCLC), it may also present as an organ-specific autoimmune disorder (NCA-LES) in the absence of cancer. The diagnosis of LES is often challenging and is frequently delayed owing to its protean symptoms and varying weakness.

2. CLINICAL PRESENTATION

2.1. Symptoms

Patients with LES typically experience gradual onset of proximal lower extremity weakness, fatigue, and dry mouth. Some patients report that the weak muscles are sore and tender. Although ocular and bulbar symptoms are generally not prominent (O'Neill, Murray, and Newsom-Davis 577-96;Tim, Massey, and Sanders 2176-78;Wirtz et al. 766-68), clinical presentations suggesting myasthenia gravis (MG) with prominent ocular and bulbar weakness have been reported (Burns et al. 270-73;Titulaer et al. 86-87). LES may initially present with prolonged apnea and ventilator dependence following use of neuromuscular blocking agents for surgery (Anderson, Churchill-Davidson, and Richardson 1291-93). However, respiratory failure in LES is uncommon other than in patients with primary pulmonary disease or after paralytic agent exposure (Barr et al. 712-15;Smith and Wald 1143-45).

Autonomic symptoms are common in LES, but are not often volunteered spontaneously and must be specifically sought by the physician. Most patients have a dry mouth, and this is sometimes associated with an unpleasant metallic taste. Although less common, orthostatic hypotension may be a disabling issue in some patients. Erectile impotence in men, constipation, dry eyes, and bladder dysfunction may also occur (Waterman 145-54).

In general, the symptoms of LES evolve insidiously, although subacute weakness may develop with upper respiratory infections or diarrheal illnesses (Tim, Massey, and Sanders 823-26). CA-LES has been associated with more rapid onset and fulminant disease in some reports (Wirtz, Wintzen, and Verschuuren 226-29), but not in others (Tim, Massey, and Sanders 823-26). As in MG, weakness in LES may be increased by elevated body temperature due to fever or high ambient temperature.

2.2. Physical findings

In LES, the degree of fatigue reported may greatly exceed the amount of weakness demonstrated on clinical examination. Facilitation of muscle strength with brief exercise and decline of strength with more sustained effort may be observed, but is only demonstrated in about half of LES patients (Oh and Sher 1167-71). The distribution of weakness typically involves hip flexors and abductors with a waddling gait pattern that is rarely observed in MG. Although cholinesterase inhibitors may improve weakness, the response is not as robust or as marked as that observed in MG. Tendon reflexes are reduced or absent in most patients, although they may be preserved in early or mild disease. Facilitation of absent or hypoactive reflexes after brief contraction of the corresponding muscle is a virtually diagnostic finding (Nilsson and Rosén 350-57;Henriksson et al. 117-40;O'Neill, Murray, and Newsom-Davis 577-96;Oh and Sher 1167-71). Autonomic findings may include tonic pupils that react poorly to light (O'Neill, Murray, and Newsom-Davis 577-96;Wirtz et al. 444-45), along with orthostatic hypotension with a rapid, invariant pulse.

3. ASSOCIATION WITH CANCER

LES was originally described in a patient with lung cancer (Anderson, Churchill-Davidson, and Richardson 1291-93). In Eaton, Lambert, and Rooke's initial report, six patients with confirmed or presumed lung cancer and proximal weakness, areflexia, and dysautonomia had a neuromuscular junction disorder with electrophysiological findings distinct from MG (Lambert, Eaton, and Rooke 612-13).

In the Duke MG Registry, cancer has been present at disease onset or discovered subsequently in about 40% of LES patients since 1980 (Table 1 and Figure 1). Small cell lung carcinoma (SCLC) is by far the most common tumor type, and smoking and advanced age represent the major risk factors for this malignancy. Along with 35 patients with SCLC, six additional patients had lung tumors causally related to LES (Table 2). Five other patients had malignancy that was likely coincidental and not causally related to LES: three had breast cancer

Table 1. Demographics of 102 LES patients in the Duke MG Registry (1980-2009)

	CA-LES n=42	NCA-LES n=60	All LES n=102
M:F	22:20	25:35	47:55
VGCC +/-	14:4 (78%)	31:10 (76%)	45:14 (76%)
Age onset (years)			
Median	63	54	58
Mean, sd	62.6 +/- 10.1	49.3 +/- 17.0	54.8 +/- 15.9
min-max	40-83	8-77	8-83

CA – associated cancer detected; NCA – no associated cancer detected; VGCC – P/Q type voltage-gated calcium channel antibodies

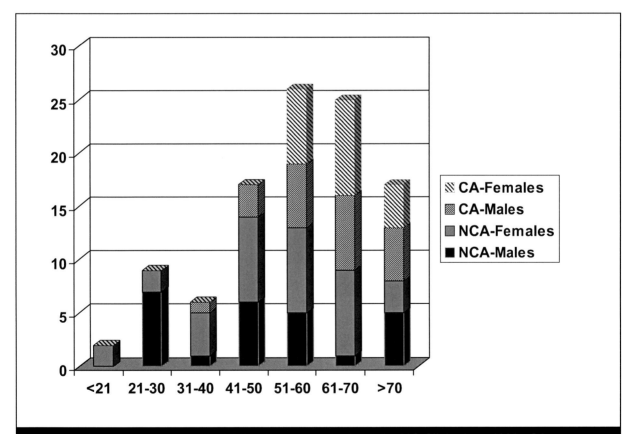

Figure 1. Age of onset age in 102 LES patients seen in the Duke MG Clinic since 1980. CA – associated cancer; NCA – no associated cancer detected. Most patients less than 50 have no associated cancer. With increasing age, more LES patients have cancer, but even over 70 years, cancer is not detected in half the patients.

Table 2. Cancer type in 102 LES patients in the Duke MG Registry

SCLC	35
Other lung cancer	6
Mixed small cell/other	2
Non-small cell	2
Carcinoid	1
Neuroendocrine tumor	1
Other tumors, not likely associated*	5
Breast	3
Prostate	1
Leukemia	1

*These tumors occurred many years before or after LES onset and were deemed to be coincidental and unrelated to the LES.

SCLC – Small cell lung carcinoma

eight and twelve years after and four years prior to LES onset, one had prostate cancer three years prior to LES onset, and one had leukemia eleven years after LES onset. Other tumors rarely associated with LES include non-Hodgkin lymphoma, leukemia, malignant thymoma, and carcinomas of the breast, colon, prostate, larynx, and gall bladder (Wirtz et al. 359-63;Sanders S63-S73;Harper and Lennon 269-91).

It is critical to determine if a patient diagnosed with LES has an underlying cancer. When present, the underlying cancer is usually found within two years of LES onset. Chronic smokers presenting with LES after age 50 nearly always have an underlying cancer, which is unlikely in younger non-smokers (O'Neill, Murray, and Newsom-Davis 577-96;Sanders and Juel 274-83). LES patients with SCLC may have additional paraneoplastic syndromes including cerebellar degeneration, inappropriate antidiuretic hormone secretion (SIADH), or sensorimotor neuropathy (Kobayashi et al. 203-06).

4. ASSOCIATION WITH AUTOIMMUNE DISEASE

The concept that LES may represent an organ-specific autoimmune disorder was suggested in an early report of a patient with longstanding NCA-LES and coexisting pernicious anemia and hypothyroidism (Gutmann et al. 354). In a large series, additional autoimmune disorders were found in 27% NCA-LES, but in only 6% CA-LES patients (Wirtz et al. 1255-59). In the Duke MG Registry, autoimmune thyroid disease is the most common coexisting autoimmune disorder, with pernicious anemia, rheumatoid arthritis, inflammatory myopathy, and systemic vasculitis also observed (Tim, Massey, and Sanders 2176-78).

Organ-specific antibodies (including parietal cell, thyroid microsomal, thyroglobulin, striated muscle, and acetylcholine receptor antibodies) are found more frequently in serum from NCA-LES patients (52-60%) than in CA-LES (24-28%) (O'Neill, Murray, and Newsom-Davis 577-96;Lennon et al. S21-S25), while non-organ specific antibodies (such as antinuclear, smooth muscle, mitochondrial, and rheumatoid factor) are more found more commonly in CA-

LES (60%) compared with NCA-LES (24%) (O'Neill, Murray, and Newsom-Davis 577-96). Immunogenetic factors common to LES and other autoimmune disorders are suggested by the increased frequency of autoimmune disease in maternal relatives of NCA-LES patients that is not observed in relatives of CA-LES patients (Wirtz et al. 1255-59). The HLA genotype is an important marker of genetic susceptibility to autoimmune disease, and highly significant associations of HLA-B8, -A1, and -DR3 haplotypes are observed in NCA-LES, but not in CA-LES patients (Wirtz et al. 230-37).

5. PATHOPHYSIOLOGY

A presynaptic neuromuscular transmission defect was initially demonstrated in LES by *in vitro* microelectrode studies of intercostal muscles (Elmqvist and Lambert 689-713;Lambert and Elmqvist 183-99). This microelectrode technique measures localized depolarizations of the muscle membrane near the endplate. Release of individual acetylcholine (ACh) quanta elicit miniature endplate potentials (MEPP) that reflect the amount of ACh released with each quantum as well as the ability of the endplate to respond to ACh. In LES, these studies demonstrate that MEPP amplitude is normal, but fewer quanta of ACh are released with each motor nerve depolarization.

Although an autoimmune cause for LES was suggested by its association with autoimmune diseases (Gutmann et al. 354) and by the improvement in strength in LES patients following treatment with plasma exchange (Newsom-Davis and Murray 480-85), intravenous immunoglobulin (Bain et al. 678-83) and corticosteroid treatment (Tim, Massey, and Sanders 823-26;Maddison et al. 212-17), direct evidence for humoral autoimmunity in LES derives from the following elegant immunopathological investigations.

Human presynaptic membrane preparations using a freeze-fracture electron microscopy technique demonstrate active zone particles (AZPs) that represent voltage-gated calcium channels (VGCC) in the presynaptic membrane. These AZPs are normally arranged in regular, parallel arrays on the presynaptic nerve terminal membrane (Figure 2A). In LES, the normal morphologic pattern of AZPs becomes disrupted, with clustering and depletion of AZPs (Figure 2B, 2C) (Fukunaga et al. 686-97).

Passive transfer of human LES sera containing IgG to mice induces electrophysiologic and morphologic features of LES in the mice. Endplate microelectrode studies in these animals demonstrate a reduction in quantal content (Lang et al. 224;Lang et al. 335-45;Kim 523-30), and ultrastructural studies show the same clustering and AZP depletion as seen in LES (Fukunaga et al. 7636-40;Fukuoka et al. 193-99). Immunoelectron microscopy localizes LES IgG to the active zones (Fukuoka et al. 200-11), and, as at the postsynaptic membrane in MG, cross-linkage of divalent antibodies is a critical component of this process (Nagel et al. 552-58).

Taken together, these studies demonstrate that the P/Q VGCC are the target of disease-causing antibodies in LES and that these antibodies downregulate VGCC expression by antigenic modulation. In combination with the demonstration of P/Q VGCC antibodies in 90% of non-immune suppressed LES patient sera (Lennon et al. 1467-74), the aforementioned studies provide conclusive evidence that LES results from humoral autoimmunity. In CA-LES, the neuroectodermal antigens expressed by SCLC cells mimic VGCC and induce production of VGCC antibodies as a paraneoplastic syndrome. In NCA-LES as in other primary autoimmune disorders, altered self-tolerance is presumed to induce production of VGCC antibodies.

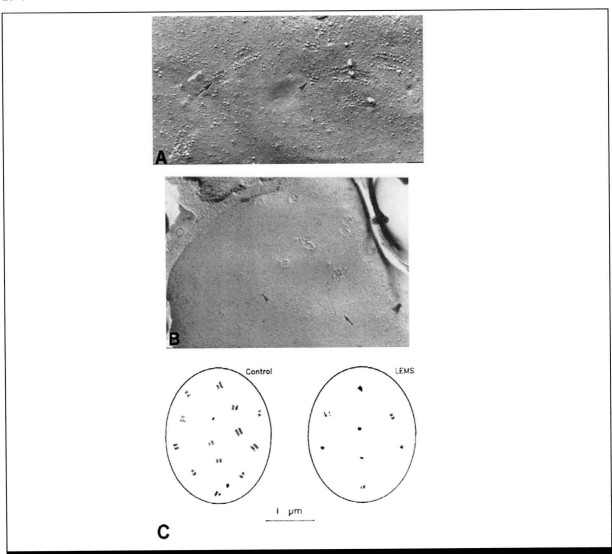

Figure 2. Electron microscopy in freeze-fractured human presynaptic membrane preparations. (Fukunaga et al., 1982) With permission from *Muscle and Nerve*.

A. Control presynaptic membrane, P-face x 55,000, Bar = 1 μm
Intramembrane particles representing VGCC are abundant and organized in active zones with double parallel rows of particles (arrows).

B. LES presynaptic membrane, P-face x 61,000, Bar = 1 μm
Active zones are markedly depleted. A solitary short active zone (arrow) is identified. The cluster of large intramembrane particles (arrowhead) may reflect cross-linkage of VGCC antibody-receptor complexes.

C. Schematic reconstruction of 5 μm² regions of presynaptic membrane P-faces based upon data from membrane preparations in 9 LES patients and 14 controls. Control membranes had a mean of 13 active zones and 2 intramembrane clusters, while LES membranes had a mean of 3 active zones and 5 intramembrane clusters.

6. EPIDEMIOLOGY

LES is rare, and it is likely underdiagnosed due to its non-specific, fluctuating symptoms and generally insidious onset. The population frequency of LES is significantly influenced by factors that determine the frequency of lung cancer (e.g. smoking and age) and susceptibility to autoimmune disease. LES usually begins in adults after age 40, although there are rare instances of childhood onset LES (O'Neill, Murray, and Newsom-Davis 577-96;Sanders and Juel 274-83). Women have an earlier age of onset and are somewhat less likely than men to have an underlying cancer (Harper and Lennon 269-91;Maddison et al. 212-17). The best epidemiological data are from the Netherlands and document an annual incidence of 0.4 cases per million and prevalence of 2.5 cases per million (Wirtz et al. 397-98). Extrapolation of this population frequency to the United States suggests that there would be fewer than 1000 U.S. LES cases at any point in time, which probably reflects an underestimate of the actual occurrence of LES. At two large university neuromuscular referral centers in the U.S., LES is diagnosed about 10% as frequently as MG (Harper and Lennon 269-91;Sanders and Juel 274-83). By comparison, the contemporary annual incidence of MG is estimated at 4 to 11 cases per million with prevalence approaching 200 cases per million (Phillips 407-12).

7. DIAGNOSTIC TESTING

In LES patients with the clinical triad of proximal weakness, attenuated or absent tendon reflexes and dry mouth, the diagnosis may be confirmed by demonstration of characteristic electrophysiological findings (See 7.1. below). In patients who lack these EMG findings, the diagnosis of LES can also be presumed when clinical weakness and abnormal neuromuscular transmission are demonstrated along with either the presence of P/Q VGCC antibodies or SCLC (Sanders and Juel 274-83).

7.1 Electrodiagnostic testing

In LES, the severity of the electrodiagnostic abnormalities often exceeds that of the clinical findings (Eaton and Lambert 1117-24), whereas the opposite is often true in MG (Lambert 380-81). The typical electrodiagnostic findings of LES include small compound muscle action potentials (CMAPs) that increase dramatically after brief (5-10 seconds) isometric muscle contraction or with high frequency (20-50 Hz) repetitive nerve stimulation (RNS) (Lambert, Eaton, and Rooke 612-13;Eaton and Lambert 1117-24;Lambert 367-84) (Figures 3 and 4). Postactivation facilitation (PAF) of more than 100% is considered to be diagnostic of LES (Lambert et al. 362-410;AAEM Quality Assurance Committee and American Association of Electrodiagnostic Medicine. 1236-38), but this may not be found in all muscles and may not be present in early or mild LES (Sanders 167-80).

In our experience (Figure 3), the most sensitive RNS finding in LES is a greater than 10% CMAP decrement to low-frequency RNS in at least one intrinsic hand muscle, which was found in 99% of patients. Although considered a more specific finding for LES, ≥100% PAF was demonstrated in at least one of three tested intrinsic hand or foot muscles in 80% patients, and was observed in all three muscles in only 37%. Although the amount of facilitation varies greatly

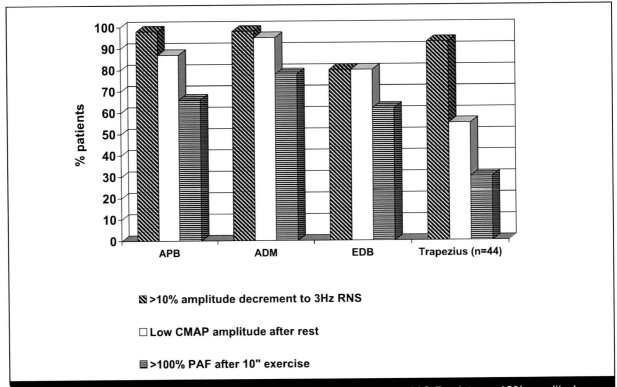

Figure 3. Electrodiagnostic findings in 76 LES patients from the Duke MG Registry. >10% amplitude decrement is the most sensitive finding for LES. While a more specific finding, >100% PAF is not observed in all muscles nor in all patients.

ADM = Abductor digiti quinti manis
APB = Abductor pollicis brevis
EDB = Extensor digitorum brevis

among muscles, it is consistently greater in distal than in proximal muscles (Tim, Massey, and Sanders 2176-78).

Some LES patients have electrodiagnostic findings indistinguishable from MG, particularly with mild or early disease (Lambert 380-81). Substantial PAF may also be seen in MG, especially in atrophic muscles. Although no electrodiagnostic criteria will discriminate between all patients with MG and LES, when PAF is greater than 400% in any muscle or greater than 100% in most tested muscles, the diagnosis of LES is confirmed.

Points of emphasis for electrodiagnosis in LES include:

- While decrement to low frequency (1-5 Hz) RNS is virtually always present, it is nonspecific and is also seen in MG, peripheral nerve, and muscle disease.
- Low amplitude CMAPs are common, but are also non-specific and seen in peripheral nerve and muscle disease.
- PAF exceeding 100% is present in 80% of patients in at least one hand or foot muscle and is most pronounced in distal muscles.
- Given the variability of findings among muscles, even in the same hand, several muscles should be tested to establish the overall pattern of abnormality.

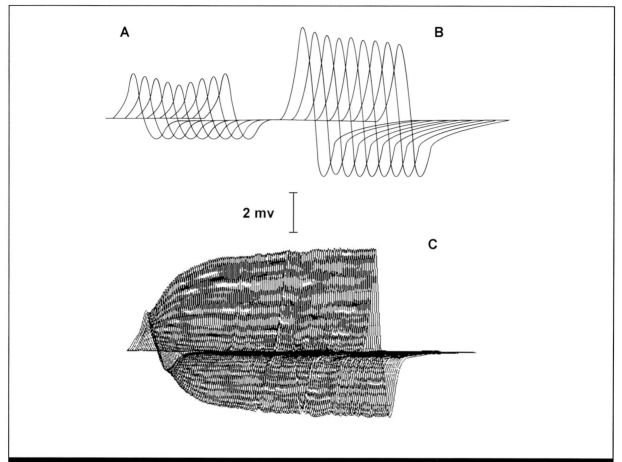

Figure 4. Repetitive nerve stimulation studies in LES. (A) CMAPs recorded from the hypothenar muscles during stimulation of the ulnar nerve at 3 per second. The initial CMAP amplitude is reduced and there is a decremental response. (B) Immediately after maximum contraction of the muscle for 10 seconds, the initial CMAP amplitude is increased by more than 100% from (A). (C) During 20/sec stimulation the CMAP amplitude falls slightly, then increases by more than 100% of the initial value. (With permission from *Journal of Clinical Neurophysiology*) Sanders, D. B. "Clinical neurophysiology of disorders of the neuromuscular junction." Journal of Clinical Neurophysiology 10 (1993): 167-80.

- When PAF exceeds 100% in most muscles studied or 400% in any muscle, the diagnosis of LES is confirmed.
- Mild or early LES may not show these findings, and repeat studies may be necessary.
- Low limb temperature, incomplete relaxation, or inadequate rest of the muscle being tested may obscure the electrodiagnostic findings.

The following electrodiagnostic strategy is suggested for cases of suspected LES. Elicit a CMAP from a rested intrinsic hand muscle warmed to 34 degrees Centigrade. If the CMAP amplitude is low, deliver a second supramaximal stimulus after 10 seconds of maximal isometric muscle contraction. If PAF is observed, perform low frequency RNS before and after 10 seconds of isometric contraction to assess for decrement and for PAF. If the findings are negative or equivocal, it may be necessary to study additional hand and foot muscles to establish the diagnosis of LES.

As in MG, needle electromyography (EMG) demonstrates motor unit potential instability or "jiggle" during muscle activation. Single-fiber EMG demonstrates increased jitter and impulse blocking. In some endplates, jitter and blocking may decrease at higher firing rates with voluntary activation or with axonal stimulation (Trontelj and Stålberg 226-32;Sanders 256-58;Trontelj and Stålberg 258). As with the other electrodiagnostic findings, these abnormalities are not observed in all muscles, nor in all LES patients.

7.1.1. Serological testing: Voltage-gated calcium channel antibodies

Small cell lung carcinoma (SCLC) and human neuronal cell lines express voltage-gated calcium channels (VGCC) that bind Ω-conotoxin from the snail *Conus geographus*. The P/Q type VGCCs are associated with ACh release and bind Ω-conotoxin with high-affinity. Immunoprecipitation assays for VGCC antibodies use SCLC or human neuroblastoma cell lines incubated with radiolabeled ^{125}I-Ω-conotoxin. These assays demonstrate VGCC antibodies in almost all patients with CA-LES and in more than 90% of NCA-LES patients (Harper and Lennon 269-91). There are no apparent clinical differences between LES patients with or without P/Q VGCC antibodies, except that somewhat fewer CA-LES patients are seronegative (Nakao et al. 1773-75). Low titers of VGCC antibodies have been reported in patients with systemic lupus erythematosus, rheumatoid arthritis, conditions associated with high levels of circulating immunoglobulins (Lang et al. 382-93), and in up to 5% of patients with MG (Harper and Lennon 269-91). Patients who are seronegative early in the course of LES may seroconvert later, and repeat antibody testing may be useful in such cases. Although VGCC antibody titers do not correlate with disease severity among different patients, antibody levels within individual patients fall with clinically improved disease and with immunosuppression (Leys et al. 307-14). In a small contemporary series, antibodies against domain IV of the alpha 1A subunit of the P/Q type VGCC were more commonly found in NCA-LES (38%) than in CA-LES (5%) (Pellkofer et al. 136-39). Further development of this assay may help to guide surveillance for cancer in patients who have no apparent cancer at the time of LES diagnosis.

7.1.2. Serological testing: SOX1 antibodies

Patients with lung cancer related paraneoplastic disorders frequently have an anti-glial nuclear antibody (AGNA) (Graus et al. 166-71). SOX1, a transcription factor involved in neural development, is a highly immunogenic tumor antigen recognized by AGNA-positive sera in CA-LES patients with SCLC. In a recent series, SOX1 antibodies predicted the presence of SCLC, being found in 64% CA-LES with SCLC, 32% of Hu-antibody positive paraneoplastic neurological syndromes with SCLC, 22% of patients with SCLC only, and 0% of NCA-LES (Sabater et al. 924-28). Although the assay remains a research tool, the presence of SOX1 antibodies in LES may eventually help clinicians to pursue a rigorous evaluation for underlying cancer.

7.2. Other testing

When autonomic function is studied formally, most LES patients exhibit abnormal findings even if they are not symptomatic (Waterman 145-54;Khurana 506-11). Both sympathetic and parasympathetic dysfunction may be seen (Waterman 145-54;Khurana 506-11;Baker, Low, and

McEvoy A220;O'Suilleabhain, Low, and Lennon 88-93). Skeletal muscle biopsies may demonstrate non-specific type 2 fiber atrophy, as in disuse (O'Neill, Murray, and Newsom-Davis 577-96).

8. DIFFERENTIAL DIAGNOSIS

LES patients commonly receive an initial incorrect diagnosis (Wirtz et al. 397-98). When there are minimal findings on examination, the protean symptoms of LES may be dismissed. In CA-LES, symptoms and findings are often attributed to cachexia, peripheral neuropathy, and/or the effects of cancer treatment. In LES patients without evident cancer, the symptoms and findings may be attributed to neuropathy, myopathy, or myasthenia gravis.

Although the clinical presentations of LES and MG have been noted to be quite distinct (Wirtz et al. 766-68), there may be similarities in some cases (Rudnicki 1863-64;Burns et al. 270-73). Findings that suggest MG include prominent ocular weakness, limb weakness with predominant upper limb involvement, and normal tendon reflexes. Findings that suggest LES include prominent lower limb weakness, hypoactive or absent tendon reflexes, and dry mouth.

When neuromuscular transmission is abnormal, serum acetylcholine receptor (AChR) antibodies or muscle specific tyrosine kinase (MuSK) antibodies confirm the diagnosis of MG, and P/Q-type VGCC antibodies confirm LES. AChR antibodies have been reported to be elevated in up to 13% of LES patients, usually in low concentrations (Lennon S23-S27), but we have not found elevated AChR antibodies in our LES patients outside of the context of MG/LES overlap syndrome.

9. MG/LES OVERLAP SYNDROME

Although there are many reports of patients with overlapping clinical and electrophysiological features of MG and LES, there are very few reported patients with a true overlap syndrome with antibodies to both AChR and VGCC. Electrophysiological findings of low amplitude CMAP responses with marked facilitation are not unique to presynaptic disorders, and may also be observed in postsynaptic dysfunction as with curare (Hutter 216-27), some congenital myasthenic syndromes (Harper 1687-95), and MG with severe muscle atrophy. RNS findings in mild or early LES may resemble those seen in MG (Lambert 380-81), and do not represent a true overlap syndrome.

Among 102 patients with LES seen in the Duke Neuromuscular Clinic since 1980, AChR and VGCC antibodies were elevated in only one. This patient also had clinical and electrophysiological findings that represented an overlap between MG and LES, and six other such patients have been reported with a true MG/LES overlap syndrome (Newsom-Davis et al. 452-53;Katz et al. 470-75;Kanzato et al. 1727-30;Oh and Sher 1167-71). It has been suggested that these patients may represent outliers of MG or LES with nonpathogenic antibodies against an additional epitope (Katz et al. 470-75), or simply that they represent coexisting autoimmune disorders (Sanders and Juel 274-83). As most treatments are similar for both disorders, save for thymectomy in MG and cancer surveillance in LES, establishing the ultimate diagnosis in patients with overlapping features of MG and LES may be largely academic.

10. TREATMENT

Treatment in LES must be individualized based on the presence or suspected presence of underlying cancer, medical comorbidities, and the degree of disability.

10.1. Underlying cancer

Only about 2% of SCLC patients have LES (Wirtz et al. 230-37;Maddison et al. 117-18), and LES onset may precede the diagnosis of cancer in up to 69% of CA-LES patients (Titulaer et al. 153-58). The underlying cancer is diagnosed within one year of LES diagnosis in 96% of CA-LES patients (Titulaer et al. 153-58). LES may remit with effective treatment of an underlying cancer (Chalk et al. 1552-56;Jenkyn et al. 1123-27), thus it is essential to aggressively evaluate all LES patients for cancer. Since the underlying cancer is in the lung in nearly all patients, the initial evaluation should include at least a chest CT scan. Iodinated contrast agents should be used with great caution in LES, particularly in patients with respiratory weakness. These agents can exacerbate the weakness, even to the point of respiratory crisis (van den Bergh et al. 206-07). Bronchoscopy (Titulaer et al. 153-58) or whole body PET scanning (Titulaer et al. 153-58;Rees et al. 2223-31) should be considered when the chest CT is normal and there is a significant risk for lung cancer (e.g. in smokers, rapid onset disease, suspicious findings on chest imaging).

If no tumor is found initially, surveillance for occult cancer should be repeated at intervals determined by the patient's risk factors for cancer. Patients less than 50 years old without a history of chronic smoking have a low risk for cancer, particularly if they have other autoimmune diseases and have had LES symptoms for several years. Chronic smokers with LES onset after age 50 should be evaluated for cancer as delineated above every four to six months.

When cancer is demonstrated, the initial LES treatment should be directed toward the underlying cancer. In some patients, no additional LES treatment is needed (Chalk et al. 1552-56;Jenkyn et al. 1123-27). In our experience, immunotherapy for LES without effective treatment of underlying cancer usually does not improve strength in CA-LES. Theoretically, immunosuppressive therapy could also reduce the innate immunologic suppression of tumor growth. Immunotherapy is more readily justified in NCA-LES.

10.2. Cholinesterase inhibitors

Pyridostigmine bromide (PB) frequently reduces dry mouth and may reduce subjective fatigue in LES, but usually does not improve strength. We begin PB 30-60mg every 4 to 6 hours while awake, and increase to a maximum of 480mg/day. The response should be assessed after several days of treatment at each dosage. We also use PB to enhance the effect of 3,4-diaminopyridine (DAP), which may permit the use of lower DAP doses (see below).

10.3. Guanidine

Guanidine inhibits mitochondrial calcium uptake, increases intracellular calcium concentration, and thus increases acetylcholine release at cholinergic nerve terminals with improved strength in many LES patients. In an open-label trial of low dose guanidine in combination with pyridostigmine, improved strength and CMAP amplitude were demonstrated, although one-third of the patients dropped out of the trial due to gastrointestinal side effects (Oh et al. 1146-52).

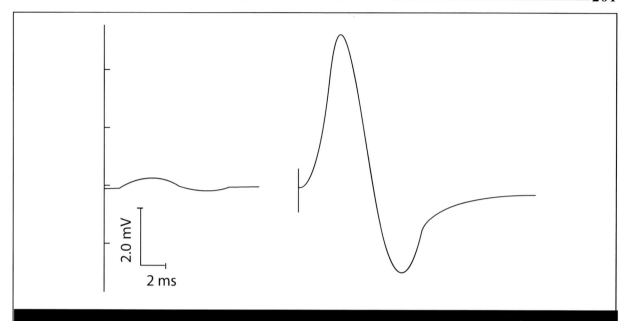

Figure 5. Compound muscle action potentials in LES elicited before (left) and immediately after (right) maximum voluntary contraction of abductor digiti quinti manis for 10 seconds. (With permission from Elsevier/Churchill Livingstone) Sanders, D. B. "Electrophysiologic Study of Disorders of Neuromuscular Transmission." Ed. M. J. Aminoff. 5 ed. Philadelphia : Elsevier Chruchill Livingstone, 2005. 335-55.

Treatment with guanidine hydrochloride begins at 5-10 mg/kg/day in divided doses while awake, increasing to a maximum of 30 mg/kg/day based on improvement in strength. The therapeutic response of guanidine may be augmented by pyridostigmine, which permits the use of lower guanidine dosages.

The side effects of guanidine are many and severe, and limit its clinical utility. These include bone marrow suppression, renal tubular acidosis, chronic interstitial nephritis, cardiac arrhythmia, hepatic toxicity, pancreatic dysfunction, peripheral paresthesias, ataxia, and encephalopathy. Surveillance hematologic, hepatic and renal function testing must be performed frequently during treatment with guanidine.

10.4. 3,4-diaminopyridine (DAP)

Aminopyridines augment neurotransmitter release at central and peripheral nervous system synapses by blocking the delayed potassium conductance (Yeh et al. 519-35). 3,4-diaminopyridine (DAP) is more effective than 4-aminopyridine in augmenting neuromuscular transmission (Molgó, Lundh, and Thesleff 25-34), less readily crosses the blood-brain barrier (Lemeignan et al. 166-69), and is less likely to produce seizures (Lechat et al. 345-49). Two randomized, placebo-controlled trials have demonstrated improved strength and autonomic function in LES patients receiving DAP (McEvoy et al. 1567-71;Sanders et al. 603-07;Maddison and Newsom-Davis CD003279). In our experience, more than 85% LES patients experience significant clinical benefit with DAP, and in more than half, the benefit is marked (Tim, Massey, and Sanders 2176-78).

A small, controlled trial assessing muscle strength and CMAP amplitude in LES patients receiving DAP, pyridostigmine bromide, or combined therapy showed that only patients receiving

3,4-DAP showed significant increases in strength and CMAP amplitude (Wirtz et al. 44-48). Although this study showed no additional benefit from combined therapy, many of our patients feel that taking pyridostigmine along with DAP allows them to space their DAP doses farther apart, and thus require less total DAP.

DAP is administered in an oral dose of 5 to 25 mg three to four times a day. The optimal dosing schedule must be individualized for each patient and is generally between 15 and 60 mg per day in divided doses. Side effects include perioral and digital paresthesias with doses in the therapeutic range. Seizures may occur at dosages greater than 100 mg per day, and asthma attacks have been precipitated in patients with pre-existing asthma. There is a theoretical risk for prolonged QT intervals with increased risk for cardiac arrhythmia, although this has not been reported, and no ECG changes were observed in a controlled trial of DAP (Sanders et al. 603-07). A LES patient who took six times the therapeutic dose of DAP (60 mg six times a day) had seizures and cardiac arrhythmia that resolved within 24 hours without apparent sequelae (Boerma et al. 249-51). There have been no reports of organ toxicity despite more than ten years of DAP exposure in many patients. Nevertheless, given the limited experience and the small number of patients who have received DAP, periodic surveillance testing of hematologic, renal, and hepatic function is recommended.

DAP is a safe and effective treatment for LES with or without associated cancer, and represents the mainstay of symptomatic treatment of LES in Europe (Maddison and Newsom-Davis CD003279). Although not formally approved for clinical use in the United States, it is available to physicians for individual patients on a treatment use basis. Information about the application process can be obtained from Jacobus Pharmaceutical Co., Inc., Princeton, NJ, USA, Fax 609-799-1176.

10.5. Immune modulation

When weakness or autonomic dysfunction is severe and refractory or when respiratory function is compromised, intravenous immunoglobulin (IVIG) or plasma exchange (PEX) may induce rapid, although temporary improvement in LES. Observational studies suggest that treatment with PEX produces short-term improvement in strength, although repeated courses may be necessary to sustain the improvement (NIH Consensus Conference Statement 1333-37) (Newsom-Davis and Murray 480-85). Small randomized trials have demonstrated short-term improvement with IVIG infusions, although it is unclear whether repeated infusions induce sustained improvement. Maximum improvement is observed at two to four weeks following each infusion, with a corresponding decline in serum VGCC antibody titers (Bain et al. 678-83).

10.6. Immune suppression

Immune suppressants may be a therapeutic consideration in LES patients refractory to DAP or in order to sustain benefit following PEX or IVIG infusions. In patients with CA-LES, agents that suppress T-lymphocyte function could theoretically compromise the host immune response to the underlying cancer. In such patients, aggressive treatment of the underlying cancer should be pursued initially. Prednisone or prednisolone used alone or in combination with azathioprine have shown benefit in observational studies (Maddison et al. 212-17). As in MG, mycophenolate and cyclosporine may also be useful, but evidence for efficacy in LES is very limited (Newsom-Davis 191-98) (Skeie et al. 691-99).

11. AGENTS THAT MAY WORSEN LES

Medications that increase weakness in MG may have a similar effect in LES (Pascuzzi). The first reported patient with LES had prolonged apnea following administration of succinylcholine (Anderson, Churchill-Davidson, and Richardson 1291-93). As with MG, competitive neuromuscular blocking agents such as pancuronium and d-tubocurarine have a profound, potentiated effect in LES. Iodinated contrast material (van den Bergh et al. 206-07) or magnesium (Gutmann and Takamori 977-80;Streib 175-76) may also dramatically worsen weakness in LES, even to the extent of precipitating respiratory crisis.

12. PROGNOSIS

The factors determining prognosis in LES include the presence, type, and staging of underlying cancer in CA-LES, the presence and type of additional autoimmune diseases in NCA-LES, and the distribution and severity of weakness in both groups. In CA-LES, effective treatment of the underlying cancer induces improvement or even remission in some patients. SCLC has been reported to have a more favorable prognosis when associated with LES (Maddison et al. 117-18), perhaps because of earlier cancer detection, more effective immune surveillance, or both. In NCA-LES, initial muscle strength assessments correlate with long-term outcome, but serological or electrophysiological findings do not (Maddison et al. 117-18). Despite carefully chosen treatment utilizing symptomatic and immune suppressant agents, many patients with LES continue to have significant disability.

REFERENCES

1. AAEM Quality Assurance Committee and American Association of Electrodiagnostic Medicine. Practice parameter for repetitive nerve stimulation and single fiber EMG evaluation of adults with suspected myasthenia gravis or Lambert-Eaton myasthenic syndrome: summary statement. *Muscle & Nerve* 24 (2001): 1236-38.

2. Anderson, H. J., H. C. Churchill-Davidson, and A. T. Richardson. "Bronchial neoplasm with myasthenia. Prolonged apnea after administration of succinylcholine. *Lancet* ii (1953): 1291-93.

3. Bain, P. G. et al. Effects of intravenous immunoglobulin on muscle weakness and calcium-channel autoantibodies in the Lambert-Eaton myasthenic syndrome. *Neurology* 47 (1996): 678-83.

4. Baker, M. K., P. A. Low, and K. M. McEvoy. Quantification of autonomic dysfunction in Lambert-Eaton syndrome by composite autonomic scoring scale. *Neurology* 44 (Supp 2): (1994): A220.

5. Barr, C. W. et al. Primary respiratory failure as the presenting symptom in Lambert-Eaton myasthenic syndrome. *Muscle & Nerve* 16 (1993): 712-15.

6. Boerma, C. E. et al. Cardiac arrest following an iatrogenic 3,4-diaminopyridine intoxication in a patient with Lambert-Eaton myasthenic syndrome. *J Toxicol Clin Toxicol* 33 (1995): 249-51.

7. Burns, T. M. et al. Oculobulbar involvement is typical with Lambert-Eaton myasthenic syndrome. *Annals of Neurology* 53 (2003): 270-73.

8. Chalk, C. H. et al. Response of the Lambert-Eaton myasthenic syndrome to treatment of associated small-cell lung carcinoma. *Neurology* 40 (1990): 1552-56.

9. Eaton, L. M. and E. H. Lambert. Electromyography and electric stimulation of nerves in diseases of the motor unit. *Journal of the American Medical Association* 163 (1957): 1117-24.

10. Elmqvist, D. and E. H. Lambert. Detailed analysis of neuromuscular transmission in a patient with the myasthenic syndrome sometimes associated with bronchogenic carcinoma. *Mayo Clinic Proceedings* 43 (1968): 689-713.

11. Fukunaga, H. et al. Passive transfer of Lambert-Eaton myasthenic syndrome with IgG from man to mouse depletes the presynaptic membrane active zones. *Proc Natl Acad Sci* 80 (1983): 7636-40.

12. Fukunaga, H. et al. Paucity and disorganization of presynaptic membrane active zones in the Lambert-Eaton myasthenic syndrome. *Muscle & Nerve* 5 (1982): 686-97.

13. Fukuoka, T. et al. Lambert-Eaton myasthenic syndrome: I. Early morphological effects of IgG on the presynaptic membrane active zones. *Annals of Neurology* 22 (1987): 193-99.

14. Fukuoka, T. et al. Lambert-Eaton myasthenic syndrome: II. Immunoelectron microscopy localization of IgG at the mouse motor endplate. *Annals of Neurology* 22 (1987): 200-11.

15. Graus, F. et al. Anti-glial nuclear antibody: marker of lung cancer-related paraneoplastic neurological syndromes. *Journal of Neuroimmunology* 165 (2005): 166-71.

16. Gutmann, L. et al. The Eaton-Lambert syndrome and autoimmune disorders. *American Journal of Medicine* 53 (1972): 354.

17. Gutmann, L. and M. Takamori. Effect of Mg^{++} on neuromuscular transmission in the Eaton-Lambert syndrome. *Neurology* 23 (1973): 977-80.

18. Harper, C. M. Congenital Myasthenic Syndromes. Ed. W. F. Brown, C. F. Bolton, and M. J. Aminoff. Philadelphia: W.B. Saunders Company, 2002. 1687-95.

19. Harper, C. M. and V. A. Lennon. The Lambert-Eaton Myasthenic Syndrome. Ed. H. J. Kaminski. Totowa, NJ: Humana Press, 2002. 269-91.

20. Henriksson, K. G. et al. Clinical, neurophysiological and morphological findings in Eaton Lambert syndrome. *Acta Neurologica Scandinavica* 56 (1977): 117-40.

21. Hutter, O. F. Post-tetanic restoration of neuromuscular transmission blocked by d-tubocurarine. *Journal of Physiology* 118 (1952): 216-27.

22. Jenkyn, L. R. et al. Remission of the Lambert-Eaton syndrome and small cell anaplastic carcinoma of the lung induced by chemotherapy and radiotherapy. *Cancer* 46 (1980): 1123-27.

23. Kanzato, N. et al. Lambert-Eaton myasthenic syndrome with ophthalmoparesis and pseudoblepharospasm. *Muscle & Nerve* 22 (1999): 1727-30.

24. Katz, J. S. et al. Acetylcholine receptor antibodies in the Lambert-Eaton myasthenic syndrome. *Neurology* 50 (1998): 470-75.

25. Khurana, R. K. Paraneoplastic Autonomic Dysfunction. Ed. P. A. Low. Boston: Little, Brown Co., 1993. 506-11.

26. Kim, Y. I. Passively transferred Lambert-Eaton syndrome in mice receiving purified IgG. *Muscle & Nerve* 9 (1986): 523-30.

27. Kobayashi, H. et al. Bronchogenic carcinoma with subacute cerebellar degeneration and Eaton-Lambert syndrome; an autopsy case. *Jpn J Med* 27 (1988): 203-06.

28. Lambert, E. H. Defects of neuromuscular transmission in syndromes other than myasthenia gravis. *Annals of the New York Academy of Sciences* 135 (1966): 367-84.

29. Lambert, E. H. General discussion. *Annals of the New York Academy of Sciences* 505 (1987): 380-81.

30. Lambert, E. H., L. M. Eaton, and E. D. Rooke. Defect of neuromuscular conduction associated with malignant neoplasms. *American Journal of Physiology* 187 (1956): 612-13.

31. Lambert, E. H. and D. Elmqvist. Quantal components of end-plate potentials in the myasthenic syndrome. *Annals of the New York Academy of Sciences* 183 (1971): 183-99.

32. Lambert, E. H. et al. Myasthenic Syndrome Occasionally Associated With Bronchial Neoplasm: Neurophysiologic Studies. Ed. H. R. Viets. Springfield: Charles C. Thomas, 1961. 362-410.

33. Lang, B. et al. Autoantibody specificities in Lambert-Eaton myasthenic syndrome. *Annals of the New York Academy of Sciences* 681 (1993): 382-93.

34. Lang, B. et al. Antibodies to motor nerve terminals: an electrophysiological study of human myasthenic syndrome transferred to mouse. *Journal of Physiology* 344 (1983): 335-45.

35. Lang, B. et al. Autoimmune etiology for myasthenic (Eaton-Lambert) syndrome. *Lancet* 2 (1981): 224.

36. Lechat, P. et al. Toxicité aiguë composee de quelques aminopyridines in vivo (souris) et in vitro (cultures cellulaires). *Ann Pharmac Fr* 26 (1968): 345-49.

37. Lemeignan, M. et al. Evaluation of 4-aminopyridine and 3,4-diaminopyridine penetrability into cerebrospinal fluid in anesthetized rats. *Brain Research* 304 (1984): 166-69.

38. Lennon, V. A. Serological profile of myasthenia gravis and distinction from the Lambert-Eaton myasthenic syndrome. *Neurology* 48 (Suppl 5) (1997): S23-S27.

39. Lennon, V. A. et al. Calcium-channel antibodies in the Lambert-Eaton syndrome and other paraneoplastic syndromes. *New England Journal of Medicine* 332 (1995): 1467-74.

40. Lennon, V. A. et al. Autoimmunity in the Lambert-Eaton syndrome. *Muscle & Nerve* 5 (1982): S21-S25.

41. Leys, K. et al. Calcium channel autoantibodies in the Lambert-Eaton myasthenic syndrome. *Annals of Neurology* 29 (1991): 307-14.

42. Maddison, P. et al. Long term outcome in Lambert-Eaton myasthenic syndrome without lung cancer. *Journal of Neurology, Neurosurgery & Psychiatry* 70 (2001): 212-17.

43. Maddison, P. and J. Newsom-Davis. "Treatment for Lambert-Eaton myasthenic syndrome. *Cochrane Database of Systematic Reviews.* (2005): CD003279.

44. Maddison, P. et al. Favourable prognosis in Lambert-Eaton myasthenic syndrome and small-cell lung carcinoma. *Lancet* 353 (1999): 117-18.

45. McEvoy, K. M. et al. 3,4-Diaminopyridine in the treatment of Lambert-Eaton myasthenic syndrome. *New England Journal of Medicine* 321 (1989): 1567-71.

46. Molgó, J., H. Lundh, and S. Thesleff. Potency of 3,4-diaminopyridine and 4-aminopyridine on mammalian neuromuscular transmission and the effect of pH changes. *European Journal of Pharmacology* 61 (1980): 25-34.

47. Nagel, A. et al. Lambert-Eaton myasthenic syndrome IgG depletes presynaptic membrane active zone particles by antigenic modulation. *Annals of Neurology* 24 (1988): 552-58.

48. Nakao, Y. K. et al. Seronegative Lambert-Eaton myasthenic syndrome: study of 110 Japanese patients. *Neurology* 59 (2002): 1773-75.

49. Newsom-Davis, J. "Therapy in myasthenia gravis and Lambert-Eaton myasthenic syndrome. *Seminars in Neurology* 23 (2003): 191-98.

50. Newsom-Davis, J. et al. Immunological evidence for the co-existence of the Lambert-Eaton myasthenic syndrome and myasthenia gravis in two patients. *Journal of Neurology, Neurosurgery & Psychiatry* 54 (1991): 452-53.

51. Newsom-Davis, J. and N. M. Murray. Plasma exchange and immunosuppressive drug treatment in the Lambert- Eaton myasthenic syndrome. *Neurology* 34 (1984): 480-85.

52. NIH Consensus Conference Statement. The utility of therapeutic plasmapheresis for neurological disorders. *Journal of the American Medical Association* 256 (1986): 1333-37.

53. Nilsson, O. and I. Rosén. The stretch reflex in the Eaton-Lambert syndrome, myasthenia gravis and myotonic dystrophy. *Acta Neurologica Scandinavica* 57 (1978): 350-57.

54. O'Neill, J. H., N. M. Murray, and J. Newsom-Davis. The Lambert-Eaton myasthenic syndrome. A review of 50 cases. *Brain* 111 (1988): 577-96.

55. O'Suilleabhain, P., P. A. Low, and V. A. Lennon. Autonomic dysfunction in the Lambert-Eaton myasthenic syndrome: serologic and clinical correlates. *Neurology* 50 (1998): 88-93.

56. Oh, S. J. et al. Low-dose guanidine and pyridostigmine: relatively safe and effective long-term symptomatic therapy in Lambert-Eaton myasthenic syndrome. *Muscle & Nerve* 20 (1997): 1146-52.

57. Oh, S. J. and E. Sher. MG and LEMS overlap syndrome: case report with electrophysiological and immunological evidence. *Clinical Neurophysiology* 116.5 (2005): 1167-71.

58. Pascuzzi, R. M. Medications and myasthenia gravis: A reference for health care professionals. 2007.

59. Pellkofer, H. L. et al. Lambert-Eaton myasthenic syndrome differential reactivity of tumor versus non-tumor patients to subunits of the voltage-gated calcium channel. *Journal of Neuroimmunology* 204 (2008): 136-39.

60. Phillips, L. H. The epidemiology of myasthenia gravis. *Ann.N.Y.Acad.Sci.* 998 (2003): 407-12.

61. Rees, J. H. et al. The role of [18F]fluoro-2-deoxyglucose-PET scanning in the diagnosis of paraneoplastic neurological disorders. *Brain* 124 (2001): 2223-31.

62. Rudnicki, S. Lambert-Eaton myasthenic syndrome with pure ocular weakness. *Neurology* 68 (2007): 1863-64.

63. Sabater, L. et al. SOX1 antibodies are markers of paraneoplastic Lambert-Eaton myasthenic syndrome. *Neurology* 70 (2008): 924-28.

64. Sanders, D. B. The effect of firing rate on neuromuscular jitter in Lambert- Eaton myasthenic syndrome. *Muscle & Nerve* 15 (1992): 256-58.

65. Sanders, D. B. Clinical neurophysiology of disorders of the neuromuscular junction. *Journal of Clinical Neurophysiology* 10 (1993): 167-80.

66. Sanders, D. B. Lambert-Eaton myasthenic syndrome: Clinical diagnosis, immune-mediated mechanisms, and update on therapy. *Annals of Neurology* 37(S1) (1995): S63-S73.

67. Sanders, D. B. and V. C. Juel. Lambert-Eaton Myasthenic Syndrome. Ed. A. G. Engel. Series 3 ed. *Handbook of Clinical Neurology*. Elsevier, 2008. 274-83.

68. Sanders, D. B. et al. A randomized trial of 3,4-diaminopyridine in Lambert-Eaton myasthenic syndrome. *Neurology* 54 (2000): 603-07.

69. Skeie, F. et al. Guidelines for the treatment of autoimmune neuromuscular transmission disorders. *European Journal of Neurology* 13 (2006): 691-99.

70. Smith, A. G. and J. Wald. Acute ventilatory failure in Lambert-Eaton myasthenic syndrome and its response to 3,4-diaminopyridine. *Neurology* 46 (1996): 1143-45.

71. Streib, E. W. Adverse effects of magnesium salt cathartics in a patient with the myasthenic syndrome (Lambert-Eaton syndrome). *Annals of Neurology* 2 (1977): 175-76.

72. Tim, R. W., J. M. Massey, and D. B. Sanders. Lambert-Eaton myasthenic syndrome (LEMS). Clinical and electrodiagnostic features and response to therapy in 59 patients. *Annals of the New York Academy of Sciences* 841 (1998): 823-26.

73. Tim, R. W., J. M. Massey, and D. B. Sanders. Lambert-Eaton myasthenic syndrome. Electrodiagnostic findings and response to treatment. *Neurology* 54 (2000): 2176-78.

74. Titulaer, M. J. et al. The Lambert-Eaton myasthenic syndrome 1988-2008: A clinical picture in 97 patients. *Journal of Neuroimmunology* 201 (2008): 153-58.

75. Titulaer, M. J. et al. Lambert-Eaton myasthenic syndrome with pure ocular weakness. *Neurology* 70 (2008): 86-87.

76. Trontelj, J. V. and E. Stålberg. Single motor end-plates in myasthenia gravis and LEMS at different firing rates. *Muscle & Nerve* 14 (1991): 226-32.

77. Trontelj, J. V. and E. Stålberg. The effect of firing rate on neuromuscular jitter in Lambert-Eaton myasthenic syndrome: a reply. *Muscle & Nerve* 15 (1992): 258.

78. van den Bergh, P. et al. Intravascular contrast media and neuromuscular junction disorders. *Annals of Neurology* 19 (1986): 206-07.

79. Waterman, S. A. Autonomic dysfunction in Lambert-Eaton myasthenic syndrome. *Clinical Autonomic Research* 11 (2001): 145-54.

80. Wirtz, P. W. et al. Associated autoimmune diseases in patients with the Lambert-Eaton myasthenic syndrome and their families. *Journal of Neurology* 251 (2004): 1255-59.

81. Wirtz, P. W. et al. Tonic pupils in Lambert-Eaton myasthenic syndrome. *Muscle & Nerve* 24 (2001): 444-45.

82. Wirtz, P. W. et al. Differences in clinical features between the Lambert-Eaton myasthenic syndrome with and without cancer: an analysis of 227 published cases. *Clinical Neurology & Neurosurgery* 104 (2002): 359-63.

83. Wirtz, P. W. et al. Difference in distribution of muscle weakness between myasthenia gravis and the Lambert-Eaton myasthenic syndrome. *Journal of Neurology, Neurosurgery & Psychiatry* 73 (2002): 766-68.

84. Wirtz, P. W. et al. The epidemiology of the Lambert-Eaton myasthenic syndrome in the Netherlands. *Neurology* 63 (2004): 397-98.

85. Wirtz, P. W. et al. Efficacy of 3,4-diaminopyridine and pyridostigmine in the treatment of Lambert-Eaton myasthenic syndrome: a rondomized, double-blind, placebo-controlled, crossover study. *Clin Pharmacol Ther* 86 (2009): 44-48.

86. Wirtz, P. W. et al. HLA and smoking in prediction and prognosis of small cell lung cancer in autoimmune Lambert-Eaton myasthenic syndrome. *Journal of Neuroimmunology* 159 (2005): 230-37.

87. Wirtz, P. W., A. R. Wintzen, and J. J. Verschuuren. The Lambert-Eaton myasthenic syndrome has a more progressive course in patients with lung cancer. *Muscle & Nerve* 32 (2005): 226-29.

88. Yeh, J. Z. et al. Dynamics of aminopyridine block of potassium channels in squid axon membrane. *J Gen Physiol* 68 (1976): 519-35.

III

Congenital Myasthenic Syndrome

Congenital Myasthenic Syndromes

Bruno Eymard M.D., PhD. & Daniel Hantaï M.D., PhD

1. INTRODUCTION

Congenital myasthenic syndromes (CMSs) form a heterogeneous group of genetic diseases characterized by a dysfunction of neuromuscular transmission. This dysfunction causes muscle weakness, which is increased by exertion and usually starts during infancy/childhood. CMSs are much more uncommon than autoimmune myasthenia (1). The prevalence of CMSs was initially estimated at one in 500.000 in Europe, but they are probably more frequent because they are underdiagnosed. Presently in the French national CMS network, more than 200 cases have been diagnosed.

Knowledge of the mechanisms underlying CMSs has increased considerably in the past 30 years, thanks to the pioneering work undertaken by the group of Andrew Engel. Acetylcholinesterase (AChE) deficiency was the first CMS identified based on the lack of the enzyme at neuromuscular junctions (2). Progressively, the pathophysiological heterogeneity of CMSs was demonstrated: besides synaptic CMS caused by acetylcholinesterase deficiency, pre- and postsynaptic CMSs were described. Microelectrophysiological studies in intercostal biopsy, applied since 1980, were crucial to separate pre- and postsynaptic CMS and to describe acetylcholine receptor (AChR) kinetic abnormalities (3). In the past 20 years, many gene mutations responsible for CMS have been identified. Twelve different genes have been discovered to date, the latest being *LAMB2*, which encodes the laminin β2 chain and was reported in 2009 (4) **(Figure 1)**. Among identified CMSs, 85 % are postsynaptic, with three main genes encoding respectively the ε-subunit of AChR, rapsyn and downstream-of-kinase 7 (Dok-7), 10 % synaptic, due mostly to mutations within *COLQ* encoding the collagen tail of AChE and 5 % presynaptic, due to mutations in *CHAT* encoding choline acetyl-transferase (ChAT). Causative mutations and/or genes are still unknown for half of the patients.

From a pathophysiological point of view, CMSs, like all other myasthenic syndromes, are due to neuromuscular transmission loss of safety margin, but two aspects are original: 1) the multiplicity of defective molecules, each of them responsible for a type of CMS, 2) due to the key and very early roles of several molecules involved in CMSs (as MuSK, rapsyn and Dok-7), the impaired organization and development of the neuromuscular junction and innervation may cause early symptoms very close to a severe congenital myopathy with poor fetal mobility, arthrogryposis and severe muscle atrophy. Conversely, mutations affecting the AChR ε-subunit, which is expressed late in fetal life (32nd week), have less negative effect on synaptogenesis, with generally no fetal symptoms or myopathic features. It is not uncommon in CMS that the lifelong duration of impaired neuromuscular transmission causes synaptopathy with ongoing severe synaptic functional and structural alterations, explaining why many patients suffer from progressive muscle wasting. Several reviews have been devoted to CMS, the most recent by Müller et al. (5).

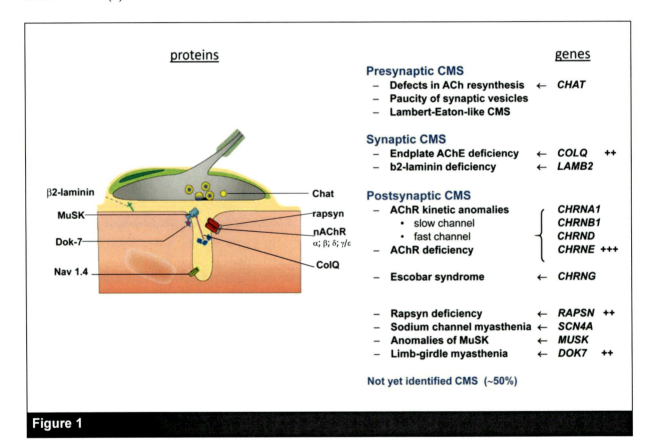

Figure 1

2. CLINICAL EXPRESSION OF CMS

The various CMSs share a common clinical presentation (**Figure 2**). The onset is generally early: birth or infancy. Antenatal onset with reduced fetal mobility, hydramnios, arthrogryposis multiplex may be present, preferentially in *RAPSN* CMS (see infra). Late appearance of the symptoms

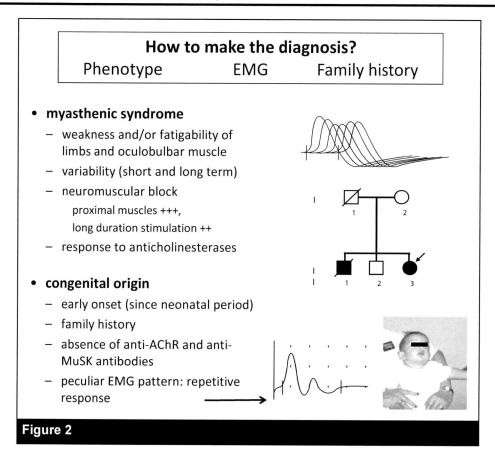

How to make the diagnosis?

Phenotype   EMG   Family history

- **myasthenic syndrome**
  - weakness and/or fatigability of limbs and oculobulbar muscle
  - variability (short and long term)
  - neuromuscular block
    - proximal muscles +++,
    - long duration stimulation ++
  - response to anticholinesterases

- **congenital origin**
  - early onset (since neonatal period)
  - family history
  - absence of anti-AChR and anti-MuSK antibodies
  - peculiar EMG pattern: repetitive response

Figure 2

during adolescence, or even in adulthood, is more rarely reported. Hypotonia is common, and some clinical signs suggest an anomaly of neuromuscular transmission: ophthalmoplegia and ptosis, dysphonia and swallowing disturbance, facial paresis, and muscle fatigability. In the young child, ptosis is not easy to recognize because hypotonia, poor mimicry, suction disorders, and weakness of the cry are in the foreground. Worsening by exertion is characteristic of the disease, as is the occurrence of spontaneous bouts. A particularly long duration of exacerbation period (months to years) is not uncommon in patients with CMS. The favorable effect of cholinesterase inhibitors is a significant argument in favor of a myasthenic syndrome. However, several types of CMSs are worsened by cholinesterase inhibitors (see infra). Often associated with the proper myasthenic signs are myopathic signs: amyotrophy, tendinous retractions, facial malformation and scoliosis. The severity of CMS is variable, depending upon the severity of the walking deficit, the bulbar disorders and the respiratory difficulties. Acute respiratory failure may occur, triggered by infectious episodes, and is frequent in the first months of life. In the absence of respiratory assistance, the risk of death is high.

A family history of the disease is an essential argument in favor of the genetic origin of myasthenic syndrome. Most CMSs are of autosomal recessive inheritance. Slow channel syndrome is the only autosomal dominant CMS characterized hitherto. The progression patterns of CMSs are highly variable, transient worsening with or without return to previous state, regularly progressive deterioration or improvement, stability. The course may change in a given patient, at various periods of life. Myasthenic bouts are frequently triggered by infectious episodes, pregnancy and even menstrual periods. Progressive worsening of the disease may occur late in adulthood, with the appearance of respiratory insufficiency and/or wheelchair-dependency. A favorable progression during childhood or adolescence is possible after a severe neonatal onset, spontaneously or due to treatment. Therapies facilitating neuromuscular transmission have often improved prognosis.

3. POSTSYNAPTIC CONGENITAL MYASTHENIC SYNDROMES ARE FROM FAR THE MOST FREQUENT CMSs (85 % OF IDENTIFIED CMSs)

Five postsynaptic molecules have identified as a primary cause of CMS, in decreasing order of frequency: AChR and its different subunits, rapsyn, Dok-7, MuSK, and the α-subunit of the voltage-gated sodium channel type 4 (Nav 1.4). Two categories of CMSs due to AChR have been described: CMS in connection with a kinetic anomaly and, much more frequent, CMS with a decreased number of AChRs (but without kinetic anomaly) at the neuromuscular junction.

3.1. CMS caused by AChR kinetic anomalies

3.1.1. Slow channel syndrome is the most frequent kinetic anomaly of the AChR. Of autosomal dominant inheritance, it is characterized by a prolonged opening time of the AChR (3). About nineteen autosomal dominant missense point mutations causing a gain of function of the AChR have been identified. Although most mutations have been found in the AChR α subunit, other subunits are also concerned (6). The mutations are located in two transmembrane domains taking part in the formation of the AChR pore through which passes the sodium flux, M1 for mutations of the α, β and? ε subunits and M2 for those, more frequent, affecting the α, β, δ ?and ε subunits (7) and the area of the extracellular domain of the a subunit close to the acetylcholine binding site (mutations α G153S and α V156M). The functional consequences of the various mutations were studied in intercostal muscle biopsy specimens or by expressing the mutation in cell systems (8). The prolonged opening time of the AChR is dependent either on the slowed closing of the channel or on the increased affinity of the AChR for its ligand (9). Clinical expression may vary from early onset and severe to late onset and moderate (3, 10, 11). The arguments in favor of the diagnosis are autosomal dominant heredity, although a peculiar case of recessive transmission occurring in a consanguineous family was once reported (12): no response to esterase inhibitors, repetitive compound muscle action potential (CMAP) after a single stimulation, selectivity of muscle involvement with a prevalent atrophic deficit of the finger extensors and of the cervical muscles. Remodeling of the ultrastructure of the endplate is observed with calcium deposits, destruction of the postsynaptic folds, vacuolizations and tubular aggregates (3). Quinidine and fluoxetine, acting as blocking agents able to normalize the AChR opening time, are used for treatment (13, 14) (see infra).

   3.1.2. Fast channel syndromes are of autosomal recessive transmission, although a case of autosomal dominant transmission was reported recently (15). Clinical severity is variable. Arthrogryposis was reported in one case (16). The patients are responsive to the combination of 3,4-diaminopyridine (3,4-DAP) and cholinesterase inhibitors. Unlike slow channel syndrome, fast channel may not be suspected on a clinical basis or by conventional electrophysiology showing myasthenic decrement without specific features. The diagnosis is made by microelectrophysiology of intercostal or anconeus muscle biopsy or in HEK cells expressing mutations showing a shortening of the AChR opening time (6, 17). Thirteen mutations were identified affecting α, δ and ε subunits and are located in the extracellular domain, the M3 transmembrane domain (mutation α V285I), or in the cytoplasmic loop between the M3 and M4 domains (ε mutations only). Different mechanisms underlie fast channel syndromes: diminished affinity for acetylcholine, impaired gating efficiency and destabilization of channel kinetics (18).

3.2 Congenital myasthenic syndromes with predominant AChR deficiency (with no or only slight kinetic anomalies)

This category accounts for approximately half of all identified CMS patients (19). More than 60 different mutations have been reported in the AChR, most of them located within the ε subunit gene. Mutations in this gene will be first described. A founder effect has been demonstrated in Gypsies (ε1267delG mutation) with a carrier rate of 3.74 (20), and in the North African population (ε 1293insG mutation) (21). Besides these two ethnic mutations, there are about 60 different other mutations reported, most of them are located in the extracellular NH2 terminal region and in the M3/M4 loop **(Figure 3)**. The described mutations are numerous, either homozygous or

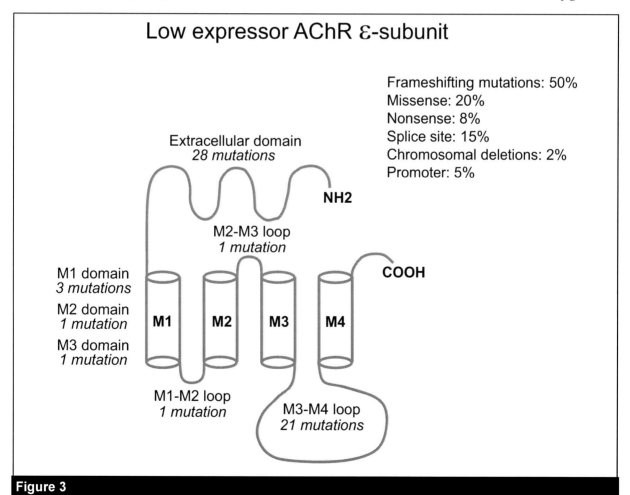

Figure 3

heterozygous. They are of all types: missense (25%), frameshifting, splice-site and nonsense mutations as well as microdeletions. Mutations in the promoter have also been described (22). More rarely, AChR ?α, β and δ ?subunits are involved. The preponderance of mutations of the e ?subunit may be caused by the possibility of re-expression of the γ fetal AChR isoform in the case of null mutations of *CHRNE* (19). No peculiar clinical or electrophysiological findings point to this category of CMS (autosomal recessive transmission, typical myasthenic syndrome with oculobulbar involvement including ptosis and ophthalmoparesis, variable severity, myasthenic decrement without repetitive CMAP, positive effect of cholinesterase inhibitors and 3,4-DAP with additional benefit). Myopathic features are uncommon and antenatal symptoms are not present.

3.3. CMS due to defective MuSK- Dok-7-rapsyn pathway

MuSK is a muscle-specific receptor tyrosine kinase, detectable very early (from myoblast proliferation). It activates signaling cascades responsible for all aspects of neuromuscular junction formation: organization of a primary post-synaptic scaffold and later proper synaptic differentiation and innervation. MuSK, which is activated by agrin released by motoneurons, triggers AChR aggregation via another 43kDa postsynaptic protein called rapsyn and promotes synapse-specific transcription (23-26). MuSK is activated by a cytoplasmic activator, Dok-7. Mice with MuSK or Dok-7 ablated genes present with aberrant innervation and lack of postsynaptic differentiation, absence of AChR clusters in diaphragmatic muscle and die shortly after birth (23, 27). In rapsyn-deficient mice, no AChR clusters form in culture, even in the presence of saturating amounts of agrin, but the neuromuscular junction is not as drastically perturbed as in MuSK- or Dok-7-deficient mice, and subsynaptic myonuclei selectively transcribe AChR genes (22, 28). Rapsyn and Dok-7 CMSs are much more frequent that MuSK CMS.

3.3.1. CMSs with mutations of the rapsyn gene

CMSs with mutations of the rapsyn gene were first identified in 2002 in four patients with CMS due to three recessive *RAPSN* mutations (29). Antenatal involvement was present in 3 cases and severity was variable. Endplate studies in these patients showed decreased staining for rapsyn and AChR. Since these first cases were published, many other cases have been reported (30-34). Rapsyn is a postsynaptic cytoplasmic protein which participates in AChR assembly at the neuromuscular junction (35) and allows its anchoring to the cytoskeleton by β-dystroglycan among other molecules (36). In the first report by Ohno, all patients harbored the N88K missense mutation, either homozygous, orr heterozygous, in chromosome 11p11. Subsequent studies confirmed that this mutation, located in the second of the seven tetratricopeptide repeats that mediate rapsyn self-association **(Figure 4)**, was present in nearly all patients. Half of the patients bore the homozygous N88K. The other half displayed N88K on one allele and a second mutation on the other allele. The high frequency of the N88K mutation may lead to cases of pseudo-dominant inheritance. A founder effect of the frequently identified N88K mutation is likely at least in the European or Indo- European population (37). The second mutation can be localized all along the rapsyn molecule **(Figure 4)**. More than 30 different mutations have been described. Missense mutations predominate (approximately two thirds of cases). When the second mutation is not identified by direct sequencing, search for a chromosomal microdeletion of *RAPSN* is recommended (38). Molecular pathophysiology has been elucidated by expression studies of several mutations. N88K mutation decreases colocalization of AChR and rapsyn in HEK and TE671 cells; in rapsyn-/- myotubes expressing N88K mutant rapsyn and treated by agrin, the number of AChR clusters is only mildly reduced, but 5 hours after agrin wash the number of clusters is highly diminished, contrarily to the control, indicating a negative effect of the mutation on AChR stability (34). The effect on clustering of rapsyn in TE671 cells is variable: R91L

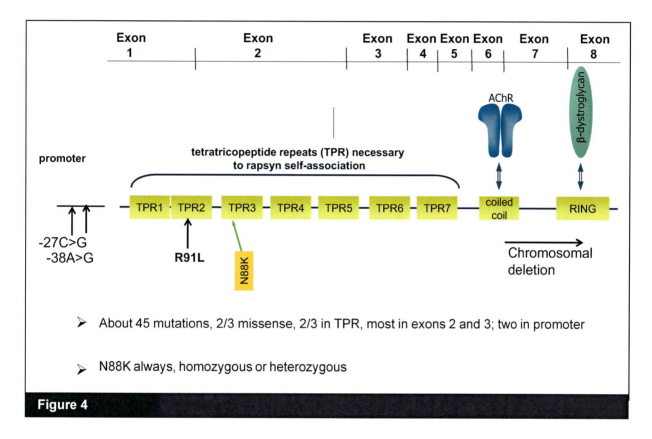

Figure 4

mutation located in the TPR2 domain **(Figure 4)** abrogates clustering of rapsyn in TE671 cells; other mutations have no effect such as N88K, A25V, K273del, respectively located in TPR2, TPR1 and Ring-H2 domains (34).

Analysis of the corpus of clinical observations confirms the existence of two phenotypes: (1) a neonatal form, with acute respiratory failure, and severe progression of the disease; an antenatal involvement with arthrogryposis multiplex congenita is not rare; and (2) mild forms beginning during childhood or in adulthood (30-34). It is not rare that the most severe symptoms present during neonatal period or in infancy (such as respiratory crises), and resolve partly or completely in the childhood or adolescence (33, 39). Diagnosing late-onset cases is crucial in order to avoid improper immunotherapy. Patients with rapsyn gene mutations respond well to cholinesterase inhibitors (30-34) or to the combination of cholinesterase inhibitors and 3,4-DAP (40). According to most authors, patients heteroallelic for N88K and a different missense mutation may be affected more severely than homozygous cases (30-34). Except one case (33), all patients presenting with mild and late disease are homozygous for the N88K mutations (30-34), but homozygous N88K patients may have an early onset, with severe symptoms and even arthrogryposis (33,34).

A set of patients completely different for clinical and molecular features has been reported by Ohno and collaborators in 2003 (41). Two homozygous E-box mutations were identified in the rapsyn promoter. Seven of the eight reported patients originated from the Jewish population of Iraq and Iran and had already been described for their peculiar clinical phenotype: benign CMS (fatigable eye-lid ptosis without ophtalmoparesis, facial weakness, nasal speech, without limb weakness) with facial malformations (mandibular prognathism, elongated face, high-arched palate). They harbor a homozygous founder mutation 38A>G. The eighth patient, a North American woman with moderate fatigable weakness involving eyelid, facial and limb muscles, carries -27C>G mutation. Both mutations attenuate a reporter gene expression in C2C12 myotubes. The -27C>G mutation additionally attenuates reporter gene in MyoD-or myogenin transfected HEK cells and attenuates the enhancer activity on an E-box on an SV40 promoter. On the whole impaired transcriptional activities of the *RAPSN* promoter region reduced rapsyn expression and endplate AChR deficiency (41).

3.3.2. *DOK7* mutations are a major cause of CMS. In 2006, Okada et al. (27) demonstrated that Dok-7 can induce the aneural activation of MuSK and subsequent clustering of AChR in cultured myotubes. Shortly after, Beeson's group reported *DOK7* mutations in 27 patients from 24 kinships in autosomal recessive CMS without tubular aggregates (42, 43). Mutation 1124_1127 dupTGCC was present in 20 out of 24 kinships. Other series were subsequently published: 14 patients from 12 kinships by Müller et al. (44), 6 unrelated patients by Anderson et al. (45), 16 patients by Selcen et al. (46). In our French network, we identified 15 patients. The clinical features are the followings: in one third, onset at birth, with hypotonia, feeding difficulties, respiratory distress, two thirds in infancy and early childhood with limb-girdle weakness/ fatigability, difficulties in walking; in 5%, the onset occurs later during adolescence or early adulthood. Limb weakness is constant. Additional features are mild finger extensor weakness, ptosis in 75% of patients, ophthalmoparesis in 30%, facial paresis in 70%, respiratory involvement in 70% of patients, ranging from mild decreased vital capacity to severe ventilatory insufficiency requiring ventilation with or without tracheostomy, bulbar involvement in 60% (swallowing problems). Fluctuations are frequent, with good and bad periods (over weeks or even months), more than in daytime. Respiratory problems and crises are frequent. The disease course is often progressive and may lead to loss of ambulation in adulthood (44). Decrement without double motor response is nearly constant, if looked for in proximal muscles. Anticholinesterase benefit is rare and, if present, only transitory; more often this approach is inefficient or even worsens the condition. 3,4-DAP may be beneficial (43,44). Biopsy may show type I predominance, type II atrophy without tubular aggregates. At the endplates (EP) level, if some EP regions appear normal, the following abnormalities are frequently evidenced: reduced size of the EPs, reduced postsynaptic foldings, alteration of innervation in several cases, absence of nerve terminal (46, 47). No consistent correlation between conformational changes at EPs and the clinical states was detected (46). Dok-7 expression was localized in EP-containing cryostat sections available from 5 patients by Selcen and collaborators: the protein was present in some patients and markedly attenuated in others, without a consistent correlation between the clinical states (46). AChR number per EP is decreased in most studied biopsies (from intercostal or quadriceps muscle) (42,46). No consistent modification of quantal content and of kinetic properties of AChR was evidenced by *in vitro* electrophysiological studies (42, 46). Ephedrine is the most efficient therapy. More than 35 mutations have been reported (5 new ones in our series), half of them in exon 7 **(Figure 5)**. Several mutations are identifiable only in complementary DNA or cloned complementary DNA (46). The C-terminal frameshift 1124_1127 dup TGCC is present in most patients, homozygous or in association with another mutation. It does not disrupt Dok-7-MuSK interaction in HEK 293 cells. In C2C12 myotubes, the 1124-1127 dup TGCC mutation impairs MuSK activity: decreased number of AChR clusters, reduced phosphorylation of MuSK and of AChR β subunit (42, 48). The frequency of mutations is as follows: frameshift > missense > nonsense and splice site. Mutations are located along the gene: the main 1124_1127 dup TGCC and more than 10 other mutations are located in the C-terminal domain; a few mutations are within the pleckstrin–homology (PH) domain in the N-terminal moiety, and others in the phosphotyrosine-binding (PTB) domain (**Figure 5**). For instance, the 158Q missense mutation located in the PTB domain induces a failure to bind DoK-7 with MuSK in HEK cells and to activate MuSK in myotubes (48). PH and PTB domains are indispensable for the activation and phosphorylation of MuSK. No obvious genotype-phenotype correlations have been established.

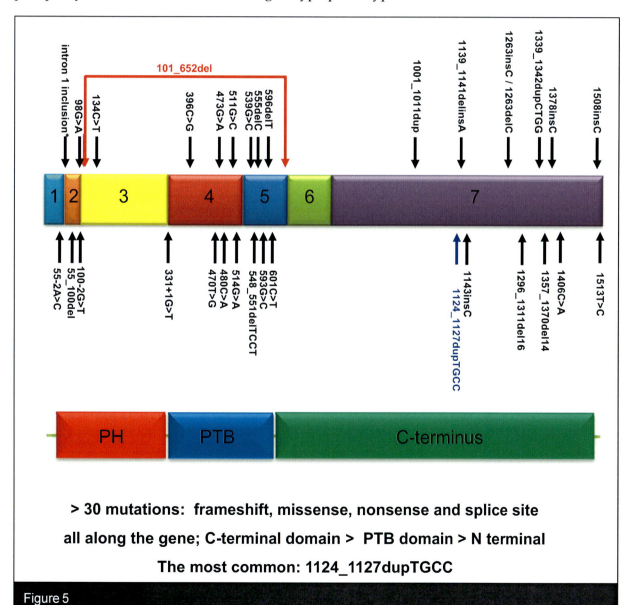

Figure 5

Patients with homozygous for 1124_1127 dup TGCC may have a mild and late-onset disease (44) but other patients may have an early onset and /or a severe disease (43).

    3.3.3. A few cases of CMS due to *MUSK* mutations have been identified but only one case has been published (49). A female patient presented with ptosis and respiratory distress in the neonatal period, very mild ptosis and fatigability during exercise in childhood and adolescence and strong exacerbation of weakness and disabling bulbar symptoms during pregnancy. A similarly affected brother died during a respiratory crisis at 1.5 year of age. EMG showed decrement. Biopsy of the patient revealed decreased expression of MuSK and AChR ε. Gene analysis identified two heteroallelic mutations, a frameshift mutation c.220insC in the Ig-like extracellular domain and a missense mutation V790M located in the kinase domain. The missense mutation did not affect MuSK catalytic kinase activity, but diminished expression and stability of MuSK leading to decreased agrin-dependent AChR aggregation in MuSK -/- myotubes. In electroporated mouse muscle, overexpression of the missense mutation induced a phenotype similar to that of the patient muscle biopsy.

3.4 Other rare post-synaptic CMSs

A congenital myasthenic syndrome caused by a mutation in the sodium channel Nav 1.4 (SCN4A) was reported in a 20-year-old patient presenting since birth with very short bouts (3–30 min) of respiratory distress and bulbar paralysis (50). The diagnosis was made by electrophysiology of the intercostal muscle, which revealed the impossibility of evoking an action potential after nerve stimulation. Two mutations of *SCN4A* were identified, including only one (V1442E) located in the S3/S4 extracellular domain, which was found to be pathogenic when expressed in HEK cells.

    Plectin is a highly preserved structural protein of the cytoskeleton expressed in several cell types, including skeletal muscle, postsynaptic membrane, and skin. Plectin deficiency was described in a patient presenting with progressive myopathy, associated with myasthenic syndrome (involving facial, limb, oculomotor muscles), and epidermolysis bullosa (51). The pathophysiology of this CMS is poorly understood.

3.5 Fetal akinesia and multiple pterygium syndromes may be caused by *CHRNG* and *RAPSN* mutations

Multiple pterygium syndromes (MPSs) comprise a group of multiple congenital anomaly disorders characterized by webbing of the neck, elbows and/or knees, and joint contractures. MPSs are phenotypically and genetically heterogeneous but are divided into prenatally lethal and nonlethal types (Escobar) types. Recently, mutations in the embryonic AChR γ-subunit were identified in approximately 30% of lethal MPS, and also in nonlethal Escobar variant MPS (52, 53). Deficiency of embryonic AChR γ-subunit, which is present at the fetal neuromuscular junction till gestation week 31 and is then replaced by adult AChR ε-subunit, explains fetal akinesia. A baby with Escobar syndrome does not show marked muscle weakness or myasthenic syndrome because the γ-subunit is not required postnatally. Recently, a mutational analysis of MPS without *CHRNG* mutations has been reported: no *CHRNA1*, *CHRNB1*, or *CHRND* mutations were found, but a homozygous *RAPSN* frameshift mutation (c.1177-1178 del A) was identified in a family with three members affected by lethal fetal akinesia (54).

4. PRESYNAPTIC CMS

Three categories of presynaptic CMS are reported: the most frequent and the only molecularly elucidated is caused by *CHAT* mutations, the second category defined on the basis of morphological features is CMS with vesicle paucity, and lastly, Lambert-Eaton-like CMS with electrophysiological features similar to autoimmune Lambert-Eaton myasthenic syndrome (LEMS).

4.1. Congenital myasthenic syndromes caused by *CHAT* mutations

Ohno et al. (55) described the first mutations in *CHAT*, the gene encoding ChAT and located in10q11.2. ChAT is a presynaptic protein localized in the nerve terminals, where it catalyzes acetylcholine production. Onset of these autosomal recessive CMSs is either neonatal from birth after an uneventful pregnancy or infantile. The clinical symptoms are hypotonia, ptosis, bulbar weakness and recurrent episodic apneas (56) or even sudden death (57). In infantile onset cases, exercise intolerance and proximal weakness are common. Apneic crises triggered by fever, fatigue and overexertion are very brief -a few minutes- and may be misdiagnosed as seizures. They may cause hypoxic brain damage with severe psychomotor delay. Apart from these brief bouts, the myasthenic signs are often modest or not present. Cholinesterase inhibitors are very effective, useful in preventing crises and well tolerated. In spite of cholinesterase inhibitors, a significant proportion of patients suffers in later childhood or in adolescence from increasing proximal weakness and may need a wheelchair. Five-minute 10 Hz stimulation may be necessary before classic 3 Hz stimulation to reveal the neuromuscular block. Microelectrophysiology shows, after prolonged 10 Hz repetitive stimulation, a reduction in amplitude of the miniature endplate potentials. These anomalies are characteristic of a defect in the resynthesis of acetylcholine or in the (re)filling of synaptic vesicles (56). Most mutations are private and of the missense type (55, 57-59). The I336T mutation was found in three independent Turkish families and may indicate a founder effect. As shown in knockout mice (60), mutations lead to a reduction in or even abolition of the catalytic capacity of the enzyme.

4.2. Other presynaptic myasthenic syndromes still incompletely characterized

Paucity of synaptic vesicles was described in one patient with early-onset CMS. The density of acetylcholine synaptic vesicles was reduced by 80% and the number of quanta released was drastically reduced (61). The exact cause of this CMS is still unknown. Two cases of Lambert-Eaton-like CMS have been reported: one at the Mayo clinic and the other in France (62). Both had electrophysiological anomalies identical to those of a LEMS, i.e. diminished action potentials markedly potentiated by tetanic stimulation and quantal content was decreased by 90% in the Mayo clinic case. A few other cases with decreased quantal release but without LEMS features (absence of small CMAP and potentiation) have been reported (63,64). No mutation was found in the gene coding for the presynaptic calcium channel or in various presynaptic candidate molecules.

5. SYNAPTIC CONGENITAL MYASTHENIC SYNDROMES

5.1. CMSs caused by acetylcholinesterase deficiency

AChE deficiency causes around 10% of identified CMSs and was first described in 1977. AChE was absent from the endplates by enzyme cytochemical and immunocytochemical criteria (2).

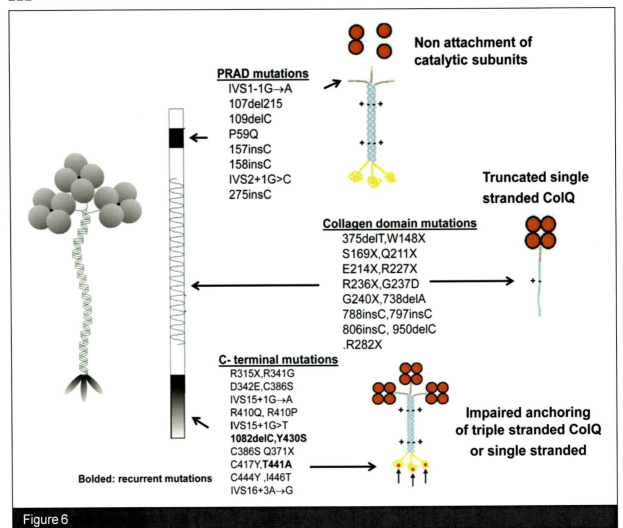

Figure 6

Twenty one years later, the molecular pathophysiology was elucidated by two groups : AChE deficiency is related to mutations in *COLQ* coding for the collagen tail (65,66). At the neuromuscular synapse, AChE is present as asymmetric AChE, which is made up of three homotetramers, each comprising four globular catalytic subunits linked together by a collagen tail (ColQ; Col for collagen and Q for 'queue' in French, which means 'tail') of trimeric helicoidal structure **(Figure 6)**. The collagen tail concentrates and anchors the enzyme within the synaptic basal lamina. Hutchinson and collaborators have described in 1992 a series of 5 patients (67). A recent paper reports 22 new patients/20 *COLQ* mutations, with a review of previous cases (68). The disease onset is typically at birth or during infancy. Muscle hypotonia, ptosis, ophthalmoparesis, bulbar symptoms and respiratory insufficiency are the presenting symptoms, with a significant lethal risk, and delay in motor developmental milestones is frequently observed. However, the disease may start later, during childhood, with weakness/ fatigability and it is not so severe. Some patients may have severe disease onset at birth or during infancy, with improvement during adolescence. Slow pupillary light response is pathognomonic, but is found in less than one third of patients. Several observations point to the diagnosis of AChE deficiency: autosomal recessive heredity, repetitive CMAP after single stimulation (66 to 92% of patients) (**Figure 2**), the absence of response to cholinesterase inhibitors, present in all patients. Diagnosis using muscle biopsies is guided by the absence or the poor visualization of acetylcholinesterase at the neuromuscular junction. More than 35 different recessive mutations have been described to date located all along the gene (68,69) (**Figure 6**). Some mutations are recurrent: 1082delC, Y430S, T441A (66, 68, 69). Most mutations are homozygous, and the majority of them are frameshift or missense, but nonsense and splice-site mutations are also found. Depending on their localization, *COLQ* mutations have different consequences: in the N-terminal proline-rich attachment domain (PRAD) they prevent attachment of the AChE catalytic subunits to the collagen tail; in the mid-part they prevent the trimerization of the collagen tail; in the C terminal domain they most often impair anchoring of the enzyme within the synaptic basal lamina (69-71) (**Figure 6**). While no correlation can generally be established between the location of mutations and disease severity, the patients with C-terminal mutation (homozygous) Y430S have a milder disease with persistent asymmetric AChE, and in T441A (homozygous) with residual A8 and A4 activity. Therapy is difficult because of the inefficacy of esterase inhibitors; 3,4-DAP may be useful and ephedrine is the most effective molecule for the disease (68).

5.2 CMS due to laminin β2-chain mutations

Maselli et al. recently reported a case of CMS due to two frame-shifting heteroallelic mutations within *LAMB2* (4). The patient experienced during the neonatal period several episodes of respiratory distress and she was found to have persistently constricted pupils and severe renal disease with nephritic syndrome due to microcystic nephrosis requiring kidney transplant at 15 months. During childhood, the patient developed ophthalmoplegia with bilateral ptosis, severe proximal limb weakness without bulbar deficit, and scoliosis requiring surgery. Electromyography showed significant decrement. Anconeus muscle biopsy demonstrated abnormal architecture and function of the neuromuscular junction similar to that in mice lacking laminin β2-subunit: reduction of axonal terminal size, widening of primary synaptic cleft, simplification of postsynaptic folds, reduced quantal content. Western blot analysis of muscle and kidney tissue showed no laminin β2 expression. Cholinesterase inhibitors were not tolerated, but ephedrine was effective.

6. INCOMPLETELY CHARACTERIZED CMSs: LIMB–GIRDLE CMS WITH TUBULAR AGGREGATES

Tubular aggregates have been reported in sporadic or autosomal recessive "limb-girdle" CMSs (72, 73). Clinically, the absence of oculobulbar signs was remarkable. The weakness and fatigability involved the limb-girdle. The peculiarity of this not yet understood myasthenia was recently stressed with the publication of five cases, in which all patients presented with tubular aggregates on muscle biopsy and responded favorably to cholinesterase inhibitors (73).This CMS is associated with tubular aggregates on histological muscle examination. The case of three sisters presenting with a slowly progressive myopathy beginning in early childhood associated with cardiomyopathy was reported (71). A favorable response to cholinesterase inhibitors was noted (74). In the absence of thorough investigations of neuromuscular transmission, the classification of these cases remains difficult, especially as the presence of tubular aggregates is not specific and can be associated with isolated myopathy, painful cramps and with slow channel syndromes (10).

7. STRATEGY FOR CMS DIAGNOSIS, DIFFERENTIAL DIAGNOSIS

Two complementary stages are necessary for a proper diagnosis in CMS patients: first to relate the symptoms and signs to a CMS and second to characterize the defective neuromuscular junction molecule responsible for the disease. The main clues are presented in **Figures 2 and 7.**

In many cases, the diagnosis is more difficult: late onset (adolescence, adulthood), no response to anticholinesterase, no family history (most CMSs are autosomal recessive), myopathic features (permanent weakness, atrophy, scoliosis, contractures), confusing muscle biopsy with type I predominance and type II atrophy or with lipidosis, atypical EMG pattern with myogenic features. The main alternative diagnoses wrongly proposed in CMS patients are congenital myopathy, metabolic myopathy if lipid overload at biopsy, and autoimmune seronegative

Pathophysiological characterization

- **Clinical data**
  - Autosomal -dominant: only slow channel
  - No anticholinesterase response: **slow channel, AChE deficiency, *DOK7, LAMB2***
  - Slow pupil response to light: **AChE deficiency**
  - Ethnic context: ***CHRNE*** founding mutations Gypsies and in the North African population
  - Arthrogryposis: preferentially ***RAPSN***
  - Prominent limb-girdle involvement: ***DOK7, COLQ***
  - microcystic nephrosis , miosis, hypoplasic macula area: ***LAMB2***
- **Conventional EMG**:
  - repetitive response →

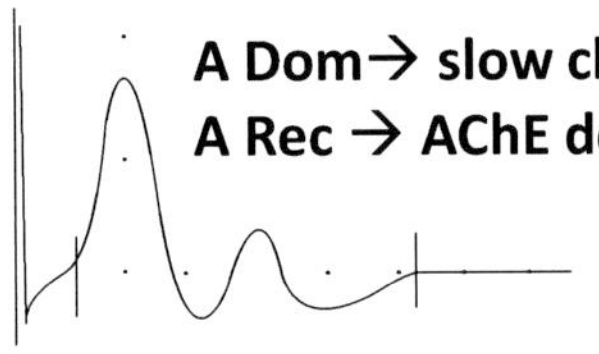

A Dom → slow channel
A Rec → AChE deficiency

- **Microelectrophysiological study**:
  - intercostal, anconeus: MEPPs, quantal content, kinetic AChR properties
- Biopsy
  -if suspected **AChE deficiency**: reduced/absent AChE staining
- **Molecular genetics:**
  - if autosomal recessive or sporadic: first ***CHRNE, RAPSN, DOK7***

Figure 7

myasthenia gravis in late-onset cases. The best clue to CMS diagnosis is a careful electromyographic study of neuromuscular transmission testing many proximal and distal nerves. Autoimmune neonatal myasthenia gravis affecting 10 to 20% of babies from mothers with myasthenia gravis differs from CMS by the presence of anti-AChR ore more rarely anti-MuSK antibodies and recovery after birth. Exceptional cases have been reported with fetal features mimicking CMS due to anti-AChR antibody directed against fetal (γ) subunit (75,76).

8. PHENOTYPE–GENOTYPE CORRELATIONS

The genotype-phenotype correlation in CMS is complex. Mutations in different synaptic proteins give similar clinical pictures: apnoeic episodes in early childhood initially reported in CMSs with a deficit in ChAT, may be found in CMS due to deficit in rapsyn, AChE or in AChR (particularly in δ subunit). If arthrogryposis is very common in CMS caused by mutations in the gene encoding rapsyn [31, 33, 34], it has also be shown in CMS due acetylcholine receptor δ subunit [16]. Prominent Limb-Girdle involvement is found in CMSs due *DOK7* and *COLQ* mutations, and in tubular aggregates CMS. The same mutation could lead to very different clinical phenotypes: for example, the homozygous N88K rapsyn mutation leads either to a very severe neonatal form or to a late onset and benign form [27, 33]. Finally, interfamilial variability is not uncommon in CMS.

9. PROGNOSIS

CMS Prognosis is difficult to assess. A favorable outcome is possible in cases of CMS initially thought to be severe because of respiratory or bulbar bouts (particularly, in CMS due to rapsyn deficiency). In contrast, motor and respiratory degradation occurring late in adulthood has been reported in patients initially only slightly affected; late-onset deterioration in patients with CMS due to mutations in *COLQ*, *DOK7* and *RAPSN* . Thus knowledge of the primary molecular anomaly of CMS does not enable prediction of disease progression. The response to treatments known to ameliorate neuromuscular transmission is a significant prognostic factor and the absence of response to cholinesterase inhibitors or any other drug may be alarming.

10. THERAPY

Treatment approaches to CMSs are summarized in **Figure 8**. Nonspecific measures are essential: immediate treatment of respiratory distress, the prevention of infections and of malnutrition as a result of swallowing disorders, and orthopedic surveillance of spinal complications and retractions. Drug contraindications must be respected as for any other myasthenic syndrome. In the case of CMS, there is no reason to implement the immunosuppressive therapy used for myasthenia gravis. Cholinesterase inhibitors are efficient in most CMSs, with the exception of slow channel syndrome, AChE deficiency, Dok-7 and β2-laminin deficiency, which they can even worsen. 3, 4-DAP, whose mode of action is presynaptic, is often effective in pre- or postsynaptic CMSs (77). A potential synergy with cholinesterase inhibitors may be found in CMS due to AChR deficiency without kinetic abnormality, fast-channel syndrome, MuSK deficiency, and primary rapsyn deficiency. Patients suffering from slow channel syndrome benefit from the regulatory action of AChR blockers—

Therapy in Congenital Myasthenic Syndromes

- <u>AChE</u> : Ephedrine[1], if not obtainable 3,4-DAP[2]; avoid AChE-inhibitors
- <u>AChR deficiency</u> : AChE-inhibitors[3]; if necessary, add 3,4-DAP[2]
- <u>AChR Fast-channel</u> : AChE-inhibitors[3]; if necessary, add 3,4-DAP[2]
- <u>AChR Slow-channel</u> : Quinidine sulfate[4]; if not obtainable Fluoxetine[5]; avoid AChE-inhibitors
- <u>ChAT</u> : AChE-inhibitors[1]; if necessary, add 3,4-DAP[2]
- <u>Dok7</u> : Ephedrine[1], if not obtainable 3,4-DAP[2] avoid AChE-inhibitors
- <u>Laminin β2</u> : Ephedrine[1]; avoid AChE-inhibitors,
- <u>MuSK</u> : AChE-inhibitors[3] and 3,4-DAP[2]
- <u>Rapsyn</u> :AChE-inhibitors[3]; if necessary, add 3,4-DAP[2]

[1]Ephedrine : 3 mg/kg/day in 3 divided doses; begin with 1 mg/kg; not obtainable in several countries
[2] 3,4-DAP: 1mg/kg/day in 4 divided doses, up to 60 mg/day in adults
[3] pyridostigmine bromide (Mestinon) 4 to 5 mg/kg/day in 4-6 divided doses
[4] Quinidine sulfate : in adults, begin for one week with 200 mg, 3 times a day; gradual increase to maintain a serum level of 1 to 2.5μg/ml; in children 15-60 mg/kg/day in 4-6 divided doses; not obtainable in several countries
[5] Fluoxetine : 80 - 100 mg/day in adults

Figure 8

---

quinidine and fluoxetine—which correct the prolonged opening of the AChR (13,14,78). Ephedrine may be useful in CMS due to Dok-7 (43, 44), AChE deficiency (68) and β2-laminin deficiency (4). Therapeutic aspects have been recently reviewed (79, 80).

11. CONCLUSION

In the two last decades major advances have been made in understanding of CMSs: strategy for diagnosis, clinical characterization, molecular elucidation with 12 genes identified, therapy and genetic counseling. However, much work remains to be done in the years to come in order to characterize epidemiology better and to identify new genes (half of CMSs remained unclassified). Collaboration between clinicians, morphologists, geneticists, and neurobiologists is essential for a complete characterization of CMSs and for understanding of the fundamental mechanisms of neuromuscular transmission based on human disease.

The first case of a CMS due to a mutation in AGRN, the gene encoding again, has recently been published (63)

REFERENCES

1   Millichap JG, Dodge PR.1960. Diagnosis and treatment of myasthenia gravis in infancy, childhood, and adolescence. *Neurology* 10: 1007–1014.

2   Engel AG, Lambert EH, Gomez MR. 1977. A new myasthenic syndrome with end-plate acetylcholinesterase deficiency, small nerve terminals, and reduced acetylcholine release. *Ann Neurol. 1: 315-330.*

3   Engel AG, Lambert EH, Mulder DM,Torres CF, Sahashi K, Bertorini TE, Whitaker JN. 1982. A newly recognized congenital myasthenic syndrome attributed to a prolonged open time of the acetylcholine- induced ion channel. *Ann Neurol.* 11: 553–569.

4   Maselli RA, Ng JJ, Anderson JA, Cagney O, Arredondo J, Williams C, Wessel HB, Abdel-Hamid H, Wollmann RL. 2009. Mutations in *LAMB2* causing a severe form of synaptic congenital myasthenic syndrome. *J. Med. Genet.* 46, 203-208.

5   Müller JS, Mihaylova V, Abicht A, Lochmüller H. 2007. Congenital myasthenic syndromes: spotlight on genetic defects of neuromuscular transmission. *Expert Rev Mol Med.* 9(22):1-20.

6   Engel AG, Sine SM. 2005. Current understanding of congenital myasthenic syndromes. *Curr Opin Pharmacol.* 5: 308-321.

7   Milone M, Wang HL, Ohno K, Fukudome T, Pruitt JN, Bren N, Sine JM, Engel AG.1997. Slow-channel syndrome caused by enhanced activation, desensitization, and agonist binding activity due to mutation in the M2 domain of the acetylcholine receptor alpha subunit. *J Neurosci.* 17: 5561-5565.

8   Croxen R, Newland C, Beeson D, Oosterhuis H, Chauplannaz G, Vincent A, Newsom-Davis J. 1997. Mutations in different functional domains of the human muscle acetylcholine receptor alpha subunit in patients with the slow-channel congenital myasthenic syndrome. *Hum Mol Genet* 6: 767–774.

9   Engel AG, Ohno K, Milone M, Whang HL, Nakano D, Bouzat C, Pruitt JN, Hutchinson DO, Brengman JM, Sieb JP, Sine SM. 1996. New mutations in acetylcholine receptor subunit genes reveal heterogeneity in the slow-channel congenital myasthenic syndrome. *Hum Mol Genet.* 5: 1217–1227.

10   Sine SM, Ohno K, Bouzat C, Auerbachn A, Milone M, Pruitt JN, and Engel AG. 1995. Mutation of the acetylcholine receptor alpha subunit causes a slow-channel myasthenic syndrome by enhancing agonist binding affinity. *Neuron* 15: 229–239.

11   Oosterhuis H, Newsom-Davis J, Wokke JH, Molenaar PC, Weerden TV, Oen BS, Jennekens FG, Veldman H, Wray DW, Prior C, Murray N M F.1987. The slow channel syndrome. Two new cases. *Brain.* 110: 1061–1079.

12   Croxen R, Hatton C, Shelley C, Brydson M, Chauplannaz G, Oosterhuis H, Vincent A, Newsom-Davis J, Colguhoun D. 2002. Recessive inheritance and variable penetrance of slow-channel congenital myasthenic syndromes. *Neurology.* 59: 162–168.

13   Harper CM, Engel AG. 1998. Quinidine sulfate therapy for the slow-channel congenital myasthenic syndrome. *Ann Neurol.* 43: 480-484.

14   Harper CM, Engel AG, Fukudome T. 2003. Treatment of slow channel congenital myasthenic syndrome with fluoxetine. *Neurology.* 60: 1710– 1713.

15   Webster R, Brydson M, Croxen R, Newsom-Davis J, Vincent A, Beeson D. 2004. Mutation in the AChR ion channel gate underlies a fast channel congenital syndrome. *Neurology;* 62: 1090–1096.

16   Brownlow S, Webster R, Croxen R, Brydson M, Neville B, Lin JP, Vincent A, Newsom-Davis J, Beeson D. 2001. Acetylcholine receptor delta subunit mutations underlie a fast-channel myasthenic syndrome and arthrogryposis multiplex congenita. *J Clin Invest.* 108: 125–130.

17   Uchitel O, Engel AG, Walls TJ, Nagel A, Atassi MZ, Bril V. 1993. Congenital myasthenic syndromes: A syndrome attributed to abnormal interaction of acetylcholine with its receptor. *Muscle Nerve.* 16:1293–1301.

18   Sine SM, Wang HL, Ohno K, Shen XM, Lee WY, Engel AG. 2003. Mechanistic diversity underlying fast channel congenital myasthenic syndromes. *Ann NY Acad Sci.* 998:128–137.

19   Engel AG, Ohno K, Bouzat C, Sine SM, Griggs RC. 1996b. End-plate acetylcholine receptor deficiency due to nonsense mutations in the epsilon subunit. *Ann Neurol.* 40: 810–817.

20   Morar B, Gresham D, Angelicheva D, Tournev I, Gooding R, Guergueltcheva V, Schmidt C, Abicht A, Lochmüller H, Tordai A, Kalmar L, Nagy M, Karcagi V, Jeanpierre M, Herczegafvi A, Beeson D, Ventkataraman V, Warwick C, Reeve J, de Pablo R, Kucinskas V, Kalaydjieva L. 2004. Mutation history of the Roma/Gypsies. *Am J Hum Genet.* 75: 596–609.

21   Richard P, Gaudon K, Haddad H, Ammar AB, Genin E, Bauché S, Paturneau-Jouas M, Müller JS, Lochmüller H, Grid D, Hamri A, Nouioua S, Tazir M, Mayer M, Desnuelle C, Barois A,Chabrol B, Pouget J, Koenig J, Gouider Khouja N, Hentati F, Eymard B, Hantaï D. 2008. The *CHRNE* 1293insG founder mutation is a frequent cause of congenital myasthenia in North Africa. *Neurology* 71: 1967-1972.

22   Nichols P, Croxen R, Vincent A, Rutter R, Hutchinson M, Newsom-Davis J, Beeson D. 1999. Mutation of the acetylcholine receptor epsilon-subunit promoter in congenital myasthenic syndrome. *Ann Neurol* 45: 439–443.

23   De Chiara TM, Bowen DC, Valenzuela dm? Simmons MV, Poueymirou WT, Thomas S, Kinetz E, Compton DL, Rojas E, Park JS, Smith C, DiStefano PS, Glass DJ, Yancopoulos GD. 1996. The receptor tyrosine kinase MuSK is required for neuromuscular junction formation in vivo. *Cell.* 85: 501-512.

24   Apel ED, Glass DJ, Moscoso LM, Yancopoulos GD, Sanes JR. 1997 Rapsyn is required dor MuSK signaling and recruits synaptic components to a MuSK-containing scaffold.*Neuron.* 18 : 623-635.

25   Glass DJ, Apel ED, Shah S, Bowen DC, DeChiara TM, Stitt TN, Sanes JR, Yancopoulos GD. 1997; Kinase domain of the muscle –specific receptor tyrosine kinase (MuSK) I s sufficient for phosphorylation but not clustering of acetylcholine receptors : required role for the MuSK ectodomain ? *Proc Natl Acad Sci USA.* 94 : 8848-8853

26   Bezakova G, Rüegg MA.2003. New insights in the roles of agrin. *Nat Rev Mol Cell Biol* .4: 295-298.

27   Okada K, Inoue A, Okada M, Murata Y, Kakuta S, Jigami T, Kubo S, Shiraishi H, Eguchi K, Motomura M, Akiyama T, Iwakura Y, Higuchi O, Yamanashi Y. 2006. The muscle protein Dok-7 is essential for neuromuscular synaptogenesis. *Science.* 312(5781):1802-1805.

28   Gautam M, Noakes PG, Mudd J, Nichol M, Chu GC, Sanes JR, Merlie JP. 1995. Failure of postsynaptic specialization to develop at neuromuscular junctions in rapsyn-deficient mice. *Nature.* 377: 232-236.

29   Ohno K, Engel AG, Shen XM, Selcen D, Brengman J, Harper CM, Tsujino A, Milone M. 2002. Rapsyn mutations in humans cause endplate acetylcholine-receptor deficiency and myasthenic syndrome. *Am J Hum Genet.* 70: 875–885.

30   Richard P, Gaudon K, Andreux F, Yasaki E, Prioleau C, Bauché S, Barois A, Ioos C, Mayer M, Routon MC, Mokhtari M, Leroy JP, Fournier E, Hainque B, Koenig J, Fardeau M, Eymard B, and Hantaï D. 2003. Possible founder effect of rapsyn N88K mutation and identification of novel rapsyn mutations in congenital myasthenic syndromes. *J Med Genet.* 40: e81–e85.

31   Müller JS, Mildner G, Müller-Felber W,Schara U, Krampfl K, Petersen B, Petrova S, Stucka R, Mortier W, Bufler J, Kurlemann G, Huebner A, Merlini L, Lochmüller H, Abicht A. 2003. Rapsyn N88K is a frequent cause of congenital myasthenic syndromes in European patients. *Neurology.* 60: 1805–1810.

32   Dunne V, Maselli RA. 2003. Identification of pathogenic mutations in the human rapsyn gene. *J Hum Genet.* 48: 204-207.

33   Burke G, Cossins J, Maxwell S, Owens G, Vincent A, Robb S, Nicolle M, Hilton-Jones, Newsom-Davis J, Palace J, and Beeson D. 2003. Rapsyn mutations in hereditary myasthenia. Distinct early and late-onset phenotypes. *Neurology.* 61 : 826-828.

34   Cossins J, Burke G, Maxwell S, Spearman H, Man S, Kuks J, Vincent A, Palace J, Fuhrer C, and Beeson D. 2006. Diverse molecular mechanisms involved in AChR deficiency due to rapsyn mutations. *Brain.* 12 : 2773-2783.

35   Ramarao MK, Bianchetta MJ, Lauken J, and Cohen JB. 2001. Role of rapsyn tetratricopeptide repeat and coiled-coil domains in self association and nicotinic acetylcholine receptor clustering. *J Biol Che.* 9: 7475–7483.

36   Cartaud A, Coutant S, Petrucci TC, and Cartaud J. 1998. Evidence for in situ and in vitro association between beta-dystroglycan and the subsynaptic 43 K rapsyn protein. Consequence for acetylcholine receptor clustering at the synapse. *J Biol Chem.273*: 11321–11326.

37   Müller JS, Abicht A, Burke G,Cossins J, Richard P, Baumeister SK, Stucka R, Eymard B, Hantaï D, Beeson D, and Lochmüller H. 2004. The congenital myasthenic syndrome (CMS) mutation RAPSN N88K derives from an ancient Indo-European founder. J Med Genet 41: e104–e106.

38   Müller JS, Abicht A, Christen HJ, Christen HJ, Stucka R, Schara U, Mortier W, Huebner A, and Lochmüller H. 2004. A newly identified chromosomal deletion in of the rapsyn gene causes a congenital myasthenic syndrome. *Neuromusc Disord.* 14: 744-749.

39   Ioos C, Barois A, Richard P, Eymard B, Hantaï D, and Estournet-Mathiaud B. 2004. Congenital myasthenic syndrome due to rapsyn deficiency: three cases with artrogryposis and bulbar symptoms. *Neuropediatrics.* 35: 246-249.

40   Banwell BL, Ohno K, Sieb JP, and Engel A. 2004. Novel truncating *Rapsyn* mutations causing congenital myasthenic syndrome responsive to 3,4-diaminopyridine. *Neuromusc Disord.*14 : 202-207.

41   Ohno K, Sadeh M, Blatt I, Brengman JM, and Engel AG. 2003. E-box mutations in the RAPSN promoter region in eight cases with congenital myasthenic syndrome. *Hum Mol Genet.* 12: 739-748.42 Beeson D, Higuchi O, Palace J, Cossins J, Spearman H, Maxwell S, Newsom-Davis J, Burke G, Fawcett P, Motomura M, Müller JS, Lochmüller H, Slater C, Vincent A, and Yamanashi Y. 2006. Dok-7 mutations underlie a neuromuscular junction synaptopathy. *Science.* 313:1975-1978.

43 Palace J, Lashley D, Newsom-Davis J, Cossins J, Maxwell S, Kennett R, Jayawant S, Yamanashi Y, and Beeson D. 2007. Clinical features of the DOK7 neuromuscular junction synaptopathy. *Brain.* 130:1507-1515.

44 Müller JS, Herczegfalvi A, Vilchez JJ, Colomer J, Bachinski LL, Mihaylova V, Santos M, Schara U, Deschauer M, Shevell M, Poulin C, Dias A, Soudo A, Hietala M, Aärimaa T, Krahe R, Karcagi V, Huebner A, Beeson D, Abicht A, and Lochmüller H. 2007. Phenotypical spectrum of DOK7 mutations in congenital myasthenic syndromes. *Brain* 130 :1497-1506.

45 Anderson JA, Ng JJ, Bowe C, McDonald C, Richman DP, Wollmann RL, and Maselli RA. 2008. Variable phenotypes associated with mutations in DOK7. *Muscle Nerve.* 37:448-456.

46 Selcen D, Milone M, Shen XM, Harper CM, Stans AA, Wieben ED, and Engel AG. 2008. Dok-7 myasthenia: phenotypic and molecular genetic studies in 16 patients. *Ann Neurol.* 64(1):71-87

47 Slater CR, Fawcett PR, Walls TJ, Lyons PR, Bailey SJ, Beeson D, Young C, and Gardner-Medwin D. 2006. Pre- and post-synaptic abnormalities associated with impaired neuromuscular transmission in a group of patients with 'limb-girdle myasthenia'. *Brain.* 129 :2061-20

48 Hamuro J, Higuchi O, Okada K, Ueno M, Iemura S, Natsume T, Spearman H, Beeson D, and Yamanashi Y. 2008. Mutations causing DOK7 congenital myasthenia ablate functional motifs in Dok-7. *J Biol Chem.* 283:5518-5524.

49 Chevessier F, Faraut B, Ravel-Chapuis A, Richard P, Gaudon K, Bauché S, Prioleau C, Herbst R, Goillot E, Ioos C, Azulay JP, Attarian S, Leroy JP, Fournier E, Legay C, Schaeffer L, Koenig J, Fardeau M, Eymard B, Pouget J, and Hantaï D. 2004. *MUSK*, a new target for mutations causing congenital myasthenic syndrome. *Hum Mol Genet.* 13 :3229-3240.

50 Tsujino A, Maertens C, Ohno K, Shen XM, Fukuda T, Harper CM, Cannon SC, and Engel AG. 2003. Myasthenic syndrome caused by mutation of the SCN4A sodium channel. *Proc Natl Acad Sci U S A.* 100: 7377–7382.

51 Banwell BL, Russel J, Fukudome T, Shen XM, Stilling G, and Engel A. 1999. Myopathy, myasthenic syndrome, and epidermolysis bullosa simplex due to plectin deficiency. *J Neuropathol Exp Neurol.* 58:832–846.

52 Hoffmann K, Müller JS, Stricker S,Megarbane A, Rajab A, Lindner TH, Cohen M, Chouery E, Adaimi L, Ghanem I, Delague V, Bolltshauser E, Talim B,Horvath R, Robinson PN, Lochmüller H, Hübner C, and Mundlos S. 2006. Escobar syndrome is a primary myasthenia caused by disruption of the acetylcholine receptor fetal gamma subunit. *Am J Hum Genet.* 79: 303-312.

53 Morgan NV, Brueton LA, Cox P, Greally MT, Tolmie J, Pasha S, Aligianis IA, Von Bokhoven H, Marton T, Al-Gazali L, Morton JE, Oley C, Johnson CA, Tremblath RC, Brunner HG, and Maher ER. 2006; Mutations in the embryonnic subunit of the acetylcholine receptor (*CHRNG*) cause lethal and Escobar variants of multiple pterygium syndrome. *Am J Hum Genet.* 79: 390-395.

54 Vogt J, Harrison BJ, Spearman H, Cossins J, Vermeer S, ten Cate LN, Morgan NV, Beeson D, and Maher ER. (2008). Mutation analysis of *CHRNA1, CHRNB1, CHRND*, and *RAPSN* genes in multiple pterigium syndrome/fetal akinesia. *Am J Hum Genet.* 82: 222-227.

55   Ohno K, Tsujino A, Shen XM, Brengmann JM, Harper CM, Bajzer Z, Udd B, Beyring R, Robb S, Kirkam FJ, and Engel AG. 2001. Choline acetyltransferase mutations cause myasthenic syndrome associated with episodic apnea in humans. *Proc Natl Acad Sci U S A*. 98: 2017–2022.

56   Mora M, Lambert EH, and Engel AG. 1987. Synaptic vesicle abnormality in familial infantile myasthenia. *Neurology.* 37: 206–214.

57   Byring RF, Pihko H, Shen XM, Tsujino A, Shen XM, Gustafsson B, Hackman P, Ohno K, and Udd B. 2002. Congenital myasthenic syndrome associated with episodic apnea and sudden infant death. *Neuromusc Disord* 12: 548–553.

58   Schmidt C, Abicht A, Krampfl K, Voss W, Stucka R, Mildner G, Petrova S, Schara U, Mortier W, Bufler J, Huebner A, and Lochmüller H. 2003. Congenital myasthenic syndrome due a novel missense mutation in the gene encoding choline acetyltransferase. *Neuromusc Disord.* 13: 245–251.

59   Maselli RA, Chen D, Mo D, Bowe C, Fenton G, and Wollmann RL. 2003. Choline acetyltransferase mutations in myasthenic syndrome due to deficient acetylcholine resynthesis. *Muscle Nerve.* 27: 180–187.

60   Misgeld T, Burgess RW, Lewiss RM, Cunningham JM, Lichtman JW, and Sanes JR. (2002). Roles of neurotransmitter in synapse formation: development of neuromuscular junctions lacking choline acetyltransferase. *Neuron.* 36: 635–648.

61   Walls TJ, Engel AG, Nagel AS, Harper CM, and Waisburg HA. 1993. Congenital myasthenic syndrome associated with paucity of synaptic vesicles and reduced quantal release. *Ann NY Acad Sci.* 681: 461–468

62   Bady B, Chauplannaz G, and Carrier H. 1987. Congenital Lambert–Eaton myasthenic syndrome. *J Neurol Neurosurg Psychiatry.* 50:476–478.

63.   Huzi C, Bauche S, Richard P, Chevessier F, Goikot E, Gaudon K, Ben Ammar A, Chaboud A, Grosjean I, Lecuyer HA, Bernard V, Rouche A, Alexandri N, Kuntzer T, Fardeau M, Fournier E, Brancaccio A, Ruegg MA, KoenigJ, Eymard B, Schaeffer L, Hantai D. l 2009. Identification of an again mutation that causes congenital myasthenia and affects synapse function. *Arm J Hum Genet* 85: 155-167

IV

Experimental Autoimmune Myasthenia Gravis

Mechanisms of Tolerance in Experimental Models of Myasthenia Gravis

Earlanda L. Williams Ph.D, Sue Stacy Ph.D, Anthony J. Infante MD.,
Ph.D & Ellen Kraig Ph.D

1. INTRODUCTION

Myasthenia gravis (MG) is an autoimmune disorder often characterized by the development of autoantibodies against the nicotinic acetylcholine receptors (AChR) at the neuromuscular junctions (1). The consequent disruption in signaling results in progressive and debilitating skeletal muscle weakness that worsens with fatigue. Although the symptoms of MG are the direct consequence of autoantibodies produced by the reactive B cells, there is a large body of evidence also implicating T cells in the disease pathogenesis. For example, MG shows an HLA-linked genetic susceptibility; this suggests that antigen presentation to T cells plays a critical role in the regulation of tolerance/immunity to the muscle autoantigens (2). In addition, many patients present with either thymomas or thymic hyperplasias (3) and it has been proposed that these thymic abnormalities contribute to disease etiology through disruption of central tolerance and/ or altered antigen presentation to maturing T cells. Lastly, MG can be induced in SCID mice by the passive transfer of anti-AChR CD4[+] T cells from patients with MG (4). Collectively, these data support essential roles for both B and T lymphocytes in regulating MG pathology. Therefore, immune tolerance to this autoantigen could be controlled by mechanisms that target autoreactive T cells, B cells, or both.

In order to unravel the characteristic features of tolerance to AChR, rodent experimental models of myasthenia gravis (EAMG) have been used extensively. Typically, EAMG is generated in rats or mice by immunization with AChR from the electric fish Torpedo californica (TAChR) (5). The immunized animals produce both B cells and T cells specific for TAChR and muscle weakness develops in susceptible strains (5-8). As in human MG, the symptoms are due to antibodies that bind AChR at the neuromuscular junction (1). Moreover, susceptibility to EAMG is regulated by the MHC haplotype and T cell reactivities control pathogenesis (6-8). On the other hand, the thymic abnormalities often observed in human MG subjects (3) have never been seen in the immunized rodents, so the thymic contribution to disease progression can not be fully addressed in these models. Nonetheless, the rat and mouse EAMG models have provided tremendous insights into immune-based interventions capable of re-establishing tolerance to AChR and ameliorating MG symptoms. As we will discuss, this "acquired" tolerance largely targets the reactive T cells with the consequence that autoantibody production also decreases. However, the responding T cells are, for the most part, not specific for self peptides and would not have been susceptible to the immune tolerance mechanisms that function during T cell ontogeny. In order to begin to elucidate the mechanisms of developmentally-acquired tolerance, it has been necessary to turn to transgenic models. In one such system from our lab, the mice express the immunodominant TAChR α chain as a "self" protein and as expected, T cell tolerance results (9). In addition, a T cell receptor (TCR) transgenic animal has been generated that is specific for the TAChR α chain immunodominant epitope (10,11). In this chapter, insights into the mechanisms regulating B cell tolerance and central and peripheral mechanisms of T cell tolerance have been addressed using both the classical and genetically-modified rodent EAMG models. In addition, the effects of aging on immune tolerance to AChR and the implications for late onset myasthenia gravis are presented.

2. RODENT MODELS OF INDUCED TOLERANCE TO ACHR

2.1 EAMG model in the rat and studies of induced tolerance to AChR

MG can be induced in Lewis rats, or other susceptible strains, by inoculation with TAChR emulsified in complete Freund's adjuvant (CFA). The immunized animals produce antibodies to the Torpedo-derived AChR, some of which cross-react with the rat receptor, causing muscle weakness (12). In addition, T cells specific for the immunogen are elicited against several different peptides of the TAChR molecule. However, the response is dominated by one epitope of the TAChR α chain, amino acids 100-116 (13). Although this peptide shares significant similarity with the homologous region of the rat AChR α chain, there are several differences as well (Figure 1A). Thus, p100-116 is not identical to the endogenous self polypeptide and the immunodominance of T cells to this peptide could be influenced by partial tolerance generation during development.

The EAMG model in Lewis rats has been used extensively to test protocols for inducing "acquired" tolerance to AChR (some of these are summarized in Table 1). For example, it has been shown that oral administration of TAChR prevents the development of clinical EAMG in response to subsequent immunization with TAChR/CFA (14,15,17,31). It was further demonstrated that the numbers of anti-AChR antibody secreting B cells were reduced in the orally tolerized animals, relative to control rats (17); this could be due either to a tolerizing effect on the B cells or more likely, to suppression of the requisite helper T cells.

Tolerance can be similarly induced by nasal administration of TAChR; delivery of the tolerogen by this route is even more effective and requires a significantly lower dose of antigen (32). Nasally induced tolerance to TAChR in rats can be reversed by simultaneous administration of IFN-γ, suggesting that cytokines and the method of delivery may be important for tolerance

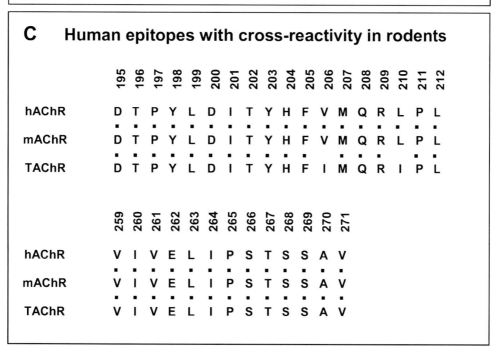

Figure 1: Sequences of homologous regions for the immundominant peptides of AChR.

induction (23). In fact, a decrease in the number of IFN-γ secreting T cells in the lymph nodes (22, 23) and an increase in the proportion of TGF-β mRNA producing cells was seen (14). As discussed in more detail later in this chapter, several recent studies have demonstrated a role for CD25+ regulatory T cells (Tregs) in mediating the tolerance to AChR; given the cytokine profiles seen, Tregs are likely to be implicated in both oral and nasal tolerance induced in rats with TAChR.

Table 1. Rat models used in studying tolerance to AChR

Induced Tolerance-Lewis rat model				
Route / Manipulation	Tolerogen		Conclusion	Ref
Oral	TAChR	foreign	Tolerant if given prior to TAChR; Lower Ig titers	14-17
	Hα1-205	foreign	Tolerant if given prior to TAChR; EAMG suppressed	18
	Hα1-210 manipulated to lack B cell epitopes	foreign	Tolerant; Ongoing MG suppressed; Lower Ig titer	19
	Rα1-205	self	Tolerant; Ongoing EAMG suppressed	20-21
Nasal	TAChR	foreign	Tolerant; High dose alleviates ongoing MG	22
	TAChR and IFN-γ	foreign	Tolerant if TAChR given alone or with IFN-γ (i.p.); Not tolerant if TAChR given with IFN-γ nasally	23
	TAChR peptides	foreign	Not tolerant	24
Intraperitoneal injection	Blocking CD40L	foreign	Tolerant; EAMG suppressed; Lower antibody titers	25
	Blocking IL-18	self	Tolerant; EAMG prevented or suppressed	26
	Blocking TNF-α	self	Suppressed EAMG induction and development	27
Subcutaneous injection	TAChR-pulsed DCs	foreign	Tolerant when given before TAChR; Lower Ig titers	28
	IFN-γ-treated DCs	n.a.	Tolerant when given after TAChR immunization	29
Intravenous injection	Syngeneic bone marrow stromal cells	n.a	Tolerant when given after R-AChR 97-116 immunization; EAMG suppressed	30

Table 2. Mouse models used to study the mechanisms of tolerance to AChR

Induced Tolerance-C57BL/6 mouse models				
Route / Manipulation	Tolerogen		Conclusion	Ref
Neonatal	TAChR or Tα146-162	foreign	Tolerant as adults	45
Nasal	Peptide pool: Tα150-169, 181-200, 360-378	foreign	Tolerant CD4+T cells can transfer tolerance to IL4-/-	46-48
Oral	TAChR	foreign	Tolerant; TGFβ Tregs involved	49
	TAChR	foreign	Tolerant	50
	Tα146-162	foreign	Tolerant	50
Intraperitoneal injection	High dose of Tα146-162/IFA	foreign	Tolerant; Epitope spread beyond p146-162	51
	mPEG- Tα125-148	foreign	Tolerant; Epitope specific	52
Subcutaneous injection	Peptide pool or TAChR	foreign	Tolerogenic if given prior to TAChR immunization	53
	MHC I-Aβ peptide	foreign	T cell and Ig responses down; EAMG down	54
Altered DCs – IV	DCs (RelB knockdown)/ Tα146-162	foreign	Tolerance induced in ongoing MG; Tregs	55
Altered DCs – IP	DCs - GM-CSF	n.a.	Tolerant; effective in ongoing MG, Tregs	56-57
Altered NKs	NK-T agonist	n.a.	Tolerance induced in ongoing MG, Tregs	58
Induced Tolerance-SJL mouse model				
Subcutaneous, Oral, or IP	Dual altered peptide ligand of human AChR p195-212 and 259-271	foreign, with self-reactivity	Tolerant; Tregs and anergy suggested	59-60
Transgenic mouse models for studying development of tolerance to AChR				
TCR transgenic	TCR to Tα146-162	foreign	Not tolerant	10-11
TAChR α transgenic	Expresses TAChRα	neo-self antigen	Tolerant to Tα146-162	9,44

Although effective in rats, oral tolerance has not proven very efficacious in humans. This may be due, at least in part, to complexities of immune regulation in response to protein immunogens. For example, although exposure of rats to intact TAChR was protective, nasal administration of several immunodominant TAChR peptides (α 61-76, α 100-116, α 146-162, α 261-277, and α 354-367) had no such effect (33). This suggests that the intact molecule, possibly in a native configuration, is providing a tolerogenic signal to cells that are not necessarily induced by the immunodominant epitopes (33). This could imply that B cell tolerance is important as well, or that adequate T cell help can be directed at multiple specificities. Another limitation to the rat model used is that there are sequence differences between the tolerogen, TAChR, and the self antigen, rat AChR (Figure 1A) and thus responses to "foreign" versus "self" epitopes are not easily distinguished.

To circumvent these potentially confounding factors, a number of studies have used recombinant alpha chain proteins from mammalian sources, either human or rat, to induce tolerance in Lewis rats. For example, oral administration of the human AChR-α subunit extracellular domain (Hα1-205) has been shown to protect against EAMG induction if given prior to TAChR immunization. Moreover, this protocol can suppress EAMG symptoms if the tolerogen is given after disease induction (18, 21). In addition, the syngeneic rat AChR-α subunit (Rα1-205) has been shown to suppress ongoing EAMG if given orally after TAChR immunization (20) and this treatment resulted in reduced mRNA expression of IFN-γ, TNF-α, and several other cytokines and chemokines (20,34). Thus, tolerance in this model appears to elicit epitope spread to TAChR epitopes not represented in the rat molecule. On the other hand, the syngeneic rat AChR alpha chain immunogen did not elicit TGF-β or regulatory T cells; this was noteworthy since the xenogeneic human AChR alpha chain tolerogen had increased the numbers of Tregs (20). Thus, minor differences in sequences, like those seen in Figure 1A, can bias the responding T cell populations. The immunized rats do apparently discriminate between "self" and "almost self". Although both rat and human antigens, when delivered through the mucosal route, are tolerogenic, the mechanisms may be distinct (20). Further support for the hypothesis that several tolerance mechanisms may be operating in concert is found in recent studies where tolerance was induced by the introduction of modified dendritic cells (29) or bone marrow stromal cells (30). Presumably, tolerance in these models was due to altered presentation of the TAChR or peptide immunogen and may involve mechanisms that are distinct from those mediating oral or nasal tolerance.

2.2 EAMG models in C57BL/6 mice and studies of induced tolerance to AChR

MG can be similarly induced in C57BL/6 mice, the prototypic susceptible strain, by immunization with TAChR in CFA (5,6). Both antibodies and T cells are produced against the immunogen and muscle weakness is observed in some animals; this suggests that a subset of the anti-TAChR antibodies cross-react with the mouse's own AChR (1). Our laboratories and many others have used this conventional EAMG (Experimental Autoimmune Myasthenia Gravis) model to investigate the role of immune components in regulating responsiveness to AChR and in some cases, on the development of MG (35-39).

Immunization of C57BL/6 mice elicited T cells specific for several different TAChR peptides, but the vast majority of the responding T cells were directed at a single epitope on the α chain, p146-162 (37,40). T cell reactivity to this immunodominant peptide has been shown to play a critical role in MG disease susceptibility in this rodent model. For example, congenic B6.C-H-2^{bm12} mice, which express an I-A^b molecule that differs from the C57BL/6 I-A^b in only 3 amino acid residues, failed to generate a T cell response to p146-162 and did not induce pathogenic B cells (6,7). Moreover, disease incidence was reduced in C57BL/6 animals that had been tolerized to p146-162 as neonates (41) or injected with tolerizing high doses of this peptide even after TAChR immunization (42). Thus, T cell reactivity to p146-162 is required for MG in C57BL/6 mice. For this reason, T cells with this specificity have been extensively characterized. They express a relatively restricted TCR repertoire; the TCR β chain is most often encoded by BV6 and contains an acidic amino acid (Glu or Asp) within its CDR3 region (36,43); this conserved acidic residue likely interacts with the lysine at position 155 in the immunodominant peptide (residue circled in Figure 1B). When purified recently-activated (CD4^{high}) T cells from TAChR immunized mice were examined, the Vβ6 population was greatly enriched (38). In addition, when the CD4^{high} T cells were expanded in vitro, they were shown to express TCR β chains encoded by Vβ6 with the conserved acidic amino acid within CDR3. Immunodominance of this population was partially explained by a four-fold higher avidity for p146-162 when compared to non Vβ6 clones (38). Thus, this restricted T cell response dominates in TAChR immunized mice. Importantly, T cells that express this canonical TCR and recognize TAChRp146-162 do not cross-react with the murine alpha chain (37,40). Studies with modified peptides showed that T cell recognition required a lysine at position 155; this residue is not present in the endogenous mouse sequence (Figure 1B). Thus, these reactive T cells are not directed against a self peptide, they do not proliferate in response to murine AChR, and they would not be susceptible to the T cell tolerance mechanisms that function during T cell maturation. This system has nonetheless proven very useful in testing many different routes of tolerance induction post-maturation (summarized in Table 2).

In order to generate a model where the tolerogen is related more closely to "self", Mozes and colleagues have inoculated SJL mice with a peptide tolerogen comprised of two mutated T cell epitopes from the human AChR alpha sequence (59-60). As shown in Figure 1C, these peptides show significant similarity across species and they elicit cross-reactive T cell responses in rodents. Both anergy and Tregs appear to play roles in controlling these autoreactive responses.

2.3 TCR transgenic model

To facilitate the analysis of peripheral mechanisms operating in the "induced" tolerance models, Lenardo and colleagues generated a TCR transgenic line expressing the antigen receptor derived from a TAChR-reactive T cell clone (10-11). In these animals, the majority (>90%) of the T cells recognize p146-162 of the TAChRα chain and display vigorous *in vitro* proliferation to p146-162 and purified TAChR (10,11). While the TCR α/β transgenic mice fail to develop spontaneous EAMG, disease can be induced upon TAChR immunization. These TCR transgenic T cells should be susceptible to induced tolerance protocols and may be useful in dissecting the mechanisms controlling these responses. However, since C57BL/6 mice do not express the ligand recognized by this TCR, "developmentally" regulated tolerance can not be directly assessed in these mice and towards this end, other useful transgenic lines have been generated (as described in the next section).

3. MODELS OF DEVELOPMENTALLY ACQUIRED TOLERANCE TO AChR

3.1 Tolerance to β-galactosidase expressed from the AChR promoter

Studies of developmentally induced tolerance to AChR have been hampered by the use of xenogeneic tolerogen or antigen. Although several groups have isolated AChR directly from rodents, it is difficult to purify sufficient quantities for studies of tolerance. Efforts to use recombinant mammalian AChR polypeptides have proven informative, but still suffer from complications due to non-native conformations and complex subunit structures. As an alternate approach, genetically manipulated mice are being developed that will facilitate studies of immune tolerance to AChR and other skeletal muscle proteins. For example, Salmon et al. produced transgenic mice in which two different length constructs of the chicken AChRα promoter were driving the β-galactosidase reporter gene (61). β-galactosidase was shown to be expressed in the thymic cortical epithelium and muscle-like myoid cells within the thymic medulla of mice generated using the 3300 bp promoter, but expression was predominantly limited to myoid cells when the shorter 842 bp promoter was used. Mice generated using the longer promoter had a higher level of β-galactosidase expression in the thymus and were more tolerant, as measured by decreased T cell proliferation and anti-β-galactosidase antibody production, than the transgenic mice resulting from the shorter promoter. Thus, the level and location of antigen expressed in the thymus likely influenced central tolerance induction in these two models (61). However, since β-galactosidase is not naturally produced by either the thymus or muscle of mice, these conclusions may not be generalizable to AChR or other muscle autoantigens.

3.2 Tolerance to TAChR in transgenic mice expressing the alpha chain as "self"

The mouse EAMG models discussed thus far have provided important insights into the regulation of B and T cell immunity against AChR. Yet, they are not appropriate for studies of tolerance to endogenous "self" AChR since the majority of the T cells recognize an epitope of the Torpedo molecule that is not conserved in mice. In fact, CD4+ T cells from C57BL/6 mice showed no responsiveness when tested against a panel of overlapping mouse AChRα peptides at time points up to 16 weeks following a single TAChR immunization (62). To circumvent this limitation in the studies of tolerance, transgenic mice expressing the alpha chain of the TAChR have been generated (9). As discussed in more detail below, both B cell and T cell responses to alpha chain determinants are diminished in these animals so immune tolerance to AChR had developed during ontogeny.

The construct used in generating the TAChR transgenic mice has been described in detail elsewhere (9); it included the cDNA sequence for the intact TAChR α subunit under the regulation of the proximal 842 bp chicken AChRα chain promoter. Two different transgenic founder lines were derived, Tg1 has been well characterized and previously published (9); these mice express levels of the TAChR α chain which are equivalent to the normal murine AChR α chain mRNA. In addition, a second transgenic founder, Tg3, has been more recently derived; it expresses 3-5-fold higher levels of TAChR α chain mRNA. The tissue distribution of transgenic mRNA expression recapitulates AChR α chain transcription in both humans and mice: muscle > brain >> thymus (9 and Williams, et al., manuscript in preparation).

In order to determine whether T cells maturing in these transgenic animals have been tolerized, mice were immunized with the immunodominant peptide, TAChR α chain p146-162, and proliferation assays were performed using lymph node cells harvested seven days later. Both Tg1 and Tg3 animals showed tolerance as evidenced by diminished T cell responses to the immunodominant peptide and to intact TAChR (ref. 9 for Tg1; Williams, et al., manuscript in preparation for Tg3). Limiting dilution analysis of the p146-162-responding T cells in Tg1 revealed a 6-fold reduction in the number of responding T cells (9). As expected, the tolerance was specific for the transgenic α chain; immunization with intact TAChR produced T cell responses to the other TAChR polypeptides (β, γ) and δ (9). Additionally, for Tg1, when immunized with recombinant TAChR α chain extracellular domain, residues 1-210, the resulting antibody titers were negligible; thus, T cell help is required for B cell reactivity in this system (9).

To better understand how tolerance was generated during ontogeny in the TAChRα transgenic mice, Standifer et al. isolated antigen-reactive CD4^{high} T cells from transgenic and non-transgenic mice. As expected, T cells from peptide immunized transgenic mice had fewer CD4^{high} Vβ6+ T cells and produced lower levels of the Th1 cytokines IFN-γ and TNFα when stimulated in vitro (44). In addition, TCR beta chain CDR3 regions from CD4^{high} Vβ6+ T cells of transgenic mice included fewer sequences with the canonical acidic residue (44). The high avidity antigen-specific T cells had been deleted and lower avidity T cells were hyporesponsive, thereby accounting for the T cell tolerance seen in these mice (44). As described in the following sections, the TAChRα transgenic mice provide an additional system for studying tolerance and it is the only one in which the generation of tolerance to AChR during ontogeny can be addressed.

4. B CELL TOLERANCE

Very few studies have focused on B cell tolerance to AChR, largely because the models used involve immunization with a foreign molecule, TAChR, which elicits a polyclonal response directed at both linear and conformational determinants within the TAChR molecule. Only a subset of these antibodies will cross-react with the rodent receptor and this produces the myasthenic symptoms seen. However, some of the TAChR determinants recognized will not be conserved in the rodent molecule, so a subset of the antibodies are not directed at "self". In order to measure specifically the autoreactive component, it would be desirable to use a rodent AChR for detection of autoantibodies in ELISA assays. While this approach has been successful in some cases, the quantity of AChR obtainable from rodent (particularly mouse) muscle, is generally a limiting factor. Thus, several laboratories have generated recombinant mammalian AChR α chain fragments and used these in ELISAs to measure the fraction of this response that is cross-reactive with "self". This approach is also limited since it entirely discounts those antibodies recognizing conformational determinants or epitopes created from more than one AChR polypeptide. To demonstrate this directly, we performed ELISAs with sera from TAChR-immunized mice using three different coating antigens: i) intact TAChR, ii) recombinant TAChR α1-210 (the extracellular domain), and iii) the extracellular domain from the endogenous mouse AChR α chain. As expected, the titers to either recombinant polypeptide were significantly lower than the titers measured to the intact molecule (Williams et al., manuscript in preparation). To determine whether the subset that was detected with the recombinant alpha chains was of physiological significance, sera from transgenic (tolerant) and nontransgenic (reactive) mice were compared; there was little difference in their reactivity profiles to mouse vs. Torpedo alpha chains. Thus, the recombinant alpha chains may not be able to discriminate pathogenic from benign anti-AChR antibodies.

To circumvent this limitation with the current model in which sera from TAChR immunized mice or rats are assessed using ELISAs with recombinant alpha chains, some studies have directly immunized the rodents with mammalian AChR produced in a prokaryotic expression system. Interestingly, this protocol often results in tolerance, presumably due to the similarity between the immunogen and "self"; a greater proportion of the antibodies made should however recognize "self" epitopes. When Lewis rats were orally or nasally tolerized to TAChR prior to EAMG induction with TAChR, lower serum anti-AChR antibodies were detected compared to control animals (14). More recently, a recombinant alpha chain tolerogen was designed to be free of B cell epitopes; it was also successful in reducing AChR-specific B cell responses. Since the immunodominant B cell epitopes had been deleted, tolerance is presumed to have been elicited entirely through its effects on T cells (19). Similarly depressed B cell responses were elicited following subcutaneous injection of AChR-pulsed or IFN-γ-treated dendritic cells prior to TAChR immunization (28,29). In most of the experiments just described, the rats were immunized with TAChR and although tolerance was observed, there were still possible confounding effects due to "foreign" epitopes on the immunogen that were not present on the tolerogen.

Transgenic mice expressing the TAChR alpha chain were immunized with the recombinant TAChR extracellular domain (alpha chain p1-210), which should be seen as "self" in this model. In non-transgenic littermates, a significant antibody response is detected, but it was largely eliminated in the transgenic mice (9). Thus, it is possible that expression of the TAChR alpha chain transgene directly tolerized the reactive B cells. We consider it more likely that the decreased antibody response actually reflected tolerance of the helper T cells that would have been required to drive the B cell response. In summary, there is no conclusive demonstration of B cell tolerance to AChR; the B cell response to AChR is tightly regulated by T cells which will also be tolerized in a rodent (or human) expressing self AChR. Use of adoptive transfer of T cells from the TCR transgenic mouse may be useful in efforts to delineate whether B cell tolerance is necessary.

5. CENTRAL MECHANISMS IN GENERATING T CELL TOLERANCE TO ACHR

Over 70% of MG patients have thymic abnormalities, including thymomas and thymic hyperplasias, and it has been postulated that these aberrations disrupt the normal thymic architecture and alter the regulated expression of self antigens that is required for proper negative selection. Although thymic abnormalities are not seen in the EAMG rodent models, negative selection mediated by thymic expression of AChR subunits is nonetheless likely to contribute to immune tolerance to AChR, as discussed in the following section.

5.1 Expression of AChR subunits in the thymus

AChR genes have been shown to be transcribed and translated at low levels in the thymus in both humans and mice (63-69). The mRNAs for the α, β, Δ, γ and å chains have been demonstrated in normal human thymi. Transcripts for AChR α chain have similarly been detected in the mouse thymus. It has been suggested that AChR expression in thymomas of MG patients is involved in the breakdown of central tolerance leading to an autoimmune response. However, for most peripheral antigens, low level expression in the thymus is tolerogenic as the reactive T cells are deleted through negative selection. Therefore, the thymus may normally function in generating tolerance to AChR, but when normal thymic architecture is disrupted, it could also become the initial site of autoimmune activation.

5.2 Role of Aire in controlling central tolerance to AChR

It has been well documented that developing T cells encounter a vast number of peripheral self antigens, like AChR subunits, which are expressed at low levels in the thymic medulla (70-71). Expression of many of these proteins in the thymus has been shown to be controlled by the transcription factor, Aire, the autoimmune regulator gene (72,73). When Aire is not present, the set of regulated proteins is absent from the thymus and negative selection does not occur (74,75). The consequence of Aire-deficiency, in both humans and mice, is an autoimmune syndrome which targets several organs, particularly affecting the skin and endocrine systems (76). Aire deficiency is not known to cause MG.

Although it is known that AChR is transcribed at low levels in the thymus and recent evidence suggests that Aire plays an indirect role in AChR expression (77,78), the role of Aire in T cell tolerance to AChR had not yet been elucidated. We generated TAChR α chain transgenics (both Tg1 and Tg3) on the Aire-knockout background and asked whether T cell tolerance would be affected; it was not (Williams, et al., manuscript in preparation). Thus, tolerance to AChR does not require the Aire protein, a transcription factor previously shown to be critically important for central tolerance to a number of other peripheral antigens (74-76). Alternatively, it is possible that central tolerance contributes, but is not required when peripheral mechanisms are functioning properly. Using thymus transplant approaches, we have obtained preliminary data to suggest that this is precisely the case for AChR (Williams, et al., unpublished observation).

Thymic expression of AChR could be eliciting tolerance through another pathway that is not Aire-regulated. For example, while negative selection in the thymus is primarily mediated via apoptosis of potentially autoreactive T cells and Aire has been shown to play a fundamental role in this process, some thymocytes are not deleted but are instead rendered anergic. This would occur in instances were T cells may encounter their self-peptide/MHC in the thymus, but on an inappropriate cell, like the myoid cell. If so, the thymocyte might become anergic since it did not receive proper costimulation (79). Similarly, AChR-reactive regulatory T cells (Tregs) could be specifically activated in the thymus. These possibilities have not yet been directly addressed.

6.0 PERIPHERAL T CELL TOLERANCE TO AChR

Once T cells have matured and left the thymus, potentially autoreactive T cells that have escaped thymic negative selection are subjected to a host of other tolerance generating mechanisms operating in the periphery. These mechanisms include anergy (inactivation), deletion, ignorance, and suppression (80-85). Studies of induced tolerance in rats (Table 1) and mice (Table 2) have provided many insights into the peripheral mechanisms that can contribute to immune tolerance to AChR. In addition, as described below, the TAChR transgenic model has allowed us to explore which of these mechanisms function in tolerance generation during development.

6.1 Evidence for peripheral tolerance from induced rodent models

While the immune response to some proteins is tolerized by peripheral expression of antigen, the relative roles of muscle (peripheral) versus thymic (central) expression in generating tolerance to AChR and other skeletal muscle proteins has not been fully addressed. There is a significant body of evidence that peripheral tolerance to AChR can be induced in rodents by immunization with fragments, subunits, peptides, or intact AChR if delivered under tolerizing conditions. For example, administration of the immunodominant T cell epitope, p146-162 of the TAChRα chain, to neonates can suppress subsequent EAMG-induction (41). Similarly, oral or nasal exposure to the antigen, either TAChR or the mammalian alpha chain, was tolerogenic (summarized in Tables 1 and 2). In several, but not all, of these model systems, regulatory T cells have been implicated. For example, Sheng et al. reported that EAMG in mice can be suppressed by GM-CSF (granulocyte-macrophage colony-stimulating factor) administration and this treatment also led to increased CD4+CD25+ Tregs (86,87).

In rat, some of the epitopes seen are shared between the immunogen, TAChR, and the "self" AChR, so generation of peripheral tolerance in these models may be more physiological. Several groups have shown that the administration of antibodies to specific cytokines before or after TAChR immunization can suppress both acute and chronic EAMG symptoms (21,26,27). For example, administration of anti-IL-18 antibodies leads to decreased T cell responses in EAMG-induced rats, and injection of anti-CD40L antibodies results in lower antibody titers (21). In both cases, disease symptoms were consequently diminished as well. These results and others summarized in Tables 1 and 2 are consistent with a pivotal role for T cell regulation in tolerance induction to AChR.

6.2 Mechanisms of peripheral tolerance to self AChR (developmentally acquired tolerance)

Since the induced rodent models can not be used to assess the mechanisms of tolerance that would be functioning efficiently to block development of MG in healthy individuals, we collaborated with Dr. Michael Lenardo whose laboratory had generated the TCR transgenic in which most T cells were specific for p146-162 of the TAChRα chain (10-11). Fluorescently-labeled TCR transgenic T cells were transferred into TAChRα transgenic and non-transgenic hosts. Analysis of the donor T cells by FACS indicated that the T cells continued to divide and did not appear to be deleted in the TAChRα transgenic hosts, a result similarly observed in other models (83,88). These experiments argue that anergy and deletion are not likely to be involved in the generation or maintenance of peripheral tolerance to AChR in the TAChRα transgenic mice.

Other rodent studies have implicated peripheral deletion for the "induced" tolerance models. For example, Deng et al. (89) demonstrated that administration of a high dose of the AChRα chain peptide, p146-162, after TAChR immunization resulted in apoptosis of Vβ6+ T cells; they suggested that Fas-mediated activation induced cell death may play a role in tolerance to AChR-specific T cells. The mechanisms may well differ when the tolerogen is seen as "self". Indeed, in the transgenic mice expressing the TAChR alpha chain, thymic transplant experiments have shown that peripheral tolerance alone can suffice and that it is not likely to involve either deletion or anergy (Williams et al., in preparation).

6.3 Regulatory T cells as a peripheral tolerance mechanism for AChR

Much attention has been given to natural, thymically derived T regulatory cells (Tregs) expressing the co-receptors CD4, CD25 (the higher affinity IL-2 receptor) and the forkhead/winged-helix transcription factor Foxp3 (Tregs) which contribute to about 5-10% of the peripheral blood CD4+ T cell population in mice and 1-2% in humans (90). In addition to expressing CD4 and

CD25, this particular subset of Tregs also expresses a number of other cell surface markers characteristic of activated and/or memory T cells, including CTLA-4, CD45RB[low], glucocorticoid-induced TNFR (GITR), and CD62L (91-92), but the expression of Foxp3 allows Tregs to be distinguished from these other cells (93-95).

Tregs have been implicated in maintaining and/or re-establishing peripheral tolerance to AChR in many different systems, both in humans and in rodent models. Numerous studies have reported that CD4+CD25+ Tregs are decreased in number and/or functionally defective in human MG patients (96-99). Specifically, Luther et al. reported that the number of CD4+CD25[hi] Tregs was significantly decreased in thymomas of MG patients but not in peripheral blood samples (98). These findings suggest that a defect in the thymoma tumor microenvironment may affect the thymic development of these regulatory cells. Balandina and colleagues reported that the number of CD4+CD25+ Tregs in MG patients was not significantly decreased but that they were functionally impaired and this correlated with a two-fold decrease in Foxp3 mRNA (96). However, the MG-associated changes in the CD25+ Treg population do not appear to correlate with the thymic abnormalities seen in some subjects and the frequency of circulating CD4+CD25[hi] Tregs was roughly equivalent in MG patients in the presence or absence of thymic abnormalities compared to healthy controls although again, there were functional differences (100).

A critical role for Tregs in modulating tolerance to AChR has also been suggested from the rodent studies (101-103). For example, isolated splenic CD4+CD25+Foxp3+ Tregs, expanded ex vivo, were able to halt the progression of MG when adoptively transferred into affected hosts (101). Further investigation demonstrated that Treg treatment effectively reduced anti-AChR specific IgG1 and IgG2 antibody responses as measured by ELISA, and quantitative real-time PCR revealed reduced expression of the Th1 cytokine IL-18 and the Th2/Treg cytokine IL-10 (101). Similarly, Sheng et al. reported that the suppression of EAMG by GM-CSF was mediated by CD4+CD25+ Tregs (102-103).

Given the findings in humans and in the induced rodent models, we asked whether Foxp3+CD4+CD25+ Tregs contributed to tolerance in our transgenic models. To assess the role of these cells in maintaining B cell tolerance to AChR we employed scurfy (Foxp3[sf]) mice which lack functional Tregs (104). TAChR α transgenic scurfy mice (Foxp3-/Y) showed elevated levels of endogenous serum autoantibodies recognizing TAChR, even without immunization (Williams and Carlisle, in preparation). Thus, Tregs do appear to be involved. These data encouraged us to further explore the role of CD25+Foxp3+ T regulatory cells in maintaining T cell tolerance to the TAChR. Towards this end, anti-CD25 antibody was used to treat TAChRα transgenic mice prior to immunization with p146-162. Abrogation of Treg function resulted in a loss of T cell tolerance in both Tg1 and Tg3 mice (Williams et al, manuscript in preparation). Therefore, Tregs are likely involved in tolerance to this muscle autoantigen and further support a predominant role for peripheral mechanisms in tolerance to AChR.

7. LATE ONSET MYASTHENIA GRAVIS AND IMMUNE TOLERANCE WITH AGING

There is mounting evidence that immune tolerance might be affected by aging. For example, the levels of circulating autoantibodies to rheumatoid factor, ssDNA, dsDNA, cardiolipin, and other antinuclear antibodies have been reported to increase with age (105-109). In addition, some autoimmune disorders such as Sjogren syndrome, pernicious anemia and myasthenia gravis have peaks of incidence later in life (108,110). The increase in autoreactivity is somewhat paradoxical since older individuals show a significant decline in overall immunocompetence, as evidenced by decreased effectiveness of vaccines and an increased susceptibility to infections and cancer (111-113). Thus, a shift in the balance between immunity and autoimmunity in the elderly may be associated with the age-related changes in immune regulation. While many MG patients present with disease symptoms before the age of 40, over 50% of patients develop the disease later in life (after the age of 50) (110, 114). Interestingly, there are a number of ways in which the early and late onset forms of MG differ. For example, they show distinct gender predilections, different HLA-linked susceptibilities, and some differences in the antibody fine specificity profiles.

Many factors have been implicated in the loss of immune tolerance with age. For instance, thymic involution leads to a drastic decrease in the number of naïve T cells exported from the thymus, which may explain why older individuals do not respond well to foreign antigens and are more prone to infection (115). On the other hand, the peripheral T cell pool is maintained by proliferation of memory T cells resulting in a more restricted TCR repertoire (116).

7.1 Late onset MG can be induced in mice by immune memory recall to AChR

When old and young C57BL/6 mice were immunized with TAChR, the responses in the older animals were significantly lower than in the younger cohort (117). The primary responses could be boosted with subsequent immunizations, but old animals never achieved sufficient titers to develop MG symptoms (117). On the other hand, when young mice were immunized several times and then aged and re-immunized with TAChR when they were old, a more youthful B cell response was evident and in some cases MG was induced in the older mice (117). This observation was not surprising given that memory B and T cells do survive aging. Thus, we speculated that one cause of increased autoimmunity in older individuals may be the loss of tolerance to self antigens first encountered when young.

7.2 T cell tolerance to AChR is maintained with age

To assess directly whether T cell tolerance to AChR is lost with aging, Tg1 transgenic mice expressing the TAChR a-chain were aged. When these old transgenic mice were tested, T cell tolerance to p146-162 had been maintained (Stacy et al., in preparation). Had central tolerance predominated in this model, one might have presumed that tolerance would have been lost with age-associated thymic involution, yet this was not the case. Thus, we asked whether peripheral tolerance and particularly Tregs were maintained with aging in these transgenic animals. In fact, the proportion of Tregs increases with age, as has been widely reported and was also noted in the transgenic mice (Stacy et al., in preparation). Thus, immune tolerance mechanisms do survive aging which suggests that late onset autoimmune disorders may be induced by a specific insult that disrupts immune homeostasis. Using the rodent models now available it should be feasible to undertake studies that can begin to dissect these complex regulatory networks.

8. CONCLUSIONS

The molecular mechanisms involved in generating and maintaining immune tolerance to the nicotinic acetylcholine receptor, the autoantigen in most individuals with MG, have yet to be clearly delineated. B cell tolerance to AChR has been presumed to be involved, but direct supporting evidence is lacking. Mechanistic studies of tolerance to AChR have largely focused on the T cell compartment where both central and peripheral mechanisms have been implicated. Whether one mechanism is predominantly disturbed in human MG remains to be answered, although recent studies have focused on the potential role of Tregs. Experimental hurdles to working with mammalian AChR have prevented detailed studies of tolerance in unmaniplulated animals. For this reason, we and others have focused on transgenic models where heterologous AChR or other antigens are expressed under the control of the AChR promoter. Consistent with studies of tolerance to various antigens, factors such as the thymic microenvironment and the level and location of AChR expression influence the success of central tolerance induction. The maintenance of peripheral tolerance to AChR appears to be mediated mostly by regulatory T cells. Future studies involving animals carrying both heterologous AChR and corresponding TCR transgenes should be able to further dissect the mechanisms involved in the generation, maintenance, and breakdown of tolerance to AChR. These transgenic models should also allow us to determine whether early and late onset MG are due to disruption of the same immune tolerance networks and to what extent age-associated changes in tolerance affect the outcomes. These approaches might then lead to novel therapeutic approaches designed to re-establish tolerance and ameliorate MG symptoms in humans as well as providing insight into which therapies are most likely to be effective in a given subject.

REFERENCES

1. Conti-Fine, B.M., M. Milani and H.J. Kaminski. (2006) Myasthenia gravis: past, present, and future. *J Clin Invest.* 116:2843-2854.

2. Bell, J., L. Rassenti, S. Smoot, K. Smith, C. Newby, R. Hohlfeld, K. Toyka, H. McDevitt and L. Steinman. (1986) HLA-DQ beta-chain polymorphism linked to myasthenia gravis. Lancet. 1:1058-1060.

3. Levinson, A.I. and L.M. Wheatley. (1996) The thymus and the pathogenesis of myasthenia gravis. *Clin Immunol Immunopathol.* 78:1-5.

4. Wang, Z.Y., P.I. Karachunski, J.F. Howard, Jr. and B.M. Conti-Fine. (1999) Myasthenia in SCID mice grafted with myasthenic patient lymphocytes: role of CD4+ and CD8+ cells. *Neurology.* 52:484-497.

5. Berman, P.W. and J. Patrick. (1980) Experimental myasthenia gravis. A murine system. *J Exp Med.* 151:204-223.

6. Christadoss, P., J.M. Lindstrom, R.W. Melvold and N. Talal. (1985) Mutation at I-A beta chain prevents experimental autoimmune myasthenia gravis. *Immunogenetics.* 21:33-38.

7. Infante, A.J., P.A. Thompson, K.A. Krolick and K.A. Wall. (1991) Determinant selection in murine experimental autoimmune myasthenia gravis. Effect of the bm12 mutation on T cell recognition of acetylcholine receptor epitopes. J Immunol. 146:2977-2982.

8. Milani, M., N. Ostlie, H. Wu, W. Wang and B.M. Conti-Fine. (2006) CD4+ T and B cells cooperate in the immunoregulation of Experimental Autoimmune Myasthenia Gravis. *J Neuroimmunol.* 179:152-162.

9. Stacy, S., B.E. Gelb, B.A. Koop, J.J. Windle, K.A. Wall, K.A. Krolick, A.J. Infante and E. Kraig. (2002) Split tolerance in a novel transgenic model of autoimmune myasthenia gravis. *J Immunol.* 169:6570-6579.

10. Lobito, A.A., B. Yang, M.F. Lopes, A. Miagkov, R.N. Adams, G.R. Palardy, M.M. Johnson, H.I. McFarland, M. Recher, D.B. Drachman and M.J. Lenardo. (2002) T cell receptor transgenic mice recognizing the immunodominant epitope of the Torpedo californica acetylcholine receptor. *Eur J Immunol.* 32:2055-2067.

11. Miagkov, A., A.A. Lobito, B. Yang, M.F. Lopes, R.N. Adams, G.R. Palardy, M.M. Johnson, H. McFarland, M.J. Lenardo and D.B. Drachman. (2003) Production and characterization of a T cell receptor transgenic mouse recognizing the immunodominant epitope of the Torpedo californica acetylcholine receptor. *Ann N Y Acad Sci.* 998:379-383.

12. Graus, Y.M. and M.H. De Baets. (1993) Myasthenia gravis: an autoimmune response against the acetylcholine receptor. *Immunol Res.* 12:78-100.

13. Fujii, Y. and J. Lindstrom. (1988) Specificity of the T cell immune response to acetylcholine receptor in experimental autoimmune myasthenia gravis. Response to subunits and synthetic peptides. *J Immunol.* 140:1830-1837.

14. Ma, C.G., G.X. Zhang, B.G. Xiao, Z.Y. Wang, J. Link, T. Olsson and H. Link. (1996) Mucosal tolerance to experimental autoimmune myasthenia gravis is associated with down-regulation of AChR-specific IFN-gamma-expressing Th1-like cells and up-regulation of TGF-beta mRNA in mononuclear cells. *Ann N Y Acad Sci.* 778:273-287.

15. Wang, Z.Y., J. Qiao and H. Link. (1993) Suppression of experimental autoimmune myasthenia gravis by oral administration of acetylcholine receptor. *J Neuroimmunol.* 44:209-214.

16. Drachman, D.B., S. Okumura, R.N. Adams and K.R. McIntosh. (1996) Oral tolerance in myasthenia gravis. *Ann N Y Acad Sci.* 778:258-272.

17. Wang, Z.Y., J. Huang, T. Olsson, B. He and H. Link. (1995) B cell responses to acetylcholine receptor in rats orally tolerized against experimental autoimmune myasthenia gravis. *J Neurol Sci.* 128:167-174.

18. Im, S.H., D. Barchan, S. Fuchs and M.C. Souroujon. (1999) Suppression of ongoing experimental myasthenia by oral treatment with an acetylcholine receptor recombinant fragment. *J Clin Invest.* 104:1723-1730.

19. Yi, H.J., C.S. Chae, J.S. So, S.J. Tzartos, M.C. Souroujon, S. Fuchs and S.H. Im. (2008) Suppression of experimental myasthenia gravis by a B-cell epitope-free recombinant acetylcholine receptor. *Mol Immunol.* 46:192-201.

20. Maiti, P.K., T. Feferman, S.H. Im, M.C. Souroujon and S. Fuchs. (2004) Immunosuppression of rat myasthenia gravis by oral administration of a syngeneic acetylcholine receptor fragment. *J Neuroimmunol.* 152:112-120.

21. Souroujon, M.C., P.K. Maiti, T. Feferman, S.H. Im, L. Raveh and S. Fuchs. (2003) Suppression of myasthenia gravis by antigen-specific mucosal tolerance and modulation of cytokines and costimulatory factors. *Ann N Y Acad Sci.* 998:533-536.

22. Shi, F.D., X.F. Bai, H.L. Li, Y.M. Huang, P.H. van der Meide and H. Link. (1998) Nasal tolerance in experimental autoimmune myasthenia gravis (EAMG): induction of protective tolerance in primed animals. *Clin Exp Immunol.* 111:506-512.

23. Li, H.L., F.D. Shi, X.F. Bai, Y.M. Huang, P.H. van der Meide, B.G. Xiao and H. Link. (1998) Nasal tolerance to experimental autoimmune myasthenia gravis: tolerance reversal by nasal administration of minute amounts of interferon-gamma. *Clin Immunol Immunopathol.* 87:15-22.

24. Zhang, G.X., F.D. Shi, J. Zhu, B.G. Xiao, M. Levi, B. Wahren, L.Y. Yu and H. Link. (1998) Synthetic peptides fail to induce nasal tolerance to experimental autoimmune myasthenia gravis. *J Neuroimmunol.* 85:96-101.

25. Im, S.H., D. Barchan, P.K. Maiti, S. Fuchs and M.C. Souroujon. (2001) Blockade of CD40 ligand suppresses chronic experimental myasthenia gravis by down-regulation of Th1 differentiation and up-regulation of CTLA-4. *J Immunol.* 166:6893-6898.

26. Im, S.H., D. Barchan, P.K. Maiti, L. Raveh, M.C. Souroujon and S. Fuchs. (2001) Suppression of experimental myasthenia gravis, a B cell-mediated autoimmune disease, by blockade of IL-18. *FASEB J.* 15:2140-2148.

27. Duan, R.S., H.B. Wang, J.S. Yang, B. Scallon, H. Link and B.G. Xiao. (2002) Anti-TNF-alpha antibodies suppress the development of experimental autoimmune myasthenia gravis. *J Autoimmun.* 19:169-174.

28. Xiao, B.G., R.S. Duan, H. Link and Y.M. Huang. (2003) Induction of peripheral tolerance to experimental autoimmune myasthenia gravis by acetylcholine receptor-pulsed dendritic cells. *Cell Immunol.* 223:63-69.

29. Adikari, S.B., H. Lian, H. Link, Y.M. Huang and B.G. Xiao. (2004) Interferon-gamma-modified dendritic cells suppress B cell function and ameliorate the development of experimental autoimmune myasthenia gravis. *Clin Exp Immunol.* 138:230-236.

30. Kong, Q.F., B. Sun, S.S. Bai, D.X. Zhai, G.Y. Wang, Y.M. Liu, S.J. Zhang, R. Li, W. Zhao, Y.Y. Sun, N. Li, Q. Wang, H.S. Peng, L.H. Ji and H.L. Li. (2009) Administration of bone marrow stromal cells ameliorates experimental autoimmune myasthenia gravis by altering the balance of Th1/Th2/Th17/Treg cell subsets through the secretion of TGF-beta. *J Neuroimmunol.* 207:83-91.

31. Wang, Z.Y., H. Link, A. Ljungdahl, B. Hojeberg, J. Link, B. He, J. Qiao, A. Melms and T. Olsson. (1994) Induction of interferon-gamma, interleukin-4, and transforming growth factor-beta in rats orally tolerized against experimental autoimmune myasthenia gravis. *Cell Immunol.* 157:353-368.

32. Ma, C.G., G.X. Zhang, B.G. Xiao, J. Link, T. Olsson and H. Link. (1995) Suppression of experimental autoimmune myasthenia gravis by nasal administration of acetylcholine receptor. *J Neuroimmunol.* 58:51-60.

33 Zhang, G.X., F.D. Shi, J. Zhu, B.G. Xiao, M. Levi, B. Wahren, L.Y. Yu and H. Link. (1998) Synthetic peptides fail to induce nasal tolerance to experimental autoimmune myasthenia gravis. *J Neuroimmunol.* 85:96-101.

34. Feferman, T., S.H. Im, S. Fuchs and M.C. Souroujon. (2003) Epitope spreading to hidden cytoplasmic regions of the acetylcholine receptor in experimental autoimmune myasthenia gravis. *Ann N Y Acad Sci.* 998:388-390.

35. Yang, B., K.R. McIntosh and D.B. Drachman. (1998) How subtle differences in MHC class II affect the severity of experimental myasthenia gravis. *Clin Immunol Immunopathol.* 86:45-58.

36. Kraig, E., J.L. Pierce, K.Z. Clarkin, N.E. Standifer, P. Currier, K.A. Wall and A.J. Infante. (1996) Restricted T cell receptor repertoire for acetylcholine receptor in murine myasthenia gravis. *J Neuroimmunol.* 71:87-95.

37. Wall, K.A., J.Y. Hu, P. Currier, S. Southwood, A. Sette and A.J. Infante. (1994) A disease-related epitope of Torpedo acetylcholine receptor. Residues involved in I-Ab binding, self-nonself discrimination, and TCR antagonism. *J Immunol.* 152:4526-4236.

38. Standifer, N.E., E. Kraig and A.J. Infante. (2003) A hierarchy of T cell receptor motifs determines responsiveness to the immunodominant epitope in experimental autoimmune myasthenia gravis. *J Neuroimmunol.* 145:68-76

39. Infante, A.J., H. Levcovitz, V. Gordon, K.A. Wall, P.A. Thompson and K.A. Krolick. (1992) Preferential use of a T cell receptor V beta gene by acetylcholine receptor reactive T cells from myasthenia gravis-susceptible mice. J Immunol. 148:3385-3390.

40. Oshima, M., T. Yokoi, P. Deitiker and M.Z. Atassi. (1998) T cell responses in EAMG-susceptible and non-susceptible mouse strains after immunization with overlapping peptides encompassing the extracellular part of Torpedo californica acetylcholine receptor alpha chain. Implication to role in myasthenia gravis of autoimmune T-cell responses against receptor degradation products. *Autoimmunity.* 27:79-90.

41. Shenoy, M., M. Oshima, M.Z. Atassi and P. Christadoss. (1993) Suppression of experimental autoimmune myasthenia gravis by epitope-specific neonatal tolerance to synthetic region alpha 146-162 of acetylcholine receptor. *Clin Immunol Immunopathol.* 66:230-238.

42. Wu, B., C. Deng, E. Goluszko and P. Christadoss. (1997) Tolerance to a dominant T cell epitope in the acetylcholine receptor molecule induces epitope spread and suppresses murine myasthenia gravis. *J Immunol.* 159:3016-3023.

43. Pierce, J.L., K.A. Zborowski, E. Kraig and A.J. Infante (1994) Highly conserved TCR beta chain CDR3 sequences among immunodominant acetylcholine receptor-reactive T cells in murine myasthenia gravis. *Int Immunol.* 6:775-783.

44. Standifer, N., S. Stacy, E. Kraig and A.J. Infante. (2007) Discrete T cell populations with specificity for a neo-self antigen bear distinct imprints of tolerance. *J Immunol.* 178: 3544-3550.

45. Shenoy, M., M. Oshima, M.Z. Atassi and P. Christadoss. (1993) Suppression of Experimental Autoimmune Myasthenia Gravis by Epitope-Specific Neonatal Tolerance to Synthetic Region α 146-162 of Acetylcholine Receptor. *Clin. Immunol Immunopathol.* 66: 230-238.

46. Karachunski, P.I., N.S. Ostlie, D.K. Okita and B.M. Conti-Fine. (1997) Prevention of experimental myasthenia gravis by nasal administration of synthetic acetylcholine receptor T epitope sequences. *J Clin Invest.* 100:3027-3035.

47. Monfardini C., M. Milani, N. Ostlie, W. Wang, P.I. Karachunski, D.K. Okita, J. Lindstrom and B.M. Conti-Fine. (2002) Adoptive protection from experimental myasthenia gravis with T cells from mice treated nasally with acetylcholine receptor epitopes. *J Neuroimmunol.* 123:123-134.

48. Karachunski P.I., N.S. Ostlie, D.K. Okita, and B.M. Conti-Fine. (1998) Nasal administration of synthetic acetylcholine receptor T epitopes affects the immune response to the acetylcholine receptor and prevents experimental myasthenia gravis. *Ann N Y Acad Sci.* 841:560-564.

49. Shi, F.D., H. Li, H. Wang, X. Bai, P. H. van der Meide, H. Link and H.G. Ljunggren. (1999) Mechanisms of nasal tolerance induction in experimental autoimmune myasthenia gravis: identification of regulatory cells. *J Immunol.* 162: 5757-5763.

50. Baggi, F., F. Andreetta, E. Caspani, M. Milani, R. Longhi, R. Mantegazza, F. Cornelio and C. Antozzi. (1999) Oral administration of an immunodominant T-cell epitope downregulates Th1/Th2 cytokines and prevents experimental myasthenia gravis. *J Clin Invest.* 104:1287-1295.

51. Wu, B., C. Dent, E. Coluszki and P. Christadoss. (1997) Tolerance to a dominant T cell epitope in the acetylcholine receptor molecule induces epitope spread and suppresses murine myasthenia gravis. *J Immunol.* 159: 3016-3023.

52. Atassi, M.Z., K.H. Ruan, K. Jinnai, M. Oshima and T. Ashizawa. (1992) Epitope-specific suppression of antibody response in experimental autoimmune myasthenia gravis by a monomethoxypolyethylene glycol conjugate of a myasthenogenic synthetic peptide. *Proc Natl Acad Sci.* 89: 5852-5856.

53. Karachunski P.I., N.S. Ostlie, D.K. Okita, R. Garman and B.M. Conti-Fine. (1999) Subcutaneous administration of T-epitope sequences of the acetylcholine receptor prevents experimental myasthenia gravis. *J Neuroimmunol.* 93:108-121.

54. Oshima, M., P. Dettiker, T. Ashizawa and M.Z. Atassi. (2002) Vaccination with a MHC class II peptide attenuates cellular and humoral responses against tAChR and suppresses clinical EAMG. *Autoimmunity.* 35: 183-190.

55. Zhang, Y., H. Yang, B. Xiao, M. Wu, W. Zhou, J. Li, G. Li and P. Christadoss. (2009) Dendritic cells transduced with lentiviral-mediated Re1B-specific ShRNAs inhibit the development of experimental autoimmune myasthenia gravis. *Mol Immunol.* 46: 657-667.

56. Meriggioli, M., J. Sheng, L. Li and B.S. Prabhakar. (2008) Strategies for Treating Autoimunity: Novel Insights from Experimental Myasthenia Gravis. *Ann N Y Acad Sci.* 1132: 276-282.

57. Sheng, J.R., L.C. Li, B.B. Ganesh, B.S. Prabhakar and M.N. Meriggioli. (2008) Regulatory T cells induced by GM-CSF suppress ongoing experimental myasthenia gravis. *Clin Immunol.* 128: 172-180.

58. Liu, R., A. La Cava, X.F. Bai, Y. Jee, M. Price, D.I .Campagnolo, P. Christadoss, T.L. Vollmer, L.Van Kaer and F.D. Shi. (2005) Cooperation of invariant NKT cells and CD4+CD25+ T regulatory cells in the prevention of autoimmune myasthenia. *J Immunol.* 175: 7898-7904.

59. Paas-Rozner, M., M. Sela and E. Mozes. (2001) The nature of the active suppression of responses associated with experimental autoimmune myasthenia gravis by a dual altered peptide ligand administered by different routes. Proc. Natl. Acad. Sci. 98: 12642-12647.

60. Paas-Rozner, M., M. Sela and E. Mozes. (2003) A dual altered peptide ligand down-regulates myasthenogenic T cell responses by up-regulating CD25- and CTLA-4-expressing CD4+ T cells. Proc Natl Acad Sci. 100: 6676-6681.

61. Salmon, A.M., C. Bruand, A. Cardona, J.P. Changeux and S. Berrih-Aknin. (1998) An acetylcholine receptor alpha subunit promoter confers intrathymic expression in transgenic mice. Implications for tolerance of a transgenic self-antigen and for autoreactivity in myasthenia gravis. *J Clin Invest.* 101:2340-2350.

62. Ostlie N., M. Milani, W. Wang, D. Okita and B.M. Conti-Fine. (2003) Absence of IL-4 facilitates the development of chronic autoimmune myasthenia gravis in C57BL/6 mice. *J Immunol.* 170:604-612.

63. Wheatley, L.M., D. Urso, Y. Zheng, E. Loh and A.I. Levinson. (1993) Molecular analysis of intrathymic nicotinic acetylcholine receptor. *Ann N Y Acad Sci.* 681:74-82.

64. Hara, H., K. Hayashi, K. Ohta, N. Itoh and M. Ohta. (1993) Nicotinic acetylcholine receptor mRNAs in myasthenic thymuses: association with intrathymic pathogenesis of myasthenia gravis. *Biochem Biophys Res Commun.* 194:1269-1275.

65. Navaneetham, D., A.S. Penn, J.F. Howard, Jr. and B.M. Conti-Fine. (2001) Human thymuses express incomplete sets of muscle acetylcholine receptor subunit transcripts that seldom include the delta subunit. *Muscle Nerve.* 24:203-210.

66. Bruno, R., L. Sabater, E. Tolosa, M. Sospedra, X. Ferrer-Francesch, J. Coll, M. Foz, A. Melms and R. Pujol-Borrell. (2004) Different patterns of nicotinic acetylcholine receptor subunit transcription in human thymus. *J Neuroimmunol.* 149:147-159.

67. Wheatley, L.M., D. Urso, K. Tumas, J. Maltzman, E. Loh and A.I. Levinson. (1992) Molecular evidence for the expression of nicotinic acetylcholine receptor alpha-chain in mouse thymus. *J Immunol.* 148:3105-3109.

68. Okumura, M., Y. Fujii, H. Shiono, M. Inoue, M. Minami, T. Utsumi, Y. Kadota and Y. Sawa. (2008) Immunological function of thymoma and pathogenesis of paraneoplastic myasthenia gravis. *Gen Thorac Cardiovasc Surg.* 56:143-150.

69. Maclennan, C.A., A. Vincent, A. Marx, N. Willcox, N.E. Gilhus, J. Newsom-Davis and D. Beeson. (2008) Preferential expression of AChR epsilon-subunit in thymomas from patients with myasthenia gravis. *J Neuroimmunol.* 201-202:28-32.

70. Kyewski, B., J. Derbinski, J. Gotter and L. Klein. (2002) Promiscuous gene expression and central T-cell tolerance: more than meets the eye. *Trends Immunol.* 23:364-371.

71. Derbinski, J., A. Schulte, B. Kyewski and L. Klein. (2001) Promiscuous gene expression in medullary thymic epithelial cells mirrors the peripheral self. *Nat Immunol.* 2:1032-1039.

72. Anderson, M.S., E.S. Venanzi, L. Klein, Z. Chen, S.P. Berzins, S.J. Turley, H. von Boehmer, R. Bronson, A. Dierich, C. Benoist and D. Mathis. (2002) Projection of an immunological self shadow within the thymus by the aire protein. *Science.* 298:1395-1401.

73. Derbinski, J., J. Gabler, B. Brors, S. Tierling, S. Jonnakuty, M. Hergenhahn, L. Peltonen, J. Walter and B. Kyewski. (2005) Promiscuous gene expression in thymic epithelial cells is regulated at multiple levels. *J Exp Med.* 202:33-45.

74. Liston, A., S. Lesage, J. Wilson, L. Peltonen and C.C. Goodnow. (2003) Aire regulates negative selection of organ-specific T cells. Nat Immunol. 4:350-354.

75. Liston, A., D.H. Gray, S. Lesage, A.L. Fletcher, J. Wilson, K.E. Webster, H.S. Scott, R.L. Boyd, L. Peltonen and C.C. Goodnow. (2004) Gene dosage—limiting role of Aire in thymic expression, clonal deletion, and organ-specific autoimmunity. *J Exp Med.* 200:1015-1026.

76. Bjorses, P., J. Aaltonen, N. Horelli-Kuitunen, M.L. Yaspo and L. Peltonen. (1998) Gene defect behind APECED: a new clue to autoimmunity. Hum Mol Genet. 7:547-553.

77. Giraud, M., R. Taubert, C. Vandiedonck, X. Ke, M. Levi-Strauss, F. Pagani, F.E. Baralle, B. Eymard, C. Tranchant, P. Gajdos, A. Vincent, N. Willcox, D. Beeson, B. Kyewski and H.J. Garchon. (2007) An IRF8-binding promoter variant and AIRE control CHRNA1 promiscuous expression in thymus. *Nature.* 448:934-937.

78. Scarpino, S., A. Di Napoli, A. Stoppacciaro, M. Antonelli, E. Pilozzi, R. Chiarle, G. Palestro, M. Marino, F. Facciolo, E.A. Rendina, K.E. Webster, S.A. Kinkel, H.S. Scott and L. Ruco. (2007) Expression of autoimmune regulator gene (AIRE) and T regulatory cells in human thymomas. *Clin Exp Immunol.* 149:504-512.

79. Schonrich, G., F. Momburg, G.J. Hammerling and B. Arnold. (1992) Anergy induced by thymic medullary epithelium. *Eur J Immunol.* 22:1687-1691.

80. Falb, D., T.J. Briner, G.H. Sunshine, C.R. Bourque, M. Luqman, M.L. Gefter and T. Kamradt. (1996) Peripheral tolerance in T cell receptor-transgenic mice: evidence for T cell anergy. *Eur J Immunol.* 26:130-135.

81. van Parijs, L., V.L. Perez and A.K. Abbas. (1998) Mechanisms of peripheral T cell tolerance. Novartis Found Symp. 215:5-14; discussion 14-20, 33-40.

82. Lenardo, M., K.M. Chan, F. Hornung, H. McFarland, R. Siegel, J. Wang and L. Zheng. (1999) Mature T lymphocyte apoptosis—immune regulation in a dynamic and unpredictable antigenic environment. Annu Rev Immunol. 17:221-253.

83. Ohashi, P.S., S. Oehen, K. Buerki, H. Pircher, C.T. Ohashi, B. Odermatt, B. Malissen, R.M. Zinkernagel and H. Hengartner. (1991) Ablation of "tolerance" and induction of diabetes by virus infection in viral antigen transgenic mice. Cell. 65:305-317.

84. Coleman, C.A., M.C. Muller-Trutwin, C. Apetrei and I. Pandrea. (2007) T regulatory cells: aid or hindrance in the clearance of disease? *J Cell Mol Med.* 11:1291-1325.

85. Mellanby, R.J., D.C. Thomas and J. Lamb. (2009) Role of regulatory T-cells in autoimmunity. Clin Sci (Lond). 116:639-649.

86. Meriggioli, M.N., J.R. Sheng, L. Li and B.S. Prabhakar. (2008) Strategies for treating autoimmunity: novel insights from experimental myasthenia gravis. *Ann N Y Acad Sci.* 1132:276-282.

87. Sheng, J.R., L.C. Li, B.B. Ganesh, B.S. Prabhakar and M.N. Meriggioli. (2008) Regulatory T cells induced by GM-CSF suppress ongoing experimental myasthenia gravis. *Clin Immunol.* 128:172-180.

88. Calbo, S., H. Delagreverie, C. Arnoult, F.J. Authier, F. Tron and O. Boyer. (2008) Functional tolerance of CD8+ T cells induced by muscle-specific antigen expression. *J Immunol.* 181:408-417.

89. Deng, C., E. Goluszko and P. Christadoss. (2001) Fas/Fas ligand pathway, apoptosis, and clonal anergy involved in systemic acetylcholine receptor T cell epitope tolerance. *J Immunol.* 166:3458-3467.

90. La Cava, A. (2008) T-regulatory cells in systemic lupus erythematosus. Lupus. 17:421-425.

91. Jiang, H. and L. Chess. (2004) An integrated view of suppressor T cell subsets in immunoregulation. *J Clin Invest.* 114:1198-1208.

92. Fehervari, Z. and S. Sakaguchi. (2004) Development and function of CD25+CD4+ regulatory T cells. Curr Opin Immunol. 16:203-208.

93. Fontenot, J.D., M.A. Gavin and A.Y. Rudensky. (2003) Foxp3 programs the development and function of CD4+CD25+ regulatory T cells. Nat Immunol. 4:330-336.

94. Khattri, R., T. Cox, S.A. Yasayko and F. Ramsdell. (2003) An essential role for Scurfin in CD4+CD25+ T regulatory cells. *Nat Immunol.* 4:337-342.

95. Hori, S., T. Nomura and S. Sakaguchi. (2003) Control of regulatory T cell development by the transcription factor Foxp3. Science. 299:1057-1061.

96. Balandina, A., S. Lecart, P. Dartevelle, A. Saoudi and S. Berrih-Aknin. (2005) Functional defect of regulatory CD4(+)CD25+ T cells in the thymus of patients with autoimmune myasthenia gravis. *Blood.* 105: 735-741.

97. Li, X., B.G. Xiao, J.Y. Xi, C.Z. Lu and J.H. Lu. (2008) Decrease of CD4(+)CD25(high)Foxp3(+) regulatory T cells and elevation of CD19(+)BAFF-R(+) B cells and soluble ICAM-1 in myasthenia gravis. *Clin Immunol.* 126:180-188.

98. Luther, C., S. Poeschel, M. Varga, A. Melms and E. Tolosa. (2005) Decreased frequency of intrathymic regulatory T cells in patients with myasthenia-associated thymoma. *J Neuroimmunol.* 164:124-128.

99. Strobel, P., A. Rosenwald, N. Beyersdorf, T. Kerkau, O. Elert, A. Murumagi, N. Sillanpaa, P. Peterson, V. Hummel, P. Rieckmann, C. Burek, B. Schalke, W. Nix, R. Kiefer, H.K. Muller-Hermelink and A. Marx. (2004) Selective loss of regulatory T cells in thymomas. *Ann Neurol.* 56:901-904.

100. Zhang, Y., H.B. Wang, L.J. Chi and W.Z. Wang. (2009) The role of FoxP3+CD4+CD25hi Tregs in the pathogenesis of myasthenia gravis. *Immunol Lett.* 122: 52-57.

101. Aricha, R., T. Feferman, S. Fuchs and M.C. Souroujon. (2008) Ex vivo generated regulatory T cells modulate experimental autoimmune myasthenia gravis. *J Immunol.* 180:2132-2139.

102. Meriggioli, M.N., J.R. Sheng, L. Li and B.S. Prabhakar. (2008) Strategies for treating autoimmunity: novel insights from experimental myasthenia gravis. *Ann N Y Acad Sci.* 1132:276-282.

103. Sheng, J.R., L.C. Li, B.B. Ganesh, B.S. Prabhakar and M.N. Meriggioli. (2008) Regulatory T cells induced by GM-CSF suppress ongoing experimental myasthenia gravis. Clin Immunol. 128:172-180.

104. Brunkow, M.E., E.W. Jeffery, K.A. Hjerrild, B. Paeper, L.B. Clark, S.A. Yasayko, J.E. Wilkinson, D. Galas, S.F. Ziegler and F. Ramsdell. (2001) Disruption of a new forkhead/ winged-helix protein, scurfin, results in the fatal lymphoproliferative disorder of the scurfy mouse. Nat Genet. 27:68-73.

105. Attanasio, R., K.M. Brasky, S.H. Robbins, L. Jayashankar, R.J. Nash and T.M. Butler. (2001) Age-related autoantibody production in a nonhuman primate model. Clin Exp Immunol. 123:361-365.

106. Ioannidis, J.P., G.E. Katsifis, E.D. Stavropoulos, M.N. Manoussakis and H.M. Moutsopoulos. (2003) Evaluation of the association of autoantibodies with mortality in the very elderly: a cohort study. *Rheumatology* (Oxford). 42:357-361.

107. Manoussakis, M.N., A.G. Tzioufas, M.P. Silis, P.J. Pange, J. Goudevenos and H.M. Moutsopoulos. (1987) High prevalence of anti-cardiolipin and other autoantibodies in a healthy elderly population. *Clin Exp Immunol.* 69:557-565.

108. Mishra, N. and G.M. Kammer. (1998) Clinical expression of autoimmune diseases in older adults. *Clin Geriatr Med.* 14:515-542.

109. Xavier, R.M., Y. Yamauchi, M. Nakamura, Y. Tanigawa, H. Ishikura, T. Tsunematsu and S. Kobayashi. (1995) Antinuclear antibodies in healthy aging people: a prospective study. Mech Ageing Dev. 78:145-154.

110. Aarli, J.A. (2008) Myasthenia gravis in the elderly: Is it different? Ann N Y Acad Sci. 1132:238-243.

111. Arreaza, E.E., J.J. Gibbons, Jr., G.W. Siskind and M.E. Weksler. (1993) Lower antibody response to tetanus toxoid associated with higher auto-anti-idiotypic antibody in old compared with young humans. *Clin Exp Immunol.* 92:169-173.

112. Ginaldi, L., M.F. Loreto, M.P. Corsi, M. Modesti and M. De Martinis. (2001) Immunosenescence and infectious diseases. *Microbes Infect.* 3:851-857.

113. Webster, R.G. (2000) Immunity to influenza in the elderly. *Vaccine.* 18:1686-1689.

114. Somnier, F.E. (2005) Increasing incidence of late-onset anti-AChR antibody-seropositive myasthenia gravis. *Neurology.* 65:928-930.

115. Aspinall, R. and D. Andrew. (2000) Thymic involution in aging. *J Clin Immunol.* 20:250-256.

116. Mackall, C.L., C.V. Bare, L.A. Granger, S.O. Sharrow, J.A. Titus and R.E. Gress. (1996) Thymic-independent T cell regeneration occurs via antigen-driven expansion of peripheral T cells resulting in a repertoire that is limited in diversity and prone to skewing. *J Immunol.* 156: 4609-4616.

117. Stacy, S., A.J. Infante, K.A. Wall, K. Krolick and E. Kraig. (2003) Recall immune memory: a new tool for generating late onset autoimmune myasthenia gravis. *Mech Ageing Dev.* 124:931-940.

14

Effector Functions of IgG Isotypes in Myasthenia Gravis

Joost Van den Broeck,MSc, Alejandro Gomez,MSc, Kathleen Vrolix,MSc, Pilar Martínez-Martínez,PhD, Peter Molenaar,PhD, Marc H. De Baets, M.D. PhD, and Mario Losen, PhD

1. INTRODUCTION

Myasthenia gravis (MG) is an autoimmune disease caused by autoantibodies against proteins located in the postsynaptic membrane of the neuromuscular junction (NMJ) [1, 2]. MG is one of the best understood autoimmune diseases. It has a prevalence of 20 per 100 000 persons [3]. Several lines of evidence have clearly demonstrated that antibodies against the acetylcholine receptor (AChR) cause the disease in approximately 85% of MG patients [4]. Autoantibodies against the muscle specific tyrosine kinase (MuSK) have been demonstrated in up to 70% of MG patients without autoantibodies against the AChR [5]. MuSK plays an important role in the differentiation of the NMJ [5, 6]. Together, AChR-MG and MuSK-MG cover more than 90% of MG cases. The remaining patients also have an autoimmune disorder, since they benefit from immunosuppression or plasmapheresis. Historically, the term "seronegative MG", was used for MG without anti-AChR antibodies, but with the discovery of MuSK antibodies in some, but not all seronegative patients, this term has become confusing. Therefore, the following nomenclature will be used in this review: "AChR-MG" for myasthenia with anti-AChR antibodies; "MuSK-MG" for myasthenia with anti-MuSK antibodies; "idiopathic MG" for patients with (autoimmune) MG, but (thus-far) undetectable levels of anti-AChR or anti-MuSK antibodies (Table 1). The pathogenesis of chronic disease processes in AChR-MG and MuSK-MG is discussed in Section 2. A transient form of MG occurs when autoantibodies are passively transferred from a mother to the unborn child [7, 8], which is discussed in Section 3.

Table 1. Myasthenia gravis and related animal models

MG in humans		MG in animals	Animal models	
chronic	transient	chronic	Active immunization	Passive immunization
AChR-MG human IgG1, human IgG3	Neonatal AChR-MG [9-12]	**AChR-MG** dogs, cats [13,14]	**AChR-EAMG** rabbit [15] rats, guinea pigs [16], rhesus monkeys [17]	**passive transfer AChR-MG** mice [18], rhesus monkeys [19], rats [20]
MuSK-MG human IgG4 **Idiopathic MG** "seronegative MG"	Neonatal MuSK-MG [21, 22]		**MuSK-EAMG** rabbits [23] mice [24]	**passive transfer MuSK-MG** mice [25]

Findings that the NMJ of AChR-MG patients contained different activated components of the complement system [26-28] suggested an important role of the classical complement pathway in the NMJ damage. Moreover, autoantibodies can block and modulate the AChR and induce loss of AChR-associated proteins. The effector functions strongly depend on the IgG subclass properties which are discussed in Section 4.

Animal models have contributed significantly to elucidate the pathogenesis of MG and are discussed in detail in Section 5. AChR-immunization induced MG is used as an MG animal model termed experimental autoimmune myasthenia gravis (EAMG). Moreover, injection of MG patient sera or monoclonal anti-AChR antibodies also induce muscle weakness in animals and this model is termed passive transfer MG [18].

Similarly, MG can be induced in animals by active immunization with MuSK [23, 24] or by passive transfer with serum from MuSK-MG patients [25]. In this review, these models are referred to as "MuSK-EAMG" and "passive transfer MuSK-MG", respectively (Table 1).

MG models have been crucial for understanding the role of the different IgG isotypes in the pathology and severity of MG. This knowledge provides a basis to innovate the current therapies for MG patients into more specific and effective treatment approaches. Strategies that use this knowledge to curb the pathogenic effects of pro-inflammatory IgG subclasses are also discussed in Section 5.

2. NEUROMUSCULAR JUNCTION ORGANIZATION AND PATHOGENIC CHANGES IN ACHR-MG, MUSK-MG AND IDIOPATHIC MG

The AChR is a ligand-gated ion channel, which is located at the postsynaptic membrane of the NMJ and functions as a receptor for the neurotransmitter acetylcholine (ACh) [29]. Binding of ACh to the AChR opens the channel for cations, thereby causing local depolarization of the postsynaptic membrane [30]. The subsequent opening of voltage-gated cation channels (Na^+ and K^+) generates an action potential that spreads along the muscle fiber. The action potential triggers the release of calcium from intracellular stores and consequently muscle fiber contraction. In AChR-MG patients, the anti-AChR antibodies induce loss of the AChRs, leading to an impaired neuromuscular transmission with muscle weakness as a result [31]. The breakdown of the AChR is known to be mediated by complement-mediated lysis of the postsynaptic membrane [27] and by cross-linking the AChR in the membrane, leading to its internalization and degradation. This process is also known as antigenic modulation, because AChR internalization is believed to be initiated by an antibody-induced conformational change of the antigen [32].

Antibodies against many other antigens are frequently found in AChR-MG patients (Table 2). Their role in the pathogenesis and their contribution to the clinical symptoms are not completely understood. Many of these antibodies also occur in patients with other autoimmune diseases. In addition, some autoantibodies are associated with malignancies of the thymus (thymoma). Thymic abnormalities such as hyperplasia and thymoma are significant risk factors for AChR-MG [33].

MuSK is known to initiate aggregation of the AChR during synapse formation via the agrin/Lrp4/MuSK/rapsyn/AChR clustering pathway (Figure 1), but MuSK is also expressed at the mature NMJ. MuSK autoantibodies have the potential to alter the MuSK function at the adult NMJ, and they may not only inhibit MuSK function directly, but also increase the turnover of MuSK, thereby further reducing its activity [5, 6]. In contrast with AChR antibody-positive patients, there is no evidence of loss of junctional folds, no apparent loss of AChR density and generally no complement deposition [120, 121] in muscle biopsies of MuSK-MG patients. These findings suggest that MuSK-MG may be different in etiological and pathological mechanisms, compared to AChR-MG [41].

In about 5% to 10% of MG patients no autoantibodies against the AChR or MuSK are found [86]. These idiopathic MG patients may also have an antibody-mediated disease since they respond well to plasma exchange and to immunosuppression. This suggests that the autoantibodies might be directed against other neuromuscular proteins in idiopathic MG patients [122]. Idiopathic MG is more similar to AChR-MG than to MuSK-MG regarding thymic pathology [123] and clinical features [124]. Since idiopathic MG patients have the same clinical presentation as patients with AChR-MG, it is also possible that they produce AChR autoantibodies at a very low level or with low affinity, which makes these autoantibodies undetectable for conventional AChR antibody assays [125, 126].

3. NEONATAL MG

Passive transfer of MG autoantibodies can occur form mother to the unborn child [9]. About 21% of infants of mothers with MG develop at birth a transient myasthenic syndrome called neonatal myasthenia gravis (NMG) [11]. In the worst case autoantibodies impair muscle and joint development [7, 8] leading to joint contractures (arthrogryposis). Antibodies against the fetal form of the AChR [127] are particularly dangerous for the unborn child, since they affect the development of the neuromuscular junction while at the same time only causing mild MG symptoms in the mother [128]. Mild cases of NMG are characterized by a short postnatal period of muscle weakness and respiratory impairment. However, it is not clear why some children become ill while others remain asymptomatic, even though they have detectable levels of anti-AChR antibodies. Symptoms usually appear within hours after birth and disappear spontaneously after two to three weeks. The delay of symptoms may be due to anticholinesterase drugs given to the mother; they can cross the placenta and therefore protect the baby for several hours after

Table 2. Auto-antigens reported in MG patients

Auto-antigen	Prevalence in MG	Association with other disease	Main IgG isotype	Reference
AChR	~85%	-	IgG1, IgG3	[4, 34-39]
MuSK	4-70% *	-	IgG4	[5, 6, 40-48]
Titin	30-75% **	Thymoma	IgG1, IgG4	[49-57]
RyR	50-90% **	Thymoma, myositis	IgG1, IgG3	[52, 54, 58-66]
DHPR	37% **	-	/	[67]
TRPC3	36%	-	/	[66]
Tropomyosin	32%	-	/	[68, 69]
Actin	3%	-	/	[69-71]
Myosin	36-48%	-	IgG1, IgG2, IgG4	[69-72]
Actomyosin	/	-	/	[71]
α-Actinin	23%	-	/	[69-71]
Troponin	29%	-	/	[69]
Filamin	77-100% (ocular)	-	/	[68]
Vinculin	/	-	/	[68]
Rapsyn	12-13%	-	/	[73, 74]
VGKC	12-28%	Acquired neuromyotonia		[57, 62, 75]
AChE	5-36%	-	IgG1	[76-78]
PsmR	~ 50%	-	/	[79-81]
Thyroid	27-40%	HT, GD	/	[82-84]
Thyroglobulin	5-26%	HT, GD	/	[77, 84-86]
Thyroperoxidase	19%	HT, GD	/	[86]
TSH	7%	HT, GD	/	[87]
Nuclear antigen	6-60%	SLE	/	[83, 88-93]
Cardiolipin	20-40%	Anti-phospholipid syndrome, SLE	/	[94-96]
Muscarinic AChR	28%	LEMS	/	[97]
Neuronal AChR	4-8%	AAG	/	[98, 99]
Adrenergic receptor	18-27%	Dilated cardiomyopathy	IgG2, IgG4	[100, 101]
Cytokines	3-90%	-	IgG1	[33, 50, 102-105]
Heat shock protein	30-80%	-	/	[106, 107]
C1q	/	-	/	[108]
Thrombocyte	20%	NAT, SLE	/	[109]
Growth hormone	2%	-	/	[110]
Neuroblastoma cells	40-60%	-	/	[111-113]
Thymus	40-75%		/	[114, 115]
Alkaline phosphatase	9%	-	/	[116, 117]
Gravin	18-31%	-	/	[118, 119]

Ep: epinephrine, NE: norepinephrine, HT: Hashimoto's thyroiditis, GD: Graves' disease, NAT: Neonatal alloimmune thrombocytopenie, AAG: autoimmune autonomic ganglionopathy, LEMS: Lambert-Eaton myasthenic syndrome, TSH: thyroid stimulating hormone
/: not available or not applicable; -: absent; +: present
*: of AChR-antibody negative MG; **: of late onset and thymoma MG

birth until the level of the drug diminishes [129]. The severity of NMG is highly variable, ranging from mild hypotonia to respiratory distress requiring assisted mechanical ventilation. The disease severity is not correlated to the clinical status of the mother [10], but to the anti-AChR antibody levels [10]. Despite considerable variability in absolute anti-AChR antibody levels, the anti-fetal AChR/anti-adult muscle AChR antibody titer ratio remains relatively stable and a high value of that ratio predicts the transmission of disease from mother to newborn child in first pregnancy [12, 130].

4. IgG ISOTYPES IN MG

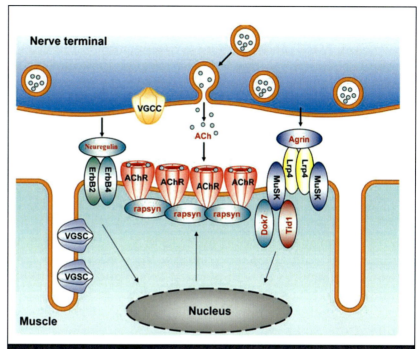

Figure 1: Scheme of the neuromuscular junction. ACh – acetylcholine; AChR-acetylcholine receptor; Dok7 – docking protein 7; ErbB2/4 erythroblastic leukemia viral oncogene homolog 2/4; Lrp4 - low density lipoprotein receptor-related protein 4; MuSK – muscle specific tyrosine kinase; rapsyn – receptor associated protein of the synapse; Tid1 - tumorous imaginal discs; VGSC – voltage gated sodium channel; VGCC – voltage gated calcium channel.

MG is mediated by circulating antibodies of the IgG class directed to the AChR, MuSK or possibly other, still unknown autoantigens in the NMJ of striated muscle.

Four human IgG isotypes exist which have very similar amino acid sequences, but differ in their ability to activate the complement system. IgG1 and IgG3 are effective complement activators, IgG2 fixes complement poorly and IgG4 is completely deficient in the ability to activate complement via the classical pathway [131, 132]. The structure responsible for the differential ability of human IgG isotypes to activate complement is located at the carboxy-terminal part (residues 292-340) of the CH2 domain [133] (Figure 2). The hinge region also has a minor contribution to the complement activation [134].

In AChR-MG patients, the complement-fixing IgG1 and IgG3 isotype of AChR-specific antibodies predominate, whereas IgG2 and IgG4 are present in lower concentrations [38, 135, 136]. Generally, the autoantibody concentration does not correlate well with the severity of the disease [137], although in individual patients there is a relation between antibody titer and clinical condition after immunotherapy [138]. Since IgG autoantibody subclasses have distinct immunological properties, a possible explanation for this weak correlation could be variations in the isotype distribution. Interestingly, anti-AChR IgG1 (but not IgG2, IgG3 and IgG4) concentration was found to be significantly correlated to severity of disease [38]. These results suggest that binding of IgG1 may play a key role in the pathogenesis of AChR-MG

[38]. In rhesus monkeys, passive transfer of human IgG1, but not IgG4 anti-AChR antibodies caused MG [19].

Anti-MuSK antibodies are predominantly of the IgG4 isotype [41] and therefore they do not cause substantial complement deposition, morphological damage or AChR loss at the NMJ [120, 121]. These findings imply differences between MuSK-MG and AChR-MG in their pathological mechanisms. The mechanism in MuSK-MG may involve downstream changes in the function and distribution of key molecules at the NMJ. It has been suggested that the postsynaptic machinery becomes structurally and functionally disorganized by a significant reduction of AChR clustering [139]. The presence of a pathogenic antibody in MuSK-MG was demonstrated by passive transfer of IgG from anti-MuSK-positive MG patients into adult mice. This passive transfer reduced the level of AChRs in the postsynaptic membrane and caused changes in the presynaptic and postsynaptic elements of the synapse leading to muscle weakness [25]. In addition, passive transfer caused a decrease of the safety factor of neuromuscular transmission and the size of endplates in regenerating muscles of adult mice [140]. Mice actively immunized with MuSK also showed the characteristic symptoms of MG [24]. However, the pro-inflammatory (i.e. complement-fixing and cross-linking) anti-MuSK antibodies that are produced in MuSK-EAMG do not closely resemble human MuSK-MG with anti-inflammatory IgG4 antibodies. Therefore, the pathological mechanisms of the MuSK-EAMG model might differ from MuSK-MG.

In idiopathic MG patients, it has been shown that the autoantibodies belong to the IgG1 subclass. In addition, they induced complement deposition on the AChR clusters which demonstrates C1q binding and activation of the classical complement pathway [126]. This strongly suggests that the autoantibodies of idiopathic MG can be directed towards the AChR, but bind only when the AChRs are densely clustered [126].

4.1. IgG interaction with neonatal Fc receptor (FcRn)

IgG1, IgG2 and IgG4 molecules have a much longer half-life relative to other serum proteins. This half-life is dependant on the overall concentration of IgG and decreases when total IgG concentration is high. These subclasses of immunoglobulins are protected from catabolism by an intracellular recycling route that selectively recycles endocytosed IgG back to the circulation by binding to the saturable neonatal Fc receptor [141]. In this way, binding of IgG to FcRn protects IgG from breakdown [142]. Knocking-out the α2-microglobulin gene, which is an essential component of FcRn [143], shortens the half-life of IgG. Interestingly, high dose immunoglobulin treatment (IVIg) of MG patients increases the turnover of anti-AChR IgG1 antibodies by saturation of FcRn, thereby reducing the anti-AChR antibody titers [144].

4.2. Effector functions of IgG autoantibody subclasses in MG

4.2.1. Antigenic modulation

Antibodies from patients with MG accelerate the degradation of AChRs in cultured muscles and *in vivo* at intact NMJs [32, 145, 146]. Antibody-accelerated degradation of the AChR, also termed antigenic modulation, is a consequence of the bivalent nature of the IgG1, IgG2 and IgG3 autoantibodies. These AChR-specific antibodies are able to cross-link adjacent highly clustered

AChR molecules in the postsynaptic membrane of the muscle. The antibody-linked AChRs are rapidly internalized by endocytosis and then degraded [147]. Serum IgG from approximately 90% of patients increased the degradation rate of the AChR two to three fold [148]. Thus, if accelerated degradation is not sufficiently compensated by increased AChR synthesis, it will lead to a reduction of the available AChR molecules at the NMJ. This reduction of AChR at the NMJ can be used as a useful diagnostic test for MG [149]. However, not all anti-AChR antibodies can cause antigenic modulation. The epitope location on the AChR surface may restrict the ability of antibodies to cross-link a second AChR molecule [150]. Moreover, IgG4 antibodies are functionally monovalent, i.e. they do not cross-link two identical antigens.

4.2.2. IgG4 Fab arm exchange

All IgGs are composed of two heavy chain / light chain pairs (half-molecules), which are connected *via* inter-heavy chain disulfide bonds situated in the hinge region (Figure 2), as well as by non-covalent bonds mostly situated between the third constant domains (CH3). IgG antibodies mediate pro-inflammatory activities with the exception of IgG4 which has anti-inflammatory activity. IgG4 represents approximately 4% of the total IgG in serum of adults and significant IgG4 titers are generated by prolonged antigenic stimulation. The anti-inflammatory activity includes a poor ability to induce complement and immune-cell activation because of a low affinity for C1q and Fc receptors. Moreover, IgG4 does not form immune complexes due to a posttranslational modification, known as Fab-arm exchange. IgG4 exchanges Fab arms by swapping a heavy chain and attached light chain with a heavy and light chain from another antibody (Figure 3). Antibodies from the IgG4 subclass have been shown to be dynamic molecules, undergoing Fab arm exchange both *in vivo* and *in vitro*. The ability to engage in Fab arm exchange appears to be an inherent feature of IgG4 that involves the third constant domain in addition to the hinge region and this posttranslational modification only requires a reducing environment to be activated [19].

Kinetic studies on the inter-heavy chain disulfide bond formation of the IgG4 molecule showed that the inter-heavy chain disulfide bonds were formed slowly and that they were unstable [151]. Both inter- and intra-heavy chain disulfide bonds exist in IgG4 antibodies and these forms are in equilibrium (Figure 4). This phenomenon is facilitated by a substitution of single amino acid in the hinge of IgG4 compared to IgG1: a proline in IgG1 is replaced by a serine in IgG4 [152]. Nevertheless, simply mixing IgG4 molecules *in vitro* does not result in Fab arm exchange. The mechanism by which IgG4 Fab arm exchange occurs *in vivo* likely requires the reducing environment in blood or at cell surfaces to facilitate the breaking of bonds between half-molecules [19].

When derived from polyclonal plasma IgG4, the Fab arm exchange reaction usually produces IgG4 molecules with two different antigen-binding sites. The resulting asymmetric antibodies are bispecific, i.e. directed against two unrelated antigens. Moreover they are unable to cross-link two identical antigens [153] and are therefore functionally monovalent [154]. Fab arm exchange, furthermore, is a dynamic process, and combinations of certain specific Fab arms are therefore only expected to exist transiently. This novel protein modification challenges the commonly accepted one antibody-one antigen paradigm and redefines our thinking about the role of IgG4 in antibody-mediated immunity and the application of IgG4 monoclonal antibodies for immunotherapy. Functionally monovalent IgG4 antibodies directed to the AChR that do not modulate the AChR or block the ACh binding are not pathogenic. Moreover, they have the potential to protect the neuromuscular junction against complement fixing IgG1 anti-AChR-autoantibodies [19] by

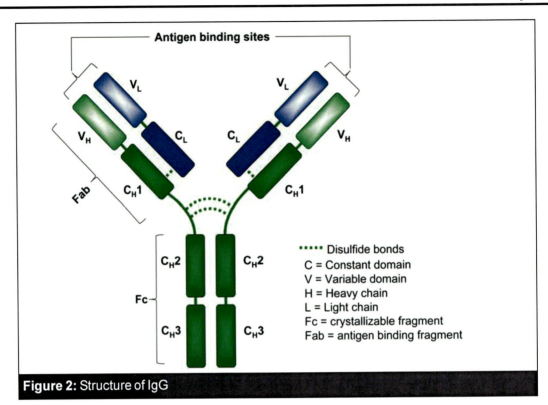

Figure 2: Structure of IgG

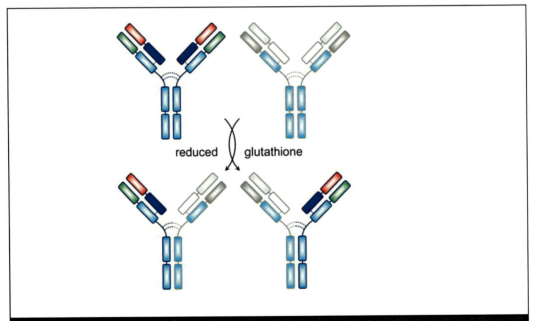

Figure 3: Fab arm exchange reaction. IgG4 molecules with different specificity interchange half-molecules resulting in chimeric bispecific antibodies [155]

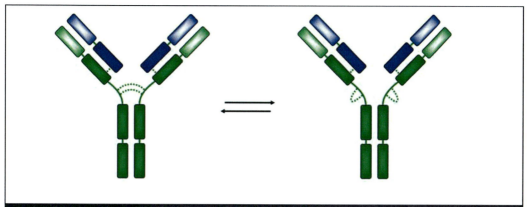

Figure 4: An appreciable fraction of wildtype IgG4 has non-covalently linked heavy chains. The instability that leads to Fab arm exchange is due to an alternatively formed intra-heavy chain disulfide bond (on the right). The inter- and intra-heavy chain disulfide bonds are in equilibrium.

competition for binding. Therefore, IgG4 has an important anti-inflammatory property and protects tissues against the biological effects of the complement-fixing IgG subclasses [153].

4.2.3. Complement activation

In the normal NMJ, AChR molecules are concentrated near the tops of the postsynaptic membrane folds, facing the nerve (Figure 1). Binding of anti-AChR antibodies to the tightly packed AChRs in this location results in very high density of bound antibody and, hence, very tightly packed Fc regions of these antibodies. Since anti-AChR antibodies belong mainly to the IgG1 and IgG3 class, this causes a highly efficient activation of the complement system and consequently the formation of the membrane attack complex (MAC) in the postsynaptic membrane. In combination with antigenic modulation of the AChR, MAC causes severe postsynaptic membrane damage [156, 157]. Stabilization of the AChR by increasing rapsyn expression prevents modulation of the AChR, even in the presence of activated complement [155, 158].

Different lines of indirect evidence support complement activation at the NMJ as a fundamental cause of AChR loss and failure of neuromuscular transmission: complement depletion with cobra venom factor [159], administration of antibodies that block a complement component [160], complement inhibitors [161] or a genetic deficit of complement components [162] make animals resistant or less susceptible to EAMG. IL-12 deficient mice develop minimal EAMG symptoms after AChR immunization in spite of robust anti-AChR antibody synthesis [163]. The lack of IL-12 prevents the production of the complement fixing IgG2a antibodies in the mouse (Table 3). NMJs in these mice contain only IgG1 antibodies, which unlike human IgG1 antibodies do not activate complement; indicating that anti-AChR antibodies, which do not activate complement, do not effectively compromise neuromuscular transmission.

Complement activation damages the postsynaptic membrane by multiple mechanisms. The membrane attack complex leads to loss of postsynaptic folding [26], loss

Table 3. IgG isotype profile and complement activation in relation to T helper subsets and cytokine production.

	Mouse			Rat			Human			
isotype	IgG1[(1)]	IgG2a[(2)]	IgG2b[(2)]	IgG1[(1)]	IgG2a[(1)]	IgG2b[(2)]	IgG1	IgG2	IgG3	IgG4
complement activation	no	yes	yes	yes	yes	yes	yes	no	yes	no
Cytokines involved in class switching and IgG production	IL4 [(a,b)] IL5 [(b)] IL6 [(b)] IL10 [(b)]	IL2 [(b)] IFNγ [(a,b)] IL12 [(d)]	TGFβ1 [(a)]	IL4 [(c)] IL10 [(f)]		IL2 [(c)] IFNγ [(c)] IL12 [(c)]	IL2 [(g)] IL4 [(a)] IL6 [(g)] IL10 [(a)] IL21 [(e)]	IL2 [(g)] IFNγ [(h)]	IL2 [(g)] IL4 [(a)] IL6 [(g)] IL10 [(a)] IL21 [(e)]	IL2 [(g)] IL4 [(a)] IL6 [(g)] IL12 [(i)] IL13 [(a)]
Th control and effector function	Th2 Anti-inflammatory	Th1 Pro-inflammatory	Pro-inflammatory	Th2 Pro-inflammatory	Pro-inflammatory	Th1 Pro-inflammatory	Pro-inflammatory	Anti-inflammatory	Pro-inflammatory	Anti-inflammatory

(1) Mouse IgG1 is homologous to rat IgG1 and rat IgG2a [166].
(2) Mouse IgG2a and mouse IgG2b are homologous to rat IgG2b [166].
(a) [167]; (b) [168]; (c) [169]; (d) [170]; (e) [171]; (f) [172]; (g) [173]; (h) [174]; (i) [175].

of membrane potential [164] and, in conjunction with antigenic modulation of the AChR, to loss of AChR-associated proteins [165].

4.2.4. Loss of AChR-associated proteins

MG is characterized by a reduction of AChR and utrophin at the motor endplate [176, 177]. Utrophin is localized primarily at the NMJ [178], while the homologous protein dystrophin [179] is expressed throughout the muscle fibre [180]. Utrophin is found closely co-localized to the AChR both in the adult NMJ [181] and throughout development [182], suggesting that it helps to stabilize the AChR clusters during development [183]. However, studies of utrophin-deficient mice indicate that utrophin is not essential for NMJ formation or for precise localization of AChRs at the NMJ [184, 185]. The reduction of utrophin in MG patients is probably secondary to the loss of AChR.

The receptor-associated protein of the synapse (rapsyn) is required for anchoring and stabilizing the AChR in the postsynaptic membrane of the NMJ during development. The AChR clustering by rapsyn is activated by agrin [186], which acts via LDL-receptor-related protein 4 (lrp4) and MuSK [187]. The expression of rapsyn increases with age and thereby stabilizes the AChR [188]. In a passive transfer rat model for MG, increased expression of rapsyn at the NMJ induces resistance against anti-AChR antibodies [158] by reducing antibody-induced AChR internalization. Conversely, rapsyn upregulation has a detrimental effect in chronic EAMG where endplates are already substantially damaged. In chronic EAMG, increased rapsyn expression increases the postsynaptic membrane turnover by anti-AChR antibodies [165]. It is of interest that a modest reduction of rapsyn expression already causes substantial changes, showing that the amount of rapsyn is critically related to the AChR levels and to the structure of the endplate [189].

It seems likely that loss of AChR-associated proteins, including rapsyn, utrophin and voltage gated sodium channels aggravate the disease and delay repair processes [165, 189].

4.2.5. Functional AChR blockade

Serum IgG from 50 to 88% of patients with MG has been shown to block the ACh-binding sites of AChRs in cultured mammalian muscle cells [149]. Antibodies with the ability to block the ACh-binding site of the AChR cause acute and severe muscle weakness in rodents without inflammation or necrosis at the NMJ [190]. Many MG patients have low levels of these antibodies. They might block the AChR in spite of their low concentrations and contribute to acute myasthenic crises [191].

5. ANIMAL MODELS FOR MG

EAMG can be induced in a large number of animal species by active immunization or by passive transfer of auto-antibodies. Depending on the model used, different immunological mechanisms are operational. In the active immunization model, the T cell is pivotal in directing the antibody production towards pro-inflammatory, cross-linking and complement fixing antibodies. Injection of anti-AChR or anti-MuSK antibodies alone is sufficient to induce passive transfer MG and specific cell-mediated immune responses are not important in the effector phase of the diseases. Major differences between these models and human MG are the absence of an acute phase in the human disease and the absence of thymic abnormalities in the animal models.

5.1 EAMG after active immunization

Patrick and Lindstrom were the first to induce MG in rabbits by immunization with AChR from the electric organ of electric eels (*Electrophorus electricus*) in complete Freund's adjuvant. They immunized these rabbits with purified AChR to obtain antibodies for the biochemical analysis of the AChR but all animals became paralyzed and eventually died [15]. Active immunization of experimental animals (including mice, rats, guinea pigs and monkeys) with AChR -with or without adjuvant- induced chronic EAMG within 30 days after immunization [16, 17, 192]. The animals mount an active immune response against injected AChR. The disease is caused by antibodies cross-reacting with the animals' own AChR. In the AChR-EAMG model, many immunological aspects of MG can be studied, such as AChR processing, antigen- presentation, the role of MHC, T cell subsets and cytokines [193].

The course of active immunization is biphasic in rats. About one week after immunization, animals develop a short-lived acute phase, occurring at the time the serum titer of anti-AChR antibody is just beginning to rise. This phase lasts only a few days and is characterized by weakness and muscle endplate necrosis, with infiltration of macrophages into the NMJ. The second, or chronic, phase develops two weeks later with weakness progressing in many cases to death. During this phase, inflammatory cells are absent from the NMJ. Instead, ultrastructural analysis reveals simplification of the endplate membrane folds and reduction in the amount of AChR normally found at the peaks of the folds, similar to the findings in MG [194].

Myasthenia can also be induced in animals by immunization with the extracellular domain of MuSK protein. Rabbits or mice immunized with MuSK manifested MG-like muscle weakness with a significant reduction of AChR clustering at the NMJ. At this point it is still unclear if MuSK-EAMG is caused by blocking the agrin signaling pathway [23, 24] or by inducing complement mediated damage resulting from pro-inflammatory anti-MuSK antibodies in these animal models. The use of passive transfer models of MuSK-MG is a promising alternative to elucidate auto-antibody effector functions.

5.2. Passive transfer MG

Toyka et al. have transferred purified IgG from MG patients to mice, which subsequently developed MG symptoms [18]. This passive transfer EAMG model is relevant for MG in order to study the effector phase of the disease. Antibodies against the main immunogenic region (MIR) of the AChR induce myasthenia within 8 to 48 hours, depending on the dose and affinity of the antibody for AChR [195]. The source of antibodies can be serum of MG patients, serum from chronic EAMG animals or monoclonal antibodies produced in cell culture [196]. The immunopathological mechanisms are antigenic modulation [197] and complement-mediated focal lysis of the postsynaptic membrane for anti-MIR antibodies [159]. Antibodies against the ACh-binding sites induce an acute paralysis within 15 to 30 minutes [198].

A passive transfer model also exists for MuSK-MG. Passive transfer of IgG from anti-MuSK-positive MG patients into adult mice reduced the level of AChR in the postsynaptic membrane and caused changes in the presynaptic and postsynaptic elements of the synapse leading in some cases to muscle weakness [25, 140].

5.3. Regulation of IgG subclass production in EAMG

MG and EAMG are typical antibody-mediated diseases. The production of the pathogenic antibodies by B cells depends on T helper cells. The pathogenic anti-AChR antibodies are high affinity IgGs, whose synthesis requires interaction of activated T cells with B cells that synthesize low-affinity anti-AChR antibodies [199]. T cells can be divided into T helper-one (Th1) and T helper-two cells (Th2) depending upon their cytokine profile. Cytokine signaling is crucial for development, modulation and downregulation of immune responses, and therefore influences the initiation and evolution of the anti-AChR response in EAMG. The regulation of Th cells by cytokines is important, because it affects the isotype profile of stimulated B-cells. Th1 cells have a pathogenic role in EAMG because they stimulate the synthesis of anti-AChR antibodies that fix complement and therefore cause destruction of the NMJ [200]. In contrast, Th2 cells induce anti-AChR antibodies that do not fix complement in mice (Table 3). In rats, both Th1 and Th2 cells are able to induce pathogenic anti-AChR antibodies [169].

5.4. Experimental immunotherapies in AChR-EAMG and passive transfer AChR-MG – use of competitor IgG antibodies

Monovalent anti-AChR antibodies or antibody fragments without complement binding capacity are not pathogenic. Since they can compete with pathogenic autoantibodies for binding to the AChR, they can prevent autoantibody binding at the NMJ. In passive transfer AChR-MG mouse and rat models, monovalent Fab fragments have been demonstrated to protect the AChR against the action of intact pathogenic antibodies [201, 202]. Fab antibody fragments can be produced recombinantly in bacteria, or by digestion of antibodies with papain. However, Fab fragments have a short half-life *in vivo*. To overcome the problem they can be linked to a molecule with a long half-life, such as human albumin [203] or polyethyleneglycol [204]. A potential safety concern is the *in vivo* aggregation of the injected monomeric Fab fragments, since these aggregated fragments still have some pathogenic potential by means of antigenic modulation and increased internalization of the AChR.

Monovalent binding to antigens is not limited to Fab fragments, but also IgG4 antibodies are functionally monovalent, as discussed in Section 4.2.2. IgG4 has many favorable properties for potential immunotherapy, such as long half-life *in vivo*, low immunogenicity, no capacity of complement activation and inability to cross-link antigens. IgG4-637 is an anti-AChR antibody derived from a pathogenic MG patient autoantibody. The coding sequences of this antibody were isolated from a phage display library prepared from the thymus of an MG patient [205]. While the corresponding IgG1-637 isotype induced moderate muscle weakness in a passive transfer MG model in rhesus monkeys, the IgG4 had no pathogenic properties in this model. Interestingly, also Fab arm exchange occurred in this model, suggesting that the rhesus monkey has an IgG4 like subclass [19].

When monkeys received the non-pathogenic IgG4-637 prior to challenge with the MG-inducing IgG1-637, the induction of both muscle weakness and clinical symptoms was prevented. These results indicated that IgG1 anti-AChR antibodies are sufficient to induce muscle weakness and IgG4 can prevent the pathogenic effects of IgG1 autoantibodies in non-human primates due to reduced antigenic modulation of AChR. A competitive recombinant antibody that protects the AChR is a promising agent to treat a myasthenic crisis and no such treatment has been tested in preclinical trails. For the treatment of MG patients, the efficacy of such an immunotherapy with IgG4 anti-AChR antibodies will also depend on variable factors including affinity, concentration and epitope specificity of autoantibodies.

Also in chronic AChR-EAMG models the isotype profile of autoantibodies can be altered by experimental treatments. Cytokines such as IL-4 stimulate Th2 cells and antagonize the action of Th1 cells, possibly by inducing regulatory T-cells [206]. In mice, manipulation of the balance in favor of Th2 cells protects against EAMG [170], because only Th1 related cytokines induce the complement activating IgG2b antibodies. In rats, both Th1 and Th2 cells are able to induce pathogenic anti-AChR antibodies (see Table 3) and manipulation of the Th1/Th2 balance does not affect the severity of disease [169]. The different requirements for Th1-dependent responses in rats and mice are therefore correlated to the capacity of complement activation by antibody subclasses. In humans, it is not yet clear if the Th1/Th2 balance affects the production of complement-binding antibodies. It would be very interesting to study how an isotype switch of IgG1 towards IgG4 can be induced in autoreactive B-cells for the treatment of AChR-MG.

REFERENCES

1. Conti-Fine, B.M., M. Milani, and H.J. Kaminski, Myasthenia gravis: past, present, and future. *J Clin Invest*, 2006. 116(11): p. 2843-54.

2. McConville, J. and A. Vincent, Diseases of the neuromuscular junction. Curr Opin Pharmacol, 2002. 2(3): p. 296-301.

3. Phillips, L.H., 2nd, The epidemiology of myasthenia gravis. *Ann N Y Acad Sci*, 2003. 998: p. 407-12.

4. Lindstrom, J.M., et al., Antibody to acetylcholine receptor in myasthenia gravis. Prevalence, clinical correlates, and diagnostic value. *Neurology*, 1976. 26(11): p. 1054-9.

5. Hoch, W., et al., Auto-antibodies to the receptor tyrosine kinase MuSK in patients with myasthenia gravis without acetylcholine receptor antibodies. *Nat Med*, 2001. 7(3): p. 365-8.

6. Evoli, A., et al., Clinical correlates with anti-MuSK antibodies in generalized seronegative myasthenia gravis. *Brain*, 2003. 126(Pt 10): p. 2304-11.

7. Jacobson, L., A. Polizzi, and A. Vincent, An animal model of maternal antibody-mediated arthrogryposis multiplex congenita (AMC). *Ann N Y Acad Sci*, 1998. 841: p. 565-7.

8. Jacobson, L., et al., Plasma from human mothers of fetuses with severe arthrogryposis multiplex congenita causes deformities in mice. *J Clin Invest*, 1999. 103(7): p. 1031-8.

9. Eymard, B., et al., Anti-acetylcholine receptor antibodies in neonatal myasthenia gravis: heterogeneity and pathogenic significance. *J Autoimmun*, 1991. 4(2): p. 185-95.

10. Morel, E., et al., Neonatal myasthenia gravis: a new clinical and immunologic appraisal on 30 cases. Neurology, 1988. 38(1): p. 138-42.

11. Papazian, O., Transient neonatal myasthenia gravis. *J Child Neurol*, 1992. 7(2): p. 135-41.

12. Vernet-der Garabedian, B., et al., Association of neonatal myasthenia gravis with antibodies against the fetal acetylcholine receptor. *J Clin Invest*, 1994. 94(2): p. 555-9.

13. Shelton, G.D., Acquired myasthenia gravis: what we have learned from experimental and spontaneous animal models. *Vet Immunol Immunopathol*, 1999. 69(2-4): p. 239-49.

14. Shelton, G.D., A. Schule, and P.H. Kass, Risk factors for acquired myasthenia gravis in dogs: 1,154 cases (1991-1995). *J Am Vet Med Assoc*, 1997. 211(11): p. 1428-31.

15. Patrick, J. and J. Lindstrom, Autoimmune response to acetylcholine receptor. Science, 1973. 180(88): p. 871-2.

16. Lennon, V.A., J.M. Lindstrom, and M.E. Seybold, Experimental autoimmune myasthenia: A model of myasthenia gravis in rats and guinea pigs. *J Exp Med*, 1975. 141(6): p. 1365-75.

17. Tarrab-Hazdai, R., et al., Experimental autoimmune myasthenia induced in monkeys by purified acetylcholine receptor. *Nature*, 1975. 256(5513): p. 128-30.

18. Toyka, K.V., et al., Myasthenia gravis: passive transfer from man to mouse. Science, 1975. 190(4212): p. 397-9.

19. van der Neut Kolfschoten, M., et al., Anti-inflammatory activity of human IgG4 antibodies by dynamic Fab arm exchange. *Science*, 2007. 317(5844): p. 1554-7.

20. Lindstrom, J.M., et al., Pathological mechanisms in experimental autoimmune myasthenia gravis. II. Passive transfer of experimental autoimmune myasthenia gravis in rats with anti-acetylcholine recepotr antibodies. *J Exp Med*, 1976. 144(3): p. 739-53.

21. Behin, A., et al., Severe neonatal myasthenia due to maternal anti-MuSK antibodies. *Neuromuscul Disord*, 2008. 18(6): p. 443-6.

22. Niks, E.H., et al., A transient neonatal myasthenic syndrome with anti-musk antibodies. *Neurology*, 2008. 70(14): p. 1215-6.

23. Shigemoto, K., et al., Induction of myasthenia by immunization against muscle-specific kinase. *J Clin Invest*, 2006. 116(4): p. 1016-24.

24. Jha, S., et al., Myasthenia gravis induced in mice by immunization with the recombinant extracellular domain of rat muscle-specific kinase (MuSK). *J Neuroimmunol*, 2006. 175(1-2): p. 107-17.

25. Cole, R.N., et al., Anti-MuSK patient antibodies disrupt the mouse neuromuscular junction. *Ann Neurol*, 2008. 63(6): p. 782-9.

26. Engel, A.G., E.H. Lambert, and F.M. Howard, Immune complexes (IgG and C3) at the motor end-plate in myasthenia gravis: ultrastructural and light microscopic localization and electrophysiologic correlations. *Mayo Clin Proc*, 1977. 52(5): p. 267-80.

27. Sahashi, K., et al., Ultrastructural localization of the terminal and lytic ninth complement component (C9) at the motor end-plate in myasthenia gravis. *J Neuropathol Exp Neurol*, 1980. 39(2): p. 160-72.

28. Fazekas, A., et al., Myasthenia gravis: demonstration of membrane attack complex in muscle end-plates. *Clin Neuropathol*, 1986. 5(2): p. 78-83.

29. Changeux, J.P., A. Devillers-Thiery, and P. Chemouilli, Acetylcholine receptor: an allosteric protein. *Science*, 1984. 225(4668): p. 1335-45.

30. Katz, B. and R. Miledi, Further Observations on the Distribution of Actylcholine-Reactive Sites in Skeletal Muscle. *J Physiol*, 1964. 170: p. 379-88.

31. Drachman, D.B., Myasthenia gravis. N Engl J Med, 1994. 330(25): p. 1797-810.

32. Drachman, D.B., et al., Myasthenic antibodies cross-link acetylcholine receptors to accelerate degradation. *N Engl J Med*, 1978. 298(20): p. 1116-22.

33. Shiono, H., et al., Spontaneous production of anti-IFN-alpha and anti-IL-12 autoantibodies by thymoma cells from myasthenia gravis patients suggests autoimmunization in the tumor. *Int Immunol*, 2003. 15(8): p. 903-13.

34. Lindstrom, J., An assay for antibodies to human acetylcholine receptor in serum from patients with myasthenia gravis. *Clin Immunol Immunopathol*, 1977. 7(1): p. 36-43.

35. Vincent, A. and J. Newsom-Davis, Acetylcholine receptor antibody as a diagnostic test for myasthenia gravis: results in 153 validated cases and 2967 diagnostic assays. *J Neurol Neurosurg Psychiatry*, 1985. 48(12): p. 1246-52.

36. Lefvert, A.K., et al., Determination of acetylcholine receptor antibody in myasthenia gravis: clinical usefulness and pathogenetic implications. *J Neurol Neurosurg Psychiatry*, 1978. 41(5): p. 394-403.

37. Leite, M.I., et al., IgG1 antibodies to acetylcholine receptors in 'seronegative' myasthenia gravis. *Brain*, 2008.

38. Rodgaard, A., et al., Acetylcholine receptor antibody in myasthenia gravis: predominance of IgG subclasses 1 and 3. *Clin Exp Immunol*, 1987. 67(1): p. 82-8.

39. Andrews, P.I., J.M. Massey, and D.B. Sanders, Acetylcholine receptor antibodies in juvenile myasthenia gravis. *Neurology*, 1993. 43(5): p. 977-82.

40. Bartoccioni, E., et al., Identification of disease-specific autoantibodies in seronegative myasthenia gravis. *Ann N Y Acad Sci*, 2003. 998: p. 356-8.

41. McConville, J., et al., Detection and characterization of MuSK antibodies in seronegative myasthenia gravis. *Ann Neurol*, 2004. 55(4): p. 580-4.

42. Lee, J.Y., et al., MuSK antibody-positive, seronegative myasthenia gravis in Korea. *J Clin Neurosci*, 2006. 13(3): p. 353-5.

43. Evoli, A., Clinical aspects of neuromuscular transmission disorders. Acta Neurol Scand Suppl, 2006. 183: p. 8-11.

44. Niks, E.H., J.B. Kuks, and J.J. Verschuuren, Epidemiology of myasthenia gravis with anti-muscle specific kinase antibodies in The Netherlands. *J Neurol Neurosurg Psychiatry*, 2007. 78(4): p. 417-8.

45. Zhou, L., et al., Clinical comparison of muscle-specific tyrosine kinase (MuSK) antibody-positive and -negative myasthenic patients. *Muscle Nerve*, 2004. 30(1): p. 55-60.

46. Ohta, K., et al., MuSK antibodies in AChR Ab-seropositive MG vs AChR Ab-seronegative MG. *Neurology*, 2004. 62(11): p. 2132-3.

47. Yeh, J.H., et al., Low frequency of MuSK antibody in generalized seronegative myasthenia gravis among Chinese. *Neurology*, 2004. 62(11): p. 2131-2.

48. Padua, L., et al., Seronegative myasthenia gravis: comparison of neurophysiological picture in MuSK+ and MuSK- patients. *Eur J Neurol*, 2006. 13(3): p. 273-6.

49. Aarli, J.A., et al., Patients with myasthenia gravis and thymoma have in their sera IgG autoantibodies against titin. *Clin Exp Immunol*, 1990. 82(2): p. 284-8.

50. Buckley, C., et al., Do titin and cytokine antibodies in MG patients predict thymoma or thymoma recurrence? *Neurology*, 2001. 57(9): p. 1579-82.

51. Gautel, M., et al., Titin antibodies in myasthenia gravis: identification of a major immunogenic region of titin. *Neurology*, 1993. 43(8): p. 1581-5.

52. Romi, F., et al., Muscle autoantibodies in subgroups of myasthenia gravis patients. *J Neurol*, 2000. 247(5): p. 369-75.

53. Skeie, G.O., et al., Titin antibodies in patients with late onset myasthenia gravis: clinical correlations. *Autoimmunity*, 1995. 20(2): p. 99-104.

54. Baggi, F., et al., Anti-titin and antiryanodine receptor antibodies in myasthenia gravis patients with thymoma. *Ann N Y Acad Sci*, 1998. 841: p. 538-41.

55. Chen, X.J., et al., The significance of titin antibodies in myasthenia gravis—correlation with thymoma and severity of myasthenia gravis. *J Neurol*, 2004. 251(8): p. 1006-11.

56. Yamamoto, A.M., et al., Anti-titin antibodies in myasthenia gravis: tight association with thymoma and heterogeneity of nonthymoma patients. *Arch Neurol*, 2001. 58(6): p. 885-90.

57. Suzuki, S., et al., Classification of myasthenia gravis based on autoantibody status. *Arch Neurol*, 2007. 64(8): p. 1121-4.

58. Mygland, A., et al., Myasthenia gravis patients with a thymoma have antibodies against a high molecular weight protein in sarcoplasmic reticulum. *J Neuroimmunol*, 1992. 37(1-2): p. 1-7.

59. Mygland, A., et al., Ryanodine receptor autoantibodies in myasthenia gravis patients with a thymoma. *Ann Neurol*, 1992. 32(4): p. 589-91.

60. Mygland, A., et al., IgG subclass distribution of ryanodine receptor autoantibodies in patients with myasthenia gravis and thymoma. *J Autoimmun*, 1993. 6(4): p. 507-15.

61. Mygland, A., et al., Anti-cardiac ryanodine receptor antibodies in thymoma-associated myasthenia gravis. *Autoimmunity*, 1994. 17(4): p. 327-31.

62. Mygland, A., et al., Autoantibodies in thymoma-associated myasthenia gravis with myositis or neuromyotonia. Arch Neurol, 2000. 57(4): p. 527-31.

63. Skeie, G.O., et al., Myasthenia gravis-associated ryanodine receptor antibodies inhibit binding of ryanodine to sarcoplasmic reticulum. *Ann N Y Acad Sci*, 1998. 841: p. 530-3.

64. Skeie, G.O., et al., Myasthenia gravis sera containing antiryanodine receptor antibodies inhibit binding of [3H]-ryanodine to sarcoplasmic reticulum. *Muscle Nerve*, 1998. 21(3): p. 329-35.

65. Takamori, M., et al., Anti-ryanodine receptor antibodies and FK506 in myasthenia gravis. *Neurology*, 2004. 62(10): p. 1894-6.

66. Takamori, M., Autoantibodies against TRPC3 and ryanodine receptor in myasthenia gravis. *J Neuroimmunol*, 2008. 200(1-2): p. 142-4.

67. Maruta, T., et al., Autoantibody to dihydropyridine receptor in myasthenia gravis. *J Neuroimmunol*, 2009. 208(1-2): p. 125-9.

68. Yamamoto, T., T. Sato, and H. Sugita, Antifilamin, antivinculin, and antitropomyosin antibodies in myasthenia gravis. *Neurology*, 1987. 37(8): p. 1329-33.

69. Takaya, M., et al., Antibodies against myofibrillar proteins in myasthenia gravis patients. *Tokai J Exp Clin Med*, 1992. 17(1): p. 35-9.

70. Williams, C.L. and V.A. Lennon, Thymic B lymphocyte clones from patients with myasthenia gravis secrete monoclonal striational autoantibodies reacting with myosin, alpha actinin, or actin. *J Exp Med*, 1986. 164(4): p. 1043-59.

71. Ohta, M., et al., Anti-skeletal muscle antibodies in the sera from myasthenic patients with thymoma: identification of anti-myosin, actomyosin, actin, and alpha-actinin antibodies by a solid-phase radioimmunoassay and a western blotting analysis. *Clin Chim Acta*, 1990. 187(3): p. 255-64.

72. Mohan, S., et al., Evaluation of myosin-reactive antibodies from a panel of myasthenia gravis patients. *Clin Immunol Immunopathol*, 1994. 70(3): p. 266-73.

73. Agius, M.A., S. Zhu, and J.A. Aarli, Antirapsyn antibodies occur commonly in patients with lupus. *Ann N Y Acad Sci*, 1998. 841: p. 525-6.

74. Agius, M.A., et al., Rapsyn antibodies in myasthenia gravis. *Ann N Y Acad Sci*, 1998. 841: p. 516-21.

75. Suzuki, S., et al., Novel autoantibodies to a voltage-gated potassium channel Kv1.4 in a severe form of myasthenia gravis. *J Neuroimmunol*, 2005. 170(1-2): p. 141-9.

76. Phillips, T.M., et al., The detection of anti-cholinesterase antibodies in myasthenia gravis. *Ann N Y Acad Sci*, 1981. 377: p. 360-71.

77. Mappouras, D.G., et al., Antibodies to acetylcholinesterase cross-reacting with thyroglobulin in myasthenia gravis and Graves's disease. *Clin Exp Immunol*, 1995. 100(2): p. 336-43.

78. Tang, J., J. Yuan, and H. Hao, Anti-acetylcholinesterase antibody in myasthenic syndrome. *Chin Med J (Engl)*, 1997. 110(9): p. 698-700.

79. Lu, C.Z., et al., Anti-presynaptic membrane receptor antibodies in myasthenia gravis. J Neurol Sci, 1991. 102(1): p. 39-45.

80. Lu, C.Z., et al., Antibody-secreting cells to acetylcholine receptor and to presynaptic membrane receptor in seronegative myasthenia gravis. *J Neuroimmunol*, 1993. 43(1-2): p. 145-9.

81. Xiao, B.G., et al., Immunological specificity and cross-reactivity of anti-acetylcholine receptor and anti-presynaptic membrane receptor antibodies in myasthenia gravis. *J Neurol Sci*, 1991. 105(1): p. 118-23.

82. Cojocaru, I.M., M. Cojocaru, and C. Musuroi, Study of anti-striational and anti-thyroid antibodies in patients with myasthenia gravis. *Rom J Intern Med*, 2000. 38-39: p. 111-20.

83. Sagar, H.J., et al., Clinical and immunological associations in myasthenia gravis. 1: Autoantibodies. *J Neurol Neurosurg Psychiatry*, 1980. 43(11): p. 967-70.

84. Kiessling, W.R., et al., Thyroid function and circulating antithyroid antibodies in myasthenia gravis. *Neurology*, 1981. 31(6): p. 771-4.

85. Weissel, M., N. Mayr, and J. Zeitlhofer, Clinical significance of autoimmune thyroid disease in myasthenia gravis. Exp Clin Endocrinol Diabetes, 2000. 108(1): p. 63-5.

86. Chan, K.H., et al., Frequency of seronegativity in adult-acquired generalized myasthenia gravis. *Muscle Nerve*, 2007. 36(5): p. 651-8.

87. Kiessling, W.R., et al., Circulating TSH-binding inhibiting immunoglobulins in myasthenia gravis. Acta Endocrinol (Copenh), 1982. 101(1): p. 41-6.

88. White, R.G. and A.H. Marshall, The autoimmune response in myasthenia gravis. Lancet, 1962. 2(7247): p. 120-3.

89. Feltkamp, T.E., et al., Myasthenia gravis, autoantibodies, and HL-A antigens. Br Med J, 1974. 1(5899): p. 131-3.

90. Shoenfeld, Y., et al., Autoimmune diseases other than lupus share common anti-DNA idiotypes. *Immunol Lett*, 1988. 17(3): p. 285-91.

91. Oosterhuis, H.J., et al., HL-A antigens, autoantibody production, and associated diseases in thymoma patients, with and without myasthenia gravis. *Ann N Y Acad Sci*, 1976. 274: p. 468-74.

92. Warlow, R., M. Garlepp, and R. Dawkins, Extractable nuclear antigen autoantibodies and their association with other autoantibodies and thymoma in myasthenia gravis. *J Neuroimmunol*, 1985. 8(2-3): p. 185-97.

93. Sthoeger, Z., et al., High prevalence of systemic lupus erythematosus in 78 myasthenia gravis patients: a clinical and serologic study. *Am J Med Sci*, 2006. 331(1): p. 4-9.

94. Colaco, C.B., G.K. Scadding, and S. Lockhart, Anti-cardiolipin antibodies in neurological disorders: cross-reaction with anti-single stranded DNA activity. *Clin Exp Immunol*, 1987. 68(2): p. 313-9.

95. Sanmarco, M. and D. Bernard, Studies of IgG-class anticardiolipin antibodies in myasthenia gravis. *Autoimmunity*, 1994. 18(1): p. 57-63.

96. Kinoshita I, M., Nagasato, Ichinose, Ohishi, Takeo, Satoh, Nakamura, Yoshimura, Tsujihata, Nagataki, Antiphospholipid antibodies in patients with myastenia gravis. Acta Med. Nagasaki, 1994. 39: p. 41-44.

97. Takamori, M., et al., Autoantibodies against M1 muscarinic acetylcholine receptor in myasthenic disorders. *Eur J Neurol*, 2007. 14(11): p. 1230-5.

98. Gotti, C., et al., Anti-neuronal nicotinic receptor antibodies in MG patients with thymoma. *J Neuroimmunol*, 2001. 113(1): p. 142-5.

99. Balestra, B., et al., Antibodies against neuronal nicotinic receptor subtypes in neurological disorders. J Neuroimmunol, 2000. 102(1): p. 89-97.

100. Eng, H., et al., Beta 2-adrenergic receptor antibodies in myasthenia gravis. *J Autoimmun*, 1992. 5(2): p. 213-27.

101. Xu, B.Y., R. Pirskanen, and A.K. Lefvert, Antibodies against beta1 and beta2 adrenergic receptors in myasthenia gravis. *J Neuroimmunol*, 1998. 91(1-2): p. 82-8.

102. Meager, A., et al., Spontaneous neutralising antibodies to interferon—alpha and interleukin-12 in thymoma-associated autoimmune disease. *Lancet*, 1997. 350(9091): p. 1596-7.

103. Meager, A., et al., Spontaneously occurring neutralizing antibodies against granulocyte-macrophage colony-stimulating factor in patients with autoimmune disease. *Immunology*, 1999. 97(3): p. 526-32.

104. Meager, A., et al., Anti-cytokine autoantibodies in autoimmunity: preponderance of neutralizing autoantibodies against interferon-alpha, interferon-omega and interleukin-12 in patients with thymoma and/or myasthenia gravis. Clin Exp Immunol, 2003. 132(1): p. 128-36.

105. Yoshikawa, H., et al., Elevation of IL-12 p40 and its antibody in myasthenia gravis with thymoma. *J Neuroimmunol*, 2006. 175(1-2): p. 169-75.

106. Munakata, S., et al., The clinical significance of anti-heat shock cognate protein 71 antibody in myasthenia gravis. *J Clin Neurosci*, 2008. 15(2): p. 158-65.

107. Astarloa, R. and J.C. Martinez Castrillo, Humoral response to the human heat shock 60 kDa protein in myasthenia gravis. *J Neurol Sci*, 1996. 135(2): p. 182-3.

108. Tuzun, E., et al., Predictive value of serum anti-C1q antibody levels in experimental autoimmune myasthenia gravis. *Neuromuscul Disord*, 2006. 16(2): p. 137-43.

109. Leone, G., et al., Platelet antibody determination by platelet factor 3 assay (comparison with radiolabelled serotonin release and platelet aggregometry). Ric Clin Lab, 1978. 8(3): p. 141-7.

110. Okada, S., et al., Autoantibody to growth hormone in a patient with myasthenia gravis. *J Endocrinol*, 1990. 127(3): p. 533-8.

111. Muller, K.M. and L.C. Andersson, Antibodies against human neuroblastoma cells in the sera of patients with myasthenia gravis. *J Neuroimmunol*, 1984. 7(2-3): p. 97-105.

112. Muller, K.M., Anti-neuroblastoma antibodies in myasthenia gravis: clinical and immunological correlations. *J Neurol Sci*, 1989. 93(2-3): p. 263-75.

113. Muller, K.M., E. Nykyri, and L.C. Andersson, Effect of thymectomy and immunosuppressive therapy on anti-neuroblastoma antibody levels in patients with myasthenia gravis. *Acta Neurol Scand*, 1991. 83(5): p. 336-42.

114. Hazama, T., et al., Electrophoretic immunoblotting analysis of anti-thymus microsome antibodies in patients with myasthenia gravis. *Acta Neurol Scand*, 1989. 79(2): p. 88-96.

115. Safar, D., et al., Antibodies to thymic epithelial cells in myasthenia gravis. *J Neuroimmunol*, 1991. 35(1-3): p. 101-10.

116. Ohta, K., et al., MuSK Ab described in seropositive MG sera found to be Ab to alkaline phosphatase. *Neurology*, 2005. 65(12): p. 1988.

117. Konishi, T., et al., Anti-alkaline phosphatase antibody positive myasthenia gravis. *J Neurol Sci*, 2007. 263(1-2): p. 89-93.

118. Sasaki, H., et al., Autoantibody to gravin is expressed more strongly in younger and nonthymomatous patients with myasthenia gravis. Surg Today, 2001. 31(11): p. 1036-7.

119. Gordon, T., et al., Molecular cloning and preliminary characterization of a novel cytoplasmic antigen recognized by myasthenia gravis sera. *J Clin Invest*, 1992. 90(3): p. 992-9.

120. Shiraishi, H., et al., Acetylcholine receptors loss and postsynaptic damage in MuSK antibody-positive myasthenia gravis. *Ann Neurol*, 2005. 57(2): p. 289-93.

121. Selcen, D., et al., Are MuSK antibodies the primary cause of myasthenic symptoms? *Neurology*, 2004. 62(11): p. 1945-50.

122. Mossman, S., A. Vincent, and J. Newsom-Davis, Myasthenia gravis without acetylcholine-receptor antibody: a distinct disease entity. *Lancet*, 1986. 1(8473): p. 116-9.

123. Leite, M.I., et al., Fewer thymic changes in MuSK antibody-positive than in MuSK antibody-negative MG. *Ann Neurol*, 2005. 57(3): p. 444-8.

124. Romi, F., et al., Striational antibodies in myasthenia gravis: reactivity and possible clinical significance. *Arch Neurol*, 2005. 62(3): p. 442-6.

125. Vincent, A. and M.I. Leite, Neuromuscular junction autoimmune disease: muscle specific kinase antibodies and treatments for myasthenia gravis. *Curr Opin Neurol*, 2005. 18(5): p. 519-25.

126. Leite, M.I., et al., IgG1 antibodies to acetylcholine receptors in 'seronegative' myasthenia gravis. Brain, 2008. 131(Pt 7): p. 1940-52.

127. Mishina, M., et al., Molecular distinction between fetal and adult forms of muscle acetylcholine receptor. *Nature*, 1986. 321(6068): p. 406-11.

128. Vincent, A., et al., Arthrogryposis multiplex congenita with maternal autoantibodies specific for a fetal antigen. *Lancet*, 1995. 346(8966): p. 24-5.

129. Mier, A.K. and C.W. Havard, Diaphragmatic myasthenia in mother and child. Postgrad Med J, 1985. 61(718): p. 725-7.

130. Gardnerova, M., et al., The fetal/adult acetylcholine receptor antibody ratio in mothers with myasthenia gravis as a marker for transfer of the disease to the newborn. Neurology, 1997. 48(1): p. 50-4.

131. Bruggemann, M., et al., Comparison of the effector functions of human immunoglobulins using a matched set of chimeric antibodies. *J Exp Med*, 1987. 166(5): p. 1351-61.

132. Dangl, J.L., et al., Segmental flexibility and complement fixation of genetically engineered chimeric human, rabbit and mouse antibodies. *Embo J*, 1988. 7(7): p. 1989-94.

133. Tao, M.H., S.M. Canfield, and S.L. Morrison, The differential ability of human IgG1 and IgG4 to activate complement is determined by the COOH-terminal sequence of the CH2 domain. *J Exp Med*, 1991. 173(4): p. 1025-8.

134. Tan, L.K., et al., Influence of the hinge region on complement activation, C1q binding, and segmental flexibility in chimeric human immunoglobulins. Proc Natl Acad Sci U S A, 1990. 87(1): p. 162-6.

135. Vincent, A. and J. Newsom-Davis, Acetylcholine receptor antibody characteristics in myasthenia gravis. I. Patients with generalized myasthenia or disease restricted to ocular muscles. Clin Exp Immunol, 1982. 49(2): p. 257-65.

136. Lefvert, A.K., S. Cuenoud, and B.W. Fulpius, Binding properties and subclass distribution of anti-acetylcholine receptor antibodies in myasthenia gravis. *J Neuroimmunol*, 1981. 1(1): p. 125-35.

137. Takeo, G., et al., Effect of myasthenic IgG on degradation of junctional acetylcholine receptor. Muscle Nerve, 1993. 16(8): p. 840-8.

138. Newsom-Davis, J., et al., Long-term effects of repeated plasma exchange in myasthenia gravis. *Lancet*, 1979. 1(8114): p. 464-8.

139. Boneva, N., et al., Major pathogenic effects of anti-MuSK antibodies in myasthenia gravis. *J Neuroimmunol*, 2006. 177(1-2): p. 119-31.

140. ter Beek, W.P., et al., The effect of plasma from MuSK myasthenia patients on regenerating endplates. *American Journal of Pathology*, 2009. in press.

141. Brambell, F.W., The transmission of immunity from mother to young and the catabolism of immunoglobulins. *Lancet*, 1966. 2(7473): p. 1087-93.

142. Aalberse, R.C. and J. Schuurman, IgG4 breaking the rules. *Immunology*, 2002. 105(1): p. 9-19.

143. Junghans, R.P. and C.L. Anderson, The protection receptor for IgG catabolism is the beta2-microglobulin-containing neonatal intestinal transport receptor. Proc Natl Acad Sci U S A, 1996. 93(11): p. 5512-6.

144. Ferrero, B. and L. Durelli, High-dose intravenous immunoglobulin G treatment of myasthenia gravis. *Neurol Sci*, 2002. 23 Suppl 1: p. S9-24.

145. Kao, I. and D.B. Drachman, Myasthenic immunoglobulin accelerates acetylcholine receptor degradation. *Science*, 1977. 196(4289): p. 527-9.

146. Stanley, E.F. and D.B. Drachman, Effect of myasthenic immunoglobulin on acetylcholine receptors of intact mammalian neuromuscular junctions. *Science*, 1978. 200(4347): p. 1285-7.

147. Pumplin, D.W. and D.B. Drachman, Myasthenic patients' IgG causes redistribution of acetylcholine receptors: freeze-fracture studies. *J Neurosci*, 1983. 3(3): p. 576-84.

148. Drachman, D.B., et al., Functional activities of autoantibodies to acetylcholine receptors and the clinical severity of myasthenia gravis. *N Engl J Med*, 1982. 307(13): p. 769-75.

149. Howard, F.M., Jr., et al., Clinical correlations of antibodies that bind, block, or modulate human acetylcholine receptors in myasthenia gravis. *Ann N Y Acad Sci*, 1987. 505: p. 526-38.

150. Conti-Tronconi, B., S. Tzartos, and J. Lindstrom, Monoclonal antibodies as probes of acetylcholine receptor structure. 2. Binding to native receptor. *Biochemistry*, 1981. 20(8): p. 2181-91.

151. Petersen, J.G. and K.J. Dorrington, An in vitro system for studying the kinetics of interchain disulfide bond formation in immunoglobulin G. *J Biol Chem*, 1974. 249(17): p. 5633-41.

152. Angal, S., et al., A single amino acid substitution abolishes the heterogeneity of chimeric mouse/human (IgG4) antibody. *Mol Immunol*, 1993. 30(1): p. 105-8.

153. van der Zee, J.S., P. van Swieten, and R.C. Aalberse, Inhibition of complement activation by IgG4 antibodies. *Clin Exp Immunol*, 1986. 64(2): p. 415-22.

154. Schuurman, J., et al., Normal human immunoglobulin G4 is bispecific: it has two different antigen-combining sites. *Immunology*, 1999. 97(4): p. 693-8.

155. Losen, M., et al., Treatment of myasthenia gravis by preventing acetylcholine receptor modulation. Ann N Y Acad Sci, 2008. 1132: p. 174-9.

156. Corey, A.L., et al., Refractoriness to a second episode of experimental myasthenia gravis. Correlation with AChR concentration and morphologic appearance of the postsynaptic membrane. *J Immunol*, 1987. 138(10): p. 3269-75.

157. Engel, A.G. and K. Arahata, The membrane attack complex of complement at the endplate in myasthenia gravis. Ann N Y Acad Sci, 1987. 505: p. 326-32.

158. Losen, M., et al., Increased expression of rapsyn in muscles prevents acetylcholine receptor loss in experimental autoimmune myasthenia gravis. Brain, 2005. 128(Pt 10): p. 2327-37.

159. Lennon, V.A., et al., Role of complement in the pathogenesis of experimental autoimmune myasthenia gravis. J Exp Med, 1978. 147(4): p. 973-83.

160. Biesecker, G. and C.M. Gomez, Inhibition of acute passive transfer experimental autoimmune myasthenia gravis with Fab antibody to complement C6. *J Immunol*, 1989. 142(8): p. 2654-9.

161. Piddlesden, S.J., et al., Soluble complement receptor 1 (sCR1) protects against experimental autoimmune myasthenia gravis. *J Neuroimmunol*, 1996. 71(1-2): p. 173-7.

162. Christadoss, P., C5 gene influences the development of murine myasthenia gravis. *J Immunol*, 1988. 140(8): p. 2589-92.

163. Karachunski, P.I., et al., Absence of IFN-gamma or IL-12 has different effects on experimental myasthenia gravis in C57BL/6 mice. *J Immunol*, 2000. 164(10): p. 5236-44.

164. Mozrzymas, J.W., et al., An electrophysiological study of the effects of myasthenia gravis sera and complement on rat isolated muscle fibres. *J Neuroimmunol*, 1993. 45(1-2): p. 155-62.

165. Martinez-Martinez, P., et al., Overexpression of rapsyn in rat muscle increases acetylcholine receptor levels in chronic experimental autoimmune myasthenia gravis. *Am J Pathol*, 2007. 170(2): p. 644-57.

166. Bazin, H., Rat Immunoglobulins, in Rat Hybridomas and Rat Monoclonal Antibodies, H. Bazin, Editor. 1990, CRC press: Boca Raton. p. 5-42.

167. Zhang, K., Accessibility control and machinery of immunoglobulin class switch recombination. *J Leukoc Biol*, 2003. 73(3): p. 323-32.

168. Saoudi, A., et al., Role of the TH1-TH2 balance in the development of autoimmunity in rats. *Transplant Proc*, 1993. 25(5): p. 2824-5.

169. Saoudi, A., et al., Experimental autoimmune myasthenia gravis may occur in the context of a polarized Th1- or Th2-type immune response in rats. *J Immunol*, 1999. 162(12): p. 7189-97.

170. Moiola, L., et al., IL-12 is involved in the induction of experimental autoimmune myasthenia gravis, an antibody-mediated disease. *Eur J Immunol*, 1998. 28(8): p. 2487-97.

171. Avery, D.T., et al., IL-21-induced isotype switching to IgG and IgA by human naive B cells is differentially regulated by IL-4. *J Immunol*, 2008. 181(3): p. 1767-79.

172. Zhang, G.X., et al., Interleukin 10 aggravates experimental autoimmune myasthenia gravis through inducing Th2 and B cell responses to AChR. *J Neuroimmunol*, 2001. 113(1): p. 10-8.

173. Kawano, Y. and T. Noma, Role of interleukin-2 and interferon-gamma in inducing production of IgG subclasses in lymphocytes of human newborns. *Immunology*, 1996. 88(1): p. 40-8.

174. Kawano, Y., T. Noma, and J. Yata, Regulation of human IgG subclass production by cytokines. IFN-gamma and IL-6 act antagonistically in the induction of human IgG1 but additively in the induction of IgG2. *J Immunol*, 1994. 153(11): p. 4948-58.

175. de Boer, B.A., et al., Interleukin-12 suppresses immunoglobulin E production but enhances immunoglobulin G4 production by human peripheral blood mononuclear cells. Infect Immun, 1997. 65(3): p. 1122-5.

176. Ito, H., et al., Immunohistochemical study of utrophin and dystrophin at the motor end-plate in myasthenia gravis. *Acta Neuropathol*, 1996. 92(1): p. 14-8.

177. Slater, C.R., et al., Utrophin abundance is reduced at neuromuscular junctions of patients with both inherited and acquired acetylcholine receptor deficiencies. Brain, 1997. 120 (Pt 9): p. 1513-31.

178. Tanaka, H., et al., Expression of a dystrophin-related protein associated with the skeletal muscle cell membrane. *Histochemistry*, 1991. 96(1): p. 1-5.

179. Tinsley, J.M., et al., Primary structure of dystrophin-related protein. *Nature*, 1992. 360(6404): p. 591-3.

180. Huard, J., et al., Is dystrophin present in the nerve terminal at the neuromuscular junction? An immunohistochemical study of the heterozygote dystrophic (mdx) mouse. *Synapse*, 1991. 7(2): p. 135-40.

181. Bewick, G.S., et al., Different distributions of dystrophin and related proteins at nerve-muscle junctions. *Neuroreport*, 1992. 3(10): p. 857-60.

182. Bewick, G.S., C. Young, and C.R. Slater, Spatial relationships of utrophin, dystrophin, beta-dystroglycan and beta-spectrin to acetylcholine receptor clusters during postnatal maturation of the rat neuromuscular junction. *J Neurocytol*, 1996. 25(7): p. 367-79.

183. Phillips, W.D., et al., Clustering and immobilization of acetylcholine receptors by the 43-kD protein: a possible role for dystrophin-related protein. *J Cell Biol*, 1993. 123(3): p. 729-40.

184. Grady, R.M., J.P. Merlie, and J.R. Sanes, Subtle neuromuscular defects in utrophin-deficient mice. *J Cell Biol*, 1997. 136(4): p. 871-82.

185. Deconinck, A.E., et al., Postsynaptic abnormalities at the neuromuscular junctions of utrophin-deficient mice. *J Cell Biol*, 1997. 136(4): p. 883-94.

186. Brockhausen, J., et al., Neural agrin increases postsynaptic ACh receptor packing by elevating rapsyn protein at the mouse neuromuscular synapse. Dev Neurobiol, 2008. 68(9): p. 1153-69.

187. Kim, N., et al., Lrp4 is a receptor for Agrin and forms a complex with MuSK. Cell, 2008. 135(2): p. 334-42.

188. Gervasio, O.L. and W.D. Phillips, Increased ratio of rapsyn to ACh receptor stabilizes postsynaptic receptors at the mouse neuromuscular synapse. *J Physiol*, 2005. 562(Pt 3): p. 673-85.

189. Martinez-Martinez, P., et al., Silencing rapsyn in vivo decreases acetylcholine receptors and augments sodium channels and secondary postsynaptic membrane folding. Neurobiol Dis, 2009. 35(1): p. 14-23.

190. Gomez, C.M. and D.P. Richman, Anti-acetylcholine receptor antibodies directed against the alpha-bungarotoxin binding site induce a unique form of experimental myasthenia. Proc Natl Acad Sci U S A, 1983. 80(13): p. 4089-93.

191. Whiting, P.J., A. Vincent, and J. Newsom-Davis, Acetylcholine receptor antibody characteristics in myasthenia gravis. Fractionation of alpha-bungarotoxin binding site antibodies and their relationship to IgG subclass. *J Neuroimmunol*, 1983. 5(1): p. 1-9.

192. Berman, P.W. and J. Patrick, Experimental myasthenia gravis. A murine system. *J Exp Med*, 1980. 151(1): p. 204-23.

193. Christadoss, P., M. Poussin, and C. Deng, Animal models of myasthenia gravis. *Clin Immunol*, 2000. 94(2): p. 75-87.

194. Richman, D.P., et al., Effector mechanisms of myasthenic antibodies. *Ann N Y Acad Sci*, 1993. 681: p. 264-73.

195. Hoedemaekers, A.C., P.J. van Breda Vriesman, and M.H. De Baets, Myasthenia gravis as a prototype autoimmune receptor disease. *Immunol Res*, 1997. 16(4): p. 341-54.

196. Richman, D.P., et al., Monoclonal anti-acetylcholine receptor antibodies can cause experimental myasthenia. *Nature*, 1980. 286(5774): p. 738-9.

197. Tzartos, S.J., D. Sophianos, and A. Efthimiadis, Role of the main immunogenic region of acetylcholine receptor in myasthenia gravis. An Fab monoclonal antibody protects against antigenic modulation by human sera. *J Immunol*, 1985. 134(4): p. 2343-9.

198. Balass, M., et al., Identification of a hexapeptide that mimics a conformation-dependent binding site of acetylcholine receptor by use of a phage-epitope library. Proc Natl Acad Sci U S A, 1993. 90(22): p. 10638-42.

199. Conti-Fine, B.M., M. Milani, and W. Wang, CD4+ T cells and cytokines in the pathogenesis of acquired myasthenia gravis. *Ann N Y Acad Sci*, 2008. 1132: p. 193-209.

200. Balasa, B., et al., Interferon gamma (IFN-gamma) is necessary for the genesis of acetylcholine receptor-induced clinical experimental autoimmune myasthenia gravis in mice. *J Exp Med*, 1997. 186(3): p. 385-91.

201. Papanastasiou, D., et al., Prevention of passively transferred experimental autoimmune myasthenia gravis by Fab fragments of monoclonal antibodies directed against the main immunogenic region of the acetylcholine receptor. *J Neuroimmunol*, 2000. 104(2): p. 124-32.

202. Toyka, K.V., et al., Passively transferred myasthenia gravis: protection of mouse endplates by Fab fragments from human myasthenic IgG. *J Neurol Neurosurg Psychiatry*, 1980. 43(9): p. 836-42.

203. Paige, A.G., et al., Prolonged circulation of recombinant human granulocyte-colony stimulating factor by covalent linkage to albumin through a heterobifunctional polyethylene glycol. *Pharm Res*, 1995. 12(12): p. 1883-8.

204. Kitamura, K., et al., Chemical engineering of the monoclonal antibody A7 by polyethylene glycol for targeting cancer chemotherapy. *Cancer Res*, 1991. 51(16): p. 4310-5.

205. Graus, Y.F., et al., Human anti-nicotinic acetylcholine receptor recombinant Fab fragments isolated from thymus-derived phage display libraries from myasthenia gravis patients reflect predominant specificities in serum and block the action of pathogenic serum antibodies. *J Immunol*, 1997. 158(4): p. 1919-29.

206. Ostlie, N., et al., Absence of IL-4 facilitates the development of chronic autoimmune myasthenia gravis in C57BL/6 mice. *J Immunol*, 2003. 170(1): p. 604-12.

15

Myasthenia Gravis: The Influence of Complement and its Regulatory Proteins

Jindrich Soltys DVM, PhD & Henry J. Kaminski M.D.

1 INTRODUCTION

There is emerging information that complement regulatory proteins modulate disease severity of experimental autoimmune myasthenia gravis (EAMG) but the significance of these proteins in the human MG, in determination of disease severity, is not known. This review is focused on MG and EAMG animal models for evidence of complement injury and role of complement regulatory proteins in EAMG pathogenesis(1).

MG, and its animal model EAMG fulfill strict criteria for autoimmunity (2). To support the hypothesis of an autoimmune origin there are the following observations: i) the presence antibodies at the site of pathology, the neuromuseular junction (NMJ) (3); ii) immunoglobulin from MG patients or anti-AChR antibodies from EAMG animals cause MG manifestations when injected into rodents, (4); iii) immunization of animals with AChR reproduces the disease (5), iiii/ therapies that moderate autoantibody levels decrease the severity of weakness (6).

Compromise of the NMJ is executed by three distinct mechanisms (7): i) direct block of the AChR function primarily due to antibodies which recognize the binding site for the cholinergic ligand; ii) enhanced endocytosis and degradation of the AChR triggered by antibody crosslinking of the AChR ; iii) complement mediated lysis of NMJ. In the final pathway AChR specific autoantibodies form immune complexes and initiate the complement cascade resulting in lysis of the post-synaptic muscle membrane.

2. COMPLEMENT SYSTEM OVERVIEW

Complement is an essential component of innate immunity. Its main function is to protect against invading pathogens by mechanisms, such as cell lysis of pathogens, opsonization with complement fragments, chemotaxis of inflammatory cells and formation of the membrane attack complex (MAC) (8). For adaptive immunity, the complement system is an important modulator of cell mediated (9) and humoral immune responses (10). B cell complement receptors participate in the development of autoimmunity by affecting the survival and activation of autoreactive B cells, which produce pathogenic auto-antibodies, which then form complement fixing immune complexes (11).

The complement system involves a series of plasma and membrane proteins produced by a variety of cells and has classical, alternative and lectin pathways. The classical pathway is initiated by binding of C1 protein to the Fc region of IgG and IgM molecules that have interacted with antigen (12, 13). The alternative pathway is activated by foreign pathogens and polymeric IgA (14, 15), and lectin pathway is initiated primarily by binding of mannose-binding lectin to microbial pathogens and may also involve IgA-containing immune complexes (16, 17). Although initiated differently all three pathways lead to cleavage of C3 and activation of the C5b convertase, which leads to formation of the MAC (18).

3. COMPLEMENT REGULATION

Complement activity is modulated by regulatory proteins that prevent binding of activated complement components and thereby protect an organism from self damage (19, 20). There are several soluble and cell bound complement regulators protecting cells from the exaggerated complement activity: 1) decay accelerating factor (DAF - CD55), (21) 2) Membrane inhibitor of reactive lysis (MIRL - CD59), (22) 3) Membrane cofactor proteins (MCP – CD46), (23), 4) complement receptor 1 (CR1 - CD35), (24, 25) and 5) complement related receptor Y (Crry), a rodent specific regulator with properties of DAF and MCP(26) (Table 1).

In humans there are three cell-associated regulators: DAF, CD59 and MCP. While the human MCP has activity similar to Crry (27), DAF and CD59 act similarly to rodent homologues; therefore, results of EAMG studies of mice are likely to serve as good models of the cell surface complement regulator function in human disease. There is emerging evidence that complement regulatory proteins impact on adaptive immune responses. DAF modulates T cell proliferation, cytokine production and controls the outcome of T cell response to a given antigen (28, 29). CD59 down regulates CD4+ activity *in vitro* and in *vivo* (30) and ligation of complement receptor I-related protein Crry/p65 (Crry) has a costimulatory effect on mouse CD4+ T cell activation (31). The dual function of each regulator demonstrates that complement and complement regulatory proteins provide a means of crosstalk between innate and adaptive immunity.

4. ACHR ANTIBODIES AND COMPLEMENT ACTIVATION IN MYASTHENIA GRAVIS

AChR antibodies are heterogeneous and consist of complement fixing subclasses IgG_1, IgG_{2b}, and IgG_3 subtypes, which are efficient activators of classical complement activation pathway *in vitro* and *in vivo* (32). The antibody production is T-cell dependent and the epitope repertoire of AChR CD4+cells in MG is complex and characteristic of each individual patient (33). Similar diversity is observed in EAMG (34-36).

Table 1. Complement Regulators

Complement regulatory protein	Complement Inhibition	Distribution
Decay Accelerating factor (DAF; CD55)	induces the decay of C3 and C5 convertases preventing C3b deposition	Ubiquitous
Protectin or Membrane inhibitor of reactive lysis (MIRL; CD59)	prevents binding of C9 to C5b-9 complex and formation of membrane attack complex (MAC)	Ubiquitous
Membrane cofactor protein (MCP; CD46)	human specific, serves as a cofactor for the cleavage cell-bound C4b and C3b by the serum protease factor I	peripheral blood cells (except erythrocytes), fibroblasts epithelial and endothelial cells
Complement receptor 1 (CR1; CD35)	possess both DAF and MCP properties	peripheral blood cells, follicular and dendritic cells
Complement related protein Y (Crry)	rodent specific regulator with DAF and MCP properties protecting cells from C3 mediated cleavage	Ubiquitous

About 90% of patients with generalized MG have antibodies to the AChR and antibodies to another neuromuscular junction protein, the muscle specific kinase (MusK) are identified in 30- 70% of AChR antibody negative patients (37, 38). The remaining patients are consistently negative for both the AChR and MusK antibodies. "Double" seronegative MG resembles AChR antibody positive MG (39). Explanations could be the loss of antigenic determinants in autoantibody assays or levels of autoantibodies are below detection limits of conventional assays (40). MuSK antibodies have been found to activate complement (41).

The predominant role of complement involvement in human MG pathogenesis is supported by various studies (42-44). Neuromuscular junctions from patients have IgG, C3 and MAC deposition (3, 45, 46). Increased complement consumption *in vivo* has also been observed (47). The simplified NMJ structure is a likely consequence of complement-mediated injury (48). Overall, all results suggest that complement-activation is an important pathogenic mechanism even in patients without detectable AChR antibodies (49).

5. COMPLEMENT REGULATORY PROTEINS AND EAMG

As an innate component, complement protects the host against invading pathogens by mechanisms which include cell lysis of pathogens, opsonization with complement fragments and chemotaxis of inflammatory cells (8). In adaptive immune response complement acts as an effector system for the primary and secondary antibody responses of B cells (11, 50). Based upon identification of complement deposition at the NMJ and the expression of cell surface complement regulators at the NMJ, the influence of complement regulators on MG severity would be expected. The following sections discuss evidence for how each of the complement regulators influences EAMG severity.

5.1 DAF (CD55)

DAF inhibits complement activation by interfering with C3 and C5 convertases (51, 52). As in humans, mouse DAF is expressed on muscle fibers (53, 54) and tissues exposed to complement activation (55-57). A role for DAF as a signal transduction molecule present on T cells was originally validated by Davis et al. (58). A study by Liu (59) showed that recall responses, as measured using spleen cells from mice immunized with ovalbumin (OVA) or an MHC class II restricted MOG peptide, are more efficient in DAF deficient mice than in wild type. T cells from the DAF knockout mice produce more IFN-g and IL-2 upon antigen restimulation, whereas production of the immunosuppressive IL-10 is reduced. Hyper-responsiveness of T cells is due to lack of DAF on the T cells and no difference is observed after stimulation with superantigen. The effect of DAF deficiency on T cells is largely mediated through complement. Heeger and colleagues reported similar findings in which spleen cells of DAF-deficient mice proliferated more vigorously following *in vitro* stimulation with allogeneic cells (60).

DAF at the NMJ has been found to moderate the severity of EAMG. EAMG induced by passive transfer of monoclonal anti-AChR was found to be much more severe in DAF knockout than wild-type mice, as assessed by weakness assessment, reduced AChR level, and augmented C3b deposition at the NMJ. The expression of *Crry* and *CD59* was found to be comparable between DAF-deficient and sufficient mice (61). With passively induced EAMG DAF-deficient mice developed profound weakness within 48 hours of administration of anti-AChR antibody and showed greater complement deposition at the NMJ compared to wild-type mice. Therefore, the heightened complement activity at the NMJ caused by DAF deficiency lead to worsened disease (62).

Complement regulator alterations may play a role in the thymic pathogenesis of MG. In early-onset MG, human thymus contains lymph node-type infiltrates with frequent AChR specific germinal centers. Hyperplastic epithelial cells demonstrate an up-regulation in C5a receptor and CD59 as well as activated C3b complement component on infiltrating B cells, macrophages, and especially follicular dendritic cells. Myoid cells may be particularly vulnerable to complement since the complement regulators DAF, CD46, and CR1 are expressed low levels and CD59 was absent. Many myoid cells in the pathological thymus of seropositive and seronegative patients also have deposits of complement activation products. These observations suggest that a deficiency in DAF, and other complement regulators, may contribute to the initiation of a breakdown in tolerance in the thymus of patients with MG (63).

In passive EAMG using mice, we found evidence that complement regulator deficiency of extraocular muscle could contribute to their increased susceptibility to MG. Extraocular muscle showed significant decreases in mRNA levels of all three complement regulators in response to EAMG. Also, immunoreactivity for DAF, CD59 and Crry was highly positive at diaphragm NMJ, but less intense or absent at the extraocular muscle junctions (64, 65). The hypothesis that differential expression of complement regulatory proteins influences regional vulnerability to complement mediated damage is supported by observations of Tang and Brimijoin (66).

5.2 MIRL (CD59)

After identification that DAF protects the NMJ from passive EAMG (61), the question arose whether there were differences in degree to which complement regulators may influence EAMG disease severity. Mice deficient in DAF or CD59 mice have milder weakness compared to mice deficient in both regulators and the inhibition of MAC formation abrogates disease in double KO mice (67). One study suggests that DAF provides more protection than CD59 (62), but this was not the case in another investigation (67).

Tuzun and colleagues evaluated the influence of CD59 deficiency in active EAMG. There was no observation of greater weakness; however, CD59 knockout mice exhibited reduced IgG1, IgG2b anti-AChR antibodies. Complement levels, IL-2 production and lymphocyte proliferation responses to AChR were decreased (68). In contrast, CD59 was found to modulate antiviral CD4+ T cell activity in a complement-independent manner. *In vitro* assays showed that CD4$^+$ T cells in CD59 deficient mice proliferate more vigorously in response to stimulation with CD3 specific antibodies and antigen presenting cells (69).

5.3 Complement receptor 1 (CR1)

CR1 is expressed on many cell types including red blood cells and immune cells (25, 70). CR1 initiates the classical complement cascade, mediates phagocytosis of C3b opsonised particles, and regulates C3 and C5 activation (71). Mice deficient in early pathway components (C1q, C4 or C3) or CD21 and CD35 receptors show impaired humoral responses but activation of naive mature B cells is enhanced by an intact classical pathway (72). Therefore, CR1 and other early components of complement would be expected to influence disease course in both, MG and EAMG (73). In generalized MG, the thymus contains lymph node-type infiltrates with frequent AChR-specific germinal centers. Expression of CR1 is essentially confined to germinal centers, where deposits of activated C3b are detected (74).

CR1 binds C1q and autoantibodies to C1q have been found in several autoimmune and inflammatory diseases. Though not observed in patients, high levels of C1q antibody in EAMG mice correlate with disease severity (75). Administration of 10 mg of C1q antibody is associated with reduction of complement deposits, decreased serum complement activity and IL-6 production. In contrast, 100 mg of C1q antibody causes an augmented response. EAMG mice show greater weakness and elevated C3, IgG deposition and AChR antibodies (76). See Chapter 18 for a detailed description on the effect of anti-C1q Ab in EAMG pathogenesis.

Soluble recombinant CR1 has been found to reduce weight loss and weakness in passively induced EAMG (77) likely because of its inhibition of the complement cascade and acceleration of the decay of C3 and C5 convertases. Soluble CR1 has not been developed as a therapeutic for human use.

5.4 Complement receptor 1 – related protein y (Crry)

Crry inhibits the C3 convertases (78) and appears to be involved in communication between complement and the adaptive immune response (79-81) and is the only regulator expressed in detectable amounts on T cells of rats (82, 83). Crry influences the level of serum C3 (84), which is important in the design and interpretation of experimental studies involving continual use of soluble Crry complement inhibitor (85) since Crry influences the level of C3 the extent of inhibition *in vivo* may not be as much as expected from *in vitro* studies.

Fusion of the Crry domain to rat IgG2a has been produced and evaluated as therapeutic complement inhibitor (rCrry-Ig). The fusion leads to a compound with an extended half-life compared to a soluble Crry domain. Long term systemic administration of rCrry-Ig generates a weak predominantly IgM response, which did not neutralize Crry activity or enhance clearance of the agent. In a rat model of EAMG, injection of rCrry-Ig prevented C3 and C9 deposition at the NMJ and elliminated signs of weakness (86).

6. THERAPEUTIC COMPLEMENT INHIBITION FOR MG

The extensive studies of complement (see Chapter 18) and its regulators in EAMG have lead to consideration that therapies could be targeted against the complement system for human MG, and complement inhibitor based therapeutics are under evaluation for MG (87,88). Several complement inhibitors have been identified to moderate EAMG severity. Administration of anti-C5 (89),a tick-derived C5 inhibitor (90), anti-C6 (91), and soluble C3b receptor (CR1 or CD35) (77) have all been shown to limit EAMG. However, treatment applications that are designed to only limit complement activation at the NMJ may be found to have broader influences. With the growing evidence that complement influences adaptive immune system, complement inhibition may enhance the underlying drivers of the autoimmune process on the side of the T and B cells and prove to be overall deleterious.

REFERENCES

1. Kusner, L. L., H. J. Kaminski, and J. Soltys. 2008. Effect of complement and its regulation on myasthenia gravis pathogenesis. *Expert Rev. Clin. Immunol.* 4:43-52.
2. De Baets, M., M. Stassen, M. Losen, X. Zhang, and B. Machiels. 2003. Immunoregulation in experimental autoimmune myasthenia gravis-about T cells, antibodies, and endplates. *Ann. NY Acad. Sci.* 998:308-317.
3. Nakano, S., and A. G. Engel. 1993. Myasthenia gravis: quantitative immunocytochemical analysis of inflammatory cells and detection of complement membrane attack complex at the end-plate in 30 patients. *Neurology* 43:1167-1172.
4. Eymard, B. 2009. Antibodies in myasthenia gravis. *Rev. Neurol.* 165:137-143.
5. Link, H., and B. G. Xiao. 2001. Rat models as tool to develop new immunotherapies. *Immunol. Rev.* 184:117-128.
6. Fuchs S., T. Feferman, R. Meidler, R. Margalit, C. Sicsic, T. Brenner, O. Laub, and M. C. Souroujon 2008. Immunosuppression of EAMG by IVIG Is Mediated by a Disease-specific Anti-immunoglobulin Fraction. *Ann. NY Acad. Sci.* 1132:244-248.
7. Conti-Fine, B. M., M. Milani, and H. J. Kaminski. 2006. Myasthenia gravis: past, present, and future. *J. Clin. Invest.* 116:2843-2854.
8. Kohl, J. 2006. Self, non-self, and danger: a complementary view. Adv. Exp. Med. Biol. 586:71-94.
9. Morgan, B. P., K. J. Marchbank, M. P. Longhi, C. L. Harris, and A. M. Gallimore. 2005. Complement: central to innate immunity and bridging to adaptive responses. *Immunol. Lett.* 97:171-179.
10. Blank, M., and Y. Schoenfeld. 2007. B cell targeted therapy in autoimmunity. *J. Autoimmun.* 28:62-68.
11. Boackle, S. A. 2003. Complement and autoimmunity. *Biomed. Pharmacother.* 57:269-273.
12. Sim, R. B., and K. B. Reid. 1991. C1: molecular interactions with activating systems. *Immunol. Today* 12:307-311.
13. Quartier, P., P. K. Potter, M. R. Ehrenstein, M. J. Walport, and M. Botto. 2005. Predominant role of IgM-dependent activation of the classical pathway in the clearance of dying cells by murine bone marrow-derived macrophages *in vitro. Eur. J. Immunol.* 35:252-260.
14. Austen, K. F., and D. T. Fearon. 1979. A molecular basis of activation of the alternative pathway of human complement. *Adv. Exp. Med. Biol.* 120B:3-17.
15. Bogers, W. M., R. K. Stad, L. A. van Es, and M. R. Daham. 1991. Complement enhances the clearence of large-sized soluble IgA aggregates in rats. *Eur. J. Immunol.* 21:1093-1099.
16. Roos, A., L. H. Bouwman, D. J. van Gijlswijk-Janssen, M. C. Faber-Krol, G. L. Stahl, and M. R. Daha. 2001. Human IgA activates the complement system via the mannan-binding lectin pathway. *J. Immunol.* 167:2861-2868.
17. Thiel, S., T. Vorup-Jensen, C. M. Stover, W. Schwaeble, S. B. Laursen, K. Poulsen, A. C. Willis, P. Eggleton, S. Hansen, U. Holmskov, K. B. Rei, and J. C. Jensenius. 1997. A second serine protease associated with mannan-binding lectin that activates complement. *Nature* 386:506-510.

18. Rus, H., C. Cudrici, and F. Niculescu. 2005. The role of the complement system in innate immunity. *Immunol. Res.* 33:103-112.

19. Gasque, P. 2004. Complement: a unique innate immune sensor for danger signals. *Mol. Immun.* 41:1089-1098.

20. Unsworth, D. J. 2008. Complement deficiency and disease. *J. Clin. Pathol.* 61:1013-1017.

21. Lin, F., Y. Fukuoka, A. Spicer, R. Ohta, N. Okada, C. L. Harris, S. N. Emancipator, and M. E. Medof. 2001. Tissue distribution of products of the mouse decay-accelerating factor (DAF) genes. Exploitation of a Daf1 knock-out mouse and site-specific monoclonal antibodies. *Immunology* 104:215-225.

22. Huang, Y., C. A. Smith, H. Song, B. P. Morgan, R. Abagyan, and S. Tomlinson. 2005. Insights into the human CD59 complement binding interface toward engineering new therapeutics. *J. Biol. Chem.* 280:34073-34079.

23. Brodbeck, W. G., C. Mold, J. P. Atkinson, and M. E. Medof. 2000. Cooperation between decay-accelerating factor and membrane cofactor protein in protecting cells from autologous complement attack. *J. Immunol.* 165:3999-4006.

24. Ahearn, J. M., and D. T. Fearon. 1989. Structure and function of the complement receptors, CR1 (CD35) and CR2 (CD21). *Adv. Immunol.* 46:183-219.

25. Khera, R., and N. Das. 2009. Complement Receptor 1: disease associations and therapeutic implications. *Mol. Immunol.* 46:761-772.

26. Wu, X., D. Spitzer, D. Mao, S. L. Peng, H. Molina, and J. P. Atkinson. 2008. Membrane protein Crry maintains homeostasis of the complement system. *J. Immunol.* 181:2732-2740.

27. Lublin, D. M., M. K. Liszewski, T. W. Post, M. A. Arce, M. M. Le Beau, M. B. Rebentisch, L. S. Lemons, T. Seya, and J. P. Atkinson. 1988. Molecular cloning and chromosomal localization of human membrane cofactor protein (MCP). Evidence for inclusion in the multigene family of complement-regulatory proteins. *J. Exp. Med.* 168:181-194.

28. Heeger, P. S., P. N. Lalli, F. Lin, A. Valujskikh, J. Liu, N. Muqim, Y. Xu, and M. E. Medof. 2005. Decay-accelerating factor modulates induction of T cell immunity. *J. Exp. Med.* 201:1523-1530.

29. Lalli, P. N., M. G. Strainic, F. Lin, M. E. Medof, and P. S. Heeger. 2007. Decay accelerating factor can control T cell differentiation into IFN-gamma-producing effector cells via regulating local C5a-induced IL-12 production. *J. Immunol.* 179:5793-5802.

30. Longhi, M. P., C. L. Harris, B. P. Morgan, and A. Gallimore. 2006. Holding T cells in check - a new role for complement regulators? *Trends Immunol.* 27:102-108.

31. Jimenez-Perianez, A., G. Ojeda, G. Criado, A. Sanchez, E. Pini, J. Madrenas, J. M. Rojo, and P. Portoles. 2005. Complement regulatory protein Crry/p65-mediated signaling in T lymphocytes: role of its cytoplasmic domain and partitioning into lipid rafts. *J. Leukoc. Biol.* 78:1386-1396.

32. Lindstrom, J. 1985. Immunobiology of myasthenia gravis, experimental autoimmune myasthenia gravis, and Lambert-Eaton syndrome. *Ann. Rev. Immunol.* 3:109-131.

33. Holers, V. M. 2005. Complement receptors and the shaping of the natural antibody repertoire. *Springer Semin. Immunopathol.* 26:405-423.

34. Drachman, D. B., K. R. McIntosh, and B. Yang. 1998. Factors that determine the severity of experimental myasthenia gravis. *Ann. NY Acad. Sci.* 841:262-282.

35. Holers, V. M. 2003. The complement system as a therapeutic target in autoimmunity. *Clin. Immunol.*107:140-151.

36. Yang, H., E. Goluszko, C. David, D. K. Okita, B. Conti-Fine, T. S. Chan, M. A. Poussin, and P. Christadoss. 2002. Mapping myasthenia gravis-associated T cell epitopes on human acetylcholine receptors in HLA transgenic mice. *J. Clin. Invest.* 109:1111-1120.

37. Hoch, W., J. McConville, S. Helms, J. Newsom-Davis, A. Melms, and A. Vincent. 2001. Auto-antibodies to the receptor tyrosine kinase MuSK in patients with myasthenia gravis without acetylcholine receptor antibodies. *Nat. Med.* 7:365-368.

38. Bartoccioni, E., F. Scuderi, G. M. Minicuci, M. Marino, F. Ciaraffa, and A. Evoli. 2006. Anti-MuSK antibodies: correlation with myasthenia gravis severity. *Neurology* 67:505-507.

39. Zhou, L., J. McConville, V. Chaudhry, R. N. Adams, R. L. Skolasky, A. Vincent, and D. B. Drachman. 2004. Clinical comparison of muscle-specific tyrosine kinase (MuSK) antibody-positive and -negative myasthenic patients. *Muscle Nerve* 30:55-60.

40. Vincent, A., and M. I. Leite. 2005. Neuromuscular junction autoimmune disease: muscle specific kinase antibodies and treatments for myasthenia gravis. *Curr. Opin. Neurol.* 18:519-525.

41. Leite, M. I., S. Jacob, S. Viegas, J. Cossins, L. Clover, B. P. Morgan, D. Beeson, N. Willcox, and A. Vincent. 2008. IgG1 antibodies to acetylcholine receptors in 'seronegative' myasthenia gravis. *Brain* 131:1940-1952.

42. Lennon, V. A., M. E. Seybold, J. M. Lindstrom, C. Cochrane, and R. Ulevitch. 1978. Role of complement in the pathogenesis of experimental autoimmune myasthenia gravis. *J. Exp. Med.* 147:973-983.

43. Christadoss, P. 1988. C5 gene influences the development of murine myasthenia gravis. *J. Immunol.* 140:2589-2592.

44. Tuzun, E., B. G. Scott, E. Goluszko, S. Higgs, and P. Christadoss. 2003. Genetic evidence for involvement of classical complement pathway in induction of experimental autoimmune myasthenia gravis. *J. Immunol.* 171:3847-3854.

45. Sahashi, K., A. G. Engel, E. H. Lambert, and F. M. Howard, Jr. 1980. Ultrastructural localization of the terminal and lytic ninth complement component (C9) at the motor end-plate in myasthenia gravis. *J. Neuropathol. Exp. Neurol.* 39:160-172.

46. Barohn, R. J., and R. L. Brey. 1993. Soluble terminal complement components in human myasthenia gravis. *Clin. Neurol. Neurosurg.* 95:285-290.

47. Romi, F., E. K. Kristoffersen, J. A. Aarli, and N. E. Gilhus. 2005. The role of complement in myasthenia gravis: serological evidence of complement consumption in vivo. *J. Neuroimmunol.* 158:191-194.

48. Engel, A. G. 2004. Acquired Autoimmune Myasthenia Gravis. In *Myology*. A. G. Engel, and C. Franzini-Armstrong, eds. McGraw-Hill, New York. 1755-1789.

49. Vincent, A., M. I. Leite, M. E. Farrugia, S. Jacob, S. Viegas, H. Shiraishi, O. Benveniste, B. P. Morgan, D. Hilton-Jones, J. Newsom-Davis, D. Beeson, and N. Willcox. 2008. Myasthenia gravis seronegative for acetylcholine receptor antibodies. *Ann. NY Acad. Sci.* 1132:84-92.

50. Blank, M., and Y. Shoenfeld. 2007. B cell targeted therapy in autoimmunity. *J. Autoimmun.* 28:62-68.

51. Medof, M. E., T. Kinoshita, and V. Nussenzweig. 1984. Inhibition of complement activation on the surface of cells after incorporation of decay-accelerating factor (DAF) into their membranes. *J. Exp. Med.* 160:1558-1578.

52. Fujita, T., T. Inoue, K. Ogawa, K. Iida, and N. Tamura. 1987. The mechanism of action of decay-accelerating factor (DAF). DAF inhibits the assembly of C3 convertases by dissociating C2a and Bb. *J. Exp. Med.* 166:1221-1228.

53. Navenot, J. M., M. Villanova, B. Lucas-Heron, A. Malandrini, D. Blanchard, and J. P. Louboutin. 1997. Expression of CD59, a regulator of the membrane attack complex of complement, on human skeletal muscle fibers. *Muscle Nerve* 20:92-96.

54. Louboutin, J. P., J. M. Navenot, K. Rouger, and D. Blanchard. 2003. S-protein is expressed in necrotic fibers in Duchenne muscular dystrophy and polymyositis. *Muscle Nerve* 27:575-581.

55. Harris, C. L., N. K. Rushmere, and B. P. Morgan. 1999. Molecular and functional analysis of mouse decay accelerating factor (CD55). *Biochem. J.* 341:821-829.

56. Harris, C. L., O. B. Spiller, and B. P. Morgan. 2000. Human and rodent decay-accelerating factors (CD55) are not species restricted in their complement-inhibiting activities. *Immunology* 100:462-470.

57. Hinchliffe, S. J., N. K. Rushmere, S. M. Hanna, and B. P. Morgan. 1998. Molecular cloning and functional characterization of the pig analogue of CD59: relevance to xenotransplantation. *J. Immunol.* 160:3924-3932.

58. Davis, L. S., S. S. Patel, J. P. Atkinson, and P. E. Lipsky. 1988. Decay-accelerating factor functions as a signal transducing molecule for human T cells. *J. Immunol.* 141:2246-2252.

59. Liu, J., T. Miwa, B. Hilliard, Y. Chen, J. D. Lambris, A. D. Wells, and W.-C. Song. 2005. The complement inhibitory protein DAF (CD55) suppresses T cell immunity *in vivo*. *J. Exp. Med.* 201:567-577.

60. Pavlov, V., H. Raedler, S. Yuan, S. Leisman, W. H. Kwan, P. N. Lalli, M. E. Medof, and P. S. Heeger. 2008. Donor deficiency of decay-accelerating factor accelerates murine T cell-mediated cardiac allograft rejection. *J. Immunol.* 181:4580-4589.

61. Lin, F., H. J. Kaminski, B. M. Conti-Fine, W. Wang, C. Richmonds, and M. E. Medof. 2002. Markedly enhanced susceptibility to experimental autoimmune myasthenia gravis in the absence of decay-accelerating factor protection. *J. Clin. Invest.* 110:1269-1274.

62. Kaminski, H. J., L. L. Kusner, C. Richmonds, M. E. Medof, and F. Lin. 2006. Deficiency of decay accelerating factor and CD59 leads to crisis in experimental myasthenia. *Exp. Neurol.* 202:287-293.

63. Leite, M. I., M. Jones, P. Strobel, A. Marx, R. Gold, E. Niks, J. J. Verschuuren, S. Berrih-Aknin, F. Scaravilli, A. Canelhas, B. P. Morgan, A. Vincent, and N. Willcox. 2007. Myasthenia gravis thymus: complement vulnerability of epithelial and myoid cells, complement attack on them, and correlations with autoantibody status. *Am. J. Pathol.* 171:893-905.

64. Kaminski, H. J., Z. Li, C. Richmonds, F. Lin, and M. E. Medof. 2004. Complement regulators in extraocular muscle and experimental autoimmune myasthenia gravis. *Exp. Neurol.* 189:333-342.

65. Kusner, L. L., A. Puwanant, and H. J. Kaminski. 2006. Ocular myasthenia: diagnosis, treatment, and pathogenesis. *Neurologist* 12:231-239.

66. Tang, H., and S. Brimijoin. 2001. Complement regulatory proteins and selective vulnerability of neurons to lysis on exposure to acetylcholinesterase antibody. *J. Neuroimmunol.* 115:53-63.

67. Morgan, B. P., J. Chamberlain-Banoub, J. W. Neal, W. Song, M. Mizuno, and C. L. Harris. 2006. The membrane attack pathway of complement drives pathology in passively induced experimental autoimmune myasthenia gravis in mice. *Clin. Exp. Immunol.*146:294-302.

68. Tuzun, E., S. S. Saini, B. P. Morgan, and P. Christadoss. 2006. Complement regulator CD59 deficiency fails to augment susceptibility to actively induced experimental autoimmune myasthenia gravis. *J. Neuroimmunol.* 181:29-33.

69. Longhi, M. P., B. Sivasankar, N. Omidvar, B. P. Morgan, and A. Gallimore. 2005. Cutting edge: murine CD59a modulates antiviral CD4+ T cell activity in a complement-independent manner. *J. Immunol.* 175:7098-7102.

70. Yazdanbakhsh, K. 2005. Review: complement receptor 1 therapeutics for prevention of immune hemolysis. *Immunohematol.* 21:109-118.

71. Reid, K. B., M. Colomb, F. Petry, and M. Loos. 2002. Complement component C1 and the collectins—first-line defense molecules in innate and acquired immunity. *Trends Immunol.* 23:115-117.

72. Fearon, D. T., and M. C. Carroll. 2000. Regulation of B lymphocyte responses to foreign and self-antigens by the CD19/CD21 complex. *Ann. Rev. Immunol.* 18:393-422.

73. Willcox, N., M. I. Leite, Y. Kadota, M. Jones, A. Meager, P. Subrahmanyam, B. Dasgupta, B. P. Morgan, and A. Vincent. 2008. Autoimmunizing mechanisms in thymoma and thymus. *Ann. NY Acad, Sci.* 1132:163-173.

74. Leite, M. I., M. Jones, P. Strobel, A. Marx, R. Gold, E. Niks, J. J. Verschuuren, S. Berrih-Aknin, F. Scaravilli, A. Canelhas, P. B. Morgan, A. Vincent, and N. Willcox. 2007. Myasthenia Gravis Thymus. Complement Vulnerability of Epithelial and Myoid Cells, Complement Attack on Them, and Correlations with Autoantibody Status. *Am. J. Pathol* 171:893-905.

75. Tuzun, E., S. S. Saini, S. Ghosh, J. Rowin, M. N. Meriggioli, and P. Christadoss. 2006. Predictive value of serum anti-C1q antibody levels in experimental autoimmune myasthenia gravis. *Neuromuscul. Disord.* 16:137-143.

76. Tuzun, E., J. Li, S. S. Saini, H. Yang, and P. Christadoss. 2007. Pros and cons of treating murine myasthenia gravis with anti-C1q antibody. *J. Neuroimmunol.* 182:167-176.

77. Piddlesden, S. J., S. Jiang, J. L. Levin, A. Vincent, and B. P. Morgan. 1996. Soluble complement receptor 1 (sCR1) protects against experimental autoimmune myasthenia gravis. *J. Neuroimmunol.* 71:173-177.

78. Molina, H. 2002. The murine complement regulator Crry: new insights into the immunobiology of complement regulation. *Cell. Mol. Life Sci.* 59:220-229.

79. Fernandez-Centeno, E., G. de Ojeda, J. M. Rojo, and P. Portoles. 2000. Crry/p65, a membrane complement regulatory protein, has costimulatory properties on mouse T cells. *J. Immunol.* 164:4533-4542.

80. Antic Stankovic, J., D. Vucevic, I. Majstorovic, S. Vasilijic, and M. Colic. 2004. The role of rat Crry, a complement regulatory protein, in proliferation of thymocytes. *Life Sciences* 75:3053-3062.

81. Li, Q., K. Nacion, H. Bu, and F. Lin. 2009. Mouse CD4+ CD25+ T regulatory cells are protected from autologous complement mediated injury by Crry and CD59. *Biochem. Biophys. Res. Commun.* 382:223-226.

82. Hanna, S. M., O. B. Spiller, S. M. Linton, R. J. Mead, and B. P. Morgan. 2002. Rat T cells express neither CD55 nor CD59 and are dependent on Crry for protection from homologous complement. *Eur. J. Immunol.* 32:502-509.

83. Funabashi, K., N. Okada, S. Matsuo, T. Yamamoto, B. P. Morgan, and H. Okada. 1994. Tissue distribution of complement regulatory membrane proteins in rats. *Immunology* 81:444-451.

84. Ruseva, M. M., T. R. Hughes, R. M. Donev, B. Sivasankar, M. C. Pickering, X. Wu, C. L. Harris, and B. P. Morgan. 2009. Crry deficiency in complement sufficient mice: C3 consumption occurs without associated renal injury. *Mol. Immunol.* 46:803-811.

85. Kang, H. J., L. Bao, Y. Xu, R. J. Quigg, P. C. Giclas, and V. M. Holers. 2004. Increased serum C3 levels in Crry transgenic mice partially abrogates its complement inhibitory effects. *Clin. Exp.Immunol.* 136:194-199.

86. Hepburn, N. J., J. L. Chamberlain-Banoub, A. S. Williams, B. P. Morgan, and C. L. Harris. 2008. Prevention of experimental autoimmune myasthenia gravis by rat Crry-Ig: A model agent for long-term complement inhibition *in vivo*. *Mol. immunol.* 45:395-405.

87. Garcia-Carrasco, M., R. O. Escarcega, S. Fuentes-Alexandro, C. Riebeling, and R. Cervera. 2007. Therapeutic options in autoimmune myasthenia gravis. *Autoimmun. Rev.* 6:373-378.

88. Hillmen, P., C. Hall, J. C. W. Marsh, M. Elebute, M. P. Bombara, B. E. Petro, M. J. Cullen, S. J. Richards, S. A. Rollins, C. F. Mojcik, and R. P. Rother. 2004. Effect of Eculizumab on Hemolysis and Transfusion Requirements in Patients with Paroxysmal Nocturnal Hemoglobinuria. *N. Engl. J. Med.* 350:552-559.

89. Zhou Y., B. Gong, F. Lin, R. P. Rother, M. E. Medof, and H. J. Kaminski. 2007. Anti-c5 antibody treatment ameliorates weakness in experimentally acquired myasthenia gravis. *J. Immunol.* 179:8562-8567.

90. Soltys J., L. L. Kusner, A. Young, C. Richmonds, D. Hatala, B. Gong, V. Shanmugavel and H. J. Kaminski. 2009. Novel complement inhibitor limits severity of experimentally myasthenia gravis. *Ann. Neurol.* 65:67-75.

91. Biesecker, G., and C. M. Gomez. 1989. Inhibition of acute passive transfer experimental autoimmune myasthenia gravis with Fab antibody to complement C6. *J. Immunol.* 142:2654-2659.

Chemokines and chemokine receptors in MG and EAMG

Miriam C. Souroujon PhD, Tali Feferman PhD, Sonia Berrih-Aknin PhD,
Sara Fuchs PhD

1. INTRODUCTION

CHEMOKINES IN HEALTH AND DISEASE

Chemokines and their receptors constitute a signaling network involved in several physiological processes and in particular leukocyte chemotaxis and adhesion. In the last ten years there is accumulating evidence pointing to a critical role of chemokine networks in various pathological conditions such a several autoimmune and chronic inflammatory diseases. Chemokine signaling networks attract considerable interest from a therapeutic point of view as pharmacological tools interfering with events mediated by chemokines have a potential in modulating pathological states including autoimmune diseases.

Chemokines are composed of single polypeptide chains 70-100 amino acids in length, with 20-95% sequence identity to each other. The two main sub-families, CXC and CC chemokines are distinguished according to the position of the first two cysteins which are either separated by one amino acid (CXC) or adjacent to each other (CC). According to systematic classification principles (1), chemokine receptors are designated CXC, CC, XC and CX3C followed by R (for receptor) and a number, whereas the chemokines are designated by the same acronyms followed by L (for ligand) and a number.

Chemokines exert their biological effects by binding to and activating cell-surface receptors that belong to the G-protein-coupled receptor (GPCR) superfamily. Currently, 19 chemokine receptors have been identified (2). They are expressed on a variety of cells including immune cells, endothelial cells and neurons (3), and are either constitutively activated or induced by agents such as cytokines and lipopolysaccharides (4). Each receptor has a repertoire of chemokine ligands that can activate it. These range from CCR1, which has at least nine different ligands, to receptors such as CCR8, which have only one ligand (2). This redundancy in the chemokine system is even further accentuated by the fact that some chemokines can bind with high affinity to more than one receptor. For example, CCL5 (also known as RANTES) can bind to CCR1, CCR3 and CCR5. By contrast, other chemokines such as CCL1 (also known as I-309) bind only to a single receptor. In addition, chemokines that are agonists for one receptor can act as natural antagonists for others (5).

Chemokines and their receptors control leukocyte migration and homing throughout the body in both physiological and pathological conditions. In the context of the adaptive immune system, which requires high efficiency and control, chemokines and chemokine receptors orchestrate the localization and timing of the immune response by their involvement in T-cell recirculation between lymphoid tissues and the periphery and in selectively recruiting subsets of lymphocytes towards specific target sites. In addition to their chemotactic properties, chemokines can directly modulate T-cell responses by amplifying signals at the immune synapse and tuning Th1/Th2 polarization.

2. CHEMOKINES IN AUTOIMMUNE DISEASES

The importance of chemokines and chemokine receptors in the pathogenesis of autoimmunity has been initially suggested in a number of animal models and was later supported by genetic evidence and clinical studies in humans. Deregulated expression of chemokines and chemokine receptors have been described in the animal models of multiple sclerosis (MS), rheumatoid arthritis (RA), diabetes and lupus (4,6,7). In mouse and rat EAE – the animal model of MS - mRNA levels of MIP-1α, MIP-1ß, RANTES, TCA-3, IP-10, MCP-1, and SDF-1 were found to correlate with disease progression (8) and in mouse collagen-induced arthritis - a model for RA - mRNA levels of MIP-2, RANTES and MIP-1α were increased during the course of disease (9). Treatment of affected mice by chemokine antagonists or blocking antibodies has provided the first proof of concept attesting to the involvement of chemokines in autoimmune diseases. In addition, knockout mice have revealed that the absence of a chemokine or its receptor may prevent or attenuate the development of autoimmune diseases (10).

Consistent with results obtained in animal models, studies in humans have demonstrated that chemokine and chemokine receptor expression are significantly altered during the progression of some autoimmune diseases (4, 11-13). Accordingly, alleviation of symptoms following treatment was correlated with a reduction in the levels of formerly up-regulated chemokines (14). An abnormal expression of chemokine receptors on immune cells has been reported in a number of autoimmune conditions in humans including MS (CCR1, CCR2, CCR5, CXCR3 and CX₃CR1) , RA (CCR1, CCR2, CCR5, CXCR3), lupus (CCR2, CCR5), psoriasis (CCR1, CCR8, CXCR2, CXCR3), Crohn's disease and inflammatory bowel disease (IBD) (CCR5, CCR9) as well as diabetes (CCR2, CXCR3) (4,7,15). In autoimmune diseases which have a chronic inflammatory nature such as MS, psoriasis and RA, multiple chemokines/receptors are present within lesions. For example, synovial tissue from patients with RA expresses chemokines including MCP-1, MIP-1, IL-8, and RANTES, and infiltrating lymphocytes within synovial fluid express the chemokine receptors CXCR3 and CCR5.

Although chemokines and their receptors were first implicated in autoimmune diseases such as MS and RA, in which inflammation is a major component of the tissue damage, there is accumulating evidence for their involvement also in other autoimmune diseases. In the latter, chemokine networks seem to play a key role in trafficking of effector, and possibly also suppressive lymphocytes within central and peripheral lymphoid organs and from them towards target sites of the autoimmune attack.

3. CHEMOKINES IN MG AND EAMG

Prominent cellular infiltrates are not characteristically observed in muscles, the target organ in myasthenia gravis (MG). These however may be missed if they occur during the early stages of disease. Moreover, the involvement of chemokine networks in myasthenia may be attributed, at least in part, to transient chemoattraction of small numbers of leukocytes with cytokine-producing potential to the muscle. These may in turn lead to the production of additional cytokines, chemokines or surface structures by myocytes promoting further interactions between immune cells and the target muscle.

In this chapter we will describe and discuss the data concerning the chemokines and chemokine receptors that have been shown to date to be associated with the pathogenesis of MG and in its animal model, experimental autoimmune MG (EAMG). These data are summarized in Table 1.

3.1. CXCR receptors

There are currently seven known CXC chemokine receptors in mammals, named CXCR1 through CXCR7. The CXC chemokines are further divided into two subgroups: the chemokines belonging to the first group have a characteristic three amino acid sequence - ELR (glutamic acid-leucine-arginine) and act primarily on neutrophils as chemoattractants and activators and those belonging to the second group which lack the ELR domain and act as chemoattractants and activators of monocytes, dendritic cells (DC), T and B cells, NK cells, basophils and eosinophils. In the following we will focus on the involvement of CXCR3, CXCR4 and CXCR5 receptors and their ligands in myasthenia.

3.1.1. CXCR3 and IP-10 (CXCL10)

CXCR3 is the receptor for three chemokines that are induced by interferon gamma (IFN-γ): monokine-induced by IFN-γ (Mig/CXCL9), IFN-γ-inducible 10 kDa protein (IP-10/CXCL10), and IFN-γ-inducible T cell alpha-chemoattractant (I-TAC/CXCL11). CXCR3 is expressed on various types of leukocytes, including activated T cells, B cells, natural killer (NK) cells and monocytes (15-19). CXCL10 is a highly inducible chemoattractant for activated T cells, and has additional pleiotropic activities such as stimulation of monocytes and NK cells, bone marrow progenitor maturation, modulation of adhesion molecule expression and inhibition of angiogenesis (20).

Feferman et al., (21) have shown that IP-10 (CXCL10) and its receptor CXCR3, are overexpressed in MG patients and in rats with EAMG. In rat EAMG, IP-10 (CXCL10) and Mig (CXCL9) and their receptor CXCR3 were overexpressed as were also TNF-α and IL-1β that act synergistically with IFN-τ to induce CXCL10. These upregulations were observed in immune

Table 1: Chemokines and chemokine receptors in MG and EAMG

Chemokine receptor	Chemokines	In EAMG animals	In MG patients
CXCR3	CXCL9 (Mig) CXCL10 (IP-10) CXCL11 (I-TAC)	CXCR3 and IP-10 upregulated in LNC and muscle (21). Anti-IP-10 antibodies and a CXCR3 antagonist (T487) suppress EAMG (27)	CXCR3 and IP-10 upregulated in thymus and muscle (21, 23). CXCR3 increased in PBMC in $CD4^+$ but not in CDS^+ T cells or $CD19^+$ B cells (21) $CXCR3^+CD4^+$ T cell frequency in PBL of MG with thymorma lower than in MG with thymic hyperplasia. $CXCR3^+CD8^+$ cells unaltered (26).
CXCR4	CXCL12 (SDF-1)	CXCR4 expression in LNC incrased in correlation with disease severity (Feferman et al., unpublished).	No change in CXCR4 and SDF-1 expression in the thymus (Berrih-Aknin et al., unpublished)
CXCR5	CXCL13 (BCA-1)		CXCL13 overexpressed in thymus (23) High frequency of $CXCR5^+$ $CD4^+$ T cells in PBL in correlation with disease severity (46). CXCL13 upregulated in TEC and serum and decreased in response to glucocorticoids treatment (42).
CCR1	CCL3 (MIP-1α) CCL3L1, CCL5 (RANTES) CCL9/10 (MIP-1α) CCL14 CCL15 CCL16		CCR1 on CD4+ and CD8+ T cells upregulated in MG with thymic hyperplasia and decreased after therapy (22).
CCR2	CCL2 (MCP-1), CCL13 (MCP-4) CCL7 (MCP-3) CCL-8 (MCP-2) CCL-12 (MCP-5)	CCL2 overexpressed in lymphoid organs (48) and muscle (49, 50). CCL2-1- mice develop mild EAMG correlated with impaired anti-AChR IgG2b response. CCL2 affects Th 17 cells in secondary lymphoid organs(48)	
CCR5	CCL-8 (MCP-2,) CCL-12 (MCP-5), CCL3 (MIP-1α) CCL4 (MIP-1β) CCL3L1, CCL5 (RANTES), CCL6	RANTES, MCP, MIP-1α and MIP-2 are not overexpressed in muscle. (52).	RANTES (CCL5) augmented in TEC cultures. RANTES modulates migration of peripheral lymphocytes to thymus (51).
CCR7	CCL19 CCL21		CCL21 overexpressed in hyperplastic thymuses (23, 53, 54).

response effector cells – namely lymph node cells (LNC) and in the target organ of the autoimmune attack – the muscle of myasthenic rats and were significantly reduced after suppression of EAMG by mucosal tolerance induction with an acetylcholine receptor (AChR) fragment. The relevance of IP-10/CXCR3 signaling in myasthenia was validated by similar observations in MG patients. A significant increase in IP-10 and CXCR3 mRNA levels in both thymus and muscle was observed in myasthenic patients compared to age-matched controls (21). An increased expression of CXCL10 in the thymus of MG patients was also observed by Le Panse et al. (23).

CXCR3 expression in peripheral blood mononuclear cells (PBMC) of MG patients was markedly increased in CD4$^+$ but not in CD8$^+$ T cells or CD19$^+$ B cells. Suzuki et al., (22) have reported that the frequency of CD4$^+$ T cell expressing CXCR3 in PBL of MG patients with thymoma was lower compared with MG patients presenting thymic hyperplasia, whereas the frequencies of CXCR3 positive CD8$^+$ T cells remained normal irrespective of the thymic pathology. The cells in the periphery could thus reflect the events in the thymus since MG patients with thymic hyperplasia, but not with thymoma produce CXCR3$^+$ cells.

The results by Feferman et al. (21) not only demonstrate the involvement of IP-10/CXCR3 signaling in the pathogenesis of myasthenia but also suggest that the muscle may be involved in chemokine signaling in MG. The positive correlation observed between CXCR3 and IP-10 expression in the muscle suggests that the regulation of the genes coding for them is controlled by a common factor that affects both or that they control one another. mRNA Expression of IP-10 and Mig was also reported in myotubes of inclusion body myositis patients cultured *in vitro* (24). Although the physiological role of CXCR3 in myotubes is still not fully understood, it was shown that the binding of I-TAC caused transient mobilization of intracellular calcium as well as chemotactic migration in activated T cell lines expressing CXCR3 (25), as well as in neurons (26). It is thus possible that the calcium influx induced by the binding of IP-10 to its receptor on myotubes contributes to the contractile properties of the muscle.

In order to assess the potential of IP-10/CXCR3 signaling to serve as a drug target in MG, Feferman et al. (27) tested the effect of interference with IP-10/ CXCR3 signaling in rat EAMG. This was performed by two different approaches: a) a small synthetic CXCR3 antagonist (T487 produced by Amgen) and b) antibodies that specifically block IP-10 but not the other CXCR3 chemokines (CXCL9 and CXCL11). Treatments by both these approaches were found to be effective in suppressing ongoing EAMG. Treatment by IP-10-specific antibodies led to decreased mRNA expression of IP-10 and CXCL9 and increased expression levels of CXCR3 and the IP-10 inducer, IFN-γ but had no significant effect on AChR-specific responses. Treatment by the CXCR3 antagonist led to a reduction in humoral and cellular AChR-specific responses but had no significant effects on the expression levels of CXCR3 and its ligands. These observations in EAMG suggest that inhibitors of IP-10/CXCR3 signaling should be considered as potential treatment modalities for MG.

3.1.2. CXCR4 and SDF-1 (CXCL12)

CXCR4 is a chemokine receptor that is mainly expressed on memory T cells and most immature thymocytes and is required for migration of thymic regulatory T cells (Treg) to secondary lymphoid tissue. CXCR4 is specific for stromal-derived-factor-1 (SDF-1, CXCL12), a molecule with potent chemotactic activity for lymphocytes. But SDF-1 binds also to another receptor - CXCR7. SDF-1 is important in hematopoietic stem cell homing to the bone marrow and in hematopoietic stem cell quiescence and acts as a B cell growth factor. SDF-1 is also secreted by injured tissues, and is therefore involved in chemoattracting CXCR4$^+$ stem cells for repair and remodeling of smooth blood vessel wall muscles after injury and of infracted heart cells (28, 29). CXCR7, the other receptor for SDF-1 is expressed on marginal zone B cells, a cell type associated with autoimmune diseases, and has a role in endothelial biology and valve development (30).

Deregulated expression of CXCR4 and SDF-1 has been reported in a number of autoimmune diseases. The synovium of RA patients was shown to contain increased levels of CXCR4 and SDF-1 expressing memory T cells (31). In diabetes, CXCR4 and SDF-1 expression was elevated in inflamed pancreatic islets and CXCR4 was elevated also in pancreatic LNC (32).

In rat EAMG, CXCR4 mRNA levels start to increase when disease symptoms appear (Feferman et al, unpublished). Moreover, a good correlation was found between CXCR4 expression and severity of disease in individual rats (Fig. 1). Expression levels of SDF-1 in LNC of EAMG rats did not differ from those of CFA-injected controls. No differences in the mRNA expression levels of either CXCR4 or SDF-1 were observed in the muscles of myasthenic rats compared with control CFA-injected rats. Attempts to affect the course of EAMG by a CXCR4 inhibitor, (BKT140 produced by Biokine), which was successful in suppressing collagen-induced RA in mice (33), are now underway in our lab. In humans, CXCR4 is expressed on most thymocytes and SDF-1 is highly expressed by thymic epithelial cells (TEC). There were no significant differences in the thymic expression of CXCR4 and SDF-1 between MG patients and healthy controls. However, this analysis could not exclude minor changes that are difficult to evaluate because of the high level of expression of SDF-1 and CXCR4 in normal thymuses (Berrih-Aknin et al., unpublished).

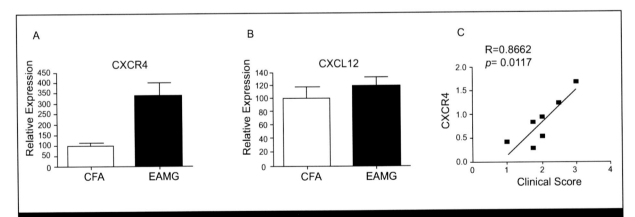

CXCR4 (A) and CXCL 12(SDF-1) expression in EAMG

Figure 1: Lymph node cells were harvested from CFA and AChR-immunized EAMG rats 8 weeks after disease induction. The mRNA expression levels of CXCR4 (A) and CXCL 12 (B) were determined by quantitative real time RT-PCR. Data are presented as relative expression values for the EAMG induced group compared with the control CFA injected group, which were assigned a value of 100. β-actin was used for normalization for each gene. (C) correlation between the expression levels of CXCR4 and disease severity in LNC of EAMG rats.

3.1.3. CXCR5 and its ligands

The chemokine receptor CXCR5 regulates lymphocyte migration and is expressed on mature B cells and on a subset of non-Th1 non-Th2 T CD4$^+$ memory T cells named follicular helper T cells (T$_{FH}$s) (34-36). It is involved in B cell migration and localization within specific compartments in lymphoid organs. Knockout mice lacking CXCR5 lack inguinal lymph nodes and possess no or only few phenotypically abnormal Peyer's patches. The migration of their lymphocytes into splenic follicles is severely impaired, resulting in morphologically altered primary lymphoid follicles (37). Both T$_{FH}$s and B cells are localized to the B follicles of secondary lymphoid organ and are attracted by CXCL13 (B cell attracting chemokine-1, BCA-1) which is produced in B follicles by follicular DC (38,39), germinal center (GC) specific CD4$^+$ CD57$^+$ T cells (40,41) and TEC (42). CXCL13 is highly attractive for B cells and is important in GC formation and maintenance under physiological conditions (43-45).

MG patients were shown to have a significantly higher frequency of CXCR5$^+$ CD4$^+$ T cells in their peripheral blood compared with controls (46). The increased CXCR5$^+$ CD4$^+$ T cell frequency correlated with disease severity but no significant differences were found between patients with thymic hyperplasia and those with thymoma. The CXCR5$^+$ CD4$^+$ T cell frequency in MG patients that were positive for other autoantibodies in addition to anti-AChR antibodies was significantly higher than in those having only anti-AChR antibodies suggesting that some MG patients have systemic abnormalities in antibody production mediated by T$_{FH}$s. After therapy by thymectomy together with glucocorticoids the CXCR5$^+$ CD4$^+$ T cell percentage decreased gradually to control levels with a significant inverse correlation between the CXCR5$^+$ CD4$^+$ T cell frequency and duration after the initiation of MG therapy.

CXCL13 was shown to be overexpressed in thymuses of seropositive MG patients with a low or high degree of hyperplasia and in thymuses of seronegative MG patients (23). The expression of CXCL13 was shown to be increased in TEC and sera of MG patients that were not treated by glucocorticoid and decreased in response to such treatment in correlation with clinical improvement (42,47). Anti-CXCL13 antibodies inhibited the chemoattracting effect that thymic extracts from glucocorticoid-untreated patients had on normal B cells (42). These observations suggest that the excess production of CXCL13 by TEC could be responsible for germinal center formation in MG thymuses and for the massive B cell infiltration into the thymus in MG patients. Furthermore, they suggest that the CXCL13 gene is a main target for corticosteroid therapy. Thus, new therapies targeting CXCL13 could be of interest for MG and other autoimmune diseases that are characterized by ectopic germinal center formation. Models of mice overexpressing CXCL13 in TEC are now under investigation (Berrih-Aknin et al., unpublished).

3.2. CCR receptors

There are currently eleven CC-specific receptors designated CCR1 to CCR11. Several lines of evidence implicate CCR1 in the pathophysiology of RA and MS (4) but its involvement in myasthenia is suggested only by the observation that MG patients with thymic hyperplasia have significantly increased expression of CCR1 on CD4$^+$ and CD8$^+$ cells that is reduced to control level after therapy. No significant changes in the frequencies of CCR2, CCR3, CCR4, and CCR5 were observed in peripheral blood T cells of MG patients (22). In the context of myasthenia we will describe here the chemokine receptors CCR2, CCR5 and CCR7.

3.2.1 CCR2, CCR5 and their ligands

CCR2 is expressed on a variety of cell types, including monocytes, basophils, activated T lymphocytes, DC, and endothelial and vascular smooth muscle cells. CCR2 also binds several chemokines: CCL2 (monocyte chemoattractant protein; MCP-1), CCL7 (MCP-3), CCL8 (MCP-2) and CCL13 (MCP-4) (10). The main function of CCR2 (also called monocyte chemoattractant protein-1 receptor) is to recruit leukocytes from the circulation into sites of trauma, bacterial and mycobacterial infection, toxin exposure and ischemia thus playing an important role in human inflammatory states. CCR2 and CCR5 interact primarily with the human CC family ligands CCL2 (MCP-1), CCL3 (macrophage inflammatory protein-1 alpha ; MIP-ld) and CCL4 (MIP-1β). CCL2 is expressed by inflammatory cells at sites of tissue injury. Its role is to direct the migration of monocytes, DC, NK and T cells and coordinates inflammatory responses during infection (15). CCR2 and its ligands have been implicated in the pathophysiology of autoimmune diseases including RA and MS (10). These studies suggest that CCR2 has an important role in monocyte recruitment and in Th1 type inflammatory diseases.

CCL2 (MCP-1) was shown to play a critical role in the pathogenesis of EAMG. CCL2 is overexpressed in mouse EAMG (48-50). CCL2$^{-/-}$ mice develop mild EAMG correlated with a reduced anti-AChR IgG2b response which is responsible for the impairment of the neuromuscular transmission. It has been suggested that CCL2 is involved in the pathogenesis of EAMG via its effect on the development of pathogenic autoreactive Th17 cells in secondary lymphoid organs (48). In addition, Reyes-Reyna et al., (50) have shown that CCL2 levels produced by a Lewis rat skeletal muscle cell line (LE1) were upregulated when exposed to IFN-γ. This was demonstrated also *in vivo* in experimental myasthenia induced by passive transfer of mAb 35 and suggests that the muscle may contribute to progression of myasthenia by producing factors that influence activities of the immune system (50) as discussed above for CXCR3 and IP-10 (21).

CCR5 and its ligands are probably also involved in the pathogenesis of myasthenia. The CCR5 ligand RANTES (CCL5) and IL-6 levels were abnormally augmented in TEC cultures derived *in vitro* from normal or hyperplastic age-matched MG thymuses, Elevation was observed at basal conditions and after induction by adhesion-related stimuli. IL-6 and RANTES were found to modulate, respectively, survival and migration of peripheral lymphocytes of myasthenic patients suggesting their involvement in the pathological remodeling of the thymus in MG (51). It should be noted that mRNA expression of the C-C chemokines RANTES, MCP, MIP-1α and MIP-2 has not been detected in muscles of EAMG rats (52).

3.2.2 CCR7 and its ligands

CCR7 is essential for the localization of naïve T cells and central memory T cells to the thymus and to secondary lymphoid organs. CCR7 ligands guide the migration of mature DC to the thymus to present antigens to T cells. CCR7$^{-/-}$ mice show morphological abnormalities in lymphoid organs and impaired homing of lymphocytes and DC to these organs. The binding of the homeostatic chemokines CCL19 (also called ELC) and CCL21 (also called secondary lymphoid-tissue chemokine, SLC) to their receptor, CCR7 is involved in lymphocyte migration to the thymus (10, 15). CCL19 and CCL21 localize in medullary vessels and act through CCR7 as their chemotactic receptor in the thymus, but they differ in their role in T cell migration. CCL21 guides the migration of developing T cells from the cortex to the medulla of the thymus, while CCL19 guides the migration of mature T cells out of the thymus.

MG thymuses presenting a high degree of hyperplasia are characterized by the presence of numerous germinal centers and an overexpression of CCL21 compared to healthy controls, to MG patients presenting low or no hyperplasia and to seronegative MG patients (23). The different chemotactic properties found in hypreplastic thymuses suggest that the specific overexpression of CCL21 in these thymuses triggers their ectopic germinal center formation (53).

The overexpression of CCL21 in MG thymuses was found especially around extralobular blood vessels where the CD44^{high} cell population accumulates (54) suggesting that DC may migrate into the hyperplastic thymus from the vascular system via mechanisms that involve CD44 and CCL21. DC may present self-antigens, such as AChR, thereby promoting the priming and/or boosting of potentially autoreactive T cells that are directed against AChR that is expressed by TEC. In contrast to the elevation of CCL21 in hyperplastic thymuses of MG patients, there were no significant differences in the levels of CCR7 and CCL19 between MG and control thymuses (54), although CCL19 was increased in highly hyperplastic thymuses of MG patients compared to healthy controls (53).

CXCL13 described earlier is upregulated in all MG groups whereas CCL21 is overexpressed in MG hyperplastic thymuses. These two chemokines may cooperate in guiding the generalized B cell infiltration and the attraction of activated T cells to the thymus. These T cells retain their activated state due to the pro-inflammatory environment in the thymus and to the defect in the suppressive activity of Treg in MG patients (47).

4. DEVELOPMENT OF NOVEL CHEMOKINE-BASED TREATMENTS FOR MG

Evidence accumulated over the past decade points to the key role of chemokines and chemokine receptor in the pathogenesis of autoimmune diseases. Chemokine networks have therefore attracted considerable interest as potential drug targets and led to the development of a rapidly expanding number of antagonists that hold promise for new treatment modalities to combat autoimmune diseases. However, in spite of the vast efforts to identify novel, safe and effective therapeutics based on chemokine network antagonists, these goals have so far not been fully achieved. A number of clinical trials have been initiated to assess the efficacy of chemokine receptor antagonists for the treatment of autoimmune diseases such as MS (CCR1, CCR2), RA (CCR1, CCR2, CCR5), irritable bowel syndrome and Croh'n disease (CCR9) and psoriasis (CXCR3) (reviewed in (4)). Some of these trials are now ongoing while others have failed due to various possible reasons (10) including the fact that some autoimmune diseases involve more than one chemokine network. An even greater challenge is posed by the great degree of redundancy in the chemokine receptor system which complicates the development of effective and selective antagonists. Some chemokines bind with high affinity to more than one receptor and some chemokines that are agonists for one receptor can be natural antagonists for others (5). This suggests that in some instances targeting of more than one receptor may be required to obtain optimal effects. The latter was demonstrated in animal models by the efficacy of combined CXCR3/CCR5 blocking of allograft rejection (55) and development of asthma (56).

Most of the studies on chemokine involvement in autoimmune diseases focus on conditions in which there is an excessive recruitment of leukocytes, the hallmark of inflammation, into the target organ or tissue. This may explain why studies on chemokine involvement in MG are so scarce. However, although prominent cellular infiltrates are not characteristically observed in the target muscles of MG patients, these could be missed since they may occur during the early onset of disease before patients seek medical help. Moreover, transient chemoattraction of small numbers of cytokine producing leukocytes to the muscle may lead to cytokine and chemokine production by myocytes or promote other interactions between leukocytes and muscle.

Chemokines govern also the traffic of immune cells between lymphoid organs and the periphery. Given the central role of the thymus in the pathogenesis of human MG, chemokines like CXCL13 and CCL21 which are overexpressed in the thymus of MG patients may be involved in the ectopic germinal center formation in the thymus of these patients. Chemokine networks may also be involved in the migration of effector and Treg cells from the bone marrow to lymphoid organs, between lymphoid organs and from them to the periphery.

The intervention in chemokine networks can be performed by interfering with either receptor or chemokine function. The ideal therapeutic would be orally administered small molecule inhibitors that would either act as receptor antagonists or as chemokine blocker. Each of these approaches has its advantages and drawbacks. Chemokine receptor antagonists enable to block all signaling by a single receptor independent of the chemokine ligand inducing it, whereas specific chemokine blockers are more ligand specific. However due to the apparent redundancy in the chemokine networks the advantage of such specificity needs to be assessed. As described above both approaches were effective in suppressing EAMG by interference in the signaling of CXCL10 with its receptor CXCR3 (27). In this study, a small molecule CXCR3 antagonist as well as anti-CXCL10 antibodies were both effective in modulating EAMG. This is to our knowledge the only report on modulation of experimental myasthenia by targeting chemokine networks. Hopefully more studies on the involvement of chemokine networks in the pathogenesis of myasthenia will be performed and will lead to chemokine-based clinical trials in MG patients.

REFERENCES

1. Zlotnik, A., and O. Yoshie. 2000. Chemokines: a new classification system and their role in immunity. *Immunity 12:121*.

2. Murphy, P. M., M. Baggiolini, I. F. Charo, C. A. Hebert, R. Horuk, K. Matsushima, L. H. Miller, J. J. Oppenheim, and C. A. Power. 2000. International union of pharmacology. XXII. Nomenclature for chemokine receptors. *Pharmacol Rev 52:145*.

3. Horuk, R. 2001. Chemokine receptors. *Cytokine Growth Factor Rev 12:313*.

4. Horuk, R. 2009. Chemokine receptor antagonists: overcoming developmental hurdles. *Nat Rev Drug Discov 8:23*.

5. Ogilvie, P., G. Bardi, I. Clark-Lewis, M. Baggiolini, and M. Uguccioni. 2001. Eotaxin is a natural antagonist for CCR2 and an agonist for CCR5. *Blood 97:1920*.

6. Proudfoot, A. E., A. L. de Souza, and V. Muzio. 2008. The use of chemokine antagonists in EAE models. *J Neuroimmunol 198:27*.

7. Ribeiro, S., and R. Horuk. 2005. The clinical potential of chemokine receptor antagonists. *Pharmacol Ther 107:44*.

8. Karpus, W. J., and R. M. Ransohoff. 1998. Chemokine regulation of experimental autoimmune encephalomyelitis: temporal and spatial expression patterns govern disease pathogenesis. *J Immunol 161:2667*.

9. Thornton, S., L. E. Duwel, G. P. Boivin, Y. Ma, and R. Hirsch. 1999. Association of the course of collagen-induced arthritis with distinct patterns of cytokine and chemokine messenger RNA expression. *Arthritis Rheum 42:1109*.

10. Proudfoot, A. E. 2002. Chemokine receptors: multifaceted therapeutic targets. *Nat Rev Immunol 2:106*.

11. Narumi, S., T. Takeuchi, Y. Kobayashi, and K. Konishi. 2000. Serum levels of IFd-inducible Protein-10 relating to the activity of systemic lupus erythematosus. *Cytokine 12:1561*.

12. Boven, L. A., L. Montagne, H. S. Nottet, and C. J. De Groot. 2000. Macrophage inflammatory protein-1alpha (MIP-1alpha), MIP-1beta, and RANTES mRNA semiquantification and protein expression in active demyelinating multiple sclerosis (MS) lesions. *Clin Exp Immunol 122:257*.

13. Simpson, J., P. Rezaie, J. Newcombe, M. L. Cuzner, D. Male, and M. N. Woodroofe. 2000. Expression of the beta-chemokine receptors CCR2, CCR3 and CCR5 in multiple sclerosis central nervous system tissue. *J Neuroimmunol 108:192*.

14. Boiardi, L., P. Macchioni, R. Meliconi, L. Pulsatelli, A. Facchini, and C. Salvarani. 1999. Relationship between serum RANTES levels and radiological progression in rheumatoid arthritis patients treated with methotrexate. *Clin Exp Rheumatol 17:419*.

15. Charo, I. F., and R. M. Ransohoff. 2006. The many roles of chemokines and chemokine receptors in inflammation. *N Engl J Med 354:610*.

16. Henneken, M., T. Dorner, G. R. Burmester, and C. Berek. 2005. Differential expression of chemokine receptors on peripheral blood B cells from patients with rheumatoid arthritis and systemic lupus erythematosus. *Arthritis Res Ther 7:R1001*.

17. Janatpour, M. J., S. Hudak, M. Sathe, J. D. Sedgwick, and L. M. McEvoy. 2001. Tumor necrosis factor-dependent segmental control of MIG expression by high endothelial venules in inflamed lymph nodes regulates monocyte recruitment. *J Exp Med 194:1375*.

18. Johnston, B., C. H. Kim, D. Soler, M. Emoto, and E. C. Butcher. 2003. Differential chemokine responses and homing patterns of murine TCR alpha beta NKT cell subsets. *J Immunol 171:2960*.

19. Qin, S., J. B. Rottman, P. Myers, N. Kassam, M. Weinblatt, M. Loetscher, A. E. Koch, B. Moser, and C. R. Mackay. 1998. The chemokine receptors CXCR3 and CCR5 mark subsets of T cells associated with certain inflammatory reactions. *J Clin Invest 101:746*.

20. Neville, L. F., G. Mathiak, and O. Bagasra. 1997. The immunobiology of interferon-gamma inducible protein 10 kD (IP-10): a novel, pleiotropic member of the C-X-C chemokine superfamily. *Cytokine Growth Factor Rev 8:207*.

21. Feferman, T., P. K. Maiti, S. Berrih-Aknin, J. Bismuth, J. Bidault, S. Fuchs, and M. C. Souroujon. 2005. Overexpression of IFN-induced protein 10 and its receptor CXCR3 in myasthenia gravis. *J Immunol 174:5324*.

22. Suzuki, Y., H. Onodera, H. Tago, R. Saito, M. Ohuchi, M. Shimizu, Y. Matsumura, T. Kondo, O. Yoshie, and Y. Itoyama. 2006. Altered expression of Th1-type chemokine receptor CXCR3 on CD4+ T cells in myasthenia gravis patients. *J Neuroimmunol 172:166*.

23. Le Panse, R., G. Cizeron-Clairac, J. Bismuth, and S. Berrih-Aknin. 2006. Microarrays reveal distinct gene signatures in the thymus of seropositive and seronegative myasthenia gravis patients and the role of CC chemokine ligand 21 in thymic hyperplasia. *J Immunol 177:7868*.

24. Raju, R., O. Vasconcelos, R. Granger, and M. C. Dalakas. 2003. Expression of IFN-gamma-inducible chemokines in inclusion body myositis. *J Neuroimmunol 141:125*.

25. Cole, K. E., C. A. Strick, T. J. Paradis, K. T. Ogborne, M. Loetscher, R. P. Gladue, W. Lin, J. G. Boyd, B. Moser, D. E. Wood, B. G. Sahagan, and K. Neote. 1998. Interferon-inducible T cell alpha chemoattractant (I-TAC): a novel non-ELR CXC chemokine with potent activity on activated T cells through selective high affinity binding to CXCR3. *J Exp Med 187:2009*.

26. Xia, M. Q., B. J. Bacskai, R. B. Knowles, S. X. Qin, and B. T. Hyman. 2000. Expression of the chemokine receptor CXCR3 on neurons and the elevated expression of its ligand IP-10 in reactive astrocytes: in vitro ERK1/2 activation and role in Alzheimer's disease. *J Neuroimmunol 108:227*.

27. Feferman, T., R. Aricha, K. Mizrachi, E. Geron, R. Alon, M. C. Souroujon, and S. Fuchs. 2009. Suppression of experimental autoimmune myasthenia gravis by inhibiting the signaling between IFN-gamma inducible protein 10 (IP-10) and its receptor CXCR3. *J Neuroimmunol*.

28. Schober, A. 2008. Chemokines in vascular dysfunction and remodeling. *Arterioscler Thromb Vasc Biol 28:1950*.

29. Czarnowska, E., M. Gajerska-Dzieciatkowska, K. Kusmierski, J. Lichomski, E. K. Machaj, Z. Pojda, M. Brudek, and A. Beresewicz. 2007. Expression of SDF-1-CXCR4 axis and an anti-remodelling effectiveness of foetal-liver stem cell transplantation in the infarcted rat heart. *J Physiol Pharmacol 58:729*.

30. Sierro, F., C. Biben, L. Martinez-Munoz, M. Mellado, R. M. Ransohoff, M. Li, B. Woehl, H. Leung, J. Groom, M. Batten, R. P. Harvey, A. C. Martinez, C. R. Mackay, and F. Mackay. 2007. Disrupted cardiac development but normal hematopoiesis in mice deficient in the second CXCL12/SDF-1 receptor, CXCR7. *Proc Natl Acad Sci U S A 104:14759*.

31. Nanki, T., K. Hayashida, H. S. El-Gabalawy, S. Suson, K. Shi, H. J. Girschick, S. Yavuz, and P. E. Lipsky. 2000. Stromal cell-derived factor-1-CXC chemokine receptor 4 interactions play a central role in CD4+ T cell accumulation in rheumatoid arthritis synovium. *J Immunol 165:6590*.

32. Aboumrad, E., A. M. Madec, and C. Thivolet. 2007. The CXCR4/CXCL12 (SDF-1) signalling pathway protects non-obese diabetic mouse from autoimmune diabetes. *Clin Exp Immunol 148:432*.

33. Tamamura, H., M. Fujisawa, K. Hiramatsu, M. Mizumoto, H. Nakashima, N. Yamamoto, A. Otaka, and N. Fujii. 2004. Identification of a CXCR4 antagonist, a T140 analog, as an anti-rheumatoid arthritis agent. *FEBS Lett 569:99*.

34. Moser, B., and L. Ebert. 2003. Lymphocyte traffic control by chemokines: follicular B helper T cells. *Immunol Lett 85:105*.

35. Moser, B., P. Schaerli, and P. Loetscher. 2002. CXCR5(+) T cells: follicular homing takes center stage in T-helper-cell responses. *Trends Immunol 23:250*.

36. Yoshie, O., T. Imai, and H. Nomiyama. 2001. Chemokines in immunity. *Adv Immunol 78:57*.

37. Forster, R., A. E. Mattis, E. Kremmer, E. Wolf, G. Brem, and M. Lipp. 1996. A putative chemokine receptor, BLR1, directs B cell migration to defined lymphoid organs and specific anatomic compartments of the spleen. *Cell 87:1037*.

38. Gunn, M. D., V. N. Ngo, K. M. Ansel, E. H. Ekland, J. G. Cyster, and L. T. Williams. 1998. A B-cell-homing chemokine made in lymphoid follicles activates Burkitt's lymphoma receptor-1. *Nature 391:799*.

39. Legler, D. F., M. Loetscher, R. S. Roos, I. Clark-Lewis, M. Baggiolini, and B. Moser. 1998. B cell-attracting chemokine 1, a human CXC chemokine expressed in lymphoid tissues, selectively attracts B lymphocytes via BLR1/CXCR5. *J Exp Med 187:655*.

40. Bowen, M. B., A. W. Butch, C. A. Parvin, A. Levine, and M. H. Nahm. 1991. Germinal center T cells are distinct helper-inducer T cells. *Hum Immunol 31:67*.

41. Kim, C. H., H. W. Lim, J. R. Kim, L. Rott, P. Hillsamer, and E. C. Butcher. 2004. Unique gene expression program of human germinal center T helper cells. *Blood 104:1952*.

42. Meraouna, A., G. Cizeron-Clairac, R. L. Panse, J. Bismuth, F. Truffault, C. Tallaksen, and S. Berrih-Aknin. 2006. The chemokine CXCL13 is a key molecule in autoimmune myasthenia gravis. *Blood 108:432*.

43. Cyster, J. G. 1999. Chemokines and cell migration in secondary lymphoid organs. *Science 286:2098*.

44. Muller, G., U. E. Hopken, and M. Lipp. 2003. The impact of CCR7 and CXCR5 on lymphoid organ development and systemic immunity. *Immunol Rev 195:117*.

45. Allen, C. D., K. M. Ansel, C. Low, R. Lesley, H. Tamamura, N. Fujii, and J. G. Cyster. 2004. Germinal center dark and light zone organization is mediated by CXCR4 and CXCR5. *Nat Immunol 5:943*.

46. Saito, R., H. Onodera, H. Tago, Y. Suzuki, M. Shimizu, Y. Matsumura, T. Kondo, and Y. Itoyama. 2005. Altered expression of chemokine receptor CXCR5 on T cells of myasthenia gravis patients. *J Neuroimmunol 170:172*.

47. Le Panse, R., G. Cizeron-Clairac, M. Cuvelier, F. Truffault, J. Bismuth, P. Nancy, N. K. De Rosbo, and S. Berrih-Aknin. 2008. Regulatory and pathogenic mechanisms in human autoimmune myasthenia gravis. *Ann N Y Acad Sci 1132:135*.

48. Bai, Y., R. Liu, D. Huang, A. La Cava, Y. Y. Tang, Y. Iwakura, D. I. Campagnolo, T. L. Vollmer, R. M. Ransohoff, and F. D. Shi. 2008. CCL2 recruitment of IL-6-producing CD11b+ monocytes to the draining lymph nodes during the initiation of Th17-dependent B cell-mediated autoimmunity. *Eur J Immunol 38:1877.*

49. Reyes-Reyna, S. M., and K. A. Krolick. 2000. Chemokine production by rat myocytes exposed to interferon-gamma. *Clin Immunol 94:105.*

50. Reyes-Reyna, S., T. Stegall, and K. A. Krolick. 2002. Muscle responds to an antibody reactive with the acetylcholine receptor by up-regulating monocyte chemoattractant protein 1: a chemokine with the potential to influence the severity and course of experimental myasthenia gravis. *J Immunol 169:1579.*

51. Colombara, M., V. Antonini, A. P. Riviera, F. Mainiero, R. Strippoli, M. Merola, G. Fracasso, O. Poffe, N. Brutti, G. Tridente, M. Colombatti, and D. Ramarli. 2005. Constitutive activation of p38 and ERK1/2 MAPKs in epithelial cells of myasthenic thymus leads to IL-6 and RANTES overexpression: effects on survival and migration of peripheral T and B cells. *J Immunol 175:7021.*

52. Li, H., F. D. Shi, X. Bai, Y. Huang, A. Diab, B. He, and H. Link. 1998. Cytokine and chemokine mRNA expressing cells in muscle tissues of experimental autoimmune myasthenia gravis. *J Neurol Sci 161:40.*

53. Berrih-Aknin, S., N. Ruhlmann, J. Bismuth, G. Cizeron-Clairac, E. Zelman, I. Shachar P. Dartevelle, N. Kerlero de Rosbo and R. Le Panse. 2009. CCL21 overexpressed on lymphatic vessels drives thymic hyperplasia in Myasthenia. *Annals of Neurology,* 66:52-31

54. Nagane, Y., K. Utsugisawa, D. Obara, M. Yamagata, and H. Tohgi. 2003. Dendritic cells in hyperplastic thymuses from patients with myasthenia gravis. *Muscle Nerve 27:582.*

55. Schnickel, G. T., S. Bastani, G. R. Hsieh, A. Shefizadeh, R. Bhatia, M. C. Fishbein, J. Belperio, and A. Ardehali. 2008. Combined CXCR3/CCR5 blockade attenuates acute and chronic rejection. *J Immunol 180:4714.*

56. Suzuki, K., T. Morokata, K. Morihira, I. Sato, S. Takizawa, M. Kaneko, K. Takahashi, and Y. Shimizu. 2007. A dual antagonist for chemokine CCR3 receptor and histamine H1 receptor. *Eur J Pharmacol 563:224.*

The Immunopathogenesis of Experimental Autoimmune Myasthenia Gravis Induced by Autoantibodies Against Muscle-specific Kinase (MuSK EAMG)

Kazuhiro Shigemoto M.D., Ph.D., Sachiho Kubo, Syuuichi Mori Ph.D., Shigeru Yamada Ph.D., Tsuyoshi Miyazaki M.D., Ph.D., Takuyu Akiyoshi M.D., and Naoki Maruyama M.D., Ph.D.

1. INTRODUCTION

Myasthenia gravis (MG) is the most common disorder of neuromuscular synapses and well-recognized for such characteristic clinical features as ptosis, fatigue and muscular weakness. Ptosis and diplopia occur early in most of these patients. With passing time, when the weakness of bulbar and respiratory muscles worsens, the disease becomes life-threatening so that intubation with mechanical ventilation is required. In 1905, Buzzard postulated that a circulating "autotoxic agent" causes the muscle weakness as lymphocytes infiltrate muscles and tumors of the thymus gland. He also believed that such muscle degeneration was closely related to Graves disease and Addison disease, both of which are now regarded as autoimmune diseases. In 1960, Simpson and, independently, Nastuk et al. proposed that MG is caused by an autoimmune mechanism.

In 1973, seminal studies done by Patrick and Lindstrom first demonstrated that autoantibodies against nicotinic acetylcholine receptors (AChRs) at neuromuscular junctions (NMJs) cause MG. This conclusion came from their work with an animal model they called experimental autoimmune myasthenia gravis (EAMG) (1). To develop this model, they inoculated rabbits with AChR protein purified from electric eels and showed that the resulting AChR antibodies induced muscle weakness and paralysis. In fact, these antibodies produced in response to the eel AChR protein cross-reacted with rabbit AChRs at the NMJs. The flaccid paralysis and results from electrophysiological studies of animals with EAMG closely resembled manifestations in patients with MG. In 1976, Lindstrom used the newly developed immunoprecipitation assay of that sera with radio-labeled human AChRs and discovered that approximately 80% of patients with MG had serum antibodies to AChRs (2). Further, histological and functional studies of NMJs in both MG patients and animals with AChR EAMG demonstrated a loss of AChR numbers and function and failure of neuromuscular transmission leading to muscle weakness (3, 4). However, ~20% of MG patients' autoantigens were never identified, although accumulating evidence showed the existence of autoantibodies against NMJs. MG patients bearing the latter autoantibodies responded well to plasma exchange and immunosuppressive therapies (5). Additionally, passive transfer of plasma immunoglobulin from such MG patients into mice caused a failure of neuromuscular transmission as shown by electrophysiological studies (6).

In 2001, Hoch and Vincent found autoantibodies against muscle-specific kinase (MuSK) in 70% of generalized MG patients who lacked antibodies to AChRs and demonstrated that MuSK antibodies in the sera inhibited MuSK functions in culture myotubes (7). MuSK is indispensable for neuromuscular development, as proven when MuSK knockout mice failed to form AChR clusters or differentiate postsynaptic regions and, therefore, died perinatally (8). Considering its performance of such functions in developing NMJs, MuSK seemed to be the long-sought autoantigen in MG patients; nevertheless, the pathogenic role of anti-MuSK antibodies has been unclear. First, no experimental animal model of MG has been induced by MuSK (9). Second, passive transfer of MuSK antisera from MG patients does not generate the equivalent disease in mice. Apparently the pathogenicity of anti-MuSK antibodies still requires proof by establishing an EAMG like that incited by AChRs (9).

In 2006, for the first time, the inoculation of rabbits with purified MuSK protein caused a loss of AChRs and muscular weakness by disrupting neuromuscular transmission (10). Next, MuSK EAMG was also successfully established in mice (11, 12). In 2008, passive transfer of a large amount of MuSK antibodies from MG patients into mice caused EAMG (13). Therefore, the pathogenicity of MuSK antibodies has now been proven by inciting MG experimentally via active immunization with MuSK and also by passive transfer of MuSK antibodies from patients with MG.

However, if we turn our attention to the clinical studies of MG patients with anti-MuSK antibodies (termed MuSK-MG patients), several complex issues remain unresolved. First, no significant loss of AChRs at NMJs was observed in biopsies from biceps brachii muscles of MuSK-MG patients (14). Second, MuSK antibodies are mainly in the IgG4 subclass, which does not activate complement (15-17), yet complement-mediated damage to postsynaptic membranes is considered a major source of pathogenicity in MG patients with AChR antibodies. Third, a number of clinical studies have shown that MuSK MG constitutes a distinct subclass of the disease (18-20). MuSK-MG patients more often develop severe muscle weakness and eventual atrophy than AChR-MG patients, and the former respond differently to therapy than persons in the latter group. Fourth, although antibodies to AChR in MuSK-MG sera have barely been detected using routine radio-immunoprecipitation assays, low affinity IgG and IgM antibodies to AChR were detected with an immunofluorescent technique in some MuSK-MG patients by using human embryonic kidney cells expressing recombinant AChR subunits on the cell surface (21). Studies of MuSK EAMG will contribute to understanding both the pathogenicity of anti-MuSK antibodies and the clinical features of MG patients.

In this chapter, we will first describe the EAMG caused by anti-MuSK antibodies and discuss the possible pathogenic roles of the antibodies associated with the clinical features of MuSK-MG patients. Finally, we suggest the wisdom of using animals with MuSK EAMG for the development of more effective medication.

2. INDUCTION OF MUSK EAMG IN ANIMALS

The first piece of evidence that active immunization with MuSK protein induced MG-like muscle weakness in animals came from experiments with rabbits (10). The muscle weakness of such rabbits resembled that observed when purified AChR was first used to induce EAMG in rabbits (1). After anti-MuSK antibodies were generated by inoculating rabbits with recombinant soluble MuSK protein, the recipients developed flaccid paralysis. Even before Hoch and Vincent reported the existence of anti-MuSK antibodies in the sera of generalized MG patients (7), the ability of these antibodies to inhibit MuSK functions had been serendipitiously studied. Recombinant proteins from the extracellular portion of mouse MuSK were generated as antigens. The extracellular segment of MuSK comprised five distinct domains, i.e., four immunoglobulin-like domains and one cysteine-rich region. The fusion protein expression construct, which consisted of the mouse MuSK ectodomain with His-tag, was generated and transfected into COS-7 cells (Figure 1). The secreted recombinant MuSK-His proteins were purified by using histidine affinity columns. New Zealand White rabbits were then immunized with 100 to 400 µg of the purified MuSK recombinant protein. After three to four injections of MuSK protein, all of six rabbits manifested flaccid paralysis (Figure 2A). Sera from the paretic rabbits contained a high titer of anti-MuSK antibodies that reacted specifically with MuSK molecules on the surfaces of C2C12 myotubes as observed in sera from MG patients who were positive for anti-MuSK antibodies (7, 10). In repetitive electromyograms from one of these paretic rabbits, the retroauricular branch of the facial nerve was stimulated at 20 Hz, and recordings were taken from adjacent retroauricular muscle. The compound muscle action potential (CMAP) showed a decremental pattern, consistent with the typical MG (Figure 2B). However, injections of acetylcholinesterase inhibitor (Neostigmine) did not significantly reverse either the CMAP defect or the paralytic symptoms in the rabbit EAMG.

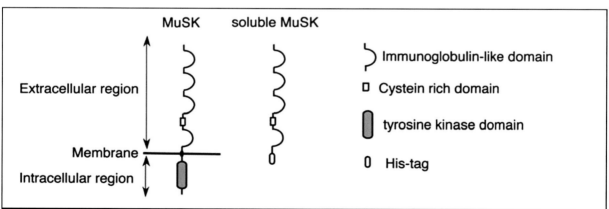

Figure 1. Schematic representation of MuSK proteins. Soluble recombinant protein of MuSK contains His-tag at the C-terminal end.

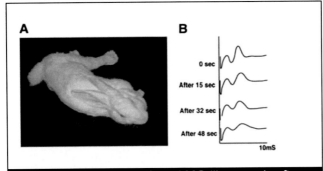

Figure 2. A rabbit manifested MG-like paresis after immunization with soluble MuSK protein (A). Electromyograms of the paretic rabbit show a decline in compound muscle action potential (CMAP) during repetitive nerve stimulation. (Reprinted with permission from Shigemoto et al., J Clin Invest 116:1016-1024).

Inoculation of MuSK protein also successfully caused MG-like weakness in mice (11, 12). In certain mouse strains, these injections with a recombinant rat-MuSK extracellular domain elicited clinical signs resembling those seen in MG patients. Additionally, the muscle weakness of MuSK-injected mice was similar to that observed in rabbits injected with purified AChR or MuSK (1, 10) and was accompanied by electrophysiological changes that resembled those of MG (Figure 3A). Injections of Neostigmine only partially reversed the CMAP defect (Figure 3B).

To assess susceptibility to muscle weakness caused by MuSK immunization in mice, four different strains of mice were injected with the same dose of MuSK proteins (11). Mice of the following strains: C57/BL6 (B6, n =25), A/J (n =15), B6.C-H-2 [bm12] (bm12, n =10) and BALB/c (n =5) were injected on days 0 and 28 with MuSK (10 μg/mouse) followed by a third injection at day 56 for mice without severe disease (23 B6, 6 A/J, 10 bm12 and 5 BALB/c mice). Muscle weakness was evaluated by an exercise test (Table 1). In three strains, B6, A/J and bm12, the majority of MuSK-injected mice responded with at least mild signs of fatigable muscle weakness after the second injection and severe signs of weakness after the third injection (Table 1).

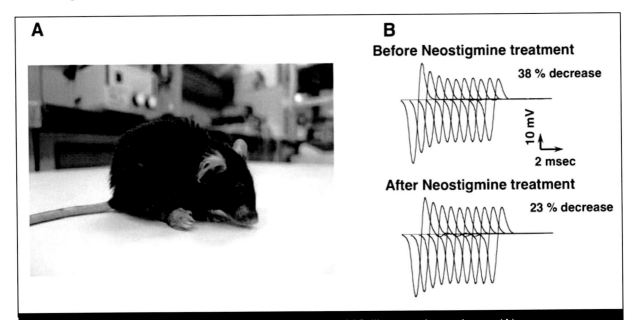

Figure 3. Injection of soluble MuSK protein mice induces MG-like muscle weakness (A). Electromyograms of the paretic mice show a decline in CMAP during repetitive nerve stimulation (B). Treatment of acetylcholine-esterase inhibitor (Neostigmine) can only partially improve the decremental response to repetitive nerve stimulation.

Table 1. Quantitative assessment of muscle weakness in four mouse strains after the second and third injections of MuSK.

Mice received injections of MuSK on days 0, 28 and 58. Grades for muscular strength were as follows: Grade 0, no weakness after exercise test consisting of 20 consecutive paw grips on cage-top steel grids; Grade 1 (moderately decreased activity), mild muscle fatigue after exercise; Grade 2 (markedly decreased activity), hunched posture at rest; Grade 3 (severe generalized weakness), loss of weight and inability to ambulate. (Reprinted from *J Neuroimmunol.* Jha et al., 175:107-117.2006 with permission from Elsevier.)

Strains	No.of injections	No. of mice	Muscle weakness MG grade				% mice showing EAMG	Average grade of all mice
			0	1	2	3		
B6 (H2^b)	2	25	8	6	8	3	68	1.24
	3	23	3	4	7	9	87	1.96
A/J (H2^a)	2	15	1	1	3	10	93	2.47
	3	6	0	1	1	4	100	2.50
bm12(H2^{bm12})	2	10	2	4	4	0	80	1.20
	3	10	2	2	3	3	80	1.70
BALB/c (H-2^d)	2	5	5	0	0	0	0	0.00
	3	5	5	0	0	0	0	0.00

Susceptibility to MG clearly differed among mouse strains. B6 and bm12 mice were highly susceptible, which coincided with their higher anti-MuSK-antibody responses. However, A/J mice were even more susceptible, and the most severely affected had lower titers of anti-MuSK antibodies compared to B6 and bm12 strains, which were clinically less affected (Table 1, Figure 4). The B6 and bm12 strains differ by only 3 amino acids in the β chain of the I-A subregion. We must note that A/J is one of the strains that develop a late onset (four to five months) progressive muscular dystrophy as a result of a homozygous retrotransposon insertion in the dysferlin (*Dysf*) gene, and phenotypes with such a mutation are natural models for limb girdle muscular dystrophy 2B (22). Thus, the A/J strain is genetically prone to muscle weakness even when myasthenia is not induced with MuSK immunization. Intriguingly, the BALB/c strain is highly resistant to both anti-MuSK-antibody production and manifestations of muscle weakness after MuSK immunization (Table1, Figure 4); therefore, genetic factors other than the Dysf gene must play a role in the regulation of this autoimmune disease in mice. An association with HLA-DR14-DQ5 (odds ratio 8.5) was found in 23 Dutch Caucasians with MuSK-MG (23), thus one genetic factor determining susceptibility or resistance to this disease might be MHC-subclass II genes, which control antibody production in mice as well as humans. Additionally, MHC-subclass II (H-2A) genes mediate immune responsiveness to AChRs in mice with EAMG (24, 25), whereas AChR MG of humans is associated with polymorphism of the HLA-DQ genes (26)

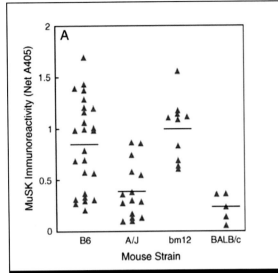

Figure 4. Immunoreactivity to Musk of antisera (dilution, 1:100,000) obtained after a second MuSK injection from individual mice. B6 and bm 12 mice produced the largest amount of anti-MuSK antibodies, followed by A/J and then by BALB/c mice. Antisera obtained after a third injection showed similar results. (Reprinted from *J Neuroimmunol.* Jha et al., 175:107-117.2006 with permission from Elsevier.)

Although active immunization of rabbits and mice with the extracellular domain of MuSK protein clearly demonstrated the pathogenicity of anti-MuSK antibodies in EAMG (10-12), the failure to incite EAMG by passive transfer of human anti-MuSK antibodies into adult mice still challenged the idea that anti-MuSK antibodies can cause MG in humans. Previous studies showed that passive transfer of anti-AChR-negative sera from MG patients into adult mice did not reduce AChRs at the postsynaptic membrane or cause myasthenia, but electrophysiological changes were present such as a reduction in miniature endplate potential amplitudes and endplate potential quantal content, which suggested the impairment of both pre- and post-synaptic transmission (5, 6, 27). In 2008, passive transfer of a large amount of IgG from MuSK MG patients into adult mice induced myasthenia with a significant reduction of AChR in the postsynaptic membrane and a decremental electromyographic trace on repetitive nerve stimulation (Figure 5) (13).

The inbred mice (C57BL/6J strains) were injected daily (intraperitoneally - IP) with 45mg human IgG from two patients (anti-MuSK-2; patient 2, and anti-MuSK-3; patient 3, in Figure 5A and B) for more than 5 days with a single IP injection of cyclophosphamide monohydrate 24 hours after the first IgG injection to suppress immune reactions against the human protein. After 14 days of injections, mice developed signs of weakness such as chin down, flaccid tail, and limb weakness with a prominent cervicothoracic hump (Figure 5D), which may reflect weak cervical extensor muscles. These features were also observed in mice with EAMG induced by MuSK immunization (11, 12). Mice injected with control IgG showed neither weight loss nor muscle weakness compared with uninjected mice (Figure 5C). Decremental electromyographies typical of MG patients were recorded in the mice injected with human anti-MuSK antibodies (Figure 5E). The evidence of EAMG from the passive transfers clearly demonstrated that anti-MuSK antibodies in MG patients cause their disease rather than being just bystander antibodies.

3. STRUCTURE OF NMJ

Before we discuss the pathogenic roles of MuSK antibodies in EAMG and patients, we should look at the structure of NMJs and MuSK functions. NMJs are the sites of synapses between motor nerves and muscle fibers (Figure 6). The NMJ comprises portions of three cells such as motor neurons, muscle fibers and Schwann cells (28, 29). The motor nerve terminal is specialized for neurotransmitter (acetylcholine:ACh) release. Synaptic vesicles storing ACh adjacent to specialized structures of the presynaptic membrane are called active zones. The active zones are

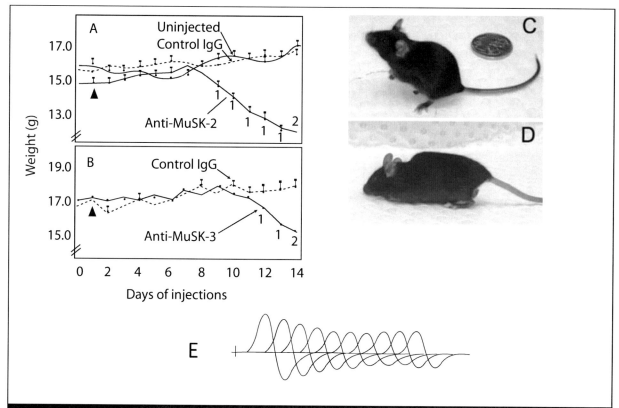

Figure 5. MG-like muscle weakness and weight loss in C57BL/6J mice after injection with anti-MuSK IgG purified from MuSK-MG patients. Mice injected with IgG from anti-MuSK-positive Patient 2 began to lose weight and develop muscle weakness from 9 to 12 days after the start of daily injections. Control IgG-injected and uninjected mice were not affected. Numbers besides symbols refer to the muscle weakness grading scale as described in Table 1. (B) In a separate experiment, mice injected with IgG from anti-MuSK-positive Patient 3 similarly lost weight and became weak. (C) Mouse after 14 days of injections with control IgG, showed no sign of weakness after the standard exercise regimen. Coin diameter was 28mm, (D) Mouse after 14 days of injections with IgG from anti-MuSK-positive Patient 2 showed muscle deterioration with chin down, flaccid tail and limb weakness. Note also the characteristic hump in the upper back. (E) Electromyography recorded from the gastrocnemius muscle of a C57BL/67 mouse injected for 14 days with IgG from anti-MuSK-positive Patient 2. Data represent means ± standard error of the mean for n=3 mice for all groups expect for mice injected with Patient 3 IgG. (B); the amount of IgG available was limited, so n=2. (Reprinted with permission from Cole et., *Ann Neurol* 63:782-7892008 C5713L/6j)

precisely opposite mouths of the postjunctional folds (30, 31). AChRs are highly concentrated, with a density of about 12,000 receptors per μm^2(32), at the post-junctional membrane nearest the fold's peak (Figure 6) (33). Rapsyn is co-localized with AChRs as a scaffold molecule and required for the clustering of AChRs (34). When the nerve action potential reaches the terminal, depolarization opens voltage-gated Ca^+ channels on the presynaptic membrane (35, 36). This allows a Ca^+ influx that triggers the fusion of synaptic vesicles with the presynaptic membrane and the release of ACh (37, 38). The postsynaptic membrane responds rapidly and dependably to ACh released from the overlying active zones in the nerve terminal. AChRs, by binding ACh, become transiently permeable to both Na^+ and K^+, then opening the associated voltage-gated ion channels in the depths of folds, which contribute to the action potential and muscle contraction

(28). The synaptic cleft between nerve terminals and the postsynaptic membrane is about 50 nm wide (39, 40). A layer of connective tissue called basal lamina (basement membrane) sheaths each muscle fiber, passes through the synaptic clef and extends into the junctional folds (29). Both the presynaptic terminal and the muscle fiber secrete molecules including collagen IV, laminin, ectactin and heparan sulfate proteoglycans (agrin, perlcan, etc.) to the basal lamina. However, synaptic portions of the basal lamina contain their distinctive isoform composition separate from that of the extrasynaptic portions. Synaptic basal lamina contains the enzyme acetylcholinesterase, which quickly inactivates the ACh released from the presynaptic terminal by hydrolyzing it to acetate and choline. Acetylcholinesterase is clustered with AChRs by association with collagen Q and MuSK at the crest of the junctional folds (41). Concentrations of released ACh in the synaptic cleft decrease rapidly by diffusion and interaction with acetylcholinesterase, upon which the neuromuscular transmission terminates.

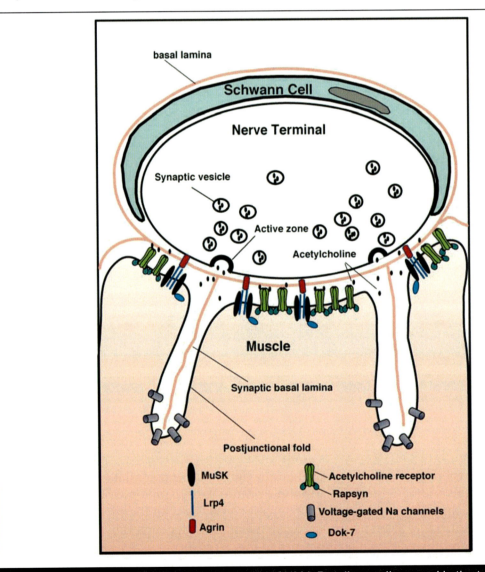

Figure 6. Structure and molecular architecture of NMJ. Details are discussed in the text.

4. MUSK FUNCTIONS IN NMJ

MuSK, which is a receptor-tyrosine kinase, is a component of the agrin receptor with the low-density-lipoprotein receptor-related protein 4 (LRP4) at the postsynaptic membrane (Figure 6) (8, 42-46). MuSK knock-out mice display devastating defects in both pre- and post-synaptic differentiation and die at birth because they cannot breathe, thus MuSK requires the formation of NMJs during neuromuscular development (8). In the knock-out mice, motor axons grow excessively and fail to form terminal arbors, and no AChR-rich clusters are present on myotubes opposing ingrowing motoneuron terminals as shown in Figure 7. Since MuSK is expressed in skeletal muscle but not in motor neurons (42), MuSK requires regulation of the retrograde signals for differentiation of pre-synaptic structures in NMJs (8).

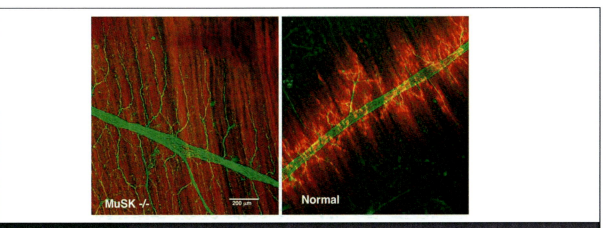

Figure 7. Aberrant Structure of pre- and postsynaptic differentiation in diaphragm muscle from MuSK-/- mutant mouse axon (green), AChR(red).

MuSK also plays multiple roles in AChR clustering during development of the postsynaptic membranes of NMJs (47, 48). Contact of the motor-nerve growth cone with the muscle induces a narrow, distinct endplate zone in the mid-muscle that is marked by a high density of AChR clustering. In this step, innervation disperses aneural AChR clusters in nonsynaptic areas via muscle activity elicited by ACh (49, 50), whereas in synaptic regions, this negative activity is overpowered by agrin delivered by motor nerve terminals to induce AChR clusters (44, 48). However, since agrin does not bind MuSK, additional components are required to activate MuSK (44, 47). Recent studies demonstrated that LRP4, a member of the LDLR family, is a long-sought receptor of agrin, forms a complex with MuSK, and mediates MuSK activation by agrin (45, 46). MuSK is also required for organizing a primary synaptic scaffold to create the post-synaptic membrane (48). Prior to muscle innervation, AChR clusters form at the central regions of muscle fibers, creating an endplate zone that is somewhat broader than that in innervated muscle (51, 52). Thus, MuSK is required for pre-patterning of AChR clustering in the absence of motor innervation. An intriguing finding is that MuSK has a cysteine-rich domain that shows homology to the Wnt receptor Frizzled (53, 54). Wnt is a family of secreted proteins that are implicated in neural development, neural outgrowth, navigation, and synaptogenesis (55-60). Wnt ligans bind to the receptor complex of Frizzled and LRP5/6 (61). Subsequently, signal is transmitted to the adaptor protein Dishevelled (Dvl), which interacts with Frizzled, to initiate intracellular canonical and noncanonical pathways. Like Frizzled, MuSK might interact on the membrane with LRP4 as a Wnt receptor and promote postsynaptic specialization at mammalian NMJ as in Zebrafish (62, 63). In fact, pre-patterning of AChR clustering disappears in LRP4 mutant mice as MuSK-deficient mice (46). Intriguingly, a number of Wnt signaling molecules including APC, β-catenin, Dvl have been implicated in MuSK signaling (63). Simultaneously or alternatively, MuSK could, thereby, form a primary scaffold molecule without activation by agrin.

The listed pleiotropic roles of MuSK in AChR clustering at developmental NMJs could also be required for the maintenance of mature NMJs throughout life. Studies performed *in vivo* have shown that synaptic AChRs intermingle among themselves completely over a period of ~four days and that many extra-synaptic AChRs are incorporated into the synapse at the mature NMJs, although the synaptic membrane in adult muscle appears macroscopically to be stable (64-66). Therefore, the mechanisms at play during AChR clustering in developing NMJs are also required in mature NMJ where postsynaptic complexes including those with AChR and MuSK dynamically turn over for the maintenance of muscle function. Furthermore, MuSK requires the development and maintenance of synaptic structures at NMJs after birth. The disassembly of NMJ structures *in vivo* can be induced by a reduction of MuSK expression using the RNA interference technology in single muscle fibers of adult rats (67). Postnatal inactivation of MuSK using the loxP/Cre system in mice also causes loss of AChRs and disassembly of the postsynaptic organization (68). The conditional inactivation of MuSK in mice during postnatal development leads to defects in NMJ maintenance and premature death. Studies of these dynamics indicated that MuSK is required for retrograde signals, so far unidentified, to maintain the pre-synaptic structure in mature NMJs (69). Moreover, histopathological studies disclosed the same changes of NMJs in mature animals with MuSK EAMG.

5. PATHOGENIC ROLES OF ANTI-MUSK ANTIBODIES IN EAMG

The establishment of MuSK EAMG, which reproduces the clinical and electrophysiological features of MG, enabled assessment of the pathogenic roles of the relevant autoantibodies in experimental animals (10). Histopathologic examination of NMJs in rabbits with MuSK EAMG revealed that anti-MuSK antibodies interfere with MuSK functions at play in the maintenance of mature NMJs described in the previous section. Reduced expression of AChRs at the NMJs was observed by using fluorescence microscopy after applying a rhodamine-conjugated AChR antagonist, α - bungavotoxin (Figure 8A and B) (10). The areas and intensity of AChR fluorescence at NMJs in muscles of paretic rabbits were significantly reduced compared with those in normal rabbits. Anti-MuSK antibodies in rabbits with EAMG blocked agrin-induced clustering of AChRs in C2C12 myotubes as well as the human antibodies, whereas absorption of the antibodies with purified MuSK products prevented this blocking effect as illustrated in Figure 9A.

To elucidate the mechanisms of AChR clustering at NMJs, numerous studies have been performed using cultured C2C12 myotubes (44). Agrin induces the clustering of AChRs in C2C12 myotubes following autophosphorylation by MuSK. *In vivo*, this event represents a major cascade of AChR clustering at the NMJs after innervation by motoneurons (42). These results showed that MuSK antibodies effectively inhibited the formation of agrin-induced AChR clustering. The monovalent Fab fragments of MuSK antibodies, from rabbits with MuSK EAMG also inhibited AChR clustering by agrin on C2C12 cells indicating that complement-mediated mechanisms are not necessarily required for such inhibition (unpublished data). In addition, the anti-MuSK antibodies in rabbits strongly inhibited AChR clustering induced by

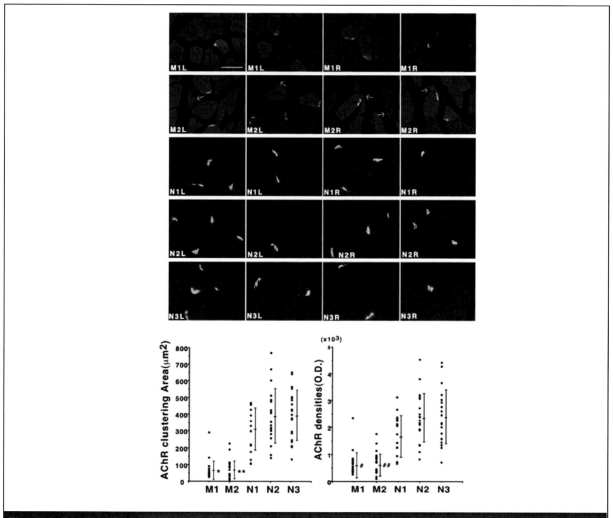

Figure 8. Reduction of the size and density of AChR clusters at NMJs in paretic rabbits with MuSK EAMG. (A) Cross sections from the soleus muscles of 2 paretic (M1 and M2) and 3 normal rabbits (N1, N2, and N3). (B) Quantification of the area and intensity of AChR clustering. (Reprinted with permission from Shigemoto et al., *J Clin Invest* 116:1016.1024.2006)

all known agrin-independent pathways as well as by agrin itself (Figure 9A) (10). Soluble laminin and the N-acetylgalactosamine (GalNAc)-specific lectin *Vicia villosa* agglutinin (VVA-B4) also induce AChR clustering on C2C12 myotubes (Figure 9A and B), without activation of MuSK (10, 70-73). Laminin can induce clustering of AChRs via a pathway that involves tyrosine kinases downstream of MuSK by association with dystroglycan and β1-integrin (Figure 9B) (74, 75). VVA-B4 selectively stains NMJs in skeletal muscles and AChR-rich portions of the C2C12 myotube surface (76, 77); however, the receptor remains to be identified (78). Laminin and VVA-B4 receptors lie downstream from and are common to agrin-mediated AChR clustering pathways (78). These receptors may be associated at postsynaptic membranes and cooperate in the maintenance of AChRs in NMJs. Without question, autoantibodies to MuSK will serve as useful tools for comprehending how MuSK functions at mature NMJs and the pathogenic mechanisms of MuSK MG.

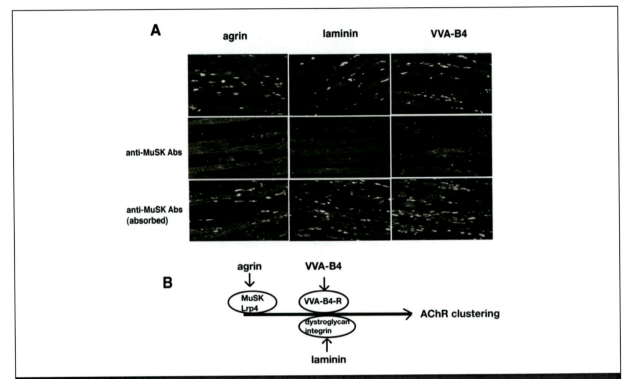

Figure 9. (A) Inhibition of agrin-induced and agrin-independent AChR clustering by MuSK antibodies. This inhibition was blocked by absorption of the MuSK antibodies with MuSK protein before treatment of the cells. (Reprinted with permission from Shigemoto et al., *J Clin Invest* 116:1016-1024. 2006) (B) VVA-B4 binds the unidentified receptors and induces AChR clustering. Laminin induces AChR clustering by binding with dystroglycan and integrin.

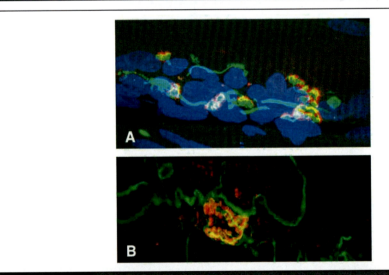

Figure 10. Disassembly of NMJs induced by anti-MuSK antibodies. Motor axon (green), AChR (red), subsynaptic nucleus (blue) NMJs in a rabbit with MuSK EAMG.

(B) NMJs in a mouse with MuSK EAMG.

In addition to the loss of AChR during EAMG, we have also noted the disassembly of NMJ structures and a reduction in the size and branching of the motor terminals in the paretic rabbits (Figure 10A). Electron microscopic observations of NMJs in rabbits with MuSK EAMG demonstrated a significant loss of complexity in the convoluted synaptic folds but not their destruction (unpublished data). Similarly, the NMJs of mice with MuSK EAMG incited by active immunization with MuSK (Figure 10B) and passive transfer of IgG from MuSK MG patients presented with the same histopathological picture (11-13). A reduction in the size and branching of the motor terminals contributes to a decreased ACh output, and a loss of AChRs and post-synaptic folding at NMJs increases the threshold for generation of muscle fiber action potential. These structural abnormalities in NMJs, including both pre- and post-synaptic structures, thus impair neuromuscular transmission in animals with MuSK EAMG (10-13, 69).

The susceptibility to muscle weakness caused by anti-MuSK antibodies may vary among animal species, since the structures of NMJs differ greatly among them (79). Human NMJs are among the smallest found in the well-studied vertebrates. Therefore, the structural factors affecting the impairment of neuromuscular transmission by anti-MuSK antibodies may also vary among animals (79). However, anti-MuSK antibodies in rabbits and mice with MuSK EAMG inhibit agrin-induced AChR clustering on C2C12 myotubes much like that in MG patients (7), indicating the commonality of anti-MuSK antibodies as a cause of MG beyond the difference of species (10, 11).

The mechanisms used by anti-AChR antibodies to cause MG are well delineated (3, 4, 27), but those mechanisms simply do not apply to MG associated with anti-MuSK antibodies. One route of pathogenicity by anti-AChR antibodies is to damage the postsynaptic membrane in NMJs, whereas antibodies to MuSK may interfere directly with the functions of MuSK required for maintaining NMJ structures (10, 12). Anti-MuSK antibodies in MG patients have been identified as predominantly IgG4, which does not activate complement (15, 16). Although the IgG1 of anti-MuSK antibodies is present in MG patients, only the titers of IgG4 were significantly associated with disease severity (17). Therefore, IgG4-antibodies binding to MuSK could accelerate the degradation of MuSK molecules (antigenic modulation) and/or inhibit MuSK functions directly (10, 69). In either case, anti-MuSK antibodies inhibit the functions of MuSK in NMJs.

We effectively generated EAMG in complement-deficient mice with severe symptoms by inoculating them with MuSK (unpublished data), whereas the deficient mice were highly resistant to EAMG from AChR immunization (80). Therefore tissue degradation by complement activation is not necessarily required for the manifestation of myasthenia by MuSK antibodies. Some MG patients with anti-MuSK antibodies also have low-affinity antibodies to AChRs found by testing with a highly sensitive immunofluorescence method (21, 81). Currently, the significance of anti-AChR antibodies in patients is not clear, but the clinical features of MuSK-MG are distinct from those for AChR-MG, thus anti-AChR antibodies may not produce visible symptoms in MuSK-MG patients.

Although significant AChR loss and structural changes in NMJs of animals with EAMG are commonly observed, those changes were not reported in the studies of biceps brachii muscles of anti MuSK-positive patients in a previous study (14). However, further histopathological analysis of NMJs in patients with severely weakened muscles would be beneficial for comparison with the animal under study for a similar condition. In such patients, the weakness and atrophy are not observed uniformly; some anti MuSK-positive patients have more focal weakness in the neck, shoulder and respiratory muscles with prominent cranial and bulbar involvement than patients with anti-AChR antibodies. The limb muscles of individuals with MuSK-MG were less severely affected and inconsistently damaged, whereas patients with generalized AChR-MG patients often suffered from clearcut limb deterioration (82, 83). The mechanisms that favor particular sites of muscle weakness are unknown, and the nature of NMJs among various muscles may not be uniform.

6. THE USE OF AMIMALS WITH EAMG TO IMPROVE MEDICATION

MuSK MG is frequently a severe disease requiring emergent and aggressive therapies. The response to therapy for MuSK MG differs from that for AChR MG (84). Experimentation with animal models of EAMG will contribute to the development of more effective medication as the underlying pharmacological mechanisms become known. Acetylcholinesterase inhibitors are often used as symptomatic treatment and are effective for AChR MG. However, patients with MuSK MG are frequently unresponsive or develop cholinergic crises characterized by increasing muscle weakness that sometimes results in dysphagia and respiratory insufficiency (19, 20, 84, 85). Thus, differentiating a cholinergic crisis from a myasthenic crisis is critical for the decision on medical care of each patient (84, 86). Abnormal sensitivity to ACh after MuSK-MG patients receive acetylcholinesterase inhibitors can sometimes be recorded by electromyography (EMG) as extra discharges occurring after the CMAP with low-frequency motor nerve stimulation, as shown in Figure 11 (86, 87). Such hypersensitivity to ACh may be caused by the interference of anchoring acetylcholinesterase to the synaptic cleft of postsynaptic membranes by MuSK (41). The same patterns of EMG showing hypersensitivity to ACh can be reproduced in mice with MuSK EAMG (unpublished data). The mechanisms of this hypersensitivity may be elucidated by studies of such animals with MuSK EAMG.

Other symptomatic therapy such as 3,4-diaminopyridine, which increases ACh release from the nerve terminal, may be worth trying in MuSK-MG patients. Congenital myasthenic syndrome due to MuSK or Dok-7 mutations has been reported to respond favorably to 3,4-diaminopyridine (88-90). Dok-7 is essential for the formation of NMJs through its interaction with MuSK (91). Patients with MuSK MG apparently do not respond to immunosuppressive therapy as well as those with AChR MG; in fact, some of the former patients who did not respond to the therapy rapidly progressed to life-threatening muscle atrophy (20, 84). However, long-term treatment with higher dose steroids to unrefractory patients may accelerate the distortion of NMJ morphology by anti-MuSK antibodies (92). In view of the clinical variables involved, studying animals with MuSK EAMG will provide important clues for developing and assessing the appropriate medication for all patients afflicted with MuSK MG.

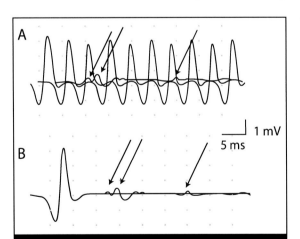

Figure 11: Extra repetitive discharge after the CMAP at low-frequency stimulation were recorded in a MuSK-MG patient with actylcholinesterase inhibitor treatments. (Reprinted with permission from et al., *Muscle Nerve* 34:111-115.2006)

REFERENCES

1. Patrick, J., and Lindstrom, J. 1973. Autoimmune response to acetylcholine receptor. *Science* 180:871-872.
2. Lindstrom, J.M., Seybold, M.E., Lennon, V.A., Whittingham, S., and Duane, D.D. 1976. Antibody to acetylcholine receptor in myasthenia gravis. Prevalence, clinical correlates, and diagnostic value. *Neurology* 26:1054-1059.
3. Conti-Fine, B.M., Milani, M., and Kaminski, H.J. 2006. Myasthenia gravis: past, present, and future. *J Clin Invest* 116:2843-2854.
4. Vincent, A., Lang, B., and Kleopa, K.A. 2006. Autoimmune channelopathies and related neurological disorders. *Neuron* 52:123-138.
5. Mossman, S., Vincent, A., and Newsom-Davis, J. 1986. Myasthenia gravis without acetylcholine-receptor antibody: a distinct disease entity. *Lancet* 1:116-119.
6. Burges, J., Vincent, A., Molenaar, P.C., Newsom-Davis, J., Peers, C., and Wray, D. 1994. Passive transfer of seronegative myasthenia gravis to mice. *Muscle Nerve* 17:1393-1400.
7. Hoch, W., McConville, J., Helms, S., Newsom-Davis, J., Melms, A., and Vincent, A. 2001. Auto-antibodies to the receptor tyrosine kinase MuSK in patients with myasthenia gravis without acetylcholine receptor antibodies. *Nat Med* 7:365-368.
8. DeChiara, T.M., Bowen, D.C., Valenzuela, D.M., Simmons, M.V., Poueymirou, W.T., Thomas, S., Kinetz, E., Compton, D.L., Rojas, E., Park, J.S., et al. 1996. The receptor tyrosine kinase MuSK is required for neuromuscular junction formation in vivo. *Cell* 85:501-512.
9. Lindstrom, J. 2004. Is "seronegative" MG explained by autoantibodies to MuSK? *Neurology* 62:1920-1921.
10. Shigemoto, K., Kubo, S., Maruyama, N., Hato, N., Yamada, H., Jie, C., Kobayashi, N., Mominoki, K., Abe, Y., Ueda, N., et al. 2006. Induction of myasthenia by immunization against muscle-specific kinase. *J Clin Invest* 116:1016-1024.
11. Jha, S., Xu, K., Maruta, T., Oshima, M., Mosier, D.R., Atassi, M.Z., and Hoch, W. 2006. Myasthenia gravis induced in mice by immunization with the recombinant extracellular domain of rat muscle-specific kinase (MuSK). *J Neuroimmunol* 175:107-117.
12. Shigemoto, K., Sachiho, K., Chen, J., Naohito, H., Yasuhito, A., Norifumi, U., Naoto, K., Kenji, K., Katsumi, M., Atsuo, M., et al. 2008. Experimentally induced myasthenia gravis with muscle-specific kinase
. *Ann N Y Acad Sci* 1132:93-98.
13. Cole, R.N., Reddel, S.W., Gervasio, O.L., and Phillips, W.D. 2008. Anti-MuSK patient antibodies disrupt the mouse neuromuscular junction. *Ann Neurol* 63:782-789.
14. Shiraishi, H., Motomura, M., Yoshimura, T., Fukudome, T., Fukuda, T., Nakao, Y., Tsujihata, M., Vincent, A., and Eguchi, K. 2005. Acetylcholine receptors loss and postsynaptic damage in MuSK antibody-positive myasthenia gravis. *Ann Neurol* 57:289-293.
15. McConville, J., Farrugia, M.E., Beeson, D., Kishore, U., Metcalfe, R., Newsom-Davis, J., and Vincent, A. 2004. Detection and characterization of MuSK antibodies in seronegative myasthenia gravis. *Ann Neurol* 55:580-584.

16. Ohta, K., Shigemoto, K., Fujinami, A., Maruyama, N., Konishi, T., and Ohta, M. 2007. Clinical and experimental features of MuSK antibody positive MG in Japan. *Eur J Neurol* 14:1029-1034.

17. Niks, E.H., van Leeuwen, Y., Leite, M.I., Dekker, F.W., Wintzen, A.R., Wirtz, P.W., Vincent, A., van Tol, M.J., Jol-van der Zijde, C.M., and Verschuuren, J.J. 2008. Clinical fluctuations in MuSK myasthenia gravis are related to antigen-specific IgG4 instead of IgG1. *J Neuroimmunol* 195:151-156.

18. Vincent, A., Bowen, J., Newsom-Davis, J., and McConville, J. 2003. Seronegative generalised myasthenia gravis: clinical features, antibodies, and their targets. *Lancet Neurol* 2:99-106.

19. Sanders, D.B., El-Salem, K., Massey, J.M., McConville, J., and Vincent, A. 2003. Clinical aspects of MuSK antibody positive seronegative MG. *Neurology* 60:1978-1980.

20. Evoli, A., Tonali, P.A., Padua, L., Monaco, M.L., Scuderi, F., Batocchi, A.P., Marino, M., and Bartoccioni, E. 2003. Clinical correlates with anti-MuSK antibodies in generalized seronegative myasthenia gravis. *Brain* 126:2304-2311.

21. Leite, M.I., Jacob, S., Viegas, S., Cossins, J., Clover, L., Morgan, B.P., Beeson, D., Willcox, N., and Vincent, A. 2008. IgG1 antibodies to acetylcholine receptors in 'seronegative' myasthenia gravis. *Brain* 131:1940-1952.

22. Bittner, R.E., Anderson, L.V., Burkhardt, E., Bashir, R., Vafiadaki, E., Ivanova, S., Raffelsberger, T., Maerk, I., Hoger, H., Jung, M., et al. 1999. Dysferlin deletion in SJL mice (SJL-Dysf) defines a natural model for limb girdle muscular dystrophy 2B. *Nat Genet* 23:141-142.

23. Niks, E.H., Kuks, J.B., Roep, B.O., Haasnoot, G.W., Verduijn, W., Ballieux, B.E., De Baets, M.H., Vincent, A., and Verschuuren, J.J. 2006. Strong association of MuSK antibody-positive myasthenia gravis and HLA-DR14-DQ5. *Neurology* 66:1772-1774.

24. Christadoss, P., Krco, C.J., Lennon, V.A., and David, C.S. 1981. Genetic control of experimental autoimmune myasthenia gravis in mice. II. Lymphocyte proliferative response to acetylcholine receptor is dependent on Lyt-1+23- cells. *J Immunol* 126:1646-1647.

25. Christadoss, P., Lennon, V.A., Krco, C.J., and David, C.S. 1982. Genetic control of experimental autoimmune myasthenia gravis in mice. III. Ia molecules mediate cellular immune responsiveness to acetylcholine receptors. *J Immunol* 128:1141-1144.

26. Bell, J., Rassenti, L., Smoot, S., Smith, K., Newby, C., Hohlfeld, R., Toyka, K., McDevitt, H., and Steinman, L. 1986. HLA-DQ beta-chain polymorphism linked to myasthenia gravis. *Lancet* 1:1058-1060.

27. Newsom-Davis, J. 2007. The emerging diversity of neuromuscular junction disorders. *Acta Myol* 26:5-10.

28. Ruff, R.L. 2003. *Neuromuscular Junction Physiology and Pathology*. Totowa, New Jersey: Humana Press.

29. Engel, A.G. 2004. *The Neuromuscular junction*. New York: McGraw-Hill, Medical Pub. Divisio.

30. Heuser, J.E., and Reese, T.S. 1973. Evidence for recycling of synaptic vesicle membrane during transmitter release at the frog neuromuscular junction. *J Cell Biol* 57:315-344.

31. Robitaille, R., Adler, E.M., and Charlton, M.P. 1990. Strategic location of calcium channels at transmitter release sites of frog neuromuscular synapses. *Neuron* 5:773-779.

32. Salpeter, M.M., and Loring, R.H. 1985. Nicotinic acetylcholine receptors in vertebrate muscle: properties, distribution and neural control. *Prog Neurobiol* 25:297-325.

33. Salpeter, M. 1987. *The Vertebrate Neuromuscular Junction.* New York: Alan R. Liss.

34. Burden, S.J., DePalma, R.L., and Gottesman, G.S. 1983. Crosslinking of proteins in acetylcholine receptor-rich membranes: association between the beta-subunit and the 43 kd subsynaptic protein. *Cell* 35:687-692.

35. Engel, A.G. 1991. Review of evidence for loss of motor nerve terminal calcium channels in Lambert-Eaton myasthenic syndrome. *Ann N Y Acad Sci* 635:246-258.

36. Pumplin, D.W., Reese, T.S., and Llinas, R. 1981. Are the presynaptic membrane particles the calcium channels? *Proc Natl Acad Sci U S A* 78:7210-7213.

37. Smith, S.J., and Augustine, G.J. 1988. Calcium ions, active zones and synaptic transmitter release. *Trends Neurosci* 11:458-464.

38. Augustine, G.J., Adler, E.M., and Charlton, M.P. 1991. The calcium signal for transmitter secretion from presynaptic nerve terminals. *Ann N Y Acad Sci* 635:365-381.

39. Engel, A.G., and Santa, T. 1971. Histometric analysis of the ultrastructure of the neuromuscular junction in myasthenia gravis and in the myasthenic syndrome. *Ann N Y Acad Sci* 183:46-63.

40. Engel, A.G., Tsujihata, M., Lindstrom, J.M., and Lennon, V.A. 1976. The motor end plate in myasthenia gravis and in experimental autoimmune myasthenia gravis. A quantitative ultrastructural study. *Ann N Y Acad Sci* 274:60-79.

41. Cartaud, A., Strochlic, L., Guerra, M., Blanchard, B., Lambergeon, M., Krejci, E., Cartaud, J., and Legay, C. 2004. MuSK is required for anchoring acetylcholinesterase at the neuromuscular junction. *J Cell Biol* 165:505-515.

42. Valenzuela, D.M., Stitt, T.N., DiStefano, P.S., Rojas, E., Mattsson, K., Compton, D.L., Nunez, L., Park, J.S., Stark, J.L., Gies, D.R., et al. 1995. Receptor tyrosine kinase specific for the skeletal muscle lineage: expression in embryonic muscle, at the neuromuscular junction, and after injury. *Neuron* 15:573-584.

43. Ganju, P., Walls, E., Brennan, J., and Reith, A.D. 1995. Cloning and developmental expression of Nsk2, a novel receptor tyrosine kinase implicated in skeletal myogenesis. *Oncogene* 11:281-290.

44. Glass, D.J., Bowen, D.C., Stitt, T.N., Radziejewski, C., Bruno, J., Ryan, T.E., Gies, D.R., Shah, S., Mattsson, K., Burden, S.J., et al. 1996. Agrin acts via a MuSK receptor complex. *Cell* 85:513-523.

45. Zhang, B., Luo, S., Wang, Q., Suzuki, T., Xiong, W.C., and Mei, L. 2008. LRP4 serves as a coreceptor of agrin. *Neuron* 60:285-297.

46. Kim, N., Stiegler, A.L., Cameron, T.O., Hallock, P.T., Gomez, A.M., Huang, J.H., Hubbard, S.R., Dustin, M.L., and Burden, S.J. 2008. Lrp4 is a receptor for Agrin and forms a complex with MuSK. *Cell* 135:334-342.

47. Strochlic, L., Cartaud, A., and Cartaud, J. 2005. The synaptic muscle-specific kinase (MuSK) complex: new partners, new functions. *Bioessays* 27:1129-1135.

48. Kummer, T.T., Misgeld, T., and Sanes, J.R. 2006. Assembly of the postsynaptic membrane at the neuromuscular junction: paradigm lost. *Curr Opin Neurobiol* 16:74-82.

49. Lin, W., Dominguez, B., Yang, J., Aryal, P., Brandon, E.P., Gage, F.H., and Lee, K.F. 2005. Neurotransmitter acetylcholine negatively regulates neuromuscular synapse formation by a Cdk5-dependent mechanism. *Neuron* 46:569-579.

50. Misgeld, T., Kummer, T.T., Lichtman, J.W., and Sanes, J.R. 2005. Agrin promotes synaptic differentiation by counteracting an inhibitory effect of neurotransmitter. *Proc Natl Acad Sci U S A* 102:11088-11093.

51. Lin, W., Burgess, R.W., Dominguez, B., Pfaff, S.L., Sanes, J.R., and Lee, K.F. 2001. Distinct roles of nerve and muscle in postsynaptic differentiation of the neuromuscular synapse. *Nature* 410:1057-1064.

52. Yang, X., Arber, S., William, C., Li, L., Tanabe, Y., Jessell, T.M., Birchmeier, C., and Burden, S.J. 2001. Patterning of muscle acetylcholine receptor gene expression in the absence of motor innervation. *Neuron* 30:399-410.

53. Saldanha, J., Singh, J., and Mahadevan, D. 1998. Identification of a Frizzled-like cysteine rich domain in the extracellular region of developmental receptor tyrosine kinases. *Protein Sci* 7:1632-1635.

54. Masiakowski, P., and Yancopoulos, G.D. 1998. The Wnt receptor CRD domain is also found in MuSK and related orphan receptor tyrosine kinases. *Curr Biol* 8:R407.

55. Burden, S.J. 2000. Wnts as retrograde signals for axon and growth cone differentiation. *Cell* 100:495-497.

56. Zou, Y. 2004. Wnt signaling in axon guidance. *Trends Neurosci* 27:528-532.

57. Ciani, L., and Salinas, P.C. 2005. WNTs in the vertebrate nervous system: from patterning to neuronal connectivity. *Nat Rev Neurosci* 6:351-362.

58. Salinas, P.C. 2003. Synaptogenesis: Wnt and TGF-beta take centre stage. *Curr Biol* 13:R60-62.

59. Yoshikawa, S., McKinnon, R.D., Kokel, M., and Thomas, J.B. 2003. Wnt-mediated axon guidance via the Drosophila Derailed receptor. *Nature* 422:583-588.

60. Lyuksyutova, A.I., Lu, C.C., Milanesio, N., King, L.A., Guo, N., Wang, Y., Nathans, J., Tessier-Lavigne, M., and Zou, Y. 2003. Anterior-posterior guidance of commissural axons by Wnt-frizzled signaling. *Science* 302:1984-1988.

61. Kikuchi, A., Yamamoto, H., and Kishida, S. 2007. Multiplicity of the interactions of Wnt proteins and their receptors. *Cell Signal* 19:659-671.

62. Jing, L., Lefebvre, J.L., Gordon, L.R., and Granato, M. 2009. Wnt signals organize synaptic prepattern and axon guidance through the zebrafish unplugged/MuSK receptor. *Neuron* 61:721-733.

63. Zhang, B., Xiong, W.C., and Mei, L. 2009. Get ready to Wnt: prepatterning in neuromuscular junction formation. *Dev Cell* 16:325-327.

64. Akaaboune, M., Culican, S.M., Turney, S.G., and Lichtman, J.W. 1999. Rapid and reversible effects of activity on acetylcholine receptor density at the neuromuscular junction in vivo. *Science* 286:503-507.

65. Akaaboune, M., Grady, R.M., Turney, S., Sanes, J.R., and Lichtman, J.W. 2002. Neurotransmitter receptor dynamics studied in vivo by reversible photo-unbinding of fluorescent ligands. *Neuron* 34:865-876.

66. Kummer, T.T., Misgeld, T., Lichtman, J.W., and Sanes, J.R. 2004. Nerve-independent formation of a topologically complex postsynaptic apparatus. *J Cell Biol* 164:1077-1087.

67. Kong, X.C., Barzaghi, P., and Ruegg, M.A. 2004. Inhibition of synapse assembly in mammalian muscle in vivo by RNA interference. *EMBO Rep* 5:183-188.

68. Hesser, B.A., Henschel, O., and Witzemann, V. 2006. Synapse disassembly and formation of new synapses in postnatal muscle upon conditional inactivation of MuSK. *Mol Cell Neurosci* 31:470-480.

69. Shigemoto, K. 2007. Myasthenia gravis induced by autoantibodies against MuSK. *Acta Myol* 26:185-191.

70. Vogel, Z., Christian, C.N., Vigny, M., Bauer, H.C., Sonderegger, P., and Daniels, M.P. 1983. Laminin induces acetylcholine receptor aggregation on cultured myotubes and enhances the receptor aggregation activity of a neuronal factor. *J Neurosci* 3:1058-1068.

71. Sugiyama, J.E., Glass, D.J., Yancopoulos, G.D., and Hall, Z.W. 1997. Laminin-induced acetylcholine receptor clustering: an alternative pathway. *J Cell Biol* 139:181-191.

72. Montanaro, F., Gee, S.H., Jacobson, C., Lindenbaum, M.H., Froehner, S.C., and Carbonetto, S. 1998. Laminin and alpha-dystroglycan mediate acetylcholine receptor aggregation via a MuSK-independent pathway. *J Neurosci* 18:1250-1260.

73. Marangi, P.A., Wieland, S.T., and Fuhrer, C. 2002. Laminin-1 redistributes postsynaptic proteins and requires rapsyn, tyrosine phosphorylation, and Src and Fyn to stably cluster acetylcholine receptors. *J Cell Biol* 157:883-895.

74. Schwander, M., Shirasaki, R., Pfaff, S.L., and Muller, U. 2004. Beta1 integrins in muscle, but not in motor neurons, are required for skeletal muscle innervation. *J Neurosci* 24:8181-8191.

75. Nishimune, H., Valdez, G., Jarad, G., Moulson, C.L., Muller, U., Miner, J.H., and Sanes, J.R. 2008. Laminins promote postsynaptic maturation by an autocrine mechanism at the neuromuscular junction. *J Cell Biol* 182:1201-1215.

76. Sanes, J.R., and Cheney, J.M. 1982. Lectin binding reveals a synapse-specific carbohydrate in skeletal muscle. *Nature* 300:646-647.

77. Martin, P.T., and Sanes, J.R. 1995. Role for a synapse-specific carbohydrate in agrin-induced clustering of acetylcholine receptors. *Neuron* 14:743-754.

78. McDearmon, E.L., Combs, A.C., and Ervasti, J.M. 2001. Differential Vicia villosa agglutinin reactivity identifies three distinct dystroglycan complexes in skeletal muscle. *J Biol Chem* 276:35078-35086.

79. Slater, C.R. 2008. Structural factors influencing the efficacy of neuromuscular transmission. *Ann N Y Acad Sci* 1132:1-12.

80. Christadoss, P. 1988. C5 gene influences the development of murine myasthenia gravis. *J Immunol* 140:2589-2592.

81. Vincent, A., Leite, M.I., Farrugia, M.E., Jacob, S., Viegas, S., Shiraishi, H., Benveniste, O., Morgan, B.P., Hilton-Jones, D., Newsom-Davis, J., et al. 2008. Myasthenia gravis seronegative for acetylcholine receptor antibodies. *Ann N Y Acad Sci* 1132:84-92.

82. Deymeer, F., Gungor-Tuncer, O., Yilmaz, V., Parman, Y., Serdaroglu, P., Ozdemir, C., Vincent, A., and Saruhan-Direskeneli, G. 2007. Clinical comparison of anti-MuSK-vs anti-AChR-positive and seronegative myasthenia gravis. *Neurology* 68:609-611.

83. Wolfe, G.I., and Oh, S.J. 2008. Clinical phenotype of muscle-specific tyrosine kinase-antibody-positive myasthenia gravis. *Ann N Y Acad Sci* 1132:71-75.

84. Evoli, A., Bianchi, M.R., Riso, R., Minicuci, G.M., Batocchi, A.P., Servidei, S., Scuderi, F., and Bartoccioni, E. 2008. Response to therapy in myasthenia gravis with anti-MuSK antibodies. *Ann N Y Acad Sci* 1132:76-83.

85. Hatanaka, Y., Hemmi, S., Morgan, M.B., Scheufele, M.L., Claussen, G.C., Wolfe, G.I., and Oh, S.J. 2005. Nonresponsiveness to anticholinesterase agents in patients with MuSK-antibody-positive MG. *Neurology* 65:1508-1509.

86. Punga, A.R., and Stalberg, E. 2009. Acetylcholinesterase inhibitors in MG: To be or not to be? *Muscle Nerve* 39:724-728.

87. Punga, A.R., Flink, R., Askmark, H., and Stalberg, E.V. 2006. Cholinergic neuromuscular hyperactivity in patients with myasthenia gravis seropositive for MuSK antibody. *Muscle Nerve* 34:111-115.

88. Chevessier, F., Faraut, B., Ravel-Chapuis, A., Richard, P., Gaudon, K., Bauche, S., Prioleau, C., Herbst, R., Goillot, E., Ioos, C., et al. 2004. MUSK, a new target for mutations causing congenital myasthenic syndrome. *Hum Mol Genet* 13:3229-3240.

89. Beeson, D., Higuchi, O., Palace, J., Cossins, J., Spearman, H., Maxwell, S., Newsom-Davis, J., Burke, G., Fawcett, P., Motomura, M., et al. 2006. Dok-7 mutations underlie a neuromuscular junction synaptopathy. *Science* 313:1975-1978.

90. Palace, J., Lashley, D., Newsom-Davis, J., Cossins, J., Maxwell, S., Kennett, R., Jayawant, S., Yamanashi, Y., and Beeson, D. 2007. Clinical features of the DOK7 neuromuscular junction synaptopathy. *Brain*.

91. Okada, K., Inoue, A., Okada, M., Murata, Y., Kakuta, S., Jigami, T., Kubo, S., Shiraishi, H., Eguchi, K., Motomura, M., et al. 2006. The muscle protein Dok-7 is essential for neuromuscular synaptogenesis. *Science* 312:1802-1805.

92. Farrugia, M.E., Robson, M.D., Clover, L., Anslow, P., Newsom-Davis, J., Kennett, R., Hilton-Jones, D., Matthews, P.M., and Vincent, A. 2006. MRI and clinical studies of facial and bulbar muscle involvement in MuSK antibody-associated myasthenia gravis. *Brain* 129:1481-1492.

V

Preclinical Trials in Myasthenia Gravis

Targeting Classical Complement Pathway And IL-6 To Treat Myasthenia Gravis

Erdem Tüzün M.D. and Premkumar Christadoss M.B.B.S.

1. INTRODUCTION

Experimental autoimmune myasthenia gravis (EAMG) induced by active immunization of mice with AChR closely mimics clinical and immunopathological features of human MG. Studies in EAMG have unravelled the immunopathogenic mechanisms underlying MG and understanding the molecular and cellular mechanisms involved in the NMJ pathology.

Two humoral elements, anti-AChR IgG and the complement system (required for assembly of membrane attack complex [MAC]), are the essential pathogenic factors in MG/EAMG. Both IgG and complement deposits at the NMJ of patients with MG and mice with EAMG are the culprits of NMJ damage (1-11). Antibodies directed against different epitopes of AChR, and binding of IgG to NMJ AChR initiates complement-dependent lysis of the postsynaptic muscle membrane. Anti-AChR antibodies might also increase AChR degradation and directly inhibit acetylcholine binding (12,13). In contrast with many other autoimmune diseases, there is minimal or no cellular infiltration at the target muscle tissue in MG or EAMG (14), and therefore, myasthenic muscle weakness is not induced by direct effects of inflammatory cells on the muscle tissue. Nevertheless, cellular immunity is still involved in MG and EAMG pathogenesis by establishing a robust antibody response against various AChR epitopes. The antigen presenting cells effectively process AChR and present AChR epitopes as autoantigens to T cells. MHC class II molecules, costimulatory molecules, proinflammatory cytokines and chemokines are required for the activation of AChR specific T and B cells (2,15). Immune cells might also be enhancing EAMG severity simply by secreting cytokines that would eventually contribute to the damage of the muscle tissue to some extent. (16,17). In this chapter we will initially review the evidence for the role of classical complement pathway (CP) activation in the destruction of NMJ AChR in mice and the role of CP in MG.

In addition to various complement factors and specific anti-AChR antibodies, non-specific circulating immune complexes (CIC) contribute to the development of EAMG and possibly MG (18-20). Therefore, immune complex associated disease mechanisms in MG/EAMG will be reviewed in the second part. Next the role of IL-6 in EAMG pathogenesis will be discussed because of its close association with the complement system and T and B cell activation.. Finally, we will discuss how MG could be effectively treated by blocking the CP activation and IL-6 inhibition.

2. THE ROLE OF THE COMPLEMENT SYSTEM IN MG

The complement system is composed of a group of proteins with a wide variety of biological functions. The activation of the complement cascade and consequent formation of MAC deposits at the target tissues can be initiated by the classical complement pathway (CP), the alternative complement pathway and the mannose binding lectin pathway (21). While the alternative and lectin pathways are usually activated by the surface molecules of microorganims and thus are generally involved in defense against pathogens, CP is mainly activated by antigen-antibody complexes and therefore is involved in the pathogenesis of a variety of immune complex and antibody associated diseases (21).

Complement system is involved in autoimmune disorders via two different mechanisms. In one group of autoimmune disorders, deficiency of CP components (C1, C2 and C4) results in defective clearance of apoptotic cells and immune complexes -as seen in immune complex associated diseases such as systemic lupus erythematosus (SLE), glomerulonephritis and vasculitis (22,23). Also, some complement factors are involved in immune tolerance induction and the absence of these factors may lead to increased immune responsiveness to self antigens and autoimmune diseases (24). Alternatively, in various complement and antibody mediated autoimmune disorders such as Goodpasture syndrome, pemphigus, dermatomyositis, Grave's disease, autoimmune hemolytic anemia and MG, increased presence rather than absence of complement deposits at the target tissue (often activated by antigen-specific antibodies via CP) gives rise to pathological and clinical findings. In these disorders, activation of the complement cascade does not only end up in formation of MAC, which disrupts the architecture of self antigen bearing tissue, but also release many break-up side products that attract the immune cells to the inflammation site, thus boosting the proinflammatory (ie. TNF, IL-6) cytokine production by lymph node cells and thereby enhance the self tissue destruction and clinical manifestations of a given autoimmune disease (25).

MG is one of the best characterized complement-associated autoimmune diseases. The pathological and clinical findings of this disease is primarily mediated by antibody and complement associated mechanisms. The complement system is involved in anti-AChR antibody positive MG, purely ocular MG, actively and passively induced forms of EAMG and the recently established ocular form of experimental MG (26-29).

2.1. The complement system in anti-AChR associated MG and EAMG

A wide range of data supports the notion that the complement system activation by anti-AChR antibodies is the major mechanism that mediates AChR loss at the NMJ. The earliest and foremost proofs for the complement involvement in MG were, (i) alterations in complement levels in MG patients' sera suggesting increased utilization of the complement system and (ii) co-localization of MAC, C3 and IgG deposits at the NMJ of MG patients and EAMG rodents demonstrated by immunohistochemistry and immunoelectron microscopy studies (6-11). In some early reports, higher amounts of complement deposits have been related with lower AChR content and decreased structural integrity of the NMJ (9,10). In a more recent study, MG patients with higher serum anti-AChR antibody levels displayed lower serum C3 and C4 concentrations suggesting in vivo complement consumption by anti-AChR antibodies. Serum C3 and C4 levels were not correlated with the clinical MG severity or presence of anti-titin or anti-ryanodin receptor (RyR) antibodies (30). In another study, plasma C3c levels were found out to be associated with the clinical severity of MG (31).

Second line of evidence comes from experimental studies showing that actively or passively induced EAMG can be effectively prevented or treated by inhibition or depletion of various complement factors. In earlier studies, muscle weakness of rodents with EAMG induced by passive transfer of anti-AChR antibodies has been shown to improve following treatment by cobra venom factor (CVF), soluble complement receptor 1 (sCR1) and anti-C6 antibody (32-34). CVF and sCR1 both inhibit classical and alternative complement pathways, while anti-C6 antibody interferes with MAC formation. Notably, CVF treated rats exhibited normal muscle AChR content and preserved neuromuscular transmission despite the presence of antibody deposits at the NMJ, suggesting that IgG deposits might not be capable of inducing NMJ damage without the aid of the complement system. In line with these studies, pathological and electrophysiological findings of NMJ damage induced by transfer of MG patients' sera or IgG to rats can be prevented by CVF treatment (35).

Passively induced EAMG of Lewis rats could be completely prevented by anti-C5 monoclonal antibody administered before transfer of anti-AChR antibody. Moreover, anti-C5 antibody treatment 24 hours after EAMG induction restored muscle strength in two thirds of the rats, while all control rats were to be terminated due to severe weakness. Clinical amelioration of anti-C5-treated mice paralleled with reduction of NMJ C9 deposits (36). Similarly, rEV576, a novel 17kDa C5 inhibiting protein prevented and treated passively induced EAMG in a dose dependent manner by reducing serum anti-AChR IgG levels and NMJ C9 deposits (37).

The method used for EAMG induction in all these experiments was passive transfer of pathogenic antibodies, which only mimics the final effector stage (destruction of muscle AChR by antibody and complement) of MG development and does not simulate the afferent limb (antigen presenting cell-T cell interaction and B cell production of antibodies) of the autoimmune response to AChR. Therefore, these studies do not provide information about the role of complements in the breakdown of self-tolerance to NMJ antigens. Nevertheless, improvement of myasthenic symptoms with in vivo inhibition of MAC or earlier components of the complement cascade strongly suggested that EAMG related pathology and muscle weakness required complement activation.

Amelioration of myasthenic symptoms following intravenous immunoglobulin (IVIg) treatment or plasmapheresis was also partially associated with the removal of various pathogenic factors (including complements and complement activating antibodies) from circulation (see Chapter 6 and 24 for IVIg mechanisms of action). In fact, a sharp decrease in circulating levels of C3 and/or C4 following plasma exchange and immunoadsorption of plasma has been invariably demonstrated (38-40) (see Chapter 26 for further readings on plasma exchange). Additionally, majority of MG patients are positive for anti-AChR IgG1 and IgG3 isotypes (41,42), both of which are strong activators of the complement system via CP.

EAMG immunopathogenesis following AChR immunization mimics human MG pathogenesis in various aspects: Both EAMG and MG, (i) display a T cell mediated and B cell dependent immune response to AChR; ,(ii) influenced by major histocompatibility complex genes, expression of IL-6, TNF-α and costimulary molecules including ICOS and B7 (1-3,29); and (iii) a simplified NMJ folds and NMJ IgG and complement deposits Following AChR immunizations in C57BL/6 (B6) mice, serum anti-AChR antibody, complement and immune complex levels rise simultaneously in a time dependent manner (19). NMJ displays C1q, C3 and MAC deposits and accumulation of complement deposits is associated with degradation of the postsynaptic NMJ, decreased miniature end-plate potential amplitude, reduced NMJ AChR content and succeeding muscle weakness (1,2,19).

Further delineation of the role of the complement system in the formation of AChR-specific immune response in addition to complement dependent lysis of the NMJ was achieved by actively induced EAMG experiments. B10.D2/nSn (C5 sufficient) and B10.D2/oSn (C5 deficient) mouse strains, which are genetically identical except in the C5 gene locus, were immunized with AChR. C5 deficient mice demonstrated significantly reduced EAMG incidence, death rate and muscle AChR loss as compared to C5 sufficient mice (43). As opposed to 78% (18 out of 23) C5 sufficient mice with EAMG, only 5% (1 out of 18) C5 deficient mice developed clinical muscle weakness. In striking resemblance to previously mentioned sCR1 and CVF treated rodents, serum anti-AChR antibody levels of EAMG resistant C5 deficient mice were not lower than those of EAMG susceptible C5 sufficient mice (43). In a recent study, AChR-immunized rats treated with a C5 inhibiting protein exhibited reduced EAMG severity (37).

Plausibly, C5 deficient mice lack both C5a and C5b components. While C5b is a MAC component, C5a is not involved in MAC formation and it is a major anaphylactic and chemotactic agent. Since the mononuclear cell infiltration and attraction of cells to the muscle tissue are generally not involved in actively induced EAMG and human MG pathogenesis, C5a may not contribute to MG pathogenesis. However, C5a is involved in various other immunological functions such as release of certain cytokines (e.g. IL-IL-1β, IL-6) that are actively involved in EAMG and possibly MG pathogenesis. As a matter of fact, C5a is involved in other antibody and complement mediated diseases such as autoimmune hemolytic anemia and anti-phospholipid syndrome and thus loss of C5a function renders mice resistant to these diseases (44). Therefore, inborn deficiency of C5a associated immunological factors could have contributed to EAMG resistance in C5 deficient mice by disabling certain immunological functions. To address this question, we investigated whether C5a receptor deficient mice were resistant to EAMG. Notably, AChR-immunized C5aR KO and wild-type (WT) mice showed identical EAMG incidences, clinical scores and grip strengths. Additionally, serum anti-AChR antibody, NMJ IgG and complement deposits and AChR-induced lymphocyte proliferation values of C5aR KO mice were comparable to those of WT mice (45). These results indicate that the inborn deficiency of C5a signaling through C5a receptor does not confer mice EAMG resistance, C5a is not involved in EAMG pathogenesis and C5 deficiency prevents EAMG induction through deficient MAC production due to absence of C5b. Nevertheless, C5a mediated mechanisms might still be in effect in passively induced EAMG model, characterized with cellular infiltrates in the muscle tissue. This assumption is supported by the finding that anti-C5 antibody treatment reduces the amount of muscular cellular infiltrates of EAMG rats, whereas EAMG rats treated with antibodies directed to C6 (which is not involved in leukocyte chemotaxis) exhibit increased amounts of cellular infiltrates as non-treated control mice (36).

In EAMG, the immunological response to AChR immunization develops as a result of the complex activities of a network of various cytokines and complement components activating or inhibiting each other's production. Many MG-associated immunological factors appear to exert their functions at least partially through activation of complement components. Removal of one of these factors from this complex network might result in partial or complete loss of complement system functions and consequent EAMG resistance. For instance, EAMG resistance of IL-5, IL-6, IL-12, ICOS, FcγRIII KO and IL-1 receptor antagonist treated mice is associated with reduced serum and/or NMJ complement content (18,46-49), further supporting the central role of the complement system in MG/EAMG pathogenesis.

2. 2. The complement system in anti-MUSK and sero-negative MG

Serum anti-AChR antibody is one of the hallmarks of MG pathogenesis and a supportive finding in MG diagnosis. However, 10-15% of the MG patients do not exhibit anti-AChR antibodies in their sera. While the role of the complement system in the anti-anti-MuSK and seronegative MG is less evident and more controversial, accumulating evidence suggests that complement factors might also be involved in these MG subtypes (see Chapter 2). MuSK is a transmembrane polypeptide that is expressed by skeletal muscle cells and is involved in AChR clustering (50). Antibodies directed against the MuSK polypeptide were discovered by Hoch et al. (51) in a group of non-anti-AChR positive patients and the subsequent research identified that anti-MuSK antibody associated MG constitutes a distinct subgroup, which is distinguished from anti-AChR antibody associated MG by clinical features, response to treatment, muscle pathology and pathogenic factors involved in muscle weakness (52) (for further readings on anti-MuSK MG, see Chapter 2). Initial studies showed that there is no substantial muscle AChR loss in anti-MuSK positive MG patients and only a small percentage of patients have complement deposits at their NMJs. Moreover, anti-MuSK antibodies are predominantly of IgG4 isotype, which is the non-complement fixing type as opposed to IgG1, IgG2 and IgG3 isotypes (52,53). However, a new antibody detection method utilizing transfected human embryonic kidney (HEK) cells to express MuSK antigens at a high density on their membranes showed that anti-MuSK antibodies were partially of IgG1 isotype and could activate C3b and MAC deposition when bound to MuSK on the cell surface (26). In the same study, it has also been shown that around two thirds of seronegative (anti-AChR or anti-MuSK negative) cases actually have low affinity anti-AChR antibodies that can not be detected with routine diagnostic assays. These antibodies strongly react with AChR/rapsyn clusters expressed on the cell surface of HEK cells, are mainly of complement-activating IgG1 isotype and can potentially induce MAC formation. Likewise, sera of seronegative MG patients with no anti-AChR or -MuSK reactivity display complement-fixing IgG1 isotype antibodies (26). Overall, these results suggest that complement-mediated NMJ destruction might at least partially be involved in pathogenesis of MG without conventional anti-AChR antibodies.

MG associated autoantibodies other than anti-AChR and anti-MuSK might also potentially activate the complement cascade. Anti-titin and anti-RyR antibodies are frequently observed in MG patients' sera and their pathogenic significance is not well known. Romi et al. demonstrated that anti-titin or anti-RyR positive sera activated the complement cascade and identified that a significant percentage of these antibodies were of complement fixing isotype (IgG1, IgG3) (54). Both titin and RyR are intracellular molecules and pathogenic antibodies directed against intracellular antigens might penetrate the cell membrane and bind their target antigens. However, lack of an apparent muscle fiber pathology in MG suggests that these antibodies are not significantly involved in MG pathogenesis. Nevertheless, in severe MG cases or during myasthenic crisis these antibodies might hypothetically induce muscle cell damage and thus contribute to overall muscle weakness primarily mediated by NMJ damage.

2.3. The complement system in ocular MG

Extraocular muscle involvement constitutes the hallmark clinical finding in MG and the preferential involvement of the extraocular muscles in MG is a very well established fact. A great majority of MG patients develop extraocular muscle weakness and usually this is the first and sometimes the only sign in the clinical course of MG. While the physiological features and high metabolic requirements of the extraocular muscles render them more susceptible to affliction in MG (28), it is now well known that these muscles are also prone to complement associated immunological damage more than other muscle types. As compared to other muscles, extraocular muscles show reduced expression of complement inhibiting decay accelarating factor (DAF, CD55) and CD59 in humans and complement receptor 1-related gene/protein y (Crry) in mice (28,55). Moreover, in mice, complement regulatory gene expression is significantly downregulated following AChR immunization or passive transfer of anti-AChR antibodies (28). Notably, while anti-C5 antibody treatment eliminates complement deposition at the NMJ of limb muscles, it can not induce a similar effect in the extraocular muscles (28,36).

Further support for the involvement of the complement system in ocular MG comes from an autoimmune model for ocular MG induced in susceptible mouse strains by human AChR α-subunit immunization. While B6, C57BL/10 and HLA-DQ8 transgenic mice are highly susceptible to ocular MG, HLA-DR3 transgenic mice show significant resistance. This differential ocular MG susceptibility is correlated with the number of IgG, C3 and MAC deposits located at the NMJ of the extraocular muscles (27). These studies imply that the complement system also plays a trivial role in purely ocular MG.

2.4. Other potential mechanisms for the complement system in MG/EAMG pathogenesis

As mentioned before, a major complement associated pathogenic mechanism is the attraction of inflammatory cells to the target tissue. Since muscle tissue does not show significant cellular infiltration in MG and EAMG induced by AChR immunization, this does not seem to be a valid mechanism for NMJ destruction in MG. However, EAMG induced by passive transfer of pathogenic antibodies is characterized with antibody and complement deposits at the NMJ as well as phagocytic cell invasion of the NMJ (29) and represents an acute form of EAMG (animals might have severe weakness in 24 hours in this model as opposed to more than one month in the immunization based model). In this model, cellular infiltration might be induced by opsonization of destroyed NMJ folds by C3 deposits (29,36). While this EAMG model does not have an exact human correlate, it has often been argued that acute myasthenic crisis (severe widespread paralysis of striated muscles including respiratory muscles often requiring assisted ventilation) might have features somewhat identical to the passively induced EAMG model (36). Whether, complement breakdown products draw phagocytic cells to the muscle tissue during a myasthenic crisis and thus enhance the muscle weakness initiated by anti-AChR and complement deposits remain to be elucidated.

Another intriguing mechanism by which the complement system is involved in MG pathogenesis could be the breakdown of tolerance to AChR at the initial stages of the disease. It has long been proposed that AChR molecules expressed by thymic medullary epithelial and myoid cells might be initiating the autoimmune response against the NMJ. This hypothesis is supported by abundant cellular infiltrates located in close proximity to thymic epithelial and myoid cells of MG patients. Various complement factors (C1q, C3b and C9) are detected at or around AChR-expressing myoid cells, indicating the presence of a robust complement attack on these cells. Absence or very low expression of complement inhibitors (CD46, DAF and CD59) by myoid cells render them particularly vulnerable to this attack. Notably, myoid cells express AChR in its native form. Thymic cellular infiltration mediated at least partially by the complement system and usually observed in earlier stages of MG might be exposing AChR molecules to the immune system and thus initiating or enhancing the anti-AChR immune response (56).

2.5. CP in MG and EAMG

CP is known to be primarily activated by immune complexes. Since EAMG is an antibody mediated disease characterized by circulating anti-AChR antibodies, we hypothesized that the complement system could plausibly be activated via CP by the pathogenic antibodies that bind to their target antigen AChR, thus forming immune complexes. Reduced serum C4 levels have been reported in patients with MG and rodents with EAMG (6,7) and in one report, patients with higher anti-AChR antibody levels have shown lower C4 levels (30), suggesting that CP proteins are excessively utilized in MG patients due to increased demand.

To demonstrate direct genetic evidence for the role of CP in EAMG, we immunized C4 deficient and sufficient littermates in the B6 background with AChR along with C3 KO and WT mice. C3 KO and C4 KO mice showed significantly reduced EAMG incidence and severity as compared to their C3 or C4 sufficient littermates. C3 or C4 heterozygous mice displayed intermediate EAMG incidences between KO and WT mice. To further clarify the anti-AChR IgG status, frozen muscle sections were double stained with BTx (to visualize the NMJ) and antibodies against IgG, C3 or MAC. As expected, C3 KO and C4 KO mice did not display C3 or MAC deposits at their NMJs, further corroborating the critical role that CP is playing in complement mediated NMJ lysis. However, C4 KO mice did have IgG deposits at their NMJ. In line with previous observations (33,42), C4 gene KO mice were EAMG resistant despite the presence of serum anti-AChR antibodies and NMJ IgG deposits, showing once again that at least in the animal model of MG, significant NMJ destruction generally requires the presence of a fully functioning complement system in addition to IgG deposition. These results represented the first direct genetic evidence for the involvement of CP in clinical EAMG development (11).

As is the case with all KO studies, the influence of the inherent deficiency of C3 or C4 gene on the immune system functioning might have influenced EAMG resistance. For instance, both C3 and C4 KO mice had reduced B cell ratios and increased apoptotic B cells in their lymph nodes following AChR immunization (11). C3 and C4 are both involved in tolerance induction to self antigens and their deficiency increases the elimination of B cells with negative selection via apoptosis associated mechanisms (57). This phenomenon, among others, might have at least partially influenced EAMG resistance in C3 or C4 KO mice.

To determine whether CP is genuinely vital for NMJ lysis and EAMG induction and that EAMG resistance of C4 KO mice is not due to some inborn immunological deficiency rather than the inactivation of CP, we initially attempted to prevent EAMG induction by blocking the CP. For this purpose, we injected B6 mice with anti-C1q antibody before AChR immunization. Anti-C1q antibody or isotype antibody treatment (i.p.) was started with two loading doses of 200 µg given on days -7 and -4 before first AChR immunization (day 0), followed by 100 µg/injection, twice weekly for 5 weeks. Anti-C1q antibody treatment protected B6 mice from developing EAMG. As opposed to 70% isotype antibody administered mice, only 20% of anti-C1q antibody treated mice developed clinical EAMG. Anti-C1q antibody treated mice also had significantly less severe EAMG and higher average grip strength than isotype antibody treated mice (18). Anti-C1q antibody exerted its EAMG preventing effect by reducing NMJ C3, IgG and MAC deposits and by diminishing lymph node cell IL-6 production in response to AChR and immunodominant peptide á146-162 challenges (18). These results also demonstrated for the first time that an autoimmune disease could be prevented by inhibition of the CP.

In therapeutic studies B6 and RIIIS/J mice treated with 10 µg of anti-C1q antibody twice weekly for 4 weeks following EAMG induction by AChR immunization had significantly reduced clinical grades and improved grip strength, as compared to isotype antibody treated control mice. In the anti-C1q antibody treated group, 62.5% of B6 mice and 60% of RIIIS/J mice clinically improved during the treatment period (showed reduced clinical severity by observation and increased muscle strength as measured by a dynamometer). None of the remaining B6 mice (0%) and only one of the remaining RIIIS/J mice (20%) clinically deteriorated. In contrast, improvement rates of isotype antibody treated B6 and RIIIS/J mice were 33.3% and 20%, respectively, while 33% B6 mice and 40% RIIIS/J mice significantly worsened (58). On the other hand, administration of anti-C1q antibody boosted serum immune complex and C3 levels in a dose dependent manner and induced a mild nephropathy characterized with kidney C3 and IgG deposits, indicating that other avenues of CP inhibiting methods should be tried in future experiments. Nevertheless, these studies showed that anti-C1q antibody treatment was capable of ameliorating myasthenic muscle weakness and an autoimmune disease could be treated by CP inhibition.

2.6. MBL and alternate pathway are not invoved in EAMG

The above studies, which showed the significant role of CP in EAMG, do not dissect the roles of lectin (also requires C4 component) and alternative complement pathways in EAMG pathogenesis. Binding of mannose binding lectin (MBL) to various pathogens triggers lectin pathway activation and this leads to cleavage of C4 and C2, which induces C3 convertase formation, C3 activation and eventually MAC formation (21). Therefore, EAMG resistance of C4 KO mice could at least partially be associated with impaired functioning of the lectin pathway. To test this assumption, we investigated whether MBL gene KO mice were susceptible to anti-AChR antibody mediated NMJ destruction in EAMG. MBL KO mice in B6 background and WT B6 mice were immunized with AChR on days 0 and 30. MBL KO mice started developing EAMG before WT mice and thus at the third week following second AChR immunization, EAMG incidence and severity and average muscle strength of MBL KO mice were significantly higher than those of WT mice. As WT mice started developing EAMG in the following days, the clinical parameters became identical in the fourth week. At termination (5th week after 2nd immunization), there were more MBL KO mice with EAMG (82%) than WT mice (62.5%). However, this difference was not statistically significant (59). This study showed that murine EAMG can be established in the absence of MBL, the lectin pathway is not required for EAMG induction and MBL deficiency even renders mice slightly more susceptible to EAMG.

MBL KO mice also had preserved immune response to AChR, as demonstrated by serum anti-AChR IgG and complement levels and NMJ IgG/complement deposits identical to those of WT mice. Interestingly, MBL KO mice showed reduced lymphocyte proliferation response to AChR or immunodominant peptide stimulation and increased circulating immune complex levels in comparison to WT mice (59). MBL is not only involved in immune system defense against pathogens but also in clearance of cellular debris, apoptotic cells and immune complexes. Therefore, MBL deficient individuals are prone to certain immune complex mediated autoimmune diseases such as SLE and rheumatoid arthritis (21). However, MBL KO mice are not susceptible to autoimmunity and no experimental autoimmune disease model has been described in MBL KO mice, so far. Our results also support the notion that lectin pathway is not significantly involved in antibody mediated autoimmune disease development.

Anti-AChR positive MG patients have reduced serum C3 and C4 levels probably due to overconsumption of these factors by antibodies bound to the NMJs (30). To investigate whether a possible overutilization of the lectin pathway could have diminished serum MBL levels in a similar manner, we compared serum MBL levels of anti-AChR positive MG patients and healthy controls. No significant difference was observed between the serum MBL levels of 77 anti-AChR antibody positive generalized MG patients and 105 healthy controls. Therefore, MBL pathway does not play a role in MG pathogenesis (59).

As a final note, alternative complement pathway, which is also primarily activated by microorganisms like lectin pathway might also have a subtle adjunctive role in MAC formation at the NMJ and thus MG development, especially taking into account that certain pathogens are often suggested to participate in the initiation of autoimmune disorders. The validity of this assumption needs to be tested with future experiments.

2.7. Complement regulators in EAMG

In addition to extensive experimental and clinical proofs corroborating the involvement of the complement system in EAMG and MG, a new line of evidence has recently started mounting on the defense mechanisms of the muscle tissue against the complement assault. Mouse skeletal muscle tissue can express various complement inhibitors such as DAF, CD59 and Crry (55) and these molecules are involved in protection of the muscle tissue against the complement assault (see Chapter 15 for further readings on complement regulators).

The initial proof for the involvement of complement regulators in EAMG came from a passive transfer study conducted using Daf1 (mouse equivalent of human DAF) KO, Daf1 and CD59 double KO mice and their WT control littermates. In this study, shortly after EAMG induction both KO strains exhibited enhanced clinical severity, increased NMJ complement deposits and damage. Moreover, inhibition of the complement cascade with a C5-inhibiting antibody abrogated disease in Daf1/CD59 KO mice (60,61). These studies clearly marked the importance of complement regulators expressed by myocytes as a defense mechanism against complement mediated NMJ lysis. In contrast with the DAF study, AChR-immunized CD59 KO mice were shown to exhibit identical susceptibility to EAMG induction as WT mice (62). This finding was supported by other reports utilizing the passively induced EAMG model in CD59 KO mice (60,63) (see Chapter 15 for more information).

CD59 and DAF do not only regulate complement activation but they are also involved in T cell proliferation and functions (64,65). Therefore, EAMG induction might be hindered in CD59 KO mice probably due to deficient T cell functioning, which is highly essential for anti-AChR immunity. Also, CD59 KO mice with EAMG show significantly reduced NMJ C3 deposition as compared to DAF KO mice (63), suggesting that DAF acitivty is adequate to prevent complement deposition and CD59 does not play a major role in protection of the NMJ against the complement attack.

3. THE ROLE OF IMMUNE COMPLEXES IN EAMG AND MG

There are various immunological factors, which are not considered as components of the complement system but are closely associated with the complement mediated disease mechanisms such as the immune complexes. The initial evidence on the role of CIC on MG pathogenesis came from clinical studies. While the earliest reports pointed out a significant increase in the serum levels of immune complexes (7), more recent ones suggested a correlation between CIC levels and the severity of muscle weakness (66). Moreover, AChR-anti-AChR antibody immune complexes were shown to enhance the AChR-specific T cell proliferation (67).

To better characterize the role of the immune complexes in MG pathogenesis, we performed a series of experiments using the B6 and RIIIS/J EAMG model. First, we found out that levels of anti-AChR IgG, C1q, C3, C1q-conjugated CIC (C1q-CIC) and C3-conjugated CIC (C3-CIC) are remarkably elevated in sera of AChR-immunized B6 mice following AChR immunization. Then, we compared all measured parameters with the clinical scores and the grip strengths of mice. Serum C3-CIC and C1q-CIC levels of AChR-immunized mice showed a weak and statistically non-significant correlation with the grip strengths of the mice (19). Nevertheless, these weak inverse correlations indicated that mice with higher CIC levels were more likely to have greater muscle weakness. We also demonstrated that RIIIS/J mice had a higher EAMG incidence and severity than B6 mice and this was associated with higher serum C3 and C1q-CIC levels. Furthermore, EAMG clinical scores of AChR-immunized RIIIS/J mice were significantly correlated with their serum C1q-CIC levels (R=0.9698, p=0.0004). In other words, just like B6 mice, RIIIS/J mice with higher CIC levels were inclined to have more severe muscle weakness (20). So far, there are no diagnostic tests available to predict the clinical severity of MG. Whether serum CIC levels can be used for this purpose needs to be substantiated by further clinical studies.

3.1. CP activation by immune complexes

The mechanisms by which CIC exert their pathogenic effects are not entirely understood. It has long been established that immune complexes are the major activators of the CP. Therefore, the major mechanism of action of AChR-anti-AChR antibody immune complexes might be activation of the complement cascade. Several reports have shown co-localization of IgG and complement deposits in MG and EAMG (9-11). Plausibly, AChR-anti-AChR antibody immune complexes bind AChR, activate CP and trigger an inflammatory response resulting in NMJ destruction and muscle weakness. This view is supported by a new line of evidence using mouse strains with defective CP functioning. As mentioned previously, genetic disruption of C4 and inhibition of C1q by antibodies before or after AChR immunization render mice resistant to EAMG induction. In both cases, anti-AChR antibody production is not compromised and IgG deposits are detected at the NMJ and yet mice do not develop significant muscle weakness (11,18).

3.2. Fcgamma receptor (FcγR) activation by immune complexes

In addition to activation of CP, immune complexes also appear to influence the disease manifestation by interacting with the FcγR. CIC mediate a variety of immune functions such as macrophage phagocytosis, neutrophil activation and immune complex clearance by interacting with FcγRIIb and III. Since FcγRIII acts in favor of antibody production, increased macrophage activity and proinflammatory cytokine production, its deficiency results in resistance to inflammatory disorders (68). Likewise, AChR-immunized FcγRIII KO mice have significant lower EAMG incidence (25% in FcγRIII KO mice vs 75% in WT mice) and severity and reduced NMJ IgG, C3 and MAC deposits as compared to WT mice. This is associated with reduced lymph node cell IL-6 production in response to AChR challenge and serum C1q, C3 and C1q-CIC levels. Notably, FcγRIII gene deficiency does not inhibit the lymphocyte proliferation and antibody production in response to AChR (18). Overall, these results show that CIC enhance the clinical severity of EAMG by stimulating IL-6 and complement production via their interaction with FcγRIII.

Due to the crucial role of FcγRIII in promoting inflammation, FcγRIII KO mice are resistant to various autoimmune disorders such as autoimmune nephritis, arthritis, Goodpasture's syndrome and corneal inflammation (18,68,69). In contrast, FcγRIIB KO mice are generally highly susceptible to autoimmune diseases indicating that FcγRIIB antagonizes the inflammatory response against self-tissue and its deficiency disrupts the inhibition of the immune system. However, most of the experimental disease models tested with FcγRIIB KO mice are autoimmune diseases primarily mediated by cellular immunity and characterized with cellular infiltration of the target tissue. As opposed to these disease models, in EAMG, a classical antibody-mediated disease, genetic deficiency of FcāRIIB protects mice against disease development, suggesting that FcāRIIB is a promoter of antibody-mediated immunity (69). Notably, FcγRIIB KO mice are patially resistant to EAMG, despite preserved anti-AChR antibody production and NMJ complement deposition. This might be at least partially be associated with reduced lymph node cell IL-6 and IL-10 production and increased CD4+CD25+ cell ratios in lymph nodes (69). Both FcγRIII KO and FcγRIIB KO mice have increased germinal center numbers, serum anti-AChR antibody and CIC levels, suggesting that FcγRIIB and FcγRIII both have an inhibitory effect on anti-AChR antibody production.

3.3. Anti-C1q antibody in EAMG

Anti-C1q antibody has been detected in sera of patients with various immune complex associated diseases such as SLE and rheumatoid arthritis (70,71). Moreover, anti-C1q antibody is a predictor of clinical severity and kidney involvement in SLE (72). We recently demonstrated anti-C1q antibodies in sera of EAMG mice and MG patients for the first time. AChR-immunized B6 mice did not only develop anti-C1q antibodies following AChR immunization but also serum levels of these antibodies significantly correlated with the muscle strength (R=-0.61, p=0.01), serum C1q-CIC levels (R=0.69, p=0.002) and serum C3-CIC levels (R=0.61, p=0.003) (19).

These results also suggest that anti-C1q antibody might be an active participant of MG pathogenesis as it is proposed to be in SLE (72). The exact mechanisms of this participation remains to be elucidated. Anti-C1q antibodies might be binding C1q molecules attached to immune complex deposits located at the NMJ (19) and thus activating the complement cascade.

A similar role has been proposed for anti-C1q antibody in kidney complications of an experimental autoimmune nephropathy model (73).

In summary, immune complexes appear to influence EAMG induction via direct and indirect mechanisms (Figure 1). Immune complexes might be directly activating the complement cascade via CP and thus enhancing the immune response against AChR. As an indirect mechanism, CIC might be modulating cytokine and complement production through their interactions with FcγRIIB and FcγRIII and thus potentiate the ongoing NMJ destruction. Additionally, anti-C1q antibodies might be contributing to NMJ destruction either by enhancing the complement activation or by some yet unknown mechanisms. Preliminary EAMG data suggest that CIC and anti-C1q antibody might be potential markers for prediction of clinical severity of MG.

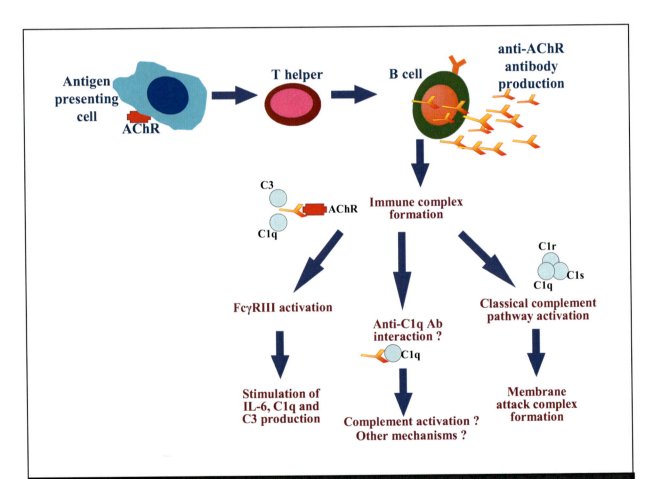

Figure 1: Hypothetical illustration depicting possible mechanisms by which immune complexes participate in EAMG pathogenesis (AChR: acetylcholine receptor). Antigen presenting cells activate T helper cells following AChR consumption. Activation of B cells by T helper cells results in anti-AChR antibody production. These antibodies form immune complexes, which affect the anti-AChR immune response by activating the complement cascade, and FcγRIII and possibly by interacting with anti-C1q antibodies. Mechanisms that are required to be further substantiated by additional experimental data were designated by question marks.

4. THE ROLE OF IL-6 IN MG

Cytokines are required in every step of production of antibodies against AChR epitopes. Presentation of AChR fragments to T helper cells, activation of T helper cells by NK cells, activation of B cells by T helper cells and proliferation and differentiation of AChR antibody producing B cells are all achieved by various cytokines (2,15). The function and significance of individual cytokines in the development of this cascade of events are mainly assessed through the use of cytokine or cytokine receptor gene KO mice or specific cytokine inhibitors. Experimental studies of the last three decades utilizing the EAMG model have shown that a wide variety of cytokines is involved in the induction of the immune response against the NMJ and both Th1 and Th2 cytokines are required for effective EAMG induction. IFN-γ, IL-12, IL-18, IL-10, TNF-α and IL-6 appear to be particularly associated with anti-AChR response and impaired functioning of one of these cytokines results in interruption of the immune response against the NMJ and thus reduced EAMG severity and frequency (47,74-77).

When all cytokine associated EAMG studies are compared, IL-6 gene deficiency seems to be particularly associated with a markedly significant reduction in EAMG incidence and severity (76). While only 20-25% of IL-6 KO mice can develop clinical EAMG, around 40-45% of IFN-γ or IL-12 KO mice, 60% of IL-10 KO mice and 70-100% of WT mice display muscle weakness following AChR-immunization (47,75,76). Extremely reduced EAMG incidence of IL-6 KO mice emphasizes the significance of this cytokine in EAMG induction.

IL-6 is a major proinflammatory cytokine involved in various autoimmune disorders and experimental autoimmune models. Among other factors, pathogenicity of IL-6 is probably most closely exercised through its contribution to antibody and complement production (78), both of which are highly essential for EAMG induction. As a matter of fact, IL-6 gene deficient mice exhibit markedly reduced serum levels of anti-AChR IgG (particularly the complement-fixing IgG2b isotype) and C3 (76). IL-6 KO mice also have reduced AChR and immunodominant peptide (α146–162)-specific lymphocyte-proliferative responses, IFN-γ and IL-10 production and splenic germinal centers as compared to WT mice (76). Since both IFN-γ and IL-10 have facilitating roles in EAMG (47,75), their deficient production by lymph node cells could plausibly be associated with EAMG resistance of IL-6 KO mice. IL-6 deficiency also leads to defective AChR-stimulated IL-17 production by CD4+ cells, which is also required for EAMG induction (79).

Additionally, IL-6 production is upregulated in thymic epithelial cells of MG patients (80) and therefore IL-6 might be contributing to MG development via thymus associated mechanisms. IL-6 is also known to exhibit directly toxic effects on neurons (81) and muscle cells (17). Immunization of EAMG-susceptible B6 mice promotes IL-6 production in muscle cells and IL-6 treated skeletal muscle cells display increased apoptotic cell death and decreased α-bungarotoxin (BTx)-binding sites (17). There results suggest that local IL-6 production by muscle cells might be contributing to muscle weakness in MG through autocrine mechanisms.

All these studies implicate that inhibition of IL-6 could effectively treat MG. Since expression of immune cell surface molecules of IL-6 KO mice is intact (76), neutralization of IL-6 would not be expected to have significant global immunosuppression. In an effort to design novel treatment methods based on inhibition of IL-6, we treated EAMG-susceptible B6 mice with a rat anti-mouse IL-6 antibody. Ten B6 mice were immunized with 20 μg of AChR on day 0 and 38. On day 1, five mice were injected i.p. with 0.5 mg anti-IL-6 and five control B6 mice were injected i.p. with PBS. A second injection of 0.5 mg of anti-IL-6 was given on day 31. Figure 2 illustrates the clinical EAMG incidence and severity of B6 mice following anti-IL-6 antibody administration. On day 18 following second AChR immunization, 100% of the AChR-immunized B6 mice injected with PBS developed clinical EAMG compared to only 20% of anti-IL-6 antibody-treated mice. Also, anti-IL-6 antibody-treated mice had less severe disease compared to PBS-treated controls. However, the treatment effect of anti-IL-6 antibody waned after day 20, implying that anti-IL-6 Ab treatment should be given more frequently for a sustained effect.

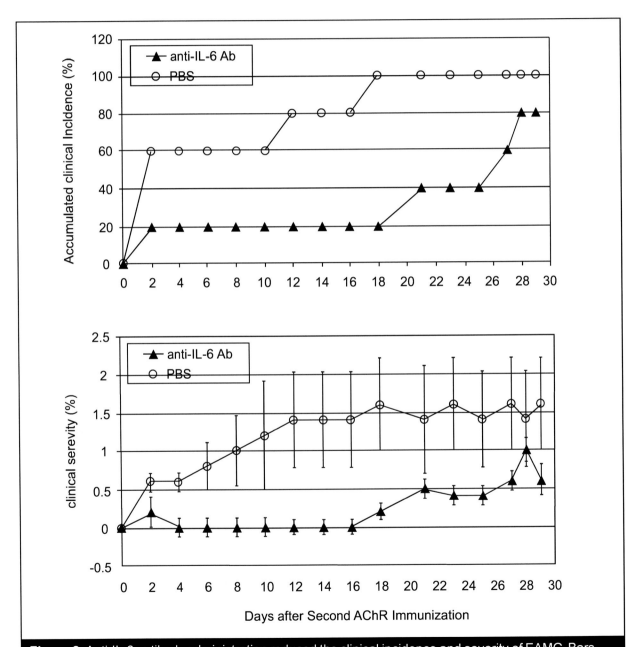

Figure 2: Anti-IL-6 antibody administration reduced the clinical incidence and severity of EAMG. Bars indicate standard errors.

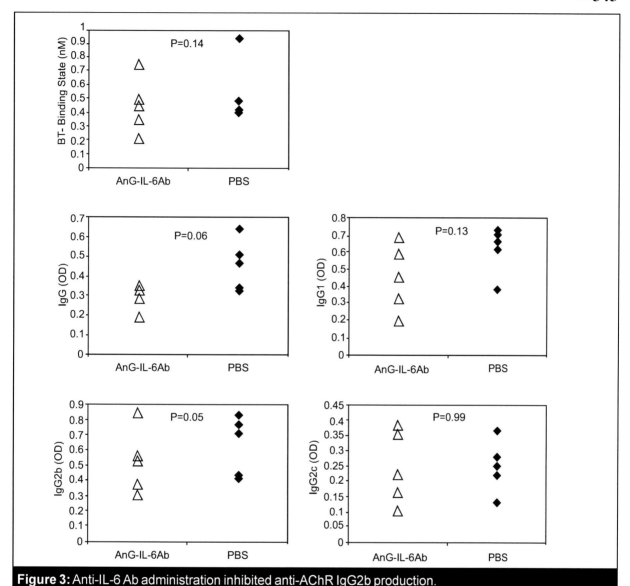

Figure 3: Anti-IL-6 Ab administration inhibited anti-AChR IgG2b production.

Sera obtained on day 60 (at termination) were tested for the level of anti-AChR IgG and IgG1, IgG2b and IgG2c isotypes. There was no statistically significant difference in the serum (1:1000) level of anti-AChR IgG1 and IgG2c between anti-IL-6 and PBS-treated mice. However, the serum anti-AChR IgG2b (complement fixing) level was significantly ($p<0.05$) reduced in anti-IL-6 antibody-treated mice (Figure 3), just as IL-6 KO mice. Anti-AChR IgG2b antibody has been implicated in EAMG pathogenesis, since this is a complement-fixing isotype in the mouse (82). Lymph node cells obtained at termination of the experiment (day 60) were evaluated for AChR and α146-162 peptide-specific lymphocyte proliferative responses, IL-2, IFN-γ, IL-10 and IL-6 production. Although all of these parameters were reduced by anti-IL-6 Ab administration, only AChR and α146-162 induced IL-2 and IL-6 responses were significantly suppressed (Figure 4). When LNC were studied for the percentages of CD3, CD4, CD8 and CD19 positive cells, only CD19+ B cells were slightly, but significantly reduced in anti-IL-6-administered mice (Figure

5) suggesting that anti-IL-6 antibody administration preserves T cells and specifically depletes a small fraction of B cells. Since anti-IL-6 administration particularly suppresses anti-AChR IgG2b, the data might suggest that part of the depleted B cell population could be anti-AChR IgG2b producing B cells. Sera obtained on day 14 and 59 after the second AChR immunization were tested for IL-6, IFN-γ, IL-10, C1q, C3 and circulating immune complexes. Anti-IL-6 treatment specifically suppressed serum C1q levels (p<0.05) but not any of the other tested parameters. In summary, suppression of clinical EAMG following anti-IL-6 antibody administration in B6 mice

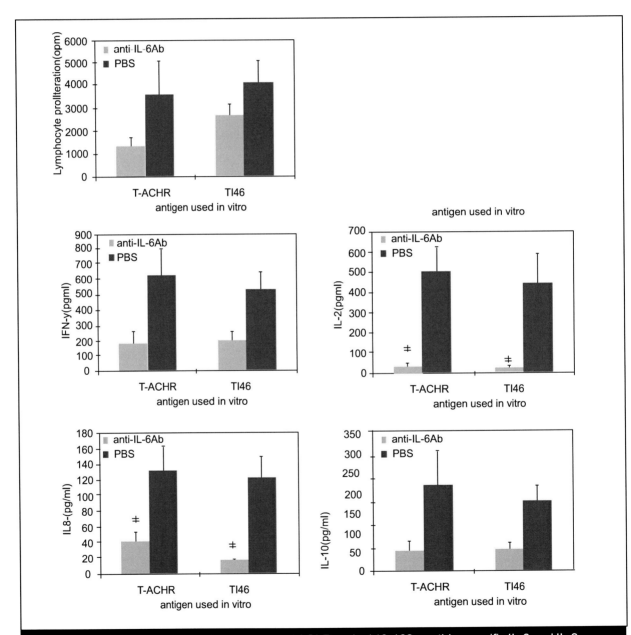

Figure 4: Anti-IL-6 Ab administration suppressed AChR and α146-162 peptide-specific IL-6 and IL-2 production. Bars indicate standard deviations. *, indicates p<0.05.

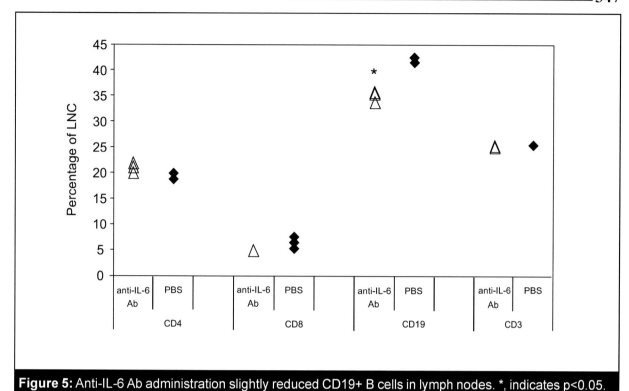

Figure 5: Anti-IL-6 Ab administration slightly reduced CD19+ B cells in lymph nodes. *, indicates p<0.05.

was associated with reduction in a) AChR and 146-162 peptide-specific IL-2 and IL-6 production, b) CD19+ B cells in the lymph nodes, and c) serum anti-AChR IgG2b and C1q levels.

5. CONCLUSION-THERAPEUTIC IMPLICATIONS

As reviewed in this chapter, the complement system has a significant importance in MG pathogenesis. Many preclinical studies (18,34,36,37,58) have already shown that preventing the formation of MAC deposits at the NMJ by monoclonal antibodies might be a very promising future treatment method for MG. The predominant role that CP plays in EAMG and presumably in MG pathogenesis (83,84) is of extreme importance. New therapeutic methods based on specific inhibition of CP may effectively treat MG without abolishing the alternative pathway, which is primarily responsible for host immune defense against invading pathogens. Treatment with specific CP inhibitors would thus be expected to prevent infections that are frequently associated with the currently available immunosuppressive medications. This strategy might also be used in other complement-associated autoimmune diseases. Since the CP factor C1q is also responsible for immune complex clearance, therapeutic CP inhibition might increase immune complex levels and induce immune complex associated autoimmune diseases. This problem can be overcome by developing reagents that specifically inhibit other CP factors such as C2.

In various MG and EAMG studies, serum immune complexes have been shown to be related with clinical muscle weakness. Immune complexes might be exerting their pathogenic effects through the activation of the CP. Therefore, CP inhibiting treatment strategies would also be expected to prevent myasthenic symptoms through the inhibition of this mechanism. However, preliminary studies suggest that immune complexes appear to modulate EAMG via FcᾱRs expressed by immune cells and therefore inhibition of CP might not completely eliminate the pathogenicity of immune complexes in MG. For this purpose, novel treatment methods based on inhibition of FcγRs might aid in effective control of MG. These treatment methods would facilitate MG treatment by preventing FcᾱR mediated production of proinflammatory cytokines and complement factors.

IL-6 is a central factor in MG pathogenesis and promotes muscle weakness by producing complement factors and anti-AChR antibodies and by exerting direct deleterious effects on muscle cells. Therefore, inhibition of IL-6, as exemplified in our preliminary studies, would be expected to treat MG by not only abolishing a major proinflammatory cytokine but also by preventing complement associated disease mechanisms. More successful treatment models for EAMG can be innovated by combined inhibition of IL-6 and the complement cascade, which appear to work in close relationship in inflammatory disorders.

REFERENCES

1. Vincent, A. 2006. Immunology of disorders of neuromuscular transmission. *Acta Neurol. Scand. Suppl.* 183:1-7.
2. Christadoss, P., M. Poussin and C. Deng. 2000. Animal models of myasthenia gravis. *Clin. Immunol.* 94:75-87.
3. Conti-Fine, B.M., M. Milani and H.J. Kaminski. 2006. Myasthenia gravis: past, present, and future. *J. Clin. Invest.* 116:2843-2854.
4. Ashizawa, T. and S.H. Appel. 1985. Complement-dependent lysis of cultured rat myotubes by myasthenic immunoglobulins. *Neurology.* 35:1748-1753.
5. Childs, L.A., R. Harrison and G.G. Lunt. 1987. Complement-mediated muscle damage produced by myasthenic sera. *Ann. N. Y. Acad. Sci.* 505:180-193.
6. Nastuk, W.L., O.J. Plescia and K.E. Osserman. 1960. Changes in serum complement activity in patients with myasthenia gravis. *Proc. Soc. Exp. Biol. Med.* 105:177-184.
7. Casali, P., P. Borzini and C. Zanussi. 1976. Immune complexes in myasthenia gravis. *Lancet.* 2:378.
8. Engel, A.G., K. Sahashi and G. Fumagalli. 1981. The immunopathology of acquired myasthenia gravis. *Ann. N. Y. Acad. Sci.* 377:158-174.
9. Sahashi, K., A.G. Engel, E.H. Lambert and F.M. Howard, Jr. 1980. Ultrastructural localization of the terminal and lytic ninth complement component (C9) at the motor end-plate in myasthenia gravis. *J. Neuropathol. Exp. Neurol.* 39:160-172.
10. Engel, A.G., E.H. Lambert and F.M. Howard. 1977. Immune complexes (IgG and C3) at the motor end-plate in myasthenia gravis: ultrastructural and light microscopic localization and electrophysiologic correlations. *Mayo. Clin. Proc.* 52:267-280.
11. Tüzün, E., B.G. Scott, E. Goluszko, S. Higgs and P. Christadoss. 2003. Genetic evidence for involvement of classical complement pathway in induction of experimental autoimmune myasthenia gravis. *J. Immunol.* 171:3847-3854.
12. Howard, F.M., Jr, V.A. Lennon, J. Finley, J. Matsumoto and L.R. Elveback. 1987. Clinical correlations of antibodies that bind, block, or modulate human acetylcholine receptors in myasthenia gravis. *Ann. N. Y. Acad. Sci.* 505:526-538.
13. Engel, A.G. and G. Fumagalli. 1982. Mechanisms of acetylcholine receptor loss from the neuromuscular junction. *Ciba. Found. Symp.* 90:197-224.
14. Shi, F.D., X.F. Bai, H.L. Li and H. Link. 1998. Macrophage apoptosis in muscle tissue in experimental autoimmune myasthenia gravis. *Muscle Nerve.* 21:1071-1074.
15. Conti-Fine, B.M., M. Milani and W. Wang. 2008. CD4+ T cells and cytokines in the pathogenesis of acquired myasthenia gravis. *Ann. N. Y. Acad. Sci.* 1132:193-209.
16. Stegall, T. and K.A. Krolick. 2000. Myocytes respond to both interleukin-4 and interferon-gamma: cytokine responsiveness with the potential to influence the severity and course of experimental myasthenia gravis. *Clin. Immunol.* 94:133-139.
17. Tüzün, E., J. Li, N. Wanasen, L. Soong and P. Christadoss. 2006. Immunization of mice with T cell-dependent antigens promotes IL-6 and TNF-alpha production in muscle cells. *Cytokine.* 35:100-106.
18. Tüzün, E., S.S. Saini, H. Yang, D. Alagappan, S. Higgs and P. Christadoss. 2006. Genetic evidence for the involvement of Fcgamma receptor III in experimental autoimmune myasthenia gravis pathogenesis. *J. Neuroimmunol.* 174:157-167.

19. Tüzün, E., S.S. Saini, S. Ghosh, J. Rowin, M.N. Meriggioli and P. Christadoss. 2006. Predictive value of serum anti-C1q antibody levels in experimental autoimmune myasthenia gravis. *Neuromuscul. Disord.* 16:137-143.

20. Tüzün, E., B.G. Scott, H. Yang, B. Wu, E. Goluszko, M. Guigneaux, S. Higgs and P. Christadoss. 2004. Circulating immune complexes augment severity of antibody-mediated myasthenia gravis in hypogammaglobulinemic RIIIS/J mice. *J. Immunol.* 172:5743-5752.

21. Szebeni, J. 2004. The complement system. Springer-Verlag New York, LLC.

22. Meyer, O., G. Hauptmann, G. Tappeiner, H.D. Ochs and F. Mascart-Lemone. 1985. Genetic deficiency of C4, C2 or C1q and lupus syndromes. Association with anti-Ro (SS-A) antibodies. *Clin. Exp. Immunol.* 62:678-684.

23. Yang, Y., E.K. Chung, B. Zhou, K. Lhotta, L.A. Hebert, D.J. Birmingham, B.H. Rovin and C.Y. Yu. 2004. The intricate role of complement component C4 in human systemic lupus erythematosus. *Curr. Dir. Autoimmun.* 7: 8-132.

24. Sohn, J.H., P.S. Bora, H.J. Suk, H. Molina, H.J. Kaplan and N.S. Bora. 2003. Tolerance is dependent on complement C3 fragment iC3b binding to antigen-presenting cells. *Nat. Med.* 9:206-212.

25. Mendell, J.R., T.S. Garcha and J.T. Kissel. 1996. The immunopathogenic role of complement in human muscle disease. *Curr. Opin. Neurol.* 9:226-234.

26. Leite, M.I., S. Jacob, S. Viegas, J. Cossins, L. Clover, B.P. Morgan, D. Beeson, N. Willcox and A. Vincent. 2008. IgG1 antibodies to acetylcholine receptors in 'seronegative' myasthenia gravis. *Brain.* 131:1940-1952.

27. Yang, H., B. Wu, E. Tüzün, S.S. Saini, J. Li, W. Allman, S. Higgs, T.L. Xiao and P. Christadoss. 2007. A new mouse model of autoimmune ocular myasthenia gravis. *Invest. Ophthalmol. Vis. Sci.* 48:5101-5111.

28. Soltys, J., B. Gong, H.J. Kaminski, Y. Zhou and L.L. Kusner. 2008. Extraocular muscle susceptibility to myasthenia gravis: unique immunological environment? *Ann. N. Y. Acad. Sci.* 1132:220-224.

29. Tüzün, E. and P. Christadoss. 2006. Unraveling myasthenia gravis immunopathogenesis using animal models. *Drug Discovery Today: Disease Models.* 3:15-20.

30. Romi, F., E.K. Kristoffersen, J.A. Aarli and N.E. Gilhus. 2005. The role of complement in myasthenia gravis: serological evidence of complement consumption in vivo. *J. Neuroimmunol.* 158:191-194.

31. Kamolvarin, N., T. Hemachudha, B. Ongpipattanakul, K. Phanthumchinda and T. Sueblinvong. 1991. Plasma C3c in immune-mediated neurological diseases: a preliminary report. *Acta. Neurol. Scand.* 83:382-387.

32. Lennon, V.A., M.E. Seybold, J.M. Lindstrom, C. Cochrane and R. Ulevitch. 1978. Role of complement in the pathogenesis of experimental autoimmune myasthenia gravis. *J. Exp. Med.* 147:973-983.

33. Piddlesden, S.J., S. Jiang, J.L. Levin, A. Vincent and B.P. Morgan. 1996. Soluble complement receptor 1 (sCR1) protects against experimental autoimmune myasthenia gravis. *J. Neuroimmunol.* 71:173-177.

34. Biesecker, G. and C.M. Gomez. 1989. Inhibition of acute passive transfer experimental autoimmune myasthenia gravis with Fab antibody to complement C6. *J. Immunol.* 142:2654-2659.

35. Howard, J.F. Jr and D.B. Sanders. 1980. Passive transfer of human myasthenia gravis to rats: 1. Electrophysiology of the developing neuromuscular block. *Neurology*. 30:760-764.

36. Zhou, Y., B. Gong, F. Lin, R.P. Rother, M.E. Medof and H.J. Kaminski. 2007. Anti-C5 antibody treatment ameliorates weakness in experimentally acquired myasthenia gravis. *J. Immunol.* 179:8562-8567.

37. Soltys, J., L.L. Kusner, A. Young, C. Richmonds, D. Hatala, B. Gong, V. Shanmugavel and H.J. Kaminski. 2009. Novel complement inhibitor limits severity of experimentally myasthenia gravis. *Ann. Neurol.* 65:67-75.

38. Ptak, J. and J. Lochman. 2005. Immunoadsorption therapy and complement activation. *Transfus. Apher. Sci.* 32:263-267.

39. Thorlacius, S., T.E. Mollnes, P. Garred, J.A. Aarli, R. Matre, O Tonder and K. Halvorsen. 1988. Plasma exchange in myasthenia gravis: changes in serum complement and immunoglobulins. *Acta. Neurol. Scand.* 78:221-227.

40. Dalakas, M.C. 2004. Intravenous immunoglobulin in autoimmune neuromuscular diseases. *JAMA*. 291:2367-2375.

41. Rodgaard, A., F.C. Nielsen, R. Djurup, F. Somnier and S. Gammeltoft. 1987. Acetylcholine receptor antibody in myasthenia gravis: predominance of IgG subclasses 1 and 3. *Clin. Exp. Immunol.* 67:82-88.

42. Engel, A.G., H. Sakakibara, K. Sahashi, J.M. Lindstrom, E.H. Lambert and V.A. Lennon. 1979. Passively transferred experimental autoimmune myasthenia gravis. Sequential and quantitative study of the motor end-plate fine structure and ultrastructural localization of immune complexes (IgG and C3), and of the acetylcholine receptor. *Neurology*. 29:179-188.

43. Christadoss, P. 1988. C5 gene influences the development of murine myasthenia gravis. *J. Immunol.* 140:2589-2592.

44. Kumar, V., S.R. Ali, S. Konrad, J. Zwirner, J.S. Verbeek, R.E. Schmidt and J.E. Gessner. 2006. Cell-derived anaphylatoxins as key mediators of antibody-dependent type II autoimmunity in mice. *J. Clin. Invest.* 116:512-520.

45. Qi, H., E. Tüzün, W. Allman, S.S. Saini, Z.R. Penabad, S. Pierangeli and P. Christadoss. 2008. C5a is not involved in experimental autoimmune myasthenia gravis pathogenesis. *J. Neuroimmunol.* 196:101-106.

46. Yang, H., E. Tüzün, D. Alagappan, X. Yu, B.G. Scott, A. Ischenko and P. Christadoss. 2005. IL-1 receptor antagonist-mediated therapeutic effect in murine myasthenia gravis is associated with suppressed serum proinflammatory cytokines, C3, and anti-acetylcholine receptor IgG1. *J. Immunol.* 175:2018-2025.

47. Karachunski, P.I., N.S. Ostlie, C. Monfardini and B.M. Conti-Fine. 2000. Absence of IFN-gamma or IL-12 has different effects on experimental myasthenia gravis in C57BL/6 mice. *J. Immunol.* 164:5236-5244.

48. Poussin, M.A., E. Goluszko, J.U. Franco and P. Christadoss. 2002. Role of IL-5 during primary and secondary immune response to acetylcholine receptor. *J. Neuroimmunol.* 125:51-58.

49. Scott, B.G., H. Yang, E. Tüzün, C. Dong, R.A. Flavell and P. Christadoss. 2004. ICOS is essential for the development of experimental autoimmune myasthenia gravis. *J. Neuroimmunol.* 153:16-25.

50. Liyanage, Y., Hoch, W., Beeson, D. and A. Vincent. 2002. The agrin/muscle-specific kinase pathway: new targets for autoimmune and genetic disorders at the neuromuscular junction. *Muscle Nerve.* 25:4-16.

51. Hoch, W., J. McConville, S. Helms, J. Newsom-Davis, A. Melms and A. Vincent. 2001. Auto-antibodies to the receptor tyrosine kinase MuSK in patients with myasthenia gravis without acetylcholine receptor antibodies. *Nat. Med.* 7:365-368.

52. Vincent, A. and M.I. Leite. 2005. Neuromuscular junction autoimmune disease: muscle specific kinase antibodies and treatments for myasthenia gravis. *Curr. Opin. Neurol.* 18:519-525.

53. McConville, J., M.E. Farrugia, D. Beeson, U. Kishore, R. Metcalfe, J. Newsom-Davis and A. Vincent. 2004. Detection and characterization of MuSK antibodies in seronegative myasthenia gravis. Ann. Neurol. 55:580-584.

54. Romi, F., G.O. Skeie, C. Vedeler, J.A. Aarli, F. Zorzato and N.E. Gilhus. 2000. Complement activation by titin and ryanodine receptor autoantibodies in myasthenia gravis. A study of IgG subclasses and clinical correlations. *J. Neuroimmunol.* 111:169-176.

55. Kaminski, H.J., Z. Li, C. Richmonds, F. Lin and M.E. Medof. 2004. Complement regulators in extraocular muscle and experimental autoimmune myasthenia gravis. *Exp. Neurol.* 189:333-342.

56. Leite, M.I., M. Jones, P. Ströbel, A. Marx, R. Gold, E. Niks, J.J. Verschuuren, S. Berrih-Aknin, F. Scaravilli, A. Canelhas, B.P. Morgan, A. Vincent and N. Willcox. 2007. Myasthenia gravis thymus: complement vulnerability of epithelial and myoid cells, complement attack on them, and correlations with autoantibody status. Am. J. Pathol. 171:893-905.

57. Carroll, M. 1999. Negative selection of self-reactive B lymphocytes involves complement. *Curr. Top. Microbiol. Immunol.* 246:21-27.

58. Tüzün, E., J. Li, S.S. Saini, H. Yang and P. Christadoss. 2007. Pros and cons of treating murine myasthenia gravis with anti-C1q antibody. *J. Neuroimmunol.* 182:167-176.

59. Li, J., H. Qi, E. Tüzün, W. Allman, V. Yýlmaz, S.S. Saini, F. Deymeer, G. Saruhan-Direskeneli and P. Christadoss. 2009. Mannose-binding lectin pathway is not involved in myasthenia gravis pathogenesis. *J. Neuroimmunol.* 208:40-45.

60. Kaminski, H.J., L.L. Kusner, C. Richmonds, M.E. Medof and F. Lin. 2006. Deficiency of decay accelerating factor and CD59 leads to crisis in experimental myasthenia. *Exp. Neurol.* 202:287-293.

61. Lin, F., H.J. Kaminski, B.M. Conti-Fine, W. Wang, C. Richmonds and M.E. Medof. 2002. Markedly enhanced susceptibility to experimental autoimmune myasthenia gravis in the absence of decay-accelerating factor protection. *J. Clin. Invest.* 110:1269-1274.

62. Tüzün, E., S.S. Saini, B.P. Morgan and P. Christadoss. 2006. Complement regulator CD59 deficiency fails to augment susceptibility to actively induced experimental autoimmune myasthenia gravis. *J. Neuroimmunol.* 181:29-33.

63. Morgan, B.P., J. Chamberlain-Banoub, J.W. Neal, W. Song, M. Mizuno and C.L. Harris. 2006. The membrane attack pathway of complement drives pathology in passively induced experimental autoimmune myasthenia gravis in mice. *Clin. Exp. Immunol.* 146:294-302.

64. Longhi, M.P., B. Sivasankar, N. Omidvar, B.P. Morgan and A. Gallimore. 2005. Cutting edge: murine CD59a modulates antiviral CD4+ T cell activity in a complement-independent manner. *J. Immunol.* 175:7098-7102.

65. Heeger, P.S., P.N. Lalli, F. Lin, A. Valujskikh, J. Liu, N. Muqim, Y. Xu and M.E. Medof. 2005. Decay-accelerating factor modulates induction of T cell immunity. *J. Exp. Med.* 201:1523-1530.

66. Mathai, A., C. Sarada and V.V. Radhakrishnan. 2000. Significance of circulating immune complexes in myasthenia gravis. *Indian J. Med. Res.* 111:180-183.

67. Melms, A., R. Weissert, W.E. Klinkert, B.C. Schalke, S. Tzartos and H. Wekerle. 1993. Specific immune complexes augment in vitro acetylcholine receptor-specific T-cell proliferation. *Neurology.* 43:583-588.

68. Dijstelbloem, H.M., J.G. van de Winkel and C.G. Kallenberg. 2001. Inflammation in autoimmunity: receptors for IgG revisited. *Trends. Immunol.* 22:510-516.

69. Li, J., E. Tüzün, X.R. Wu, H.B. Qi, W. Allman, S.S. Saini and P. Christadoss. 2008. Inhibitory IgG receptor FcgammaRIIB fails to inhibit experimental autoimmune myasthenia gravis pathogenesis. *J. Neuroimmunol.* 194:44-53.

70. Reveille, J.D. 2004. Predictive value of autoantibodies for activity of systemic lupus erythematosus. *Lupus.* 13:290-297.

71. Yoshinoya, S., Y. Mizoguchi, S. Aotsuka, R. Yokohari, K. Nishioka and T. Miyamoto. 1992. Circulating immune complex levels measured by new ELISA kits utilizing monoclonal anti-C1q and anti-C3d antibodies correlate with clinical activities of SLE but not with those of RA. *J. Clin. Lab. Immunol.* 38:161-173.

72. Marto, N., M.L. Bertolaccini, E. Calabuig, G.R. Hughes and M.A. Khamashta. 2005. Anti-C1q antibodies in nephritis: correlation between titres and renal disease activity and positive predictive value in systemic lupus erythematosus. *Ann. Rheum. Dis.* 64:444-448.

73. Trouw, L.A., T.W. Groeneveld, M.A. Seelen, J.M. Duijs, I.M. Bajema, F.A. Prins, U. Kishore, D.J. Salant, J.S. Verbeek, C. van Kooten and M.R. Daha. 2004. Anti-C1q autoantibodies deposit in glomeruli but are only pathogenic in combination with glomerular C1q-containing immune complexes. *J. Clin. Invest.* 114:679-688.

74. Im, S.H., D. Barchan, P.K. Maiti, L. Raveh, M.C. Souroujon and S. Fuchs. 2001. Suppression of experimental myasthenia gravis, a B cell-mediated autoimmune disease, by blockade of IL-18. *FASEB J.* 15:2140-2148.

75. Poussin, M.A., E. Goluszko, T.K. Hughes, S.I. Duchicella and P. Christadoss. 2000. Suppression of experimental autoimmune myasthenia gravis in IL-10 gene-disrupted mice is associated with reduced B cells and serum cytotoxicity on mouse cell line expressing AChR. *J. Neuroimmunol.* 111:152-160.

76. Deng, C., E. Goluszko, E. Tüzün, H. Yang and P. Christadoss. 2002. Resistance to experimental autoimmune myasthenia gravis in IL-6-deficient mice is associated with reduced germinal center formation and C3 production. *J. Immunol.* 169:1077-1083.

77. Goluszko, E., C. Deng, M.A. Poussin and P. Christadoss. 2002. Tumor necrosis factor receptor p55 and p75 deficiency protects mice from developing experimental autoimmune myasthenia gravis. *J. Neuroimmunol.* 122:85-93.

78. Kopf, M., S. Herren, M.V. Wiles, M.B. Pepys and M.H. Kosco-Vilbois. 1998. Interleukin 6 influences germinal center development and antibody production via a contribution of C3 complement component. *J. Exp. Med.* 188:1895-1906.

79. Bai, Y., R. Liu, D. Huang, A. La Cava, Y.Y. Tang, Y. Iwakura, D.I. Campagnolo, T.L. Vollmer, R.M. Ransohoff and F.D. Shi. 2008. CCL2 recruitment of IL-6-producing CD11b+ monocytes to the draining lymph nodes during the initiation of Th17-dependent B cell-mediated autoimmunity. *Eur. J. Immunol.* 38:1877-1888.

80. Cohen-Kaminsky, S., O. Devergne, R.M. Delattre, I. Klingel-Schmitt, D. Emilie, P. Galanaud and S. Berrih-Aknin. 1993. Interleukin-6 overproduction by cultured thymic epithelial cells from patients with myasthenia gravis is potentially involved in thymic hyperplasia. *Eur. Cytokine Netw.* 4:121-132.

81. Kaplin, A.I., D.M. Deshpande, E. Scott, C. Krishnan, J.S. Carmen, I. Shats, T. Martinez, J. Drummond, S. Dike, M. Pletnikov, S.C. Keswani, T.H. Moran, C.A. Pardo, P.A. Calabresi and D.A. Kerr. 2005. IL-6 induces regionally selective spinal cord injury in patients with the neuroinflammatory disorder transverse myelitis. *J. Clin. Invest.* 115:2731-2741.

82. Germann, T., M. Bongartz, H. Dlugonska, H. Hess, E. Schmitt, L. Kolbe, E. Kölsch, F.J. Podlaski, M.K. Gately and E. Rüde. 1995. Interleukin-12 profoundly up-regulates the synthesis of antigen-specific complement-fixing IgG2a, IgG2b and IgG3 antibody subclasses in vivo. *Eur. J. Immunol.* 25:823-829.

83. Tüzün, E., J. Li, S.S. Saini, H. Yang and P. Christadoss. 2008. Targeting classical complement pathway to treat complement mediated autoimmune diseases. *Adv. Exp. Med. Biol.* 632:265-272.

84. Christadoss, P., E. Tüzün, J. Li, S.S. Saini and H. Yang. 2008. Classical complement pathway in experimental autoimmune myasthenia gravis pathogenesis. *Ann. N. Y. Acad. Sci.* 1132:210-219.

19

CD4+CD25+ Regulatory T cells in Myasthenia Gravis

Ruolan Liu MD, PhD., Junwei Hao MD & Fu-Dong Shi MD, PhD.

1. INTRODUCTION

CD4+CD25+ regulatory T cells (Treg cells): An Overview

Several types of lymphocytes may inhibit ongoing immune processes and avoid autoimmunity depending on the stage and intensity of immune response. These lymphocytes may include NKT cells, NK cells and CD4+CD25+Foxp3+ regulatory T (Treg) cells; of which Treg cells are best characterized in terms of ontogeny, lineage-specific markers as well as mechanisms of suppressor functions. Naturally occurring Treg cells (nTreg) undergo development and maturation in the thymus before entering the circulation. Treg cells compose 1.5-3% of total lymphocytes. IL-2 and TGF-β are required for the generation of Treg cells *in vitro*; IL-2 also plays a non-redundant role in sustaining Treg cells *in vivo* (1-4). Foxp3 has been identified as lineage-defining transcription factors. Treg cells can also be generated from CD4+CD25-Foxp3- cells in other anatomical locations outside of the thymus with appropriate cytokine milieu (1, 5). These Treg cells are referred to as (inducible) iTreg cells. Understanding the biology and pathophysiology of both nTreg and iTreg cells will lead to improved understanding of disease pathogenesis and allow for the design of novel therapies to target Treg cells. Therefore, this subject has been a focus of intense scrutiny from all immunological aspects in recent years (6-8).

2. TREG CELLS IN PATIENTS WITH MG

2.1. Treg cells in circulation

Emerging studies have characterized Treg cells from patients with MG (*Table*). Multiple color flow cytometry was employed to quantify CD4+ and CD25+ double positive populations from blood. Various degrees of reduction in the frequency of Treg cells in peripheral blood has been documented in MG patients (9-11). Further, expression of the Treg cell lineage-defining transcriptional factor, Foxp3, was also determined by intracellular staining technique in some of the studies (12); it was found that the level of Foxp3 was reduced in Treg cells from these patients. Thus, similar to findings in other types of autoimmune diseases, circulating Treg cells are present in reduced numbers and levels of Foxp3 expression (13-16).

Table: Phenotype and functional analysis of Treg cells in Myasthenia Gravis[a]

Author (ref.)	MG (n)	CD4+CD25+ (%)	Foxp3+ expression	Suppressive function
Zhang (12)	21	±	↓ CD4+CD25hiFoxp3+ (%)	↓
Li (17)	75	NA	↓ CD4+CD25hiFoxp3+ (%)	±
Fattorossi (10)	38	↓	NA	NA
Huang (18)	23	±	NA	NA
Balandina (9)	17	±	↓ Foxp3 mRNA	↓↓
Xiao (19)	29	↓↓	NA	NA

[a] MG patients compared with healthy control subjects.
±: similar, no difference; ↓: decrease or defective; and NA: not available.

2.2. Treg cells and thymic abnormality

nTreg cells develop within the thymus and are released into peripheral lymphoid organs and circulation upon maturation (1, 3). The fact that a portion of MG patients posses an associated thymic abnormality suggests that the defective Treg cells observed in MG patients may be derived from thymus, in which the microenvironment for Treg cell development becomes aberrant. MG patients with thymic dysplasia or thymoma provide a unique opportunity to address this interesting hypothesis. Balandina and colleagues analyzed Treg cells in thymi from patients with MG and compared them to thymi from healthy subjects. Their data revealed that the numbers of Treg cells were normal but their regulatory functions, as reflected by their capacity to suppress the proliferation of responding cells as well as expression of Foxp3, were profoundly defective (9). Strobel and colleagues independently demonstrated that in MG patients with thymomas, from maturation to exportation, Treg cells were significantly reduced (20). These studies provide strong evidence that defective Treg cells in MG patients may be derived from thymus.

nTreg cells derived from thymus and iTreg cells derived from conversion from CD4+CD25- all contribute to the peripheral Treg cell pool. Thymectomy has beneficial effects on disease severity and course in a substantial proportion of MG patients. An interesting question arises as to whether thymectomy in MG patients can restore Treg cells. However, a study failed to demonstrate a recognizable effect of thymectomy on periphery Treg cells (18). It is noteworthy that the particular group of patients studied had no cross Treg cell defect(s), and it was not clear whether the timing chosen for quantifying Treg cells truly reflects the window at which the effects of thymectomy may be seen in the periphery. Paradoxically, thymectomy was found to augment peripheral Treg cells (10). The latter study raises an important question as to what extent the thymus contributes to the Treg cell pool in MG patients.

2.3. Responsiveness of Treg cells in MG during immunotherapy

If defective Treg cells contribute to the emergence of autoantibdoies against AChR, the beneficial effects of immune therapies may be achieved, in part, through modulating Treg cells. General immunosuppression via the use of steroid and/or azathioprine is indeed associated with an increased number of Treg cells in MG patients after a period of therapy (10). The mechanisms responsible for this finding have not been investigated. Studies suggesting that the dynamic recovery of Treg cells and T effector cells might be different (21), which lead to swift reconstitution of Treg cells during immune ablation therapy; a non-exclusive mechanism is that Treg cells are relatively resistant to immunosuppressive or cell ablation therapy (21).

In addition to immunosuppressive therapy, the immunomodulatory compounds (interferons, anti-α4 integrin, anti-TNF α, anti-CD20, etc) used in other types of autoimmune conditions are more likely to affect Treg cells. However, no studies have addressed this question in MG and other autoimmune diseases. As for MG, few attempts have been made so far to test these immunomodulatory compounds.

3. HOMEOSTASIS OF Treg CELLS IN EAMG

Progress in understanding the newly identified immunological variables for human MG is greatly aided by experimental autoimmune myasthenia gravis (EAMG). Repeated immunization of C57BL/6 mice with AChR and adjuvant induces mounting autoantibodies against AChR and chronic muscular weakness characteristic of MG. Activation and expansion of autoreactive CD4+ cells is a central process in EAMG, and perhaps in MG, as these cells coordinate a number of cascade events leading to the genesis and accumulation of pathogenic antibodies. The synchronized clinical course, as well as accessibility of the immune system, makes this model suitable for addressing the exact role played by Treg cells in EAMG and exploring strategies to use Treg cells as a therapeutic target for MG. We have quantified the frequency of Treg cells during induction, progression and the chronic stage of EAMG in lymph nodes, spleen, peripheral blood and thymus. The frequency of Treg cells was not altered during the course of the disease in all organs examined, and was similar to unimmunized control mice (our unpublished data). Furthermore, the levels of Foxp3 expression were comparable with that of control mice, and the levels of expression were constant during EAMG (our unpublished data). These results suggest that the Treg cell deficiency found in some studies in MG patients was not present in EAMG in B6 mice. Further, thymi do not appear to be involved in the disease process of EAMG. Although these facts caution against the generalization of all findings in EAMG to MG, it does not underscore the usefulness of this model for exploring pathogenesis of disease and novel immune therapies.

4. Treg CELLS MAINTAIN IMMUNE TOLERANCE TO AChR

Constant frequency of Treg cells and the stable levels of Foxp3 expression in these cells during EAMG do not preclude the outcome of manipulation of Treg cells in this model. Indeed, using anti-CD25 mAb to deplete Treg cells *in vivo* provides direct evidence supporting an inhibitory function of Treg cells which has been established in EAMG. Depletion of CD25$^+$ Treg cells leads to a pernicious clinical course of EAMG as well as augmented pathogenic antibody responses in B6 mice (22). Other evidence includes the finding that Treg cells can effectively suppress proliferation of AChR-reactive CD4$^+$ T cells in *ex vivo* experiments, and transfer of Treg cells to ameliorate severity of EAMG (23). Treg cells are likely to exhibit their inhibitory functions at multiple levels: AChR-reactive T cells, B cells or both.

5. AUGMENTATION OF Treg CELLS ATTENUATES EAMG

The powerful inhibitory role of Treg cells in the pathogenesis of EAMG, as revealed by using depletion antibodies and cell transfer approaches, establishes a foundation for manipulation of Treg cells for therapeutic purposes in MG. Since IL-2 and perhaps the related common γ-chain cytokines are crucial for homeostasis of Treg cells, administration of IL-2 is expected to augment the compartment of Treg cells. Considering direct IL-2 injection is associated with a number of side effects, our group has been searching for other means to augment Treg cells via more physiological pathways (*Figure*). Initially, we demonstrated that activation of NKT cells by a synthetic glycolipid agonist of NKT cells, a-galactosylceramide (α-GalCer), to transcribe the IL-2 gene and produce IL-2 protein. Consequently, the size of the Treg cell compartment was increased as the expression of foxp3 was augmented. α-GalCer-activated NKT cells can induce expansion of CD4$^+$CD25$^+$ Treg cells which, in turn, mediate the therapeutic effects of α-GalCer in EAMG (22).

The effect of α-GalCer/NKT cell to expand Treg cells is moderate (1.5-2.0 fold-increase in Treg cells). To seek more effective means to expand Treg cells, we employed immune complexes consisting of IL-2 and anti-IL-2 mAb (JES6-1A12) (referred to as IL-2 complexes hereafter) to augment Treg cells. Consistent with early reports in other model systems (24, 25) , we found that anti-IL-2 mAb engaged CD25 (IL-2R$_\alpha$) in the high-affinity IL-2 receptor (IL-2R$_{\alpha,\beta,\gamma_c}$), which induced a three- to four-fold expansion of Treg cells in the EAMG model. The expanded Treg cells potently suppressed autoreactive T and B cell responses to AChR and attenuated the muscular weakness that is characteristic of MG. The IL-2 dependent expansion of Treg cells is most likely via peripheral conversion of CD4$^+$CD25$^-$Foxp3$^-$ T cells (Liu et al,unpublished). Importantly, the use of IL-2 complex minimizes the dosage of IL-2 and side effects associated with IL-2 injection (Liu et al, unpublished). Independent studies suggest that general immune suppression does not occur in several experimental models where the IL-2 complex is tested (25).

Targeting Treg cells via other type IL-2 dependent and independent approaches have been explored in EAMG (*Figure*). Aricha et al showed that *ex vivo* generated Treg cells via TGF-β and IL-2 are capable of inhibiting the progression of MG in Lewis rats (23). Similarly, manipulation of Treg cells via GM-CSF (26), alteration of peptide ligand (27), and potentially transplantation of bone marrow stromal cells also ameliorates EAMG (28).

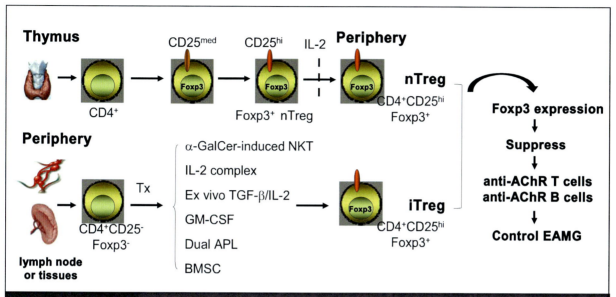

Figure: The different sources of Treg cells to suppress EAMG are shown. nTreg cells are derived from thymic CD_4^+ T cells. iTreg cells are generated and expanded from periphery $CD_4^+CD_{25}^-Foxp_3^-$ cells through various in vivo or in vitro treatments (Tx). Both nTreg and iTreg cells are capable to suppress auto-reactive AChR T Cell and B cells, resulting amelioration of EAMG.

6. SUMMARY AND FUTURE RPROSPECTS

Treg cells, as similarly compared in other autoimmune disease, were found to be deficient in the circulation and thymus from patients with myasthenia gravis. This deficiency may lead to the emergence of autoimmunity against AChR. This hypothesis has been explored in animal models of MG: EAMG. In this model, it was clearly demonstrated by multiple independent studies that Treg cells maintain tolerance to AChR expansion of Treg cells via IL-2 dependent and independent pathways which is effective in halting the progression of disease. These studies establish a solid foundation for targeting Treg cells in MG. Future investigations in this promising area should focus on mechanisms of Treg cell-mediated suppression of autoreactive T and/or B cells, identify means to induce antigen specific Treg cells while avoiding general immune suppression and maintaining these cells on a long term basis *in vivo*, and translating EAMG regime to human disease. Once we resolve these issues, our capacity in harnessing Treg cells for therapeutic purposes will be significantly enhanced.

.

REFERENCES

1. Sakaguchi, S., T. Yamaguchi, T. Nomura, and M. Ono. 2008. Regulatory T cells and immune tolerance. *Cell* 133:775-787.

2. Schwartz, R. H. 2005. Natural regulatory T cells and self-tolerance. *Nature immunology* 6:327-330.

3. Lan, R. Y., A. A. Ansari, Z. X. Lian, and M. E. Gershwin. 2005. Regulatory T cells: development, function and role in autoimmunity. *Autoimmunity reviews* 4:351-363.

4. Fontenot, J. D., J. P. Rasmussen, M. A. Gavin, and A. Y. Rudensky. 2005. A function for interleukin 2 in Foxp3-expressing regulatory T cells. *Nature immunology* 6:1142-1151.

5. Fontenot, J. D., and A. Y. Rudensky. 2005. A well adapted regulatory contrivance: regulatory T cell development and the forkhead family transcription factor Foxp3. *Nature immunology* 6:331-337.

6. Hoffmann, P., R. Eder, L. A. Kunz-Schughart, R. Andreesen, and M. Edinger. 2004. Large-scale in vitro expansion of polyclonal human CD4⁺CD25 high regulatory T cells. *Blood* 104:895-903.

7. Kretschmer, K., I. Apostolou, D. Hawiger, K. Khazaie, M. C. Nussenzweig, and H. von Boehmer. 2005. Inducing and expanding regulatory T cell populations by foreign antigen. *Nature immunology* 6:1219-1227.

8. Bluestone, J. A. 2005. Regulatory T-cell therapy: is it ready for the clinic? *Nature reviews* 5:343-349.

9. Balandina, A., S. Lecart, P. Dartevelle, A. Saoudi, and S. Berrih-Aknin. 2005. Functional defect of regulatory CD4⁺CD25+ T cells in the thymus of patients with autoimmune myasthenia gravis. *Blood* 105:735-741.

10. Fattorossi, A., A. Battaglia, A. Buzzonetti, F. Ciaraffa, G. Scambia, and A. Evoli. 2005. Circulating and thymic CD4 CD25 T regulatory cells in myasthenia gravis: effect of immunosuppressive treatment. *Immunology* 116:134-141.

11. Battaglia, A., C. Di Schino, A. Fattorossi, G. Scambia, and A. Evoli. 2005. Circulating CD4+CD25+ T regulatory and natural killer T cells in patients with myasthenia gravis: a flow cytometry study. *Journal of biological regulators and homeostatic agents* 19:54-62.

12. Zhang, Y., H. B. Wang, L. J. Chi, and W. Z. Wang. 2009. The role of FoxP3⁺CD4⁺CD25hi Tregs in the pathogenesis of myasthenia gravis. *Immunology letters* 122:52-57.

13. Gerli, R., G. Nocentini, A. Alunno, E. B. Bocci, R. Bianchini, O. Bistoni, and C. Riccardi. 2009. Identification of regulatory T cells in systemic lupus erythematosus. *Autoimmunity reviews* 8:426-430.

14. Costantino, C. M., C. Baecher-Allan, and D. A. Hafler. 2008. Multiple sclerosis and regulatory T cells. *Journal of clinical immunology* 28:697-706.

15. Vandenbark, A. A., and H. Offner. 2008. Critical evaluation of regulatory T cells in autoimmunity: are the most potent regulatory specificities being ignored? *Immunology* 125:1-13.

16. Boissier, M. C., E. Assier, J. Biton, A. Denys, G. Falgarone, and N. Bessis. 2009. Regulatory T cells (Treg) in rheumatoid arthritis. *Joint Bone Spine* 76:10-14.

17. Li, X., B. G. Xiao, J. Y. Xi, C. Z. Lu, and J. H. Lu. 2008. Decrease of CD4⁺CD25(high)Foxp3⁺ regulatory T cells and elevation of CD19⁺BAFF-R⁺ B cells

and soluble ICAM-1 in myasthenia gravis. *Clinical immunology (Orlando, Fla* 126:180-188.

18. Huang, Y. M., R. Pirskanen, R. Giscombe, H. Link, and A. K. Lefvert. 2004. Circulating CD4⁺CD25⁺ and CD4⁺CD25⁺ T cells in myasthenia gravis and in relation to thymectomy. *Scandinavian journal of immunology* 59:408-414.

19. Sun, Y., J. Qiao, C. Z. Lu, C. B. Zhao, X. M. Zhu, and B. G. Xiao. 2004. Increase of circulating CD4⁺CD25⁺ T cells in myasthenia gravis patients with stability and thymectomy. *Clinical immunology (Orlando, Fla* 112:284-289.

20. Strobel, P., A. Rosenwald, N. Beyersdorf, T. Kerkau, O. Elert, A. Murumagi, N. Sillanpaa, P. Peterson, V. Hummel, P. Rieckmann, C. Burek, B. Schalke, W. Nix, R. Kiefer, H. K. Muller-Hermelink, and A. Marx. 2004. Selective loss of regulatory T cells in thymomas. *Annals of neurology* 56:901-904.

21. Piao, W. H., R. Wong, X. F. Bai, J. Huang, D. I. Campagnolo, R. T. Dorr, T. L. Vollmer, and F. D. Shi. 2007. Therapeutic effect of anthracene-based anticancer agent ethonafide in an animal model of multiple sclerosis. *J Immunol* 179:7415-7423.

22. Liu, R., A. La Cava, X. F. Bai, Y. Jee, M. Price, D. I. Campagnolo, P. Christadoss, T. L. Vollmer, L. Van Kaer, and F. D. Shi. 2005. Cooperation of invariant NKT cells and CD4⁺CD25⁺ T regulatory cells in the prevention of autoimmune myasthenia. *J Immunol* 175:7898-7904.

23. Aricha, R., T. Feferman, S. Fuchs, and M. C. Souroujon. 2008. *Ex vivo* generated regulatory T cells modulate experimental autoimmune myasthenia gravis. *J Immunol* 180:2132-2139.

24. Boyman, O., M. Kovar, M. P. Rubinstein, C. D. Surh, and J. Sprent. 2006. Selective stimulation of T cell subsets with antibody-cytokine immune complexes. *Science (New York, N.Y* 311:1924-1927.

25. Webster, K. E., S. Walters, R. E. Kohler, T. Mrkvan, O. Boyman, C. D. Surh, S. T. Grey, and J. Sprent. 2009. In vivo expansion of T reg cells with IL-2-mAb complexes: induction of resistance to EAE and long-term acceptance of islet allografts without immunosuppression. *The Journal of experimental medicine* 206:751-760.

26. Sheng, J. R., L. C. Li, B. B. Ganesh, B. S. Prabhakar, and M. N. Meriggioli. 2008. Regulatory T cells induced by GM-CSF suppress ongoing experimental myasthenia gravis. *Clinical immunology (Orlando, Fla* 128:172-180.

27. Aruna, B. V., M. Sela, and E. Mozes. 2005. Suppression of myasthenogenic responses of a T cell line by a dual altered peptide ligand by induction of CD4⁺CD25⁺ regulatory cells. *Proceedings of the National Academy of Sciences of the United States of America* 102:10285-10290.

28. Kong, Q. F., B. Sun, G. Y. Wang, D. X. Zhai, L. L. Mu, D. D. Wang, J. H. Wang, R. Li, and H. L. Li. 2009. BM stromal cells ameliorate experimental autoimmune myasthenia gravis by altering the balance of Th cells through the secretion of IDO. *European journal of immunology* 39:800-809.

Generation of Regulatory Immune Cells Utilizing Granulocyte-Macrophage Colony-Stimulating Factor (GM-CSF) in Experimental Myasthenia Gravis

Jianrong Sheng, PhD. & Matthew N. Meriggioli, M.D.

1. INTRODUCTION

Dendritic cells (DCs) are bone marrow-derived, specialized antigen-presenting cells that play an important role in the regulation of immune responses against foreign as well as self antigens (1). While all DCs share the ability to process and present antigen to T cells, they differ in their expression of surface markers, migratory patterns, localization, immunological functions and their dependence on inflammatory stimuli for their generation (2). The nature of the immunological response generated by DCs is determined by a number of factors, including the nature of the antigen, the cytokine microenvironment, and the maturation status of the DCs themselves (3,4). A number of cytokine modulators, including granulocyte-macrophage colony-stimulating factor (GM-CSF), can influence the differentiation or maturation of DCs, under appropriate conditions (5-7).

GM-CSF is an important hematopoietic growth factor and immune modulator that has a profound effect on various circulating leukocytes (8). In particular, its effects on DC maturation and function have been the subject of recent investigation. It is used clinically to treat neutropenia in cancer patients during chemotherapy, and in patients after bone marrow transplantation. GM-CSF has also been widely used for generating DCs from bone marrow and peripheral blood precursor cells (9), and its effects are not limited to *in vitro* conditions. Accordingly, we and others have demonstrated the ability of low-dose GM-CSF to induce and maintain semi-mature, tolerogenic DCs in vivo, and have shown that treatment could suppress autoimmunity by inducing CD4⁺CD25⁺ regulatory T cells (Tregs) (10-14).

The immunopathogenesis of EAMG involves the production of high-affinity anti-AChR antibodies whose synthesis is modulated by, and dependent upon anti-AChR CD4⁺ T cells (15-18). The activation of anti-AChR T cells is, in turn, determined by their interactions with antigen-presenting cells (APCs). DCs play an important role in MG by presenting self-antigens and promoting the priming and/or boosting of anti-AChR T cells (19-21). DCs not only initiate autoantibody synthesis by activation of T cells which provide cytokines and "help" to B cells, but also directly promote antibody production and isotype switching (22,23). Recently, a number of studies have shown that autologous DCs modified in a number of different ways in vitro and administered to rodents with EAMG can have a protective effect on the development and progression of disease (24-26). Thus, the manipulation of DCs may represent an effective therapeutic strategy to restore tolerance in an antibody-mediated autoimmune disease like EAMG.

While the primary immune effectors in autoimmune myasthenia gravis (MG) and experimental MG (EAMG) are anti-AChR antibodies which bind to and destroy the neuromuscular junction (NMJ) through the activation of complement (15, 27), T cells provide help to antibody-producing B cells in MG. As noted, previous work has been published examining the potential of *in vivo* administration of GM-CSF in experimental autoimmune thyroiditis (EAT) (13,14), and in the experimental model of autoimmune diabetes (12). As effector T cells are critically involved in the immunopathogenesis and in the destruction of the target tissue in these two diseases, the generation of tolerogenic DCs by GM-CSF which leads to mobilization of Tregs, may be logically expected to down-regulate pathogenic, thyroiditis-causing or diabetogenic CD8⁺ T cells, reduce T cell infiltration of the target tissue, and thus ameliorate disease manifestations. In contrast, the effectiveness of this approach in suppressing CD4⁺ T helper cells resulting in suppression of autoantibody production in an ongoing antibody-mediated autoimmune disease has not been as extensively studied.

In this chapter, we review the biology of GM-CSF and its effects on DCs and T cell responses. We describe observations that we have made in which the differential activation of specific subsets of DCs using GM-CSF effectively protects against the induction of EAMG (10), and also exerts a potent therapeutic effect on ongoing, chronic disease (11). Furthermore, we show that these beneficial changes in clinical manifestations are accompanied by suppression of ongoing anti-AChR immune responses (both T cell *and* antibody responses), the mobilization of tolerogenic DCs, and the expansion of FOXP3⁺ Tregs capable of specifically suppressing AChR-stimulated T cell proliferation.

2.1. GM-CSF – Basic Biologic Activities

GM-CSF was first identified in mouse lung-tissue-conditioned medium by its ability to stimulate the proliferation of mouse bone marrow cells, generating colonies of granulocytes and macrophages *in vitro* (28). Depending upon its concentration, GM-CSF stimulates multipotent precursor cells differentially, having an effect on macrophage progenitors at the lowest doses, followed by granulocyte, erythroid, eosinophilic and megakaryocyte progenitors (29).The biologic activities of GM-CSF are exerted through binding to cell-surface receptors expressed on myelomonocytic cells (30). The GM-CSF receptor is composed of α- and β- chains, and expression is characterized by low number and high affinity (31).

GM-CSF is produced by a wide variety of cell types, including endothelial cells, fibroblasts, muscle cells, macrophages, and activated T cells. Inflammatory cytokines such as IL-1, IL-6, TNF-α, as well as bacterial endotoxins, are potent inducers of GM-CSF (32), while its expression can be inhibited by IL-10, IL-4, and IFN-γ. GM-CSF is produced by T cells after T cell receptor (TCR) activation along with the appropriate co-stimulatory signals (32). Over-expression of GM-CSF leads to severe inflammation and even autoimmunity (33). Patients with rheumatoid arthritis who are treated with GM-CSF to correct immunosuppressive drug-induced neutropenia, may experience exacerbations of their rheumatologic disease (34).

Surprisingly, deletion of the GM-CSF gene has no significant effect on hematopoiesis, and GM-CSF-/- mice show normal development of myeloid cells including macrophages and DCs, except for a defect in alveolar macrophage function resulting in alveolar proteinosis (35). Analysis of GM-CSF-/- mice, however, has revealed an essential role for GM-CSF in the development of autoimmune inflammatory diseases such as experimental autoimmune encephalomyelitis and collagen-induced arthritis (36,37).

It should be noted that GM-CSF levels are low in the steady state but rise during inflammation, and overproduction in certain microenvironments may lead to enhanced inflammatory responses, while lower level production may have opposite effects. This may in part explain the wide range of reported biologic effects of GM-CSF, ranging from "pro-inflammatory" to "tolerance-inducing".

2.2. GM-CSF, DCs and T cells

GM-CSF is a critical factor in the generation and development of DCs from bone marrow precursors. However, the main role attributed to GM-CSF has traditionally been that of a survival-promoting factor, rather than a differentiation-driving factor. Scattered studies have suggested a direct role for GM-CSF in driving the differentiation of human monocytoes into DCs, and one study has shown that human monocytes cultured for 24-48 hours in the presence of GM-CSF up-regulate the expression of MHC class II and of costimulatory molecules (38). Conti et al (39) have also shown that the exposure of purified blood monocytes for 5-6 days to GM-CSF alone leads to their conversion into immature DCs.

It is clear that GM-CSF can affect the proliferation, activation, and differentiation of various hematopoietic cells in vitro. However, GM-CSF deficiency in experimental animals does not appear to produce dramatic effects on steady state numbers of DCs, raising some doubt as to the importance of GM-CSF in DC development in vivo. The direct effects of GM-CSF on T cells is not clear, and very little is known about the regulation of its production by lymphocytes. Generally, the effects of GM-CSF on T cells are believed to be mediated indirectly through antigen-presenting cells, and specifically DCs (40). The outcome of an interaction between T cells and antigen-presenting DCs depends upon whether a "danger" or "tolerogenic" signal is received by the DCs. GM-CSF has been shown to be capable of either stimulating the immune response, endowing DCs with improved antigen presentation capacity (41), or alternatively suppress the immune response by favoring the development of semi-mature DCs that recruit Tr1 and Th2 cells and prevent or even suppress ongoing autoimmunity (13-15,42). Furthermore, it may have a direct effect on Tregs, as studies have shown that GM-CSF can enhance anti-CD3-induced Treg proliferation in the presence of APCs in a dose-dependent manner (43).

It is interesting that, as a hemopoietic growth factor, GM-CSF also has purported pro-inflammatory effects, and has even been suggested as a treatment to "boost" the immune response in sepsis (44). How can the same agent be used to effectively induce immune tolerance in EAMG and other animal models of autoimmunity? While this range of induced effects is most likely related to a number of factors (8,45), including the nature of any existing inflammatory response, the influence of additional stimulation (infection), and the timing of GM-CSF administration, one important determinant may be the dose of GM-CSF used. Investigators have observed that low-dose GM-CSF leads to the development of "semi-mature" DCs which are resistant to maturation stimuli in culture, compared to the development of mature, "immunogenic" DCs when high-dose GM-CSF is used (46). The finding that GM-CSF can have both immune-stimulatory and regulatory functions very likely reflects the functional plasticity of DCs and emphasizes the role of the miroenvironment in determining the balance between immune-stimulation and tolerance.

3.1. GM-CSF and immune tolerance

In murine secondary lymphoid organs, two major DC subsets are characterized by their expression of the marker CD8α (47,48), and the administration of GM-CSF can induce differential activation of these subsets (49,50). GM-CSF is a potent growth factor for CD8α DCs and has been shown to promote a Th2 response (51). Th2 cells can down-modulate immune responses, possibly by acting as growth and differentiation factors for Tregs (52,53). As noted, it has been demonstrated that the mobilization of tolerogenic DCs using GM-CSF can potently suppress induction and progression of disease in experimental autoimmune disease models including experimental autoimmune thyroiditis (EAT) (13,14), the non-obese diabetic (NOD) mouse model of autoimmune diabetes (12) - both T cell mediated diseases - as well as in the murine experimental model of MG (10,11), perhaps the best characterized antibody-mediated autoimmune disease (Table 1).

Table 1: GM-CSF in experimental autoimmunity

Disease Model	Result	Associated findings
EAT (13,14)	-Suppression of disease induction -Amelioration of ongoing disease	- ↓ Thyroid inflammation - Semi-mature DCs / ↑ Tregs
T1D (NOD) (12)	-Protection against diabetes	- ↓ Pancreatic islet inflammation - Semi-mature DCs / ↑ Tregs
EAMG (10,11)	-Suppression of disease induction -Amelioration of ongoing disease	- ↓ Anti-AChR antibodies - Semi-mature DCs / ↑ Tregs

EAT = experimental autoimmune thyroiditis, T1D (NOD) = Type 1 diabetes (Non-Obese Oiabetic), EAMG = experimental autoimmune myasthenia gravis, DC = dendritic cells, Tregs = regulatory T cells

3.2. GM-CSF suppresses induction of EAMG

We administered GM-CSF to C57BL/6 mice prior to immunization with acetylcholine receptor (AChR) protein, and observed the effect on the frequency and severity of EAMG development (10). Compared to AChR-immunized controls, mice treated with GM-CSF prior to immunization, demonstrated a significantly reduced disease incidence and severity. To determine if this relative protection from disease induction was associated with reduced production of pathogenic anti-AChR antibodies, we monitored serum anti-AChR antibody levels at different time points after AChR immunization.   Treatment with GM-CSF resulted in a decrease in total anti-mouse AChR IgG levels, and in particular, resulted in a prominent decrease in the murine complement-fixing IgG2b isotype, while IgG1 (non-complement fixing) isotypes were relatively unaffected (10).

The effects of GM-CSF treatment on DC phenotype were ascertained by analyzing the expression of CD11c, MHC class II and costimulatory molecules as well as the production of pro-inflammatory cytokines from GM-CSF-treated and untreated mice after AChR immunization. Spleens from mice treated with GM-CSF had relatively equal percentages of CD11c$^+$ cells and comparable levels of expression of MHC class II, and CD80 compared with untreated AChR-immunized mice and control (CFA) mice. GM-CSF-treated mice, however, showed an increase in CD8α^- CD11c$^+$ cells: 3.55% compared to 1.82% in the untreated group.   In addition, levels of pro-inflammatory cytokines, such as TNF-α, IL-12, and IL-1β, evaluated by RT-PCR, were low in GM-CSF-treated mice compared to untreated AChR-immunized controls (10).

To determine if treatment with GM-CSF affects the relative numbers of T cells expressing a regulatory phenotype, we tested spleen cells for expression of known Treg cell surface markers by FACS.   We found significantly increased numbers of CD4$^+$CD25$^+$ cells in mice treated with GM-CSF compared to untreated AChR-immunized control animals. We also found an expansion in the percentage of both CD25$^+$ and CD25$^-$ cells expressing the transcription factor FoxP3 in GM-CSF-treated mice compared to untreated AChR-immunized controls (10).

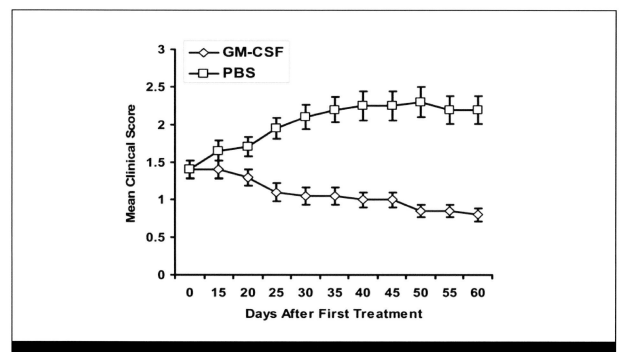

Figure 1. Severity of EAMG in GM-CSF-treated, compared to PBS-treated, AChR-immunized mice. Average clinical score during days 0-60 of the observation period is shown for the two experimental groups (n=20/group). Day 0 corresponds to initiation of treatment (GM-CSF vs. PBS). All mice had received a priming immunization and 3 booster immunizations with AChR. An additional AChR booster immunization was given on day 32, after treatment initiation. (Modified from ref. 11)

3.3. Effects of GM-CSF on Progression of Ongoing EAMG.

While interesting, effective suppression of EAMG using this approach did not guarantee effectiveness in the treatment of ongoing, well-established autoimmune disease. Therefore, in a subsequent series of experiments we have allowed mice to develop clinical EAMG before treating with GM-CSF. In one representative study, we immunized mice with AChR on days 0, 30, 60, and 90 (11). At this point greater than 90% of the animals had clear clinical signs of EAMG. We then divided the animals into two groups with an equal distribution of animals with disease grades 0, 1, and 2, and then randomly treated one group with GM-CSF (2 μg X 10 days) while the other received PBS. Both groups received a booster immunization 32 days after treatment initiation, followed seven days later by an additional 5 day course of GM-CSF. The GM-CSF-treated animals exhibited significant improvement while, as expected, the untreated group worsened (Figure 1).

Significant differences in the mean clinical score between the two groups became apparent approximately 20 days after initiating therapy. As in our "prevention" experiments with treatment prior to TAChR immunization, this amelioration of clinical disease was accompanied by down-modulation of both autoreactive T cell, and pathogenic autoantibody responses, a mobilization of DCs with a tolerogenic phenotype, and an expansion of regulatory T cells (Tregs) (11). As expected, we observed a change in DC phenotype in GM-CSF-treated animals in our study, characterized by decreased production of TNFα, IL-12, and IL1β, with no change in the expression of co-stimulatory molecules, and minimally reduced expression of MHC class II (Figure 2).

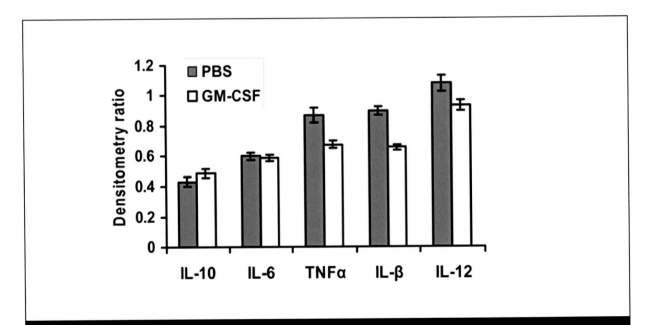

Figure 2: A multiplex RT-PCR assay was used to detect cytokine transcripts from isolated splenic dendritic cells from GM-CSF treated and untreated (PBS) mice with EAMG. Densitometry ratio of PCR products are shown for IL-10, IL-6, TNFá, IL-1â and IL-12.

This cytokine profile in DCs, in combination with the observed increase in production of IL-4 and IL-10 by splenocytes suggests a shift in the immune response to a Th2 pattern in response to GM-CSF treatment. Furthermore, the cytokine milieu in GM-CSF-treated animals clearly shifted to a Th2 polarization (Figure 2), indicating suppression of the anti-AChR Th1 response. As expected, the population of Tregs as determined by the expression of the transcription factor FOXP3 has been consistently expanded in both lymph nodes and splenocytes of EAMG mice treated with GM-CSF compared to controls (Figure 3).

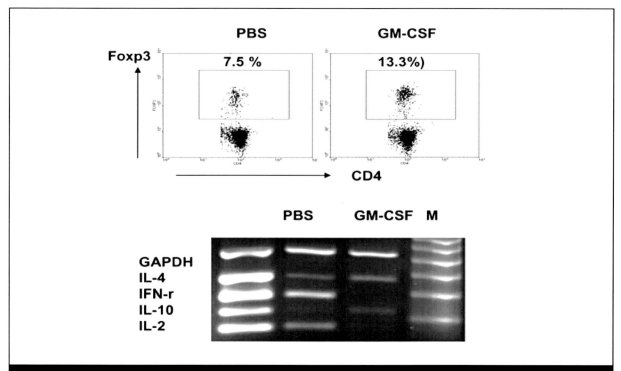

Figure 3. Effects of GM-CSF on the population of FOXP3+ T cells and Th1/Th2 cytokine responses to AChR stimulation. Representative plots showing the percentage of FOXP3+ regulatory T cells in splenocytes are shown. Gated CD4+ cells are shown and or FOXP3+ cells are marked within each inset. In the lower panel, CD4+ cells were isolated from splenocytes using a magnetic cell isolation kit, and a multiplex RT-PCR kit was used to detect Th1/Th2 cytokine transcripts.

We have examined the ability of the expanded population of Tregs to suppress AChR-stimulated T cell proliferation *in vitro*. In these experiments, CD4+ CD25+ T cells isolated from GM-CSF-treated mice potently suppressed AChR-induced proliferation, while there was no effect of addition of these CD4+ CD25+ cells on T cell responses to non-specific stimulation suggesting an antigen-specific immune modulation (Figure 4).

Furthermore, CD4+CD25+ cells from GM-CSF-treated mice inhibited T cell proliferation to a much greater degree compared to equal ratios of CD4+ CD25+ cells isolated from untreated EAMG mice (11), strongly indicating that the cells obtained from the former were composed of a higher proportion of antigen-specific Tregs. We have further demonstrated that the suppressive ability of these CD4+ CD25+ cells was dependent upon IL-10, but not TGF-β (11). These findings indicate that the Tregs mobilized in response to GM-CSF in our studies have similar functional

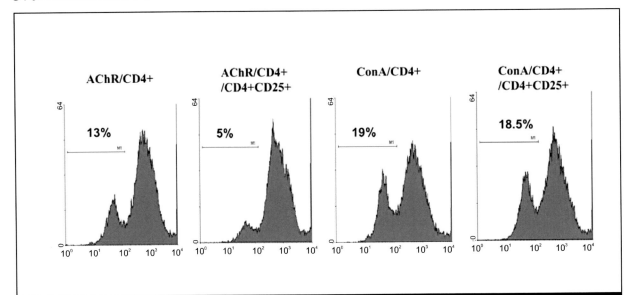

AChR/CD4+

13%

AChR/CD4+
/CD4+CD25+

5%

ConA/CD4+

19%

ConA/CD4+
/CD4+CD25+

18.5%

Figure 4. Responder CD4⁺ cells from untreated EAMG mice were stimulated with AChR (or ConA) as indicated. These cells were co-cultured with CD4⁺CD25⁺ cells from GM-CSF-treated mice. The presence of CD4⁺CD25⁺ cells from GM-CSF-treated mice resulted in a significantly lower proliferative response to stimulation with AChR. CD4⁺CD25⁺ cells from GM-CSF-treated mice did not suppress the T cell proliferative response to nonspecific (ConA) stimulation.

properties as the previously described antigen-induced T_R1 cells (54), and suggest that the Tregs induced by GM-CSF treatment are intimately involved in the down-modulation of anti-AChR immune responses.

4. MECHANISMS OF GM-CSF'S EFFECTS IN EXPERIMENTAL MG

The effects of GM-CSF are hypothesized to be explained by the mobilization of subsets of DCs which are in a steady or semimature state, which are resistant to maturation stimuli. These DCs, in turn, promote tolerance by inducing antigen-specific Tregs which suppress AChR-specific autoreactive T helper cells and impact upon their ability to provide the required help to B cells, thereby inhibiting the synthesis of anti-AChR antibodies. In support of this hypothesis, we show a significant reduction in circulating anti-AChR antibodies, specifically in pathogenic, complement-activating IgG isotypes when GM-CSF was administered to mice with active disease (11). Our studies have further shown that treatment of EAMG with GM-CSF is associated with reduced deposition of IgG and complement at the NMJ, and with maintenance of normal endplate morphology (10), indicating that all downstream aspects of the immune pathogenesis of EAMG are favorably impacted.

As noted, GM-CSF is a multifunctional cytokine which has found widespread current clinical use in the treatment of chemotherapy-induced neutropenia and in mobilizing bone marrow stem cells into the blood (55,56). Importantly, GM-CSF is a pivotal mediator of the maturation and function of DCs (57). It has been shown to mobilize "semi-mature" or tolerogenic DCs and to promote a Th2 cytokine response (51). Accordingly, in addition to the observed alteration in DC phenotype in our study, the cytokine milieu in CD4⁺ splenocytes of GM-CSF-treated animals clearly shifted from a Th1 to a Th2 polarization, indicating suppression of the anti-AChR Th1 response (11). The importance of this observed shift to a Th2 cytokine response is emphasized by the IL-10 dependent Treg suppression of AChR-stimulated T cell proliferation in GM-CSF-treated mice.

Low-dose GM-CSF favors the development of "semi-mature" DCs which are resistant to maturation stimuli in culture, compared to the development of mature, "immunogenic" DCs when high-dose GM-CSF is used (46). In our experiments, we used a dose of 2 ug/injection to effectively suppress EAMG. Our 2 μg dose is less than the 250μg /m² for up to 42 days, which is the current recommended dose (administered intravenously) for GM-CSF in the treatment and prevention of neutropenia in the setting of cancer therapy and autologous bone marrow transplantation (55). Formal dose ranging studies have not been performed, and it is not clear whether even lower doses will be effective when administered intraperitoneally, intravenously, or subcutaneously. Future studies examining the effects of different doses and routes of administration of GM-CSF are planned, but based on our observations we believe that GM-CSF treatment, as dosed in our study, induced the mobilization of tolerogenic DCs which, upon antigen capture, initiated a suppression of the anti-AChR immune response, predominantly through the activation of antigen-specific Tregs.

5. CLINICAL TRANSLATION TO HUMAN MG AND FUTURE DIRECTIONS

While the precise mechanisms of GM-CSF's therapeutic effects in established EAMG remain under investigation, we have shown that GM-CSF at the doses utilized in our studies specifically down-modulates anti-AChR T cell and antibody responses. Since GM-CSF is an approved medication currently used in the fields of oncology and organ transplantation, the translation of the above findings would appear to be relatively straightforward. However, a number of caveats must be stressed.

Firstly, while our experiments showing the more potent suppression of T cell proliferation demonstrated by Tregs from GM-CSF-treated mice compared to Tregs from untreated mice is evidence for an increased mobilization of of AChR-specific Tregs in these animals, these Tregs still probably represent a polyclonal population in terms of antigen specificity. To maximize the tolerizing effects of GM-CSF, its administration would likely have to coincide with active disease, as ongoing antigen presentation would presumably be an absolute requirement for subsequent induction of antigen-specific immune tolerance. Thus, enhancing the antigen-specificity of systemic therapy of GM-CSF in human MG will certainly require the appropriate timing of administration of the drug during active antigen presentation; but whether this should be in, for example, new onset disease or chronic but active disease is far from clear.

It must also be stressed that the current use of GM-CSF in medicine is based on its hematopoietic and immune *stimulatory* effects. It is likely that a number of factors not limited to dosing, play a role in determining whether GM-CSF's actions result in immune regulation or stimulation. From a safety point of view, the effects of GM-CSF on the immune processing and regulation of responses to foreign (infectious) agents also must be more carefully investigated. What are the effects of GM-CSF if administered under pro-inflammatory conditions such as during a systemic infection? We have seen that the functional status of DCs is intimately dependent upon the cytokine microenvironment, which is impossible to fully control in vivo.

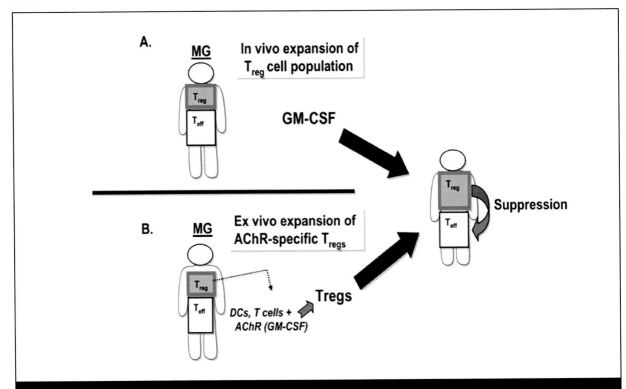

Figure 5. Strategies utilizing GM-CSF for the **A.** in vivo and **B.** ex vivo mobilization/generation of Tregs.

Alternative approaches that utilize a similar therapeutic strategy but may eliminate some of these concerns could consist of isolating and expanding DCs and Tregs *ex vivo* and then using them as cellular therapy (Figure 5B). This is currently being investigated in other autoimmune disease models, and may be readily translated to human MG using bone marrow or even peripheral blood monocytes obtained from patients. Clearly the study of GM-CSF in experimental MG will provide insight into the role of DCs and Treg cells in the regulation of autoimmune disease MG, and the mechanisms underlying their effects on autoantibody production, and antibody-mediated destruction of the muscle endplate. This knowledge may then allow for clinical application of GM-CSF or related molecules to the treatment of human MG in the future.

REFERENCES

1. Rossi, M., and Young, J.W. 2005. Human dendritic cells: Potent antigen-presenting cells at the crossroads of innate and adaptive immunity. *J. Immunol* **175**:1373-1381.

2. Banchereau J, Steinman RM. Dendritic cells and the control of immunity. *Nature* 1998;392:245-252.

3. Villadangos JA, Schnorrer P. Intrinsic and cooperative antigen-presenting functions of dendritic cell subsets in vivo. *Nat Rev Immunol* 2007;7:543-555.

4. Lutz, M.B., & G. Schuler. 2002. Immature, semi-mature and fully mature dendritic cells: which signals induce tolerance or immunity? *Trends Immunol*. 23: 445-449.

5. Zou GM, Tam YK. Cytokines in the generation and maturation of dendritic cells : recent advances. *Eur Cytokine Netw* 2002 ;13 :186-199.

6. Pulendran, B., J. Banchereau, S. Burheholder, et al. 2000. Flt3-Ligand and granulocyte colony-stimulating factor mobilize distinct human dendritic cell subsets in vivo. *J. Immunol*. 165: 566-572.

7. O'Keefe, M., H. Hochrein, D. Vremec, et al. 2002. Effects of administration of progenipoietin 1, Flt3 ligand, granulocyte colony-stimulating, and pegylated granulocyte colony-stimulating factor on dendritic cell subsets in mice. *Blood* 99: 2122-2130.

8. Hamilton, J.A. 2002. GM-CSF in inflammation and autoimmunity. *Trends Immunol* 23:403-408.

9. Conti L, Gessani S. GM-CSF in the generation of dendritic cells from human blood monocyte precursors: recent advances. *Immunobiology* 2008;213:859-870.

10. Sheng, J.R., L.C. Li, B.B. Ganesh, et. al. 2006. Suppression of experimental autoimmune myasthenia gravis (EAMG) by granulocyte-macrophage colony-stimulating factor (GM-CSF) is associated with an expansion of FoxP3+ regulatory T cells. *J. Immunol*. 177: 5296-306.

11. Sheng JR, Li L, Ganesh BB, Prabhakar BS, Meriggioli MN. Regulatory T cells induced by GM-CSF suppress ongoing experimental myasthenia. *Clin Immunol* 2008;128:172-180.

12. Gaudreau S, Guindi C, Menard M, Besin G, Dupuis G, Amrani A, Granulocyte-macrophage colony-stimulating factor prevents diabetes development in NOD mice by inducing tolerogenic dendritic cells that sustain the suppressive function of CD4+CD25+ regulatory T cells, *J. Immunol*. 179; 2007: 3638-3647.

13. Vasu, C., R.E. Dogan, M.J. Holterman, et al. 2003. Selective induction of dendritic cells using granulocyte macrophage-colony stimulating factor, but not fms-like tyrosine kinase receptor-3 ligand, activates thyroglobulin-specific CD4+/CD25+ T cells and suppresses experimental autoimmune thyroiditis. *J. Immunol*. 170: 5511-5522.

14. Gangi, E., C. Vasu, D. Cheatem D, et al. 2005. IL-10-producing CD4+CD25+ regulatory T cells play a critical role in granulocyte-macrophage colony-stimulating factor-induced suppression of experimental autoimmune thyroiditis. *J. Immunol*. 174: 7006-7013.

15. Meriggioli MN, Sanders DB. Myasthenia gravis: emerging clinical and biologic heterogeneity. *Lancet Neurol* 2009;8(5):475-90.

16. Moiola, L., M.P. Protti, A.A. Manfredi, et al. 1993. T-helper epitopes on human nicotinic acetylcholine receptor in myasthenia gravis. *Ann NY Acad Sci* 681: 198-218.

17. Protti MP, Manfredi AA, Straub C, Howard JF Jr, Conti-Tronconi BM. Immunodominant regions for T helper-cell sensitization on the human nicotinic receptor alpha subunit in myasthenia gravis. *Proc Natl Acad Sci USA* 1990;87: 7792-6.

18. Wang ZY, Okita DK, Howard J Jr, Conti-Fine BM. T-cell recognition of muscle acetylcholine receptor subunits in generalized and ocular myasthenia gravis. *Neurology* 1998;50: 1045-54.

19. Hornell TM, Beresford GW, Bushey A, Boss JM, Mellens ED. Regulation of the class II MHC pathway in primary human monocytes by granulocyte-macrophage colony-stimulating factor. *J Immunol* 2003;171:2374-2383.

20. Conti L, Cardone M, Varano B, Puddo P, Belardelli F, Gessani S. Role of the cytokine environment and cytokine receptor expression on the generation of functionally distinct dendritic cells from human monocytes. *Eur J Immunol* 2008;38:750-762.

21. Wada H, Noguchi Y, Marino MW, Dunn AR, Old LJ. T cell functions in granulocyte/macrophage colony-stimulating factor deficient mice. Proc Natl Acad Sci USA 1997;94:12557-12561.

22. Huleihel M, Douvdevani A, Segal S, Apte RN. Differential regulatory levels are involved in the generation of hematopoietic cytokines (CSFs and IL-6) in fibroblasts stimulated by inflammatory products. *Cytokine* 1993;5:47-56.

23. Kuwana, M. 2002. Induction of anergic and regulatory T cells by plasmacytoid dendritic cells and other dendritic cell subsets. *Hum. Immunol.* 63: 1156-1163

24. Kared H, Leforban B, Montandon R, Renand A, Layseca Espinosa E, Chatenoud L, Rosenstein Y, Schneider E, Dy M, Zavala F. Role of GM-CSF in tolerance induction by mobilized hematopoietic progenitors. *Blood* 112:2575-2578.

25. J. Pugin, Immunostimulation is a rational therapeutic strategy in sepsis, *Novartis Found. Symp.* 280 (2007) 21-27.

26. Tarr PE, Granulocyte-macrophage colony-stimulating factor and the immune system, *Med Oncol* 1996;13:133-40.

27. Lutz MB, Suri RM, Niimi M, Ogilvie AL, Kukutsch NA, Rossner S, Schuler G, Austyn JM, Immature dendritic cells generated with low doses of GM-CSF in the absence of IL-4 are maturation resistant and prolong allograft survival in vivo, *Eur J Immunol* 2000;30:1813-1822.

28. Maldonado-Lopez, R., T. De Smedt, B. Pajak, et al. 1999. Role of $CD8_\alpha^+$ and CD8⁻ dendritic cells in the induction of primary immune responses in vivo. *J. Leukocyte Biol.* 66: 242-246.

29. Martin P, del Hoyo GM, Anjuere F, et al. Concept of lymphoid versus myeloid dendritic cell lineages revisited: both CD8alpha(-) and CD8alpha(+) dendritic cells are generated from CD4 (low) lymphoid-committed precursors. *Blood* 2000;96: 2511-2519.

30. Daro, E., E. Butz, J. Smith, et al. 2002. Comparison of the functional properties of murine dendritic cells generated in vivo with flt3 ligand, GM-CSF and flt3 ligand plus GM-CSF. *Cytokine* 17: 119-130.

31. Daro, E., B. Pulendran, K. Brasel, et al. 2000. Polyethylene glycol-modified GM-CSF expands CD11b(high)CD11c(high) but not CD11b(low) CD11c(high) murine dendritic cells in vivo: a comparative analysis with Flt3 ligand. *J. Immunol.* 165: 49-58.

32. Arpinati, M., C.L. Green, S. Heimfeld, et al. 2000. Granulocyte-colony stimulating factor mobilizes T helper 2-inducing dendritic cells. *Blood* 95: 2484-2490.

33. Crane IJ, Forrester JV. Th1 and Th2 lymphocytes in autoimmune disease. *Crit Rev Immunol* 2005;25: 75-102.

34. Kroemer G, Hirsch F, González-García A, Martínez C. Differential involvement of Th1 and Th2 cytokines in autoimmune disease. *Autoimmunity* 1996;24: 25-33.

35. Wakkach, A., N. Fournier, V. Brun, et al. 2003. Characterization of dendritic cells that induce tolerance and T regulatory 1 cell differentiation in vivo. *Immunity* 18: 605-617.

36. Buchsel PC, Forgey A, Grape FB, Hamann SS. Granulocyte-macrophage colony-stimulating factor: current practice and novel approaches. *Clin J Oncol Nurs* 2002;6:198.

37. Hamilton JA, Anderson GP. GM-CSF Biology. Growth Factors 2004;22:225-31.

38. Pulendran BJ, Banchereau S, Burkeholder E, Kraus E, Guinet E, Chalouni C, Caron D, Maliiszewski C, Davoust J, Fay J, Palucka K. Flt3-Ligand and granulocyte-macrophage colony-stimulating factor mobilize distinct human dendritic cell subsets in vivo. *J Immunol* 2000;165:566-572.

Dendritic Cells for the Antigen Specific Therapy of Experimental Autoimmune Myasthenia Gravis

21

Yang H. M.D., PhD., & Rauniyar V. M.B.B.S.

1. INTRODUCTION

Myasthenia Gravis (MG) is an autoimmune disease of neuromuscular junction characterized by T cell dependent antibody-mediated autoimmune response to acetylcholine receptor (AChR) of the post synaptic muscle membrane. Current therapeutic options for MG are limited and non specific. They suppress the immune system in general. In an effort to find noble treatment which is specific and does not affect the other aspects of the immune system, various studies have been conducted in the past few years.

As the most potent antigen presenting cells (APC) of the immune system, DCs play an important role in MG by presenting self-Ags and promoting the priming and/or boosting of AChR-specific T cells (1). Activation of immature DCs in peripheral tissues results in an increase of their immunostimulatory capacity and migration to the draining lymph nodes where they initiate immune responses. However, DCs have been shown to have potent capabilities to tolerize T cells in an Ag-specific manner (2, 3), thereby minimizing autoreactive immune responses (4).

The immunostimulatory or immunoregulatory properties of DC depend on their maturation status, phenotype, and source of origin. Unlike mature DC (mDC), which express high levels of MHC and costimulatory molecules on their surface and induce immune responses (5), immature dendritic cells (imDC) deficient in costimulatory molecules have the potential to induce tolerance by inhibiting alloreactive T cell proliferation, inducing Ag-specific T cell anergy or triggering generation of regulatory T cells. This has prompted studies of a new strategic method of using the dendritic cells in the treatment of MG. Scores of experimental studies have yielded very impressive results that systemic administration of imDC had a protective effect on the development and progression of EAMG. These evidences present a potential for the future therapy of MG.

In this review, we first summarize the role of DC in autoimmunity. Next, we introduce several ways to achieve protective effect on the development and progression of EAMG by imDCs that is modifed with cytokines, antigens, growth factors. Finally, we focus on the immune modulation in EAMG induction by RelB-silenced dendritic cells through RNA interference, which could maintain imDC in a steady state for the induction of long-term immune tolerance in vivo.

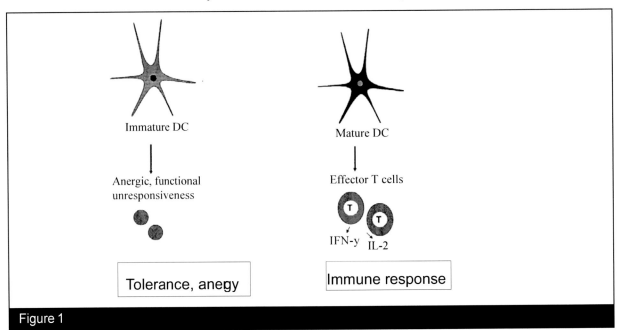

Immature DC

Anergic, functional
unresponsiveness

Tolerance, anegy

Mature DC

Effector T cells

IFN-y   IL-2

Immune response

Figure 1

2. DENDRITIC CELLS AND AUTOIMMUNITY

Autoimmunity results from a breakdown in the regulation of the immune system resulting in an inflammatory response directed at self-antigens and tissues. Loss of tolerance to self-antigens is necessary for generation of autoimmunity. It has been proposed that dendritic cells (DCs) are the critical decision-making cells in the immune system (6). Considerable experimental data support the concept that activated DC can induce autoimmune diseases. Through their role in the generation of central and peripheral tolerance, as well as in priming immune responses and stimulation of memory and effector T cells, DCs are likely to play essential roles in the initiation and perpetuation of autoimmunity and autoimmune diseases. Tolerance is actively maintained centrally in the thymus (7). Here, T cells reactive to self-antigen presented by medullary DCs are deleted by negative selection above a threshold of affinity for the antigen (8). In the periphery, tolerance may be active, through deletion or regulation of self-reactive T cells, or passive, due to ignorance of certain self-antigens. Peripheral self-reactive T cells may be controlled in a number of ways. Deletion of self-reactive cells has been shown to occur in lymph nodes draining uninflammed peripheral organs and tissues (9). In other circumstances, T-cell receptor (TCR) signaling may lead to functional unresponsiveness or anergy (10). Indeed, DC pulsed with myelin basic protein elicited experimental allergic encephalomyelitis(11), DC pulsed with thyroglobulin triggered autoimmune thyroiditis (12), and vaccination against tumor using DC pulsed with tumor antigens shared with normal host resulted in severe autoimmune disease in the experimental models (13).

3. DENDRITIC CELLS IN ANTIGEN SPECIFIC THERAPY OF EAMG

The immunopathogenesis of MG and EAMG involves the production of high-affinity anti-AChR Abs whose synthesis is modulated by, and dependent upon AChR-specific CD4+ T cells (14-16). The activation of AChR specific T cells is, in turn, determined by their interactions with APCs. As discussed earlier, being the most potent APC of the immune system, DCs present self-Ags and promote the priming and/or boosting of AChR-specific T cells (17-18) in MG.

A number of studies have shown that autologous DCs modifed in a number of different ways ex vivo and administered to rodents with EAMG can have a protective effect on the development and progression of the disease. DCs modulated by treatment with various cytokines, growth factors, antigens etc. have been used with very exciting results. Most of the studies so far are based on the principle that the maturity and development of the DCs can be altered by exposing them to various cytokines milieu, environment ex vivo so that they remain immature or tolerogenic thereby inducing tolerance.

TGF beta is a well known, potent cytokine family responsible for many pathophysiolgic processes in humans. It is crucial for differentiation and maturation of DCs as it can prevent maturation of DCs (19,20). Yarlin et al (21) demonstrated that dendritic cells exposed to TGF beta-1 in vitro ameliorate EAMG. They found that DC exposed to TGF-β1 in vitro mediate protection against EAMG. In their study, freshly prepared DC from spleen of healthy rats were exposed to TGF-β1 in vitro for 48 h, and administered subcutaneously to Lewis rats (2×10^6DC/rat) on day 5 post immunization with AChR in Freund's complete adjuvant. Control EAMG rats were injected in parallel with untreated DC (naive DC) or PBS. Lewis rats receiving TGF-β1-exposed DC developed very mild symptoms of EAMG without loss of body weight compared with control EAMG rats receiving naive DC or PBS. This effect of TGF-β1-exposed DC was associated with augmented spontaneous and AChR-induced proliferation, IFN-α and NO production, and decreased levels of anti-AChR antibody-secreting cells.

Interleukin-10 (IL-10) plays crucial role in the maturation of the dendritic cells too. It inhibits DCs of antigen presentation, enhance endocytosis and render them immature (22). It also inhibits the generation of DCs from monocyte precursors (23). Link et al (24) showed that DCs in vitro exposed to IL-10 can produce suppression of EAMG in lewis rats. They concluded that IL-10 downregulates costimulatory molecules and lower lymphocyte proliferation. This resulted in lower numbers of anti-AChr IgG antibody-secreting cells, lower affinity of anti-AChR antibodiesÿthusÿin lower clinical scores in the treated rats.Both of the experimental studies reveals an aspect of DCs modulation in a beneficial way through cytokines milieu, thereby altering the development and maturation of DCs in EAMG and subsequently resulting in beneficial outcome.

GM-CSF is an important factor in development of myeloid DCs. DCs generated in GM-CSF plus IL-4 require further stimulus for mature phenotype (25,26). In an experimental study, Li et al (27) showed that immature DCs [iMDCs] pulsed with acetylcholine receptor can induce tolerance to development of EAMG. In this study iDCs were generated in low dose of GM-CSF, and then they were pulsed with acetylcholine receptor (AChR) and transferred to allogeneic rats. After 3 weeks, all rats were immunized with AChR and complete Freund's adjuvant (CFA) and observed for the corresponding indices of MG for 7 weeks. The results showed that compared with mature DCs (mDCs) generated at high dose of GM-CSF plus additional stimulation by lipopolysaccharide, iDCs expressed significantly lower levels of MHC-II, CD80 and CD86, and the ability to stimulate proliferation of allogeneic T cells were weaker.

Similarly Adikari et al (28) showed that interferon (IFN) gamma modified dendritic cells suppress B cell function and ameliorate the development of EAMG. This study was designed to investigate the therapeutic effects of IFN-gamma modulated DC in EAMG. EAMG was induced in Lewis rates by immunization with Torpedo (T) AChR and adjuvant were injected with IFN-gamma-DC. A control group of EAMG rats received naive DC. The severity of clinical signs of EAMG was reduced dramatically in IFN-gamma- DC-treated rats compared to rats receiving naive DC. They found that the number of plasma cells secreting AChR antibodies was reduced and the expression of B cell activation factor (BAFF) on splenic and lymph node mononuclear cells (MNC) was down-regulated in rats treated with IFN-gamma -DC. Additionally, in vitro co-culture of MNC derived from EAMG rats with IFN-gamma-DC produced relatively few cells secreting AChR antibodies. They concluded that IFN-gamma- DC reduced the number of plasma cells secreting AChR antibodies and ameliorated the development of EAMG in Lewis rats. Yet in another interesting study, Sheng et al (29) showed that EAMG can be suppressed by administration of GMCSF, which modulates DCs phenotype and functional status, leading to expansion of regulatory T cells. And this was also associated with lowered serum antibody levels, reduced T cell proliferative responses to AChR as well. And they found that this suppression of EAMG was associated with an expansion of FoxP3+ regulatory T cells TRegs). See Chapter 20 for a detailed study.

In another study, Wang et al. (30) demonstrated that immature DCs pulsed with Talpha 146-162 can prevent EAMG by the negative regulation on BCR signalling. Mice were immunized with AChR in Freund's complete adjuvant on day 0, 30, 60; immature bone marrow dendritic cells were cultured and pulsed with Talpha146-162 and then injected in EAMG mice, on day 3, 33, 63, while control EAMG mice were injected in parallel with untreated DCs. At the end of the experiment, the Talpha 146-162 pulsed DCs group showed lower clinical incidence and lower severity of clinical signs of EAMG, and the suppression effect were closely correlated with the enhanced expression of the negative regulator Cbl and Cbl-b on BCR signaling pathway. This study would add another exciting result of DC modulation in the therapy of EAMG.

4. IMMUNE MODULATION IN EAMG INDUCTION BY RelB-SILENCED DENDRITIC CELLS THROUGH RNA INTERFERNCE

A major limitation of above approaches is that imDC are likely to encounter inflammatory stimuli at some stage following infusion into recipients, triggering the terminal maturation/activation of DC (31). Therefore, maintaining imDC in a steady state is critical for the induction of long-term immune tolerance in vivo (5). Recently in an interesting study, Zhang et al (32) showed that DCs transduced with lentiviral-mediated RelB-specfic ShRNAs inhibit the development of EAMG.

RelB is a NF-kappaB family member which plays a key role in the differentiation and maturation of DC. In this study, lentiviral vector expressing RelB-specific short hairpin RNAs (ShRNAs) that efficiently silenced the RelB gene in bone marrow-derived dendritic cells (BMDCs) was made. These RelB-silenced BMDCs were maturation resistant, produce low levels of IL-12, IL-23, IL-6 and could functionally decrease antigen-specific T cells proliferation.

The immune modulation of RelB-silenced BMDCs in C57BL/6 mice with EAMG was examined. They found that intravenous injection with RelB-silenced BMDCs plused with TAChR dominant peptide Talpha 146-162 decreased the incidence and severity of clinical EAMG. Additionally, they found that IFN-gamma production was suppressed and IL-10, IL-4 production was increased in vitro and in vivo, along with decreased serum anti-AChR IgG, IgG1, IgG2b Ab levels. Furthermore, the therapeutic potential of DC-SiRelB in ongoing EAMG was evaluated. Intravenous Injection of DC-SiRelB pulsed with Talpha 146-162 reduced the severity of EAMG significantly in mice, and levels of serum anti-AChR antibody as well. Th1-related markers (IFN-α, T-bet) and Th17-related markers (RORãt, IL-17) were down-regulated, whereas Th2 markers like IL-4 and GATA3 were up-regulated. In addition, DC-SiRelB promoted regulatory T cell profiles as indicated by a marked increase in FoxP3 expression. These results indicate that down-regulation of RelB by RNAi potentiate the capacity of BMDC to relieve detrimental autoimmune responses in vivo.

In conclusion, they suggested that lentiviral-mediated RNAi targeting RelB was effective method to inhibit the maturation of BMDCs and could be effectively used in the treatment of EAMG and MG.

5. PROSPECT

The use of dendritic cells in the therapy of MG has very exciting results at least in the laboratory on the animal models of MG. The modulation of the DCs in vitro with cytokines, antigens, growth factors, and RNA interference has been successful in prevention and treatment of the disease. These experimental studies points to a very bright aspect of using dendritic cells in different ways to achieve a better immunological therapy for MG. The ultimate goal is to treat the disease without hampering the general immune system as a whole. We are still a long way to see any of these treatments in clinic, nevertheless these studies confirm the very important role of DCs and their manipulation in MG. The DC modulation in vitro seems very promising option in the experimental studies on animal. We hope that the promising results shown by these studies could be used soon in near future on humans with similar excellent results and brings a new era in the treatment of MG and other autoimmune diseases as well.

REFERENCES

1. Nagane,Y., Utsugisawa,K., Obara,D., Yamagata,M., Tohgi,H.. Dendritic cells in hyperplastic thymuses from patients with myasthenia gravis. *Muscle Nerve*, 2003, 27(5): 582–9.

2. Jonuleit,H., Schmitt,E., Steinbrink, K., and Enk,A. H.. Dendritic cells as a tool to induce anergic and regulatory T cells. *Trends Immunol*, 2001, 22(7): 394–400.

3. Hackstein,H., Morelli,A. E. and Thomson,A.W.. Designer dendritic cells for tolerance induction: guided not misguided missiles. *Trends Immunol*, 2001, 22(8): 437–42.

4. Rossi,M. and Young, J.W.. Human dendritic cells: potent antigen-presenting cells at the crossroads of Innate and adaptive immunity. *J. Immunol*, 2005, 175(3): 1373–81.

5. Steinman,R.M. The Control of Immunity and Tolerance by dendritic cell. Pathol Biol (paris), 2003, 51(2): 59-60.

6. Fazekas de St Groth.B. The evolution of self-tolerance: a new cell arises to meet the challenge of self-reactivity. *Immunol* Today, 1998, 19(10): 448-54.

7. Ardavin, C. Thymic Dendritic Cells. Immunol Today, 1997,18(7): 350-61.

8. Kappler,J.W., Roehm,N., Marrack,P. T Cell tolerance by clonal elimination in the Thymus. *Cell*, 1987, 49(2): 273-80.

9. Kurts,C., Carbone,F.R., Barnden,M., Blanas,E., Allison,J., Heath,W.R., Miller,J.F.. CD+4 T cell help impairs CD+8 T cell deletion induced by cross-presentation of self-antigens and favours autoimmunity. *J Exp Med*, 1997,186(12): 2057-62.

10. Rocha,B., Tanchot,C., Von Boehmer,H. Clonal anergy blocks in vivo growth of mature T cells and can be reversed in the absence of antigen. *J Exp Med*, 1993, 177(5): 1517-21.

11. Dittel,B.N., Visintin,I., Merchant,R.M., Janeway,C.A.,Jr.. Presentation of the self antigen myelin basic protein by dendritic cells leads to experimental autoimmune encephalomyelitis. *J Immunol*, 1999, 163(1): 32-9.

12. Watanabe,H., Inaba,M., Adachi,Y., Sugiura,K., Hisha,H., Iguchi,T., Ito,T., Yasumizu,R., Inaba,K., Yamashita,T., Ikehara,S.. Experimental autoimmune thyroiditis induced by thyroglobulin-pulsed dendritic cells. *Autoimmunity*, 1999, 31(4): 273-82.

13. Ludewig,B., Ochsenbein,A.F., Odermatt,B., Paulin,D., Hengartner,H., Zinkernagel,R.M.. Immunotherapy with dendritic cells directed against tumor antigens shared with normal host cells results in severe autoimmune disease. J *Exp Med*, 2000, 191(5): 795-804.

14. Drachman,D.B.. Myasthenia gravis. N. Engl. *J. Med*, 1994, 330(25): 1797–810.

15. Christadoss,P., Poussin,M. and Deng,C. Animal models of myasthenia gravis. *Clin. Immunol*, 2000,94(2): 75–87.

16. Vincent,A. Unravelling the pathogenesis of myasthenia gravis. Nat.Rev.Im-munol, 2002, 2(10): 797–804.

17. Xiao,B.G., Duan,R.S., Link,H. and Huang,Y.M. Induction of peripheral tolerance to experimental autoimmune myasthenia gravis by acetylcholine receptor- pulsed dendritic cells. Cell. *Immunol*, 2003, 223(1): 63–9.

18. Yang,H., Kala,M., Scott,B.G., Goluszko,E., Chapman,H.A. and Christadoss, P.. Cathepsin S is required for murine autoimmune myasthenia gravis pathogenesis. *J. Immunol*, 2005, 174(3): 1729–37.

19. Geissmann,F., Revy,P., Regnault,A. et al. TGF-beta 1 prevents the noncognate maturation of human dendritic Langerhans cells. *J Immunol*, 1999, 162(8): 4567–75.

20. Lee,W.C., Qiani,S., Wan,Y. et al. Contrasting effects of myeloid dendritic cells transduced with an adenoviral vector encoding interleukin-10 on organ allograft and tumour rejection. *Immunology*, 2000, 101(2): 233–41.

21. Yarilin,D., Duan,R., Huang,Y.M., Xiao,B.G.. Dendritic cells exposed in vitro to TGF-beta 1 ameliorate EAMG . Clin.Exp.*Immunol*, 2002,127(2): 214-9.

22. Allavena,P., Piemonti,L., Longoni,D., Bernasconi,S., Stoppacciaro,A., Ruco,L., Mantovani,A.. IL-10 prevents the differentiation of monocytes to dendritic cells but promotes their maturation to macrophages. *Eur J Immunol*, 1998, 28(1): 359-69.

23. Buelens,C., Verhasselt,V., De Groote,D., Thielemans,K., Goldman,M., Willems, F.. Interleukin-10 prevents the generation of dendritic cells from human peripheral blood mononuclear cells cultured with interleukin-4 and granulocyte/macrophage -colony-stimulating factor. *Eur J Immunol*, 1997, 27(3): 756-62.

24. Link,H., Huang,Y.M., Xiao,B.. Suppression of EAMG in Lewis rats by IL-10-exposed dendritic cells. *Ann N Y Acad Sci*, 2003, 998(1): 537-8.

25. Inaba,K., Inaba,M., Romani,N., Aya,H., Deguchi,M., Ikehara,S., Muramatsu,S., Steinman,R.M.. Generation of large numbers of dendritic cells from mouse bone marrow cultures supplemented with granulocyte/macrophage colony-stimulating factor. *J Exp Med*, 1992, 176(6): 1693-702.

26. Sallusto,F., Lanzavecchia, A.. Efficient presentation of soluble antigen by cultured human dendritic cells is maintained by granulocyte/macrophage colony-stimulating factor plus interleukin 4 and downregulated by tumor necrosis factor alpha. *J Exp Med*, 1994, 179(4):1109-18.

27. Li,L., Sun,S., Cao,X., Wang,Y., Chang,L., Yin,X. Experimental study on induction of tolerance to experimental autoimmune myasthenia gravis by immature dendritic cells. *J Huazhong Univ Sci Technolog Med Sci*, 2005, 25(2): 215-8.

28. Adikari,S.B., Lian,H., Link,H., Huang,Y.M., Xiao,B.G.. Interferon-gamma-modified dendritic cells suppress B cell function and ameliorate the deve-lopment of experimental autoimmune myasthenia gravis. *Clin Exp Immun-ol*, 2004, 138(2): 230-6.

29. Sheng,J.R., Li.L., Ganesh,B.B., Vasu,C., Prabhakar,B.S., Meriggioli,M.N.. Suppression of experimental autoimmune myasthenia gravis by granulocyte-macrophage colony-stimulating factor is associated with an expansion of FoxP3+ regulatory T cells. *J Immunol*, 2006, 177(8): 5296-306.

30. Wang,R., Yang,H., Xiao,B., Zhang,L.F.. B cell activation in experimental autoimmune myasthenia graves treated with Talpha146-162-iMDCs. *Xi Bao Yu Fen Zi Mian Yi Xue Za Zhi*, 2009, 25(1): 42-5. Chinese

31. Wang,Y.Q., Peng,Y.Z., Wang,Q., Wang,Y.T., You,B.. Influence of adenovirus transfection on the maturation characteristics of human immature dendritic cells. Zhonghua Shao Shang Za Zhi, 2006, 22(6): 458-61. Chinese

32. Zhang,Y., Yang,H., Xiao,B., Wu,M., Zhou,W., Li,J., Li,G., Christadoss,P.. Dendritic cells transduced with lentiviral-mediated RelB-specific ShRNAs inhibit the development of experimental autoimmune myasthenia gravis. *Mol Immunol*, 2009, 46(4): 657-67.

Pixantrone: Preclinical Studies in EAMG

Fulvio Baggi PhD, Sara Nava PhD & Chiara Ruocco Dpharm

1. INTRODUCTION

Current therapeutic strategies for MG include corticosteroids, immunosuppressive drugs and immunomodulation by apheresis or high dose intravenous immunoglobulins (1,2). The majority of patients show a positive response to standard treatments, nevertheless some of them require long-term immunosuppression with corticosteroids and/or immunosuppressive drugs. The importance of drug-related side effects (e.g. as a consequence of long-term treatment with corticosteroids) has been underlined in MG as well as in other autoimmune disorders; in some occasions, side effects might lead to a degree of disability greater than that caused by MG itself. In this context, new immunosuppressants are needed for treatment-resistant MG, for patients with intolerable side effects or with major contraindications to prolonged high-dose corticosteroid treatment.

Pixantrone (PIX), also named BBR2778, is a novel aza-anthracenedione molecule with antiblastic properties, developed to reduce the cardiotoxic effect of its analogue Mitoxantrone (MTX). The anti-tumor activity of PIX was evaluated in various hematologic and solid tumor animal models. Compared to MTX, PIX showed better anti-tumor activity in advanced leukemias and in human prostate carcinoma, and comparable anti-tumor activity in most solid tumor models (3). Furthermore, while MTX is most active at its maximum tolerated doses (MTD), PIX showed a high level of efficacy at approximately one third of its MTD (3). Now PIX is in trial in patients with more solid tumors or leukemias such as relapsed aggressive non-Hodgking's lymphoma, in which, given as a single agent, demonstrated good activity (4-6). PIX and MTX were also proposed as antiproliferative immunosuppressant agents since the common mechanism of action might allow the control of an ongoing autoimmune process (7).

Preclinical studies in the experimental model of Multiple Sclerosis (MS) confirmed the immunosuppressive effects of PIX and suggested that the drug might be effective for treatment of patients with MS (8). Our group has recently investigated the activity of PIX in the experimental model of Myasthenia Gravis (EAMG) (9). EAMG is the animal model of human Myasthenia gravis (MG), and is characterized by the presence of T helper CD4+ cells and autoantibodies (Ab) of the IgG type, specific for the acetylcholine receptor (AChR). EAMG is routinely induced in susceptible rat and mouse strains by immunization with Torpedo AChR (TAChR); a variable proportion of anti-TAChR IgGs, induced by immunization, cross-reacts with self-AChR at the neuromuscular junction. As EAMG mimics MG in its clinical and immunological manifestations, it is considered a reliable model suitable to preclinical investigation of new therapies (10).

2. STRUCTURE AND MECHANISM OF ACTION

PIX is a novel anti-tumor drug that contains an aza-anthracenedione molecular structure, differentiating it from anthracycline drugs. Anthracyclines have been shown to be clinically very active in a number of tumor types, such as lymphoma, leukemia, and breast cancer. For these diseases, anthracycline-containing chemotherapeutic regimens are effective as first-line initial treatment. However, they may cause cumulative heart damage that limits lifetime dosage and does not allow further re-treatment. PIX has been designed to reduce the potential for heart damage compared to currently available anthracyclines or anthracenediones without a loss in anti-tumor activities.

PIX and MTX share some general similarities with anthracyclines, such as the central quinoid Ring (Ring-b in Figure 1). The main differences between the two compounds reside in Ring-a, where the typical 5,8-dihydroxy-substitution pattern of MTX is substituted with piridin ring, and in Ring-c, where both side-chains bears a 'primary' amino group more susceptible to formaldehyde activation and consequently has a greater potential to form complexes with DNA (11). These structural differences allow for a less severe toxic effects and a decrease of cardiotoxicity of PIX (12).

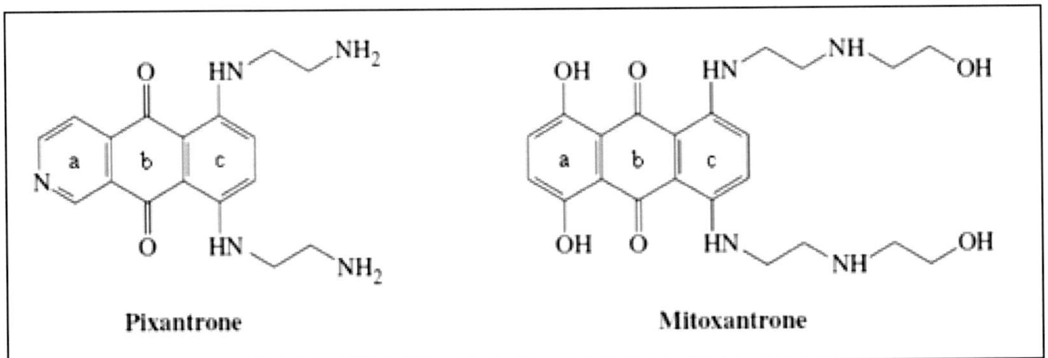

Figure 1. Chemical structures of PIX and MTX.

In vitro and *in vivo* tests demonstrated the cytotoxic effect of PIX in murine and human tumor cell lines and in tumor animal models, showing that PIX retained a high level of activity in a wide range of doses despite of its significantly reduced cytotoxicity in comparison to MTX (12). However, the mechanism of PIX cytotoxicity has not yet been well elucidated: although PIX intercalates DNA and inhibits topoisomerase II, DNA damage is not correlated with cytotoxicity (13).

DNA topoisomerase II has been identified as the target of a number of DNA intercalators, including anthracyclines (doxorubicina), anthracenediones (MTX) and aza-anthracenediones (PIX) (14). DNA topoisomerase II is associated with the nuclear matrix of interphase cells and is a major constituent of the chromosome scaffold. The latter is consistent with the enzyme's essential role in chromosome condensation and separation of daughter DNA molecules at the end of DNA replication (decatenation). Topoisomerase II is also a DNA-relaxing enzyme, which removes DNA supercoiling and torsional tension as they arise during transcription and DNA replication (14).

DNA-damage induced by PIX may result from an alternative mechanism, i.e. "poisoning" of the topoisomerase-DNA complex, that in turn prevents the formation of a cleavable complex; the topoisomerase inhibitory activity of PIX makes it a viable antitumor agent (15). Indeed, topoisomerase II inhibitors were used as immunosuppressant agents in the experimental model of arthritis (16), and MTX have been used in human MS (17-19). Due to its close chemical relationship with MTX activity, PIX has been also studied and evaluated as immunosuppressive/ antiproliferative drug since its ability to interfere with DNA structure during cell cycle and cell duplication, events that play a crucial role in immune activation processes in autoimmune conditions (16). PIX has been considered of potential interest for the treatment of autoimmune diseases. Indeed, PIX has been demonstrated to be effective in modulating the course of EAE, an animal model of MS (20,21).

3. PHARMACOKINETICS

Pharmacokinetic data for PIX in rodents indicated a multi-exponential clearance with a rapid decline in drug concentration during the distribution phase, followed by a slow and prolonged elimination phase lasting up to 192 h (22). The drug was administrated as a slow intravenous (i.v.) infusion, and a rapid distribution throughout the body with accumulation in some tissue compartments was observed. In studies with radiolabelled PIX, the highest percentages of the administered dose were found in the skeletal muscles, liver and kidneys of mice and rats. Less than 0.05% of the administered dose was found in the brain, suggesting that the drug and its metabolites do not cross the blood brain barrier. The efficiency of unchanged drug elimination from the systemic circulation was also shown to be high, but the metabolites were cleared more slowly with a greater volume of distribution. The apparent terminal half-lives of PIX and total radioactivity derived from the plasma data were 2.9 h and 78.6 h in mice and 7.1 h and 81.9 h in rats, which suggested that PIX has a large volume of distribution with a relatively slow clearance of the drug and its metabolites. PIX pharmacokinetics in human conformed to a two-compartment linear open model. HPLC assessment of PIX concentration in plasma and urine (treatment dosage of 180 mg/m^2) showed that the drug has a large volume of distribution (21.4 l/kg) and a rapid clearance (1.15 l/h/kg); its terminal half-life was 14.1 h, and PIX urinary elimination as unchanged drug was less than 10% (22).

4. TOXICITY

The acute toxicity tests of PIX in rodents after a single i.v. injection defined the doses corresponding to the LD_{10} (65.4-77.8 mg/Kg for mouse males and females, respectively) and LD_{50} (77.8-84.9 mg/Kg for mouse males and females, respectively); corresponding values for rats were: LD_{10} 98.1-100.2 mg/Kg and LD_{50} 119.5-111.5 mg/Kg (23). The main symptoms in the acute toxicity tests after i.v. injection were: dyspnea, piloerection, reduced motility, swollen snout and blue pigmentation of the skin. These symptoms lasted no longer than four days with the exception of blue pigmentation that lasted for the whole study period. Moreover the body-weight of the animals decreased in a dose-dependent manner (more evident in males) and a complete recovery was observed in females at the end of the study (23). The histopathological examinations of the organs of rats treated with high dose of PIX showed degenerative atrophy of spleen, bone marrow, gastrointestinal mucosa and renal degeneration (22). Animals receiving single or repeated toxic dosages of PIX did not present myocardial lesions typical of treatments with anthracyclines and anthracenediones (MTX); PIX was also less myelodepressive (2,15). These studies confirm the low cardiotoxicity of PIX as one of its most important features.

5. IMMUNOSUPPRESSIVE POTENTIAL OF ANTHRACENEDIONES: EAE

Immunosuppressive drugs are effective in the treatment of various autoimmune diseases; however, their prolonged use is hampered in most cases by severe side effects (24). Several lines of evidence link immunosuppression to inflammation in patients with MS and provide a rationale for the increasing use of immunosuppressive drugs in the treatment of MS (18). Various immunosuppressive agents have been tested in pre-clinical studies, resulting effective in preventing and treating EAE, and their effect on the immune responses have been elucidated (7). Pre-clinical *in vitro* and *in vivo* studies in EAE models have demonstrated that MTX is effective in reducing T- and B-cell numbers, in suppressing humoral immunity and T-helper cells (25,26); various clinical trials have been performed in MS patients confirming its immunosuppressive effect. The peculiar mechanism of action of MTX has made it extremely interesting in the treatment of MS. Compared with other immunosuppressant drugs, MTX represents an important advance: the immediate tolerance is definitely better and the treatment regimen is more comfortable for the patients (7). Furthermore, unlike other immunosuppressants, MTX induces apoptosis of B lymphocytes in peripheral blood (27,28). Moreover, *ex vivo* analysis of the cytokine profile of immune cells from MS patients treated with MTX, has revealed a long-lasting decrease of IL-10 expressed in monocytes and of IL-2R1 expressed in T cells (25). This drug has, therefore, been approved for MS treatment in the USA and Europe (19,29). Nevertheless, severe long-term side effects may be associated with its prolonged use: cardiotoxicity is the major side effect, and it is strictly dependent on the total cumulative dose. Moreover, cases of therapy-related acute leukaemia have been reported after MTX therapy for MS (30,31).

     The combination of chemical structure, mechanism of action and drug-efficacy linked to lower cardiotoxicity make PIX a good candidate for pre-clinical studies in EAE. Several studies evaluated the effect of PIX in acute and chronic EAE in rodents and the *in vitro* action on antigen- and mitogen-induced T-cell proliferation of animal cells. Potential immunosuppressive activity of PIX was first investigated in SJL mice by Dubois et al. (32). The study demonstrated that PIX prevented in a dose-related way the onset of EAE when it was given daily starting immediately after antigen inoculation. In 2004, Cavaletti and colleagues (21) indicated that PIX modified the course of acute and relapsing-remitting EAE in rats. The reduced EAE severity in PIX-treated rats was due to the marked and long-lasting effect of the drug on lymphocyte subpopulations and to the suppression of antigen-specific responses: circulating CD4+ and CD8+ cells were markedly reduced until the end of the experiment; a very evident effect was also observed on CD45RA+ B cells. PIX effect was dose-dependent and was comparable to the effect of equitoxic doses of MTX. The antigen-specific autoantibody B-cell response to myelin basic protein was also abolished by the highest dose of PIX and MTX; moreover PIX was similarly active on *in vitro* human peripheral blood cells and rat cells (21). Experimental data indicate that PIX is as potent as MTX to prevent EAE development as well as relapses in established disease (7), but the extremely favourable safety profile of PIX makes it a most promising immunosuppressant agent to be evaluated for clinical use with multiple sclerosis patients (21).

6. PIX IN THE ANIMAL MODEL OF MYASTHENIA GRAVIS

MG is probably the most thoroughly understood autoimmune disease of the nervous system (33). Current therapies aim to restore the functional pool of acetylcholine receptors (AChR) at the neuromuscular junctions, by depleting AChR specific autoantibodies and by suppressing the autoimmune attack at the T cell level (34). Again, prolonged drug treatments are required alongside the high risk of severe side effects (33). Even though treatment protocols of proven efficacy are available for the majority of MG patients, research on powerful immunosuppressive drugs is needed since a proportion of patients either does not respond to standard immuno-suppression for prolonged periods of time or have major contraindications to long-term corticosteroid treatment.

The availability of an experimental model for MG (EAMG), induced by active immunization with AChR, allows the study of innovative therapies aiming to the suppression/modulation of the disease manifestations (35). PIX efficacy has already been demonstrated in the modulation of EAE, a model of demyelinating disease in which axonal loss is the consequence of inflammation and T-cell infiltration in the nervous system. We have been interested in evaluating PIX efficacy in MG, an antibody-mediated autoimmune disorder in which the autoantibody production is considered to be T-cell-dependent, since PIX (as MTX) mediates a complex immune suppression involving both B and T lymphocytes (20). Indeed, the effects of PIX have been recently investigated by us in the EAMG model induced in Lewis rats (9).

PIX was tested *in vitro* on rat T cell lines specific for the peptide 97–116 (Rp.97-116), an immunodominant T cell epitope of the rat AChR α subunit (10). Antigen specific T cell lines, grown from Rp.97-116 immunized rats, were challenged with the peptide and with Concanavalin A (ConA) in the presence of PIX (range 0.01–10 μM). Our results showed that even if at the lowest concentration used (i.e. 10nM), a significant reduction of Ag-specific responses as well as ConA-induced T cell responses was observed (Figure 2). Micromolar PIX concentrations abrogated almost completely T cell responses.

Drug efficacy on *ex vivo* lymphocytes proliferation was tested by treating TAChR-immunized Lewis rats with PIX at a dosage of 16.25 mg/kg administered intravenously once weekly for three times. This dosage was one/fourth of the lower confidence limit of LD_{10}. Both spleens and lymph nodes (LN) were aseptically removed one week after the last treatment and total cell count and cell viability were evaluated. Total splenic cell count decreased in the PIX-treated animals compared to the vehicle-treated ones with 39.8% of reduction (mean cell number ± SE $37.13 \pm 9.07 \times 10^6$, p<0.05); PIX effect was more dramatic in draining LN, with a reduction of 77.3% of total LN cell count in

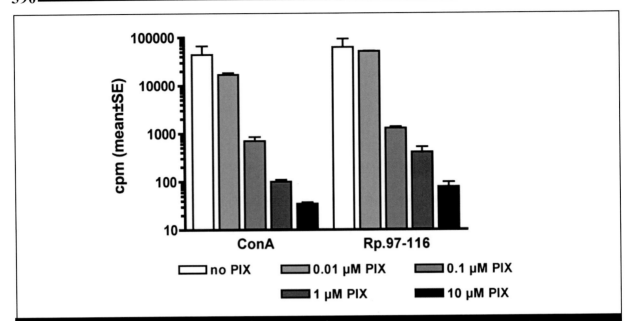

Figure 2. Effect of PIX on Rp.97–116-specific T-cell line. A CD4+ T cell line specific for peptide 97–116 of the rat AChR α subunit was challenged *in vitro* with the specific peptide (5 μg/ml) and with ConA (2 μg/ml) in the presence of increasing amounts of PIX (range 0.01–10 μM). Data are expressed as mean cpm±SE from triplicate wells on a y-axis logarithmic scale.

comparison with vehicle-treated rats (mean cell number ± SE $16.50 \pm 5.32 \times 10^6$, p<0.001). The expression of CD3, CD4, and CD8 molecules as T-cell markers was studied by FACS analysis on both spleen cell and LN cell populations; our analysis showed no differences in the percentage of expression of these T cell subsets among living cells (dead cells were excluded by FSC/SSC gate) between vehicle- and PIX-treated groups. Proliferative responses from LN cells (2×10^5 cells), challenged with TAChR (1.25 and 0.25 μg/ml), Torpedo and Rat AChR 97–116 peptides (10 μg/ml), were found reduced as compared with vehicle treated animals.

Next, we assessed PIX efficacy in the EAMG model, in a preventive treatment protocol (i.e. delaying EAMG manifestation) and in a therapeutic protocol (i.e. modulating ongoing EAMG). Only a single immunization with purified TAChR is sufficient to induce the disease; after a transient "acute" phase (at 1 week after immunization), "chronic" EAMG occurs at 4 weeks, and in 6 weeks more than 75% of animals become affected. The preventive treatment started 4 days after TAChR immunization, with PIX dosage of 16.25 mg/kg administered intravenously once weekly for three times, while the therapeutic treatment started 4 weeks after immunization. Animals were scored every other day by assessing their body weight and strength (36). Results indicated that both treatment schedules modified the course of the disease as compared with vehicle-treated EAMG rats, as shown by increased body weight and a lower EAMG score in the treated group (Figure 3, lines with filled circles and diamonds). Biochemical and immunological assays confirmed PIX efficacy: treated animals had increased muscle AChR content and mean anti-rat AChR Abs titres were significantly reduced. The latter result suggests that PIX exerts immuno-modulating function also on B cells. Proliferative LNC responses to TAChR were affected by both PIX protocols, whereas ConA-induced LNC response was unaltered. The pathological examination of hearts collected from PIX-treated and vehicle-treated rats did not show signs of cardiotoxic damage, confirming its better safe profile (9).

We then addressed whether PIX treatment *in vivo* modify T-helper (CD4+) subsets by evaluating (by qPCR) Th1/Th2/Th3 type cytokines (IFNγ for Th1, IL6 and IL10 for Th2, TGFb for Th3); we also analyzed CTLA-4 and FoxP3 transcription levels as markers of the T-cell CD4+ regulatory subset. TAChR-primed and control rats received a single PIX injection one week later, and then were sacrificed 8 days later. We observed specific up-regulation of FoxP3 transcript (mean $2^{-\Delta\Delta CT}\pm SD$ 2.991±0.811; p<0.05) and TGF-β transcript (mean $2^{-\Delta\Delta CT}\pm SD$ 8.965±0.890; p<0.05) in LN cells of treated animals after a single injection of PIX (16.25 mg/kg) as compared with vehicle-treated rats (used as calibrator); on the contrary, IFN-γ was down-regulated in PIX-treated rats (mean $2^{-\Delta\Delta CT}\pm SD$ 0.080±0.068; p<0.05). All the other cytokines were not modified following PIX treatment.

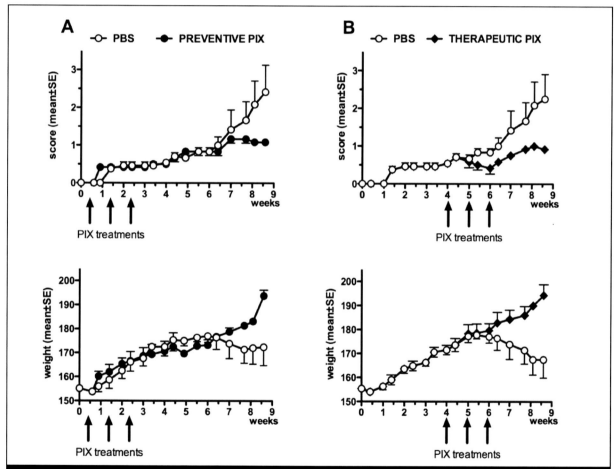

Figure 3. Comparison of the preventive (left panels) and therapeutic (right panels) PIX treatments on EAMG manifestation. Body weight and clinical score were recorded in EAMG rats twice weekly. For the preventive protocol, 4 days after TAChR immunization the animals started to receive PIX (16.25 mg/kg i.v. once weekly for three times, filled circle) or vehicle (sterile saline i.v. once weekly for three times, open circle). For the therapeutic protocol, 4 weeks after TAChR immunization the animals started to receive PIX (16.25 mg/kg i.v. once weekly for three times, filled diamond) or vehicle (sterile saline i.v. once weekly for three times, open circles). The arrows indicate PIX treatments in each protocol.

PIX is also characterised by a myelotoxic effect, and this might hamper dendritic cells (DCs) differentiation from bone marrow (BM) myeloid precursors or DC ability to present the relevant antigen to T-cells. DCs are professional antigen presenting cells, and play a crucial role in maintaining an active state of immune response, and also in inducing regulatory T-cells. Bone marrow myeloid precursors were isolated from PIX- (16.25 mg/kg, one administration) and vehicle-treated animals, and DCs were allowed to differentiate in the presence of GM-CSF and IL-4 for 7 days of culture (37). We did not observe any difference in the total number of BM precursors or in the number of differentiated DCs. DCs were analyzed in their ability to capture and present antigen to T cells, taking advantage of the availability of CD4+ T cells lines, specific for Rp.97-116. The differentiated DCs were used as antigen presenting cells (APC) in lymphocyte proliferation tests in the presence of a specific stimulation (ConA) and specific antigen (Rp.97-116). Obtained results suggested that DCs derived from animals treated with PIX were less efficient in inducing T cell proliferation in response to ConA (vehicle 20300 cpm $\pm$ 661.2 SE vs PIX 14120 $\pm$ 809.5 SE, $p<0.05$) and to Rp97-116 (vehicle 31910 $\pm$ 2009 SE vs PIX 25010 $\pm$ 1106 SE, $p<0.05$).

7. CONCLUSIONS

Corticosteroids and immunosuppressive agents represent the conventional treatments for MG patients. These drugs act on the immune system in a generalized, nonspecific manner and are effective in a large proportion of patients. However the clinical response to conventional treatments is poor in some of them and the severity of side effects is a limiting factor to the prolonged administration of generalised immunosuppressants.

MTX, an anthracenedione, is an antineoplastic pharmacological agent. Initially it was used for the treatment of adult acute myeloid leukemia and, more recently, it has been approved by FDA for the use in specific forms of MS (38-41). MTX has a broad range of effects on the immune system: it is able to suppress proliferation of T cells, B cells, and macrophages and to impair Ag presentation due to the induction of apoptosis in APC. Experimental studies in the MS animal model (EAE) showed that MTX suppresses the B cell function and Abs production. Furthermore it reduced the release of proinflammatory cytokines. These features suggest the possible use of MTX and derived antiblastic agents to control the autoimmune attack also in T cell-dependent, B cell-mediated autoimmune diseases such as MG. However the use of MTX in the treatment of chronic autoimmune diseases has a limitation due to its side effects, namely cardiotoxicity, with an increasing risk with cumulative doses above 100 mg/m^2 (42-44). The clinical experience with MTX from trials in MS suggested that the incidence of heart failure is low, but asymptomatic reduction of left ventricular ejection fraction might be common (38,42,44). Moreover, little data are yet available regarding the potential late cardiac toxicity as observed in cancer series, as well as the risk of developing leukemia (45).

PIX is an antiblastic agent structurally related to MTX, with similar mechanism of action and antineoplastic activity, but is characterised by a significant lower cardiotoxicity. The effect of PIX has been evaluated in EAE, showing that PIX can prevent the onset of EAE in SJL mice and modify the course of the ongoing disease in rats (21,20). These effects have been attributed to the long-lasting effect of PIX on lymphocyte subpopulations and on impaired Ag presentation. The observed effect was dose-dependent, and no signs of cardiotoxicity compared with MTX were observed. Interestingly, the B cell response to myelin basic protein was also inhibited, providing a further mechanism of action to explain the reduced demyelination (21).

We have recently investigated the potential immunomodulatory effect of PIX *in vitro* and *in vivo* in the TAChR-induced model of EAMG (9). We demonstrated that PIX modifies the course of the disease (improvement of clinical score and recovery of body weight). The clinical effect was associated with a marked reduction of specific anti-rat AChR Abs and increase of AChR content in rat muscles.

PIX inhibited T cell responses *in vitro* in a dose-dependent fashion, up to the complete suppression of the proliferation: LNCs response from PIX-treated TAChR-immunized rats showed that not only TAChR-specific T cell proliferation was markedly inhibited, but also LNC response to AChR derived peptides corresponding to immunodominant epitope 97–116 from both Torpedo and rat a-subunits.

The total number of spleen cells and peripheral LNC recovered in vitro was markedly reduced by PIX treatment; FACS analysis on living (gated) cells did not reveal any specific effect on CD3, CD4 or CD8 subsets involved in AChR recognition and proliferation. This finding is similar to that reported in EAE on the effect of PIX on circulating lymphocytes (21).

The inhibitory effect of PIX on immunological parameters in vitro was paralleled by improvement of EAMG clinical findings. The effect of PIX was investigated both on a preventive or a therapeutic schedule: in both conditions, PIX modified the course of the disease (Figure 3). Our data on specific Abs and muscle AChR content suggest that PIX might also be effective at the B cell level.

Our preclinical study clearly indicates that PIX might be a promising immunomodulatory agent suitable for clinical investigation in MG, due to its combined effect at both T cell and B cell level. We suggest that the principal candidates might be represented by MG patients with severe forms of the disease or with major side effects or contraindications to corticosteroids.

PIX administration schedule (i.e. every 3 - 4 weeks) might represent a further important feature of this drug, enabling us to limit the severity of side effects.

The effectiveness and the reduced cardiotoxicity make PIX a new agent with immunosuppressant activity suitable for clinical investigation in MG. Its safety profile in prolonged treatments can be evaluated in preclinical experiments. Current research in EAMG will address more precisely PIX immunomodulatory effects at multiple cellular targets (T effector cells, T regulatory cells, B cells, DCs). The effect of alternative treatment schedules, resulting in a lower cumulative dosage, is also on current investigation in the EAMG model.

REFERENCES

1. Conti-Fine B.M., Milani M., Kaminski H.J. 2006. Myasthenia gravis: past, present, and future. *J. Clin. Invest.* 116:2843-2854.

2. Vincent A., Leite M.I. 2005. Neuromuscular junction autoimmune disease: muscle specific kinase antibodies and treatments for myasthenia gravis. *Curr. Opin. Neurol.* 18:519-525.

3. Cavaletti E., Crippa L., Mainardi P., Oggioni N., Cavagnoli R., Bellini O., Sala F. 2006. Pixantrone (BBR 2778) has reduced cardiotoxic potential in mice pretreated with doxorubicin: comparative studies against doxorubicin and mitoxantrone. *Invest New Drugs.* 25(3):187-195.

4. Lim S.T., Fayad L., Tulpule A., Modiano M., Cabanillas F., Laffranchi B., Allievi C., Bernareggi A., Levine A.M. 2007. A phase I/II trial of pixantrone (BBR2778), methylprednisolone, cisplatin, and cytosine arabinoside (PSHAP) in relapsed/refractory aggressive non-Hodgkin's lymphoma. *Leuk. Lymphoma.* 48(2):374-380.

5. Engert A., Herbrecht R., Santoro A., Zinzani P.L., Gorbatchevsky I. 2006. EXTEND PIX301: a phase III randomized trial of pixantrone versus other chemotherapeutic agents as third-line monotherapy in patients with relapsed, aggressive non-Hodgkin's lymphoma. *Clin. Lymphoma Myeloma.* 7(2):152-154.

6. Borchmann P., Schnell R., Knippertz R., Staak J.O., Camboni G.M., Bernareggi A., Hiibel K., Staib P., Schulz A., Diehl V., Engert A. 2001. Phase I study of BBR 2778, a new aza-anthracenedione, in advanced or refractory non-Hodgkin's lymphoma. *Annals of Oncology.* 12:661-667.

7. Fox E.J. 2004. Mechanism of action of mitoxantrone. *Neurology.* 28; 63(12 Suppl 6):S15-8.

8. Gonsette R.E., Dubois B. 2004. Pixantrone (BBR2778): a new immunosuppressant in multiple sclerosis with a low cardiotoxicity. *J Neurol Sci.* 223:81-86.

9. Ubiali F., Nava S., Nessi V., Longhi R., Pezzoni G., Capobianco R., Mantegazza R., Antozzi C., Baggi F. 2008. Pixantrone (BBR2778) reduces the severity of experimental autoimmune myasthenia gravis in Lewis rats. *J Immunol.* 180(4):2696-2703.

10. Baggi F., Annoni A., Ubiali F., Milani M., Longhi R., Scaioli W., Cornelio F., Mantegazza R., Antozzi C. 2004. Breakdown of tolerance to a self-peptide of acetylcholine receptor alpha-subunit induces experimental myasthenia gravis in rats. *J Immunol.* 172(4):2697-2703.

11. Evison B.J., Mansour O.C., Menta E., Phillips D.N., Cutts S.M. 2007. Pixantrone can be activated by formaldehyde to generate a potent DNA adduct forming agent. *Nucleic Acids Research.* 35(11)3581-3589.

12. Beggiolin G., Crippa L., Menta E., Manzotti C., Cavalletti E., Pezzoni G., Torriani D., Randisi E., Cavagnoli R., Sala F., Giuliani F.C., Spinelli S. 2001. BBR2778, an aza-anthracenedione endowed with preclinical anticancer activity and lack of delayed cardiotoxicity. *Tumori.* 87(6):407-416.

13. Borchmann P., Reiser M. 2003. Pixantrone (Novuspharma). *IDrugs.* 6(5):486-490.

14. Pommier Y. DNA topoisomerase I , and II in cancer chemotherapy: update and perspectives. 1993. *Cancer Chemother. Pharmacol.* 32:103-108.

15. Borchmann P., Morschhauser F., Parry A., Schnell R., Harousseau J.L., Gisselbrecht C., Rudolph C., Wilhelm M., Günther H., Pfreundschuh D.M., Camboni G., Engert

A. 2003. Phase-II study of the new aza-anthracenedione, BBR 2778, in patients with relapsed aggressive non-Hodgkin's lymphomas. *Haematologica.* 88(8):888-894.

16. Verdrengh M., Isaksson O., Tarkowski A. 2005. Topoisomerase II inhibitors, irrespective of their chemical composition, ameliorate experimental arthritis. *Rheumatology (Oxford).* 44(2):183-186.

17. Hartung H.P., Gonsette R., König N., Kwiecinski H., Guseo A., Morrissey S.P., Krapf H., Zwingers T. and the Mitoxantrone in Multiple Sclerosis Study Group (MIMS). 2002. Mitoxantrone in progressive multiple sclerosis: a placebo-controlled, double-blind, randomised, multicentre trial. *Lancet.* 360:2018-2025.

18. Gonsette R.E. 2004. New immunosuppressants with potential implication in multiple sclerosis. *J. Neurol. Sci.* 223 (1): 87-93.

19. Martinelli Boneschi F., Rovaris M., Capra R., Comi G. 2005. Mitoxantrone for multiple sclerosis. *Cochrane Database Syst. Rev.* 19(4):CD002127.

20. Mazzanti B., Biagioli T., Aldinucci A., Cavaletti G., Cavalletti E., Oggioni N., Frigo M., Rota S., Tagliabue E., Ballerini C., Massacesi L., Riccio P., Lolli F. 2005. Effects of pixantrone on immune-cell function in the course of acute rat experimental allergic encephalomyelitis. *J. Neuroimmunol.* 168:111-117.

21. Cavaletti G., Cavalletti E., Crippa L., Di Luccio E., Oggioni N., Mazzanti B., Biagioli T., Sala F., Sala V., Frigo M., Rota S., Tagliabue E., Stanzani L., Galbiati S., Rigolio R., Zoia C., Tredici G., Perseghin P., Dassi M., Riccio P., Lolli F. 2004. Pixantrone (BBR2778) reduces the severity of experimental allergic encephalomyelitis. *J. Neuroimmunol.* 151(1-2):55-65.

22. Dawson L.K., Jodrell D.I., Bowman A., Ryea R., Byrne B., Bernareggi A., Camboni G., Smyth J.F. 2000. A clinical phase I and pharmacokinetic study of BBR 2778, a novel anthracenedione analogue, administered intravenously, 3 weekly. European J. of Cancer. 36:2353-2359.

23. Investigator's Brochure for BBR2778. 2002. Edition no. 6.

24. Chan A., Stüve O., Von Ahsen N. 2008. Immunosuppression in clinical practice: approaches to individualized therapy. J. Neurol. 255 (Suppl 6):22-27.

25. Gbadamosi J., Buhmann C., Tessmer W., Moench A., Haag F., Heesen C. 2003. Effects of mitoxantrone on multiple sclerosis patients' lymphocyte subpopulations and production of immunoglobulin, TNF-alpha and IL-10. *Eur. Neurol.* 49:137-141.

26. Fidler J.M., Dejoy S.Q., Gibbons J.J.Jr. 1986. Selective immunomodulation by the antineoplastic agent mitoxantrone. I. Suppression of B Lymphocyte function. *J. Immunol.* 137(2):727-732.

27. Chan A., Weilbach F.X., Toyka K.V., Gold R. 2005. Mitoxantrone induces cell death in peripheral blood leucocytes of multiple sclerosis patients. *Clinical and Experimental Immunology.* 139:152-158.

28. Bellosillo B., Colomer D., Pons G., Gil J. 1998. Mitoxantrone, a topoisomerase II inhibitor, induces apoptosis of b-chronic lymphocytes leukaemia cells. *Br. J. Haematol.* 100:142-146.

29. Gonsette R.E. 1996. Mitoxantrone immunotherapy in multiple sclerosis. *Mult. Scler.* 1(6):329-332.

30. Gonsette R.E. 2003. Mitoxantrone in progressive multiple sclerosis: when and how to treat? *J. Neurol. Sci.* 206:203-208.

31. Ghalie R.G., Mauch E., Edan G., Hartung H.P., Gonsette R.E., Eisenmann S., Le Page E., Butine M.D., Goodkin D.E. 2002. A study of therapy-related acute leukaemia after mitoxantrone therapy for multiple sclerosis. *Mult. Scler.* 8:441-445.

32. Dubois B., Gonsette R., Dillen C., Billiau A. 2001. Efficacy of a novel noncardiotoxic aza-anthracenedione (BBR2778) in acute EAE. *Mult. Scler.* 7(Suppl 1):S20 [P-010].

33. Sieb J.P. 2005. Myasthenia gravis: emerging new therapy options. *Curr. Opin. Neurol.* 5:303-307.

34. Drachman D.B., McIntosh K.R., Yang B. 1998. Factors that determine the severity of experimental myasthenia gravis. *Ann. NY. Acad. Sci.* 841:262-282.

35. Fuchs S., Bartfeld D., Eshhar Z., Feingold C., Mochly-Rosen D., Novick D., Schwartz M., Tarrab-Hazdai R. 1980. Immune regulation of experimental myasthenia. *J. Neurol. Neurosurg. Psychiatry.* 43:634-643.

36. Lennon V.A., Lindstrom J.M., Seybold M.E. 1975. Experimental autoimmune myasthenia: A model of myasthenia gravis in rats and guinea pigs. *J. Exp. Med.* 141(6):1365-1375.

37. Tiurbe G., Matuschek A., Kämmerer U., Schneider M., Thiede A., Ulrichs K., Otto C. 2009. Inhibitory effects of rat bone marrow-derived dendritic cells on naïve and alloantigen-specific CD4+ T cells: a comparison between dendritic cells generated with GM-CSF plus IL-4 and dendritic cells generated with GM-CSF plus IL-10. *BMC Research Notes.* 2:12-21.

38. Debouverie M.L., Taillandier S., Pittion-Vouyovitch, S.L., Vespignani H. 2007. Clinical follow-up of 304 patients with multiple sclerosis three years after mitoxantrone treatment. *Mult. Scler.* 13:626-631.

39. Gonsette R.E. 2007. Compared benefit of approved and experimental immunosuppressive therapeutic approaches in multiple sclerosis. *Expert Opin. Pharmacother.* 8:1103-1116.

40. Neuhaus O., Kieseier B.C., Hartung H.P. 2006. Mitoxantrone in multiple sclerosis. *Adv. Neurol.* 98:293-302.

41. Jeffery D.R., Herndon R. 2004. Review of mitoxantrone in the treatment of multiple sclerosis. *Neurology.* 63:S19-S24.

42. Paul F., Dorr J., Wurfel J., Vogel H.P., Zipp F. 2007. Early mitoxantroneinduced cardiotoxicity in secondary progressive multiple sclerosis. *J. Neurol. Neurosurg. Psychiatry.* 78:198-200.

43. Galetta S.L., Markowitz C. 2005. US FDA-approved disease-modifying treatments for multiple sclerosis: review of adverse effect profiles. *CNS Drugs.* 19:239-252.

44. Cohen B.A., Mikol D.D. 2004. Mitoxantrone treatment of multiple sclerosis: safety considerations. *Neurology.* 63:S28-S32.

45. Cartwright M.S., Jeffery D.R., Lewis Z.T., Koty P.P., Stewart W.T., Molnar I. 2007. Mitoxantrone for multiple sclerosis causing acute lymphoblastic leukemia. *Neurology.* 68:1630-1631.

Antigen-Specific Apheresis of Autoantibodies as a Treatment Strategy for Myasthenia Gravis

Paraskevi Zisimopoulou PhD, George Lagoumintzis PhD, Nikolaos Trakas PhD,
Petros Giastas PhD, Konstantinos Poulas PhD and Socrates J. Tzartos PhD

1. INTRODUCTION

Myasthenia gravis (MG), a prototypic antibody-mediated autoimmune disease, is an excellent research tool for the better understanding of the mechanisms and the development of therapies for several antibody-mediated diseases. The main advantage in the study of MG is that the main autoantigen is well characterized, since in ~90% of MG patients, antibodies against the muscle acetylcholine receptor (AChR) seem to be responsible for the disease.

The AChR is an acetylcholine-gated cation channel with a key role in communication between motor nerves and skeletal muscles and between neuronal cells in the peripheral and central nervous systems (1, 2). At the normal neuromuscular junction (NMJ), the AChR is highly concentrated postsynaptically. Its principal function is to permit the flow of current through its ion channel after binding of acetylcholine (ACh). In the central nervous system, AChRs also act presynaptically and extrasynaptically to modulate transmission by facilitating the release of several transmitters (3, 4).

The AChR and other proteins located on the cell membrane of the motor nerve or muscle endplate with an extracellular domain (ECD) accessible to circulating substances are targets for autoimmune attack. Following attack, the disruption of communication at the NMJ results in muscle weakness, the best characterized conditions being the autoimmune myasthenic disorders. Molecules in the NMJ identified as autoantibody targets include calcium and potassium channels in the motor nerve terminal, AChR and muscle specific kinase (MuSK) postsynaptically, and rapsyn, titin, and the ryanodine receptor intracellularly in the muscle cell (5).

The role of autoantibodies in MG has been established by several measures. These include the demonstration of the presence of circulating anti-AChR antibodies in nearly 80-90% of patients with MG (6), the passive transfer of several features of the disease from human to mouse with IgG (7), the localization of immune complexes (IgG and complement) on the postsynaptic membrane (8), the beneficial effects of plasmapheresis (9, 10), and the induction of experimental MG (EAMG) by immunization with AChR (11) or by transfer of anti-AChR antibodies (12). In addition, a direct proof of the pathogenicity of the human anti-AChR antibodies comes from the recent observation that EAMG is readily induced in animals injected intraperitoneally with isolated anti-AChR antibodies from some MG patients, while, in the same experiment, the serum remaining after anti-AChR antibody removal was not able to induce disease (13).

2. CURRENT TREATMENTS OF MG

Current treatments control MG by improving neuromuscular transmission or downmodulating overall immune function.

Acetylcholinesterase inhibitors remain the first-line of symptomatic MG medication. They enhance muscle strength by increasing ACh levels in the NMJ; their side effects are mostly related to enhanced cholinergic activity in tissues and organs other than the skeletal muscles. In most cases, additional pharmacological treatment is needed.

Immunosuppressive treatments include corticosteroids, which are usually effective in reducing anti-AChR antibody titer, but induce serious side effects, and non-steroidal immunosupressants, which inhibit lymphocyte proliferation, require a longer period to act, and also have serious side effects. Thymectomy, which is often used for early-onset and thymoma MG, may also be considered as an immunomodulatory treatment (14, 15).

A different therapeutic approach, plasma exchange (plasmapheresis), is used as a short term therapy, mostly in severe MG symptoms and in myasthenic crisis, as well as in cases where muscle function must be optimized, such as before surgery (including thymectomy). It produces a rapid clinical improvement regardless of whether the patients are seronegative or seropositive for anti-AChR antibodies (16). This suggests that the removal of circulating pathogenic antibodies and possibly other pathogenic agents leads to the clinical improvement. Administration of intravenous Ig (IVIg) is also used in similar circumstances to plasma exchange (17, 18). IVIg administration has been linked to adverse effects, which, however, are only minor (19-21). IVIg seems to impact on the autoimmune process by several mechanisms, including interfering with the binding of antibodies to Fc receptors on macrophages (22). Nevertheless, as with other therapies for MG, neither IVIg nor plasma exchange are specific for MG. See Chapter 5 and 6 for a detailed discussion on plasma exchange and IVIg.

3. EXPERIMENTAL THERAPEUTIC STRATEGIES

Several experimental therapeutic strategies are currently under investigation with the common aim of avoiding generalized immunosuppression. These include

- administration of phosphodiesterase inhibitors that target regulatory T cells (23),
- induction of tolerance using various AChR-derived molecules to suppress ongoing disease (24-26),

- T-cell receptor vaccination to suppress autoreactive T cells (27, 28),

- manipulation of antigen-presenting cells to make them specifically eliminate AChR-specific T cells (28, 29),

- acetylcholinesterase gene silencing using antisense oligonucleotides to selectively block alternative spliced variants of acetylcholinesterase, which cannot be blocked by pyridostigmine (30),

- the use of non-pathogenic univalent human anti-AChR Ab fragments that bind to the AChR, thereby preventing the binding of pathogenic autoantibodies (31-35),

- selective antigen-specific depletion of autoantibodies (immunoadsorption) and the return of the "cleared" plasma to the patient (Fig. 1). This might be achieved through the use of immunoadsorbent columns carrying immobilized human AChR (whole or part), which would necessitate the production and use of large amounts of recombinant AChR or AChR domains. The immobilization of such recombinant proteins on Sepharose beads and the incubation of these matrices with a variety of seropositive MG sera results in a significant reduction in the concentration of autoantibodies in these sera (36-38).

In this article, we will review our efforts aimed at the selective depletion of anti-AChR autoantibodies by immunoadsorption and propose it as a future antigen-specific therapy for MG and as a model for similar therapy for other autoantibody-mediated diseases.

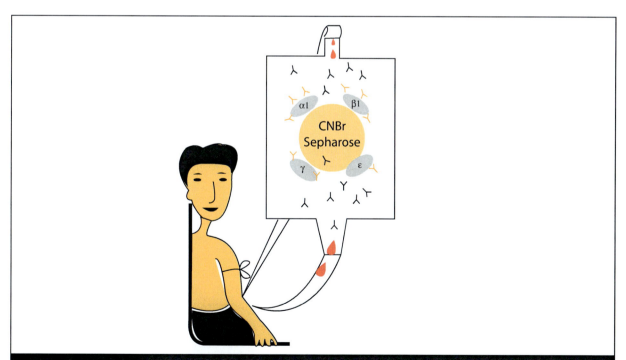

Figure 1. Proposed therapeutic immunoadsorption method using a column made from immobilized ECDs to adsorb anti-AChR antibodies. The orange and black antibodies denote antibodies binding to various ECDs or non-ECD-binding antibodies, respectively.

4. IMMUNOADSORPTION TECHNIQUES

A number of techniques have been devised as alternatives to plasmapheresis. These include, (a) adsorption of immunoglobulins using a tryptophan-linked polyvinyl alcohol gel (TR-350) that adsorbs most large proteins, including most anti-AChR antibodies, by hydrophobic interactions (39), (b) columns carrying staphylococcal protein A, which avidly binds most human immunoglobulins (40), and (c) columns carrying sheep anti-human IgG antibodies (Ig-Adsopak) to remove human IgG molecules (41); the main drawback of these approaches is their non-specificity, namely the indiscriminate removal of all, or most, immunoglobulins, including potentially useful antibodies. To this end, three alternative approaches to the development of an antigen-specific approach for the selective depletion of anti-AChR autoantibodies from MG patients' sera have been described. The first two consist of the use of columns bearing (a) a peptide corresponding to amino acids 183–200 of the Torpedo AChR α subunit (42) or (b) the ECD of the Torpedo α -subunit expressed in *E. coli* as a fusion protein with the maltose binding protein immobilized on amylase-resin; this immunoadsorbent was successfully tested on two MG sera (43). However, the majority of anti-AChR antibodies are directed against several epitopes other than that used by Takamori and Maruta, and, in the vast majority of MG patients, few autoantibodies bind to Torpedo AChR (44, 45). These facts necessitated the development of a more effective approach for selective antibody clearance. The third approach, under development by our own group, is the depletion of autoantibodies from anti-AChR antibody-positive MG sera using yeast- or *E. coli*-expressed ECDs of human muscle AChR subunits immobilized on CNBr-activated Sepharose beads as immunoadsorbents (36-38).

5. THE NATURE OF THE IMMUNOADSORBENT

Muscle AChR is present in two subtypes, a fetal subtype with an $(\alpha1)_2\beta1\tau\delta$ stoichiometry and an adult subtype with an $(\alpha1)_2\beta\epsilon\delta$ stoichiometry. Each AChR subunit consists of an N-terminal ECD, containing the characteristic 13-residue long Cys-loop of a ligand-gated ion channel, four membrane-spanning α-helices, a large cytoplasmic loop, and a small extracellular C-terminal tail (46).

The development of a specific immunoadsorption approach for the selective depletion of pathogenic autoantibodies from MG sera requires large amounts of recombinant AChR, a challenging task, as the AChR is a membrane protein and the presence of cellular factors seems to be necessary for correct assembly. However, the use of the ECD of each AChR subunit should overcome this problem, especially as the extracellular side of the AChR probably carries the full range of epitopes recognized by the pathogenic autoantibodies.

We therefore expressed and purified the ECD of each human muscle AChR subunit. The ECDs of the human α1 (amino acids 1-210), β1 (amino acids 1-221), γ (amino acids 1-218), and mutants of the ECDs of the γ, δ (amino acids 1-219), and ε (amino acids 1-219) AChR subunits were expressed in *P. pastoris*, a eukaryotic expression system (47-49). These ECDs were then used as immunoadsorbents for the specific depletion of antibodies from seropositive MG sera.

Due to the relatively moderate ECD yield in the yeast expression system (usually around 1 mg/L), we also explored the possibility of using *E. coli*-expressed ECDs as immunoadsorbents (38). The proteins were expressed in inclusion bodies and purified under denaturing conditions. As expected, the yield for all ECDs was significantly higher than that of the corresponding yeast product (around 12 mg/L).

6. CLEARANCE OF MG SERA

The average degree of immunoadsorption obtained for 40 randomly chosen MG sera using *E. coli*-produced ECDs was 24.1% using an α1 ECD column, 12.9% using a β1 ECD column, 15.8% using a γ ECD column, and 13.5% using an ε ECD column, whereas the corresponding results for the yeast *P. pastoris* ECDs "matrix" were 31%, 13.9%, 7%, and 12.7% [Fig. 2, (38)]. A different set of 50 randomly chosen MG sera tested only with yeast ECDs columns showed higher levels of immunoadsorption (Fig. 3), namely 35% for α1, 22% for β1, 20% for γ, and 15.5% for ε (36, 37). The unexpected ability of the denatured *E. coli*-expressed ECDs to immunoadsorb MG autoantibodies at considerable levels (often with a similar efficiency to that of the yeast-expressed folded ECDs) suggests that the initially unfolded *E. coli*-expressed ECDs acquire the correct conformation after immobilization on the resin and removal of the denaturing reagent. However, in the case of *E. coli*-expressed proteins, 10-fold more protein may be needed as immunoadsorbent.

Use of the δ ECD did not result in considerable immunoadsorption of autoantibodies, which suggests that either anti-δ autoantibodies are strictly conformation-dependent and not removed due to a possibly imperfect conformation of the recombinant δ ECD (*E. coli*- or yeast-expressed) or are rare in MG.

The availability of the ECDs of all AChR subunits has allowed the construction of immunoadsorption columns with improved efficiency for removing MG autoantibodies. Our data show that the combination of more than one ECD on a single immunoadsorbent leads to increased depletion of anti-AChR antibodies and, in some cases, to near-complete clearance (37).

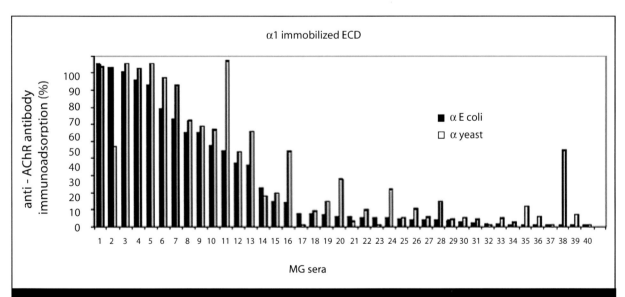

Figure 2: Immunoadsorption of anti-AChR antibodies from 40 MG sera using Sepharose-immobilized *E. coli*- or yeast-expressed α1 ECD. Randomly selected anti-AChR antibody-positive MG sera were incubated with ECD-Sepharose, then the non-bound material was assayed for anti-AChR antibodies by radioimmunoassay and the percentage of immunoadsorption calculated. The Figure shows that the efficiency of the *E. coli*-expressed α1 ECD as immunoadsorbent approaches that of the yeast-expressed ECD.

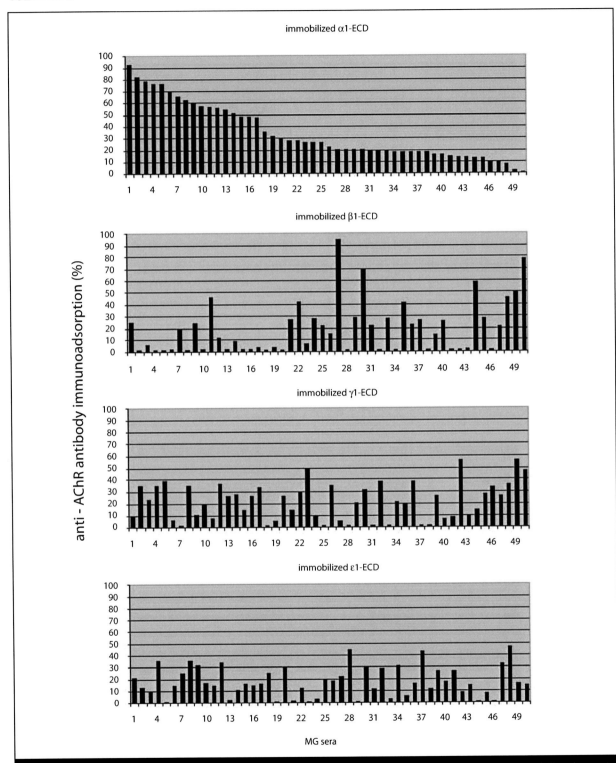

Figure 3: Immunoadsorption of anti-AChR antibodies from 50 MG sera using Sepharose-immobilized yeast-expressed ECDs. The result for the immobilized δ ECD is not shown, as the immunoadsorption using this ECD was very low.

7. CHARACTERIZATION OF THE ECD IMMUNOADSORBENTS

The potential use of the immobilized ECDs as immunoadsorbents would require them to have a set of characteristics, such as (a) a considerable capacity, (b) stability during incubation with human serum and (c) specificity for anti-AChR antibodies. Results of test for these characteristics are described below, supporting the suitability of the immobilized ECDs as immunoadsorbents for MG therapy.

The maximal amount of anti-AChR antibodies removed by α1 ECD-Sepharose was about 1.5 pmol of antibody per microgram of immobilized protein (36), while the β1 ECD-Sepharose removed 5 pmol of antibody per microgram of immobilized protein (37). These results suggest that the plasma from an adult patient (approximately 3L) containing anti-β1 antibodies, with an average anti-AChR titer of 10-50 nM, would be cleared of anti-β1 antibodies by a column bearing 10-30 mg of yeast-expressed β1 ECD. Although such amounts are already easily produced, the future use of fermentors and the establishment of optimal culture conditions could multiply the ECD yield and allow the treatment of patients with almost any anti-AChR titer.

Stability of the column is a prerequisite, since any polypeptide released from the column during immunoadsorption might act as an immunogen when introduced into the patient, despite the fact that the ECDs are of human origin and so would be only weakly immunogenic. To eliminate this possibility, we studied the stability of the columns and showed that no detectable amounts of ECD (yeast- or *E. coli*-expressed) were removed from the resin even after 24 h incubation with human serum, thus ensuring that no potentially antigenic ECD molecules would be introduced into the patient during the brief therapeutic apheresis procedure (36, 38). To further verify the safety of the immunoadsorption process, we performed preliminary studies on experimental rabbits. Two rabbits were used, one of which was not immunized and the other immunized twice with the β1 ECD. The immunized rabbit developed anti-ECD and anti-AChR antibodies, although no disease symptoms appeared. The plasma from the immunized and non immunized animals was passed through a β1-ECD column and reintroduced intravenously into the same rabbit. The procedure was repeated once more. After this process, the non-immunized rabbit did not develop any anti-AChR antibodies and the antibody titer in the immunized rabbit did not increase. More importantly, the rabbits remained healthy for a long period (50). This preliminary experiment suggests that the ECD immunoadsorption procedure may be safe for use on patients.

The specificity of the ECD resin was tested using known anti-MuSK antibody-positive sera. These experiments showed that no anti-MuSK antibody was removed after extended incubation with the ECD resin (38). Confirmation of the specificity of the binding of the anti-AChR antibodies to the ECD immunoadsorbents was provided by the finding that the antibodies did not bind to the control BSA immunoadsorbent. In addition, measurement of the total protein content in a test serum before and after immunoadsorption did not reveal any measurable reduction in protein after treatment, further verifying the specificity of immunoadsorption.

Additionally, it was found that immunoadsorption takes place in very short time (~5 min), and that the immunoadsorbents may be used repeatedly for 4-6 times, characteristics useful for the clinical application of the technique. Finally, in preliminary studies, in which 4 ml-columns of ECD-Sepharose were used, the estimated time needed to clear 1 ml of serum with a moderate titer (10-50 nM) was found less than 1 min, which means that a 50 ml ECD-column might be able to clear much more than 3L serum in an hour.

8. ACTIVITY OF ANTIBODY-DEPLETED SERA AND OF PURIFIED ANTI-SUBUNIT AUTOANTIBODIES *in vitro* AND *in vivo*.

The effectiveness of either plasmapheresis or Ig apheresis does not exclude the possibility that non-anti-AChR antibody factors in the plasma also contribute to the development of MG symptoms. If this were true, the effectiveness of selective anti-AChR antibody depletion might only be moderate. To examine this possibility, we investigated the ability of the autoantibody-depleted sera and the purified subunit-specific autoantibodies to cause both receptor loss *in vitro* and EAMG *in vivo*. More specifically, using α1 and β1 ECD immunoadsorbents, we initially depleted MG sera containing mostly anti-α1 or anti-β1 antibodies of the corresponding antibodies, then isolated the bound antibodies from the immunoadsorbents.

The ability of the "depleted" MG sera and the purified ECD-bound antibodies to cause AChR antigenic modulation (AChR loss) was initially tested *in vitro* in TE671 cell cultures (51). Sera partially depleted of anti-AChR antibodies still caused AChR antigenic modulation, but at a considerably lower level, whereas completely depleted sera did not. The autoantibodies isolated from the α1 or β1 ECD column caused dose-dependent AChR loss, with the anti-α1 autoantibodies being approximately 4 times more potent on a molar basis than the anti-β1 antibodies in triggering AChR modulation. This observation supports the notion that the α1 subunit is the main target of the pathogenic autoantibodies.

Our next aim was to determine the ability of the untreated sera, depleted sera, and isolated autoantibodies to passively transfer EAMG to Lewis rats. Two MG sera with high titers of antibodies to both human and rat AChR and with a high titer of anti-α ECD antibodies were used in preliminary *in vivo* experiments. Four- to five-week-old Lewis rats were injected once intraperitoneally with the different samples and disease severity assessed on the basis of clinical symptoms. The untreated sera and isolated anti-α1 subunit-specific antibodies were equally capable of inducing severe MG symptoms and death. Interestingly, the depleted sera, which did not contain antibodies reactive with rat AChR, did not induce any MG-like symptoms (Tzartos et al., 2008; Kordas, Sideris, Poulas and Tzartos, unpublished).

Even though the latter result remains to be confirmed using additional sera, the fact that the antibody-depleted fractions of the MG sera did not induce MG-like symptoms suggests that the anti-AChR autoantibodies are the sole pathogenic factor in these sera. Thus, the proposed therapeutic approach aimed at the depletion of anti-AChR autoantibodies from MG patients' plasma should be able to remove all, or most, of the pathogenic factors.

To try to improve and technically simplify our system, we explored the possibility of direct whole blood immunoadsorption, rather than plasma immunoadsorption. This approach is interesting, since it simplifies the procedure and bypasses complicated technology and instrumentation, such as a plasma separator circuit. Preliminary results showed that whole blood immunoadsorption may be equally efficiently applied in our system (Lagoumintzis, Zisimopoulou, Poulas and Tzartos, unpublished data). In fact, the average percentage of anti-AChR autoantibodies removed was almost identical for both methods tested (i.e. plasma immunoadsorption and whole blood immunoadsorption). Furthermore, no hemolysis was seen in whole blood immunoadsorption and no measurable reduction in total protein content after treatment was observed, verifying the safety and specificity of the technique.

Complement activation during immunoadsorption could be a potential problem in the therapeutic application of the approach. We assume that, since the amount of column-bound anti-AChR Abs in therapeutic immunoadsorption would be extremely small compared to the amount of immunoglobulin bound to immobilized protein-A or anti-Ig, which have already been successfully used instead of plasmapheresis in MG and other diseases, complement activation during selective immunoadsorption would not be significant or create a problem. However, we tested this parameter using two randomly selected MG sera and two normal human sera as controls. As expected, complement activation after immunoadsorption was negligible in all four sera tested. Thus, complement activation seems not to be a problem in therapeutic immunoadsorption with ECD-columns.

9. CONCLUSIONS

The use of columns carrying immobilized ECDs of human AChR subunits in therapeutic immunoadsorption has a number of advantages. First, it would be specific for anti-AChR antibodies, thus avoiding the removal of useful antibodies and other molecules from the patient and eliminating the need for replacement fluids. Second, it would be reasonably affordable, since the production of substantial amounts of recombinant AChR subunit ECDs, especially using the prokaryotic expression system, is now a standard laboratory procedure. Third, the immunoadsorbents are re-usable, since we showed that they can be used at least 4 times. Fourth, the titration of the immunoadsorbents showed a satisfactory efficiency in terms of the amount of recombinant ECD needed for complete clearance of serum.

The described results suggest that a mixture of either yeast- or *E. coli*-expressed human AChR ECDs immobilized on an insoluble material, such as CNBr-activated Sepharose, may be used in clinical trials for antigen-specific MG therapy as efficient immunoadsorbents of anti-AChR autoantibodies from many MG patients. Columns bearing *E. coli*-expressed ECDs (which can be produced much more economically) may be sufficient for some MG patients, whereas a combination of two columns in series (*E. coli*-expressed ECDs, followed by yeast-expressed ECDs) may be needed for others. We envisage two possible procedures, depending on the urgency of each case: a. the use of both complete columns (*E. coli* and yeast) each containing all five subunit ECDs, especially in the emergency case of a new patient, and b. an individualized approach, in which screening with the different columns must be performed prior to making a decision on which column is suitable for the specific patient. This screening would only take a couple of days, which would normally not pose a problem for the patient.

Importantly, anti-AChR autoantibody depletion was found to be sufficient for the elimination of the pathogenic factor(s) from two tested MG sera and the procedure seemed to be safe in two experimental rabbits. Finally, scaling up of the procedure is underway as a necessary step prior to proceeding to clinical trials. However, to date, our immobilized ECDs have proved to be efficient immunoadsorbents for some MG plasmas, but not for several others. Additional improvements in immunoadsorption efficiency might be achieved by the coexpression of all AChR ECDs, which might result in their assembly into a pentameric AChR ECD. Such a pentamer might also contain inter-subunit epitopes, thus binding more, or even all, anti-AChR antibodies. We are currently working towards this aim.

REFERENCES

1.   Lindstrom J., The structures of neuronal nicotinic receptors. Neuronal Nicotinic Receptors Handbook, ed. Clementi F., C. Gotti,D. Fornasari. Vol. 144. 2000, New York, Springer: Experimental Pharmacology, vol.144. *New York, Springer*. 101-162.

2.   Berg D., R. Shoop, K. Chang, e. al., Nicotinic acetylcholine receptors in ganglionic transmission. Neuronal Nicotinic Receptors Handbook. 2000: Experimental Pharmacology, vol. 144. *New York, Springer*. 247-270.

3.   Zoli M., Distributionof cholinergic neurons in the mammalian brain with special reference to their relationship with neuronal nicotinic receptors. 2000: Experimental Pharmacology, vol 144. *New York, Springer*. 13-30.

4.   Kaiser S., L. Soliokov, S. Wonnacott, Presynaptic neuronal nicotinic receptors: pharmacology, heterogeneity and cellular mechanisms. 2000: Experimental Pharmacology, vol. 144. *New York, Springer*. 193-212.

5.   Agius M. A., D. P. Richman, A. Vincent, Specific Antibodies in the Diagnosis and Management of Autoimmune Disorders of Neuromuscular Transmission and Related Diseases. 2003: *Current Clinical Neurology*: Myasthenia Gravis and Related Disorders, edited by H. J. Kaminsky. 177-196.

6.   Lindstrom J. M., M. E. Seybold, V. A. Lennon, S. Whittingham, D. D. Duane. 1976. Antibody to acetylcholine receptor in myasthenia gravis. Prevalence, clinical correlates, and diagnostic value. *Neurology*. 26:1054-9.

7.   Toyka K. V., D. B. Drachman, D. E. Griffin, A. Pestronk, J. A. Winkelstein, K. H. Fishbeck, I. Kao. 1977. Myasthenia gravis. Study of humoral immune mechanisms by passive transfer to mice. *N Engl J Med*. 296:125-31.

8.   Engel A. G., E. H. Lambert, F. M. Howard. 1977. Immune complexes (IgG and C3) at the motor end-plate in myasthenia gravis: ultrastructural and light microscopic localization and electrophysiologic correlations. *Mayo Clin Proc*. 52:267-80.

9.   Pinching A. J., D. K. Peters, J. Newsom-Davis. 1976. Remission of myasthenia gravis following plasma-exchange. *Lancet*. 2:1373-6.

10. Dau P. C., J. M. Lindstrom, C. K. Cassel, E. H. Denys, E. E. Shev, L. E. Spitler. 1977. Plasmapheresis and immunosuppressive drug therapy in myasthenia gravis. *N Engl J Med*. 297:1134-40.

11. Patrick J., J. Lindstrom. 1973. Autoimmune response to acetylcholine receptor. *Science*. 180:871-2.

12. Tzartos S., S. Hochschwender, P. Vasquez, J. Lindstrom. 1987. Passive transfer of experimental autoimmune myasthenia gravis by monoclonal antibodies to the main immunogenic region of the acetylcholine receptor. *J Neuroimmunol*. 15:185-94.

13. Tzartos S. J., K. Bitzopoulou, I. Gavra, G. Kordas, L. Jacobson, K. Kostelidou, G. Lagoumintzis, O. Lazos, K. Poulas, S. Sideris, A. Sotiriadis, N. Trakas, P. Zisimopoulou. 2008. Antigen-specific Apheresis of Pathogenic Autoantibodies from Myasthenia Gravis Sera. *Ann N Y Acad Sci*. 1132:291-9.

14. Kaminski H. J., Treatment of Myasthenia Gravis. 2003: *Current Clinical Neurology*: Myasthenia Gravis and Related Disorders. 197-221.

15. Fostieri E., K. Kostelidou, K. Poulas, S. J. Tzartos. 2006. Recent advances in the understanding and therapy of myasthenia gravis. *Future Neurol.* 1:799–801.

16. Chiu H. C., W. H. Chen, J. H. Yeh. 2000. The six year experience of plasmapheresis in patients with myasthenia gravis. *Ther Apher.* 4:291-5.

17. Gajdos P., H. D. Outin, E. Morel, J. C. Raphael, M. Goulon. 1987. High-dose intravenous gamma globulin for myasthenia gravis: an alternative to plasma exchange. *Ann NY Acad Sci.* 505:842-844.

18. Ferrero B., L. Durelli, R. Cavallo, A. Dutto, G. Aimo, F. Pecchio, B. Bergamasco. 1993. Therapies for exacerbation of myasthenia gravis. The mechanism of action of intravenous high-dose immunoglobulin G. *Ann N Y Acad Sci.* 681:563-6.

19. Brannagan T. H., 3rd, K. J. Nagle, D. J. Lange, L. P. Rowland. 1996. Complications of intravenous immune globulin treatment in neurologic disease. *Neurology.* 47:674-7.

20. Kazatchkine M. D., S. V. Kaveri. 2001. Immunomodulation of autoimmune and inflammatory diseases with intravenous immune globulin. *N Engl J Med.* 345:747-55.

21. Dalakas M. C., Immunotherapies in the treatment of neuromuscular disorders. 2002: Neuromuscular Disorders in Clinical Practice. *Boston, Butterworth Heinemann.* 364-383.

22. Samuelsson A., T. L. Towers, J. V. Ravetch. 2001. Anti-inflammatory activity of IVIG mediated through the inhibitory Fc receptor. *Science.* 291:484-6.

23. Aricha R., T. Feferman, M. C. Souroujon, S. Fuchs. 2006. Overexpression of phosphodiesterases in experimental autoimmune myasthenia gravis: suppression of disease by a phosphodiesterase inhibitor. *Faseb J.* 20:374-6.

24. Baggi F., F. Andreetta, E. Caspani, M. Milani, R. Longhi, R. Mantegazza, F. Cornelio, C. Antozzi. 1999. Oral administration of an immunodominant T-cell epitope downregulates Th1/Th2 cytokines and prevents experimental myasthenia gravis. *J Clin Invest.* 104:1287-95.

25. Im S. H., D. Barchan, T. Feferman, L. Raveh, M. C. Souroujon, S. Fuchs. 2002. Protective molecular mimicry in experimental myasthenia gravis. *J Neuroimmunol.* 126:99-106.

26. Yi H. J., C. S. Chae, J. S. So, S. J. Tzartos, M. C. Souroujon, S. Fuchs, S. H. Im. 2008. Suppression of experimental myasthenia gravis by a B-cell epitope-free recombinant acetylcholine receptor. *Mol Immunol.* 46:192-201.

27. Matsumoto Y., H. Matsuo, H. Sakuma, I. K. Park, Y. Tsukada, K. Kohyama, T. Kondo, S. Kotorii, N. Shibuya. 2006. CDR3 spectratyping analysis of the TCR repertoire in myasthenia gravis. *J Immunol.* 176:5100-7.

28. Berrih-Aknin S., S. Fuchs, M. C. Souroujon. 2005. Vaccines against myasthenia gravis. *Expert Opin Biol Ther.* 5:983-95.

29. Drachman D. B., J. M. Wu, A. Miagkov, M. A. Williams, R. N. Adams, B. Wu. 2003. Specific immunotherapy of experimental myasthenia by genetically engineered APCs: the "guided missile" strategy. *Ann N Y Acad Sci.* 998:520-32.

30. Boneva N., Y. Hamra-Amitay, I. Wirguin, T. Brenner. 2006. Stimulated-single fiber electromyography monitoring of anti-sense induced changes in experimental autoimmune myasthenia gravis. *Neurosci Res.* 55:40-4.

31. Tzartos S. J., D. Sophianos, A. Efthimiadis. 1985. Role of the main immunogenic region of acetylcholine receptor in myasthenia gravis. An Fab monoclonal antibody protects against antigenic modulation by human sera. *J Immunol.* 134:2343-9.

32. Graus Y. F., M. H. de Baets, D. R. Burton. 1998. Antiacetylcholine receptor Fab fragments isolated from thymus-derived phage display libraries from myasthenia gravis patients reflect predominant specificities in serum and block the action of pathogenic serum antibodies. *Ann N Y Acad Sci.* 841:414-7.

33. Papanastasiou D., K. Poulas, A. Kokla, S. J. Tzartos. 2000. Prevention of passively transferred experimental autoimmune myasthenia gravis by Fab fragments of monoclonal antibodies directed against the main immunogenic region of the acetylcholine receptor. *J Neuroimmunol.* 104:124-32.

34. Fostieri E., S. J. Tzartos, S. Berrih-Aknin, D. Beeson, A. Mamalaki. 2005. Isolation of potent human Fab fragments against a novel highly immunogenic region on human muscle acetylcholine receptor which protect the receptor from myasthenic autoantibodies. *Eur J Immunol.* 35:632-43.

35. Protopapadakis E., A. Kokla, S. J. Tzartos, A. Mamalaki. 2005. Isolation and characterization of human anti-acetylcholine receptor monoclonal antibodies from transgenic mice expressing human immunoglobulin loci. *Eur J Immunol.* 35:1960-8.

36. Psaridi-Linardaki L., N. Trakas, A. Mamalaki, S. J. Tzartos. 2005. Specific immunoadsorption of the autoantibodies from myasthenic patients using the extracellular domain of the human muscle acetylcholine receptor alpha-subunit. Development of an antigen-specific therapeutic strategy. *J Neuroimmunol.* 159:183-91.

37. Kostelidou K., N. Trakas, S. J. Tzartos. 2007. Extracellular domains of the beta, gamma and epsilon subunits of the human acetylcholine receptor as immunoadsorbents for myasthenic autoantibodies: a combination of immunoadsorbents results in increased efficiency. *J Neuroimmunol.* 190:44-52.

38. Zisimopoulou P., G. Lagoumintzis, K. Poulas, S. J. Tzartos. 2008. Antigen-specific apheresis of human anti-acetylcholine receptor autoantibodies from myasthenia gravis patients' sera using Escherichia coli-expressed receptor domains. *J Neuroimmunol.* 200:133-41.

39. Yamazaki Z., Y. Fujimori, T. Takahama, N. Inoue, T. Wada, M. Kazama, M. Morioka, T. Abe, N. Yamawaki, K. Inagaki. 1982. Efficiency and biocompatibility of a new immunosorbent. *Trans Am Soc Artif Intern Organs.* 28:318-23.

40. Matic G., R. E. Winkler, M. Tiess, W. Ramlow. 2001. Selective apheresis—time for a change. *Int J Artif Organs.* 24:4-7.

41. Ptak J. 2004. Changes of plasma proteins after immunoadsorption using Ig-Adsopak columns in patients with myasthenia gravis. *Transfus Apher Sci.* 30:125-9.

42. Takamori M., T. Maruta. 2001. Immunoadsorption in myasthenia gravis based on specific ligands mimicking the immunogenic sites of the acetylcholine receptor. *Ther Apher.* 5:340-50.

43. Guo C. Y., Z. Y. Li, M. Q. Xu, J. M. Yuan. 2005. Preparation of an immunoadsorbent coupled with a recombinant antigen to remove anti-acetylcholine receptor antibodies in abnormal serum. *J Immunol Methods.* 303:142-7.

44. Lindstrom J., M. Campbell, B. Nave. 1978. Specificities of antibodies to acetylcholine receptors. *Muscle Nerve.* 1:140-5.

45. Loutrari H., S. J. Tzartos, T. Claudio. 1992. Use of Torpedo-mouse hybrid acetylcholine receptors reveals immunodominance of the alpha subunit in myasthenia gravis antisera. *Eur J Immunol.* 22:2949-56.

46. Karlin A. 2002. Emerging structure of the nicotinic acetylcholine receptors. *Nat Rev Neurosci.* 3:102-14.

47. Psaridi-Linardaki L., A. Mamalaki, M. Remoundos, S. J. Tzartos. 2002. Expression of soluble ligand- and antibody-binding extracellular domain of human muscle acetylcholine receptor alpha subunit in yeast Pichia pastoris. Role of glycosylation in alpha-bungarotoxin binding. *J Biol Chem.* 277:26980-6.

48. Kostelidou K., N. Trakas, M. Zouridakis, K. Bitzopoulou, A. Sotiriadis, I. Gavra, S. J. Tzartos. 2006. Expression and characterization of soluble forms of the extracellular domains of the beta, gamma and epsilon subunits of the human muscle acetylcholine receptor. *Febs J.* 273:3557-68.

49. Bitzopoulou K., K. Kostelidou, K. Poulas, S. J. Tzartos. 2008. Mutant forms of the extracellular domain of the human acetylcholine receptor gamma-subunit with improved solubility and enhanced antigenicity The importance of the Cys-loop. *Biochim Biophys Acta.* 1784:1226-33.

50. Tzartos S. J., K. Bitzopoulou, I. Gavra, G. Kordas, L. Jacobson, K. Kostelidou, G. Lagoumintzis, O. Lazos, K. Poulas, S. Sideris, A. Sotiriadis, N. Trakas, P. Zisimopoulou. 2008. Antigen-specific apheresis of pathogenic autoantibodies from myasthenia gravis sera. Myasthenia Gravis and Related Disorders: *Ann N Y Acad Sci XIth International Conference,* Volume 1131, est. pub date May 2008.

51. Sideris S., G. Lagoumintzis, G. Kordas, K. Kostelidou, A. Sotiriadis, K. Poulas, S. J. Tzartos. 2007. Isolation and functional characterization of anti-acetylcholine receptor subunit-specific autoantibodies from myasthenic patients: receptor loss in cell culture. *J Neuroimmunol.* 189:111-7.

52. Zisimopoulou P., G. Lagoumintzis, K. Kostelidou, K. Bitzopoulou, G. Kordas, N. Trakas, K. Poulas, S. J. Tzartos. 2008. Towards antigen-specific apheresis of pathogenic autoantibodies as a further step in the treatment of myasthenia gravis by plasmapheresis. *J Neuroimmunol.* 201-202:95-103.

IVIg Treatment in Experimental Autoimmune Myasthenia Gravis

Sara Fuchs PhD, Tali Feferman PhD, Talma Brenner PhD, &

Miriam C. Souroujon PhD

1. INTRODUCTION

Intravenous immunoglobulin (IVIg) administration has been beneficially used in recent years in a variety of autoimmune diseases (1-3), although its mode of action is still not clear. Multiple mechanisms of action, not necessarily mutually exclusive, have been proposed for explaining the therapeutic effect of IVIg (4, 5). Some of the mechanisms depend on the interaction between the Fc fraction of IVIg and Fc receptors on target cells and others rely on the variable regions of IgG antibodies in the IVIg preparations. The various mechanisms proposed include modulation of expression and function of Fc receptors, interference with activation of complement and/or the cytokine network, regulation of cell growth, alteration of cellular adhesion processes, effects on the activation, differentiation and effector functions of T and B cells and of antigen-presenting cells as well as modulation of idiotype networks (4). More recently it has been demonstrated that sialylation of Fc in IVIg is mediating its anti-inflammatory effect (6, 7).

MG and its experimental model disease EAMG (experimental autoimmune myasthenia gravis) are T cell-dependent, antibody-mediated autoimmune diseases in which the acetylcholine receptor (AChR) is the main autoantigen. IVIg has been employed to treat MG for about two decades (8-11). The Chapter by Marinos Dalakas in this book (Chapter 6) gives a detailed description on IVIg treatment in human MG and the various mechanisms involved. In the preset chapter we will concentrate only on our studies on IVIg treatment in EAMG - the experimental model disease for MG.

As it is rather hard and costly to perform randomized controlled clinical trials in human autoimmune diseases, there is an advantage in studying experimental model diseases for delineating the mechanism(s) of action involved in IVIg therapy. Indeed, a great part of the available information on the mode of action of IVIg comes from studies in experimental models of autoimmune diseases such as murine experimental immune thrombocytopenia (12), experimental autoimmune encephalomyelitis (EAE) (13-16), experimental rat uveitis (17), experimental rat autoimmune myositis (18), myocarditis (19), experimental allergic neuritis (20) and experimental murine systemic lupus erythematosus (21). It should be noted that in most of these studies IVIg treatment has been initiated concomitantly with induction of the disease and therefore represents the preventive or protective potential of IVIg against the studied autoimmune disease, rather than its therapeutic effect, that is the one sought for in human autoimmune diseases.

In the following we will summarize our studies on the therapeutic effect of IVIg administration in EAMG in rats and describe the isolation and identification of a minor disease-specific fraction from IVIg preparations that is essential for the therapeutic immunosuppressive effect of IVIg preparation. IVIg has been demonstrated to be an effective reagent for preventing the induction of EAMG and immunosuppressing an ongoing disease both at its acute and chronic stages. The optimal conditions for immunosuppression of EAMG by IVIg have been established and immunological analyses suggested that IVIG modulates EAMG by suppression of Th1 and B cell proliferation but probably not by generation of regulatory T cells (22, 23). Furthermore, we have demonstrated that chromatography of pooled human IVIg on immobilized immunoglobulins, isolated from either EAMG rats or from MG patients, results in a complete depletion of the suppressive activity of the IVIg preparation that can be recovered upon reconstitution of the activity-depleted IVIg with the eluted minute IVIg fractions that had been adsorbed onto the disease-specific columns (24, 25).

2. SUPPRESSION OF EAMG BY IVIG TREATMENT

The well-characterized experimental model for MG, i.e. rat EAMG, has been employed to investigate the efficacy of IVIg in treating an existing experimental autoimmune disease and to explore the immunological mode of action of this treatment.

We have first tested the ability of IVIg pre-treatment to protect rats against EAMG induction. One course of a consecutive five-day IVIg treatment at a dose of 0.4g/kg body weight/day/rat, starting on the day of disease induction, or two such courses with a one-week interval between the first and second course were effective in protecting the rats against EAMG induction. The two-course protocol gave better protection and delayed the onset of clinical signs up to seven weeks following disease induction. This treatment was significantly effective not only in delaying the onset of disease but also in suppressing the clinical score up to at least 14 weeks following disease induction (22).

As our aim was to affect ongoing EAMG, we have treated rats with an already existing disease, starting the treatment at either the acute stage of disease, or at the chronic phase of the disease. In both cases a significant suppressive effect by IVIg treatment has been observed. For treatment at the acute phase of EAMG, treatment with IVIg has been initiated one week following disease induction by AChR immunization. This is the time when symptoms of acute EAMG are usually observed. Two 5-day courses of IVIg treatments were given. IVIg doses of 0.4g/kg/rat/day or of 0.8g/kg/rat/day were equally effective and a significant suppressive effect on EAMG was maintained for at least 14 weeks (22).

IVIg treatment at the chronic phase of EAMG is the most relevant to the treatment of human MG. For treatment experiments at the chronic phase of EAMG, IVIg treatment was initiated four weeks following disease induction. This is the time when rats start developing symptoms of chronic EAMG. Two courses of 5-day IVIg treatments of 0.8g/kg/day with a one-week interval between them, resulted in a significant suppressive effect on EAMG but the effect diminished gradually after cessation of the treatment. Therefore, four courses of IVIg (in doses of 0.4 or 0.8g/kg/day) were applied, where the additional two courses (the third and fourth) started three weeks after the end of the first two courses and were spaced by a week between them. It seems that the additional two courses of treatment were able to arrest the progression of clinical symptoms and at the high dose treatment (0.8g/kg) had also a therapeutic effect, resulting in alleviation of symptoms as reflected in the mean clinical score (Fig. 1). By analyzing the kinetics of the clinical score of individual rats during the course of treatment it has been shown that repeating IVIg treatments may have a continuous suppressive effect on EAMG and can reduce disease symptoms (22).

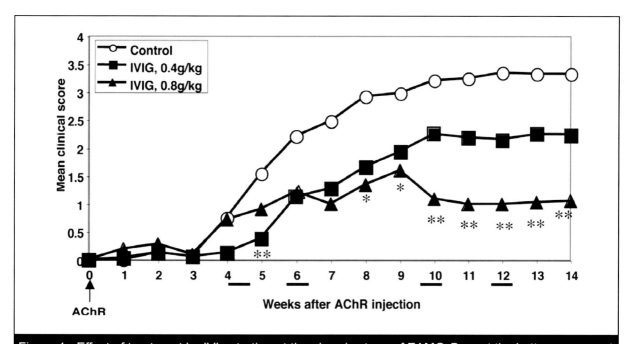

Figure 1. Effect of treatment by IVIg starting at the chronic stage of EAMG. Bars at the bottom represent each a five-day IVIg treatment. *P<0.05, ** P<0.01, compared to the control, untreated group. (From 22).

IVIg treatment has a suppressive effect on both humoral and cellular AChR-specific immune responses. The total anti-AChR IgG levels as well as specific anti-AChR IgG isotypes were markedly decreased following IVIg treatment. There was a decrease in all IgG isotypes following IVIg treatment. Interestingly, the most significant decrease in the total anti-AChR titer and in all IgG isotype levels was observed 12 weeks after disease induction, when the therapeutic effect of IVIg monitored by the clinical score, was also most prominent (Fig. 1 and (22).

Reduced antibody responses to the autoantigen have been reported in other experimental autoimmune diseases in which effective IVIg treatment has been demonstrated, such as experimental autoimmune myositis and experimental autoimmune myocarditis (18, 19) and an experimental murine model of systemic lupus erythematosus (21). There has also been a report showing that pre-treatment by IVIgM reduced serum anti-AChR antibodies in myasthenic SCID mice reconstituted with thymic cells from a myasthenia gravis patient (26).

Several possible mechanisms have been suggested for the IVIg-induced reduction in autoantibody levels. These include accelerated clearance, neutralization by anti-idiotypes and down-regulation of synthesis (27). In our studies we have observed in addition to reduced antibody levels also reduced mRNA levels of APRIL, a B cell-activating factor of the TNF family and its receptor BAFF-R (28), suggesting that down regulation of antibody synthesis may be involved.

To further investigate the possible mechanisms involved in the immune suppression of EAMG by IVIg, the expression levels of molecules that are involved in regulation of immune responses has been determined (22). These included cytokines, co-stimulatory factors, B lymphocyte stimulators and molecules expressed on regulatory T cells (Treg). IVIg treatment resulted in down-regulation of the Th1-type cytokine TNF-α, whereas the expression levels of IFN-γ and IL-2 did not change. The expression levels of the Th-2-type cytokines IL-4 and IL-10 were up-regulated.

Antigen-specific B cell responses demand a second co-stimulatory signal which is provided by cognate interactions and soluble cytokine signaling (29). We demonstrated that CD40L mRNA levels were reduced in IVIg-treated rats although CD40 levels remained unchanged (22). The role of CD40-CD40L signaling in EAMG has been demonstrated in CD40L$^{-/-}$ mice (30), which were completely resistant to EAMG. Moreover, anti-CD40L antibodies were shown by us to suppress chronic EAMG and to decrease anti-self autoantibody levels in rats (31).

It should be noted that IVIg treatment did not lead to the generation of regulatory T cells as we did not observe significant changes in the mRNA expression levels of CD25, TGF-β and Foxp3 (22), all of which are known to be associated with the development and/or function of regulatory T cells (32, 33). Thus, it seems that Treg cells are probably not involved in the *suppressive* effect of IVIG on EAMG. In this connection it should be mentioned however that it has been recently reported that the *protection* of IVIg against the induction of EAE in mice is Treg-mediated (34).

Thus, we have shown that IVIG can prevent, treat and alleviate clinical signs of EAMG effectively. Its mechanisms of action seem to involve down-regulation of rat anti-AChR autoantibody synthesis which is mediated by a shift from Th1 to Th2 regulation and by down-regulation of CD40L, BAFF-R and APRIL, all of which are involved in B cell differentiation, survival and function. CD4$^+$CD25$^+$ regulatory T cells are probably not induced by IVIg treatment of EAMG. Taken together, our data provide insight into the immunological mechanisms underlying IVIg treatment in MG in particular and in other autoimmune disorders in general.

3. ISOLATION AND IDENTIFICATION OF A DISEASE-SPECIFIC FRACTION FROM IVIG

The drawbacks of IVIg treatment include its high cost and the fact that patients are given huge amounts of protein of which only a minor fraction may be responsible for the therapeutic effect. We wondered whether there is a disease specific fraction(s) in pooled human IVIg that contributes to and responsible for its immunomodulatory therapeutic activity. In an attempt to isolate such fraction(s) and elucidate the mechanisms by which IVIg exerts its therapeutic effect we have developed a procedure for chromatographic fractionation of pooled human IVIg on immobilized immunoglobulin preparations isolated from rats with EAMG or from MG patients (24, 25). The fractionation procedure of IVIg is illustrated schematically in Fig. 2. Control columns are composed of immobilized immunoglobulin isolated from control complete Freund's adjuvant-immunized rats or from healthy patients, respectively. The various isolated fractions have been tested for their immunosuppressive effects. We have demonstrated that a minute disease-specific fraction isolated from IVIg is essential for its therapeutic activity on EAMG.

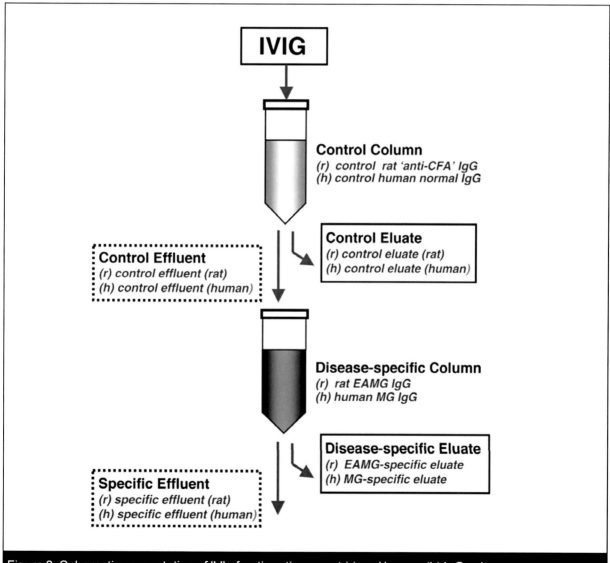

Figure 2. Schematic presentation of IVIg fractionation on rat (r) and human (h) IgG columns.

For specific fractionation, IVIg was first passed through the respective control column (rat or human) in order to remove non-specific anti-antibodies and then on the disease-specific column (rat EAMG-specific or human MG-specific, respectively). For control, IVIg was passed on the respective rat or human control column alone (see Fig. 2). The IgG adsorbed to the columns was eluted from the columns with 0.1 M Gly HCl buffer at pH 2.7 and neutralized with Tris-HCl pH 9. Only minute amounts of IVIG were depleted from the IVIG preparations following these chromatographies and were identified as immunoglobulins by gel electrophoresis and verified as IgG by its reactivity in Western blot analysis with antibodies to human IgG (23). The amount of protein (IgG) eluted from the specific EAMG and MG columns corresponded to about 100000-fold enrichment of the disease-specific fractions. It should be noted that it is quite likely that the first control columns did not deplete all the non-specific anti-immunoglobulins that are not associated with disease and therefore the specific eluates probably represents just enriched fractions and in fact the amount of the disease-specific material in these eluates may be smaller.

The therapeutic effect of the various fractions is tested in rats in which EAMG had been induced by immunization with AChR. Groups of eight AChR-immunized rats were treated with either IVIg or with a fraction derived from it. The various treatments that we have tested in several treatment experiments were as follows: 1, Unfractionated IVIg (0.4 g/ Kg/day/rat); 2, Treatment with 'control effluent' (0.4g/Kg/day/rat); 3, Treatment with the 'specific effluent' (0.4g/Kg/day/rat) i.e. the fraction obtained following chromatography first through the control and then through the disease-specific- column; 4, Treatment with a mixture of the effluent from the disease-specific column ('specific effluent', rat or human, 0.4g/Kg/day/rat), reconstituted with the eluate from the respective disease-specific column (40mg/Kg/day/rat). 5, Control treatment with the vehicle alone (20 mM sodium citrate / 120 mM NaCl, 5% maltose). Two five-day courses were usually given with a one-week interval, starting 8 days following EAMG induction. In cases in which the experiment extended over 8 weeks, a third five-day-course was sometimes given, spaced by 4 weeks from the second course (24).

In a typical experiment treatments were initiated one week following disease induction, when signs of acute EAMG are usually observed. Rats were followed for disease development and their clinical score and body weight were recorded twice a week. The results of typical experiments depicting the various treatments and using material fractionated on either the rat or human IgG columns, respectively, are depicted in Figure 3. A clear difference between the suppressive effects of the control effluent fractions and the effluents from the EAMG- or MG-specific columns is demonstrated. The 'specific effluents' obtained following chromatograpy of IVIg, first through the control column and then through the disease-specific columns, lost their therapeutic effect. EAMG in these groups had a similar pattern in terms of severity (Fig. 3) and body weight (23) to those of 'no treatment' control rats, treated by the vehicle alone. In contrast, the control effluents, obtained following chromatography through only the control columns retained the suppressive effect on EAMG.

To find out whether the suppressive activity in the IVIg preparation was retained by the EAMG- and MG-specific columns, the eluates from these columns ('EAMG specific eluate' or 'MG-specific eluate') were reconstituted each as specified above with the effluent from the respective column ('specific effluent') that had been devoid of the suppressive activity of IVIg and the resulting reconstituted mixture was applied for treatment. The therapeutic effect that had been lost in the 'specific effluents' treatment was indeed recovered following

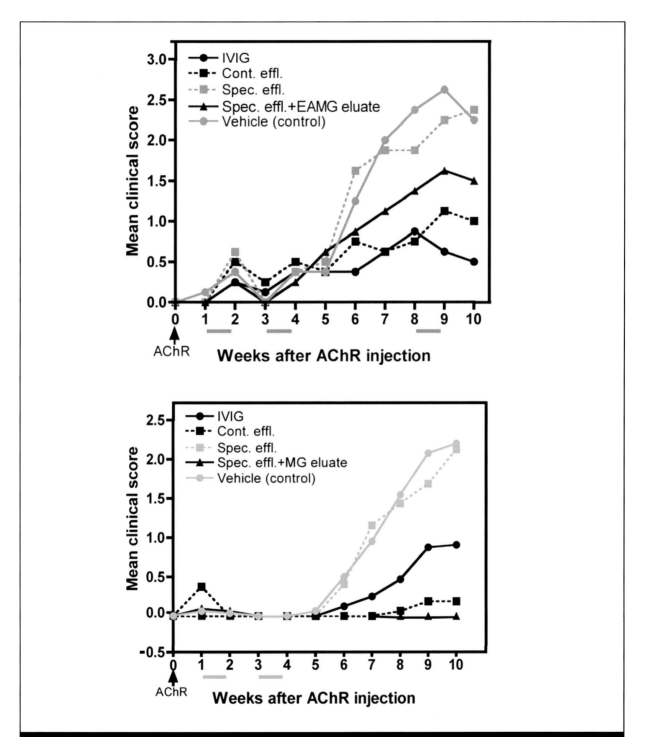

Figure 3. Fractionation and reconstitution of the suppressive activity of IVIg on EAMG following fractionation on rat (top) or human (bottom) IgG columns. (Adapted from 24, 25).

the treatment by the reconstituted samples ('specific Effluent (rat)' + 'EAMG-specific eluate' or 'specific Effluent (human)' + 'MG-specific eluate') as reflected also in the rise in the mean body weight (Fig. 3 and (24, 25). Recovery varied from 60% to 100% of the therapeutic effect of that of the unfractionated IVIg in the various experiments. Interestingly, in some experiments a marked suppressive effect, greater than that of unfractionated IVIg, was observed following treatment with a mixture of the 'specific effluent' fraction (0.4g/Kg/day/rat) reconstituted with the 'disease-specific eluate' fraction (40mg/Kg/day/rat) (see Fig.3). The marked suppression in such an experiment could be due to the use of the eluate at a large excess compared to the IVIg it was derived from, to compensate for losses during the fractionation procedures. It should be noted that reconstitution of the 'specific effluents' (rat or human, Fig. 2) with the respective 'control eluates' fractions, did not recover any of the therapeutic activity (unpublished data).

It should be noted that in this study we have employed <u>human</u> IVIg and fractions derived from it for investigating the therapeutic effect on <u>rat</u> EAMG. This is similar to previously reported studies on the application of allogeneic pooled human immunoglobulin (IVIg) for treatment of experimental autoimmune diseases in *mice* and *rats*. (12-22). The reason for using <u>human</u> immunoglobulins in allogeneic systems stems from technical difficulties of obtaining <u>rat</u> (autologous) immunoglobulins in the amounts needed for the treatment experiments. The effectiveness of experiments performed in murines (rats or mice) with human IVIg implies that there is an interspecies cross-reactivity in the active components of IVIG. Indeed, cross-species idiotypes in the anti-AChR response have been previously reported by us (35, 36). We assume that pooled *human* immunoglobulins, obtained from thousands of healthy donors contain a vast repertoire of anti-antibodies (anti-idiotypes) some of which may have interspecies cross-reactivity.

The most striking observation in this study is the ability to specifically eliminate the therapeutic activity on EAMG from the IVIg preparation by its chromatography through an EAMG- or an MG-specific column. Such a chromatography resulted in an adsorption of a very small amount of IgG from the IVIg preparation and eliminated its immunosuppressive activity on EAMG, whereas chromatography of the IVIG through the non-specific control columns did not reduce its therapeutic capability. These observations indicate that the fraction removed from IVIg by the EAMG- or MG-specific column is *essential* for the therapeutic activity of the IVIg on EAMG. This is a strong indication that only the disease-specific columns were able to adsorb and remove the disease-specific immunosuppressive fraction from the IVIG preparation. Whether it may also be *sufficient* is still not clear.

We cannot exclude the possibility that additional components in the non-active IVIg effluent fractions are required for reconstituting the full suppressive activity. Such components could include factors modulating the expression and function of Fc receptor and of complement activation, immunoglobulin molecules interacting with the specific anti-antibodies to form dimers and other factors that have been proposed to account for some of the clinical effects of IVIG (2, 4, 6). Although needed for the immunosuppressive activity of IVIg, such components that are not necessarily disease-specific may require the presence of the disease-specific anti-antibodies (anti-idiotypes) that are *essential* for the observed clinical effect on EAMG.

We assume that the specificity of the isolated anti-antibody active fraction is determined by the disease-specific immunoglobulin employed to fractionate the IVIg preparation. In our case it is only the anti-antibody fraction isolated on immunoglobulin columns from rats with EAMG or from MG patients and not on immunoglobulin columns from control animals, immunized with CFA or from normal patients, that had a therapeutic clinical effect on EAMG. Anti-antibodies with specificity for other autoimmune diseases can possibly be isolated by their selective binding to the respective disease-specific IgG. In another reported study DNA-specific antibodies from SLE patients were employed to isolate from IVIg, a fraction of anti-antibodies (anti-idiotypes) that suppressed experimental SLE (21). It is possible that the same IVIg preparation could serve for several serial fractionations of anti-antibodies *each* specific for a different disease and could thus make this therapeutic approach more specific and possibly less expensive. Moreover, a personalized fractionation of IVIg on the patient's own auto reactive immunoglobulin might in the future be considered as the treatment of choice.

REFERENCES

1. Lemieux, R., R. Bazin, and S. Neron. 2005. Therapeutic intravenous immunoglobulins. *Mol Immunol 42:839.*

2. Dalakas, M. C. 2004. The use of intravenous immunoglobulin in the treatment of autoimmune neuromuscular diseases: evidence-based indications and safety profile. *Pharmacol Ther 102:177.*

3. Kazatchkine, M. D., and S. V. Kaveri. 2001. Immunomodulation of autoimmune and inflammatory diseases with intravenous immune globulin. *N Engl J Med 345:747.*

4. Bayry, J., S. Lacroix-Desmazes, M. D. Kazatchkine, and S. V. Kaveri. 2007. Monoclonal antibody and intravenous immunoglobulin therapy for rheumatic diseases: rationale and mechanisms of action. *Nat Clin Pract Rheumatol 3:262.*

5. Gold, R., M. Stangel, and M. C. Dalakas. 2007. Drug Insight: the use of intravenous immunoglobulin in neurology—therapeutic considerations and practical issues. *Nat Clin Pract Neurol 3:36.*

6. Kaneko, Y., F. Nimmerjahn, and J. V. Ravetch. 2006. Anti-inflammatory activity of immunoglobulin G resulting from Fc sialylation. *Science 313:670.*

7. Anthony, R. M., F. Wermeling, M. C. Karlsson, and J. V. Ravetch. 2008. Identification of a receptor required for the anti-inflammatory activity of IVIG. *Proc Natl Acad Sci U S A 105:19571.*

8. Gajdos, P., H. Outin, D. Elkharrat, D. Brunel, P. de Rohan-Chabot, J. C. Raphael, M. Goulon, C. Goulon-Goeau, and E. Morel. 1984. High-dose intravenous gammaglobulin for myasthenia gravis. *Lancet 1:406.*

9. Edan, G., and F. Landgraf. 1994. Experience with intravenous immunoglobulin in myasthenia gravis: a review. *J Neurol Neurosurg Psychiatry 57 Suppl:55.*

10. Gajdos, P., S. Chevret, B. Clair, C. Tranchant, and C. Chastang. 1997. Clinical trial of plasma exchange and high-dose intravenous immunoglobulin in myasthenia gravis. Myasthenia Gravis Clinical Study Group. *Ann Neurol 41:789.*

11. Fateh-Moghadam, A., M. Wick, U. Besinger, and R. G. Geursen. 1984. High-dose intravenous gammaglobulin for myasthenia gravis. *Lancet 1:848.*

12. Samuelsson, A., T. L. Towers, and J. V. Ravetch. 2001. Anti-inflammatory activity of IVIG mediated through the inhibitory Fc receptor. *Science 291:484.*

13. Pashov, A., C. Dubey, S. V. Kaveri, B. Lectard, Y. M. Huang, M. D. Kazatchkine, and B. Bellon. 1998. Normal immunoglobulin G protects against experimental allergic encephalomyelitis by inducing transferable T cell unresponsiveness to myelin basic protein. *Eur J Immunol 28:1823.*

14. Achiron, A., F. Mor, R. Margalit, I. R. Cohen, O. Lider, and S. Miron. 2000. Suppression of experimental autoimmune encephalomyelitis by intravenously administered polyclonal immunoglobulins. *J Autoimmun 15:323.*

15. Jorgensen, S. H., and P. S. Sorensen. 2005. Intravenous Immunonoglobulin treatment of multiple sclerosis and its animal model, experimental autoimmune encephalomyelitis. *Journal of the Neuroligical Sciences 233:61.*

16. Weishaupt, A., T. Kuhlmann, L. M. Schonrock, K. V. Toyka, W. Bruck, and R. Gold. 2002. Effects of intravenous immunoglobulins on T cell and oligodendrocyte apoptosis in high-dose antigen therapy in experimental autoimmune encephalomyelitis. *Acta Neuropathol (Berl) 104:385.*

17. Saoudi, A., V. Hurez, Y. de Kozak, J. Kuhn, S. V. Kaveri, M. D. Kazatchkine, P. Druet, and B. Bellon. 1993. Human immunoglobulin preparations for intravenous use prevent experimental autoimmune uveoretinitis. *Int Immunol 5:1559.*

18. Wada, J., N. Shintani, K. Kikutani, T. Nakae, T. Yamauchi, and K. Takechi. 2001. Intravenous immunoglobulin prevents experimental autoimmune myositis in SJL mice by reducing anti-myosin antibody and by blocking complement deposition. *Clin Exp Immunol 124:282.*

19. George, J., I. Barshack, E. Malka, I. Goldberg, P. Keren, S. Laniado, and G. Keren. 2001. The effect of intravenous immunoglobulins on the progression of experimental autoimmune myocarditis in the rat. *Exp Mol Pathol 71:55.*

20. Jia, J., and M. Pollock. 2000. Treatment of rats with experimental allergic neuritis using high dose immunoglobulin. *Chin Med J (Engl) 113:1096.*

21. Shoenfeld, Y., L. Rauova, B. Gilburd, F. Kvapil, I. Goldberg, J. Kopolovic, J. Rovensky, and M. Blank. 2002. Efficacy of IVIG affinity-purified anti-double-stranded DNA anti-idiotypic antibodies in the treatment of an experimental murine model of systemic lupus erythematosus. *Int Immunol 14:1303.*

22. Zhu, K. Y., T. Feferman, P. K. Maiti, M. C. Souroujon, and S. Fuchs. 2006. Intravenous immunoglobulin suppresses experimental myasthenia gravis: Immunological mechanisms. *J Neuroimmunol 176:187.*

23. Fuchs, S., T. Feferman, K. Y. Zhu, R. Meidler, R. Margalit, N.Wang, O. Laub, and M.C. Souroujon. 2007. Suppression of experimental autoimmune myasthenia gravis by intravenous immunoglobulin and isolation of a disease-specific IgG fraction. *Ann N Y Acad Sci 1110:550.*

24. Fuchs, S., T. Feferman, R. Meidler, R. Margalit, C. Sicsic, N. Wang, K. Y. Zhu, T. Brenner, O. Laub, and M. C. Souroujon. 2008. A disease-specific fraction isolated from IVIG is essential for the immunosuppressive effect of IVIG in experimental autoimmune myasthenia gravis. *J Neuroimmunol 194:89.*

25. Fuchs, S., T. Feferman, R. Meidler, R. Margalit, C. Sicsic, T. Brenner, O. Laub, and M. C. Souroujon. 2008. Immunosuppression of EAMG by IVIG is mediated by a disease-specific anti-immunoglobulin fraction. *Ann N Y Acad Sci 1132:244.*

26. Vassilev, T., M. Yamamoto, A. Aissaoui, E. Bonnin, S. Berrih-Aknin, M. D. Kazatchkine, and S. V. Kaveri. 1999. Normal human immunoglobulin suppresses experimental myasthenia gravis in SCID mice. *Eur J Immunol 29:2436.*

27. Bleeker, W. K., J. L. Teeling, and C. E. Hack. 2001. Accelerated autoantibody clearance by intravenous immunoglobulin therapy: studies in experimental models to determine the magnitude and time course of the effect. *Blood 98:3136.*

28. Thompson, J. S., S. A. Bixler, F. Qian, K. Vora, M. L. Scott, T. G. Cachero, C. Hession, P. Schneider, I. D. Sizing, C. Mullen, K. Strauch, M. Zafari, C. D. Benjamin, J. Tschopp, J. L. Browning, and C. Ambrose. 2001. BAFF-R, a newly identified TNF receptor that specifically interacts with BAFF. *Science 293:2108.*

29. Parker, D. C. 1993. T cell-dependent B cell activation. *Annu Rev Immunol 11:331.*

30. Shi, F. D., B. He, H. Li, D. Matusevicius, H. Link, and H. G. Ljunggren. 1998. Differential requirements for CD28 and CD40 ligand in the induction of experimental autoimmune myasthenia gravis. *Eur J Immunol 28:3587.*

31. Im, S. H., D. Barchan, P. K. Maiti, S. Fuchs, and M. C. Souroujon. 2001. Blockade of CD40 ligand suppresses chronic experimental myasthenia gravis by down-regulation of Th1 differentiation and up-regulation of CTLA-4. *J Immunol 166:6893.*

32. Khattri, R., T. Cox, S. A. Yasayko, and F. Ramsdell. 2003. An essential role for Scurfin in CD4+CD25+ T regulatory cells. *Nat Immunol 4:337.*

33. Fontenot, J. D., M. A. Gavin, and A. Y. Rudensky. 2003. Foxp3 programs the development and function of CD4+CD25+ regulatory T cells. *Nat Immunol 4:330.*

34. Ephrem, A., S. Chamat, C. Miquel, S. Fisson, L. Mouthon, G. Caligiuri, S. Delignat, S. Elluru, J. Bayry, S. Lacroix-Desmazes, J. L. Cohen, B. L. Salomon, M. D. Kazatchkine, S. V. Kaveri, and N. Misra. 2008. Expansion of CD4+CD25+ regulatory T cells by intravenous immunoglobulin: a critical factor in controlling experimental autoimmune encephalomyelitis. *Blood 111:715.*

35. Souroujon, M. C., D. Barchan, and S. Fuchs. 1985. Analysis and modulation of the immune response of mice to acetylcholine receptor by anti-idiotypes. *Immunol Lett 9:331.*

36. Souroujon, M. C., and S. Fuchs. 1986. Idiotypes and anti-idiotypes in experimental autoimmune myasthenia gravis. *Ann N Y Acad Sci 475:81.*

Treatment With Anti-Sense Targeted to Acetylcholinesterase in Myasthenia Gravis and Experimental Autoimmune Myasthenia Gravis

Talma Brenner Ph.D

1. INTRODUCTION

Acetylcholine (ACh)-mediated neurotransmission is fundamental for nervous system function. Cholinergic synapses are found, among others, in brain areas associated with cognitive functions. It is responsible for transmission in the neuro-muscular junction (NMJ), where it mediates motor activation, and in the autonomic nervous system, in which it is responsible for the ganglionic transmission of the entire system and for the postganglionic transmission of the parasympathetic arm. As ACh is also found in the parasympathetic postganglionic synapses, parasympathetic over activity accounts for the majority of side effects which are reported in acetylcholinesterase inhibitors (AChEI) treated patients [1].

In addition, components of the cholinergic system are present in immune cells. Macrophages, T and B-cells posses a complete cholinergic system, termed "non-neuronal immune cholinergic system" [2]. These cells are able to synthesize ACh due to expression of the enzyme cholineacyltransferase (ChAT) and can respond to cholinergic signals through various muscarinic and nicotinic ACh receptors (mAChR and nAChR, respectively).

The ACh hydrolyzing enzyme, acetylcholinesterase (AChE), is the molecular target of approved drugs in myasthenia gravis (MG) [3] and in Alzheimer's disease (AD) [4]. AChEI can be divided into two main categories; conventional inhibitors that inhibit the catalytic activity of the enzyme such as pyridostigmine, edrophonium, donepezil, rivastigmine and tacrine, and inhibitors of the enzyme's synthesis such as the antisense EN-101 which targets exon-2 that is expressed in all the isoforms of the enzyme [5].

Anti-sense technology offers an attractive, gene-based alternative to conventional anti-AChE therapeutics. As anti-sense therapeutics target RNA rather than protein, they offer the possibility of designing highly specific drugs with effective concentration in the nanomolar range [6].

Anti-sense oligonucleotides (AS-ODN) are short synthetics DNA chains, usually 15-25 nucleotides long, that have been designed to hybridize with target mRNA according to the rule of base-pairing. The cellular uptake of oligonucleotides is not well understood. However, once inside the cell, the AS-ODN finds its complimentary mRNA and forms an RNA-ODN duplex. The action of RNAseH upon the nascent hybrid results in AS-ODN-mediated destruction of the target RNA. To protect AS-ODNs from nucleolytic degradation, chemically modified analogs have been developed that display both prolonged and enhanced anti-sense effects. Common modifications include substitution of a non-bridging oxygen in the phosphodiester backbone with sulfur (phosphorothioate modification), and replacement of the 5' and /or 3' terminal bases of the ODN with 2'-O-methyl ribonucleotides. AS-ODNs have been used to study a variety of medically relevant nervous system proteins, including ion channels, neurotransmitter receptors, neuropeptides and enzymes [7].

MG and EAMG present valuable systems for testing the involvement of the cholinergic system in the pathophysiology of NMJ disorders. The current management of MG includes the use of acetylcholinesterase inhibitors (AChEI) for temporary improvement of neuromuscular transmission, removal of anti-AChR antibodies and the use of nonspecific immunosuppression or immunomodulation [3,8-10].

2. ACETYLCHOLINESTERASE ISOFORMS AND SPECIFIC ANTI-SENSE

Termination of signaling in the cholinergic system is mediated via ACh degradation by AChE, the enzyme whose activity determines the duration and the efficacy of cholinergic neurotransmission. This enzyme has several isoforms, both membrane bound and soluble, the product of alternative splicing of its mRNA [11]. It has been documented that the AChE-synaptic (AChE-S) isoform is critical in terminating the action of ACh to prevent repeated activation of the AChR. Supporting the importance of this function is the observation that mutations of the AChE-S gene lead to cholinesterase deficiency and congenital myasthenic syndrome. The AChE-S is distributed through the primary and secondary synaptic clefts of the NMJ anchored there by a specific carboxy-terminal sequence to basal lamina. It has been found that cholinergic synapses, including the NMJ, may express the AChE-read-through (R) splice variant. Overproduction and accumulation of AChE-R occurs during stress, disease or cholinesterase inhibition [11]. The AChE-R lacks an anchoring domain and is soluble. As a consequence AChE-R serves to limit the quantity of ACh that reaches the AChR and thereby limit cholinergic overexcitation. However, accumulation of AChE-R will limit cholinergic activation, which has been shown to compromise normal synaptic function [11].

Symptomatic treatment of MG is usually begun with an orally available, non-competitive AChEI, pyridostigmine. This drug, despite its short half-life and erratic bioavailability, has served as the symptomatic therapeutic agent for decades. The amelioration of weakness seen in MG patients treated by AChEI is seldom complete, but in some instances may be sufficient to enable normal life functions without the need for further immunosuppressive treatment [1]. Side effects of AChEI include muscarinic over-activity symptoms such as abdominal cramps, diarrhea, sweating, nasal discharge, salivation, tearing, increased urination and bradycardia. Another, less common, side effect is increased muscle weakness due to NMJ receptor over-stimulation culminating in the development of a curariform (non-depolarizing) block. The resultant weakness may be quite severe, and the differentiation of such a cholinergic crisis from the more common myasthenic crisis can present a serious clinical challenge to the treating physicians.

However, it should be noted that clinicians have failed to notice that AChEI exert any immunomodulating effect under clinical settings in MG. There is no evidence to suggest that AChEI have an enhancing or regulating effect on anti-AChR titers and their effect does not linger on for more than a few hours after discontinuation of their use. While AChE inhibitors may effectively restore muscle performance in MG patients, their action is short-lived, with considerable individual variability and a poor response in some patients.

AS-ODNs to AChE have been demonstrated effective *in vitro* and *in vivo*, in the hematopoietic system [7,12-14]. First generation anti-AChE AS-ODNs were prepared in unmodified or fully phosphothioated forms and then in partially phosphorothioated form. Reducing the phosphothioate content minimized cytotoxicity without compromising activity [15]. Several anti-sense sequences including the AChE-AS-ODN EN 101 (AS3) demonstrated potent inhibition of AChE in rat pheochromocytoma PC12 cells at very low concentration [16]. In addition, the same anti-sense preparation prevented neuronal damage in a mouse model of head injury [17], and in ALS mice (Gotnik M.et al abstract presented at the 61ˢᵗ annual meeting of the American Academy of Neurology 2009). Substitution of 2'-O-methyl-modified ribonucleotides at the three terminal 3' positions conferred a wide effective range (0.02-200nM) and was used for routine configuration in the synthesis of the AChE-AS-ODN (EN101) used in our experimental and clinical studies [5,18-20].

3. RELATIONS BETWEEN ACHE AND ACHR AT THE NMJ

There is evidence that nAChR and AChE functions in the NMJ are intimately related. For example, compound mutagenesis of AChE and the á subunit gene for nAChR in zebrafish limited the severity of the impaired neuromuscular phenotype caused by ACHE disruption alone [21]. Based on this and related information, we hypothesized that disruptions in the AChE – nAChR balance may be relevant to several neuromuscular diseases. In the mammalian nerve and muscle, for example, imbalanced cholinergic neurotransmission involves changes in gene expression. These include enhanced transcription and shifted splicing options of the AChE gene, leading to overproduction and accumulation of the normally rare "readthrough" AChE-R variant [11]. In the short range, e.g. the immediate response to acute stress, elevated AChE attenuates the initial hyperexcitation [22]. However, molecular genetics has demonstrated adhesive and morphogenic non-catalytic activities for AChE [23,24], suggesting potentially detrimental long-term consequences of AChE accumulation. Such consequences are likely to be variant-specific, as the synaptic AChE-S variant forms membrane-bound multimers [25], whereas AChE-R appears as a soluble monomer [26].

4. TREATMENT OF EAMG RATS WITH ANTI-SENSE TARGETED TO ACHE mRNA

AChE inhibitors effectively restore muscle activity in MG patients; however, their action is relatively short, with considerable individual variability and a poor response in some patients, calling for the development of additional effective symptomatic therapeutic modalities. Antisense technology offers an attractive, gene-based alternative to conventional anti-AChE therapeutics. As antisense therapeutics target RNA rather than protein, they offer the possibility of designing highly specific drugs with effective concentrations in the nanomolar range [5]. Using EN 101 an AS-ODN targeted to AChE mRNA at the dose of 50 μg/Kg , we found marked improvement in the response to repetitive nerve stimulation (RNS) in EAMG rats [5]. The effect was sequence and dose dependent and lasted for at least 24 hours following intravenous or oral administration of 50 μg/Kg 2-O-methyl protected AS-ACHE-ODN (EN 101). Recording of compound muscle action potentials (CMAP) from the gastrocnemius muscle in EAMG rats showed the typical baseline decrement following RNS with 3 Hz. The decrement ranged from 10% to 36% (mean 13.0 ±2.5%). Administration of 75 μg/Kg neostigmine bromide i.p. or pyridostigmine orally rapidly corrected the CMAP decrement to 100-105%. The effects of cholinesterase blockade were evident starting 15 min after injection yet lasted only 2 hours, after which time CMAP reverted to the baseline decrement. On the other hand, EN101 treatment at doses ranging from 50-500 μg/Kg (2-20 nmole/rat) retrieved stable CMAP that lasted between 24-72 hours. 500 μg/Kg conferred 72 normalization of CMAP to 125% of baseline whereas 50 μg/Kg was effective for 24 hours.

Anti-sense agents that target the AChE mRNA transcripts can operate repeatedly, i.e. one AS-ON is responsible for hydrolysis of many mRNAs. This explains the 100 fold difference in the molar dose of AS-ON versus pyridostigmine that is effective in relieving EAMG weakness.

Furthermore, EN101 treatment lowered AChE in blood and muscle, improved survival, muscle strength and disease severity [5]. This promising findings lead to a clinical trial in MG patients and showed significant amelioration of the clinical weakness in the majority of the MG patients tested [20].

Assessment of the disease status in chronic EAMG is based mainly on clinical signs. It is often inconsistent with the results obtained from RNS, which produces a decrement of the CMAP in only a fraction of the animals and does not always reflect clinical severity [27]. We, therefore, looked for more sensitive methods of determining the response to treatment and disease severity in rats with EAMG. Applying stimulated single fiber electromyography (stimulated-SFEMG) to rats we found that EN101 treatment improved the mean consecutive difference (MCD) and blocking for 24 h and was more effective than pyridostigmine[18]. All the EAMG rats showed improved stamina 24 h following EN101 treatment. Running time in EAMG rats with mild disease increased by 2 folds, in moderately affected animals by 3.6 folds and in severely affected animals by 4.8 folds. The treadmill running time correlated with the stimulated SFEMG results present as MCD (P=0.005, r=0.77). It is important to note that despite the robust effectiveness of EN101 treatment on EAMG rat stamina, it still lags far behind the control rats. Thus, inhibiting AChE by specific antisense solves only a fraction of EAMG clinical weakness and restoration of the nAChRs remain the major therapeutic goal.

Long-term treatment of chronic EAMG rats with daily administration of oral EN 101 for one month resulted in significant improvement in survival, clinical status and stamina [5]. Eighty percent of EAMG animals under a daily EN101 (50 μg/kg) regimen showed an improved clinical status and treadmill performance one month after initiation of treatment. In contrast, placebo-saline treatment led to progressive deterioration of all the animals, with 75% mortality (Figure 1). The beneficial effect of EN 101 on clinical symptoms was also accompanied by an increase in body weight, as opposed to the control group, which lost weight [5].

A surprising finding was that lower levels of anti-rat AChR antibodies were detected in some of the EN 101-treated animals, additional to the improved clinical symptoms and muscle activity. Thus, daily EN101 administration appears also to suppress effectively the autoimmune process, perhaps via immunomodulation of the cytokine/chemokine balance.

We assume that the antisense treatment normalized neuromuscular transmission and induced a long-term stable cholinergic up-regulation that acted both at the NMJ and on the immune cells.

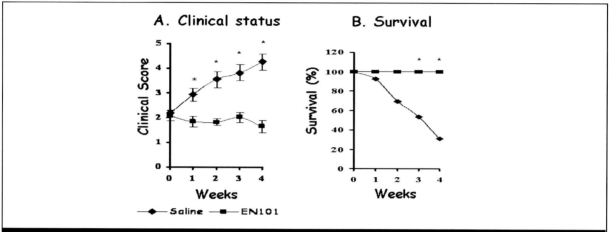

Figure1: Long-term EN 101 treatment changes the course of EAMG. (A) Clinical status, average values of the clinical score for placebo (saline) and EN 101 treated rats, (B) survival, more animals treated with EN 101 oral 50 µg/kg/day survived than the placebo group.

5. TREATMENT OF MG PATIENTS WITH EN 101

The basic experiments with EAMG rats lead to a phase 1 trial with MG patients with EN101. EN 101 given orally in 16 MG patients, resulted in significant improvement in the severity of the MG as measured by the quantitative MG (QMG) score [20]. The treated patients experienced mean improvement of six QMG score points, while an improvement of three has been found to be clinically significant [28]. The overall mean QMG change from baseline was 6.13 ±4.5 (baseline QMG score was 14.9 ±7.25) (p<0.01). Improvement of QMG score occurred with 150 µg/kg and 500 µg/kg. The QMG score lowered steadily over the time course of the study and remained lower than baseline. Furthermore, the swallowing time component of the QMG was better among treated patients. Fourteen patients reported subjective improvement with EN 101 compared with pyridostigmine. The EN 101 beneficial effects lasted for over 24 hours (and in some patients over 48 hours) supporting the notion that this therapy may reduce the need for multiple dosing [20,28].

6. EFFECT OF EN101 *IN VITRO* ON T-CELL ACTIVITY

As immune cell posses a complete cholinergic system and the nervous system is the major producer of ACh, the immune cholinergic system can mediate neuro-immune interactions, or it may serve as an internal regulator of immune responses. Termination of signaling in this system is also mediated by AChE. In addition, it has been shown that the α-7 nAChR present on macrophages and T-cells can act as an anti-inflammatory target. Activation of this receptor, both physiologically by vagal stimulation or pharmacologically with nicotinic agonists, reduced pro-inflammatory cytokine production and increased survival in a severe endotoxemia model [19,29-

32]. It appears that α-7-nAChR activation decreases NF-kb-mediated transcription, and thus may affect the secretion of various other inflammatory mediators [30].

Increasing ACh levels by EN 101 inhibited mitogen and antigen-induced lymphocyte proliferation, this inhibition was associated with reduced production of TNFα and IL-1β (Figure 2) [19]. In addition, lymphocyte activation was associated with increased expression of the α-7-nAChR, while the expression of the epsilone subunit under the same conditions was not detectable [19,31,33].

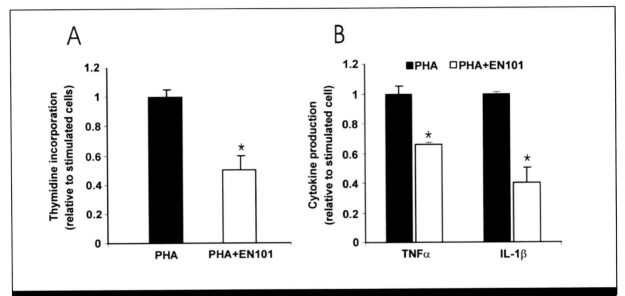

Figure 2: AChE inhibition in vitro by EN 101 reduced proliferation of activated lymphocytes (A), and the secretion of pro-inflammatory cytokines. *p< 0.05 vs PHA alone.

Experimental autoimmune encephalomyelitis (EAE) is a T-cell mediated inflammatory demyelinating CNS disease used to study human Multiple Sclerosis (MS) [34], and for the study of neuroinflammation and autoimmunity in general. Using the chronic EAE model in C57BL mice we showed recently that treatment with EN 101 at daily dose of 100 μg/kg reduced clinical severity of the disease by 90%. The clinical amelioration was accompanied by a marked reduction in CNS inflammatory infiltrates [19]. Furthermore, EN 101 treatment lowered the reactivity of T-cells involved in the pathogenesis of EAE induction and was associated with marked reduction of serum specific AChE activity [19]. Moreover, recently, we showed that the AChEI rivastigmine (the drug used for treatment in AD patients) induced anti-inflammatory and disease modifying properties in EAE mice. Rivastigmine exerted a multi-level influence on the immune responses and its anti-inflammatory effects relied on the cholinergic immune system [31].

7. CONCLUSIONS

The relatively new studies highlighting the involvement of the cholinergic balance in the regulation of innate and adaptive immune responses, broadens the targets for anticholinesterase intervention.

AS-ODN ACHE was effective in ameliorating several animal models such as EAMG, head injury, ALS, and EAE. Based on the efficacy of EN 101 in EAMG, a successful clinical trial in MG patients was initiated.

Thus, advances in our understanding of the molecular and cellular mechanisms of action of AChE allow us to postulate mechanisms explaining the limitations of conventional anticholinesterase pharmacology. These limitations may be due to non-catalytic activities of AChE isoforms or a feedback loop leading to overexpression of AChE following stress and AChE blockade. At the same time, cloning of the human ACHE gene opened the door to novel options to suppress AChE biosynthesis using anti-sense technology. This may enable us to apply AS-ODN-based drugs to anticholinesterase therapeutics such as CNS inflammation and motor-neuron disorders.

REFERENCES

1. Argov Z, Wirguin I: Drugs and the neuromuscular junction: Pharmacotherapy and adverse effects in transmission disorders. in Lisak R (ed), 1994.

2. Kawashima K, Fujii T: The lymphocytic cholinergic system and its biological function. *Life Sci* 2003;72:2101-2109.

3. Conti-Fine BM, Milani M, Kaminski HJ: Myasthenia gravis: past, present, and future. *J Clin Invest* 2006;116:2843-2854.

4. Desai AK, Grossberg GT: Diagnosis and treatment of Alzheimer's disease. *Neurology* 2005;64:S34-39.

5. Brenner T, Hamra-Amitay Y, Evron T, Boneva N, Seidman S, Soreq H: The role of readthrough acetylcholinesterase in the pathophysiology of myasthenia gravis. *Faseb J* 2003;17:214-222.

6. Galyam N, Grisaru D, Grifman M, Melamed-Book N, Eckstein F, Seidman S, Eldor A, Soreq H: Complex host cell responses to antisense suppression of ACHE gene expression. Antisense Nucleic *Acid Drug Dev* 2001;11:51-57.

7. Soreq H, Seidman S: Anti-sense approach to anticholinesterase therapeutics. *Isr Med Assoc J* 2000;2 Suppl:81-85.

8. Sathasivam S: Steroids and immunosuppressant drugs in myasthenia gravis. *Nat Clin Pract Neurol* 2008;4:317-327.

9. Dalakas MC: B cells as therapeutic targets in autoimmune neurological disorders. *Nat Clin Pract Neurol* 2008;4:557-567.

10. Gold R, Schneider-Gold C: Current and future standards in treatment of myasthenia gravis. *Neurotherapeutics* 2008;5:535-541.

11. Soreq H, Seidman S: Acetylcholinesterase—new roles for an old actor. *Nat Rev Neurosci* 2001;2:294-302.

12. Soreq H, Patinkin D, Lev-Lehman E, Grifman M, Ginzberg D, Eckstein F, Zakut H: Antisense oligonucleotide inhibition of acetylcholinesterase gene expression induces progenitor cell expansion and suppresses hematopoietic apoptosis ex vivo. *Proc Natl Acad Sci* U S A 1994;91:7907-7911.

13. Lev-Lehman E, Ginzberg D, Hornreich G, Ehrlich G, Meshorer A, Eckstein F, Soreq H, Zakut H: Antisense inhibition of acetylcholinesterase gene expression causes transient hematopoietic alterations in vivo. *Gene Ther* 1994;1:127-135.

14. Patinkin D, Seidman S, Eckstein F, Benseler F, Zakut H, Soreq H: Manipulations of cholinesterase gene expression modulate murine megakaryocytopoiesis in vitro. *Mol Cell Biol* 1990;10:6046-6050.

15. Ehrlich G, Patinkin D, Ginzberg D, Zakut H, Eckstein F, Soreq H: Use of partially phosphorothioated "antisense" oligodeoxynucleotides for sequence-dependent modulation of hematopoiesis in culture. *Antisense Res Dev* 1994;4:173-183.

16. Grifman M, Soreq H: Differentiation intensifies the susceptibility of pheochromocytoma cells to antisense oligodeoxynucleotide-dependent suppression of acetylcholinesterase activity. *Antisense Nucleic Acid Drug Dev* 1997;7:351-359.

17. Shohami E, Kaufer D, Chen Y, Seidman S, Cohen O, Ginzberg D, Melamed-Book N, Yirmiya R, Soreq H: Antisense prevention of neuronal damages following head injury in mice. *J Mol Med* 2000;78:228-236.

18. Boneva N, Hamra-Amitay Y, Wirguin I, Brenner T: Stimulated-single fiber electromyography monitoring of anti-sense induced changes in experimental autoimmune myasthenia gravis. *Neurosci Res* 2006;55:40-44.

19. Nizri E, Hamra-Amitay Y, Sicsic C, Lavon I, Brenner T: Anti-inflammatory properties of cholinergic up-regulation: A new role for acetylcholinesterase inhibitors. *Neuropharmacology* 2006;50:540-547.

20. Argov Z, McKee D, Agus S, Brawer S, Shlomowitz N, Yoseph OB, Soreq H, Sussman JD: Treatment of human myasthenia gravis with oral antisense suppression of acetylcholinesterase. *Neurology* 2007;69:699-700.

21. Behra M, Cousin X, Bertrand C, Vonesch JL, Biellmann D, Chatonnet A, Strahle U: Acetylcholinesterase is required for neuronal and muscular development in the zebrafish embryo. *Nat Neurosci* 2002;5:111-118.

22. Kaufer D, Friedman A, Seidman S, Soreq H: Acute stress facilitates long-lasting changes in cholinergic gene expression. *Nature* 1998;393:373-377.

23. Darboux I, Barthalay Y, Piovant M, Hipeau-Jacquotte R: The structure-function relationships in Drosophila neurotactin show that cholinesterasic domains may have adhesive properties. *Embo J* 1996;15:4835-4843.

24. Sternfeld M, Ming G, Song H, Sela K, Timberg R, Poo M, Soreq H: Acetylcholinesterase enhances neurite growth and synapse development through alternative contributions of its hydrolytic capacity, core protein, and variable C termini. *J Neurosci* 1998;18:1240-1249.

25. Massoulie J: The origin of the molecular diversity and functional anchoring of cholinesterases. *Neurosignals* 2002;11:130-143.

26. Seidman S, Sternfeld M, Ben Aziz-Aloya R, Timberg R, Kaufer-Nachum D, Soreq H: Synaptic and epidermal accumulations of human acetylcholinesterase are encoded by alternative 3'-terminal exons. *Mol Cell Biol* 1995;15:2993-3002.

27. Seybold ME, Lambert EH, Lennon VA, Lindstrom JM: Experimental autoimmune myasthenia: clinical, neurophysiologic, and pharmacologic aspects. *Ann N Y Acad Sci* 1976;274:275-282.

28. Kaminski HJ: Restoring balance at the neuromuscular junction. *Neurology* 2007;69:629-630.

29. Borovikova LV, Ivanova S, Zhang M, Yang H, Botchkina GI, Watkins LR, Wang H, Abumrad N, Eaton JW, Tracey KJ: Vagus nerve stimulation attenuates the systemic inflammatory response to endotoxin. *Nature* 2000;405:458-462.

30. Barnes PJ, Karin M: Nuclear factor-kappaB: a pivotal transcription factor in chronic inflammatory diseases. *N Engl J Med* 1997;336:1066-1071.

31. Nizri E, Irony-Tur-Sinai M, Faranesh N, Lavon I, Lavi E, Weinstock M, Brenner T: Suppression of neuroinflammation and immunomodulation by the acetylcholinesterase inhibitor rivastigmine. *J Neuroimmunol* 2008;203:12-22.

32. Brenner T, Nizri E, Irony-Tur-Sinai M, Hamra-Amitay Y, Wirguin I: Acetylcholinesterase inhibitors and cholinergic modulation in Myasthenia Gravis and neuroinflammation. *J Neuroimmunol* 2008;201-202:121-127.

33. Wang H, Yu M, Ochani M, Amella CA, Tanovic M, Susarla S, Li JH, Wang H, Yang H, Ulloa L, Al-Abed Y, Czura CJ, Tracey KJ: Nicotinic acetylcholine receptor alpha7 subunit is an essential regulator of inflammation. *Nature* 2003;421:384-388.

34. Steinman L, Zamvil SS: How to successfully apply animal studies in experimental allergic encephalomyelitis to research on multiple sclerosis. *Ann Neurol* 2006;60:12-21.

VI

Clinical Trials in Myasthenia Gravis

The Rationale for Tumor Necrosis Factor Antagonism (Etanercept) in the Treatment of Autoimmune Myasthenia Gravis

Julie Rowin M.D.

1. INTRODUCTION

Myasthenia gravis (MG) is one of the most thoroughly understood human autoimmune diseases. The symptoms are known to be due to an antibody-mediated, T-cell dependent, autoimmune attack directed against the acetylcholine receptors at the neuromuscular junction (1). Current treatments for MG include cholinesterase inhibitors, thymectomy, corticosteroids, long-term immunosuppressant agents, intravenous immune globulin, and plasmapheresis (2). The existing options for treatment of MG are limited due to variable patient response and both short and long term side effects. Thus, there remains a need for the development of new treatment strategies.

It is generally accepted that prednisone is an effective treatment for MG (3), although no controlled clinical trials of prednisone in MG have been carried out. A number of patients with MG become dependent upon long-term moderate to high dose corticosteroid therapy for disease control. There are major concerns regarding the side effects of chronic prednisone therapy that are shared by patients and their treating physicians (4). There are few prospective data on the side effects associated with steroid use in MG, but the potential toxicities of long-term prednisone therapy are well known and include osteoporosis, hypertension, hyperglycemia, skin atrophy, impaired wound healing, congestive heart failure and peptic ulcer disease (5). Although prednisone is a relatively inexpensive medication, the potential costs of treating these side effects are substantial.

Currently, there are several immunosuppressant agents that are used in MG patients to limit their cumulative exposure to corticosteroids (2). These *steroid-sparing* agents include azathioprine, cyclosporine, mycophenolate mofetil, and tacrolimus. Azathioprine is the more commonly used agent, and is the only agent in which a steroid-sparing effect has been demonstrated by a randomized controlled trial (RCT) (6). In this study, azathioprine was administered in combination with high dose daily prednisone in generalized MG, and patients receiving azathioprine had a lower cumulative exposure to prednisone over three years as compared to placebo. Importantly, this effect was not present until the second year of treatment, and there was no evidence that azathioprine had any discernable effect on prednisone dosing during the first year of high dose therapy. Additionally, azathioprine has potential risks of its own, including hepatotoxicity, myelosuppression, an idiosyncratic allergic/systemic reaction (10-15% of MG patients), and a possible increased risk for the development of certain malignancies (7,8).

Other immunosuppressive medications used as steroid-sparing agents in MG are associated with significant limitations. Although the effectiveness of cyclosporine has been confirmed in an RCT (9), its use is limited due to its expense, and toxicity, including hypertension, renal toxicity, and possibly an increased risk of certain malignancies (10). The emergence of mycophenolate mofetil in the treatment of MG was initially heralded by observations that it was less toxic and had a more rapid onset of action compared to azathioprine (11,12). Unfortunately, two recently published RCTs indicated that mycophenolate mofetil was no more effective than low dose daily prednisone as initial immunotherapy (13), and had no steroid-sparing effect when used in combination with corticosteroid treatment (14). Critics of these studies point out that neither one was of sufficient duration, but this point highlights the more recent feeling that if mycophenolate mofetil has therapeutic efficacy in MG, its true onset of action is probably comparable to azathioprine. While mycophenolate mofetil is generally thought to have a relatively favorable side-effect profile compared to azathioprine and cyclosporine, even this potential advantage must be viewed with caution given recent reports of an association with progressive multifocal leukencephalopathy (15). Newer or evolving treatments include tacrolimus (16,17) and ritiximab (18), but the true efficacy of these agents remain to be demonstrated and their long-term safety in MG must be confirmed. Finally, chronic treatment with intravenous immune globulin (IVIg) or plasma exchange is extremely expensive and impractical in all but the most severe refractory MG patients.

In summary, there exists a significant subgroup of MG patients who respond partially to treatment with corticosteroids, usually requiring chronic treatment with high to moderate doses to maintain the clinical benefit. These patients frequently develop side effects associated with chronic steroid use, which are potentially severe. The existing options for steroid-sparing therapies are limited to agents that either have a markedly prolonged onset of clinical benefit and/or have significant potential side effects. Furthermore, some patients are unable to tolerate treatment with immunosuppressant agents or are resistant to all current therapeutic combinations. Thus, there is a strong rationale for developing therapies for MG that are more effective, faster acting and better tolerated than the existing options. Despite the unfortunate long list of potential side effects, prednisone remains the most effective, fastest acting and most reliable chronic immunosuppressive treatment in MG

The concept of treating MG by blockade of tumor necrosis factor α (TNF-α), and specifically using the agent etanercept, grew out of this need for an effective and safe treatment alternative with a more rapid onset of action. The rationale, preclinical data, and preliminary clinical evidence for the use of TNF-α blockade in MG will be presented in this Chapter.

2. RATIONALE FOR TNF-α BLOCKADE IN MG

2.1. TNF-α

Tumor necrosis factor (TNF) is a trimolecular cytokine derived primarily from cells of the monocyte/macrophage lineage, which is known to stimulate the production of multiple mediators that drive the inflammatory process (19,20). Members of the TNF and TNF receptor superfamily are important regulators of immune cell proliferation, survival, differentiation and apoptosis (20,21). As a key pro-inflammatory cytokine, TNF-α has been implicated in the pathogenesis of a number of T-cell mediated autoimmune diseases, including Crohn's disease, rheumatoid arthritis, and multiple sclerosis (MS) (22). Blockade of TNF-α has also been shown to have an impact on memory B cells, suggesting a possible role in antibody-mediated autoimmune diseases (23,24).

In MG, the production of anti-AChR antibodies is regulated by cytokines produced by Th cells (25), and there is evidence that TNF-α likely plays a role in the regulation of these cells (26). A transient increase in the mRNA expression of TNF-α in muscle cells can be detected in the early stages of experimental autoimmune myasthenia gravis (EAMG) (27). Furthermore, TNF receptor deficiency protects mice from the development of EAMG (28,29). Linomide, a synthetic compound that inhibits systemic TNF-α production, suppresses the development of EAMG, and is accompanied by a reduced TNF-α mRNA expression in muscle (30).

2.2. Pre-clinical studies of TNF antagonism in EAMG

It has been demonstrated that the administration of recombinant human TNF:F_C suppresses ongoing experimental MG in mice (31). In these studies treated mice showed a significant improvement in clinical grading of disease severity compared to control mice. Overall, 75% of treated mice showed improvement compared to 16% of mice receiving PBS; only 8% of treated mice had worsening of their clinical condition compared to 41% in the control group. A reduction in TNF-α serum level of approximately 45% at the end of the treatment period was observed compared to baseline serum levels prior to the first injection. Anti-AChR antibody levels were no different between the two experimental groups.

Anti-TNF-α antibodies have been shown to suppress the development of EAMG in rats (32). In these studies, anti-TNF-α antibodies were administered twice per week for 5 weeks from the day of immunization with AChR. Treatment resulted in a lower incidence and delayed onset of EAMG, and a suppression of AChR-specific lymphocyte proliferation. Unlike the findings in EAMG mice, anti-AChR antibody levels were decreased in animals treated with anti-TNF-α antibodies (32).

2.3. TNF-α and human MG

TNF-α has also been implicated in the pathogenesis of human MG (33). Patients with MG have been shown to have increased numbers of TNF-α mRNA expressing cells among blood mononuclear cells compared to controls (34), and T-cells from MG patients have significantly more TNF-α receptors (33). TNF polymorphisms have been observed in MG patients (35), and peripheral blood mononuclear cells from patients with thymic lymphoid follicular hyperplasia secrete higher levels of TNF upon stimulation (36). Since TNF is also involved in the formation of germinal centers (37), these data imply that TNF may play a role in the development of germinal centers in the thymic glands of MG patients.

While the precise role of TNF in the immunopathogenesis of MG is not entirely clear, the existing evidence would suggest that TNF plays a role in promoting the disease by acting in concert with other cytokines and influencing the immune response, and by "helping" production of anti-acetylcholine receptor antibodies (26). Therefore, TNF down-regulation may represent an effective strategy in the treatment of patients with autoimmune MG.

3. TNF-α BLOCKERS: CURRENT CLINICAL USE AND SAFETY

3.1. TNF-α antagonists

There are currently three approved TNF monoclonal antibodies (infliximab, adalimunab, and certolizumab), and one soluble TNF receptor (etanercept) (22). Infliximab is administered by intravenous infusion, while certolizumab, adalimunab, and etanercept are administered by subcutaneous injection. Worldwide over a million patients have been treated with TNF-α antagonists for a variety of indications including rheumatoid arthritis, inflammatory bowel disease, psoriasis, and ankylosing spondylitis and have been shown to be safe and effective in controlled clinical trials (22,38-40). The clinical benefits have been shown to be rapid in onset and maintained with long-term treatment (22,41). As there is preliminary clinical data examining the use of etanercept in MG, this agent will be the focus for the remainder of this chapter.

3.2. Etanercept

Etanercept is an artificial bioengineered molecule derived from Chinese hamster ovary cells grown in tissue culture (24). It is a dimeric protein consisting of the extracellular ligand-binding portion of the human TNF receptor (TNFR) linked to the Fc portion of human IgG1 (TNF: Fc). Etanercept binds to both TNF-α and TNF-β and blocks their interaction with cell surface TNF receptors. The biologic activity of etanercept is dependent upon its binding to the TNFR on the cell surface. Therefore, etanercept renders TNF inactive. Etanercept can also modulate biological responses that are induced by TNF such as expression of adhesion molecules that regulate lymphocyte migration, serum levels of cytokines (e.g., IL-6) and matrix metalloproteinase-3 (MMP-3) (24).

Etanercept is approved for the treatment of rheumatoid arthritis, psoriatic arthritis, psoriasis, juvenile rheumatoid arthritis, and ankylosing spondylitis (22). It is administered once or twice weekly by subcutaneous injection. Clinical data reviewed for etanercept in the treatment of rheumatoid arthritis and psoriasis have shown good efficacy, tolerability and a low adverse event profile (22,42).

3.3. Safety of TNF-α antagonism

Increasing use of these agents have led to a recognition of the range of toxicities, as well as a lack of efficacy or even a disease-exacerbating effect in certain conditions such as heart failure and multiple sclerosis (22). As TNF plays a complex role in innate immunity and host defense, particularly against mycobacterial infections, it is not surprising that etanercept and other TNF antagonists have been associated with an increased risk of mycobacterial and other intracellular microbial infections (43), probably as a result of interference with innate immunity. New cases of active tuberculosis continue to be reported in patients treated with all anti-TNF agents, leading to recommendations for prevention of latent tuberculosis infection. Less clear are the effects of TNF antagonists on host defense against malignancies, particularly lymphomas (44). Whereas data from large registries of patients with RA clearly indicate that disease activity, rather than TNF antagonism, is likely to be responsible for the observed increased risk for lymphoma, there is still some debate about this issue.

TNF antagonists have mixed effects on autoantibody production, suppressing some responses and enhancing others. These observations may relate to the occurrence of antinuclear (ANA) and anti-dsDNA antibodies with anti-TNF use (45), and the reports of autoimmune conditions, including vasculitis, glomerulonephritis and psoriasis presenting during treatment (22). Furthermore, CNS demyelinating disease (46) and immune demyelinating polyneuropathies (47) have been reported with the use of TNF-α-blockers. Induction as well as exacerbation of psoriasis (48), and even a single case report of anti-AChR-positive MG (49) have been recently observed. Strategies for the prevention and management of these significant adverse events continue to evolve as experience with these agents grows.

4. ETANERCEPT IN HUMAN MG

4.1. Trial design and results.

Rowin et.al. (50) conducted an open-label, pilot trial of etanercept in the treatment of autoimmune MG. Eleven patients with corticosteroid-dependent MG were enrolled in the study. The baseline characteristics of the patients is summarized in Table 1. All patients were judged to be corticosteroid-dependent (as defined by a minimal steroid dosage with either persistent symptoms of MG or a demonstrated tendency for disease exacerbation with attempts to taper the steroid dose), and most were previously treated unsuccessfully with other immunosuppressant medications.

The primary outcome measure was the change in the Quantitative Myasthenia Gravis Score (QMG score) (52) at six months compared to baseline. Etanercept (25 mg twice weekly) was given by subcutaneous injection with at least 72 hours between doses. Patients were seen one month after beginning treatment, and again at 2, 4, and 6 months post-treatment. At each visit, quantitative MG (QMG) score (52), manual muscle testing (MMT) (53), prednisone dose, MG activities of daily living score (MG-ADL) (54), complete blood count, chemistry panel, and adverse events were evaluated. A change of 3 or more units on the QMG score was considered a significant change (52). Prednisone taper was carried out using a standard protocol that allowed a maximum monthly decrease of 10 mg every 48 hours, and required either improvement or stability in two of the three remaining outcome measures (QMG, MMT, MG-ADL). Plasma levels of circulating anti-acetylcholine receptor antibodies and TNF-α were measured by standard alpha bugarotoxin radioimmunoassay, and ELISA, respectively, at baseline, two months post-treatment, and six months post-treatment.

Eight out of eleven subjects completed the study. Three subjects were withdrawn. Two subjects were withdrawn due to disease worsening, one of which was acute and severe at 3 weeks of treatment and required emergent plasma exchange. The other patient's worsening was associated with taper of prednisone at 4 months of treatment. This patient improved clinically after the previous prednisone dose was re-instituted. One patient was withdrawn due to a diffuse erythematosus skin rash that resolved after discontinuation of the etanercept.

Table 1: Baseline Characteristics: Etanercept in MG (Rowin et al, 2004)

Patient #	Age	MGFA class (51)	Duration of MG (years)	QMG	MMT	Prior Immunotx
1/F	48	IVa	37	17	27	AZA, MM Cyclo
2/F	40	IIa	15	9	11	AZA,MM
3/F	54	IIIa	6	12	26	MM
4/F	41	IIIa	33	14	13	AZA, MM
5/M	47	IVa	29	21	27	AZA, IVIg
6/F	29	IIIa	2	11	6	AZA
7/F	26	IIa	10	15	17	MM, IVIg
8/F	61	IIIa	14	15	17	MM
9/F	38	IIa	1	16	12	AZA, IVIg
10/F	51	IIIa	23	15	6	None
11/F	48	IVb	4	20	36	AZA
Mean	44		16	15	18	

AZA= azathioprine, Cyclo= cyclosporine, F= female, Immunotx=Immunotherapy, IVIg= intravenous Immunoglobulin, M= male, MGFA= Myasthenia Gravis Foundation of America, MM= mycophenolate mofetil, MMT= manual muscle testing score, QMG= quantitative myasthenia gravis score. Reprinted with permission Wolter Kluwer Health from Rowin et al. Neurology 2004, 62 supplement 5: A 185.

Five out of the eight remaining patients improved on the primary outcome measure. Six of eight improved based on at least two of the following: improved QMG of 3 or more points, improved MMT of 2 or more points, and/or a decrease in prednisone dose by 50% or more. There was no significant change in the levels of TNF-α or anti-AChR antibodies. The mean changes in QMG, MMT and MG-ADL were significant (see Table 2).

Table 2. Summary of Results: Etanercept in MG (Rowin et al, 2004)

ΔQMG mean	ΔMMT mean	% of baseline prednisone dose mean	ΔMG-ADL Mean
2.9	8.4	80.4%	2.75
(SD 2.6)	(SD 8.0)	(SD 43.9%)	(SD 2.2)
p=0.04*	p=0.02*	p=0.07	p=0.02*

* =Statistically significant
Δ=Change
SD= standard deviation

Adverse events included erythema at the injection site in 4 patients. Headache after injection occurred in one patient. Diffuse erythematous rash in 1 patient and worsening myasthenic symptoms in 2 patients. Seven out of eight patients opted to continue etanercept after study completion.

4.2. Analysis of Results

In summary, six of eleven MG patients enrolled in this pilot study improved after treatment with etanercept administered twice weekly, based on objective measures of muscle strength and the ability to successfully taper prednisone doses. Patients enrolled in this study had chronic (average disease duration 15.8 years), steroid-requiring disease, and in most cases, were previously treated unsuccessfully with one or more other immunosuppressive medications.

The small numbers and open-label design of the study prohibits definitive assessment of efficacy. In addition, a synergistic effect with previous immunotherapies, although unlikely, cannot be excluded. Despite these limitations, the clinical improvement observed in patients with largely refractory MG suggests that etanercept may be effective in certain patients with chronic, steroid-dependent disease. Etanercept did not significantly affect anti-AChR antibody levels or peripheral T or B cell counts, suggesting no inhibition of anti-AChR antibody production or T or B cell suppression due to treatment.

Furthermore treatment with etanercept did not significantly change circulating levels of TNF-α (55). However in the one patient noted to experience a severe acute clinical worsening related to etanercept treatment, a prominent change in TNF-α levels was observed. This patient did not have a significant increase in circulating anti-AChR antibody titers, but did show a pronounced rise in TNF-α levels (baseline level 13.13 pg/ml, exit level 3716.48 pg/ml). Upregulation of the production of TNF-α has been observed with etanercept treatment of other autoimmune diseases (56), possibly due to a counterregulatory mechanisms or inability to distinguish plasma free TNF-α from TNF-α bound to administered soluble TNFR: Fc. This suggests that in certain patients, etanercept treatment may upregulate the cytokine response and since some of these "proinflammatory" cytokines are crucial for MG pathogenesis, these patients may worsen during treatment.

The results of this study indicate that etanercept may be effective in a subset of patients with corticosteroid-dependent MG. Based on these findings, a randomized controlled trial of etanercept in steroid-dependent MG has been considered (57). Limitations related to the cost of the study drug and concerns regarding the safety of this agent in MG have prevented further study. Future clinical trials of etanercept in MG must take into account the risk of symptom exacerbation as was observed in one subject in the pilot clinical trial, and should include more detailed immunological analyses to better characterize the mechanism of etanercept's effect and to possibly identify patients who may be at risk for disease exacerbation.

5. FUTURE DIRECTIONS

Given the critical role of TNF-α in the pathogenesis of MG and EAMG, regulation of this cytokine remains a reasonable target for therapeutic manipulation. The concerns regarding the potential for disease exacerbation might be addressed by measurement of plasma cytokine levels and recognition that patients with high plasma IL-6, IFN-α, and TNF-α levels may be more prone to paradoxical clinical worsening (56). Measurement of pro-inflammatory cytokines prior to initiation of treatment may enhance the feasibility of prescribing TNF antagonists in MG. Unfortunately, it is likely that plasma cytokine levels, particularly TNF-α, fluctuate widely (58), and there may be little correlation between these levels and clinical disease severity. Clearly, a better understanding of the mechanisms of effect of TNF antagonism in MG and EAMG may help to clarify a therapeutic approach utilizing these agents (59). Along these lines, recent reports that TNF downregulates regulatory T cells (Tregs), and that TNF antagonists restore Treg function (60) suggest that their use might promote tolerance in autoimmune conditions like MG, as these Tregs may suppress autoreactive T cells or other cells that drive inflammation in immune-mediated diseases. It is conceivable that if this finding is confirmed, the choice of the particular TNF-blocking agent, dose, and route of administration might be optimized to maximize this effect.

Finally, it is becoming increasingly apparent that autoimmune MG may be categorized into a number of clinical subtypes based on clinical presentation, autoantibody profile, and thymic pathology, and that clinical course and response to various therapeutic interventions may differ according to subtype (2). The role of TNF-α may differ substantially between subtypes, so that TNF antagonism may be most effective in certain subgroups of MG patients while not effective or even deleterious in others. Along these lines, given the significant role of TNF-α in germinal center formation, antagonism of TNF-α could prove to be a more useful strategy in early-onset MG with thymic hyperplasia. Clearly, clinical strategies for the most safe and effective use of these agents will be improved as our understanding of the role of TNF in the immunopathogenesis of MG and MG subtypes evolves.

REFERENCES

1. Vincent A, Drachman DB. Myasthenia gravis. Adv *Neurol* 2002;88: 159-88.

2. Meriggioli MN, Sanders DB. 2009. Autoimmune myasthenia gravis: emerging clinical and biological heterogeneity. *Lancet Neurol* ;8:475-450.

3. Pascuzzi RM, Coslett HB, Johns TR. Long-term corticosteroid treatment of myasthenia gravis: report of 116 patients. *Ann Neurol* 1984;15: 291-98.

4. Boumpas DT, Chrousos GP, Wilder RL, Cupps TR, Balow JE. Glucocorticoid therapy for immune-mediated diseases: basic and clinical correlates. *Ann Intern Med* 1993;119:1198-1208.

5. Frauman AG. An overview of the adverse reactions to adrenal corticosteroids. *Adverse Drug React Toxicol Rev* 1996;15: 203-06.

6. Palace J, Newsom-Davis J, Lecky B. A randomized double-blind trial of prednisone alone or with azathioprine in myasthenia gravis. Myasthenia Gravis Study Group. *Neurology* 1998;50: 1778-83.

7. Kissel JT, Levy RJ, Mendell JR, Griggs RC. Azathioprine toxicity in neuromuscular disease. *Neurology* 1986;36:35-39.

8. Hohlfeld R, Michels M, Heininger K, Besinger U, Toyka KV. Azathioprine toxicity during long-term immunosuppression of generalized myasthenia gravis. *Neurology* 1988;38:258-261

9. Tindall RSA, Phillips JT, Rollins JA, Wells L, Hall K: A clinical therapeutic trial of cyclosporine in myasthenia gravis. *Ann NY Acad Sci* 1993; 681:539-551.

10. Ciafaloni E, Nikhar NK, Massey JM, Sanders DB. Retrospective analysis of the use of cyclosporine in myasthenia gravis. *Neurology* 2000;55: 448-50.

11. Ciafaloni E, Massey JM, Tucker-Lipscomb B, Sanders DB. Mycophenolate mofetil for myasthenia gravis: An open-label pilot study. *Neurology* 2001;56:97-99.

12. Meriggioli MN, Ciafaloni E, Al-Hayk KA, Rowin J, Tucker-Lipscomb B, Massey JM, Sanders DB. Mycophenolate mofetil for myasthenia gravis: an analysis of efficacy, safety, and tolerability. *Neurology* 2003;61:1438.

13. The Muscle Study Group. A trial of mycophenolate mofetil with prednisone as initial immunotherapy in myasthenia gravis. *Neurology* 2008;71: 394-99.

14. Sanders DB, Hart IK, Mantegazza R, Shukla SS, Siddiqui ZA, DeBaets MH, Melms A, Nicolle MW, Solomons N, Richman DP. An international, phase III, randomized trial of mycophenolate mofetil in myasthenia gravis. *Neurology* 2008;71: 400-06.

15. Neff RT, Hurst FP, Falta EM, Bohen EM, Lentine KL, Dharnidharka VR, Agodoa LY, Jindal RM, Yuan CM, Abbott KC. Progressive multifocal leukoencephalopathy and use of mycophenolate mofetil after kidney transplantation. *Transplantation* 2008;86:1474-8.

16. Ponseti JM, Gamez J, Lopez-Cano M, Vilalloga R, armegol M. Tacrolimus for myasthenia gravis : a clinical study of 212 patients. *Ann N Y Acad Sci* 2008 ;1132 :254-63.

17. Konishi T, Yoshiyama Y, Takamori M, Saida T. Long-term treatment of generalized myasthenia gravis with FK506(tacrolimus). *J Neurol Neurosurg Psychiatry* 2005 ;76 :448-50.

18. Tandan R, Potter C, Bradshaw DY. Pilot trial of rituximab in myasthenia gravis. *Neurology* 2008; 70 Suppl 1:A301.

19. Brennan FM, Feldmann M. Cytokines in autoimmunity. *Curr Opin Immunol* 1992;4:754-759.

20. Wajant H, Pfizenmaier K, Scheuruch P. Tumor necrosis factor signaling. *Cell Death Differ* 2003 ;10 :45-65.

21. Baud V, Karin M. Signal transduction by tumor necrosis factor and its relatives. *Tendss Cell Biol* 2001;11:373-77.

22. Lin J, Ziring D, Desai S, Kim S, Wong M, Korin Y, Braun J, Reed E, Gjertson D, Singh RR. TNFα blockade in human disease: An overview of efficacy and safety. *Clin Immunol* 2008;126:13-30.

23. Daridon C, Burmester GR, Dorner T. Anticytokine therapy impacting on B cells in autoimmune disease. *Curr Opin Rheumatol* 2009;21:205-10.

24. Tracey D, Klareskog L, Sasso EH, Salfeld JG, Tak PP. Tumor necrosis factor antagonist mechanism of action: a comprehensive review. *Pharmacol Ther* 2008;117:244-79.

25. Hohlfeld R, Toyka KV, Tzartos SJ, Carson W, Conti-Tronconi BM. Human T-helper lymphocytes in myasthenia gravis recognize the nicotinic receptor alpha subunit. Proc Natl Acad Sci U S A. 1987;84(15):5379–5383.

26. Zhang GX, Navikas V, Link H. Cytokines and the pathogenesis of myasthenia gravis. *Muscle & Nerve* 1997;20:543

27. Li H, Shi FD, Bai XF, Huang Y, Diab A, He B, Link H. Cytokine and chemokine mRNA expressing cells in muscle tissues of experimental autoimmune myasthenia gravis. *J Neurol Sci* 1998;161:40-46.

28. Wang HB, Li H, Shi FD, Chambers BJ, Link H, Ljunggren HG. Tumor necrosis factor receptor-1 is critically involved in the development of experimental autoimmune myasthenia gravis. Int Immunol 2000;12:1381-88.

29. Goluszko E, Deng C, Poussin MA, Christadoss P. Tumor necrosis factor receptor p55 and p75 deficiency protects mice from developing experimental autoimmune myasthenia gravis. *J Neuroimmunol* 2002;122:85-93.

30. Zhang GX, Yu Y, Shi FD, Xiao BG, Bjork J, Hedlund G, Link H. Linomide suppresses both Th1 and Th2 cytokines in experimental autoimmune myasthenia gravis. *J Neuroimmunol* 1997;73:175.

31. Christadoss P, Goluszko E. Treatment of experimental autoimmune myasthenia gravis with recombinant human tumor necrosis factor receptor F$_C$ protein. *J Neuroimmunol* 2002;122:186-190.

32. Duan RS, Wang HB, Yang JS, Scallon B, Link H, Xiao BG. Anti-TNF-α antibodies suppress the development of experimental myasthenia gravis. *J Autoimmun* 2002;19:169-174.

33. Bongioanni P, Ricciardi R, Pellegrino D, Romano MR. T-cell tumor necrosis factor-alpha binding in myasthenic patients. *J Neuroimmunol* 1999;93:203

34. Matusevicius D, Navikas V, Palasik W, Pirskanen R, Fredrikson S, Link H. Tumor necrosis factor-alpha, lymphtoxin, interleukin (IL)-6, IL-10, IL-12 and perforin mRNA expression in mononuclear cells in response to acetylcholine receptor is augmented in myasthenia gravis. *J Neuroimmunol* 1996;71:191.

35. Hjelmstrom P, Peacock CS, Giscombe R, Pirskanen R, Lefvert AK, Blackwell JM, Sanjeevi CB. Polymorphism in tumor necrosis factor genes associated with myasthenia gravis. *J Neuroimmunol* 1998;88:137-143.

36. Huang DR, Pirskanen R, Matell G, Lefvert AK. Tumor necrosis factor-alpha polymorphism and secretion in myasthenia gravis. *J Neuroimmunol* 1999;94:165-171.

37. Matsumoto M, Fu YX, Molina H, Chaplin DD. Lymphotoxin-alpha-deficient and TNF-receptor-1-deficient mice define developmental and functional characteristics of germinal centers. *Immunol Rev* 1997;156:137-144

38. Brandt J, Khariouzov A, Listing J, Haibel H, Sorensen H, Grassnickel L, Rudwaleit M, Sieper J, Braun J. Six-month results of a double-blind, placebo-controlled trial of etanercept treatment in patients with active ankylosing spondylitis. *Arthritis Rheum* 2003;48(6):1667-75.

39. Moreland LW, Baumgartner SW, Schiff MH, Tindall EA, Fleischmann RM, Weaver AL, et al. Treatment of rheumatoid arthritis with a recombinant tumor necrosis factor receptor (p75)-Fc fusion protein. *N Engl J Med* 1997;337:141-147.

40. Moreland LW, Schiff MH, Baumgartner SW, Tindall EA, Fleischmann RM, Bulpitt KJ, Weaver AL, Keystone EC, Furst DE, Mease PJ, Ruderman EM, Horwitz DA, Arkfeld DG, Garrison L, Burge DJ, Blosch CM, Lange ML, McDonnell ND, Weinblatt ME. Etanercept therapy in rheumatoid arthritis. A randomized, controlled trial. *Ann Intern Med* 1999;130(6):478-86.

41. Moreland LW, Cohen SB, Baumgartner SW, Tindall EA, Bulpitt K, Martin R, Weinblatt M, Taborn J, Weaver A, Burge DJ, Schiff MH. Long-term safety and efficacy of etanercept in patients with rheumatoid arthritis. *J Rheumatol* 2001;28(6):1238-44.

42. Chen YF, Jobanputra P, Barton P, Jowett S, Bryan S, Clark W, Fry-Smith A, Buris A. A systematic review of the effectiveness of adalimunab, etanercept and infliximab for the treatment of rheumatoid arthritis in adults and an economic evaluation of their cost-effectiveness. *Health Technol Assess* 2006;10:1-229.

43. Wallis RS. Tumor necrosis factor antagonists: structure, function and tuberculosis risks. *Lancet Infect Dis* 2008;8:601-11.

44. Wolfe F, Michaud K. Lymphoma in rheumatoid arthritis: the effect of methotrexate and anti-tumor necrosis factor therapy in 18,572 patients Arthritis Rheum 2004;50:1740-51.

45. Eriksson C, Engstrand S, Sundqvist KG, Rantapaa-Dahlqvist S. Autoantibody formation in patients with rheumatoid arthritis treated with anti-TNF alpha. *Ann Rheum Dis* 2005;64:403-407.

46. Mohan N, Edwards ET, Cupps TR, Oliverio PJ, Sandberg G, Crayton H, Richert JR, Siegel JN. Demyelination occurring during anti-tumor necrosis factor alpha therapy for inflammatory arthritides. *Arthritis Rheum* 2001;44:2862-2869.

47. Lozeron P, Denier C, Lacroix C, Adams D. Long-term course of demyelinating neuropathies occuirring during tumor necrosis factor-alpha-blocker therapy. *Arch Neurol* 2009;66:490-7.

48. Ko Jm, Gottlieb AB, Kerbleski JF. Induction and exacerbation of psoriasis with TNF-blockade therapy: a review and analysis of 127 cases. *J Dermatolog Trerat* 2009;20:100-108.

49. Fee DB, Kasarskis EJ. Myasthenia gravis associated with etanercept therapy. *Muscle Nerve* 200;39(6):866-870.

50. Rowin J, Meriggioli MN, Tuzun E, Christadoss P. A pilot trial of etanercept in the treatment of steroid-dependent, generalized autoimmune myasthenia gravis. *Neurology* 2004;62(7) suppl 5:A185.

51. Jaretski A 3rd, Barohn RJ, Ernstoff RM, Kaminski HJ, Keesey JC, Penn AS, Sanders DB. Myasthenia gravis: recommendations for clinical research standards. Task force of the Medical and Scientific Advisory Board of the Myasthenia Gravis Foundation of America. *Neurology* 2000;55:16-23.

52. Barohn RJ, McIntire D, Herbelin L, Wolfe GI, Nations S, Bryan WW. Reliability testing of the quantitative myasthenia gravis score. Ann NY Acad Sci 1998;841:769-772.

53. Sanders DB, Tucker-Lipscomb B, Massey JM. A simple manual muscle test for myasthenia gravis. Validation and comparison with the QMG score. *Ann NY Acad Sci* 2003;998:440-444.

54. Wolfe GI, Herbelin L, Nations SP, Foster B, Bryan WW, Barohn RJ. Myasthenia gravis activities of daily living profile. *Neurology* 1999;52:1487-1489.

55. Tuzun E, Meriggioli MN, Rowin J, Yang H, Christadoss P. Myasthenia gravis patients with low plasma IL-6 and IFN-gamma benefit from etanercept treatment. *J Autoimmun* 2005:24:261-8.

56. Zou JX, Rudwaleit M, Brandt J, Thiel A, Braun J, Sieper J. Up regulation of the production of tumour necrosis factor alpha and interferon gamma by T cells in ankylosing spondylitis during treatment with etanercept. *Ann Rheum Dis* 2003;62:561-564.

57. Rowin J. Etanercept treatment in myasthenia gravis. *Ann NY Acad Sci* 2008:1132:300-304.

58. Lee JS, Joo IS, Seok JI. Widely varying TNF-α levels in patients with myasthenia gravis. *Neurol Sci* 2009;Feb 13 [Epub ahead of print].

59. Kremer JM. Rational use of new and existing disease-modifying agents in rheumatoid arthritis. *Ann Intern Med* 2001;134:695-706.

60. Nadkarni S, Mauri C, Ehrenstein MR. Anti-TNF-alpha therapy induces a distinct regulatory T cell population in patients with rheumatoid arthritis via TGF-beta. *J Exp Med* 2007;204:33-39.

Myasthenia Gravis and Rituximab

William Sewan Baek, MD

1. MYASTHENIA GRAVIS

Acquired myasthenia gravis is a relatively uncommon but treatable condition, with prevalence rates approximating 20 per 100,000 in the United States (1).

The clinical diagnosis is based on the classic presentation of fatiguable, fluctuating weakness in limbs or cranial muscles with or without respiratory involvement. The diagnosis can be supported by serological testing for antibodies, repetitive nerve stimulation and single-fiber electromyography (EMG). Pharmacological management consists of cholinesterase inhibitors, steroids, immunosuppressants, IVIG and plasmapheresis (discussed in detail in chapter 1 & 4).

1.1. Immunopathogenesis of myasthenia gravis (MG)

B cells, T cells and autoantibodies together herald the immunopathogenesis of myasthenia gravis.

1.2. Role of B cells in myasthenia gravis (MG)

B cells can

1. Function as antigen-presenting cells, and that 100-1000 times more potent than other antigen-presenting cells, such as macrophages or dendritic cells (2).
2. Activate T cells: B-cell depleted mice exhibit a dramatic decrease in numbers of CD4+ and CD8+ T cells, and a tenfold inhibition of memory CD8+ T cells.

3. Produce cytokines: interleukins 1, 4, 6, 10, 12, 23, 16, tumor necrosis factor (TNF) and macrophage inflammatory protein (MIP) 1α and 1β (3, 4).
4. Produce autoantibodies by differentiating into autoantibody-secreting plasma cells (5).
5. Evolve into autoreactive memory cells, remaining dormant for prolonged periods awaiting re-activation by sequestered autoantigens (6).
6. Multiply through clonal proliferation (7).

1.3. Autoantibodies and myasthenia gravis (MG)

There are two types of autoantibodies directly involved in the pathogenesis of MG and the assay kits are currently commercially available in the United States.

The first one is the classic acetylcholine receptor antibody (AChR-Ab), which is directed towards the skeletal muscle nicotinic AChRs. This results in a loss of functional AChRs, thus bringing the endplate potential towards the threshold depolarization of the muscle fiber. The number of generated muscle fiber action potentials decreases, which results in skeletal muscle weakness (8).

Anti-AChR-binding antibodies are detected in approximately 80-85% of patients with generalized MG, but at best 55% of those with purely ocular symptoms (9).There is suggestion that the thymus gland may contribute to both the initiation and maintenance of the immune dysregulation directed against the AChR at least in a subset of patients with MG. More than 50% of patients positive for such antibodies have thymic hyperplasia and 10-15% have thymic tumors. A detailed discussion on the role of thymus in MG pathogenesis will be found in chapter 7 & 8.

The second antibody is the muscle-specific receptor tyrosine kinase antibody (MuSK-Ab). MuSK mediates agrin-induced clustering of AChRs during synapse formation and is also expressed at the mature neuromuscular junction.

The agrin/MuSK signaling pathway likely maintains the normal functional integrity of the neuromuscular junction, and current evidence shows that anti-MuSK antibodies may alter the density of post-synaptic acetylcholine receptors (10).

Thus based on current serological testing, myasthenics can be subclassified into 4 different groups; 1. those positive for AChR only, 2. those positive for MuSK only, 3. those positive for both AChR and MuSK, and 4. those who are double-negative; i.e., negative for both acetylcholine receptor and MuSK antibodies

Approximately 40% of patient with anti-AChR-antibody-negative generalized MG have anti-MuSK antibodies (11).

Both AChR and MuSK antibody-positive MG differ not only with respect to the immunological target but also in their pathogenic pathways. In AChR MG, complement fixing IgG1("Th1-like")and IgG3 subclasses predominate, and in MuSK MG the antibodies are mainly of the IgG4 subclass ("Th2-like") (11, 12).

There is suggestion that MuSK+ MG patients have a more severe form of the disease and may be more refractory to conventional medical treatment than AChR+MG patients (13-19).

2. RITUXIMAB

2.1. Key pharmacological features of rituximab

Rituximab is a chimeric mouse-human monoclonal antibody consisting of human IgG_1 and kappa constant regions and a mouse variable region. It was derived from a human CD20-directed hybridoma. CD20 is a 33-37kDa, 297-amino acid transmembrane phosphoprotein with 4 transmembrane regions and a 44 amino acid extracellular loop (20, 21). (Figure 1)

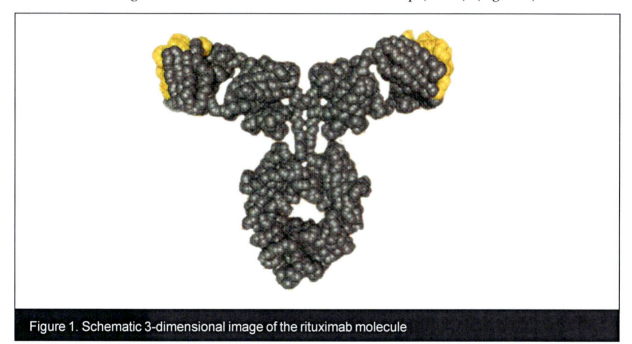

Figure 1. Schematic 3-dimensional image of the rituximab molecule

CD20 is present on all cells of B-cell lineage except for stem cells, pro-B cells and plasma cells (22). CD20 is not secreted, shed nor endocytosed when exposed to rituximab (23). The true function of CD20 is unclear, and CD20 knockout mice do not exhibit B-cell deficits (23). The average half-life of rituximab is 21 days. The adequacy of peripheral B cell depletion depends on achieving high and sustained serum rituximab concentrations.

2.2. Immunomodulatory effects of rituximab

Rituximab eliminates B cells through 3 mechanisms:

1. Antibody-dependent cellular cytotoxicity (ADCC): antibody-coated cells bind to the Fc receptors of macrophages or natural killer cells (24).
2. Complement-dependent cytotoxicity: activation of the membrane attack complex on B cells (24).
3. Induction of apoptosis:activation of phospholipase C pathways (25), leading to DNA degradation and cell death (26).

There is suggestion that clinically rituximab may also alter cell migration or interact with inhibitory receptors (27) and indirectly decrease T cell activation (28).

By downregulating CD40 and CD80 costimulatory B cell molecules, rituximab could induce generation of regulatory T cells, which could help control the autoimmune process (29).

2.3. Current indications of rituximab

Rituximab is indicated for Non-Hodgkin's Lymphoma (NHL) and rheumatoid arthritis (30).

2.4. Adverse effects of rituximab

Rituximab is generally well-tolerated, although mild hypotension and anaphylactic reactions (fever, chills, dyspnea) can occur. The most important serious adverse reactions of rituximab are fatal infusion reactions, tumor lysis syndrome (TLS), severe mucocutaneous reactions, progressive multifocal leukoencephalopathy (PML), hepatitis B reactivation with fulminant hepatitis, other viral infections, cardiovascular events, renal toxicity, and bowel obstruction and perforation.

The most common adverse reactions of rituximab (incidence ≥ 25%) observed in patients with non-Hogdkin's lymphoma (NHL) are infusion reactions, fever, chills, infection, asthenia, and lymphopenia. The most common adverse reactions of rituximab observed in patients with rheumatoid arthritis are hypertension, nausea, upper respiratory tract infection, arthralgia, pruritus, and pyrexia.

This can be addressed by stopping antihypertensives on the day of infusion and premedicating with antihistamines (30).

3. CLINICAL TRIALS OF RITUXIMAB IN MYASTHENIA GRAVIS (MG)

To date there are no large, randomized, double-blinded placebo-controlled studies to support the use of rituximab in myasthenia gravis.

There have been a number of case reports providing anecdotal evidence of rituximab being effective in myasthenia gravis (Table I).

Table 1 Case reports providing anecdotal evidence of rituximab being effective in myasthenia gravis

Age/Gender Reference	Medical conditions	Prior therapies	Rituximab + other therapies	Results
27/M Zaja et al.(36)	AChR+MG, GVHD post-BMT for AML	CSA, PYR, IVIG, methylprednisolone	260 mg/m^2 weekly x 4 weeks + PYR + methylprednisolone	Improved performance status and decreased anti-AChR antibodies after 4 weeks. Steroid and PYR doses gradually reduced over 6 months. No adverse effects noted at 5 month follow-up period.
9/F Wylam et al.(37)	AChR+MG	Prednisone, IVIG, PYR, AZA, PE, thymectomy	375mg/m^2 weekly x 4 weeks + 6MP + monthly IVIG	Increased pulmonary function and strength after 1 month. Attainment of near-normal lung volumes and maximal negative respiratory pressure after 5 months. Decreased anti-AChR antibodies. Weaned off steroids and able to perform all physicial activities without weakness. No adverse effects noted.
79/F Gajra et al.(38)	AChR+MG, NHL	Thymectomy, PYR	CTX + prednisone initially then with disease progression, Rituximab 375mg/m^2 weekly x 4 weeks followed by 6 cycles of CVP chemotherapy	After first course of rituximab, PR of maxillary lymphoma. 3 weeks after first course of rituximab: improvement in muscle weakness and fatiguability; resolution of diplopia for 5 months;

			Second course of rituximab 375mg/m² weekly x 4 weeks 10 months after initial course(patient treated for lymphoma)	discontinuation of PYR for almost 3 months. Decrease in anti-AChR antibodies from 12 to 5 nmol/L over 10months. After second course of rituximab, resolution of all sites of lymphoma except one; clinical improvement of MG lasting for more than 4 months and decrease in anti-AChR antibodies to 3.66 nmol/L. No adverse effects noted.
38/F Vandergheynst et al. (39)	MG	Methylprednisolone, Thymectomy, AZA, CSA, CTX, PE	375mg/m²(duration unclear), followed by high dose CTX x 4 days	Mild improvement in weakness based on peak flow. Patient developed septic arthritis of hip.
51/F Takagi et al.(40)	AChR+MG, NHL	Steroids, Thymectomy, PE	375mg/m² weekly x 4 weeks followed by 2 cycles of R-CHOP chemotherapy(treated for lymphoma)	After 4 weeks, anti-AChR antibodies decreased to 9.7nmol/L. After 2 cycles of CHOP, anti-AChR antibodies decreased to 6.0nmol/L and PR of lymphoma. No worsening of lymphoma and no adverse effects.
56/F Hain et al.(41)	MuSK+ AChR- MG	PYR, prednisolone, IVIG, AZA, MMF, PE, thymectomy	375mg/m² weekly x 4 weeks then monthly x 5 months, then every 10 weeks for total of 12 months + PYR + MMF	Improved dyspnea, swallowing and ADL score up to 5 points after 2 months. Clear speech, normal swallowing, resolution of ocular symptoms, FVC = 2L, and ADL score

Age/Gender Reference	Medical conditions	Prior therapies	Rituximab + other therapies	Results
27/M Zaja et al.(36)	AChR+MG, GVHD post-BMT for AML	CSA, PYR, IVIG, methylprednisolone	260 mg/m² weekly x 4 weeks + PYR + methylprednisolone	Improved performance status and decreased anti-AChR antibodies after 4 weeks. Steroid and PYR doses gradually reduced over 6 months. No adverse effects noted at 5 month follow-up period.
9/F Wylam et al.(37)	AChR+MG	Prednisone, IVIG, PYR, AZA, PE, thymectomy	375mg/m² weekly x 4 weeks + 6MP + monthly IVIG	Increased pulmonary function and strength after 1 month. Attainment of near-normal lung volumes and maximal negative respiratory pressure after 5 months. Decreased anti-AChR antibodies. Weaned off steroids and able to perform all physicial activities without weakness. No adverse effects noted.
79/F Gajra et al.(38)	AChR+MG, NHL	Thymectomy, PYR	CTX + prednisone initially then with disease progression, Rituximab 375mg/m² weekly x 4 weeks followed by 6 cycles of CVP chemotherapy	After first course of rituximab, PR of maxillary lymphoma. 3 weeks after first course of rituximab: improvement in muscle weakness and fatiguability; resolution of diplopia for 5 months;

40/F Gardner et al.(45)	AChR+ Intractable MG	Oral steroids, thymectomy, IVIG, AZA, MMF, CSA	Rituximab(dose unclear) given initially at a 2 week-interval followed by one dose every 10 weeks.	year on therapy. Symptoms improved after rituximab treatment. Patient was clinically stable for more than1 year on therapy. No adverse effects noted.
50/F Kerkeni et al.(46)	AChR+MG, RA	Gold salts, hydroxychloroquine, MTX, prednisone, AZA, IVIG, PE	$375mg/m^2$ weekly x 4 weeks x 4 weeks + AZA Second course of rituximab 1g on days 1 and 14 at 13 months after first course due to presence of CD19+ cells. MTX+AZA started 1 year after second rituximab course due to joint symptoms. Third course of rituximab 1 g on days 1 and 14 at 17 months after initiation of MTX + AZA due to reactivation of RA.	After first course of rituximab, gradual improvement of joint and muscle symptoms, decrease in AChR antibodies, decrease in steroids. MG and RA controlled 1 month after second rituximab course; steroids discontinued. Good RA response after third course of rituximab. No adverse effects noted.

Abbreviations:

AchR: acetylcholine receptor

AML: acute myelogenous leukemia

AZA: azathioprine

BMT: bone marrow transplant

CSA: cyclosporine

CTX: cyclophosphamide

CVP: cyclophosphamide, vincristine, prednisone

FVC: forced vital capacity

GVHD: graft-versus-host disease

IVIG: intravenous immunoglobulin

MG: myasthenia gravis

MMF: mycophenolate mofetil

MTX: methotrexate

MuSK: muscle-specific tyrosine kinase

NHL: non-Hodgkin's lymphoma

PE: plasma exchange/plasmapheresis

PR: partial response

PYR: pyridostigmine

RA: rheumatoid arthritis

R-CHOP: rituximab, cyclophosphamide, doxorubicin, vincristine, prednisolone

6-MP: 6-mercaptopurine

3.1. Serological evidence of efficacy of rituximab in myasthenia gravis (MG)

Rituximab effectively reduces circulating B-cell counts and, based on its potential to eliminate autoreactive B-cell clones, may have a therapeutic role in antibody-mediated autoimmune diseases, such as myasthenia gravis.

There have been a number of case reports and small studies reporting the successful use of rituximab in treatment of patients with either acetylcholine receptor antibodies (AChR-Ab), MuSK antibodies(MuSK-Ab) or neither, who had failed intravenous gammaglobulin(IVIG), plasmapheresis as well as conventional immunosuppressive therapy, such as prednisone, cyclosporine, azathioprine, mycophenolate mofetil (see Table 1).

Prednisone reduced the levels of AChR-Ab within the first months but did not have any effect on the MuSK-Ab.

Rituximab selectively targets B-cells compared with such medications, which makes rituximab an attractive treatment choice for MG. Two studies showed that rituximab improved the patient's clinical status and decreased MuSK-Ab by roughly 80% and AChR-Ab by 50% 2 months after infusion (31, 32).

A decline in antibody titers were seen in both AChR and MuSK antibody positive MG. This was significantly better in MuSK+ MG patients as opposed to AchR+ MG patients at 9 months and correlated with a more sustained clinical improvement (33). The decrease in MuSK antibodies was faster than expected based on the supposed half-life of most peripheral mature plasma cells (1-2 months) and of IgG(3 weeks) in one study (34), which was attributed to previous treatment with plasmapheresis.

3.2. Rituximab infusion protocols in MG

At the moment there are no official guidelines with regard to the dosage, frequency and duration of rituximab infusion for MG. Rituximab is given as 1gram IV on day 1 and 15 premedicated with methylprednisolone 100 mg IV as FDA approved for rheumatoid arthritis, but for NHL this is given as $375mg/m^2$ of various doses and frequencies depending on the cell type, monotherapy vs polytherapy and whether chemotherapy was given previously or not (30).

Most protocols used in case reports of MG consist of administering $375mg/m^2$ once a week for 4 weeks as induction therapy, followed by monthly infusions. The total duration of monthly infusions varied among studies.

Relapses after being treated with rituximab and lower doses of immunosuppressive agents associated with increased AChR antibody titers has been reported, but not in patients with MuSK-Ab (32). CD19+ cell levels can be followed as measure of the immunosuppressant effect of B cell depletion, which is unique for rituximab (33); however, there is no data to suggest that this is necessary even in rheumatoid arthritis.

3.4. Future clinical trials of rituximab in myasthenia gravis (MG)

Recently there was a pilot study of rituximab in MG(34); further large scale, prospective, randomized, double-blinded, placebo-controlled studies are needed to further delineate the efficacy, safety, and tolerability of rituximab in MG.

REFERENCES

1. Phillips LH, Torner JC. Epidemiologic evidence for a changing natural history of myasthenia gravis. *Neurology.* 1996; 47:1233-1238.

2. Lanzavecchia A. Receptor-mediated antigen uptake and its effect on antigen presentation to class II-restricted T lymphocytes. *Annu Rev Immunol.* 1990. 8: 773-793.

3. Lund FE. Regulartory roles for cytokine-producing B cells in infection and autoimmune disease. *Curr dir Autoimmun.* 2005; 8:25-54.

4. Duddy ME. Distinct profiles of human B cel effector cytokines: a role in immune regulartion? *J Immunol.* 2004; 172: 3422-3427.

5. Hohlfeld R, Wekerle H. Reflections on the "intrathymic pathogenesis" of myasthenia gravis. *J of Neuroimmunol.* 201-202; 21-27.

6. Gregg J, Silverman GJ, Weisman S. Rituximab therapy and autoimmune disorders: Prospects for anti-B cell therapy. *Arthritis & Rheumatism.* Vol 48(6): 1484 – 1492

7. Sims GP, Shiono H, Willcox N, Stott DI. Somatic hypermutation and selection of B cells in thymic germinal centers responding to acetylcholine receptor in myasthenia gravis. *J. Immunol.* 2001; 167: 1935–1944.

8. Goodman BE. Channels active in the excitability of nerves and skeletal muscles across the neuromuscular junction: basic function and pathophysiology. *Advan. Physiol. Edu.* 2008; 32: 127-135.

9. Keesey JC. Clinical evaluation and management of myasthenia gravis. *Muscle Nerve* 2004 ;29(4):484-505.

10. Moore C, Leu M, Müller U, Brenner HR. Induction of multiple signaling loops by MuSK during neuromuscular synapse formation. *Proc Natl Acad Sci U S A.* 2001; 98(25): 14655–14660.

11. McConville John, Farrugia Maria Elena, Beeson David, Kishore Uday, Metcalfe Richard, Newsom-Davis John, Vincent Angela. Detection and characterization of MuSK antibodies in seronegative myasthenia gravis. *Ann Neurol.* 2004; 55(4):580–584.

12. Lebrun C, Bourg V, Tieulie N, Thomas P. Successful treatment of refractory generalized myasthenia gravis with rituximab. *European Journal of Neurology* 2009, 16: 246-250.

13. Evoli A, Tonali PA, Padua L, Monaco ML, Scuderi F, Batocchi AP, Mariapaola Marino M, Bartoccioni E. Clinical correlates with anti-MuSK antibodies in generalized seronegative myasthenia gravis. *Brain.* 2003; 126(10): 2304-2311.

14. Illa I, Díaz-Manera JA, Juárez C, Rojas-García R, Molina-Porcel L, Aleu A, Pradas J, and Gallardo E . Seronegative" myasthenia gravis and anti-MuSK positive antibodies: description of Spanish series. [Article in Spanish].*Med Clin (Barc)* 2005; 125 : 100 -2.

15. Sanders DB, El-Salem K, Massey JM, McConville J, Vincent A. Clinical aspects of MuSK antibody positive seronegative MG. *Neurology.* 2003 Jun 24;60 (12):1978–1980.

16. Stickler DE, Massey JM, Sanders DB. MuSK-antibody positive myasthenia gravis: clinical and electrodiagnostic patterns. *Clin Neurophysiol.* 2005;116(9):2065-8.

17. Vincent A, Bowen J, Newsom-Davis J, McConville J. Seronegative generalised myasthenia gravis: clinical features, antibodies, and their targets. *Lancet Neurol.* 2003;2(2):99–106

18. Vincent A, Leite MI. Neuromuscular junction autoimmune disease: muscle specific kinase antibodies and treatments for myasthenia gravis. *Curr Opin Neurol.* 2005; 18:519–25

19. Zhou L, McConville J, Chaudhry V, Adams RN, Skolasky RL, Vincent A, Drachman DB. Clinical comparison of muscle-specific tyrosine kinase (MuSK) antibody-positive and -negative myasthenic patients. *Muscle Nerve.* 2004; 30(1):55–60)

20. Einfeld DA, Brown JP, Valentine MA, Clark EA, Ledbetter JA Molecular cloning of the human B cell CD20 receptor predicts a hydrophobic protein with multiple transmembrane domains. EMBO. 1988; 7(3): 711-717.

21. Nadler LM, Ritz J, Hardy R, Pesando JM, Schlossman SF, Stashenko P. A unique cell surface antigen identifying lymphoid malignancies of B cell origin. *J Clin Invest* 1981; 67: 134-140.

22. Dalakas MC. B cells as therapeutic targets in autoimmune neurological disorders. *Nature Clinical Practice Neurology.* 2008; 4: 557-567.

23. Peggs K, Segal N, Allison J. Targeting Immunosupportive Cancer Therapies: Accentuate the Positive, Eliminate the Negative. *Cancer Cell,* Vol 12(3): 192-199.

24. Clynes, R.A., Towers, T.L., Presta, L.G. & Ravetch, J.V. Inhibitory Fc receptors modulate in vivo cytoxicity against tumor targets. *Nature Medicine,* 6, 443–446.

25. Alas S, Emmanouilides C, Bonavida B. Inhibition of Interleukin 10 by Rituximab Results in Down-Regulation of Bcl-2 and Sensitization of B-cell Non-Hodgkin's Lymphoma to Apoptosis. *Clinical Cancer Research.* 2001; 7: 709-723

26. Maloney DG, Smith B, Appelbaum FR. The anti-tumor effect of monoclonal anti-CD20 antibody (mAb) therapy includes direct anti-proliferative activity and induction of apoptosis in CD20 positive non-Hodgkin's lymphoma (NHL) cell lines. *Blood* 1996; 88 (Suppl 1): 637.

27. Clark E, Ledbetter J. How does B cell depletion therapy work, and how can it be improved? *Ann Rheum Dis.* 2005; 64 (Suppl 4): iv77–iv80.

28. Raju R, Rakocevic R, Chen Z, Hoehn G, Semino-Mora C, Shi W, Olsen R, Dalakas MC. Autoimmunity to GABAA-receptor-associated protein in stiff-person syndrome. *Brain* 2006; 129(12):3270-3276.

29. Tokunaga M, Fujii K, Saito K, Nakayamada S, Tsujimura S, Nawata M, Tanaka Y. Down-regulation of CD40 and CD80 on B cells in patients with life-threatening systemic lupus erythematosus after successful treatment with rituximab. *Rheumatology* 2005; 44(2):176-182.

30. www.rituxan.com. Genetech, Inc.

31. Díaz-Manera J, Rojas-García R, Gallardo E, Juárez C, Martínez-Domeño A, Martínez-Ramírez S, Dalmau J, Blesa R, Illa I. Antibodies to AChR, MuSK and VGKC in a patient with myasthenia gravis and Morvan's syndrome. *Nature Clinical Practice Neurology* 2007; 3: 405-410.

32. Illa I, Diaz-Manera J, Rojas-Garcia R, Pradas J, Rey A, Blesa R, Juarez C, Gallardo E. Sustained response to rituximab in anti-AChR and anti-MuSK positive myasthenia gravis patients. J of *Neuroimmunology* 2008; 201-202: 90-94.

33. Lebrun C, Bourg V, Tieulie N, Thomas P. Successful treatment of refractory generalized myasthenia gravis with rituximab. *European Journal of Neurology.* Vol. 16(2): 246 – 250.

34. McLaughlin P, Grillo-Lopez A, Link BK, Levy R, Czuczman MS, Williams ME, Heyman MR, Bence-Bruckler I, White CA, Cabanillas F, Jain V, Ho AD, Lister J, Wey K, Shen D, Dallaire BK. . Rituximab chimeric anti-CD20 monoclonal antibody therapy for relapsed indolent lymphoma: half of patients respond to a four-dose treatment program. *J Clin Oncol* 1998; 16: 2825-2833.

35. Rup T, Potter C, Bradshaw Y. Pilot trial of rituximab in myasthenia gravis. *Neurology* 2008; 70: (Suppl.1): A 301

36. Zaja F, Russo D, Fuga G, Perella G, Baccarani M . Rituximab for myasthenia gravis developing after bone marrow transplant. *Neurology* 2000; 55: 1062-1063.

37. Wylam ME, Anderson PM, Kuntz NL, Rodriguez V. Successful treatment of refractory myasthenia gravis using rituximab: a pediatric case report. *J Pediatr* 2003; 143: 674-677.

38. Gajra A, Vajpayee N, Grethlein SJ. Response of myasthenia gravis to rituximab in a patient with non-Hodgkin's lymphoma. *Am J Hematol* 2004; 77: 196-197.

39. Vandergheynst F, Robin V, Vandermergel X, Decaux G . Refractory myasthenia gravis successfully treated with rituximab followed by immunoablative treatment with high dose cyclophosphamide. *Acta Clin Belg* 2004; 59: 320.

40. Takagi K, Yoshida A, Iwasaki H, Inoue H, Ueda T. Anti-CD2- antibody(rituximab) therapy in a myasthenia gravis patient with follicular lymphoma. *Ann Hematol* 2005; 84: 548-550.

41. Hain B, Jordan K, Deschauer M, Zierz S . Successful treatment of MuSK antibody-positive myasthenia gravis with rituximab. *Muscle Nerve* 2006; 33: 575-580.

42. Baek WS, Bashey A, Sheean GL. Complete remission induced by rituximab in refractory, seronegative, muscle-specific kinase-positive myasthenia gravis. *J Neurol Neurosurg Psychiatry* 2007; 78: 771.

43. Chan A, Lee DH, Linker R, Mohr, A., Toyka, K.V. and Gold, R. Rescue therapy with anti-CD20 treatment in neuroimmunologic breakthrough disease. *J Neurol.* 2007;254:1604-6.

44. Thakre M, Inshasi J, Marashi M. Rituximab in refractory MuSK antibody myasthenia gravis. *J Neurol.* 254 (2007), pp. 968–969.

45. Gardner R, Pestronk A, Al-Lozi M. Intractable myasthenia gravis responding to rituximab treatment. Presented at the 60th Annual Meeting of the American Academy of Neurology in Chicago, IL; April 12-19, 2008. AAN abstract # P06.003.

46. Kerkeni S, Marotte H, Miossec P. Improvement with rituximab in a patient with both rheumatoid arthritis and myasthenia gravis. *Muscle Nerve* 2008; 38: 1343-1345.

The Collaborates

Takuyu Akiyoshi, M.D
Tokyo Metropolitan Institute of Gerontology
Research Team for Geriatric Medicine
Sakaecho 35-2, Itabashi-ku
Tokyo 173-0015
Japan
akiyoshi-tki@umin.ac.jp

Carlo Antozzi, MD
Neuroimmunology and Muscle Pathology
Unit
Neurological Institute Foundation "Carlo
Besta"
Via Celoria 11, 20133
Milan
Italy
antozzi@istituto-besta.it

William S. Baek, MD
Dept of Neurology
Kaiser Permanente Fontana Medical Center
9985 Sierra Ave
Fontana, CA 92335
william_s_baek@hotmail.com

Mark DeBaets, MD, PhD
Neuroimmunology group
Department of Neuroscience
School of Mental Health and Neuroscience
Maastricht University
P.O. Box 616
6200 MD Maastricht
The Netherlands
m.debaets@maastrichtuniversity.nl

Sonia Berrih-Aknin, PhD
CNRS UMR 8162
IPSC
UPS
Hôpital Marie Lannelongue
92350
Le Plessis-Robinson

France
sonia.berrih-aknin@u-psud.fr

Jacky Bismuth
CNRS UMR 8162
IPSC
UPS
Hôpital Marie Lannelongue
92350
Le Plessis-Robinson
France
jacky.bismuth@u-psud.fr

Talma Brenner Ph.D
Laboratory of Neuroimmunology
Department of Neurology
Hadassah University Hospital
and
Hebrew University Medical School
Jerusalem, Israel
POB 12000
Jerusalem 91120
Israel
Brenner@cc.huji.ac.il

J. Van den Broeck, MSc
Neuroimmunology group
Department of Neuroscience
School of Mental Health and Neuroscience
Maastricht University
P.O. Box 616, 6200
MD Maastricht
The Netherlands.
j.vandenbroeck@maastrichtuniversity.nl

Premkumar Christadoss M.B.B.S
Department of Microbiology and
Immunology,
University of Texas Medical Branch,
Galveston, TX, 77555-1070,
USA
pchrista@utmb.edu

Wen-Yu Chuang MD
Department of Pathology
Chang Gung Memorial Hospital
College of Medicine
Chang Gung University
5 Fu-Hsing Street
Kwei-Shan
Taoyuan 333, Taiwan
s12126@adm.cgmh.org.tw,
wychuang0266@yahoo.com.tw

Marinos C. Dalakas MD,
Imperial College, London
Burlington Danes Building
Hammersmith Hospital Campus
Office E517
Du Cane Rd
London W12 0NN
m.dalakas@imperial.ac.uk

Amelia Evoli, MD
Neuroscience Department
Catholic University
Largo F. Vito,1 - 00168 Roma, Italy
a.evoli@rm.unicatt.it

Bruno Eymard MD, PhD
Neuromuscular Clinics
Myology Institute
La Salpêtrière Hospital
Paris
anne-marie.maronne@psl.aphp.fr

Tali Feferman PhD
Department of Immunology
The Weizmann Institute of Science
Rehovot 76100
Israel.
tali.feferman@weizmann.ac.il

Sara Fuchs PhD
Department of Immunology
The Weizmann Institute of Science
Rehovot 76100
Israel
sara.fuchs@weizmann.ac.il

Baggi Fulvio PhD
Neuroimmunology and Muscle Pathology
Unit
Neurological Institute Foundation "Carlo
Besta"
Via Celoria 11, 20133
Milan
Italy
baggi@istituto-besta.it

Henri-Jean Garchon MD.PhD
Inserm and Université Paris Descartes
Institut Cochin
27, rue du Faubourg Saint-Jacques
75014 Paris
France
henri-jean.garchon@inserm.fr

Petros Giastas, PhD
Department of Biochemistry
Hellenic Pasteur Institute
127, V. Sofias Ave.
GR11521
Athens
Greece
pegias@pasteur.gr

Felicitas Gonzales, B.S.
Wayne State University
Department of Neurology
3141 Elliman Building
421 E. Canfield Ave.
Detroit, MI 48201
fgonzale@med.wayne.edu

A. Gomez, MSc
Neuroimmunology group
Department of Neuroscience
School of Mental Health and Neuroscience
Maastricht University
P.O. Box 616
6200 MD Maastricht
The Netherlands
a.gomez@maastrichtuniversity.nl

Junwei Hao MD
Center for Neurologic Diseases,
Tianjin Medical University General Hospital,
Tianjin 300071, China
and
Barrow Neurological Institute
St. Joseph's Hospital and Medical Center
Phoenix, AZ 85013
USA
junwei.hao@chw.edu

Daniel Hantaï, MD, PhD
Inserm U 975 and Université Pierre et Marie
Curie
Myology Institute
La Salpêtrière Hospital
Paris
daniel.hantai@upmc.fr

Anthony J. Infante, MD, PhD
Pediatrics
University of Texas Health Science Center at
San Antonio
7703 Floyd Curl Drive
San Antonio, TX 78229-3900
infantea@uthscsa.edu

Henry J. Kaminski, MD
Department of Neurology & Psychiatry
Saint Louis University
1438 South Grand Blvd
St. Louis, MO 63104
hkaminsk@slu.edu

Nicole Kerlero de Rosbo PhD
CNRS UMR 8162
IPSC
UPS
Hôpital Marie Lannelongue
92350
Le Plessis-Robinson
France
nicole.kerlero-de-rosbo@u-psud.fr

Ellen Kraig PhD
Cellular and Structural Biology MC #7762

University of Texas Health Science Center at
San Antonio
7703 Floyd Curl Drive
San Antonio, TX 78229-3900
kraig@uthscsa.edu

Sachiho Kubo
Tokyo Metropolitan Institute of Gerontology
Research Team for Geriatric Medicine
Sakaecho 35-2, Itabashi-ku
Tokyo 173-0015. Japan
kubosa@tmig.or.jp

Linda L. Kusner, PhD
Departments of Ophthalmology and
Pharmacological & Physiological Sciences
Saint Louis University
1438 South Grand Blvd
St. Louis, MO 63104
LKusner@slu.edu

George Lagoumintzis PhD
Department of Pharmacy
University of Patras
Rio, GR26500
Patras
Greece
glagoum@upatras.gr

Rozen Le Panse
CNRS UMR 8162
IPSC
UPS
Hôpital Marie Lannelongue
92350
Le Plessis-Robinson
France
rozen.lepanse@u-psud.fr

Yanfeng Li, M.S.
Wayne State University
Department of Neurology
3141 Elliman Building
421 E. Canfield Ave.
Detroit, MI 48201
ay3925@wayne.edu

Robert Lisak, MD
Wayne State University
Department of Neurology
8D - University Health Center
4201 St. Antoine
Detroit, MI 48201
rlisak@med.wayne.edu

Ruolan Liu, MD, PhD;
Center for Neurologic Diseases,
Tianjin Medical University General Hospital,
Tianjin 300071, China
and
Barrow Neurological Institute
St. Joseph's Hospital and Medical Center
Phoenix, AZ 85013
USA
ruolan.liu@chw.edu

M. Losen, PhD
Neuroimmunology group
Department of Neuroscience
School of Mental Health and Neuroscience
Maastricht University
P.O. Box 616
6200 MD Maastricht
The Netherlands
m.losen@maastrichtuniversity.nl

Uladzimir Luchanok, MD, PhD
Department of Neurology & Psychiatry
Saint Louis University
1438 South Grand Blvd
St. Louis, MO 63104
luchanok@yahoo.com

Renato Mantegazza, MD
Neuroimmunology and Muscle Pathology
Unit
Neurological Institute Foundation "Carlo
Besta"
Via Celoria 11, 20133
Milan
Italy
rmantegazza@istituto-besta.it

P. Martinez-Martinez, PhD
Neuroimmunology group
Department of Neuroscience
School of Mental Health and Neuroscience
Maastricht University
P.O. Box 616
6200 MD Maastricht
The Netherlands
p.martinez@maastrichtuniversity.nl

Naoki Maruyama MD, PhD
Tokyo Metropolitan Institute of Gerontology
Research Team for Geriatric Medicine
Sakaecho 35-2, Itabashi-ku
Tokyo 173-0015
Japan
naomaru@tmig.or.jp

Alexander Marx MD
University Medical Center Mannheim
Institute of Pathology
University of Heidelberg
Theodor-Kutzer-Ufer 1.3
D-68135 Mannheim
Germany
alexander.marx@umm.de

Matthew N. Meriggioli, MD
Department of Neurology and Rehabilitation
University of Illinois College of Medicine
Chicago, IL 60612
mmerig@uic.edu

Tsuyoshi Miyazaki MD, Ph.D
Tokyo Metropolitan Institute of Gerontology
Research Team for Geriatric Medicine
Sakaecho 35-2, Itabashi-ku
Tokyo 173-0015
Japan
miyazak14@tmig.or.j

P. Molenaar, PhD
Neuroimmunology group
Department of Neuroscience
School of Mental Health and Neuroscience
Maastricht University

P.O. Box 616
6200 MD Maastricht
The Netherlands
p.molenaar@maastrichtuniversity.nl

Syuuichi Mori Ph.D
Tokyo Metropolitan Institute of Gerontology
Research Team for Geriatric Medicine
Sakaecho 35-2, Itabashi-ku
Tokyo 173-0015
Japan
shuuichi@tmig.or.jp

Sara Nava
Neuroimmunology and Muscle Pathology
Unit
Neurological Institute Foundation "Carlo
Besta"
Via Celoria 11, 20133
Milan
Italy
sara.nava@istituto-besta.it

Konstantinos Poulas PhD
Department of Pharmacy
University of Patras
Rio, GR26500
Patras
Greece
kpoulas@upatras.gr

Samia Ragheb, PhD
Wayne State University
Department of Neurology
3128 Elliman building
421 E. Canfield Ave.
Detroit, MI 48201
sragheb@med.wayne.edu

Vivek K Rauniyar, MB BS
Department of Neurology
Xiangya Hospital
Central South University
87 Xiangya road ,Changsha 410008
Hunan,China
vkrauniyar@hotmail.com

Julie Rowin, MD
University of Illinois at Chicago
Department of Neurology and Rehabilitation
912 South Wood Street (MC 796)
Room 855N
Chicago Illinois 60612
rowin@uic.edu

Chiara Ruocco
Neuroimmunology and Muscle Pathology
Unit
Neurological Institute Foundation "Carlo
Besta"
Via Celoria 11, 20133
Milan
Italy
chiararuocco@gmail.com

Jianrong Sheng, PhD.
Department of Neurology and Rehabilitation
Department of Microbiology and
Immunology
University of Illinois
College of Medicine
Chicago, IL 60612
jiashe@uic.edu

Fu-Dong Shi, MD, PhD
Center for Neurologic Diseases,
Tianjin Medical University General
Hospital,
Tianjin 300071, China
and
Barrow Neurological Institute
St. Joseph's Hospital and Medical Center
Phoenix, AZ 85013
USA
fshi@chw.edu

Kazuhiro Shigemoto MD, Ph.D
Tokyo Metropolitan Institute of Gerontology
Research Team for Geriatric Medicine
Sakaecho 35-2, Itabashi-ku
Tokyo 173-0015 Japan
kazshige@tmig.or.jp

Jindrich Soltys, DVM, PhD
Department of Neurology & Psychiatry
Saint Louis University
St. Louis, MO 63104
JSoltys@slu.edu

Miriam C. Souroujon PhD
Department of Natural Sciences
The Open University of Israel
1 University Rd
Raanana 43107
Israel
and
Department of Immunology
The Weizmann Institute of Science
Rehovot 76100
Israel
miriso@openu.ac.il

Sue Stacy, PhD
Cellular and Structural Biology MC #7762
University of Texas Health Science Center at
San Antonio
7703 Floyd Curl Drive
San Antonio, TX 78229-3900
stacys@uthscsa.edu

Philipp Strobel MD
University Medical Center Mannheim
Institute of Pathology
University of Heidelberg
Theodor-Kutzer-Ufer 1.3
D-68135 Mannheim
Germany
philipp.stroebel@umm.de

Nikolaos Trakas
Department of Biochemistry
Hellenic Pasteur Institute
127, V. Sofias Ave.
GR11521
Athens
Greece
ntrakas@pasteur.gr

Jaya R. Trivedi, MD
Univ. of Texas Southwestern Medical Center
Dept. of Neurology, 5323 Harry Hines Blvd.
Dallas, TX 75390-8897
jaya.trivedi@utsouthwestern.edu

Frédérique Truffault
CNRS UMR 8162
IPSC
UPS
Hôpital Marie Lannelongue
92350
Le Plessis-Robinson
France
frederique.truffault@u-psud.fr

Erdem Tüzün MD
Department of Neurology
Istanbul Faculty of Medicine
University of Istanbul
Çapa, Istanbul, 34390
Turkey.
drerdem@yahoo.com

Socrates J. Tzartos PhD
Department of Biochemistry
Hellenic Pasteur Institute
127, V. Sofias Ave.
GR11521, Athens
Greece
and Department of Pharmacy
University of Patras
Rio, GR26500
Patras
Greece
tzartos@pasteur.gr and tzartos@upatras.gr

Angela Vincent , FRCPath
Department of Clinical Neurology
West Wing
John Radcliffe Hospital and Neurosciences
Group Weatherall Institute of Molecular
Medicine Oxford OX3 9DS
angela.vincent@imm.ox.ac.uk

K. Vrolix, MSc
Neuroimmunology group
Department of Neuroscience
School of Mental Health and Neuroscience
Maastricht University
P.O. Box 616
6200 MD Maastricht
The Netherlands
k.vrolix@maastrichtuniversity.nl

Earlanda L. Williams, PhD
Cellular and Structural Biology MC #7762
University of Texas Health Science Center at
San Antonio
7703 Floyd Curl Drive
San Antonio, TX 78229-3900
williamse2@uthscsa.edu

Gil I. Wolfe, MD
University of Texas Southwestern Medical
Center
Dept. of Neurology, 5323 Harry Hines Blvd.
Dallas, TX 75390-8897
gil.wolfe@utsouthwestern.edu

Shigeru Yamada Ph.D
Tokyo Metropolitan Institute of
Gerontology
Research Team for Geriatric Medicine
Sakaecho 35-2, Itabashi-ku
Tokyo 173-0015
Japan
shyamada@tmig.or.jp

Huan Yang, MD,PhD
Department of Neurology
Xiangya Hospital
Central South University
87 Xiangya road,Changsha 410008
Hunan,China
yangh69@yahoo.com

Paraskevi Zisimopoulou PhD
Department of Biochemistry
Hellenic Pasteur Institute
127, V. Sofias Ave.
GR11521
Athens
Greece
zisimopoulou@pasteur.gr